NOTABLE MUSLIMS

Muslim Builders of
World Civilization and Culture

NOTABLE MUSLIMS

Muslim Builders of
World Civilization and Culture

NATANA J. DELONG-BAS

ONEWORLD

OXFORD

NOTABLE MUSLIMS

A Oneworld Book

First published by Oneworld Publications, 2006
First published in paperback, 2008

Copyright © Natana J. DeLong-Bas 2006

ISBN 978–1–85168–567–7

Cover design by Nita Ybarra
Typeset by Jayvee, Trivandrum, India
Printed and bound in the United States of America

Oneworld Publications
185 Banbury Road
Oxford OX2 7AR
England
www.oneworld-publications.com

Learn more about Oneworld. Join our mailing list to
find out about our latest titles and special offers at:

www.oneworld-publications.com

To the glory of God
and
To the building of bridges of interfaith
and intercultural understanding

Contents

Preface

I would like to thank all of those profiled who so graciously gave of their time and attention in granting interviews and reviewing and commenting on the biographies: Oussama Cherribi, Kadiatou Diallo, Farid Esack, H.R.H. Princess Haifa Al Faisal, Muzaffar Haleem, Asma Gull Hasan, Rana Husseini, Lobna Ismail, Kevin James, Aasma Khan, Zakia Mahasa, Dr. Laila al-Marayati, Shazia Mirza, Thoraya Ahmed Obaid, A.D. Pirous, Ahmed Rashid, Joshua Salaam, Muhammad Nejatullah Siddiqi, H.R.H. Sultan bin Salman Al Saud, Zainab Al-Suwaij, Tayyibah Taylor, Hajjah Maria Ulfah, Amina Wadud, Michael Wolfe, Mohamed Zakariya, and Ahmed Zewail. Without their life examples, dedication, and generosity, this book would not exist.

Thanks are also due to those who facilitated interviews or served as liaisons with the interviewees and reviewed the biographies – Kenneth M. George, Anne K. Rasmussen, Halah Al-Jubeir, Jessica Minton, Nahedah Ziad, Dr. Mukhtar Ikhsan, Vickie Lindsay, Holli Semetko, Mohammed Abdul Aleem, and Xheladin and Bethani Ann DeLong Vehapi – as well as to the staff of the Tyngsborough Public Library for their assistance in obtaining various materials.

Thanks are due to John L. Esposito and John O. Voll for their reviews and recommendations of the people to be included and for providing contact information for some of them.

Finally, I would like to express my deepest gratitude to my family for their encouragement in seeing this project through to the end and for their love and support. Thanks are due to Dad, Ruth, and Zedeka for providing child care and space to write in peace. My husband, Christophe, has provided his usual good humor, encouragement, and unconditional support and has served as an important sounding board for the ideas and visions the book encompasses. He has also provided the love, environmental support, and faith in my work that makes my writing possible. Our children, Aurora and Gabriel, have endured the completion of yet another book with fortitude, courage, and just a little impatience, asking daily, "Is your book done yet?" and making certain that I take the time to appreciate the opportunities each day offers for spending with friends, playing outside, and exploring the wonders of life.

Introduction

Notable Muslims was conceived in the summer of 2001 to build greater Western understanding and appreciation of Islam and the role of Muslims in building world civilization and culture. The need for such a book became more pronounced in the aftermath of 9/11 as images and impressions of Islam and Muslims became increasingly associated in both the media and the minds of the Western public with terrorism and hatred. The hijacking of the image of the faith of more than 1.2 billion people globally by a handful of militant extremists has resulted in increased fear and suspicion of Islam and Muslims at a time when Islam is the world's fastest-growing and second-largest religion. Muslims form significant minorities in both the United States and Europe, as well as strong majorities throughout the Middle East, South and Southeast Asia, and large portions of Africa. The strong global presence of Islam requires greater understanding of Islam as a faith and source of inspiration and constructive motivation in the lives of individual believers.

The 100 Muslims of *Notable Muslims* provide examples of Sunnis, Shiis, and Sufis, both women and men, of a variety of age groups, who have made, or are making, significant contributions to their communities, countries, and causes at both the grassroots and public levels – locally, regionally, nationally, and internationally. They are both royals and commoners, officials and civilians, government leaders and dissidents, historical (15%) and contemporary figures (85%). They include athletes, architects, artists, businesspeople, community activists, economists, entertainers, environmentalists, filmmakers, human rights activists, humanitarians, journalists, judges, media figures, musicians, philanthropists, politicians, scholars, scientists, social workers, theologians, women's rights activists, and writers. They represent thirty-seven countries, including Afghanistan, Albania, Algeria, Austria, Bahrain, Bangladesh, Bosnia, Egypt, France, Guinea, India, Indonesia, Iran, Iraq, Jordan, Kashmir, Kosovo, Lebanon, Malaysia, Morocco, the Netherlands, Nigeria, Pakistan, Qatar, Saudi Arabia, Somalia, South Africa, Spain, Switzerland, Syria, Trinidad, Tunisia, Turkey, the United Arab Emirates, the United Kingdom, the United States of America, and Uzbekistan. The scope of coverage provides examples not only of Muslim contributions in a variety of fields, but also of issues defined by Muslims as areas of concern both domestically and internationally, including the environment, humanitarian work, women's and human rights, eradication of poverty, and preservation and building of history, architecture, and culture. The result is a window onto how Muslims view themselves, their communities, and their problems, as well as onto how

1

they are working to build their communities, societies, countries, and relations with others, often due to the inspiration they derive from their faith.

Individuals profiled were selected due to the significance of their contributions, as marked by national and international recognition of their work, receipt of prestigious awards, grants, honors, titles, or prizes, and the public impact on the individual's work on an issue of critical importance. The inclusion of an equal number of women and men (fifty of each) redresses traditional tendencies to profile male accomplishment, with only tangential or token coverage of female accomplishment. As the profiles demonstrate, female Muslim accomplishment is prevalent in a variety of fields, from service to the United Nations to winning the Nobel Prize for Peace and the Goldman Prize for the Environment. Some are famous international figures. Others are not as well known, but have been the first to achieve a significant representative accomplishment, such as election or appointment to an important public office. The primary criterion for selection was accomplishment in or contribution to a given field or profession. A secondary criterion of public or community service was also required in order to demonstrate that accomplishment does not occur in a vacuum, but is intended to have an impact on others. The Muslims profiled in this collection have put their achievements to work for the greater good not only of fellow Muslims, but also of the rest of humanity. Many have dedicated themselves to building bridges between the Third World and the most highly advanced societies, science, and technology.

In many cases, religious views and content are included in the biographies because the individuals themselves have identified Islam as a motivating factor in their work or as the source of the worldview that inspired them to pursue a given field. For some, Islam served as a source of comfort and renewal during a difficult personal crisis, enabling them to return to their work with greater dedication to achieve and accomplish. In other cases, religion is mentioned only tangentially or not at all, either because the individual did not identify Islam as an important motivation for his/her work or because the individual considers religion a private matter to be kept separate from his/her public activities. The presentation of Islam in these biographies should therefore be understood as a matter of individual choice and perspective in self-representation as provided in interviews or in autobiographical materials. Religious coverage is not intended as proselytization or apologetics, but to demonstrate the variety of ways in which people interpret, explain, and live out their faith, whether personally or professionally. Furthermore, although all of the individuals profiled are Muslim, they are not all religious leaders or scholars by profession or reputation. A few religious leaders are included where they have identified and made major contributions to new interpretations of Islam, such as pluralism, liberation theology, or Sufism. However, they do not constitute the majority of those covered.

Similarly, terrorists, jihadists, and otherwise notorious Muslims are absent from this book. This should not be misinterpreted to mean that terrorists and jihadists do not exist or that they do not have influence over some Muslims to varying degrees. Clearly, such realities do exist and constitute an issue of global importance. The purpose in focusing on those who have chosen positive, constructive avenues of expressing and being motivated by their faith is to demonstrate that there are many Muslims who base their value-systems and worldviews on Islam without endorsing or engaging in terrorism. Through their life examples, they provide practical illustrations of individual adherence to Islam leading to constructive avenues for fighting the ugly realities of poverty, war, discrimination, greed, and oppression without resorting to armed conflict.

Many of those profiled here have repeatedly and publicly affirmed that they reject violence and terrorism and have denounced the perpetrators of the 9/11 attacks for hijacking not only airplanes, but also the very image of Islam and Muslims for nefarious purposes. In some cases, 9/11 marked the moment when an individual asserted a public voice or founded an organization to protest terrorism. In others, it served to expand opportunities to reach out in interfaith work and to promote diversity, pluralism, and multiculturalism. As the most pivotal event in the lifetimes of many Muslims around the world, 9/11 marked a turning point of recognition of the need to condemn terrorism publicly and unequivocally while reclaiming Islam as a faith. Many of the individuals profiled here dedicated themselves to denying legitimacy to the interpretations of jihadists by asserting their own more peaceful, tolerant, and inclusive interpretations of Islam, often in ways that emphasized democracy, women's rights, minority rights, and pluralism.

Because it covers a variety of fields, this collection is not intended to represent the 100 most important or influential Muslim thinkers or religious leaders. Rather, it is intended to present a portrait of Islam as it is lived and practiced by real people in their daily lives in many different nations and fields across a multiplicity of ethnicities and languages. This mosaic reflects the demographic realities of contemporary Islam, most notably that South and Southeast Asia – especially Pakistan, Indonesia, and Malaysia – contain the largest Muslim populations in the world, with Arab countries representing only about 20% of the world's Muslims. The strong inclusion of American and European Muslims reflects the dual reality of immigration of Muslims from a variety of nations to these countries and the phenomenon of Western converts to Islam. Conversions, in particular, provide reflections of what contemporary Muslims are searching for in a faith tradition, as well as what they define as issues that need to be addressed and reformed. Again, the inclusion of both male and female converts of different racial and ethnic backgrounds presents a variety of perspectives on these complex issues.

Emphasis in this collection was given to contemporary figures because of the need for positive, concrete, contemporary examples of Muslims who are working to build world civilization and culture at a time when popular understandings of Islam and Muslims tend to focus only on 9/11, the ongoing crisis between Israelis and Palestinians, and the insurgency in Iraq that daily claims the lives of both Iraqis and Americans at the hands of terrorists. Although individuals were not chosen according to age groups, the under-thirty generation (those born in 1974 and after: Jemima Goldsmith, Asma Gull Hasan, Amel Larrieux, Samira Makhmalbaf, Shazia Mirza, Mos Def, and Joshua Salaam) is included to show that Islam is not the exclusive purview of older generations, but that youth are also capable of making significant and important contributions in new ways and can serve as role models for other young people.

One other trend that became apparent after research and interviews were completed but that had not been a criterion for selection was that of education. Of the eighty-five contemporary Muslims included in the collection, twenty-one (25%) were educated in Europe, one (1%) in Canada, and forty-six (54%) in the United States. Otherwise stated, sixty-six (78%) were educated in the West (Benazir Bhutto and Atiq Raza were educated in both Europe and the United States), suggesting that one of the most important investments the West, particularly the United States, has made in the Muslim world is the granting of student visas and scholarships for study. Although some of these former students chose to remain in the United States, many of them returned to their home countries, taking with them not only the knowledge gained in the university disciplines studied, but also practical experience of life in America and the building of person-to-person contacts with Americans. At a time when student visas from the Muslim world, particularly the Arab Muslim world, are being restricted in unprecedented ways, the impact that Western, particularly American, education has had for the generation born in the 1940s and 1950s back in the Muslim world, and in terms of relations between the Muslim world and the West, raises serious questions about the long-term impact of visa and study restrictions. The biographies included in this collection suggest that the opportunity to be educated and experience life in the United States and Europe is one of the most important long-term investments possible for building relations between the Muslim world and the West, even as Islam is increasingly a part of the Western landscape.

Regrettably, not all Muslims at the top of their respective fields and commitments could be included. One of the disadvantages of covering contemporary figures is that changes in time, circumstances, and context bring new people to attention, making it impossible to capture all Muslim achievers in a single volume. This work should therefore be understood as an invitation to examine the accomplishments of other Muslims in the identified fields, as well as to consider other fields not represented here.

The entries are organized alphabetically. They begin with a brief statement of the person's significance, followed by basic biographical information including date and place of birth, parental occupations, pivotal childhood events, and education before providing in-depth coverage of the person's work. The entries conclude with mentions of awards or prestigious honors the person has received. Because this book is intended to be accessible to the general public, it does not rely on foreign terminology (where given, it is defined) or assume any prior knowledge of either the topics covered or of Islam. Care has been taken to provide a context in which the importance of the person's work can be understood, including the impact of their faith where specified by the person. Bibliographies are included with each entry to provide guidance in additional readings. A select bibliography appears at the end of the book with suggestions for further readings on major topics, as well as on individuals. In every case, an effort has been made to include both written materials and reliable internet sites. Many of the individuals profiled have been interviewed either orally or in writing. To facilitate flow and readability, footnotes and citations have not been included within individual entries. The bibliographies at the end of each entry indicate the sources used in writing the articles.

It is hoped that this volume will contribute to greater interfaith and intercultural understanding, as well as to recognition and appreciation of the achievements of Muslims around the world.

A

Kareem Abdul-Jabbar (b. 1947)

Basketball champion, N.B.A. legend, and actor, Kareem Abdul-Jabbar has investigated and documented African-American accomplishments and contributions to American history since retiring from professional sports.

Kareem Abdul-Jabbar was born Ferdinand Lewis Alcindor, Jr., on April 16, 1947, in New York, NY. Known as Lew, Abdul-Jabbar was the only child of Cora and Ferdinand "Al" Alcindor, both natives of the Caribbean island of Trinidad.

Abdul-Jabbar was raised in what he describes as a strict Roman Catholic home where the importance of a good education and earning good grades were emphasized. He pursued both academics and musical training as a child, developing a particular love of reading. Both parents taught him strong family values, including the beliefs that power is derived from knowing and understanding one's heritage and origins – particularly the hardships faced by, and accomplishments of, one's ancestors – and that courage is a moral act and a measure of one's character.

Abdul-Jabbar spent his early childhood in Harlem. The family later moved north to multilingual and multicultural Inwood. Because of the diversity surrounding him, he recalls being puzzled by the relative invisibility of black people in American history other than as ignorant slaves who supposedly contributed nothing to American life or society. This neglect inspired him both to accomplish and achieve at a personal level and to rediscover black accomplishment in American history.

Abdul-Jabbar began his education at the private Catholic St. Jude's School and transferred to Holy Providence boarding school in Philadelphia in the fourth grade. Frequently teased and sometimes physically abused because of his excellent academic performance, he began playing basketball as a refuge and source of solitude. Despite his lack of knowledge and skills, his height earned him a place on the eighth-grade basketball team when he was in the fifth grade. He also joined the track team, which helped him to develop his basketball style. As a seventh grader, he was tall enough to jump and reach the edge of the basketball rim. By the eighth grade, he was a confident player, scoring an unprecedented thirty-three points in a single game. At fourteen, he was able to dunk the basketball from a jump height that brought both his hand and the ball above the basket so that he could push it through the netting.

Because the center jumps for the ball at the beginning of the game and is responsible for working close to the basket, Abdul-Jabbar was chosen to play the center position. He recalls that it took both time and practice to learn to play the position well. He also had to learn to take passes from teammates, make shots, pick up on rebounds if teammates shot and missed, and block potential shots by the other team's center. Although he excelled at basketball, his parents insisted that he also continue to work hard academically.

Abdul-Jabbar received his high-school education at Power Memorial Academy. He credits his high-school basketball coach, Jack Donohue, with helping him to develop his game until he understood the sport, dedicating himself to his players as both athletes and students, and teaching him the importance of teamwork. Abdul-Jabbar made the varsity team by his sophomore year and led his teammates through the season with no losses, marking their first successful season. The team's opponents were often jealous of their success and singled Abdul-Jabbar out for harassment. During one game, he was assaulted by an opposing player who tried to bite him. His skill also resulted in increased public and media attention, although Coach Donohue refused to allow reporters to speak to him so that he could concentrate on basketball and schoolwork.

During his high-school years, Abdul-Jabbar was chosen three times consecutively for all-city and all-American. He also attended some professional games at Madison Square Garden with Coach Donohue, where he was inspired by players such as Wilt Chamberlain, Bill Russell, and Bob Cousy. He did not believe that he would ever play basketball professionally himself.

During the summer following his junior year of high school, Abdul-Jabbar was hired by the Harlem Youth Action Project as a journalist, an experience that he believes taught him to write well. He researched local architecture, discovering the Schomburg Center for Research in Black Culture where he learned about Harlem Jazz and the age of the 1920s that had produced numerous prominent African-American artists, musicians, intellectuals, writers, painters, and dancers. Learning about Harlem and the people it had produced helped Abdul-Jabbar to develop a sense of pride and respect for himself and his community. It was also during this time that he developed an interest in civil rights, racism, and African-American culture. His personal experience of the race riots of July 1964 in Harlem opened his eyes to the reality of racism and made him angry against whites for their treatment of blacks. Although he did not subscribe to Martin Luther King, Jr.'s philosophy of non-violence at the time, he came to realize later in life that this was probably the only effective way of achieving an end to racism.

Abdul-Jabbar ended his high-school career as the most sought-after recruit in the country. He decided to attend the University of California at Los Angeles (U.C.L.A.) not only because he was impressed by the record of its basketball team, which had won two national championships in the early 1960s, but also because he liked the campus and people. He was particularly impressed by Coach John Wooden and believed that he could help him achieve his goal of playing professional basketball.

Abdul-Jabbar excelled both as a student and as a basketball player. As a freshman, he was particularly touched by reading *The Autobiography of Malcolm X*, which described Islam as a religion in which all people were equal and judged on the basis of their actions, rather than their race. In a profile in *Ebony* magazine, he recommended the book to all Americans, both white and black, as essential reading.

As an athlete, Abdul-Jabbar often found himself tired during his college career because he continued to grow, finally reaching his full height of seven feet two inches. While in college, he practiced jumping to reach a line eighteen inches above the basketball rim. He also developed his trademark skyhook shot, an elevated shot that flew through the air and sank into the net – one that no other player has perfected. The shot was effective because it was made with Abdul-Jabbar's back to the man guarding him, thus protecting the shot with his body. Because he was able to jump so high, no one was able to stop him from scoring once he had the ball. However, as a team player, Abdul-Jabbar did not engage in a one-man show. He always passed the ball to someone else if he was unable to score.

Abdul-Jabbar began to play on the Varsity team during his sophomore year at U.C.L.A. He had not played as a freshman because freshmen were barred from the Varsity team. He scored a U.C.L.A. record early in the season during a game against the University of Southen California (U.S.C.) when he scored fifty-six points. In a later game, U.S.C. assigned three players to guard Abdul-Jabbar to prevent him from scoring. Unfazed, he scored nineteen points and used numerous opportunities to pass the ball to teammates who then scored to win the game. By playing as a true teammate, Abdul-Jabbar demonstrated his dedication to a team victory rather than personal glory. The team was undefeated that season and went on to win the National Collegiate Athletic Association (N.C.A.A.) Tournament. Abdul-Jabbar was selected Most Outstanding Player.

During the summer after his sophomore year, Abdul-Jabbar worked for the New York City Housing Authority teaching basketball to children. Although the job did not pay well, he found that he enjoyed working with children and could have a positive impact on their lives.

When he returned to U.C.L.A. in the fall, Abdul-Jabbar was surprised to learn that the College Basketball Rules Committee had made dunking the ball illegal

during the summer, a ruling that became popularly known as "the Alcindor Rule" because he had been the first player to make extensive use of the move. Because this had been one of his best moves, he had to learn to use different shots. Although he was initially angry about the change, he later recognized that being pushed to learn new shots made him a more effective player professionally when he had to use a variety of shots to score. An eye injury during the season kept him out of several games, which the team lost. However, it recovered with his return and won its remaining games, as well as the N.C.A.A. Tournament. Abdul-Jabbar was again selected Most Outstanding Player.

Despite his success in basketball and academics, Abdul-Jabbar had not found spiritual satisfaction. Disillusioned with the Roman Catholic faith of his parents, he began searching for a new religion that would allow him to maintain his belief in monotheism (a single God) and continue to be a person of high moral character while living a good life. A friend, recalling how he had been inspired by *The Autobiography of Malcolm X*, suggested that he read the Quran. Impressed by the Quran's declaration of the equality of all believers, Abdul-Jabbar spent the summer of 1968 studying Islamic cultures. He attended the mosque to learn more about Islam, how to prepare for Friday prayers, and to memorize the Quran. After a month of study, he proclaimed the Muslim declaration of faith (*shahadah*) that "There is no god but The God and Muhammad is the Messenger of God," and became a Muslim. He was given the name Abdul-Kareem, or "Servant of the Generous," at the mosque for religious purposes, but remained Lew Alcindor at school and on the basketball court. The split of name usage reflected the identity crisis he felt at this time.

Abdul-Jabbar was also profoundly influenced by a friend, Hamaas Abdul-Khaalis, who taught him to judge others by how they lived their lives and not to base criticism on ethnicity or color. He taught Abdul-Jabbar to care about others if they were good people and to realize that some people from every group will always live without morals or values, but that judging them on the basis of their skin color is wrong. Thanks to Khaalis, Abdul-Jabbar was finally able to let go of his anger against whites. Shortly afterward, he received the name Jabbar and became Kareem Abdul-Jabbar, or "Noble and Generous Servant of the All-Powerful God." He also became more ritually observant, avoiding alcohol and pork, performing ritual ablutions, praying five times daily, and taking off his shoes prior to entering someone's home. He took charitable giving seriously, providing a down-payment for a mosque and community center in Washington, DC, as well as contributing money to other Muslims in need and caring for his parents.

Abdul-Jabbar's conversion was met with open hostility by his parents, who were profoundly hurt by his rejection of their faith. He has commented that it took many years to overcome the hurt and divisions his conversion generated within the family, but that his parents ultimately came to terms with it. His conversion also led to his increasing isolation at U.C.L.A. He endured a lonely senior year during which he had no other Muslims with whom to communicate, no one with whom he could share his new ideas and beliefs, and discuss his religious devotion. Even harder was the realization that he no longer enjoyed playing basketball.

During his senior year, Abdul-Jabbar made an important new friend, the martial artist Bruce Lee. Abdul-Jabbar learned martial arts, which helped him to be more polished and graceful on the basketball court. Lee also encouraged Abdul-Jabbar during his last year at U.C.L.A., where he led the team to its third consecutive N.C.A.A. championship and was selected Most Outstanding Player for the third consecutive year. With Abdul-Jabbar on the team, U.C.L.A. broke the record for the most consecutive N.C.A.A. titles and for the most consecutive tournaments won. Out of the ninety games played with Abdul-Jabbar on the team, U.C.L.A. had lost only two. He became the highest scorer in U.C.L.A. history.

Abdul-Jabbar turned to professional basketball in 1969 when he was drafted by the Milwaukee Bucks. Because he had not yet made his conversion known, he continued to live a double life. Socializing was difficult because he neither drank nor gambled. Professional basketball also presented some major changes in terms of playing style and strategy. College basketball typically uses zone defense as a strategy. Professional basketball does not permit zone defense. Instead, teams play man to man. Professional basketball is also more physically interactive than college basketball. Abdul-Jabbar was not accustomed to being pushed on court.

Abdul-Jabbar's new teammates quickly learned that he could be counted on to score, so the team based its strategies on getting the ball to him. If they failed and the other team got the ball, the plan was for Abdul-Jabbar to block the shot. It took the team one half-season to perfect its strategy. The Bucks finished the season second in the division and Abdul-Jabbar was named Rookie of the Year.

The team's strategy was changed in the 1970–1971 season due to the addition of Oscar Robertson, who excelled in assists. The new strategy was based on getting the ball to either Robertson or Abdul-Jabbar. Although it was only Abdul-Jabbar's second year playing professionally, the Bucks won the N.B.A. Championship, sweeping the series in just four games. Abdul-Jabbar was named the N.B.A.'s Most Valuable Player and earned the reputation of the best player in the center position.

The 1971–1972 season was slightly less successful for the team, which lost to the LA Lakers. Despite the loss, Abdul-Jabbar was again named Most Valuable Player. He publicly announced his conversion to Islam in the fall of 1971 and legally changed his name. He also married Habiba (formerly Janice Brown), with whom he had a daughter, Habiba, in 1972.

The year 1973 was one of tragedy for Abdul-Jabbar. In January, his friend Khaalis's home was attacked. The perpetrators shot everyone they found, resulting in the deaths of several people, including some of Khaalis's children. Khaalis himself was not home. Threats were also made against Abdul-Jabbar, who took on a police escort, left the country, and traveled around the world. Although he enjoyed his travels and learning about the traditions of different cultures, his personal life remained in turmoil. He and his wife separated and divorced, and his friend Bruce Lee died. Abdul-Jabbar decided to pour all of his energy and frustration into basketball.

The 1974–1975 season proved difficult. Although the Bucks had the best record in the league, they lost the N.B.A. Championship, in part because Abdul-Jabbar had been sidelined by injuries, including a broken bone in his hand and an eye injury caused by another player. After this incident, he wore protective glasses to play. Changes on the team, including Oscar Robertson's retirement and the trade of several players, led Abdul-Jabbar to ask to be traded, as well. He was traded to the LA Lakers for the 1975–1976 season.

The return to Los Angeles boosted Abdul-Jabbar's spirits, leading him to turn in one of the best seasons of his career. He led the league in rebounds and blocked shots, was second in scoring, and was chosen as the Most Valuable Player for the fourth time. Despite his phenomenal performance, the team finished fourth in the division. The next season was better, but the team still did not win the championship.

After his big-screen debut in 1978 in a martial arts film – *Game of Death* with Bruce Lee – Abdul-Jabbar points to 1979 as a pivotal year in both his personal and professional life. He met his second wife, Cheryl Pistano, who helped him to learn to appreciate his fans and their admiration for how he played basketball. Professionally, the 1978–1979 season ended in frustration as the team lost the championship again. Recognizing Abdul-Jabbar's discouragement, T.V. sportscaster Ted Dawson organized a public drive encouraging people to send telegrams and letters to Abdul-Jabbar and the Lakers to let them know how much they were appreciated. Abdul-Jabbar recalls that, within days, the mail was piling up in stacks. The support meant so much to him that he kept every letter he received. He also began to work on his public image and offer more of himself as he realized how much people liked him.

The elusive N.B.A. championship finally came to the Lakers in 1980, after Earvin "Magic" Johnson joined the team. Abdul-Jabbar was injured during game five of the championships, but had the doctor tape his ankle so he could finish the game. Despite the pain and inability to jump, he scored forty points, the last five of which won the game. After the game, he finally headed to the hospital for X-rays. He was unable to play the final two games because of his injuries, but was still selected Most Valuable Player that year.

During the off-season, Abdul-Jabbar became a Hollywood star playing the part of Roger the co-pilot in the movie *Airplane*. However, tragedy also struck while he was on the road, as his house caught on fire and he lost everything he owned, including his jazz albums and four priceless Qurans from the Middle Ages. His wife, Cheryl, and son, Amir, had been home asleep when the fire broke out, but escaped. He was overwhelmed by the worldwide public outpouring of affection that resulted.

Although most professional basketball players retire in their early thirties, Abdul-Jabbar was still a strong player at thirty-eight. During the 1984–1985 season, some had expressed concern about his age after the Lakers lost the first game of the season finals. Before the second game, Abdul-Jabbar personally apologized to the team for not having played as well as he could have during the first game. He promised to do a better job during the second game, inspiring his teammates to pull together to win the game and, ultimately, the finals. Abdul-Jabbar scored thirty points during the game, breaking the record for the most points scored in the playoffs by a single player. He was named Most Valuable Player and the team was greeted by a welcome parade upon its return to Los Angeles, a moment that Abdul-Jabbar considers to be one of the highlights of his career.

Abdul-Jabbar played his final year as a professional in the 1988–1989 season at the age of forty-two after twenty years of professional basketball – an all-time record. A six-time Most Valuable Player, he had led his teams to six N.B.A. Championships. A special ceremony was held for him at Madison Square Garden, where he received numerous gifts and was visited by old teammates stretching as far back as high school. He was toasted by his coach as "the greatest player ever" and was honored in Philadelphia, Boston, New York, and Los Angeles, where a street was named for him. Before the last game of the regular season, the entire city of Los Angeles honored him with a tribute. He was given a Rolls Royce by his teammates and received a telegram from the President of the United States. His final game was attended by his parents and children. His son, Amir, sang the national anthem. Every player wore protective goggles like his for the game.

Immediately following his retirement, Abdul-Jabbar withdrew from basketball.

Considered one of the greatest players of all time, he was elected to the Basketball Hall of Fame in 1995 and was selected one of the fifty Greatest Players in N.B.A. History in 1996. He holds the N.B.A. record for the most minutes played (57,446), the most points scored (38,387), and the most field goals (15,837).

Retirement from basketball freed Abdul-Jabbar to pursue another life-long interest – the restoration of African-Americans to American history. He worked on two documentaries, one about African-American troops who had helped to liberate the Nazi death camps at the end of World War II and one about civil rights activist Vernon Johns. He also wrote four books, including two autobiographies and a series of biographies of prominent African-Americans designed to make information about African-American heroes available and accessible to young people and to demonstrate the positive role African-Americans have played in American history.

After more than ten years away from the N.B.A., Abdul-Jabbar resumed contact with basketball by spending a season coaching high-school basketball on an Apache reservation. He chose the reservation both because he is a quarter Native American (his mother was half-Cherokee) and because he hoped to draw attention to the conditions of poverty that exist on reservations and to open opportunities for colleges to welcome reservation children into their athletics programs. He has offered his support to the expansion of the N.B.A. to include European players and is an advocate of the W.N.B.A. (Women's National Basketball Association). He has been a leading voice in the call for greater accountability of players on issues such as public drunkenness, violence during games, and drug abuse, and in encouraging schools to play a stronger role in highlighting the violence, death, and loss that accompany such lifestyles.

Abdul-Jabbar is a frequent speaker at schools and basketball camps, encouraging children to work on being solid on the fundamentals of basketball before concentrating on more specialized moves. He recommends that they learn to play in all positions, rather than setting their sights on a particular one, and encourages them to play, even if they make mistakes, believing that mistakes present opportunities to learn. Most importantly, he calls upon children to set educational goals and dreams for themselves, as well as sports ambitions. He founded Kareem's Kids to encourage children to stay in school and is involved with a variety of literacy groups.

Further reading

Abdul-Jabbar, Kareem. *Giant Steps*. New York: Bantam Books, 1983
—— *A Season on the Reservation: My Sojourn with the White Mountain Apache*. New York: William Morrow & Company, 2000
Abdul-Jabbar, Kareem and Alan Steinberg. *Black Profiles in Courage: A Legacy of African-American Achievement*. New York: Avon Books, 1997
Knapp, Ron. *Top Ten Stars of the N.C.A.A. Men's Basketball Tournament*. Berkeley Heights, NJ: Enslow Publishers, Inc., 2001
Kneib, Martha. *Kareem Abdul-Jabbar: Basketball Hall of Famers*. New York: Rosen Publishing Group, Inc., 2002
"Talk with Kareem Abdul-Jabbar," transcript from Time.com Special Report: Black History Month, February 25, 1999, www.time.com/community/transripts/1999/022599jabbar.html

Abdus Salam (1926–1996)

The first Muslim to win a Nobel Prize, Abdus Salam was a prominent physicist who used his status as a Nobel Prize winner to call for scientific and technological development and support for scientific research in the Third World.

Abdus Salam was born in Jhang in pre-partition India (later in Pakistan), on January 29, 1926. He credits his father, an official in the Department of Education, with teaching him the Islamic values that he put to use throughout his career and with providing him with the foundations of a Western education. His belief in the compatibility of faith and science and in moral responsibility drove his dedication to Third World development.

An outstanding student by the age of fourteen, Abdus Salam earned the highest marks ever recorded for the matriculation exam at the University of Punjab. He was awarded a scholarship to the Government College of the University of Punjab, where he received his master's degree in 1946. Although this would normally have led to a job in the civil service, he was offered a scholarship to St. John's College in Cambridge, from which he graduated with honors with a bachelor's degree with a double first in mathematics and physics in 1949. In 1950, he was awarded the Smith's Prize from Cambridge University for the most outstanding pre-doctoral contribution to physics. Although he worked for a time in experimental physics, he preferred theoretical physics because it required creativity. He completed his Ph.D. in theoretical physics at Cambridge University. The publication of his doctoral thesis on quantum electrodynamics in 1951 earned him an international reputation.

Following graduation, Abdus Salam returned to Pakistan, where he taught mathematics at Government College in Lahore. He became the head of the mathematics department at Punjab University in 1952. Although he had returned to Pakistan with the goal of establishing a school for research, this proved impossible in a country that was only five years old. His closest colleague lived in Bombay and there were no conferences for him to attend to meet with other colleagues. Because Pakistan was working to establish colleges that could produce well-rounded students, professors were expected not only to teach, but also to take on responsible positions for extracurricular activities. Frustrated by the lack of time to pursue his research, he went abroad again, vowing to establish his school at a later date. He accepted a lectureship at Cambridge University in 1954 and became a full professor of theoretical physics at Imperial College, London, in 1957. He served there until his death in 1996, but continued to visit Pakistan as an adviser on science policy.

Abdus Salam's contributions in the physics of elementary particles span forty years and include the two-component neutrino theory; the prediction of the inevitable parity violation in weak interaction; the gauging of the unification of weak and electromagnetic interactions; the prediction of the existence of weak neutral currents and W,Z particles before their experimental discovery; the discovery of the symmetry properties of elementary particles and unitary symmetry; the renormalization of meson theories; the discovery of the role of gravity theory in particle physics; the unification of electroweak with strong nuclear forces; grand unification; and related prediction of proton-decay; the formulation of supersymmetry theory, in particular the formation of superspace and the formalism of superfields; development of the Kaluza–Klein theories; and work on superstrings.

Abdus Salam was jointly awarded the Nobel Prize for Physics in 1979 for his work on the "Weinberg-Salam Theory," described as "the mathematical and conceptual synthesis of electromagnetic and weak interactions." The award was unusual in that it was granted for theoretical work that had not yet been proven experimentally, although later experimentation proved the theory correct. That same year, he was also awarded the Einstein Medal by U.N.E.S.C.O. for his dedication to building world science. He was the youngest fellow of Britain's Royal Society and published about two hundred and fifty papers on the physics

of elementary particles, as well as a number of papers on scientific and educational policies for developing countries, particularly Pakistan. He received numerous international awards and medals for his scientific work, including the Hopkins Prize at Cambridge University for the most outstanding contribution to physics during 1957–1958; the Adams Prize (Cambridge University) in 1958; the first Maxwell Medal and Award from the Physical Society of London in 1961; the Hughes Medal from the Royal Society of London in 1964; the J. Robert Oppenheimer Memorial Medal and Prize at the University of Miami in 1971; and the Guthrie Medal and Prize from the Institute of Physics, London. He received thirty-six honorary degrees from universities throughout the world and was a member of many international scientific academies, societies, and orders.

In addition to his scientific research, Abdus Salam worked to develop a variety of scientific fields in Pakistan, including health, agriculture, mathematics, physics, and chemistry. He served as a member of the Pakistan Atomic Energy Commission, was a member of the Scientific Commission of Pakistan, and was the chief scientific adviser to the president from 1961 until 1974. For his service to Pakistan, Abdus Salam received the Sitara-i Pakistan in 1959, the Pride of Performance Medal and Award in 1959, and the Order of Nishan-e Imtiaz (the highest civilian award) in 1979.

Abdus Salam worked throughout his professional life to encourage the sharing of First World science and technology with Third World countries. He was driven by his belief that there should be no permanent domination of science by a single nation because scientific thought is the heritage of all of humanity. He was disturbed by widespread poverty and hunger in the twentieth century despite the existence of sufficient technical, scientific, and material resources to eliminate disease, poverty, and premature death across the globe. He considered the raising of living standards everywhere to a "decent human level" to be the most important global goal, constituting a collective world responsibility and moral issue. He called on humanity to rise above economic self-interest to the rational consideration of the needs of the world that he believed should result in a broader and fairer distribution of the world's wealth. He particularly called for an end to the arms race by the superpowers, which he believed represented an obscene waste of resources in the promotion of death and destruction at a time when both were already abundantly present in the Third World. Rather than arms, he called on the superpowers to invest in the eradication of poverty, hunger, and disease, the creation of jobs, the provision of food, and the improvement and expansion of education in the Third World as a wiser, lasting, and more far-reaching investment.

Abdus Salam's convictions led him to formulate and support a variety of initiatives promoting Third World development. He served on a number of United Nations committees concerned with the advancement of science and technology in developing countries, including the U.N. Conference for the Peaceful Use of Atomic Energy, the U.N. Advisory Committee on Science and Technology, the U.N. Panel and Foundation Committee for the United Nations University, and the Council for the University for Peace. Although he later realized how weak and fragile the U.N. was, he remained dedicated to the concept of an organization that brought together all of humanity to work for peace and betterment for the entire world. He was also a proponent of the concept of "world taxation" introduced in the 1970s, according to which international trade would be taxed in order to give the proceeds to the poorest and least developed countries, part of which he believed should be invested in programs for scientific research.

In addition to his international calls for action, Abdus Salam worked at a personal level to provide more resources for scientific research and development in the Third World. He created new physics centers and summer and winter schools in Pakistan, Peru, Jordan, Sudan, and Colombia and new centers for research in mathematics and physics in Benin, Morocco, Malaysia, and Tanzania. His most important endeavor was the creation of the International Centre for Theoretical Physics (I.C.T.P.) in Trieste, Italy, in 1964, for which he served as founder and director. Established as a research school for scientists from the developing world, the I.C.T.P. brings together scientists from a variety of countries for the purpose of conducting and discussing research. Supported by the U.N.D.P. and the Italian Government, the I.C.T.P. is both a U.N.E.S.C.O. organization and a branch of the International Atomic Energy Agency (I.A.E.A.). It has played a pivotal role in technology transfer to the Third World.

Because of his personal experience as a scientist from a developing country, Abdus Salam knew first hand the difficulties of finding both institutional and financial support for scientific research. His goal in establishing the I.C.T.P. was to provide deserving Third World scientists with the same stimulating atmosphere that American and European scientists enjoyed. The provision of associateships during summer vacations was designed to provide Third World scientists with the opportunity to work among their peers in research and leaders in the field in order to help them advance, recharge, and be refreshed for their return to their own countries to teach and continue their research.

Abdus Salam's concern for Third World development led him to call for the establishment of the Third World Academy of Sciences (T.W.A.S.). T.W.A.S. was launched in 1985 as the first international forum to promote science in the Third World by recognizing and supporting excellence in scientific research by Third World scientists, promoting contact between researchers from developing countries and the global scientific community, and encouraging scientific research on major Third World problems. In 1988, T.W.A.S. established the Third World Network of Scientific Organizations (T.W.N.S.O.) to promote the development of the historically underdeveloped South. In the South, T.W.N.S.O. encouraged greater cooperation and investment in science, technology, and institutional and legal support both to promote indigenous development and to discourage the continued brain drain of qualified scientists from Third World countries. It also called for an expanded public-affairs role for scientists in national decision making. The North was asked to participate through financial investment, the provision of free access to scientific literature, and the establishment of additional U.N. agencies and international centers for science.

Abdus Salam was widely recognized for his contributions toward peace and the promotion of international scientific collaboration. He received the Atoms for Peace Medal and Award from the Atoms for Peace Foundation in 1968; the Peace Medal from Charles University in Prague in 1981; the Premio Umberto Biancamano in Italy in 1986; the Dayemi International Peace Award from Bangladesh in 1986; and the Genova Sviluppo dei Popoli Prize from Italy in 1988.

Although he was widely decorated for both his scientific and development work, Abdus Salam never used any of his prize money for himself or his family, favoring instead his causes. The monetary award that accompanied the Atoms for Peace Medal and Award was used to set up a fund for young Pakistani physicists to visit the I.C.T.P. The Nobel Prize money was used exclusively for the benefit of physicists from developing countries. Having set the example, Abdus

Salam called upon his fellow Muslims, particularly the oil-wealthy countries of the Gulf, to contribute $1 billion annually to the creation of a fund for physics for Islamic, Arab, and developing-country scientists in order to make the best possible use of high-level talented scientists. He asserted the need for Muslims, as one-fifth of the world's population, to recover their past role as major contributors to the development of science and medicine as a matter of self-respect. He hoped to set up an Islamic science foundation sponsored by Muslim countries and run as a non-political, scientific institution by eminent scientists and technologists from the Muslim world.

Abdus Salam died in 1996.

Further reading

Lai, C.H. and Azim Kidwai, eds. *Ideals and Realities: Selected Essays of Abdus Salam*, 3rd ed. Singapore: World Scientific Publishing Co. Pte. Ltd., 1989
www.ictp.trieste.it/ – website for the I.C.T.P.
www.nobel.se – website for the Nobel Prize

Rabia al-Adawiyya, or Rabia the Mystic (c. 717–801)

A mystic and saint credited with introducing the theme of the selfless love of God into the Islamic mystical tradition, Rabia al-Adawiyya has long been revered as one of the greatest teachers and practitioners of Sufism.

Rabia al-Adawiyya was born around 717 in Basra (in contemporary Iraq), where she spent most of her life. Most of what is known about her comes from biographies written several centuries after her death and records of her prayers and other religious teachings. There are no known contemporary biographies. As is typical of the histories of the lives of saints in both the Muslim and Christian traditions, legend and fact are intertwined in her life's history.

Rabia is believed to have been the fourth daughter of a poor family.

According to legend, the family was so poor that there were no lamps, oil, or swaddling cloths in the home when she was born. As a Sufi (mystic), her father relied exclusively on God for his needs. Upon Rabia's birth, he had a vision of the Prophet Muhammad telling him to send a letter to the Emir of Basra to admonish him for failing to fulfill his vow to pray. Upon receiving the letter, the emir sent money to Rabia's father and made a donation to the poor, thus providing sustenance for Rabia.

Rabia's parents are believed to have died during a widespread famine when she was very young. She is believed to have been captured and sold as a slave. According to what is probably legend, one day, while engaged in work, she was approached by a stranger. In order to avoid him, she ran away, slipped, fell and dislocated her wrist. As she lay in the dust, she prayed to God to assert that she sought only to serve Him and to ask if she was satisfying Him. In response, she heard a voice assuring her that she would rank with those nearest to God in Heaven. After this experience, Rabia returned to the household of her master where she fasted and carried out her appointed tasks during the day and prayed and served God during the night. One night, her master woke up in the middle of the night and saw her praying, enveloped by light in a manner indicating her status as a saint. He set her free the next morning.

Rabia journeyed into the desert for a time and then obtained a cell for herself where she engaged in devotional worship. She later returned to Basra where she built her own retreat for prayer and carrying out acts of piety. She remained celibate for her entire life. None of her biographies mention a teacher for her mystical pursuits, indicating that her life was a true reflection of the individual's pursuit of the Divine.

Rabia lived to be almost ninety years old, despite her ascetic lifestyle. Although she was physically weak in her old age, she remained mentally strong and was able to serve as both guide and spiritual director to those who sought her counsel. She always prayed with her shroud in sight so as to be constantly reminded of death, which she understood as an opportunity for eternal joining with the Divine. Her trembling at the thought of death was thus an expression of joy, rather than fear or apprehension. Similarly, her lifelong fear of fire was not due to fear of physical burning in Hell, but because Hell represented an eternity of separation from the Divine.

Rabia's reputation as a saint was due to two critical factors: her complete renunciation of the world and worldly matters, including marriage, in order to serve God exclusively; and her addition of the concept of selfless love of God into the Sufi tradition. These combined factors led her admirers to describe her as a woman of outstanding character who led a life of blameless holiness. She enjoyed a reputation as a gifted mystic during her lifetime. Although her admirers liked to credit her with miracles and the ability to distribute blessings, Rabia herself denied these abilities, fearing that an enhanced reputation might lead to egotism on her part or cause her to be distracted from her service to and love of God.

Rabia's reputation as a miracle worker was a standard part of the credentialing process to sainthood. Accounts of her life indicate that the miracles that occurred in her life benefited her alone and were considered reflections of God's favor upon and care for her. They also served to justify her dedication to complete reliance on God alone for all of her needs. The miracles of her life typically involved provisions of food and other necessities.

Rabia's choice of a celibate life was unusual for a Muslim woman of her time. Normally, a Muslim woman would have married and raised a family. Rabia, however, feared that marriage and children would have distracted and hindered her from her service and love of God. Because she believed that she had passed out of phenomenal existence into a purely spiritual existence, she saw no need for marriage, despite receiving numerous offers from a variety of admirers, including fellow Sufis, founders of Sufi monastic orders, and the Emir of Basra. Although all had offered her maintenance and a more comfortable existence, Rabia preferred to live in poverty, relying only on God to provide for her. She feared that physical comfort would distract her from her service of God. Nevertheless, most of her associates were male disciples and friends. There is little information in the historical records about her relationships with other women apart from her female servant.

Besides rejecting marriage and material wealth, Rabia also rejected and resisted her physical needs, such as food and sleep. She ate only what God provided for her and considered sleep a temptation. Accounts of her life unanimously record her existence as a life of prayer, both day and night. She was reported to have prayed a thousand prostrations each day and night, not to request forgiveness, but so that, on the Day of Resurrection, the Prophet Muhammad would be able to say of her that this had been her work. For Rabia, prayer was not an opportunity to make supplications on behalf of herself or others, but a moment for "loving conversation" with God in which communion with God and perfect satisfaction in His presence could be achieved.

Rabia refused to give in to illness in her pursuit of service to God, believing that even illness and suffering were part of God's will for her and thus to be endured with fortitude. Her capacity to make herself oblivious to physical comfort and pain and to rise above them were typical hallmarks of ascetics. She explained her refusal to give in to sleep and illness as the result of a serious illness that caused her to sleep at night. Afterwards, she had a vision that chastised her for allowing her physical needs during illness to overshadow her dedication to prayer. Ever after, she refused to sleep at night, using the night to pray and test her fortitude and determination to serve God. She allowed herself only a light sleep at dawn from which she would awake in fear of giving in to the temptation to sleep some more.

Although she considered worldly goods and benefits to be sources of temptation, Rabia's dedication to service of God was not undertaken due to a sense of gloom, doom or misery, as was the habit of other ascetics. Rather than the mortification of the flesh associated with other ascetics, she undertook her service with joy and radiance, reflecting her love of God and the peace that accompanied it. In her most famous prayer, she asked, "O Lord, if I worship You out of fear of Hell, burn me in Hell, and if I worship You in hope of Paradise, exclude me from Paradise, but if I worship You for Your own sake, do not deny me Your beauty."

Rabia's service of God was based on an individualistic approach that emphasized the need for closeness between God and the believer, rather than academic learning. Consequently, her teachings are not heavily based on the Quran or example of the Prophet Muhammad (*Sunna*). There is also no attention given to community building, relationships between human beings or business transactions. Her exclusive focus on the desired direct relationship between the individual and God required no intermediary.

Rabia's life and teachings reflect the stages that guide Sufis on the Way to the Divine. The first stage is repentance, which requires remorse for disobedience, determination not to sin again, and immediate abandonment of sin. Although Rabia had a strong sense of sin and the need to repent and be forgiven, she considered the true hurtfulness of sin to be the separation it caused between the believer and God, rather than its potential for resulting in punishment in the Afterlife. She considered repentance to be a gift because it provided a way to remove the barrier between the believer and God.

The second stage is patience, which helps the adept hold out for greater reward in the midst of adversity. Rabia taught patience through her own example, demonstrating that those who are patient will be cared for by God. Her example further demonstrated that gratitude is a complementary quality to patience. She believed that gratitude should be expressed for both blessings and chastisements because both reflected God's attention to the believer. For Rabia, gratitude was to focus on the Giver, rather than the gift. Thus, true gratitude could best be expressed by constant thanksgiving for God's goodness, regardless of one's life circumstances.

The third stage for Rabia was poverty, which she defined as complete self-loss and lack of dependence on material things. Because she considered Paradise to be a state of contemplation of the Face of God, rather than a physical garden of sensual delights, living a life of poverty on Earth simply served to prepare for the eternal activity of pure contemplation and adoration of God.

The final stage is love, which includes seeing God in His beauty and experiencing the satisfaction, longing, and fellowship that result from the mystic union of the believer and God. Although Rabia was not the first Sufi to realize that the Way to God must be sought through love, she was the first to stress the theme of love and combine it with the unveiling of the Divine at the end of the Way. She was also the first to teach the doctrine of disinterested love of God which sought only God's glory and the carrying out of the Divine Will.

The attention given to Rabia in the historical literature is important not only because it demonstrates the important role that a woman played in the development of Sufism, but also because it reflects a broad trend in Sufism of recognizing that God bestows His favor upon both men and women alike. Historically, Sufism declared the responsibilities of men and women to be equal and encouraged both to join. Women who joined a Sufi order were often freed of the responsibilities of marriage and child-bearing and rearing, enjoying instead the independence and freedom that came with celibate life. Women saints are prominent in Sufi literature and are typically credited with the performance of good deeds and miracles, engaging in acts of charity, and pursuing religious learning. Their shrines are spread throughout the Muslim world, particularly in North Africa, and serve as popular sites for pilgrimage. In their devotion to Sufism, women and men alike had the opportunity to attain the rank of sainthood. However, because their lifestyles and activities did not fit the norms of orthodox visions of Islam and Muslim life, particularly where women were concerned, Sufis were often denounced by conservatives who believed that according such status to human beings was inappropriate, if not heretical.

As the greatest of Islam's women mystics and the woman who made the most significant contributions to Sufism, Rabia was held in high esteem by later Sufis and is considered an authoritative teacher of Sufism along with the great male Sufis. Her high status is reflected in the prominence of the writers who mentioned her. For many Sufis, Rabia was a "second spotless Mary" who exemplified the mystical tradition of Islam. She died in 801 and was buried in Basra.

Further reading

Arberry, A.J., trans. *Muslim Saints and Mystics*. New York: Oxford University Press, 1966

Chittick, William C. *Sufism: A Short Introduction*. Oxford: Oneworld Publications, 2000

Sedgwick, Mark J. *Sufism: The Essentials.* Cairo: American University in Cairo Press, 2000

Smith, Margaret. *Muslim Women Mystics: The Life and Work of Rabi'a and Other Women Mystics in Islam.* Oxford: Oneworld Publications, 2001

Trimingham, J. Spencer. *The Sufi Orders in Islam*, with foreword by John O. Voll. New York: Oxford University Press, 1998

The Aga Khan, Prince Karim IV (b. 1936)

The spiritual leader of the Ismaili Muslim community, the Aga Khan is recognized internationally as a philanthropist who has promoted development and architecture around the world through the Aga Khan Foundation.

Popularly known as the Aga Khan, Prince Karim Aga Khan IV was born on December 13, 1936, in Geneva, Switzerland. His mother, Princess Tajuddawlah Aly Khan, was the daughter of a British peer. His father, Prince Aly Khan, served as Pakistan's ambassador to the United Nations and was best known in the United States for his marriage to the American actress Rita Hayworth. The Aga Khan spent his early childhood in Nairobi, Kenya. He received his elementary and secondary education at the Le Rosey School in Switzerland.

The Forty-Ninth Imam of the Ismaili Muslims, The Aga Khan traces his ancestry to the Prophet Muhammad. He inherited his title and position from his grandfather in 1957 after both his father and grandfather are said to have recognized his exceptional gifts and potential. At the time, he was a twenty-year-old undergraduate student at Harvard University. He earned a B.A. in Islamic history with honors in 1958. A resident of Chantilly, France, he is married with three children, all of whom are active in the imamate's development and cultural activities. He is frequently accompanied by his daughter, Princess Zahra, as a sign of his support for raising the status of Muslim women.

As its spiritual head, the Aga Khan is responsible for overseeing the welfare and progress of the Ismaili Muslim community, which numbers about 20 million and is scattered throughout twenty-five countries, with concentrations in West and Central Asia, Africa, the Middle East, North America, and Western Europe. Historically, the Ismailis have made important contributions to Islamic civilization, including the founding of Al-Azhar University, the oldest university in the Middle East, and Dar al-Ilm (the Academy of Science) in Egypt. As major patrons of science, medicine, and astronomy, the Ismailis have a long history of encouraging intellectual freedom, education, self-reliance, solidarity, character, and tolerance. The current Aga Khan has been faithful to this tradition, supporting a variety of educational causes, working to build relationships between various Muslim communities and between Muslims and non-Muslims, and charging his followers to believe in God and be good citizens of whatever country they live in. Because he has interpreted Islam as a thinking, spiritual faith that teaches compassion, tolerance, and the inherent dignity of human beings, the Aga Khan's own teachings emphasize social commitment and intellectual inquiry as the appropriate means of solving problems of modernity and faith.

The Ismailis consider the Aga Khan to be God's representative on earth who works on God's behalf. They pay dues to him, which serve as the source of his wealth. Some have criticized the accumulation of such wealth in the hands of a single individual. However, the Aga Khan has used a large portion of this wealth to fund a variety of philanthropic and humanitarian causes throughout the world. He is known internationally for his support of architecture, education, human welfare and well-being, and the flourishing of culture. He has personally undertaken restoration of some of the great monuments of Islamic civilization. Much of his work is accomplished through the Aga Khan Foundation.

The Aga Khan Foundation was established in 1967 as a private, nondenominational, philanthropic, international development agency seeking to relate Islam's humanitarian philosophy to modern development. Funded by the Aga Khan, the Ismaili community, and a variety of foundations, individuals, partners, and local and international donor agencies, the foundation has put the ethics and ideals of Islam to use in addressing the socio-economic needs of the developing world, both Muslim and non-Muslim, including the promotion and strengthening of community participation and the development of women, the family, and the environment. It specifically focuses on health, development, and education in underserved and poor communities. Headquartered in Geneva, the foundation has programs on four continents: Africa (Uganda, Tanzania, and Kenya); Asia (Bangladesh, Pakistan, and India); Europe (the United Kingdom and Portugal); and North America (the United States and Canada). It is particularly active in rural areas of Pakistan, India, and Bangladesh.

His desire to alleviate poverty and human suffering through development also led the Aga Khan to found the Aga Khan Development Network to improve living conditions and opportunities in the developing world while maintaining a balance between material and spiritual needs. One of the world's largest private development institutions, the network works for the common public good of the location, regardless of the religious affiliation or country of origin of its inhabitants, and supports projects related to education, health, rural development, architecture, and the development of the private sector. Major projects include the 1985 founding of the Aga Khan University in Pakistan as a center for higher education and research on the health needs of the developing world and the establishment of the Aga Khan Hospital in Karachi, Pakistan, to provide health care for people of all classes, races, and faiths. In the late 1990s, the network became involved in development and international aid in Central Asia, a region shattered by the collapse of the Soviet Union, civil wars, and the rise of militant Islamic extremism in the face of poverty, political oppression, and joblessness. In addition to a developmental program in Gorno-Badakhstan, Tajikistan, it has worked to establish a Central Asian University to study the social and economic needs of the populations of the mountainous regions. The Aga Khan personally provided $33,000 to pay for studies by Kazakh students from needy families. He has also sponsored courses on Islamic civilization at a variety of American educational institutions.

One of the network's most famous programs is the Aga Khan Award for Architecture, which was launched in 1977 to encourage the use of Islamic cultural resources in the contemporary built environment. The award grew out of the Aga Khan's construction of schools, hospitals, community centers, and community buildings throughout the Muslim world and in countries with substantial Muslim minorities. He sought to build structures that were culturally meaningful, regionally appropriate, and materially authentic, and to make contemporary architecture as creative and powerful as it had been in the past. Ideally, he hoped to encourage continuity with the rich Islamic heritage of the past while reinterpreting it for a modern context and modern purposes, particularly with respect to urban environments. However, when he prepared to give instructions to the architects, he had difficulty finding the appropriate terms of reference.

The Aga Khan assembled a team of historians and architects to study

Islamic architecture from the past and contemporary building methods and considerations, particularly the changes in physical environment, in order to establish the criteria he desired for his own projects. As the team engaged in its work, it became clear that the Muslim community over time had lost both some of its competence in and knowledge of architecture. The award was thus founded to promote a synthesis of restoration, renewal, and contemporary needs to project Islamic architecture into the twenty-first century by questioning how and what inherited and new competencies should be used. The goal was to encourage social and economic development and cultural continuity through the construction of contemporary structures, such as airports, hotels, universities, and buildings related to the leisure industry. The Aga Khan has expressed the hope that, in the future, greater attention will be given to the use of nature, including landscape architecture, public spaces, parks, and use of the natural environment.

The award is issued only once every three years. Nominees are evaluated by an international team of historians, architects, and philosophers, on the basis of the aesthetics, philosophy, and spiritual value of the construction. Winning structures typically focus on community, social, development, or environmental concerns in both urban and rural environments and tend to reflect local art, traditions, and expressions. Although the award typically goes to projects generated within an Islamic context, the constructions are not limited to Muslim use, other than the Hajj Terminal in Saudi Arabia and mosques. One of the most unusual aspects of the award is that it does not go strictly to the structure's planner. In recognition of the team nature of architectural expression, the $500,000 prize and the honors associated with it are generally awarded to the team responsible for the actual construction, rather than just to the individual who designed it.

In addition to the prize, the Aga Khan has provided academic support for his architectural ventures through the financing of the Aga Khan Program for Islamic Architecture at Harvard University and the Massachusetts Institute of Technology. He has also worked to emphasize the interconnection between buildings and their surrounding environment through projects designed to restore and revitalize historically important cities, including Cairo, Samarkand, Karimabad, and Zanzibar. These cities were chosen both because of their historical, social, economic, and cultural importance and because of their potential for becoming self-sustaining centers of economic well-being that carry the capacity for a ripple effect into the peripheral populations by expanding trade and tourism without degrading the environment. By setting the example, he hopes to encourage a more environmentally sound approach to the construction of commercial and industrial buildings while rehabilitating the depreciated and poor areas of cities. Many of his projects have been undertaken with the support of the World Bank.

The Aga Khan has also provided funding for a cultural and musical venture, the Yo-Yo Ma Silk Road Project, which is designed to preserve and spread the culture and music of Central Asia. As part of the project, a group of musicians from the United States, India, Iran, Jordan, and Germany perform together as the Silk Road Ensemble. Through their diversity, the group hopes to serve as tangible proof of the potential for cooperation between Muslims and the West.

The Aga Khan's various philanthropic endeavors and development activities have earned him international recognition. In 1984, he was awarded the University of Virginia's Thomas Jefferson Memorial Foundation Medal in Architecture for his patronage of architecture and the American Institute of Architects Honor for his "unique and inspired contributions to architecture." In 1987, he received the Gold Medal of the Higher Council of Spanish Architects from King Juan Carlos. In 1991, he was awarded the Medaille d'Argent from the Academie d'Architecture of France and was made an honorary fellow of the Royal Institute of British Architects. In 1996, he received the Hadrian Award from the World Monuments Fund for his contributions to the restoration and conservation of historic buildings. In 2002, he was awarded the State Reward of Peace and Progress of the First President of the Republic of Kazakhstan for his "strengthening of peace and friendship, mutual confidence between nations, preservation of historical and cultural valuables, and development of social progress." He remains dedicated to the responsible development of impoverished and underprivileged areas of the world.

Further reading

Aga Khan Foundation International Strategy, 1991–1999. Geneva: Aga Khan Foundation, 1992

Bartolucci, Marisa. "Who is the Aga Khan?" Magazine Metropolis, September, 1997

Campbell, Robert. "Khan Awards Bridge Cultural Gap," Boston Globe, November 29, 2001

Gregorian, Vartan. "Introduction of his Highness the Aga Khan," Brown University, June 5, 1996, www.brown.edu/Administration/News_Bureau/1995-96/95-147i.html

Khan, S.S. and M.H. Khan. Rural Change in the Third World: Pakistan and the Aga Khan Rural Support Program. New York: Greenwood Publishing Group, 1992

Nanji, Azim A. "Aga Khan," in The Oxford Encyclopedia of the Modern Islamic World, editor-in-chief John L. Esposito, vol. 1. New York: Oxford University Press, 1995

—— "Aga Khan Foundation," in The Oxford Encyclopedia of the Modern Islamic World, editor-in-chief John L. Esposito, vol. 1. New York: Oxford University Press, 1995

Schmertz, Mildred F. "Interview with the Aga Khan: The Past and Future of the Aga Khan Award for Architecture: Reflections on the First Twenty Years," August 25, 1998, www.amana.org/agakhan/interview.htm

Welch, Anthony and Stuart Cary Welch. Arts of the Islamic Book: The Collection of Prince Sadruddin Aga Khan. Ithaca: Syracuse University Press, 1982

ismaili.net – provides current news on the Aga Khan and Ismaili community

www.akdn.org – Aga Khan Development Network site

www.amana.org – provides information on the Aga Khan's activities and the Ismaili community

Moustapha Akkad (1935–2005)

An award-winning filmmaker best known in the United States for producing the *Halloween* series of horror movies, Moustapha Akkad has also put his filmmaking skills to use to explain Islam to a Western audience.

Moustapha Akkad was born in Aleppo, Syria, in 1935. His father was a government employee who worked for Customs. Inspired by the films of Alfred Hitchcock, Akkad dreamed of becoming a Hollywood film director from his early childhood.

Akkad received his secondary education at the American College in Aleppo where his American theater-arts teacher, Douglas Hill, helped him gain admission to the University of California, Los Angeles (U.C.L.A.). Akkad worked for a year to earn enough money to pay for his plane ticket. He left Syria in 1954 with $200 and a copy of the Quran.

Akkad had chosen U.C.L.A. because it was reputed to have the best film program in the United States, including three productions per semester. He studied methods of staging motion pictures and television production prior to graduating in 1958 with a B.A. in theater arts. He then attended the University of Southern California (U.S.C.) for graduate school. Although U.S.C. was a smaller, less wealthy program, it taught New Wave filmmaking, a more realistic and documentary approach to filmmaking than he had learned at U.C.L.A. Akkad completed three years of study at U.S.C. and earned an M.A. in film in 1961.

After graduation, Akkad applied to seven major film studios, television stations, and advertising agencies for work. One director called him about making a movie about the Algerian revolution, but the project was canceled when Algeria achieved its independence shortly afterward in 1962. Akkad then worked with director Sam Peckinpah on a movie for M.G.M. called *Ride the High Country*, for which he served as production assistant.

When his career stalled shortly afterward, Akkad began thinking about ideas for a television program. Recalling his days at U.C.L.A. when he was frequently invited into the homes of Americans and asked about his impressions of the country as a foreigner, he proposed a program called *As Others See Us*, which featured African, European, Asian, and Latin American foreign students invited to discuss a different topic each week with an American moderator. The purpose of the program was to help the United States understand how it was viewed and understood abroad. Akkad made a small presentation of his idea to three television stations. He received offers from both C.B.S. and N.B.C. to feature it as a public-affairs program for Sunday afternoons. N.B.C. offered him $400 per week for the show, but no producer credit. C.B.S. offered $100 per week, but with producer credit. Akkad's initial reaction was to take the offer that paid more, but, after consulting with Peckinpah, decided to take the producer credit instead. It turned out to be a wise career move and one that Akkad counseled young filmmakers seeking to break into the industry to pursue.

The production of *As Others See Us* led to Akkad's formation of Akkad International Productions, Inc., for which he produced and directed a variety of documentary programs, features, and television series. He embarked on another television series, a syndicated travel show

called *Caesar's World*, hosted by Caesar Romero. The show visited a different country each week and was syndicated by over one hundred television stations in the United States. It was also aired overseas. Akkad subsequently opened offices in London and Beirut in addition to his office in Hollywood.

Akkad's next project was *The Message*, a documentary on Islam designed to promote understanding of Islam in the West. After seeking and securing financing from the Arab world, he decided to change the format to a feature film. *The Message* details the coming of the Prophet Muhammad and the revelation of the Quran. Released in 1976 and starring Anthony Quinn in the lead role, it won an Oscar nomination for best original score as composed by Maurice Jarre. *The Message* followed the Muslim tradition of never showing Muhammad, using subjective angles instead of direct representation. This adherence to custom resulted in the film not being as popular with American audiences as it was in the Arab world, although the film was still well received in the United States. *The Message* was Akkad's first major film success. It has continued to sell well on video and is commercially available via the internet.

After the success of *The Message*, Akkad made a film about the Italian occupation of Libya, *The Lion of the Desert*, released in 1980. It tells the story of the occupation through the biography of Omar Mukhtar, a teacher who moonlighted as a freedom fighter, again played by Anthony Quinn. Financed by Libyan leader Muammar al-Qadhdhafi, for $35 million, *The Lion of the Desert* was one of the worst financial disasters in filmmaking, grossing only $1 million worldwide. Although the reviews and critiques of the film were good, audiences did not go to see it and Akkad had a hard time finding a distributor. He has speculated that the film's commercial failure at the time was due to the negative publicity surrounding Qadhdhafi. Although Qadhdhafi had no control over the film and the film was not about him, it was nevertheless politicized in unintended ways.

While he was filming *The Lion of the Desert*, Akkad was approached by John Carpenter about another film project requiring a $300,000 budget. Akkad recalls laughing when he heard the budget, which was the equivalent of what he was spending each day on *The Lion of the Desert*. He also recalls stopping laughing when he heard the story line – "babysitter to be killed by the bogeyman." A lifelong fan of horror films, Akkad recognized the mass appeal of the story because it was based on a situation "everyone could relate to." He agreed to finance the film with his profits from *The Lion of the Desert*. With Akkad's financial support and Akkad as executive producer, Carpenter's film was made and distributed to individual theaters as *Halloween* in 1978.

Halloween broke all box-office records for an independent film, grossing $60 million. Not only was it subsequently listed as number 68 on the list of the 100 greatest thrillers of all time by the American Film Institute, it also sparked a series of sequels that span more than twenty years of filmmaking. Akkad was initially reluctant to make a sequel because it was a film, rather than television, and because he had not intended to make any sequels. However, because his lawyer had stipulated Akkad's ownership of the franchise in exchange for financing the first of the series, he agreed to make a sequel. *Halloween II* was successfully released in 1981. *Halloween III: Season of the Witch*, released in 1982, was not successful because the pivotal character, Michael Myers, had been left out – against Akkad's advice. For the fourth film, *Halloween 4: The Return of Michael Myers*, released in 1988, Akkad insisted on the restoration of Michael Myers to the series. Noting that "everyone hates Michael Myers," Akkad believed that Myers' presence was critical to keeping the film realistic, which was

ultimately what made it scary. *Halloween 4* was the biggest hit of the series. Although the original *Halloween* movie had made the most money (due, in part, to the low budget for production), *Halloween 4* had the most paying customers. *Halloween 5: The Revenge of Michael Myers*, released in 1989, and *Halloween 6: The Curse of Michael Myers*, released in 1995, did not do well. However, *Halloween H2O: Twenty Years Later (Halloween 7)*, released in 1998, was the biggest box office hit of the series. *Halloween 8: Resurrection*, starring supermodel Tyra Banks and Muslim hip-hop artist Busta Rhymes, was released in 2002, grossing $23 million within one month of being released.

In addition to the sequels, Akkad has also served as the producer of *Sky Bandits*, *Free Ride* (1986), and *Appointment with Fear* (1987), and was the still photographer for a television documentary entitled *Halloween: A Cut Above the Rest*, on the making of the *Halloween* series.

Akkad devoted most of his time to the *Halloween* franchise. He relied on the use of cinema and cinematic language combined with human and believable characters, rather than blood, gore or special effects, to make the films scary. The major changes that have occurred as the series has continued have to do with expansion of the budget and the high-level promotion the films have received.

The *Halloween* movies are deliberately geared toward teenagers because teenagers are the most likely to go to the movie theater to see them. The rise of home entertainment systems has resulted in adults preferring to watch movies at home. Teenagers, however, still view moviegoing as an opportunity to go out with friends or on dates. In order to keep the movies accessible to teenagers, Akkad typically asked his children for their reactions to ideas. One of his sons, Malek Akkad, worked with him in the film industry and was responsible for filming *Psychic Murders*.

Although Akkad was unusual as a Muslim executive producer in Hollywood and the president of Trancas International Films, Inc., he did not believe that this was a reflection of discrimination against Muslims or Arabs as executive producers. In fact, he received more discouragement for his dreams from his family and in the Middle East than he had ever encountered in the United States, a reality that, to him, reflected the importance of the constitution that guaranteed the right of every person to practice their faith. Akkad recognized that he enjoyed greater freedom as a Muslim filmmaker in Hollywood than would have been the case if he had been in the Arab or Muslim worlds. Instead, he attributed the relative lack of Muslim representation in the film industry to the fact that it was a field that was generally difficult to break into. He believed that knowledge, reputation, and creative material were more important than ethnicity, noting that Arab-American filmmakers were responsible for some highly successful films, including Arab Christian Mario Kassar's *First Blood*, *Total Recall*, *Terminator 2: Judgment Day*, *Terminator 3*, and *Basic Instinct*.

Akkad hoped that his own success would serve to inspire others to follow their dreams and to know that they could succeed if they knew what they were doing and were sufficiently determined. At the same time, he acknowledged the tendency of Hollywood to cast Arabs into stereotypical bad-guy roles as Muslim terrorists, hijackers, kidnappers, and religious fanatics, particularly throughout the 1980s and 1990s as the vilification of other ethnic groups, such as Native Americans, African-Americans, and Russians, became less politically correct. Because the vilification of ethnic groups historically has reflected news headlines, the existence of terrorists who kill in the name of Islam and who represent a genuine threat in international politics is reflected in the film industry. Nevertheless, Akkad felt that this minority of extremists should not be turned into an image claiming to represent the majority. Instead, he encouraged the balancing of those negative images with images that reflect Arabs and Muslims as normal human beings with families.

As a Muslim, Akkad was deeply concerned by the rise of militant religious extremism, as well as the negative portrayals of Islam and Muslims post- 9/11. Believing that a more accurate portrayal of Islam was needed in the West, he sought to resurrect a long-standing project, an epic film on the Muslim hero of the Crusades, SALADIN, with Sean Connery in the title role. Akkad noted that the Crusades were a religious war filled with terrorism, but that Christianity had not been blamed for the acts of a few adventurers. He hoped to show the same for Islam through the example of a Muslim hero known for his protection of religious freedom and chivalry. He believed that this film would fill an important gap in American culture by providing a broader understanding of Islam and Muslim history. Akkad was in the process of filming the $80 million dollar movie when he and his daughter, Rima, were killed in a terrorist bombing of the Grand Hyatt Hotel in Amman, Jordan in 2005.

Akkad's epic films have enjoyed longevity in part due to recognition that Americans need better to understand Islam and Muslims. The U.S. Army and the State Department have purchased *The Message* and *The Lion of the Desert* as required viewing for both employees and military troops heading to the Middle East.

Akkad's achievements as a film producer have led to international recognition for his work. He is considered a star in the Arab and Muslim worlds because of his success in Hollywood, was honored by the Council on American–Islamic Relations-N.Y. at an annual dinner for his film achievements, and received a lifetime achievement award from *Fangoria* magazine in 2000.

Further reading

Cain, Sandi. "Breaking In," *Arab-American Business*, October 20, 2002
Goodstein, Laurie. "Hollywood Now Plays Cowboys and Arabs," New York *Times*, November 1, 1998
Interview with Luke Ford, March 26, 2002, www.lukeford.net/profiles/profiles/mousta pha_akkad.htm
Shaheen, Jack. *Reel Bad Arabs: How Hollywood Vilifies A People*. N.p.: Interlink Publishing Group, 2001
www.cair-ny.com – website for C.A.I.R.-N.Y.
www.halloweenmovies.com – website for the Halloween movie series
www.imdb.com – website for Internet Movie Data Base providing filmography and biographies of directors, producers, etc.

Mohammed Jasim al-Ali
(b. early 1950s)

Managing director of Al-Jazeera television network, the Qatar-based satellite television channel commonly referred to as "the C.N.N. of the Arab world," Mohammed Jasim al-Ali has become one of the most important media leaders in the Arab world.

Mohammed Jasim al-Ali was born in the early 1950s and has been active in television production since 1974. He worked for Qatar Television beginning as assistant director and was later promoted to director. He also worked on the launching of Qatar Television's English channel in 1979, beginning as general program controller. He left Qatar for two years to launch Sharjat TV in the United Arab Emirates, then returning to Qatar to be assistant director and then managing director of Qatar Television. Al-Ali has also worked professionally in Japan, Germany, England, and the United States. He is best known for his affiliation with Al-Jazeera television network. He served as a member of the board when the network was initiated and has since become the managing director.

Al-Ali was one of the visionaries behind the creation of Al-Jazeera and personally handled its financing and launching. Al-Jazeera was originally intended to be a joint venture between the British B.B.C. Arab service and the Saudi satellite company Orbit. When the Saudi monarchy insisted on editorial control over the broadcasts, al-Ali turned to the Emir of Qatar, Sheikh Hamad bin Khalifa al-Thani, who offered a $140 million start-up grant in exchange for avoiding certain sensitive domestic topics. The grant money enabled al-Ali to hire a staff representing almost every Arab country and political tendency. Almost all of them had been trained by the B.B.C., giving Al-Jazeera a professional staff capable of providing immediate in-depth and informed coverage, expert knowledge and understanding of Arab politics and audiences, and the ability to raise provocative political issues in a professional manner. Al-Jazeera began with six-hour news coverage in 1996. It expanded to twenty-four-hour coverage in 1999 and could be viewed globally by 2001.

Al-Jazeera first earned international recognition in 1998 with its exclusive coverage of the Desert Fox air war in Iraq, followed by the first broadcast interview with Osama bin Laden ever given in 1999, and the March 2001 coverage of the Taliban's destruction of ancient Buddha statues in Afghanistan. It achieved international fame following the 9/11 attacks when it broadcast the first footage of bin Laden making his case to a global audience, followed by a series of exclusive broadcasts of additional bin Laden material. Estimated to reach about 35 million people around the world through its broadcasts and recording about 300,000 hits daily on its website, Al-Jazeera has become the most controversial and most watched station in the region, uniting Arab audiences globally.

Al-Jazeera's proclaimed goal is to encourage democratic and free-market transformations and the strengthening of civil society through the provision of news, analysis, and discussion of regional and domestic issues. It has introduced freedom of the press and freedom of speech in a part of the world that has known neither. Touting its role as a forum for the exchange of ideas, medium of education, and public platform for the development and empowerment of the individual, al-Ali has promoted both female and male media personalities who are intellectually stimulating and articulate.

Known for presenting "the opinion and the other opinion," Al-Jazeera presents a variety of perspectives on issues and news, most popularly through its talk show *The Opposite Direction*, which is modeled on C.N.N.'s *Crossfire*. The show presents viewpoints from opposite ends of the spectrum. Viewers can call in to express their opinions on topics that are often so controversial that no other media service is willing (or permitted) to cover them. By encouraging serious and courageous discussions of topics that are typically considered off-limits in the Arab world, the network has given Arabs a voice while teaching them the civic responsibilities of open discussion and debate. It has also served as an outlet for the accumulated frustrations of decades of oppression and lack of freedom that some analysts believe are responsible for the rise of militant religious extremism.

As managing director, al-Ali's first major task was to win the trust of Al-Jazeera's Arab audience, a job that was complicated by the audience's experience of state-controlled news and information services as propaganda tools and its anticipation of entertainment and public relations announcements, rather than substance. Concerns about censorship, closure, and imprisonment had encouraged obedience, rather than critical thinking, in the past. Those who sought independent, substantive news tended to listen to foreign news broadcasts. Al-Jazeera produced the first substantive reporting in Arabic, making it accessible to the Arab masses.

Al-Ali also sought to harness developing technology as an asset for Al-Jazeera and searched for a financial sponsor interested in a satellite channel. Before satellites and the internet, it was fairly easy for governments to control information by blocking radio broadcasts and print literature, including newspapers, from abroad. The advent of satellite channels made it more difficult to hide and control news. Al-Jazeera broadcasts include reports from journalists using video and satellite phones.

Al-Jazeera has often been criticized within the Arab world. Some governments have complained that the coverage is too critical and some have recalled their ambassadors from Qatar in protest. Others have tried to limit Al-Jazeera broadcasts, for example by arranging power blackouts during sensitive broadcasts, arresting scheduled participants to prevent their appearance on shows or denying them the right to travel, and disconnecting the telephone lines of both participants and the network. In addition, some program participants have been accused of engaging in a political act simply by appearing on a show. The network has also been criticized for inviting Israeli journalists and scholars to participate in various programs and for interviewing Israeli leaders. Al-Ali has personally come under fire for his determination to discuss controversial and sensitive issues. He was heavily criticized for programs addressing the Lebanese civil war and the 1970 Black September clashes between the Jordanian army and Palestinian commandos. Many viewers found these issues too sensitive and painful to see. Al-Ali had decided to air them in order to push the public into facing the issues honestly and to promote healing.

Al-Jazeera has also been criticized by the West, particularly the United States, for its coverage of the war in Afghanistan, Al Qaida, and Osama bin Laden and for airing what the United

States claims is anti-American and anti-Zionist coverage. Al-Ali has defended Al-Jazeera's airing of some of the bin Laden videos as responsible reporting about breaking issues of global interest. He also notes that only certain newsworthy videos were selected and that these were aired within the context of a relevant panel discussion and commentary from both Arab and Western analysts. He has defended Al-Jazeera's broadcasting of images of casualties and destruction caused by the U.S. bombing campaign against Afghanistan as a matter of responsible reporting that covers a variety of perspectives on the war. Pointing to the irony of theoretical American support for freedom of speech and freedom of the press accompanied by U.S. blocking of certain Al-Jazeera broadcasts and demands that Al-Jazeera engage in self-censorship, al-Ali has refused to violate professional journalistic standards by allowing biased reporting in either direction. He defends Al-Jazeera's coverage of the Israeli–Palestinian conflict as a matter of presenting a more balanced and complex view of issues that are of direct and popular interest to the network's audience than can be found in Western broadcasts, which are seen to be biased in favor of Israel. Coverage of the Palestinians has resonated powerfully within the Arab and Muslim worlds, as viewers have the impression of experiencing the uprising, including human rights violations, first hand. The result has been an increased demand for the just and comprehensive resolution of a crisis that is now personal and tangible for viewers.

Al-Ali has also worked to make Al-Jazeera fiscally solvent and, thereby, completely independent of government censorship, control, manipulation, and scrutiny. Because many corporations have been reluctant to advertise due to concerns about alienating or offending certain governments, Al-Jazeera has focused more on licensing and distribution rights, renting technical equipment, gaining subscriptions, making joint productions, and buying and selling programs as alternative income-generating activities. It earns some income from cable operators and selling pictures and has successful relationships with A.B.C., Fox, A.R.D., C.N.N., and organizations in Malaysia, China, and Australia. It has also invested in new projects, including an English-language channel and a documentary channel.

In the future, al-Ali foresees competition as the main game, given that satellite television has expanded and other news channels are being developed in the Arab and Islamic worlds to compete with Al-Jazeera. However, rather than being worried by this development, he notes that competition is healthy and will push the stations to upgrade their services constantly. Although he questions how free the other stations will be in their broadcasting, he believes that Al-Jazeera has made its point about the demand for intelligent newscasting that presents a variety of perspectives and the need to strengthen this important institution of civil society in the Arab world.

Further reading

"A Dialogue with Mohammed Jasim al-Ali, Managing Director, Al-Jazeera," T.B.S. *Archives*, no. 5, Special Issue: The Arab World, fall/winter 2000, www.tbsjournal.com/Archives/Fall00/al-Ali.htm

Gabriel, Judith. "Al Jazeera Remains in the Hot Seat," *Aljadid*, vol. 7, no. 37, fall 2001

Jurkowitz, Mark. "A Sharp Look Behind Al-Jazeera's Cameras," *Boston Globe*, July 10, 2003

Mernissi, Fatima. "The Satellite, the Prince and Sheherezade: The Rise of Women as Communicators in Digital Islam," in *Fantasies de l'harem I noves Xahrazads*, Centre de Cultura Contemporania de Barcelona, 2003, www.mernissi.net/books/articles/rise_of_women.html

El-Nawawy, Mohammed and Adel Iskandar. *Al-Jazeera: How the Free Arab News Network Scooped the World and Changed the Middle East*. Boulder, CO: Westview Press, 2002

Schleifer, S. Abdallah. "Interview with Mohamed Jasim Al Ali, Managing Director, Al Jazeera," T.B.S. no. 10, spring/summer 2003, www.tbsjournal.com/jasim.html

"T.B.S. Focus: Al-Jazeera: Mohammed Jasim Al-Ali," T.B.S. *Archives*, no. 7, fall/winter 2001, www.tbsjournal.com/Archives/Fall01/Jazeera_al-ali.html

Wide Angle: Exclusive to Al-Jazeera, P.B.S. documentary on Al-Jazeera produced by Ben Anthony

english.aljazeera.net/NR/exeres/E4D19123–9DD3–11D1–B44E–006097071264.htm – English website of Al-Jazeera

www.tbsjournal.com – website for Transnational Broadcasting Studies, published by the Adham Center for Television Journalism, the American University in Cairo; provides monthly interviews with a variety of Arab news networks

Muhammad Ali (b. 1942)

The world heavyweight boxing champion, Muhammad Ali became an American cultural icon for his athletic achievements and for symbolizing black pride and power during the civil rights era.

Muhammad Ali was born Cassius Clay, Jr., in Louisville, KY, on January 17, 1942. His father, Cassius Clay, Sr., was an artist whose commissioned works included advertisements and church paintings. His mother, Odessa, worked as a cleaning lady, cook, and babysitter, earning just enough money to pay for daily groceries and bus fare for herself to get to work. Although he recalls always having enough food to eat as a child, Ali notes that his parents struggled financially. Most of his clothes and shoes came from Good Will and the family home was in constant need of repairs. Because there was rarely enough money to pay for bus fare for both Ali and his brother, Rudy, to go to school, Ali frequently raced the bus to school in the mornings. This early physical training regimen helped him to develop his habit of running and daily training that made him a world-class athlete.

Ali's childhood was filled with awareness of racism. In his home town, African-Americans were not allowed to stay in hotels. Movie theaters were strictly segregated, and there was only one "black" movie theater. Most downtown stores refused to serve food or drink to blacks. The combined experiences of discrimination and awareness of white hatred of and violence against black people, as symbolized for Ali by the lynching of Emmett Till over a supposed insult to a white woman, led him to admire blacks who overcame racism through achievement. He looked to the black boxing champions of the past, particularly Joe Louis, Sugar Ray Robinson, and Jackie Robinson, as role models, finding inspiration in both their athletic prowess and the courage and confidence they displayed as black fighters who overcame racism to achieve as athletes.

From his earliest childhood, Ali dreamed of becoming the world heavyweight champion. Believing that he did not have the intelligence necessary to be a scholar or to pursue other sports such as basketball or football which would have required going to college, Ali started training as a boxer when he was in his mid-teens, sacrificing sleep and leisure time for the sake of his sport. Because he also had to work part time in order to ensure the family's financial survival, his training had to come after both school and work. Ali's daily routine involved going to school, working for four hours, training at Martin's gym from 6 until 8 P.M., and training at Stoner's gym from 8 P.M. until midnight. The demands of his work and training schedules left little time for schoolwork. He never comfortably mastered reading and admits that he sometimes cheated.

Ali's self-described methodology of boxing was to focus on defense, rather than offense. He found that opponents tended to wear themselves out by being overly aggressive. His approach of "dancing," or leaning back, stepping away, and sidestepping, often leaning against the ropes, helped him to study the timing and motions of his opponents. Dancing was considered a lightweight strategy, while heavyweight boxers tended to rely more on punching strength and remaining still. Ali was the first heavyweight to introduce dancing at his level, a technique that resulted in his having few serious injuries from boxing matches. The broken jaw he received in the 1973 fight with Ken Norton was an exception. Dancing also gave Ali freedom of movement while his opponents wore themselves out with punches that didn't connect and with having to chase him around the ring.

Ali's defense was rooted in two key abilities: to gauge an opponent's punch, and to lean just far enough away to avoid being punched while remaining close enough to strike back when his opponent's punch failed to connect. The most visually striking aspect of his fighting style was his eyes, which never seemed to close, blink or tip off an opponent. His eyes registered an opening simultaneously with his hands firing punches. His lightning-quick reflexes amazed opponents and judges alike. Ali's speed overshadowed his size and strength. Ironically, it also led to his being underrated as a boxer for years.

Ali set himself apart from other boxers through his constant training and self-control. He never took breaks from training between matches. Instead, he always tried to stay in top form. Also, unlike many athletes, he was totally focused on becoming a champion boxer. He didn't date, drink alcohol or do drugs. He was careful about nutrition, avoiding even soda. His self-control was also reflected by the fact that he never used his boxing skills outside of the ring. Despite his abstention from women and partying, Ali remained a man who enjoyed being surrounded by people. He preferred to train in the city, rather than in a private camp in solitude, because he liked to be able to go out and see people.

Ali became known for both his athleticism and his bravado. He has said that his claims to be the prettiest and the greatest were not acts of mere bragging – they were done deliberately to capture and keep the public's attention. Many people hated Ali because of his bravado. They were therefore willing to pay for someone to silence him in a fight. As he noted, the more people hated him and were fed up with his bragging, the more people wanted to see him beaten. Ali and his manager counted on this in order to set up strings of important fights, particularly as he sought to make a comeback after his exile from professional boxing. To add further fuel to the fire, he wrote poems before each match predicting in which round his opponent would fall. He was almost always right. While some were amused by Ali's poems, others, particularly white supremacists whose notion of white racial superiority had no space for a black champion, issued death threats in response.

As an amateur boxer, Ali recorded 161 wins in 167 fights. His amateur career was capped by his victory in the Golden Gloves Championship in 1959, followed by another Golden Gloves Championship and an Olympic gold medal in 1960. Proud of having represented his country, Ali hoped that his Olympic victory would mark a new level of acceptance and appreciation for African-Americans in the United States. However, after the initial euphoria, it was clear that the majority of Americans did not see his Olympic victory as relevant to the major racial discussions that were taking place.

After his Olympic victory, white managers and financiers lined up to offer their services and to talk to Ali about what they could do for his career. However, the bottom line was also that the overwhelming majority of the prize winnings went to the managers and financiers, not to Ali. With no other viable alternatives, Ali signed with a group of Louisville millionaires who offered a six-year contract with a $10,000 advance. Ali used most of the advance to pay for repairs to the family house and to finish paying the mortgage. Although the contract was a business arrangement, the media portrayed it as an act of charity on the part of the backers, conveniently leaving out the pertinent data about how much money they earned in the process.

The theme of the white establishment attempting to control Ali – who he fought against, what his financial terms would be, and how he presented himself – recurred throughout his career. It was precisely because he refused to subordinate himself to the expectations of white America that he became such a figure of bitter controversy. Recognizing that not even an Olympic gold medal could buy him the respect, equality, and human dignity that he sought in America, he changed tactics at the conclusion of his contract with the millionaires. He signed on with the black manager of an all-black promotion company, Main Bout, Inc.

Ali's new manager was Herbert Muhammad, the son of Nation of Islam's prophet and leader, Elijah Muhammad. Ali's contractual arrangement with Muhammad marked both his membership of Nation and the entrance of black powerholders into the field of boxing, which had traditionally been dominated by the Mafia. Muhammad's management brought Ali's earnings to a much higher level than had been the case under his prior contract. From 1960 to 1966 when he was managed by the Louisville Sponsoring Group, Ali's gross earnings were $2,376,115. With Herbert Muhammad as manager from 1966 to 1967 and 1970 to 1975 (he was, as he put it, in exile from 1967 to 1970), his gross earnings were $27,375,000.

In his early years, Ali was not an activist. His rising activism was the direct product of his increasing exposure to Nation of Islam, largely through Malcolm X. Although Ali had been raised as a Christian, he was attracted to Nation's teachings of black pride, separatism, discipline, bearing, self-respect, manhood, hierarchy, dignity for both men and women, and avoidance of smoking, drinking, and partying. Malcolm X suggested that Ali's role as a boxer should be understood as part of the larger ongoing struggle Nation believed was occurring between Muslims and Christians. Ali had always been reluctant to participate in the civil rights movement because he believed that blacks should not have to beg for rights that were naturally theirs. Membership in Nation marked Ali's assertion of those natural rights as a matter of fact. However, Nation rejected professional sports, particularly boxing, because it considered sports to be another means of keeping the black population segregated and disenfranchised while providing entertainment and wealth to white men. Nation changed its stance with Ali because it realized the potential for communicating its message to a wider audience through a man who embodied black heroism, pride, and masculinity. Through Ali, Nation had an impact on the domestic struggle for civil rights and established links with Muslim communities around the world. Nation labeled any criticism of Ali as religious persecution and hatred of Muslims. However, when Ali was no longer as malleable or useful to Nation, it quickly dropped him and returned to its prior denunciation of organized sports.

Although Ali and Malcolm X became close friends, Ali had not made his conversion public until his fight against Sonny Liston for the world heavyweight title on February 25, 1964. This fight was more than a boxing match – it was also about Ali's right to practice his religion. Unknown to his then sponsors, Ali had invited Malcolm X to the fight. Ali had not announced his conversion to Islam because he feared that he would not be allowed to fight for the heavyweight title if his religious orientation was made public. When Malcolm X's presence became known, Ali's white sponsors insisted that he get rid of both Malcolm X and all of the black Muslims in his entourage. They also demanded that he denounce Nation of Islam because of the negative image black Muslims had among whites at this time. Ali refused, declaring that he would rather cancel the fight than denounce his religion. He also stated that his membership in Nation was more than a matter of religious belief. It was also a means of participating in the liberation of black people from subjugation and slavery to freedom, equality, and justice. Rather than denouncing Nation, Ali decided to make his religion public, changing his name as a symbol of his break with a past dominated by whites and his claiming of responsibility for his own destiny. He began praying publicly in his corner prior to his fights. When the press asked him about his status as a black Muslim, Ali explained that Islam is a religion of peace that recognizes the equality of all believers, regardless of race. Both issues were important to him because of the racism and violence experienced by blacks at that time in America.

Ali's relationship with Nation made him even more suspicious to white America. Not only did he represent black opposition to white power, he also symbolized in the eyes of some a Muslim challenge to Christian hegemony. Some of his major fights, such as that against Floyd Patterson, were portrayed by the press as a battle between Christianity and Islam. Although the press and the white population clearly expected Patterson to win the fight and "prove" that Christianity was the "superior" religion, Ali emerged victorious, creating a powerful new symbolic victory of black Islam over white Christianity.

Ali was an effective public face for Nation, as well as a generous donor. He worked consistently with children and the black community. In 1967, he was the single largest black contributor to U.N.I.C.E.F. He was particularly fond of public school appearances which enabled him to provide children with experience with a "real live black hero" to offset the images of exclusively white heroes on television and the radio. His popularity among the black community led to a regular column in Nation's official newspaper, *Muhammad Speaks*, called "From the Camp of the Champ." The column, which ran from 1965 to 1969, detailed Ali's routines, daily activities, personal philosophies, and speaking engagements. Ali also had a powerful impact on other black athletes, particularly black college students. In 1968, he met with other prominent black athletes, including Jim Brown, Bill Russel, and Lew Alcindor (see also KAREEM ABDUL-JABBAR), to discuss the New York Athletic Club boycott, the proposed Olympic boycott, and Ali's refusal to be drafted.

While Nation had influence over Ali, it never controlled him. He never completely absorbed portions of Nation's philosophy, particularly its demonization of whites. He always had both blacks and whites in his entourage and trusted both, believing that the critical issue was not the color of their skin, but how they treated other people. In his eyes, any white person who treated other people with respect also deserved to be treated with respect.

Ali came into conflict with Nation over other issues. In an act that he deeply regretted later, he was pressured to turn his back on Malcolm X as he distanced himself from Nation's inconsistent doctrines and became more secularly active. Malcolm X was assassinated in 1965 before Ali had a chance to make amends. Relations between Ali and Nation soured further in 1969 when Ali declared his intent to return to the ring for financial reasons. Nation promptly suspended him, claiming that he was too interested in money and not enough in the spiritual platform of Islam. Nation further accused him of wasting the money he had earned, ignoring the fact that the majority of that money had gone to Nation and to support the black community. Nation dismissed Ali not only as a Muslim, but also as a fighter, reflecting the power struggle between a young, charismatic, popular black athlete and the aging leader of a politically charged religious organization.

As a boxer, Ali became well known for off-the-cuff remarks he made before and following major fights. He never used a spokesperson, believing that he needed to speak for himself. He regretted only one remark, made to a Russian reporter following his Olympic victory in which he asserted that he preferred life in America to life in Africa, which he portrayed as consisting of fighting off snakes and alligators while living in mud huts. His later travels to Africa demonstrated to him the degree to which he had absorbed white stereotypes of Africa and Africans. His time in Africa was both humbling and empowering as he learned about the levels of culture, education, and linguistic ability many Africans possessed. He also gained a deeper appreciation of Africa's contributions to world civilization, which had been arrested by slavery and colonization.

Ali's most famous remarks were made in reference to the Vietnam War. Prior to this, he had believed what he had been taught in school – that every war in which America had fought was for freedom, peace, or to make the world safe for democracy. For Ali, as for many Americans, Vietnam changed that perception. When he was asked for his opinion about the Vietnam War in 1966, Ali honestly replied that he had no quarrels with the Viet Cong because no Viet Cong had ever called him "nigger." The remarks galvanized an already divided America. For those who supported the war, Ali's denunciation of the war and subsequent refusal to be drafted reflected cowardice and a lack of patriotism on his part.

Many whites claimed it was "unfair" that Ali escaped the draft while white boys were dying in Vietnam – despite the fact that the overwhelming majority of American soldiers in Vietnam were black. Opponents of the war, on the other hand, were pleased to hear a public figure state so clearly and succinctly what many of them felt. After his remarks, Ali was routinely invited to speak at colleges and universities.

Ali made headlines in 1967 for his refusal to serve in the draft on religious grounds. Claiming the status of conscientious objector, he wrote that bearing arms and killing was against his religion and that he could not participate in any war that involved killing people. Instead of accepting his request, the government chose to make an example of him. His refusal to be drafted cost him everything he had worked to achieve. Even though he was considered unequaled in his boxing skills at that time, he was stripped of his world heavyweight title, his boxing license was revoked, and his passport was confiscated to prevent him from boxing abroad. He was sentenced to five years in jail and a $10,000 fine, rendering him unable to fight during the prime years of his boxing career. It took three years and a fight to the Supreme Court to overturn Ali's conviction unanimously.

Ali's exile from boxing was the most far-reaching boycott against a performer in American history. His eventual return to the boxing ring was complicated not only by the boycott, but also by the belief of many that he could not hope to return to championship boxing after having spent so much time out of competition. Some also believed that the public had lost interest in him. Ali proved them wrong on both counts. His entourage labeled his return from exile "The Resurrection" as he proceeded to do what no other fighter before him had accomplished: reclaiming his title after three years away from the ring. It was also at this time that the press finally started to treat Ali with more respect, having recognized the winds of change from the civil rights movement and collective protests against the Vietnam War. Whereas it had previously dismissed him as a "loudmouth slacker" and as a Muslim, his popularity and the popularity of the causes he had supported forced the press to stop punishing him for his religion and his refusal to serve in Vietnam.

Ali's goal was to fight then-world heavyweight champion Joe Frazier to prove that he was still a world-class fighter. In order to prove public interest in the fight, he publicly challenged Frazier, attracting such a huge crowd that the police had to be called in for crowd control. Ali fought both Jerry Quarry and Oscar Bonavena before the famed Frazier–Ali fight.

Just before the Bonavena fight, Ali met a man whose story touched him deeply: Judge Aaron. Aaron was a fellow African-American who had been assaulted and had his testicles cut off by whites as a warning to "uppity" blacks not to get involved in the civil rights movement. Ali subsequently began to dedicate his fights. He dedicated the Bonavena fight to "the unprotected people, to the victims." When the Governor of Atlanta encouraged citizens to boycott the later fight against Frazier, Ali dedicated his fight to the black fighters of the past who had inspired him, paved the way for him, and faced similar racism. Ali's victory was thus perceived as the triumph of black athleticism in the face of vehement racism, tying his fight to the struggles of the past.

The 1971 Frazier–Ali fight, which was widely considered the greatest heavyweight fight of all time, offered the largest purse ever: $5 million. The fight itself was a rarity in that it featured two undefeated heavyweight champions who met in the ring for the first time. It was also the first major sporting event that riveted Americans in a combination of sports, ideology, and values. Frazier won the fight –

one of only two losses in Ali's career in fifty-one fights between 1960 and 1975. (The other occurred in the 1973 fight against Ken Norton.)

A rematch with Frazier took place in 1974. This time, Ali emerged as the winner, evening the score. A third rematch in 1975 also resulted in victory for Ali, ending after fourteen rounds with Ali's first total knock-out (T.K.O.) of another fighter. Although the media often portrayed him as "streaked with savagery" and a "practicing sadist" in accordance with stereotypes of blacks, Ali maintains that he never punished or hurt his opponents more than was necessary to win the fight. The fact that he had so few T.K.O.'s reflects this personal philosophy.

The biggest and most difficult fight of Ali's career occurred in 1974 when he fought against George Foreman in Zaire for a $10 million purse – the largest purse in boxing history. The fight was billed as the homecoming of two African boys. For Ali, the experience of training and fighting in a part of Africa where blacks held power was particularly profound. Foreman was favored to win both because he was younger than Ali and because he had the highest knock-out percentage in boxing history. The Ali–Foreman fight was portrayed as another epic fight between Islam and Christianity.

Ali did not appear to be a strong contender during the fight. He spent a great deal of time against the ropes, taking body punches from Foreman, who was widely acclaimed as the hardest hitter of all time. Although spectators, including his own team, perceived his stance as a display of weakness, Ali claimed that he deliberately allowed Foreman to engage in heavy punching as a strategy to wear him out. He knew that he could go for more rounds than Foreman. Because Foreman was such a strong puncher and pounded on his opponent from the beginning, he rarely fought for many rounds. Ali's strategy proved victorious. He recovered his heavyweight title and received a long-awaited invitation to the White House. Ali later lost his title, but regained it one final time in 1978. His last fights occurred in 1981.

Ali's boxing career spanned some of the most turbulent years in American history, running from the Kennedy assassination through the Vietnam War and the civil rights movement. He dominated both headline and sports news because of his athletic achievements and his affiliation with Nation of Islam. Simultaneously admired and reviled as an accomplished African-American Muslim professional athlete and American citizen who publicly protested the draft in a way previously unimaginable for an African-American, Ali was perceived as simultaneously courageous, frightening, entertaining, and threatening. His refusal to give in to critics and opponents in particular marked him as a man of integrity at a time when America had lost its other major cultural symbols of integrity – President John F. Kennedy, Senator Robert Kennedy, and the Rev. Martin Luther King, Jr. – to assassination. In many ways, Ali helped America to move through a period of despair by challenging the status quo, refusing to apologize for his existence, and demanding recognition on the basis of his achievements. He could not be ignored because he refused to be silenced. A leader of social change, Ali has remained a powerful symbol of the civil rights era and of African-American athleticism. He also helped to change the American perception of Islam from a marginal, frightening black nationalist movement to an acceptable mainstream religion.

Despite the onset of Parkinson's disease, Ali was selected to light the Olympic torch for the 1996 Atlanta games. He was named Sportsman of the Century by *Sports Illustrated* and was the subject of a number of books. In 1974, he was featured by D.C. Comics, portraying a fight with Superman which Ali won. A 1996 documentary of the Ali–Foreman fight, *When we were Kings*, won a 1997 Oscar. A critically acclaimed full-length movie, *Ali*, starring Will Smith, was nominated for two Academy Awards.

In the aftermath of 9/11, Ali returned to the public stage, appearing on the televised *Tribute to Heroes* to reassure America that Islam is a peaceful religion and to assume the role of national healer. He remained the most visible American Muslim celebrity post-9/11, going to Ground Zero shortly after the terrorist attacks and appearing on the *Oprah Winfrey Show* to assert Islam as a religion of peace. He was recruited by Hollywood to bolster America's image abroad and agreed to make a one-minute public broadcast announcement for overseas networks to assure Muslims around the world that American Muslims are free to practice their faith and that America's "war on terrorism" was not against Islam. For his work, commitment, and support in promoting coexistence and inclusion in all walks of life, Ali was awarded the Kahlil Gibran Spirit of Humanity Award in 2004.

Further reading

Ali, Muhammad with Richard Durham. *The Greatest: My Own Story*. New York: Random House, 1975

Bingham, Howard. "GOAT – A Tribute To Muhammad Ali," Taschen, 2004

Caldwell, Deborah. "Muhammad Ali: The Reassuring Face of American Islam," in *Taking Back Islam: American Muslims Reclaim their Faith*, ed. Michael Wolfe and the Producers of Beliefnet. Emmaus, PA: Rodale Inc. and Beliefnet, Inc., 2002

Jurkowitz, Mark. "Capturing Ali's Legend and Times On-screen," *Boston Globe*, December 16, 2001

Remnick, David. *King of the World: Muhammad Ali and the Rise of an American Hero*. New York: Random House, 1998

Rutenberg, Jim. "Hollywood Enlists Ali's Help to Explain War to Muslims," *New York Times*, December 23, 2001

Smith, Maureen. "*Muhammad Speaks* and Muhammad Ali: Intersections of the Nation of Islam and Sport in the 1960s," in *With God on their Side: Sport in the Service of Religion*, ed. Tara Magdalinksi and Timothy J.L. Chandler. London and New York: Routledge, Taylor & Francis Group, 2002

Yaphett El-Amin (b. 1971)

The first American Muslim woman elected to serve in state government and the first Muslim woman to serve as a legislator in the state of Missouri, Yaphett El-Amin made history with her November, 2002 election to the Missouri House of Representatives.

Yaphett El-Amin was born Yaphett Johnson on March 30, 1971, in St. Louis, MO. She was the third of eight daughters born to a lower-middle-class African-American family. Her education began at one of Clara Muhammad's preschools run by Nation of Islam. She then entered the St. Louis public school system. From seventh through twelfth grade, she was bused to St. Louis County as part of the area's school-desegregation program because her parents wanted her to have better resources, facilities, and quality of education. She graduated from Mehlville High School, a predominantly white school, and then attended the historically black University of Arkansas in Pine Bluff. The first generation of her family to attend college, she graduated in 1994 with a B.A. in political science. She began graduate studies in public administration at Southern Illinois University, Edwardsville, but left upon marriage to Talibdin El-Amin. After having a child, she entered politics.

El-Amin's interest in politics stems from her experiences as a college freshman when she became active in the college community and fought for student rights. She volunteered to serve as an assistant to the student government, traveling throughout Arkansas. With self-confidence stemming from her strong academic performance, she continued to work with the student government throughout her college career, realizing that students needed to be empowered in order to implement change and achieve self-determination. She credits this experience with preparing her to serve her constituents at the state level.

Although she did not wish to govern the student body, El-Amin realized that she could be most effective in making student voices heard by serving in a higher-level capacity with more power. She ran for student vice-president during her junior year, earning her first election victory. She chose the mandatory student activities fee as her main issue. All students were required to pay the fee, but the authority for dispersing the funds remained with the director of student services. Because the director had the power to withhold money at will, some programs deemed to be of interest by the student body were refused funding. El-Amin believed that it was wrong for one individual to have the right to curtail the range of activities available to students when the student body as a whole had approved them. She therefore engaged the director in a series of confrontations to gain greater student control over distribution of the funds. The confrontations were caricatured in the student newspaper.

When El-Amin returned to St. Louis, she began to take note of the major problems in her community. She decided to join political campaigns to work toward resolving these problems, volunteering to serve as a Democratic committeewoman for St. Louis in 1997. She also served as the 62nd District legislative assistant to Representative Charles Quincy Troupe and started working in Missouri's Youth Services Division, helping juvenile boys who had committed crimes. The combination of social and political work made her realize that, like college students, everyday people need to have someone who cares about them and a voice to represent them. It was at that time that she decided to run for state representative, knowing that the higher she was placed, the more power she would have to influence decision making.

El-Amin based her campaign on promises of strong results in education both because she believes that education is the key to a better and more productive society and because the St. Louis public schools are notorious for their consistently low test scores. In fact, many of the schools have only provisional accreditation status, which means that they must either improve their standardized test scores or face loss of accreditation. El-Amin therefore made educational achievements for her district the center of her campaign and work.

El-Amin ran for election as state representative for the 57th District of St. Louis in November, 2002. She won 56% of the vote, earning her an eight-year term, in addition to her continuing work as a volunteer committeewoman. The district is about ninety-five percent African-American, although very few of them (about twenty people) are Muslims. Most of the population is lower income.

Because she believes that poverty is a breeding ground for drinking, drugs, crime, and lack of education, El-Amin set the eradication of poverty as her most important goal. Other priorities included providing better access to health care for her residents and attracting retail outlets to the area to boost the economy and provide jobs. She kept her campaign promise of focusing on education by serving on the state's education committee, which is responsible for channeling legislation pertaining to schooling, including controversial issues such as charter schools, voucher programs, and school choice. Despite the prevalence of low incomes, one of the schools in her district has the highest math and science scores in the state. El-Amin attributes the success to a return to basics and traditional African-American community methods, such as community involvement, volunteerism, home visits in cases of absenteeism, and

working as a "communal community." Community support has also made a reward system possible – students with perfect attendance receive bicycles.

In addition to her work on education, El-Amin serves on three other committees: the Job Creation and Economic Development Committee, the Tourism and Cultural Affairs Committee, and the Health, Mental Health, and Social Services Appropriations Committee. The Job Creation and Economic Development Committee addresses the loss of jobs and businesses in the community and has explored incentives such as tax increment financing, which provides businesses with ten years of tax abatement if they open shop in economically distressed areas, to try to address poverty issues in the district. In her work for the Tourism and Cultural Affairs Committee, El-Amin has sought to develop more state cultural institutions reflecting the positive contributions of African-Americans to both the state and the country. The Health, Mental Health, and Social Services Appropriations Committee hears testimony from state residents about ways in which government spending impacts their daily lives, including disability services and alcohol- and drug-treatment programs. The difficulty is that, like other states, Missouri faces major budget deficits on this type of program.

During her first year as legislator, El-Amin was pivotal in passing legislation such as the Amber Alert bill, which links state and local law-enforcement agencies in tracking missing persons statewide. The bill was controversial both because the state was already facing a budget deficit and because a similar system already existed via the executive order of Missouri's governor. El-Amin believed that leaving such an important program as an executive order was too risky because executive orders can be changed by the next administration. Making it into a law requires another act of legislation to cancel it. She therefore lobbied to make sure that Missouri state law mandated the participation of all state law-enforcement agencies. Although some of her colleagues were reluctant to pass the legislation because of the costs involved in the program, El-Amin insisted that the issue should be the provision of the best quality program, regardless of the cost, noting that there is no price for a missing child.

El-Amin attributes her pursuit of excellence to her pride in her African-American heritage and her sense of responsibility as a Muslim. Although some of her political opponents have tried to use her Muslim faith to turn voters away from her, they have not been successful. For example, during her campaign for state representative, one of her opponents claimed that if El-Amin were elected, she would not be able to work with churches. He also falsely claimed that she opposed non-Muslim religious beliefs. El-Amin responded by refusing to engage in a mud-slinging campaign and by focusing instead on the issues of concern to her constituency. The tactic not only won her the election, but also impressed and won the confidence of voters who were more concerned about substantive issues, such as fighting discrimination and prejudice, than about negative campaigning. Because many had personal experience with such issues, they were not willing to discriminate against El-Amin on the basis of her religion, even post-9/11. The positive role played by Nation of Islam in the lives of many African-Americans helped many of them to perceive her Muslim faith as non-threatening.

El-Amin has not made religion the central focus of her political career. She observes hijab by covering her hair and wearing loose, flowing clothing out of respect for her faith. She does not believe, however, that how she dresses is as substantive as the issue of delivering much-needed legislation to improve the lives of her constituents. She does not subscribe to the idea that women should remain home or focus exclusively on child rearing, noting that her husband provides critical support with housework and child care so that she can work. She herself has a two-hour commute to work one way on an average day that begins with breakfast meetings with individuals or organizations in need of services or trying to raise awareness of issues, followed by hearings and sessions for debate and passing bills coming out of various committees.

Contrary to the concerns voiced by her opponents, El-Amin works closely with local churches out of a belief that society needs a strong spiritual foundation. She enjoys the support of the Archbishop of St. Louis, who has pledged the support of every church under his jurisdiction for her efforts to improve the conditions of their shared community. She believes that the universal values of religion should be emphasized in the public sphere so that religion is put to the service of the public good, rather than serving as a tool for exclusion or discrimination. She has called on legislators to find ways to work together regardless of their differences and prejudices, believing that working with a diverse group is the most effective way of helping people to set aside their pre-existing misconceptions.

American Muslims consider El-Amin's election to be an important historical moment for the American Muslim community as a whole. Her presence in the state legislature helps to make the Muslim voice heard in the American political system and reflects the reality of diversity in Missouri, where there are approximately forty thousand Muslims living in St. Louis City and County combined. El-Amin's campaign was supported by Muslims throughout the United States.

Further reading

Apalategui, Inigo. "First Female Muslim Legislator Seeks Improving her Community." *Missouri Digital News*, May 8, 2003

Ulen, Eisa. "Making Herstory," *Azizah* magazine, winter 2002
www.mdn.org (*Missouri Digital News*)

Rina Amiri (b. 1968/1969)

An academic dedicated to peace, the expansion of women's rights, and the improvement of the lives of refugees, Rina Amiri returned to her native Afghanistan after the 2001 fall of the Taliban to help rebuild her country and the lives of Afghan women.

Rina Amiri was born in Afghanistan in either 1968 or 1969. She is uncertain of her exact age because birth dates were not recorded in Afghanistan at that time. Her father was a physician who ran a government hospital.

Amiri's family fled Afghanistan in 1973 after a bloodless coup displaced King Mohammad Zahir Shah, who is her third cousin. She recalls the terror, anger, confusion, and hardship of her family and other refugees as they sought shelter in other countries. She has commented that she knows first hand what it means to go from living in security and warmth to losing not only control over one's life, but also one's position as a member of a well-respected family.

Amiri's family migrated initially to Bombay, India, then to Pakistan, and finally to San Francisco, CA, where she grew up. Like many Afghans living in exile, Amiri's family continued to live as Afghans at home, speaking only Farsi, listening to Afghan music, eating Afghan food, and maintaining traditional Afghan weddings. The purpose of living in what she describes as a "frozen culture" was to maintain their Afghan cultural traditions and Islamic spirituality. The approach preserved Afghan culture among exiles during the more than twenty years that Afghanistan was engulfed by war. Amiri never thought of herself as an American until she went to college.

Amiri's parents insisted on the importance of a strong Western education and the development of professional skills, including mastery of English. She completed college and entered pre-medical school, but decided to pursue studies that could be put to use in rebuilding Afghanistan. She studied Central and Southwestern Asian politics at Tufts University's Fletcher School of Law and Diplomacy. She also developed her conflict-resolution skills and began working as a senior research associate for the Women and Public Policy Program at Harvard University's Kennedy School of Government, where she became a central participant in the Women Waging Peace program's annual colloquium.

Women Waging Peace is a network of women activists representing a variety of professions from conflict areas around the globe who work for peace by calling for a diversity of perspectives and dialogues in engaging both formal and informal peace processes. They promote the participation of all sectors of society, including women, in the prevention, management, and resolution of conflict and in reconstruction negotiations, but do not advocate political views. As an academic, Amiri's role was to provide research and analysis to support policy advocacy.

Amiri came to the media spotlight in the aftermath of the 9/11 attacks. Initially afraid that she and other Afghans would become objects of fear and hatred and might even be expelled from the United States, she stepped forward as a spokesperson for Afghanistan in response to a statement made by Senator John Kerry about Muslims hating America. Amiri asserted that not all Muslims hate America given that many of them live in the United States and that the color of a person's hair or skin does not reflect what is in their heart or mind. She was subsequently approached by reporters. She became one of the leading voices for women's rights and refugee assistance in Afghanistan, appearing on television news programs, granting radio interviews, participating in a variety of forums questioning the fate and future of Afghanistan, writing opinion pieces, and giving lectures.

Amiri recalls 9/11 as a major turning point in her life because it pushed her to define what she was willing to live and die for. Her lifelong vow to help rebuild her native country led her to place herself at the frontline of the conflict where she felt she could be most effective. First, she raised attention to the dire situation of the millions of Afghan refugees displaced, traumatized, and robbed of their identity through the lengthy wars and the American-led bombings against the Taliban. Seeing herself in the images of Afghan refugee children clinging to their parents as they made their way into exile, she sought to make people aware of the scope of the humanitarian crisis in the hope of preventing a situation similar to that which had accompanied the Soviet withdrawal in 1989 and ultimately led to the rise of the Taliban. She feared that Western indifference to the plight of the refugees could serve to inflame resentment and create greater political instability, all of which could have created a new generation of terrorists. Amiri's work on behalf of refugees includes service as an adviser on refugee relief efforts for the Afghan Women's Educational Fund and as a representative of the Afghan Women's Network, both based in Pakistan.

Second, Amiri returned to Kabul in 2002 to participate in the reconstruction project, advocating the restoration of women's participation as critical to the peaceful future of Afghanistan. She has called for the expansion of women's participation in the political, economic, and educational sectors in ways that are appropriate to Afghan culture, history, and religion. Since her return to Kabul, she has helped to mobilize and prepare women for participation in the elections and served as one of the election monitors. She was also one of the women in the delegation that greeted the former king upon his return.

Amiri has become a figure of admiration in the West for her courage in returning to a land of instability and ongoing sporadic violence. Within Afghanistan, however, reactions to her work are mixed. Some believe that her public stance is inappropriate for an Afghan woman and are concerned that her support for women's rights means that she will be pushing a pro-Western agenda. She has argued that women's rights are not necessarily Western in origin and, in fact, have strong cultural bases in Afghanistan. She believes that Afghan history clearly demonstrates that Afghan women have been reduced to symbols and pawns in the various struggles between pro-Western elites and more religiously rooted traditionalists because women are considered the culture-bearers and the heart of Afghan identity. Thus, Amiri sees that the status of women in twentieth-century Afghanistan has been caught between the modernist-led periods, where women represented more than sixty percent of the educated and professional population, and traditionalist rule, where women were powerless – most notably under the Taliban, as symbolized by the requirement that they wear the burqa and remain invisible in the public sphere.

Amiri has not spent her time fighting against the burqa, although out of consideration for Muslim standards of modesty, she began wearing a simple veil to cover her hair upon her return to Kabul; she did not don the burqa, as a subtle and silent encouragement for other women to discard theirs. She believes that the underlying issues of hunger, poverty, illiteracy, and the broader repression of women, as rooted in Afghan tribal culture, are more important than the superficial covering the burqa represents. Amiri notes that the conditions in Afghanistan following so many wars and drought had led to a general culture of violence that particularly targeted women. Broad social problems, such as high rates of illiteracy and unemployment, were particularly pronounced among women. In addition, Afghanistan had the second-highest rate of deaths related to childbirth in the world and, consequently, one of the lowest female life expectancies globally. Women further lacked inheritance and economic rights. Fully eighty-five percent of Afghan women did not have identity cards, suggesting that they did not legally exist.

Amiri sees in the debates about women's status and rights in Afghanistan reflections of the most important issues facing the contemporary Muslim world as societies increasingly discuss and debate the appropriate role for women. In the West, the emancipated Muslim woman is supported and encouraged as a sign of progress, development, and modernity; yet, within the Muslim world, she is often viewed as a symbol of Westernization and, therefore, a threat to the integrity and authenticity of Islam and Islamic culture. In order to move away from these unhelpful stereotypes and the conflicts they necessarily engender, Amiri has proposed a reinterpretation of Islam that is not inherently anti-woman. Because Islam is the only source of political and social legitimacy in Afghanistan, she believes that it is imperative for women's rights to be addressed from within an Islamic framework, rather than from Western definitions and methods that come from without. Refusal to do so can only lead, in her opinion, to opposition that would harm Afghan women and their position in the new Afghan society. She has pointed to Iran as a strong example to follow, noting that women participate in both civic and professional life, constitute the majority of university students, participate in the reinterpretation of the Quran, and vote and run for office. Although she admits that Iranian women still face some challenges, she notes that Iran demonstrates through its actions the legitimacy of Muslim women being active in public life.

Amiri believes that part of the reason why the Taliban were so repressive against women was the fact that the Soviet Union had the specific goal of destroying Afghan tribal culture, of which the status of women was one of the most powerful symbols. It was precisely because the Soviet Union had pressed so hard for women's political participation and literacy programs that the Taliban did away with them. Thus, while many Western activists believe that women's literacy and political activism are major signs of progress, many Afghans see simply a return to Soviet-era policies and a continued threat to native Afghan culture. Amiri therefore believes that the real challenge for Afghan women in the post-Taliban era is to find a balance between tradition and modernity, urban and rural culture that allows for the development of a common and authentic Afghan identity within which the gender issue can be addressed. She has cautioned against forceful and blatant Western pressure on the issue because of its potential to backfire and result in an even more limited and traditional role for women.

Amiri has proven particularly effective in working on cultural and gender issues because of her sensitivity to the discussions and the knowledge and personal experience she brings to them. The fact that she is not associated with any political party and is herself Afghan helps people to understand her as taking the side of the people, rather than taking a side in the war. She has also proven an important voice in presenting the Afghan situation credibly and poignantly to Western audiences at both the academic and policy levels.

Amiri's combined abilities, training, and experience led to her appointment as gender adviser for U.N.E.S.C.O. in Kabul. She considers her job to be more than a matter of "restoring" women's rights to what they were prior to the Taliban regime because women's rights had already been limited by the combination of war, successive *mujahidin* governments' restrictions, and brutal acts of mass violence and rape that have led women to fear the future in the absence of security and peace. Many women particularly fear a potential return to Taliban-style leadership and are afraid not only to remove their burqas but also to become more active in public life, believing that such actions could result in future reprisals.

In April 2003, Amiri pointed to evidence of progress for Afghan women. In Kabul, girls had returned to school, women had returned to the workplace, and had also made some important recoveries in public space, such as the revival of beauty parlors, which had been forbidden by the Taliban. However, she also cautioned that these positive developments have not occurred throughout Afghanistan and that the peace remains fragile. Major problems such as poverty, devastation, land mines, and the ongoing humanitarian crisis remain. In some places outside of Kabul, schoolgirls have been attacked and women have limited their public activities out of fear for their personal safety and in deference to cultural constraints. She remained hopeful that future elections would bring greater stability, end warlordism, develop the economy, and build up the country's infrastructure, but warned that such measures could succeed only with the ongoing assistance and financial support of the international community.

Amiri plans to remain in Afghanistan indefinitely to continue her efforts to bring peace and stability, particularly through resolution of the refugee crisis and the continued expansion of women's rights and access to public space. She derives inspiration from the courage of Afghan women who, after six years of extreme repression and being confined to their homes, have seized the opportunities for employment and education to rebuild their country. She continues to advise the United Nations on political matters and to work with women's organizations throughout Afghanistan toward these goals.

Further reading

Amiri, Rina. "The Fear Beneath the Burka," New York *Times*, March 20, 2002

—— "Inching Toward Normalcy and Freedom," *Boston Globe*, April 20, 2003

—— "Muslim Women as Symbols – and Pawns," New York *Times*, November 27, 2001

Crossette, Barbara. "Hope for the Future, Blunted by a Hard Past," New York *Times*, December 2, 2001

Lakshmanan, Indira A.R. "New Year Holds Special Promise for Women," *Boston Globe*, March 20, 2002

—— "A Royal Welcome for an Exiled Afghan," *Boston Globe*, April 19, 2002

Leonard, Mary. "Groups Seek Role for Women in Post-Taliban Government," *Boston Globe*, November 14, 2001

MacQuarrie, Brian. "Answering the Call: Afghan Activist Steps up to the Microphone to Help Other Women," *Boston Globe*, November 16, 2001

Rashid, Ahmed. *Taliban: Militant Islam, Oil and Fundamentalism in Central Asia.* London: I.B. Tauris, 2000

www.womenwagingpeace.net – website for Women Waging Peace

Muhammad Asad (1900–1992)

One of the most prominent twentieth-century Muslim scholars and thinkers, Muhammad Asad was one of the main theoreticians for the foundation of Pakistan, as well as one of the most prominent twentieth-century Jewish converts to Islam.

Muhammad Asad was born Leopold Weiss in July, 1900, in Lvov, Poland, which was then part of the Austro-Hungarian Empire. He was descended from a long line of rabbis. His father, Akiva, was the first male in several generations to break with the family tradition by becoming a barrister after secretly studying a secular curriculum at night. His mother, Malka, was the daughter of a wealthy local banker. She died in 1919.

At his paternal grandfather's insistence, Asad was educated to enter the family's traditional occupation. He received a thorough religious education and became proficient in Hebrew at an early age. He was also familiar with Aramaic and had a deep knowledge of the Talmud and Bible. However, his own parents were not very religious and did not adhere to Jewish rituals. Asad himself was uncomfortable with the traditional interpretation of Judaism that he learned formally because he found its worldview to be overly narrow. He personally did not believe that God was concerned about rituals or the destiny of a single ethnic or religious group. He understood God to be the creator and sustainer of all of humanity, rather than a tribal deity, and focused on the essence and purpose of religion.

Asad's family moved to Vienna when he was fourteen years old, at the outbreak of World War I. He ran away from school and tried to join the Austrian army, but was unsuccessful. He was officially drafted in 1919 just before the collapse of the empire. He then studied philosophy and art history at the University of Vienna. Although he enjoyed the intellectual stimulation of the city, his studies left him unfulfilled. He left Vienna in 1920 to travel through Central Europe. He eventually arrived in Berlin and worked at the United Telegraph news agency before becoming a journalist.

Like many of his generation, Asad had come to consider himself an agnostic. His religious views began to change in 1922 when he left Europe to visit an uncle in Jerusalem. During his time in Jerusalem, he came to know and respect many of the Arabs living there. He wrote that he was particularly struck by the meaning, spiritual strength, and peace Islam provided to their daily lives. From Jerusalem, Asad became a correspondent for the German newspaper *Frankfurter Zeitung*.

His writings from this time reflect his opposition to Zionism and the British, as well as support for Muslim and Arab nationalism.

While in Palestine, Asad met Chaim Weizman, the leader of the Zionist movement. Concerned for the then-majority Arab population of Palestine, Asad questioned the justice of a large influx of immigrants assisted by a great foreign power whose declared objective was the formation of a new majority and dispossession of the people already living there. He remained disturbed for the rest of his life that a group of people who had suffered so much historically in the diaspora could single-mindedly pursue their own goal at the cost of inflicting a similar wrong on others. He was never able to reconcile the Zionist solution with his recognition of the creative intelligence of the Jewish people.

Over the next four years, Asad traveled extensively and met Muslim intellectuals and heads of state in Palestine, Egypt, Iran, Iraq, Syria, Transjordan, and Afghanistan, all of which served to increase his interest in and contact with Islam. He later published his despatches as a book entitled *The Unromanticized East*. Although impressed by Islam as a way of life, he did not convert.

Asad returned to Berlin in 1926 as one of the most outstanding foreign correspondents in Central Europe and a source of interest to Orientalist scholars. His return by train from Afghanistan took him through Russia, Turkestan, Samarkand, Bukhara, Tashkent, the Turkmen steppes, the Ural Mountains, and Moscow where he observed the antireligious stance of the Soviet government, particularly against Muslims. Upon his return to Berlin, he gave a series of lectures at the Academy of Geopolitics. At twenty-five, he was the youngest person ever to receive such an honor.

In Berlin, Asad was struck one day while traveling on the subway by the realization that the well-dressed, well-fed people surrounding him all appeared to be unhappy and suffering. His impression was confirmed when he reached his home and read a passage of the Quran that he understood to describe this phenomenon. Convinced of the cohesion between Islam's moral teachings and the practical guidance it provided for daily life, he converted, choosing the names Muhammad in honor of the Prophet and Asad, which means "lion," in honor of his own given name. His conversion marked a rupture with his prior life. He quit his job and married his longtime girlfriend, a German painter named Elsa, who also converted. Shortly afterward, the couple went to Mecca for the Hajj pilgrimage.

Asad's pilgrimage resulted in several major life changes. Nine days after they arrived in Mecca, Elsa died from a tropical ailment. Shortly afterward, Asad had a chance encounter with Prince (later King) Faisal bin Abd al-Aziz Al Saud, resulting in an invitation to meet King Abd al-Aziz, the founder of contemporary Saudi Arabia. Asad spent the next six years studying Arabic, the Quran, the *hadith* (sayings of the Prophet), and Islamic law in Mecca and Medina, giving him a solid grounding in the sources of Islam and an interest in regenerating Islam. He also married in 1928, and again in 1930 following a divorce. His third wife, Munira, bore him a son, Talal, who became a professor of anthropology.

It is not known exactly why Asad left Saudi Arabia in 1932, although it has been speculated that he became disillusioned by the king's failure to implement the kind of progressive and value-oriented Islamic revival that Asad desired. Asad left Saudi Arabia for India,where he met Muhammad Iqbal, the poet-philosopher who became the religious ideologue for the foundation of Pakistan. Asad had planned to continue his travels to eastern Turkestan, China, and Indonesia, but Iqbal convinced him to remain in India to help establish the intellectual premises for the future state of Pakistan. Asad and Iqbal shared a dedication and vision to found Pakistan as a homeland for Muslims in which national unity would be based on adherence to a common faith and ideology. Asad became actively engaged in writing, studying, and lecturing, acquiring a reputation as an expert and dynamic interpreter of Islamic law and culture.

Asad's interest in the regeneration of Islam was based in part on his own disenchantment with materialism and secularism and in part on his belief in the practicality of Islam's teachings. He believed that the true values of Islam were generosity and readiness for self-sacrifice for the common good. His understanding of Islam as a spiritual and social phenomenon that served as the greatest driving force ever experienced by humanity was tempered by his realization of the deficiencies of Muslims themselves who he believed had ceased to follow the spirit of Islam's teachings in favor of narrow-mindedness and the love of an easy life. He sought to return Islam's spirit by gearing his interpretation toward action and engagement with the world, rather than passivity and asceticism.

In 1935, Asad made peace with his estranged father who had disowned him following his conversion to Islam. Although they corresponded continuously afterward, Asad never saw his father again. Asad returned to Europe briefly in the spring of 1939 to try to save his family from Nazi persecution. By the time he arrived, Austria had been annexed by Nazi Germany and the confiscations, persecutions, pogroms, and deportations of Jews had already started. Unable to rescue his family, Asad returned to India where he was incarcerated by the British as an "enemy alien." He remained imprisoned for six years. Upon his release in August 1945, he learned that his father, stepmother, and sister had been deported from Vienna in 1942 and had died in Nazi concentration camps.

Asad moved to Pakistan in 1947. He organized and directed the Department of Islamic Reconstruction, playing a pivotal role in the elaboration of the ideological Islamic concepts of statehood and community for the government. He also provided the theoretical foundation for an Islamic state as a liberal, multiparty parliamentary democracy in which sovereignty belongs to God and the believers conduct all affairs of state and community in consultation. He declared that Islam possessed the flexibility and features necessary for parliamentary democracy and rule of law. To his disappointment, many of his proposals were never implemented. One important exception was the constitutional provision that the head of government could be either male or female, setting the stage for BENAZIR BHUTTO's rise to power in 1988.

Asad's interpretation of Islam, Islamic law, and Islamic government was based upon knowledge of and respect for tradition without blind adherence to past decisions or dogma. He consistently argued for mercy and understanding in the application of Islamic law, rather than what he described as "cold justice." Believing that both Islamic law and Islamic political theory were critical to the success of the Muslim community, he called for the use of independent reasoning (*ijtihad*) as critical to providing enough flexibility for the system to adapt to an ever-changing world and context and the use of the Quranic principle of consultation (*shura*) for social and political issues not specifically determined by the Quran or *hadith*. He opposed totalitarian systems of government as anti-Islamic.

Part of Asad's ongoing impact on Muslim thought lies in the fact that he worked independently as a scholar. Because he neither founded nor participated in an organized movement, he did not leave behind disciples who carried out his thought. Muslims today derive inspiration from his methodology for interpreting scripture and Islamic law. Accessible to both Muslims and non-Muslims alike, Asad's writings offer a critical examination of the causes of the decline of Muslims, as well as the problems and issues they face, combined with an attempted synthesis of Islam and modernity that reconciled religion and modernization without blindly imitating Western values and mores.

Asad directed the department for two years before being transferred to the Foreign Ministry, where he was appointed head of the Middle East Division and worked to strengthen ties between Pakistan and the rest of the Muslim world. In 1952, he became Pakistan's minister plenipotentiary to the United Nations and moved to New York City. He divorced Munira shortly afterward and married an American convert to Islam, Pola Hamida.

Asad resigned his position in 1954 to write his autobiography, *The Road to Mecca*, which traces the psychological process by which he became a Muslim and adopted Muslim culture. Written in part by Asad and in part by Pola, *The Road to Mecca* has been translated into numerous European languages and remains popular throughout the Muslim world.

In 1955, Asad left New York and lived in different locations in Europe, including Switzerland, Portugal, and, ultimately, Spain. During this time, he embarked on what he considered to be the most important work of his life, his translation and exegesis of the Quran entitled *The Message of the Qur'an*, which took seventeen years to complete. *The Message of the Qur'an* continues to be considered one of the best English-language translations and interpretations of the Quran.

Over the years, Asad became saddened by what he perceived to be the intellectual insularity of the Muslim world and the intolerance of extremists. As an advocate of women's rights and human rights and a supporter of Islamic values, he believed that fundamentalists had taken the wrong approach to the implementation of Islamic law by beginning with the *hudud* punishments, rather than by focusing on creating a more Islamic society based on Islamic values. Asad's own writings demonstrate Islam as a faith for educated, rational people in the most advanced parts of the world.

Asad died in Spain in 1992 and was buried in the Muslim cemetery in Granada.

Further reading

Asad, Muhammad. "Becoming Muslim," www.usc.edu/dept/MSA/newmuslims/asad.html

—— *Islam at the Crossroads*. Chicago: Kazi Publications, 1995

—— *The Message of the Qur'an*. Gibraltar: Dar al-Andalus, 1980

—— *Principles of State and Government in Islam*. Berkeley: University of California Press, 1961

—— *The Road to Mecca*. New York: Simon & Schuster, 1954

Nawwab, Ismail Ibrahim. "Berlin to Makkah: Muhammad Asad's Journey into Islam," *Saudi Aramco World*, vol. 53, no. 1, February, 2002

Rahim, Hasan Zillur. "Muhammad Asad: Visionary Islamic Scholar," *Washington Report on Middle East Affairs*, September, 1995

Wolfe, Michael. *One Thousand Roads to Mecca: Ten Centuries of Travelers Writing about the Muslim Pilgrimage*. New York: Grove Press, 1999

video: *Tribute to Muhammad Asad*, Islamic Publications International, 1988

B

Benazir Bhutto (b. 1953)

The first democratically elected female prime minister of a Muslim-majority country, Benazir Bhutto is often pointed to as a symbol of the progress of women in the Muslim world.

Benazir Bhutto was born on June 21, 1953, into a politically active family. Her grandfather, Sir Shah Nawaz Khan Bhutto, founded the first political party in Sindh in 1947. Her father, Zulfikar Ali Bhutto, served as a lawyer and government minister in Karachi prior to founding the People's Party of Pakistan (P.P.P.). He was later elected prime minister of Pakistan. Her mother, Nusrat, was elected to the National Assembly and helped to carry out her husband's political work. As a child and young woman, Bhutto frequently traveled with her father and accompanied him to meetings with foreign dignitaries. She considers her father to have been the single greatest influence over her life, thought, and political goals. She has one sister and two brothers.

In accordance with her parents' expectation that all of their children receive a strong and equal education, Bhutto was enrolled at the Lady Jennings Nursery School when she was three years old. When she was five, she transferred to the Irish Catholic Convent of Jesus and Mary, where she was instructed in English. At the age of ten, she began boarding school from where she established a lifelong pattern of correspondence with her father, resulting in her practical political education. This correspondence continued through her formative years of higher education at Radcliffe and Oxford University.

Bhutto entered Radcliffe in 1969. There she perceived what she describes as the powerlessness of Third World countries in the face of self-interested superpowers. Her first-hand experience of the Watergate scandal and Nixon's subsequent impeachment led her to a direct understanding of what is meant by the "rule of law." She came to appreciate the importance and power of nationally accepted laws, rather than whimsical or arbitrary laws imposed by individuals, and the accountability of every individual before the law, regardless of status, gender, wealth, or political connections. She also came into contact with many women who did not set marriage and the raising of children as their primary goals in life.

Although she would have preferred to pursue her graduate studies in the United States, Bhutto's father insisted that she attend Oxford University in England. Bhutto entered Oxford in 1973 and earned a graduate degree in P.P.E.

(philosophy, politics, and economics). During her fourth year, she studied international law and diplomacy. She also joined the Oxford Union Debating Society, which was renowned as a training ground for future politicians, with the express goal of harnessing the power of oratory for herself for future use in a hoped-for career in the Foreign Service back in Pakistan. She was elected as its president in 1976.

Bhutto's life changed dramatically in 1977 when her father and his government were overthrown in a military coup led by General Zia ul-Haq. Bhutto herself was arrested for the first time on September 29, 1977, and was held in detention for fifteen days. She credits her father with teaching her the necessary skills and endurance to withstand repeated detentions and lengthy stays in solitary confinement as punishment for her active involvement in opposition politics.

While her father was in detention between 1977 and 1979, Bhutto worked with him to fight the charges leveled against him. She brought to public and international attention the injustice of the trial, including failure to adhere to the law, a code of ethics, and the judicial process during the trial, such as the prosecution's failure to present sworn testimonies. While her father was imprisoned, Bhutto began her own career as a politician and public speaker, carrying out her father's defense and spreading his message in order to stir up popular support for his cause.

Bhutto was devastated by her father's execution on April 3, 1979. Upon her release from detention, she retired to the family's farm in Larkana, where she took over its management. The situation allowed her to transcend some of Pakistan's gender traditions because she needed to meet with the male managers and overseers to discuss issues ranging from accounting to fertilization and planting crops. During this time, she also took over the role of "elder" in dispensing tribal justice to the inhabitants and farm workers, a role for which she was admittedly ill prepared. Her failure to understand rural custom and symbolism led some of her critics to charge her with elitism and a lack of contact with and understanding of the masses.

Bhutto made use of her time at the farm to continue her opposition politics by working with her father's political party, the P.P.P., to support the constitution and push for elections and the restoration of democracy. The P.P.P. swept local elections in September, 1979. Fearing a P.P.P. victory in the national elections scheduled for October, Zia canceled them and imprisoned both Bhutto and her mother.

Zia's constant posturing led Bhutto to agree to a coalition between the P.P.P. and the P.N.A. (Pakistan National Alliance) in the fall of 1980 in order to oppose him. The result was the establishment of the Movement to Restore Democracy (M.R.D.), which joined together ten different political parties to protest the injustices of martial law and unseat Zia by forcing elections. Zia responded by placing Bhutto in solitary confinement from March until December, 1981. Throughout her confinement, she repeatedly refused to renounce her political activities or to meet with administrators because she believed that the first would have meant betraying her father and her followers and the second would have entailed recognition of a regime that she regarded as illegitimate. Bhutto recalls this time as a physical and psychological challenge. She developed anorexia nervosa and an ear condition that cost her a portion of her hearing. She also experienced gynecological problems that required surgery and hospitalization. She claims that Zia intended to have her die on the operating table. She was ultimately sent abroad to England in 1983 to have her ear condition treated.

Bhutto's persecution by Zia's regime proved politically beneficial in the end. Her years in detention combined with her family's suffering served to elevate her status in the eyes of the Pakistani people as the credible successor to her father. They also allowed her to speak first hand about human rights abuses and the need to restore democracy in Pakistan when meeting with Western officials abroad. From her exile in London, Bhutto began a letter-writing campaign to address human rights abuses and the issue of political prisoners. She traveled throughout Europe to promote her campaign and began publishing a magazine, *Amal* (*Action*), about events in Pakistan to keep expatriates informed and to lift the morale of political prisoners by letting them know that they and their causes had not been forgotten. She focused on issues of national importance, rather than traditional provincial politics, and emphasized the need to fight the common enemy – the Zia regime – rather than each other.

From 1984 to 1988, Bhutto headed the opposition to Zia's government, first from abroad and then, following her return from England in April, 1986, from within Pakistan. Other than Zia's practice of detaining people for their political convictions, she was particularly angered by Zia's Islamization measures that took away many of the rights women had been given under her father's regime. When she was greeted by a crowd of over one million people upon her return to Pakistan, she used her mass popularity to call for democratic elections and to urge the people to refrain from violence. Although she believes that the masses who welcomed her upon her return did so because they supported her personally, critics and analysts have noted that this support was more likely due to the fact that she represented the most credible and potent opposition to the by-then-unpopular Zia regime. Although she proved to be a charismatic leader and had a powerful family name, she lacked a strong, effective party program and organization, a

point that became apparent when she was in power.

Recognizing that he was losing control over the country, Zia finally called for democratic elections for October, 1988. In the interim, he tried to reconsolidate his legitimacy by declaring Islamic law as the law of the land and proposing a deal with the P.P.P., which the P.P.P. refused. Ultimately, the power structure and political struggle changed when Zia and many of his senior staff and ministers were killed in a plane crash on August 17, 1988, leaving the country in a political vacuum. Bhutto responded to these events by again calling for a return to democracy via fair and impartial elections.

The P.P.P. won the largest portion of the vote in 1988, although the margin of their victory was small. Bhutto was named prime minister and was called upon to form a government. At thirty-five she was one of the youngest heads of government in the world and the first woman to lead a modern Muslim nation. One of her first acts as prime minister was to declare amnesty for all remaining political prisoners jailed by Zia. She served as prime minister until 1990 and then again from 1993 until 1996.

Bhutto's first years in office were spent focusing largely on political survival, rather than achieving the reforms she had hoped to enact, particularly the reformation of democracy and the role of Islam in the state. She had hoped to establish a secular democracy, but the general Islamic climate of Pakistani politics begun by her father and exploited and expanded by Zia proved to be insurmountable. Despite her campaign promises, she was unable significantly to dismantle their Islamic legacy. In fact, she herself ultimately had to embrace Islamic rhetoric in order to gain and remain in power. She justified her leadership of Pakistan through references to strong Muslim women leaders of the past and compared the suffering of her family for the sake of democracy to the martyrdom of the Prophet Muhammad's grandson Husayn. Shortly after her election, she made the lesser pilgrimage (*umra*) to Mecca, a pilgrimage that she has repeated annually.

Unable to initiate substantive reform for women's rights and pressured to respect tradition as a matter of political survival, Bhutto covered her head in public, agreed to an arranged marriage with Asif Zardari in 1987, and raised three children. She justified acceding to Pakistani norms for marriage and having children by noting that her previous repeated detentions and confinements had not been conducive to marriage earlier or to selecting her own spouse. She noted that her marriage was traditional in form, but not entirely in content. She made certain that her husband was aware that her primary commitment would always be to Pakistan and that her marriage and family would always come second. She broke with the Pakistani tradition of a lavish wedding celebration and gifts in favor of a simple ceremony and celebration, noting that many families on the Indian subcontinent enter into massive debt for wedding ceremonies. By setting a more practical and affordable example and by inviting the poor of Karachi, Bhutto hoped to inspire other Pakistani women and families to do the same.

Although Bhutto and her political ambitions were encouraged and strongly supported by the West, particularly the United States, many Pakistanis questioned the appropriateness of her political goals for Pakistani culture and politics. It was precisely because she appeared to be reliant upon the United States for her position that many Pakistanis felt that she lacked authority and was unable to rule effectively. Although Bhutto has claimed that she had the mandate of the people to carry out her program, political analysts note that her party, the P.P.P., had to form alliances with other political parties in order to achieve sufficient strength for election.

Domestically, Bhutto's tenure was plagued by ethnic and regional conflicts, particularly provincial demands for greater autonomy. An epidemic of violence and lawlessness followed. By late 1990, the province of Sindh had deteriorated into a region of lawlessness, kidnappings, riots, lootings, bombings, and massacres. Her regime was further hampered by charges of corruption in both her family and government. Accused of lacking a coherent strategy for rule and a clear political program, Bhutto's government was dismissed on August 6, 1990, on charges of corruption and incompetence.

Although Bhutto was reelected in 1993, her government was dismissed again in November 1996, once more on charges of corruption and incompetence. She faced numerous problems: a stagnant economy; lawlessness; continued and endemic corruption; ethnic and sectarian violence; a growing culture of drugs and guns due to Pakistan's involvement in Afghanistan; an influx of Afghan refugees; and the apparent threat of Islamic fundamentalism. Bhutto's government ultimately succumbed again to the breakdown of law and order, resulting in charges of rampant corruption (including against her husband and close associates) and mismanagement.

Although Bhutto has remained active as a voice of opposition politics in Pakistan, she has not returned to politics since the suspension of democracy that followed the coup d'état led by General Pervez Musharraf. After corruption charges were filed against her and she was sentenced to prison, she fled to exile, living in London and the United Arab Emirates while planning her eventual return to politics. Her husband has remained in prison in Pakistan on charges of corruption.

Further reading

Akhund, Iqbal. *Trial and Error: The Advent and Eclipse of Benazir Bhutto*. New York: Oxford University Press, 2000

Bhutto, Benazir. *Daughter of Destiny: Benazir Bhutto, an Autobiography.* New York: Simon & Schuster, 1989

"Bhutto Pursues a Pakistani Comeback, in India," New York *Times* International, November 30, 2001

Esposito, John L. *Islam and Politics,* 4th ed. Syracuse, NY: Syracuse University Press, 1998

Esposito, John L. and John O. Voll. *Islam and Democracy.* New York: Oxford University Press, 1998

Nasr, S.V.R. "Islamic Opposition in the Political Process: Lessons From Pakistan," in *Political Islam: Revolution, Radicalism, or Reform?,* ed. John L. Esposito. Boulder, CO: Lynne Rienner Publishers, Inc., 1997

Abu Rayham Muhammad al-Biruni (973–1048)

Considered one of the greatest and most important Muslim scientists of all time, Abu Rayham Muhammad al-Biruni was an expert in mathematics, astronomy, geography, mineralogy, metallurgy, geology, botany, pharmacology, astrology, history, and philosophy.

Abu Rayham Muhammad al-Biruni was born on September 15, 973, in Jurjaniyya, near Kath, Khwarazm (in contemporary Uzbekistan). He began his formal studies at a very early age under the renowned astronomer and mathematician Abu Nasr Mansur, who remained his mentor and colleague for the rest of his life.

Al-Biruni was engaged in serious scientific work from the time he was seventeen years old. In 990, he computed the latitude of Kath by observing the maximum altitude of the sun. By the age of twenty-two, he was a veteran of serious theoretical work, having already written a number of short works, including one on map projections entitled *Cartography,* which presents a wide selection of map projections invented by other people and includes his own projection of a hemisphere onto a plane.

Al-Biruni's quiet scholarly career was disrupted by the cataclysmic political events of 995, during which the region he lived in was engulfed by civil wars generated by the overthrow of the ruling Banu Iraq. He fled the area, although it is not known where he went. It is speculated that he might have gone to Rayy (close to the contemporary city of Tehran, Iran) because he was known to have been there several years later and to have conversed with the astronomer al-Khujandi at the major observatory in Rayy. Al-Biruni disputed al-Khujandi's measurements and latitudes, observing that his sextant did not operate correctly because of its heavy weight. During this time, al-Biruni is also believed to have traveled to Gilan because he dedicated a work written during this time to Gilan's ruler, Ibn Rustam.

Al-Biruni eventually returned to his home. He is known to have been in Kath in 997 because of a description of an eclipse of the moon he recorded there on May 24, 997. He corresponded with a Baghdadi astronomer, Abu al-Wafa, who also viewed the eclipse. The comparison of timings enabled al-Biruni to calculate accurately the difference in longitude between the cities. However, he did not remain sedentary. He traveled frequently in his pursuit of scientific knowledge. In 1000, he was known to be in Gurgan, where he was supported by the Ziyarid ruler, Qabus, to whom he dedicated his *Chronology.* He was also in Gurgan on February 19, 1003, and August 14, 1003, where he observed eclipses of the moon.

On June 4, 1004, al-Biruni was in his native Jurjaniyya, where he observed an eclipse of the moon. By this time, he enjoyed the patronage and generous support of his local ruler, Abu al-Abbas Mamun. This support enabled him to build an instrument at Jurjaniyya to observe solar meridian transits. He made fifteen observations with the instrument between June 7 and December 7, 1016.

This observational data was used to create astronomical tables.

Al-Biruni left his native region in 1017 when the Afghan Ghaznavid ruler Mahmud conquered it. Whether he left of his own volition or as a prisoner is unclear. Although he received some support from Mahmud for his scientific work, Mahmud was reportedly personally cruel to him. Despite the working conditions, al-Biruni continued his astronomical research and observations, observing an eclipse in Kabul (in contemporary Afghanistan) on October 14, 1018, creating his own instruments from materials he had on hand, and an eclipse of the sun in Lamghan (north of Kabul) on April 8, 1019. He also made observations from Ghazna (in contemporary Afghanistan) between 1018 and 1020, permitting him to make an accurate determination of its latitude.

Al-Biruni's status as Mahmud's de facto prisoner led to his inclusion in Mahmud's entourage when he made military excursions into India. It is unclear how many visits he made, but his trips to northern India covered a range of twenty years and resulted in observations that enabled him to determine the latitudes of eleven towns around the Punjab and the borders of Kashmir. One of his most famous works, *Kitab al-Hind* (*The Book of India*), was written on the basis of his direct studies there. The book describes the religion, philosophy, astronomy, astrology, calendar, marriage customs, caste system, systems of writing and numbers, and geography of India.

Athough he was a native Persian speaker, al-Biruni studied Indian literature in its original Sanskrit, some of which he translated into Arabic, which was the universal scientific language at that time. He wrote several treatises on Indian astronomy and mathematics, as well as a book entitled *Kitab al-Saydana*, which is a compilation of Arabic and Indian knowledge of medicine. He was well read in Sanskrit and possessed knowledge of Sanskrit texts on astronomy, astrology, geography, chronology, medicine, mathematics, grammar, philosophy, religion, and weights and measures, enabling him to introduce Hindu knowledge into Arabic science. He was also responsible for the transmission of Arabic scientific knowledge into Sanskrit, including his own translation of Euclid's works.

Mahmud's death in 1030 led to the succession of his son, Masud, who was kinder to al-Biruni and allowed him to travel freely. Al-Biruni continued his scientific pursuits and prolific writing up until his death on December 13, 1048 in Ghazna.

Al-Biruni is believed to have written at least 146 works, totalling more than thirteen thousand pages and covering essentially all of what was known about science during his lifetime. Only about one-third of his works have survived. He was most interested in the study of observable phenomena in both nature and humanity, as well as mathematical analysis. He was a keen observer of both history and culture, making his works important for a number of fields.

Al-Biruni's writings are characterized by a methodical approach to his topic. He typically began with a critical overview of older theories and mathematical methods, followed either by the selection of one of these theories or the presentation of a new theory. His work as a whole constitutes a critical assessment of the state of the mathematical knowledge of astronomy through the early eleventh century. This provision of a solid and complete foundation laid the ground for future scientists to move in new directions and to devise new strategies and topics of research.

Al-Biruni's scientific achievement includes the command of Hindu, Greek, and Arabic astronomy and science, which he synthesized in his major work *al-Qanun al-Masudi*, a work that is comparable to the Greek astronomer

Ptolemy's major work on astronomy, *Almagest*. The book is an important source of information about the contributions of earlier astronomers and includes discussions of several theorems of astronomy, trigonometry, and solar, lunar, and planetary motions, as well as the obligatory determination of the direction for prayer (*qibla*), although through a novel combination of the ancient Menelaus theorem and the newer sine rule. Its most important contribution was the introduction of techniques for measuring the earth and distances on it through triangulation, a mathematical method for determining the height and depth of objects and widths of obstacles, such as rivers, that could not be measured directly. It includes a table with the coordinates of 600 places and a measurement of the radius of the earth of 6,339.6 kilometers, a value not obtained in the West until the sixteenth century.

Al-Biruni's major contribution to astronomy came through his rejection of Aristotelian physical axioms, such as the notion that heavenly bodies have an inherent nature. He believed that motion could be compulsory and maintained that no observable evidence ruled out the possibility of vacuum. Although he admitted that observation appeared to confirm Aristotle's claim that the motion of heavenly bodies was circular, he held that there was no inherent "natural" reason why such movement could not be elliptical. What was significant in this hypothesis was not so much the content of his objections as his methodology of argumentation. Reflecting the emergence of the recognition of the connection between science and other forms of knowledge, al-Biruni's methodology of argumentation applies systematic, rigorous mathematical reasoning to astronomy and nature. Because he considered only observational and mathematical evidence to be "true" evidence, he clearly distinguished between philosophers and mathematicians, or metaphysicians and

scientists. This distinction was made most clearly in his correspondence with the Muslim philosopher Ibn Sina (Avicenna), eighteen letters of which have survived, addressing philosophy, physics, and astronomy. Al-Biruni's scientific methodology of observation also distinguished him from Ptolemy because, whereas Ptolemy did not include observations that did not fit his theories in his discussions, al-Biruni treated errors scientifically, providing justifications and explanations as to why he believed some observations to be more reliable than others. He also was conscientious about rounding his errors in his calculations and about observing quantities that required a minimum of manipulation in order to produce answers, thus providing examples of controlled experimentation.

Like many astronomers of his time, al-Biruni compiled some astrological manuals because of their cultural importance, but personally had little confidence in astrology as a science, seeing it as a means of providing support for his serious scientific work, rather than a serious scientific occupation. His astrological manuals are important both as a source of information about the state and practice of astrology during his lifetime and also because of the diagrams of lunar eclipses he included.

He wrote a major mathematical book entitled *Shadows* around 1021, which included the Arabic nomenclature of shade and shadows, descriptions of strange phenomena involving shadows, gnomonics, the history of tangent and secant functions, shadow observations for the solution of various astronomical problems, shadow-determined times for Muslim prayers, and applications of shadow functions to the astrolabe and other instruments. This book is a particularly important source of the history of astronomy, physics, and mathematics and contains ideas such as use of three rectangular coordinates to define a point in three-dimensional space, the connection of acceleration with non-uniform motion, and ideas that anticipated the introduction of polar coordinates. The book also details al-Biruni's mathematical contributions, including theoretical and practical arithmetic; the rule of three; irrational numbers; the summation of series; combinatorial analysis; ratio theory; algebraic definitions; Archimedes' theorems; geometry; a method for solving algebraic equations; the trisection of the angle and other problems that cannot be solved through the use of a ruler and compass alone; conic sections; trigonometry; stereometry; stereographic projection; solving spherical triangles; and the sine theorem in the plane.

In addition to these important contributions to astronomy and mathematics, al-Biruni was a keen observer of mechanical devices and processes, including a mechanical calendar and the processing of gold ores via water-drive trip hammers. His observations indicate that water power was used in a variety of industries by the early eleventh century. He also wrote about methods of casting iron and making steel and completed a treatise on minerals entitled *Kitab al-Jamahir*.

Other scientific and mathematical contributions include the compilation of an accurate table of specific gravities on the basis of experimentation, the observation that the speed of light is faster than the speed of sound, and an accurate description of the Milky Way as "a collection of countless fragments of the nature of nebulous stars." He wrote several treatises on the astrolabe and calculated the ratios between the densities of gold, lead, mercury, brass, bronze, silver, copper, iron, and tin. He studied hydrostatics and accurately explained the workings of natural springs and artesian wells by the hydrostatic principles of communicating vessels. He investigated a number of curiosities, including the phenomenon of Siamese twins and the observation that flowers have three, four, five, six or eighteen petals, but never seven or nine. He also wrote a book entitled *al-Athar al-Baqia*, in which he tried to connect the ancient history of nations and related geographical knowledge and discussed the rotation of the earth.

Al-Biruni's writings reflect the work of a man who was a careful observer and leading exponent of the experimental method, rather than a great innovator of original theories. His linguistic ability enabled him to read first hand an enormous body of literature, which, in turn, helped him to see the development of science as part of a historical process that was to be considered contextually. His writings are of interest to both scientists and historians of science.

Al-Biruni's writings also reflect a spirit of tolerance. He demonstrated no prejudice against different religious sects or races – he considered Christianity to be a "noble," although impractical, philosophy – although he had strong opinions about acts committed by people of a variety of backgrounds and persuasions. He was known during his lifetime as a devout Muslim who combined a critical spirit, love of truth, and scientific approach with tolerance.

Further reading

Anderson, Margaret J. and Karen F. Stephenson. *Scientists of the Ancient World*. Berkeley Heights, NJ: Enslow Publishers, Inc., 1999

Dallal, Ahmad. "Science, Medicine, and Technology: The Making of a Scientific Culture," in *The Oxford History of Islam*, editor-in-chief John L. Esposito. New York: Oxford University Press, 1999

Hill, Donald R. *Islamic Science and Engineering*. Edinburgh: Edinburgh University Press, 1993

Turner, Howard R. *Science in Medieval Islam: An Illustrated Introduction*. Austin: University of Texas Press, 1995

www-gap.dcs.st-and.ac.uk/~history/Mathematicians/Al-Biruni.html

Djamila Bouhired (b. 1937)

Heroine and symbol of Algerian women's participation in the Algerian war for independence, Djamila Bouhired is popularly known as the "Arab Joan of Arc." She has been active in the struggle for women's rights in Algeria since the 1960s.

Djamila Bouhired was born in 1937 in Algeria. Her father was a businessman. Her mother was a seamstress who raised the children full-time and made all of their clothing. She has five older brothers.

Bouhired's exposure to the Algerian national struggle for independence stems from her early childhood. Although her parents were not directly involved in the independence movement led by the National Liberation Front (F.L.N.), her uncles were and were frequently questioned by authorities.

Bouhired grew up believing that she was French. From the age of six, she attended a French school (Ecole Dauvidan), learned French lessons from French teachers, and spoke French at school. Her main language for communication, even as an adult, was French. Although she spoke the Algerian dialect of Arabic, she never learned to read or write in Arabic. Envisaging a future as a seamstress in which she planned to help her mother, she attended a vocational school.

Her early dreams were shattered by the increasing levels of violence surrounding her. At fifteen, she became conscious of possessing a dual (Algerian and French) identity. Two major events catapulted her Algerian identity to the forefront, radicalizing her to engage in the struggle for Algerian independence. The first was a massacre in the Qasbah section of Algiers where her family lived. The French military had recognized the Qasbah as a hotbed of Algerian activism and routinely searched the area for those involved in a series of deadly bombings in Algiers in order to break the resistance.

Up until the time of the massacres, Bouhired's involvement with the F.L.N. was limited to the distribution of pamphlets and the collection of contributions. However, both of her parents and one of her uncles were killed during the massacres, leaving her an orphan with a hatred of French rule. The second event was the death of her friend Aminah, who was one of the many Algerian women involved in the bomb-throwing campaigns in Algiers that began in September, 1956. These bombings targeted cafes and other public places frequented by the French occupation forces. Aminah carried the bombs in a fashionable French handbag, leading French police and guards to assume that she was going shopping or was on her way to meet a friend. When Aminah's activities were discovered, she committed suicide by ingesting poison, rather than risking imprisonment and torture by the French.

After these events, Bouhired became more actively involved in the struggle for independence, taking on the role of bomb thrower. She became both famous and infamous for her role in the 1957 battle of Algiers. Because she could pass for a European woman when wearing Western dress, she was chosen to place a bomb in the Bar Simone at a time when French soldiers and their girlfriends were dancing there. The purpose of the bombing was the assassination of Officer Bayard, who had led the massacre in the Qasbah that had killed Bouhired's parents. Bouhired was arrested when she was returning from the mission she had just completed, although she was not carrying a bomb at the time of her arrest. On her way to her uncle's house in the Qasbah, she heard French soldiers calling to her. Seeking escape, she started to walk faster, but was shot in the shoulder and fell to the ground. She was subsequently taken to the Barbarossa prison, where she was interrogated – even during the removal of the bullet fragments from her shoulder – incarcerated, and tortured, including the use of electrodes on her body, over a period of seventeen days in an effort to have her name her accomplices. Her refusal to betray her comrades under torture and subsequent trial and sentencing made her an international symbol of militant resistance to French rule and of Algerian women's active and public involvement in the struggle for independence.

Bouhired went on military trial in July 1957. Although she acknowledged her membership in the F.L.N., she denied participation in the fatal bombing in which she was charged. Her attorney, Jacques Verges, charged that the trial had been filled with irregularities, such as his being denied access to essential documents and the right to enter a final plea in her defense. The most incriminating testimony against Bouhired came from a female witness who showed numerous signs of mental instability – something that normally would have raised questions about the credibility of her testimony. Despite the trial's irregularities, Bouhired was found guilty and sentenced to death.

Bouhired's trial and sentence made her a *cause célèbre* for French leftists and human rights activists, who decried both the conduct of the trial and the increasingly commonplace use of torture on Algerian prisoners. Bouhired's story was publicized throughout the Arab world, where she became a symbol of Algerian women and a heroine of the revolution. Her attorney co-published a pamphlet entitled *Pour Djamila Bouhired* to publicize her case in France. In the Arab world, she became the subject of books, a movie, and a number of poems. Although she has commented that these are works of legend, rather than pure fact, the legend has been taught as history to generations of Algerian boys and girls, as well as Arab children throughout the Middle East.

In Algeria, the F.L.N. commander of the Algiers Qasbah, Saadi Yacef, ordered a new round of bombings and threatened to engulf the city in violence if Bouhired's sentence was carried out. Although Yacef was captured by the French in August 1957, demonstrations in Algiers continued, reaching their zenith at the end of the appeals process for Bouhired in March 1958. French president Coty responded to heavy Algerian and international pressure by commuting Bouhired's sentence to life imprisonment. She was transferred to France and remained incarcerated there until Algeria won independence in 1962.

After independence, Bouhired returned to Algeria and ran unsuccessfully for a seat in Algeria's first National Assembly. She later edited *Revolution africaine* until the purge of communists from Algerian public life forced her from her position in 1963. At this time, she withdrew from public life, married Jacques Verges, and raised a family. The couple eventually divorced.

After her withdrawal from public life, Bouhired worked to improve social conditions at the neighborhood level. She believed that this work was also a kind of heroism because the role of heroes does not end at the conclusion of the battle, but continues in the example one sets for others in ordinary life and day-to-day actions. Although she remained a self-defined militant, Bouhired shifted her use of militance from fighting the French to fighting poverty and working to protect orphans and war widows.

The revolution that led to independence is known in Algeria today as "the revolution of the million martyrs." Algerian women who fought as *mujahidat* (holy warriors) were important symbols in the construction of the new Algeria. Although Bouhired was widely praised as a particularly important symbol, she was a reluctant one, noting that she was only one of many Djamilas who had carried bombs in their handbags and thrown them into cafes. She also commented that there were many other women in prison with her who were

subjected to even harsher methods of torture and died from it or were executed by
the French, yet, like her, refused to betray
their comrades. Because she believes that
every Algerian had a national duty to be
a hero during the revolution, Bouhired
considers her own actions to be neither
more nor less than what every other
Algerian national was expected to do.
For her, it is the principle in which the
group believes and for which they are
willing to fight, rather than the individual
activists, that is important. The F.L.N.
sought revolution and independence,
both of which they achieved.

Because of their pivotal contributions, it
was anticipated that Algerian women
would be included in discussions of the
welfare and future of Algeria that followed independence. Family law reforms
and the expansion of women's legal rights
were widely expected. However, these
changes did not occur. Many prominent
female militants, exhausted by the personal cost of the war, withdrew into private life to raise their families. Believing
that the rebuilding of the nation and
national identity were more important
than gender issues and that men would
remember their contributions to independence, they did not cohere to formulate an
agenda for women's rights. Bouhired herself noted that Algerian women were not
concerned about sexual problems, issues
or freedom at that time because they considered the construction of Algeria to be a
greater and more important task.

Like many Algerian women, Bouhired
was surprised and disturbed by the
marginalization of women post-
independence. Believing that women
have an important role to play in the
quest for justice, freedom, and peace, she
wrote an open letter to then-President
Chadli Benjedid entitled "No to the
Betrayal of the Ideals of November 1,
1954" in 1981. She then led women to
participate in demonstrations against the
government at a time when men didn't
dare to. It was the first instance of open
and public confrontation of the state and
its single party since independence.

The letter also had a major impact on
the Algerian feminist movement during
the 1990s as Algerian women began to
articulate their own rights, including
reaching legal majority at the same age as
men; having the unconditional right to
work; enjoying equality in marriage and
divorce; calling for the abolition of
polygamy; demanding an equal division
of common inheritances; and insisting
that abandoned children be properly
protected and that single mothers be
given legal status. These issues have civil
rights, rather than feminism, as their
focal point. The fact that the campaign
was led by the heroine of the Algerian
war for independence forced the government to give in and grant some of the
rights demanded.

Bouhired remains one of the most
respected women in Algerian public life
because of her role in the struggle for
independence. She continues to serve as a
powerful symbol for women's rights,
courage, and achievement.

Further reading

Charrad, Mounira M. *States and Women's
Rights: The Making of Postcolonial Tunisia,
Algeria, and Morocco*. Berkeley: University
of California Press, 2001
Horne, Alistair A. *A Savage War of Peace:
Algeria, 1954–1962*, rev. ed. New York:
Penguin Group U.S.A., 1987
"Interviews with Jamilah Buhrayd, Legendary
Algerian Hero," in *Middle Eastern Muslim
Women Speak*, ed. Elizabeth Warnock
Fernea and Basima Qattan Bezirgan. Austin:
University of Texas Press, 1977
Perkins, Kenneth J. "Bouhired, Djamila," in
*The Oxford Encyclopedia of the Modern
Islamic World*, editor-in-chief John L.
Esposito, vol. 1. New York: Oxford Univer-
sity Press, 1995

Hassiba Boulmerka (b. 1968)

Winner of the gold medal in the 1992
Barcelona Olympic Games for the
1,500-meter race, Hassiba Boulmerka

became the first Algerian and only the second Arab or Muslim woman ever to win an Olympic gold medal. She was the first woman from an Arab or African country to win a world track championship.

Hassiba Boulmerka was born on July 10, 1968, in Constantine, Algeria. Her determination to pursue sports has always been an act of courage because she was raised in a country that had once debated banning women completely from participation in athletics. Boulmerka credits her family with providing the necessary emotional support for her athletic career.

Boulmerka began running during her high-school days in Constantine where she first exhibited her trademark qualities of speed and endurance. Her abilities were first confirmed at the Algerian National Athletic Games in 1985, although she remained relatively unknown. Shortly after the games, she began training at the M.O.C. in Constantine, where she remained until 1988. She placed first in the Junior Arab Championships in 1986 and took first place in the Arab Championships for the 800-meter race in 1987. Despite these victories, she was eliminated from the 1988 Olympics in the 800- and 1500-meter races. Those defeats inspired her to train harder.

Boulmerka quickly emerged at the front of a group of African women distance runners that began to have an impact on international competitions in the 1990s. She won a double title in the African Championships in the 800- and 1500-meter races in both 1988 and 1989. Despite these victories, she realized that she was not yet ready for stronger international competition. She therefore transferred to the C.R.B. for a short time. Her next transfer was to the Institut des Sciences et de la Technologie du Sport where she teamed up with coach Amar Bouras. Working with Bouras led her to international competitiveness.

Bouras found that Boulmerka had good endurance, a good technical base, a good mentality for achieving a high performance, that she was disciplined, and that she desired only to work to advance more. Her only drawback was not having a special base of strength. Bouras nevertheless believed that he could place her in the top ten runners in the world. They worked on this objective with the ultimate goal of a medal in the Barcelona Olympics in 1992, perfecting a racing style characterized by an even, sustained pace and a careful expenditure of energy.

Boulmerka's strongest race was the 1500 meters. They therefore worked to reduce her running time. Within a year, she had shaved a full ten seconds from her running time, completing the 1500 meters in four minutes. Ranked thirty-fourth in the world in 1989, she moved into eleventh place by 1990 and then to second in 1991. She took first place in the 800- and 1500-meter races in the North African Championships in 1990 and held the African record for the 1500-meter race from 1990 to 1992. She also held the African record for the mile in 1991.

Boulmerka set the stage for her victory with gold medals in the 800- and 1500-meter races in the 1991 Mediterranean Games in Athens. She won international acclaim two months later with her victory in the World Track and Field Championships in Tokyo, Japan, marking the first time an Algerian had won this event. In a moment immortalized by sports photographers, Boulmerka broke through the tape at the finish line, buried her hands in her hair, and screamed. She later said that her screaming was a combination of "joy and shock, for Algeria's pride, Algeria's history, for every Algerian woman, and for every Arab woman." The achievement made her both a heroine and a figure of controversy for many Algerians.

Like other runners, Boulmerka wore the clothing of her sport – shorts and a sleeveless top designed for running. Some people denounced her as a heretic for showing her bare legs, claiming that this violated a traditional conservative interpretation of Islam that asserts that women should be covered from head to toe in public. For these conservatives, Boulmerka had shown herself not to be a "proper" Muslim woman. She responded to her critics by confirming that she was a practicing Muslim. However, she was also an athlete. Conservative Islamic clothing and a headscarf would have slowed her speed. She also noted that she had worn baggy, male-style shorts, rather than the form-fitting Lycra worn by her opponents – already a concession that may have slowed her somewhat. She charged that the uproar over her choice of attire was a reflection of male tyranny, rather than Islamic standards, correctly pointing out that harsh treatment of women is not supported by the Quran or by the Prophet Muhammad's example. Boulmerka has always maintained that her participation in athletic competitions does not contradict her commitment to her Muslim faith and values.

It was precisely because of Boulmerka's gender that the controversy ensued. In many developing countries, women's bodies are the sites of struggle for cultural authenticity, tradition, and connection to the past. They also become caught in the power struggles between various political groups seeking to define the nation. For conservatives, Boulmerka's choice of dress in the international arena represented a loss of control and failure of belief that, in their opinion, tarnished Algeria's international image.

Boulmerka's victory coincided with major political upheavals in Algeria. In 1991, the Islamist-oriented Islamic Salvation Front (F.I.S.) had won major political victories. The secular government, fearing Islamists in power, canceled their democratically won election victory, sparking a civil war between Islamists and the government, as supported by the military, that has claimed more than a hundred thousand lives. Boulmerka, as a figure of controversy, became an instant political symbol, supported and applauded by secularists and vehemently denounced by conservatives.

After her victory, Boulmerka was awarded a national Medal of Merit for her athletic achievements and was proclaimed a national heroine. Her reception by the President of Algeria, where he kissed her publicly on the forehead, made her even more controversial. Extremist elements issued death threats against her for portraying an international image of Algeria that they considered to be immodest and anathema to their interpretation of Islam. Like her fellow countrywomen whose wearing of Western dress has led to assaults on their personal safety by extremists, Boulmerka feared for her safety while training. She decided to move to Italy to train in peace.

Believing that victory was more important symbolically than ever, Boulmerka trained hard for her major goal – representing her deeply divided, war-torn nation, particularly Algerian women, in the 1500-meter race at the 1992 Olympics. The night before her race, she stayed up until midnight. Her coaches were concerned about her mental state, thinking that she was fearful and nervous. However, she responded that she was engaged in positive thinking, celebrating the gold medal in advance. In the race the following day, Boulmerka initially trailed Russia's Lyudmila Rogacheva. However, she broke ahead in the last 200 meters to win the gold in a personal best time of 3 minutes 55.3 seconds. It was the first gold medal ever won by an Algerian. Her performance was the best of the year and the fifth world record for the women's 1500 meters. The race was the first in which four women finished in less than four minutes.

Although she prefers athletics to politics, Boulmerka issued a political statement following her Olympic victory by dedicating her medal to assassinated president Mohammed Boudiaf. She also criticized militant Islamists for their repression of women and their manipulation of Islamic cultural norms for political gain. Citing her victory as an achievement not only of Algeria, but of an Algerian woman in particular, she declared that she would not give in to the "blackmail of extremists" and that she remained optimistic that Algeria would be saved by its women.

After these important victories, 1993 was a difficult year for Boulmerka. Although she won the 800-meter race in the Mediterranean Games, her performance in the 1500 meters was devastating. Thinking she had won the race, she slowed down just before the finish line, not realizing there was another runner just behind her. The runner passed her, claiming first place, much to Boulmerka's embarrassment. The Algerian press and public were unforgiving and accused her of having forfeited her victory. The resultant loss of morale proved impossible to conquer that year. Her ranking dropped to twentieth in the world. She placed a disappointing third in the World Championships. Always a fighter, she swore to recover her title and re-establish her presence on the international running scene.

Boulmerka achieved a partial victory in this regard in 1994 when she won first place in the World Cup, as well as numerous Arab, Mediterranean, and African titles. She moved up in the rankings to fourth in the world. She recovered her World Championship title in 1995, making her the most decorated woman in the history of the 1500-meter race. Encouraged by her recovery, she trained for the 1996 Olympics, hoping to win a second medal. Unfortunately, rather than being a continuation of victory, the Olympics marked the beginning of the end of her running career. In the last quarter of the final lap, she was bumped by another runner, not only resulting in her dropping out of the race, but also leaving her injured. Although she should have had several

more years of competitive running, the combination of injury, the high sacrifice demanded at this level of competition, and the reality of aging parents who needed her care led to her retirement.

Although retired from competitive running, Boulmerka did not retire from sports altogether. She was one of the first people to be directly elected to the Athletes' Commission of the International Olympic Committee (I.O.C.) in 1996. In this capacity, she has worked to improve opportunities for women's participation in sports and to exclude politics from sports. In 1999, she demanded that the I.O.C. place pressure on countries that discriminate against women competitors, particularly singling out Mexico and Pakistan for criticism. She also ran in the World Championships, hoping to win a medal to symbolize the abilities of Algerian women at a time when they were no longer allowed to drive cars. Although she not did win a medal, she proved a major challenge to younger runners. She has been particularly active in the rebuilding of sports in post-Taliban Afghanistan and pressed hard for Afghan participation in the 2004 Olympics. She has served on the Algerian National Olympic Committee's Athletes' Commission and the I.O.C.'s Women and Sports Working group since 2000.

Boulmerka's athletic achievements were recognized by *Sports Illustrated*, *Sports Illustrated for Women*, and C.N.N./S.I., who named her one of the top 100 women athletes on the basis of her on-field performance and achievements, as well as her contribution to women's sports. She was awarded a prize for her "spirit of justice and tolerance" in 1998 by Le Web de l'Humanite's "Remarkable Dimensions of Sports." In her acceptance speech, she reiterated her belief that athletes have an important message to carry – that of humanity. She has expressed concern about the increasing commercialization of sporting events, believing that the emphasis should be on the competition, rather than the sponsors.

Although the environment of her home country remains hostile to women in sport, Boulmerka's example continues to inspire young Algerian women athletes and to give them hope. She is an icon not only for them, but also for the Algerian expatriate population scattered around the world. Although she is a woman, she remains a powerful symbol of Algerian identity and success.

Further reading

"BOULMERKA Hassiba: Le premier titre olympique pour l'Algerie c'est elle," www.geocities.com/algeriathle/photoBOULMERKA.html

"La dimension remarquáble de Hassiba Boulmerka," Le Web de l'Humanite, June 1, 1998, www.humanite.presse.fr/journal/1998–06–01/1998–06–01–355231

Hargreaves, Jennifer. *Heroines of Sport: The Politics of Difference and Identity*. London and New York: Routledge, 2000

"Hassiba Boulmerka, Track and Field," www.sportsillustrated.com/siforwomen/top_100/70/

Magdalinksi, Tara and Timothy J.L. Chandler, eds. *With God on their Side: Sport in the Service of Religion*. London and New York: Routledge, Taylor & Francis Group, 2002

Robson, Victoria. "Hassiba Boulmerka Main Page," Profiles in the Contemporary Africa Database, people/africadatabase.org/people/profiles/profilesforperson10860.html

C

Mustafa Ceric (b. c. 1955)

The Grand Mufti of Bosnia and Herzegovina, Mustafa Ceric has promoted national healing in the aftermath of the 1992–1995 civil war that devastated Bosnia and has become an internationally recognized leader in Muslim–Christian dialogue.

Mustafa Ceric was born around 1955 in Bosnia. He received his secondary education at the Medressa in Sarajevo and completed his undergraduate education at Al-Azhar University in Cairo, Egypt. He then returned to Bosnia and became an imam. Ceric spent several years as the Imam of the U.S. Islamic Cultural Center while earning a Ph.D. in Islamic theology at the University of Chicago in 1981. He credits his time in the United States with helping him to speak fluent English and understand American culture. It also gave him the opportunity to work with the minority American Muslim community in teaching other faiths about Islam while learning about the challenges facing new converts. In addition to expanding, improving, and providing financial support for the center's school curriculum and buildings, Ceric worked to bring diverse groups together to build a common, harmonious future.

Ceric left the United States to lecture in Islamic studies at the University of Kuala Lumpur, Malaysia. In 1987, he moved to Zagreb, Croatia, where he served as the imam of a learning center. He returned to Bosnia in 1991 as the outbreak of civil war loomed. His goal was to provide spiritual leadership and unity to the Muslim community.

The war that broke out between Bosnia, Serbia, and Croatia between 1992 and 1995 was the bloodiest conflict seen in Europe since World War II. Approximately two hundred thousand people were killed in the Serb–Croatian campaign of ethnic cleansing. The overwhelming majority of the victims were Muslims. Bosnian Muslim men were targeted for indiscriminate mass killing while Muslim women and girls were gang raped by Serb soldiers in order to impregnate and disgrace them. (See also DR. LAILA AL-MARAYATI.) These acts were classified as genocide and the major leaders of the Serbs and Croats have been tried for crimes against humanity. In addition to the killing, approximately two million people out of a population of 3.5 million were displaced from their homes and between seventy and eighty percent of the homes in Bosnia were either damaged or destroyed. Bosnia became a *cause célèbre* in the Muslim world, which was outraged both by Western failure to stop the conflict and by the international arms embargo that rendered Bosnians unable to defend themselves, ultimately contributing to the genocide.

The genocide in Bosnia came as a particular shock because of its long history of tolerance. A part of the Ottoman Empire from 1463 until 1878, Bosnia had long enjoyed broad religious freedom. As a Muslim-majority country in the heart of Europe, it had served as an example of the peaceful combination of European culture, Muslim religious identity, modernity, democracy, tolerance, and separation of mosque and state.

As the spiritual leader of Bosnia's Muslims, Ceric appealed to the country's history of interfaith and interethnic tolerance and cooperation as the key to national reconstruction and the foundation of a lasting peace. Because Bosnian Muslims coexist with a variety of other faith and ethnic communities in a small geographic region, contacts between the groups are inevitable. Ceric believes that a spirit of openness and cooperation is both productive and an accurate reflection of Bosnian identity. He points to the location of mosques, churches, and synagogues within a few blocks of each other in Sarajevo as evidence of the interconnectedness of the faith and ethnic communities. Although some view the multiplicity of faiths in Bosnia as a perversion and weakness, Ceric sees it as a sign of regional strength. He has consistently denounced terrorism and racism, both reflecting and reinforcing the views of those he leads.

In addition to serving as the Grand Mufti, Ceric serves as the president of the Council of Muslim Scholars, a body founded in Bosnia and Herzegovina to replace the leadership of the Ottoman Empire after the caliphate was abolished in 1924. Historically, the purpose of the council was to give Bosnian Muslims official leadership and control over their own religious affairs. As the oldest official Islamic institution in Europe, the council has an elected president, a constitution and by-laws, and runs its own schools, colleges, mosques, and societies. As such, it is a reflection of Bosnia's combined Muslim and European heritage and identity. Under Ceric's leadership, the council has engaged in a historical review of regional events to determine where Bosnian Muslims are headed in the future. Ceric also seeks to make the Islamic Studies College a model for all Muslims in Europe.

Ceric's vision of Bosnia's future and interpretation of Islam differs sharply from those that call for the establishment of an Islamic state or the implementation of a conservative and literal interpretation of Islamic law. Recognizing the multiplicity of faiths in Bosnia and the fact that Muslims are a simple, rather than overwhelming, majority (44% of the population), Ceric has called for Islamic realism, rather than Islamic superiority. Upholding the principle of justice in which all faiths hold equal national recognition, he believes that religious pluralism is the only safeguard against another genocide.

Ceric's leadership of the Muslim community has focused on Muslim–Christian dialogue as the key to a shared future in Europe. Observing that both faiths have tended to concentrate on troubling memories and events from the past, he has proposed an alternative and more hopeful vision of interfaith interaction that focuses on positive history. His interpretation of history begins with the assertion that consideration of Europe as a historically Christian continent is false because it has also long been home to large Jewish and Muslim communities stretching from the Iberian Peninsula to the Balkans. The existence of these communities resulted in their significant contributions to European culture and life. He points to the example of the Christian scholar Thomas Aquinas (1224–1274), whose self-examination and actualization of the spirit of Christianity grew out of his study of the Muslim theologian and philosopher

Avicenna (Ibn Sina, 980–1037). Ceric believes that the lesson to be learned from Aquinas's example is that respecting and valuing the beliefs and writings of another faith group can lead to a deeper appreciation of one's own faith tradition. Similarly, disrespect for the religious other tends to lead to disagreement and judgmentalism, such as was the case for Dante Alighieri (1265–1321) who relegated the Muslim philosopher Averroes (Ibn Rushd, 1126–1198) to Hell for his promotion of Aristotelian philosophy. Ceric rejects judgmentalism as remaining overly focused on past realities, rather than working to design new realities based on a spirit of reflection.

For Ceric, the pursuit of Muslim–Christian dialogue is a reflection of some of the most important lessons taught by the Quran: that an inclusive, rather than exclusive, approach should be taken to faith; that no one has a monopoly on the Truth; and that the Truth is open to everyone. He believes that these lessons must be put to use in overcoming the history of intolerance between faiths and competition on the basis of the assertion of the superiority of one's scripture or beliefs in favor of competition in doing good works and designing new values of righteousness, knowledge, and human decency. He believes that designing, rather than judging, should be the task of the true faith community because designing seeks to move into the future by creating new paths and opportunities, rather than remaining mired in the past. He also believes that designing is the appropriate use of religion's power to motivate people because it focuses on bringing people closer together in the quest for justice, peace, and tolerance for all of humanity. He has called for an end to the destruction of the monuments and places of worship of other faiths, noting that the destruction of a monastery no more makes a person a better Muslim than the destruction of a mosque makes a person a better Christian. He believes that people can become better Muslims and Christians by helping each other maintain their religious identities as the source of personal and collective security.

Tied to this vision of a new world order built on human trust and morality is Ceric's call for stopping the spread of nuclear weapons and weapons of mass destruction. He proposes joining the wisdom popularly associated with the East with the rationality typically associated with the West to create the moral "man of faith" who can build the human trust necessary to bring tribes and nations together to cooperate in justice, truth, peace, and reconciliation. He believes that the future of Europe lies in a morality that leads to freedom from fear and material and spiritual poverty, a trust that leads to recognition that God lives and cares for all people, a tolerance that leads to the revival of the spirit in sharing in a common good life that celebrates the diversity of religions and cultures, an active opposition to nuclear danger, ecological disaster, and violent religious, ethnic, and social conflicts, and a tangible support for peace with nature, nations, religions, God, and human beings.

Ceric derives inspiration from civil rights leaders, notably the Rev. Dr. Martin Luther King, Jr., and Mahatma Gandhi, in promoting non-violence in a region that has had little experience of peace in recent years. In a paraphrase of King, Ceric has declared his hope for a day when his three children will live in a world where they will be judged not by the faith of their hearts, but by the content of their characters. He has called for the development of an "Islamic avant-garde" that will promote human rights and democracy while opposing literalism, extremism, and terrorism and has cautioned Muslims against using the term jihad because most non-Muslims associate the term with extremism and holy war against non-Muslims.

Ceric's calls for peaceful coexistence, intra- and interreligious cooperation, and tolerance have been denounced by extremists who have alternatively called for expanded intra-Muslim self-defense and support. Critics have noted that it was the Arab fighters who came from Afghanistan who defended the Muslim population of Bosnia during the Serb–Croatian genocide when the West did nothing to stop the ethnic cleansing other than place an embargo on arms exports. With these fighters came a more militant and extremist interpretation of Islam. Ceric has noted that most Bosnians have rejected such extremism, but remains concerned that some of these fighters have remained in the region and have tried to implement a more literal, intolerant, and ritual-oriented interpretation of Islam. He has also expressed concerns about Muslims being targeted as potential terrorists until proven otherwise and the raids on Islamic charities with purported links to terrorist activities.

Ceric's pivotal role as a national healer and peacemaker was recognized by his inclusion on the board of advisers for the World Policy Institute of New School University, Dialogues: Islamic World–U.S.–the West, which promotes greater communication among and about the Islamic world, the United States, and the West. Launched as a structured forum for sustained dialogue involving religious, intellectual, economic, and political voices from Islamic and Western/American societies, the board includes non-elite Islamic figures, such as Ceric, who are credible voices in their own communities but are not always heard in the West. In many ways, the institute's goals parallel those of Ceric: the facilitation and promotion of dialogue, communication, and consultation toward the promotion of peace. (See also Chandra Muzaffar and Nurcholish Madjid.)

In addition to Ceric's religious leadership in Bosnia, he has worked to build and strengthen ties between Bosnian Muslims and other Muslim communities around the world. He is the author of numerous books in Bosnian and is a frequent speaker at conferences in the West and the Muslim world on Muslim–Christian dialogue and the need for tolerance, peaceful coexistence, and cooperation between faith groups.

Further reading

Ceric, Mustafa. "Conflict and Healing Memories," speech presented to the Islam in Europe Committee at the conference Christians and Muslims in Europe: Responsibility and Religious Commitment in the Pluralist Society, September 12–16, 2001, Sarajevo, www.ccee.ch./english/fields/Ceric.rtf

—— "Major Challenges in Europe to Common Living," speech presented to Religions for Peace, November 11, 2002, Oslo, www.religionsforpeace.net/Europe…/111201_EUROPEAN_CRL_Mustafa-Ceric.html

Mills, Nicolaus and Kira Brunner, eds. *The New Killing Fields: Massacre and the Politics of Intervention*. New York: Basic Books, 2002

Swidler, Leonard. and Paul Mojzes. "Sarajevo: A Journey to an Interreligious Future," *Journal of Ecumenical Studies*, December, 1995, astro.temple.edu/~dialogue/Bosnia/journey.htm

"We are Muslims First and Europeans Second," interview with Dr. Mustafa Ceric, *Al-Daawah*, no. 21, July 2003

Whitmore, Brian. "Bosnia Offers Lesson in Nation Building," *Boston Globe*, October 12, 2003

—— "Muslim Leader in Bosnia Preaches Need for Tolerance," *Boston Globe*, July 28, 2002

www.ccee.ch – website for Islam in Europe Committee

www.islamuswest.org – website for World Policy Institute of New School University, Dialogues: Islamic World–U.S.–the West

www.religionsforpeace.net

Oussama Cherribi (b. 1959)

The first Muslim ever to be elected to the Dutch parliament, Oussama Cherribi has become known internationally for his support for human rights, activism as a bridge-builder

64

between communities, and expertise in the political and religious uses of cyberspace.

Oussama Cherribi was born in 1959 in Morocco. He is the oldest of five children. His father, Si Mohamed Cherribi, taught French and became headmaster of a group of primary schools first near Marrakesh and later in Kenitra, which was home to the largest U.S. military base in Africa at the time. His mother, Aicha Filali, designed women's clothing and had her own shop on the ground floor of the family's home. Cherribi absorbed an interest in art, design, color, and cuisine from his mother. His parents also encouraged his early interests in theater, performance, and public speaking. Both his parents and grandparents placed great value on education. His maternal grandfather was a judge and taught at Al Qarawiyin University. His paternal grandfather had served in the French military and fought against the Germans during both world wars.

Cherribi was educated at the University of Rabat, where he earned a B.A. in philosophy and sociology in 1982. He began traveling to Amsterdam to visit his uncle's family during the summers. Fascinated by the tradition of tolerance and cosmopolitan intellectual inheritance he found there, he emigrated to the Netherlands after graduation. He began working as a policy researcher in the home of seventeenth-century French philosopher René Descartes, located next to the Anne Frank house. He decided to attend graduate school, working in French restaurants during evenings and weekends to support himself. He earned an M.A. at the University of Amsterdam in 1987 and a Ph.D. at the School of Social Science Research, University of Amsterdam, in 2000, both in sociology. His dissertation focused on Arabic-speaking imams in Europe, their sermons, and their views on Western societies in the early 1990s.

Cherribi's life-long experience with diversity – cultural, religious, and linguistic – has resulted in a commitment to bridging differences between cultures, religions, and societies. He encourages people not only to talk to each other, but, more importantly, to listen. He also encourages them to "see the citizen in the immigrant, and not the immigrant in the citizen" out of belief that individuals should not be reduced to a single aspect of group identity, such as way of dress or skin color. As a self-defined liberal and secular Muslim, he firmly believes in the separation between religion and state.

Cherribi made history in the Netherlands when he became the first Muslim to be elected to the Dutch parliament in 1994. He was reelected in 1998 and served until the national election in May, 2002 when 80 of the 150 seats in the Dutch parliament changed hands. As an M.P., Cherribi served on committees dealing with foreign affairs, Africa and Europe, technology, interior affairs, education, welfare, and health. He gained policy expertise in information and computer technology; development; conservation and environmental issues in Africa; European policies toward Africa; European and domestic issues of science, culture, and education, health and welfare, ethnic groups and youth; and small business and entrepreneurs. He put this expertise to use in organizing educational initiatives both with technology firms in Europe and with youth and ethnic groups, including Amsterdam's Chinatown. Cherribi served on the National Committee for the Reform of Health Care Policy, the board of directors for the Amsterdam Art Council, Radio North-Holland, Migrant T.V., and the "Taalunie" Belgian–Dutch Council for Language Policy, and participated in meetings of directors of the Dutch National Science Foundation (N.W.O.), the Royal Netherlands Academy of Sciences (K.N.A.W.), and major Dutch companies such as Shell and Philips. He also worked on a number of projects with the former leader of his party, Frits Bolkestein, who has been European commissioner since 1998.

Long fascinated by modern technology, Cherribi decided to harness its power to promote transparency and accountability in the national government while improving communication between citizens and representatives. He created and developed the Dutch parliament's first website and co-founded Den Haag-Online. A proponent of "e-democracy" in the Netherlands, he also created his own personal political website: www.cherribi.nl, which was the first of its kind. He won the ICT Award for Cyberpolitician in 1999. In 2001, he represented the Dutch delegation at the first worldwide convention on cybercrime.

Cherribi's work as an M.P. focused on expanding the role of the Netherlands in both the European and international communities. In 1998 and 2001, he served as an official observer at the United Nations and met delegates at U.N. sessions. He represented the Netherlands as a member of the Assembly of the West European Union (W.E.U.), which conducted parliamentary scrutiny for decisions made by European countries and associate member countries such as Turkey and Ukraine in matters of security and defense. He also served on the W.E.U.'s Political Committee and the Committee on Aerospace, Administration, and Budget.

Cherribi represented the Netherlands as a member of the Assembly of the Council of Europe (C.o.E.) for eight years, negotiating with other nations, particularly on human rights issues, and scrutinizing the decisions of the European Union's Council of Ministers. He served on the C.o.E.'s Committee on Culture, Science, and Education, which conducted hearings on human rights abuses of journalists in Ukraine, Russia, and other former Soviet countries, and on the Committee on Agriculture and Environment.

He was the reporter for a number of C.o.E. and W.E.U. policy documents and worked with the North–South Institute in Lisbon to bring European aid to Africa and Asia. Cherribi is a member of the Maison Descartes French Cultural Association, Parliamentarians for Global Action (a United Nations N.G.O.), and Amsterdamse Kring (a group of key business executives, politicians, and public intellectuals). He was invited by the mayor of Amsterdam to serve on the Expenditure Review Committee on European Union Funding for Urban Renewal 2002–2006.

As an expert on European issues, migration, and Muslims in Europe, Cherribi speaks frequently on topics such as how Muslim immigrants in Europe are contributing to the development of their homelands and what European political elites think about Muslims in Europe. His studies of the Muslim communities in Europe led to grave concerns about the status of Muslims following the 9/11 attacks as European politicians began publicly to express concerns about the growth of the Muslim community and its impact on the European way of life. Many also raised questions about the security threats associated with Muslim populations, forgetting in the process that the majority of Muslims are law-abiding citizens who deplore violence and are attached to their adopted countries. In order to help counteract these negative images and demonstrate Muslim outrage against these attacks, Cherribi visibly displayed his solidarity with and support for the victims of the attacks. On September 18, 2001, during the queen's speech opening parliament, Cherribi wore a dark suit and tie with red, white, and blue and the stars and stripes of the American flag. Most of his colleagues were amused, but one M.P. from an extreme right-wing Christian party became hostile and told him that he should have worn an orange tie at a royal event. However, Cherribi was photographed and interviewed extensively by the national press for his symbolic statement, in large part because he is Muslim. He commented that no religion or belief could justify such horrible acts and that terrorists are no one's friends. He received many positive responses from the Dutch public and media who were pleased that a Muslim had taken such a strong pro-Western stand.

In addition to his show of solidarity, Cherribi worked to defuse the heightening tensions between the Jewish, Christian, and Muslim communities in the Netherlands post-9/11 by bringing together rabbis, pastors, and imams for a public forum and by speaking to large groups of liberal Jews about cross-cultural dialogue, including the impact of the Palestinian–Israeli conflict on Muslim–Jewish relations in Europe. Although he was initially concerned about 9/11's potential for negatively disrupting the social integration of Muslims in Europe, Cherribi has since recovered his optimism because most European Muslims he knows admire human rights, democracy, and their right to practice their religion freely.

Although his term as an M.P. ended in 2002, Cherribi remained on his party's list as a potential candidate for the European Parliament. Because of his party's newly adopted policy on internal democracy, an electronic voting procedure for party members resulted in his move up the list to the number ten position in early 2004. This unprecedented shift encouraged him to run a highly visible campaign in the two weeks before the European Parliament elections in June 2004. He conducted a bus tour throughout the Netherlands to meet potential voters, resulting in reports in the main evening news and in the Dutch press that he was running an "American-style" campaign. Overall, support for his free-market Liberal Party declined, reducing their number of seats in the European Parliament

from six to four. Most political observers attributed the drop in support to attacks by the party's former leader on the current leader just days before the vote, along with the publication of embarrassing photos of the party's minister of education which led to her resignation. Only 39% of the voting population of the Netherlands participated in the elections, a rate that Cherribi described as "abysmally low" compared to the typical turnout of between 70 and 80% for Dutch national elections. He attributed the low turnout to a general lack of interest in the European Parliament.

Cherribi has published extensively in Dutch, French, and English, both in newspapers and in articles and book-length studies. He frequently appears on Dutch and international television and radio. He is the author of a number of public policy reports and is a frequent speaker at public events and conferences. He has been particularly active in Europe, serving as a moderator and reporter for the Council of Europe Conference on Cultural Cooperation between Europe and North Africa in 2002, the keynote speaker at educational workshops for Albanian and Western and Southern African parliamentarians and members of the opposition in 2002, and scientific adviser to a conference on the future of the European Union. Cherribi frequently speaks about political participation, building democracy, science and technology, immigrants, human rights, and the state of Europe. Since 2003, he has lectured at Emory University in Atlanta, GA, where he also serves as assistant to the Provost and liaison to the Carter Center, which works in partnership with Emory on social action initiatives.

Further reading

Cherribi, Oussama. "The Council of Europe's Human Rights Perspective on the Media," in *Studies in Communications*, vol. 6: *Human Rights and Media*, ed. Diana

Papademas. New York: Elsevier Science Publishers, 2003

—— "The Global Aspects of the Internet," in *Encyclopedia of International Media and Communications*, ed. Donald H. Johnston. New York: Academic Press, 2003

—— "The Growing Islamization of Europe," in *Modernizing Islam: Religion in the Public Sphere in Europe and the Middle East*, ed. John L. Esposito and Francois Burgat. Newark and London: Rutgers University Press & Hurst, 2003

—— *Internet and Information Society*. Public policy document for Council of Europe, 1997

—— *Overcoming Obstacles to E-Business*. Public policy document for Council of Europe, 2001

Haddad, Yvonne Yazbeck, ed. *Muslims in the West: From Sojourners to Citizens*. New York: Oxford University Press, 2002

Nielsen, Jorgen. *Muslims in Western Europe*, 2nd ed. Edinburgh: Edinburgh University Press, 1995

O'Hara, John and Ousssama Cherribi. *Developing a European Space Observation Capability to Meet Europe's Security Requirements*. Public policy document for Western European Union, 2002

Pedersen, Lars. *Newer Islamic Movements in Western Europe* (Research in Migration and Ethnic Relations). London: Ashgate, 1999

Valleix, Jean and Oussama Cherribi. *Anti-Missile Defence: The Implications for European Industry*. Public policy document for Western European Union, 2001

Vertovec, Steven and Ceri Peach, eds. *Islam in Europe: The Politics of Religion and Community*. London: Macmillan, 1997

Interview with the author, June 21, 2004

www.cherribi.nl – Cherribi's website

Tansu Ciller (b. 1946)

The first female prime minister of Turkey, Tansu Ciller played an important role in Turkish politics during the 1990s and has remained an influential voice behind the scenes.

Tansu Ciller was born in 1946 in Istanbul, Turkey. Her father was a wealthy provincial governor who prepared his daughter for a career in public service. Ciller was educated at Robert College, a private American school in Istanbul catering to the wealthy and elites of Turkish society. She married another graduate, Ozer Ciller, and completed a degree in economics at Bogazici University.

The Cillers moved to the United States in the late 1960s. Ciller completed a Ph.D. in economics at the University of Connecticut and post-doctoral studies at Yale University. She became an associate professor in 1978 and achieved the rank of full professor in 1983. She is fluent in Turkish, English, and German. She has two children.

Ciller entered Turkish politics in 1990 as a member of the True Path Party, which was headed by Suleyman Demirel. Her stated goal was to prevent the spread of Islamic fundamentalism and to defend Turkey's secular state. She was elected as a member of parliament from Istanbul in 1991 and became the deputy chairperson of the True Path Party. When the True Path Party and the Social Democratic Populist Party formed a coalition government following the elections, she became the state minister for the economy. During her tenure as minister, she was an active member of the cabinet and came to be admired by her contacts in the West. At the same time, she was a figure of controversy in Turkey with critics questioning her economic plans and the truth of some of her press releases, such as a claim in 1992 that the World Bank had offered Turkey unconditional support when, in reality, it had outlined conditions for its assistance to Turkey. Ciller's tendency to use government funds for personal expenses such as flowers, travel, special foods, and coffee were questioned by the opposition parties. Her knowledge also came into question over issues such as her inability to remember the names of heads of state and which countries belonged to N.A.T.O.

Despite the controversies, Ciller was admired in Turkish society and was elected Woman of the Year in 1992. She was praised by Libyan leader, Muammar al-Qadhdhafi, as a model for all Muslim women. Many Turkish women imitated her personal style, including wearing her trademark flowing, colorful neck scarves and her favorite perfume. She was particularly effective during her visits abroad.

Ciller became Turkey's first female prime minister in 1993 after the death of President Turgut Ozal and the transfer of power to Demirel as the new president. Ciller's campaign to become the new prime minister earned the media's support. She achieved her goal when her party received the highest number of votes in the elections. Ciller's election was important not only because it brought a woman to the position of head of government, but also because she was the first woman to lead a Muslim-majority country without following in her father's footsteps. (See also BENAZIR BHUTTO; SHEIKH HASINA WAZED.) For many, Ciller, as a Western-oriented woman, represented a fresh voice in politics and a symbol of change from the old system of government with which many Turks were dissatisfied. Europeans hailed her as "the Symbol of Modern Turkey." Ciller served as prime minister from 1993 until 1996.

Political analysts have observed a variety of changes in Ciller's image as a politician. Prior to 1993, she had projected herself as an urban liberal. Following her ascent to the position of prime minister, her image became more traditional and nationalist. She also claimed the mantle of "mother of the country," noting that she was capable of providing both a mother's love and a mother's authority to the country. In both cases, her image was that of a secular, rather than religious, leader. She was openly opposed to Islamism and Islamist parties. As late as 1995, she publicly referred to Islamists as "murderous merchants of religion."

Ciller considers her major accomplishments as prime minister to have been the constant reworking of political alliances,

a loosening of the limitations on freedom of expression, and her push for Turkey to join the European Customs Union. She hoped that success in these ventures would strengthen both the secular democratic forces in Turkey's government at the expense of the Islamists and Turkey's ties to Westernization, secular government, liberalization, and Europe. For Ciller, Turkey's inclusion in the E.U. was pivotal in maintaining the secular nature of the state and in encouraging Turkey to follow the model of Europe, rather than the model of Iran. Her vision was of a Turkey capable of serving as a bridge between two continents and two cultures. She campaigned for Turkey's membership in the E.U. on the basis of its economy, the most open and sophisticated in the region, as well as her success in transferring some power from the central government to local governments, reduction of the voting age to eighteen, expansion of freedom of speech, and opening of the media to expand the number of public and local television channels. She noted that she had fulfilled the terms of new freedom of speech legislation by releasing seventy-nine people from custody and dropping more than a thousand court cases. Having fulfilled the pre-requisites of the E.U., Turkey joined the Customs Union in 1996.

Despite these successes, Ciller's tenure as prime minister was marked by political scandals, economic difficulties, and repeated failures to keep her campaign promises. During her time in office, the Turkish stock market and currency collapsed, she had difficulty passing constitutional reforms designed to make the country more democratic and liberal, ethnic conflicts erupted within Turkey and neighboring countries, and she was opposed by the Islamists, who were the major opposition in parliament. Ciller's inability to control and contain Kurdish separatists in southeast Turkey led to her developing close ties to the police department and secret service. She ordered the lifting of the parliamentary immunity of Kurdish members of parliament who belonged to the D.E.P. Party and had them arrested in front of the parliament buildings in police vans. She ultimately asserted that she had broken the back of the Kurdish rebellion in southeast Turkey and that the conflict had shifted into northern Iraq. She claimed to have achieved security for Turkey. At the same time, there was a sudden increase in political murders in the spring of 1994.

By the summer of 1994, Ciller's extensive personal wealth had become headline news, in part because she had failed to declare her assets in the United States – which included four houses, a boat, some land, and a car – as part of her property on the official application form she used to run for her seat in parliament. When her American assets became public knowledge, the opposition parties called for a parliamentary investigation into her wealth. She defeated the motion by bargaining with individual party leaders and announcing that she would donate a large portion of her wealth to charity before the 1995 elections.

In 1995, Ciller campaigned on the platform of Turkey's membership in the European Union and the need to fight against both Kurdish opposition and the Islamist party. The elections did not yield a clear winner. Although the Islamists had the highest number of votes (21%), no party had won a true majority. In order to hold on to her power, Ciller's party formed a coalition with the Motherland Party in a final attempt to block the Islamists from power, despite the fact that Ciller and the leader of the Motherland Party, Mesut Yilmaz, openly detested each other. The coalition was short-lived. When Yilmaz joined the opposition in voting to establish three parliamentary commissions to investigate Ciller's alleged corruption, she responded by announcing she would join in a no-confidence vote against Yilmaz. Yilmaz resigned in June 1996, four months after the alliance was formed.

Dissatisfied with being kept out of high office despite having won the highest number of votes and increasingly concerned about government corruption and failure to provide the services needed by the Turkish people, the Islamists continued their investigation of Ciller's wealth, ultimately raising questions about a large amount of money that had disappeared from a secret slush fund the day before she left office as a member of parliament. Combined with the revelation that some of her closest associates were tied to organized crime and right-wing death-squad killings, the scandal resulted in the collapse of Ciller's political alliance in 1996 and forced her to leave office.

The collapse of the alliance finally pushed Ciller into opening negotiations with the Islamists in 1996. She formed a coalition government with the Welfare Party led by Necmettin Erbakan in June. Erbakan served as Turkey's first Islamist prime minister with Ciller as his deputy and minister of external affairs. Political analysts believed that the corruption allegations had forced her into the coalition, observing that the charges were either dropped or cleared following the formation of the alliance with the Welfare Party. In addition, the Welfare Party blocked the motion by the Social Democratic Party related to the missing slush-fund money.

Ciller's history of denunciation of the Islamists made the alliance awkward. Erbakan's subsequent moves to expand the freedom of expression of religion in public life angered powerful members of the military establishment and resulted in defections from Ciller's True Path Party. She changed her image again to reflect a new, religious persona who prayed in public, carried prayer beads, and covered her head. Although this image was in keeping with the Welfare Party's desired public image, it cost Ciller the support of many of her former admirers – not only in Turkey, but also in Europe and the United States – who questioned both her alliance with the Islamists and her wealth and shady connections, as she continued to increase her investments in the United States.

Despite the shortcomings of her governments and alliances and the personal scandals surrounding her, Ciller has retained enough power in Turkish politics to influence whether a minority government stays or falls. The multiplicity of political parties in Turkey renders it difficult to win a true majority, thus leading to the variety of alliances between parties that is the source of Ciller's power. In 1999, she offered her support to the Democratic Left Party led by Bulent Ecevit. She continues to play an important role behind the scenes.

Further reading

Ciller, Tansu, Karsten Prager, and James Wilde. "Dancing with the Wolves: Ciller Tells Europe That Now, it's Either Yes or No," *Time* magazine, November 20, 1995

Ertugrul, Kurkcu. "The Crisis of the Turkish State," *Middle East Report*, April–June, 1996

Esposito, John L. and John O. Voll. *Islam and Democracy*. New York: Oxford University Press, 1998

"Former Turkish Leader Cleared of Remaining Graft Charge," Reuters Information Service, January 15, 1997

Makovsky, Alan. "Turkey and 'The Refah Problem,' " *Policywatch*, June 19, 1996

Reinhart, Ustun. "Ambition for All Seasons: Tansu Ciller," *MERIA Journal*, vol. 3, no. 1, March, 1999

Sakallioglu, Umit Cizre. "Liberalism, Democracy and the Turkish Centre-Right: Identity Crisis of the True Path Party," *Middle East Studies*, April, 1996

Salt, Jeremy. "Nationalism and the Rise of Muslim Sentiment in Turkey," *Middle Eastern Studies*, vol. 31, no. 1, January, 1995

"Tansu Ciller to Take Over as Turkey's PM," Indian Express Newspapers (Bombay) Ltd., June 3, 1997

White, Jenny. "Islam and Democracy: The Turkish Experience." *Current History*, vol. 94, no. 588, January, 1995

www.mfa.gov.tr – website of the Ministry of Foreign Affairs, Turkey

D

Kadiatou Diallo (b. 1959)

The mother of police-brutality victim Amadou Diallo, Kadiatou Diallo has turned the tragedy of her son's murder into an opportunity for promoting greater understanding and cooperation between Africa and the United States through the establishment of the Amadou Diallo Foundation.

Kadiatou Diallo was born in 1959 in the African nation of Guinea. Her father, Amadou, was the son of a wise man and the grandson of a king. A nursing assistant in a public hospital when Diallo was born, he later worked in trade and then as a tax accountant for the government. He was the first member of his family to receive a Western education. Her mother, Diaraye, had no formal education, but was knowledgable about traditional medicine. According to tradition, she was expected to raise the children and run the household. The couple had a total of nine children, of whom Kadiatou was the fourth.

Although her father refused to allow her mother to be educated, he insisted that all of his children go to school for both Quran memorization and a Western education. Diallo excelled in academics, plays, dances, and recitals and was an entrepreneur from her early childhood. Married to a wealthy businessman and trader, Seikou Diallo, at the age of thirteen, she had four children, the first of whom was a son, Amadou. Throughout her marriage, she lived in a variety of African and Asian countries, including Liberia, Guinea, Togo, and Bangkok, according to her husband's business ventures. She learned both gemology and buying and trading to support herself and the children, particularly after her husband divorced her. Her most successful business ventures involved exporting clothing and trading in staples.

The onset of the 1990–1991 Gulf War led to the collapse of Diallo's business ventures by 1996. At this time, she and three of her children returned to their native Guinea where she remarried in 1998. The exception was Amadou, who decided to go to the United States to work while going to college and to save money to send for his siblings. He worked initially processing orders for a computer company, but soon reverted to the family trade of buying and selling as a street vendor. In 1998, he applied for asylum, which he received in 1999, making him eligible for a college scholarship and a bank account in his own name. He sent Diallo a photograph of a girl, asking her to arrange a marriage. Shortly afterward, on February 4, 1999, Amadou was shot dead by police in New York City in an apparent case of mistaken identity.

Tensions were high in the area at that time because the police were searching for a serial rapist. The police claimed that Amadou had a wallet in his hand that was mistaken for a gun. Citing his "suspicious" and "agitated" manner and "unpredictable" behavior, they fired at him forty-one times, striking him with nineteen bullets and leaving thirty-five holes in his body. Although the police claimed that they were under threat from Amadou, only four of the bullets struck him in the front. The other fifteen hit him in the back and sides. The first bullet appears to have passed through his left lung and hit his spine, instantly paralyzing him and causing him to fall, explaining why there were entry wounds in the soles of his feet. The killing of the man typically described by the media as an uneducated, "unarmed West African street vendor" who came from a poor family and spoke little English galvanized the African-American community, which turned out in several rallies in New York City in support of Amadou. Diallo appeared at several of the rallies in an effort to present a more accurate portrayal of Amadou as an educated, hard-working man who spoke English well, albeit with a stutter, and who had had no reason to be armed.

Diallo returned Amadou's body to Guinea, where he was buried in his grandfather's village. A trial one year later found the police not guilty in his death and the criminal case was closed. Disturbed by the fact that the jury never saw the murder scene; never questioned why the police officers, after shooting, turned the apartment inside out searching for something illegal; why his roommates were questioned about whether Amadou had a gun or smoked; or why the police asked if Amadou had any enemies, Diallo was unwilling to accept that no one was responsible for her son's murder. She filed a civil suit against New York City for wrongful death.

With Amadou's death, Diallo joined the ranks of mothers who have lost their sons to violence, drugs, and police shootings. Although she shares the anger and fear of many Africans and African-Americans in the United States, she did not call for revenge. Instead, she called for building bridges of understanding and knowledge between communities, races, and nations – and between police forces and communities. She has become a prominent voice for immigrant rights, knowing first hand and from others the harsh experience of discrimination faced by most immigrants when they first arrive in the United States. She notes that most immigrants come to the United States with the expectation and desire to work hard and obtain an education. The major obstacle is gaining legal permission to do so. She has therefore called for more legal opportunities for immigrants in order to allow them to claim legal status in the United States, believing that they can make important contributions to American society while pursuing experience and education that can also be put to use back in their home countries. Her recognition of the need for development and opportunities for Africans, as well as her desire to ensure that Amadou's legacy is one of positive construction, inspired her to speak out about these issues.

Since 2001, Diallo has toured the United States, lecturing about her son's experience. She also created the Amadou Diallo Foundation in his memory to promote racial healing through education and to increase understanding and co-operation between the United States and Africa. Through scholarships, mentorships, and support for research, programs, and community development, the foundation seeks to build and maintain safe, healthy, and productive communities and promote greater understanding between ethnicities, races, and cultures. The foundation is funded in part by the $3 million settlement of the civil suit against New York City. Additional funding has been provided by Diallo's speaking fees and the royalties from her autobiography, *My Heart Will Cross This Ocean*, as well as other donors.

Diallo has continued to speak out in support of immigrant rights. She considers her work for the foundation as a positive, constructive contribution to both the United States and Africa, as well as a way of ensuring that Amadou lives on.

Further reading

Diallo, Kadiatou and Craig Wolff. *My Heart Will Cross This Ocean: My Story, My Son, Amadou*. New York: One World Ballantine Books, 2003
Interview with the author, October 10, 2003
www.amadoudiallo.org – website for the Amadou Diallo Foundation

Assia Djebar (b. 1936)

An award-winning novelist, poet, and filmmaker, Assia Djebar has received international acclaim for her portrayal of the struggles of Algerian women for liberation and expanded rights.

Assia Djebar was born Fatima-Zohra Imalayen in Cherchell, Algeria, on June 30, 1936. Her father was an elementary-school teacher. Because her family did not observe conservative, traditional Muslim traditions, such as seclusion, Djebar was free to go out at will as a child. She credits this freedom with leading her to writing and non-conformity.

Like many Algerians of her generation, Djebar is the product of French and Algerian education. She attended both Quran school and a French boarding school where she was one of only three or four Algerians in a class of 400–500 girls and was typically the only Algerian girl in her classes because she chose the most difficult and elite syllabus. She became interested in literature during her third year. She had hoped to study Arabic as a foreign language, but the school did not permit it. Although she speaks the Algerian dialect of Arabic, Djebar speaks and writes in French, mirroring her perception of French and Arabic language, societies, and cultures existing side by side but never fully understanding each other.

In 1954, Djebar moved to Paris, France, to attend first Lycée Fenelon and then the Ecole Normale Supérieure. She was the first Algerian woman to be accepted there and was admitted on a full scholarship. During her time in France, she completed her first novel, *The Mischief*, which was published in 1957. Only twenty years old at the time, she was too young to sign her own publishing contract. The novel was not received well in Algeria, in part because it had been written by a woman. However, it met with success in both the United States and France and resulted in a photo shoot for *Elle* magazine. The novel represented the first time Djebar used her pseudonym. She changed her birth date and cut her hair for the article, hoping that her family would not recognize her, as she had written the novel when she was supposed to have been studying for her exams. Furthermore, it was a story about erotic self-indulgence, which was not considered an appropriate topic for a young, unmarried woman of good family.

Like many young women of her generation, Djebar had always rebelled against society's expectations of her. The success of her first novel made her a source of controversy that reflected some of the most important social debates of the time. The French held her up as an example of the success of their *mission civilisatrice*, claiming they had succeeded in turning her into one of them. Algerians rejected her as a brazen and shameless hussy who ignored Algerian culture and traditions, as well as the realities of war, suffering, and courage – traits that were becoming increasingly important as the war for Algerian independence from France loomed.

Djebar was expelled from school in 1958 for political reasons. Her then-husband, Ahmed Ould-Rouis, was a member of the Resistance to French rule and was wanted by the French police. Her younger brother was also in jail. The French sought to expel Algerian women from France because of the role they had played in starting the Algerian war for independence. (See also DJAMILA BOUHIRED.) Djebar tried to return home to Algeria, but was stopped in Tunisia. She remained in Tunis for several years, working with refugees and writing for a revolutionary newspaper. She also resumed her studies and completed the equivalent of a master's thesis on a twelfth-century Tunisian woman saint, synthesizing in her mind the precolonial past of North Africa and the role of women in shaping and transmitting that past. She completed a second novel, *The Impatient Ones*, which was received as poorly in Algeria as the first because it told the story of a young woman trapped in a family environment of domineering men and frustrated women, another social taboo.

Djebar left Tunis for Morocco where she wrote her third novel, *Children of a New World*, which won the French Culture Prize in 1962. She chose Morocco because of its support for the Algerian revolution. Like many of her generation, Djebar hoped that the war for independence would lead to a more just society. An opponent of First World intervention in the Third World, she increasingly challenged French colonial rule, while addressing the broader question of gender in the new Algeria, noting the symbolic impact of women's participation in the war of liberation.

Djebar returned to Algeria in 1962 on the day before independence from France was declared. She resided in her mother-in-law's home, a traditional environment that made clear her own gaps in language and culture. She had become accustomed to the openness of Western society and frequently asked the Algerian women with whom she came into contact direct questions about personal details and opinions, violating the cultural practices of women neither being heard nor talking

about themselves and of youth remaining silent in the face of age. Djebar asked these questions because she was disturbed by the way Algerian society had turned against the women who had led the war for independence. She was personally embittered by the laxity with which women and their achievements and efforts were dispensed with by the ruling National Liberation Front (F.L.N.) that had employed them.

Djebar worked as a lecturer at the University of Algiers. Although she had been a prolific writer in her twenties, she suffered from writer's block in Algeria. Hoping to overcome this, she returned to France in the early 1970s, where she turned her attention to drama, working first in an experimental theater on the outskirts of Paris in the 1970s and then in cinema.

Djebar wrote, directed, and produced her first feature-length film, *Celebration of the Women from Mount Chenoua*, in 1976. A documentary about the women from her tribe sponsored by the Algerian state, the film won the International Critics Prize at the Venice Film Festival in 1979. She considered making a second film, about urban women in Algiers, but declined after realizing that it would require living in Algeria for two years. Divorced by then, she returned to writing and married Malek Alloula, an Algerian poet living in Paris.

Having spent ten years away from publishing engaged in personal turmoil and self-enforced silence, Djebar found that filmmaking had not only given her a new vision and appreciation for sound, but also a clearer and broader vision of what she was trying to accomplish. She credits the success of her first film with giving her the courage to begin exploring the gender conflict she saw exploding around her.

Djebar is the only writer of her gender and generation to have written both before and after independence. In her early years, she preferred not to talk about herself as a reflection of her conscious attempts to divorce herself and her experiences from her writings and her reluctance to expose herself both as a woman and as an Algerian. Her works deal broadly with issues of both colonial and postcolonial culture, such as the definition of national literature, the debate over cultural authenticity, the problematic question of national language, and the female subject in patriarchal culture. Her novels, all of which are written in French, reflect the split personality evident in so many French-speaking Algerians writing about Algerian cultural issues through Western terms of social analysis, particularly with respect to "women's liberation." These themes come across most clearly and powerfully in her most famous novel, *Women of Algiers in their Apartment*.

Women of Algiers was written in 1979 with support from the National Endowment for the Humanities and covers the period from 1958 until 1978, or from the beginning of the Algerian war for independence until sixteen years after independence was achieved. Refusing to sit on the sidelines and watch helplessly as women's rights were eroded or to complain without taking action, Djebar used her pen to insert her voice into the battle over where the country was headed and what role women would play in it. Although the book was never published in Algeria, its first printing of 15,000 copies sold out rapidly in France and went through two printings in Italy.

Women of Algiers documents the birth of the feminist voice in Algeria through the depictions of the plight of ordinary Algerian women. It also raises issues about the cost of the war to both genders, as their human dignity and integrity are denied when one group of people is made to be subservient to the personal and political needs of another. The narrative of *Women in Algiers* is deliberately fragmented as a reflection of the fragmentation of the lives of Algerians during this

time and of the painful questions they continued to ask but to which they received no answers. The major story of the novel is a dialogue between a European woman and an Algerian woman in which the Algerian woman comes to the European woman's aid. Djebar used this set-up to question Western assumptions that Muslim women must learn uncritically from the West while having nothing to teach the West themselves. Rather than serving as the object of the narrative, the Algerian self serves as the subject.

Djebar stated that the novel presented her personal voice and analysis of the situation in Algeria at that time, particularly with respect to the status of women. Although harems had been abolished following independence, women remained segregated from men and many continued to veil. For Djebar, the veil represented hypocrisy. It was supposed to protect women from male lust, but her perception of social reality was that it simply perpetuated male domination of women by giving them access to masculine space in a manner that suggests that women are thieves of and fugitives in such space. Djebar believes that the veil is not simply about the protection of male honor, but also about preventing women from seeing the outside world and seeking their own liberation to participate in it. Thus, for Djebar, the discarding of the veil was the most visible and important sign of women's evolution in Algerian society.

Djebar was frustrated that women's contributions toward independence remained unrewarded, ignored, and marginalized as late as 1978. The war for independence had cost over a million Algerian lives, or ten per cent of the population, and included suffering the use of napalm, torture, the destruction of entire villages, and the forcible regrouping of people into squalid refugee camps. Women had particularly suffered incarceration, execution, and torture, particularly through rape and electrocution of their breasts and genitals, yet their contributions had not been rewarded. In fact, Djebar argues that the Algerian officials who took over after the colonial era simply perpetuated the policies of the French by continuing to seclude, hide, and torture women. She notes that the only "choice" Algerian women had in the postrevolutionary era was either death from insanity or death by annihilation of the will to that of the master through marriage.

From a social perspective, Djebar noted that women had two means of empowerment: becoming mothers, or using their voices. She has compared the act of martyrdom to the loss of a woman's virginity on her wedding night and the act of childbirth, both of which leave open wounds on the woman's body as she engages in her religious duty of procreation. She has denounced the limitation of women to a physical function that permits them to exist and have a voice only through others, whether husbands or children. She believes that women need to have the right to their own voices restored because the voice is the key to power. Observing that women are encouraged to be silent, from the time they are children when their parents speak for them, through marriage when the husband takes over this role, Djebar notes that Algerian culture in general has robbed women of their voices and, thus, their potential to contribute to society other than through their reproductive function. She has rebelled against this vision of women by never giving the women of her fiction children.

Djebar's writing represents her own brand of feminism that declares her voice in her own words and language, rather than the official Arabic of the current Algerian regime. She considers forced adherence to a national language to be another expression of authoritarianism and male control because Arabic is the language of men and power.

As an act of rebellion and an attempt to record living history, Djebar wrote and directed her second feature-length film, *Zerda and the Songs of Forgetting*, in 1982. *Zerda* is a colloquial word meaning "popular festival" or "occasion for merrymaking." The film celebrates the retrieval of history through the collective memories of individuals about cultural celebrations. The film marked a moment of introspection for Djebar as she tried to look at the French conquest of Algeria from both sides and included violence committed by both sides. Although the film was not well received by the French, who objected to her presentation of colonial history, it received a special prize for the best historical film in Berlin in 1982.

Djebar had planned to make a third feature-length film about the life of a Kabyle woman in the 1990s, but had to abandon the project due to civil unrest and the rise of a militant form of Islamism that sought to eradicate the un-Islamic and pre-Islamic past. She has been disturbed by the rise of this kind of Islamism because it has targeted women as the culture-bearers of Islam and silenced them even more by denying them the right to engage their voices even in cultural celebrations, such as weddings and funerals. For Djebar, the loss of folksinging is more than a loss of native Algerian culture; it also represents the ongoing and systematic silencing of women in a way that reflects twentieth-century political agendas, rather than Algerian history. She notes that Algerian history is filled with women who played strong public roles and were revered even without their veils. She points to nude statues of women dating from the Roman period that were looted from Algerian soil by the French during the colonial era as evidence of a past that does not include the veiling and seclusion of women.

Djebar took on the phenomenon of Islamism in her 1991 study, *So Far from Medina*, a meditation on Islamic history prompted by the bloody street riots of 1988. The book serves as a reminder of the prominence of Muslim women during the lifetime of the Prophet Muhammad and of their courageous role in assuring that Islam survived. As with many of Djebar's works, *So Far from Medina* received a mixed reaction in Algeria. Riots in the streets of Algeria and Morocco by both supporters and opponents occurred when excerpts of the book were published. She was denounced by the F.L.N. regime for her failure to support the regime and was opposed by Islamists for her use of French to liberate herself from her father and brothers as the guardians of what she refers to as her physical and intellectual harems. The book later became the subject of a documentary film shown on French television and was distributed throughout Europe.

Although she has written a variety of works, including poetry, a play, short stories, newspaper articles, and critical essays, Djebar is most famous for her novels, which have been translated into many languages and enjoy broad readerships in the United States and Europe. She is admired by specialists in Third World studies and is considered by some to be the most gifted twentieth-century woman writer in the Muslim world. Her novels have won several prizes, including the Franco-Arab Friendship Prize in Literature for *Love and Fantasia* in 1985; the Liberatur Prize for the best novel by a woman in 1989; the Maurice Maeterlink International Prize in 1995; the International Literary Neustadt Prize, World Literature Today, in 1996; the Fonlon-Nichols Prize from the African Literature Association and the Marguerite Yourcenar Prize for Literature in 1997; the International Prize of Palmi, Italy, in 1998; the Medal of Francophony from the Academie Française de Paris in 1999; and the International Peace Prize of the German Book Trade Association in 2000. She was elected to the Belgian Royal Academy of French Language and Literature in 1999 and became a Commandeur des Arts et des Lettres in France in 2001. She

has received several honorary doctorates. A film about her life was produced for French television.

Djebar divides her time between Paris and Baton Rouge, LA, where she serves as the director of the Center for French and Francophone Studies at Louisiana State University.

Further reading

Djebar, Assia. *Love and Fantasia*. Paris: Albin Michel, 1995 [1985]

—— *The Mischief*, trans. Frances Frenaye. New York: Simon & Schuster, 1958

—— *So Far from Medina*. London: Quartet Books, 1994

—— *Sultana's Shadow*. London: Quartet Books, 1989

—— *Women of Algiers in their Apartment*. Charlottesville, VA: University Press of Virginia, 1992

Zeidan, Joseph. *Arab Women Novelists: The Formative Years and Beyond*. Albany: State University of New York Press, 1995

www.artsci.lsu.edu/cffs/Djebar1.html – home page at Louisiana State University with current information on awards, prizes, and publications

www.culturbase.net – database of international artists with biographical information and descriptions of their work

www.kirjasto.sci.fi/indeksi.htm – international index of writers for whom biographies are provided

Shajarat al-Durr
(thirteenth century)

Sultana of Egypt and heroine of the Crusades who led her troops to victory against French king Louis IX, Shajarat al-Durr was one of the great medieval warrior queens of Islam.

Shajarat al-Durr's birthdate is unknown. She was born a Mamluk (white slave) in Egypt and was in the harem of the eighth Ayyubid sultan, al-Malik al-Salih Najm al-Din Ayyub. Renowned for a combination of beauty and intelligence, she became the sultan's favorite wife. An avid reader, she was also his chief confidante and adviser.

The Ayyubid dynasty had been founded a century earlier by the Muslim hero of the Crusades, Salah al-Din al-Ayyubi. (See also SALADIN.) Sultan al-Malik al-Salih was an important Mamluk military leader. The Mamluks were a special military caste of slaves whose purpose was to protect the monarch and defend Islam. They received both military and religious educations and served apprenticeships before being named to important posts in the military hierarchy and aristocracy. Although they were slaves, their positions were considered highly desirable as an alternative to a lifetime of hard labor. The criteria for selection as a Mamluk included having white skin, living in the north or northeast Islamic countries, being a child or pre-pubescent adolescent, and having been born a non-Muslim (Muslims could not be sold as slaves by other Muslims). The Mamluks of Egypt proved to be such an effective military machine that they alone remained independent, holding off the Mongol hordes that overtook the rest of the Muslim world and ended the Abbasid caliphate.

During the lifetime of her husband, Shajarat al-Durr was active in the court, closely following events in the highest echelons of power, particularly in the military. When her husband was killed in battle in 1250, the military looked to her to make decisions. Her first act was to keep her husband's death a secret. Believing that news of his death would lead to trouble, she decided to focus on a more pressing problem: the invasion of Egypt by the French Crusader king, Louis IX. Working with military leaders to plan operations to defeat the French, she led the battle herself, not only conquering the French, but also capturing and imprisoning King Louis. Only then did she turn her attention to the succession issue.

The sultan had a son, Turan Shah, who had been absent from Cairo at the time of his father's death. Shajarat al-Durr sent emissaries to him, asking him to return to Cairo immediately. Upon his arrival, she turned power over to him. However, Turan Shah proved to be an incapable leader. Unable to direct the troops, he alienated his key military officers. The conflict between Turan Shah and the military officers ultimately resulted in Turan Shah's assassination in 1250. It was after this event that the Mamluks decided officially to place Shajarat al-Durr on the throne.

Believing that she had proven herself a capable leader not only by her victory against the French Crusaders but also by her attempt to turn power over to the heir-apparent who had proved less capable, Shajarat al-Durr and her supporters believed that she should be recognized as the Egyptian head of state. She requested official recognition from the Abbasid caliph, al-Mustaqim. Al-Mustaqim, however, refused the request because she was a woman. Instead of recognizing her sovereignty, he sent back a message offering to send any number of capable men to Egypt to rule there as there didn't appear to be any in Egypt if they had to resort to choosing a woman as leader. Shajarat al-Durr, deeply insulted, decided to ignore the caliph's instructions. Believing that she had the military might to defy him, she gave herself the title "Queen of the Muslims."

Despite her political and military prowess, Shajarat al-Durr held onto her throne for only eighty days. The lack of a husband and the caliph's support led some to question the wisdom of allowing her to rule. Ultimately, the military, under pressure from the Abbasid caliph, withdrew their support. Although they still admired and respected her, they believed that the dynasty's need for recognized authority was greater than their need for her leadership. The great paradox of her removal from power was that she, an able military leader who helped to fend off both the Mongols and the Crusaders, succumbed to the will of a caliph who proved so weak militarily that both he and the caliphate ended with the Mongol conquest of Baghdad in 1258.

Undeterred, Shajarat al-Durr, unwilling to cede power altogether, devised a new scheme to retain the throne. She learned the name of the general who had been chosen by the army to succeed her and decided to marry him. Her new husband, al-Muizz Aybak al-Turkomani, was the most powerful of the Mamluk generals. More importantly, he had the confidence and approval of both the army and the caliph. Although Shajarat al-Durr was no longer directly in control of Egypt's affairs, she continued to be deeply involved in the political scene. That the royal couple ruled jointly is confirmed by the mention of both names during the sermons preached on Fridays in all the mosques in Cairo, as well as the inclusion of both their names on the new coins that were struck and on all official documents issued by the palace.

Shajarat al-Durr's strategy of retaining power via her second husband was rooted in the principle that the marriage would remain monogamous. She had insisted that her husband divorce his other wife in order to marry her and take over the kingdom. The couple ruled together for seven years before the marriage was disrupted by al-Turkomani's decision to take a second wife – the daughter of the atabeg of Mosul. Shajarat al-Durr decided to have her husband murdered. He was killed in the baths on April 12, 1257.

The murder of the sultan by his own wife put the army into disarray as members split over whom to support. Although Shajarat al-Durr's supporters remained by her side, she was transferred out of Cairo to another location where she was assassinated later that year. Her half-naked body was tossed from a cliff where it remained exposed to the elements for several days before being buried.

Shajarat al-Durr was buried in Cairo in the courtyard of a school she had established. A monument was built over her tomb, along with a mosque. Her burial site has become a popular pilgrimage site for those wishing to pay homage to the heroines of Islamic history.

Further reading

Hambly, Gavin R.G., ed. *Women in the Medieval Muslim World*. New York: St. Martin's Press, 1998

Mernissi, Fatima. *The Forgotten Queens of Islam*, trans. Mary Jo Lakeland. Cambridge: Polity Press, 1993

Smith, Margaret. *Muslim Women Mystics: The Life and Work of Rabi'a and Other Women Mystics in Islam*. Oxford: Oneworld Publications, 2001

E

Shirin Ebadi (b. 1947)

A former judge, attorney, law professor, writer, human rights activist, and proponent of women's and children's rights, Shirin Ebadi became the first Muslim woman and the first Iranian to win the Nobel Prize, in 2003.

Shirin Ebadi was born in 1947 in Iran. She received her law degree from the University of Tehran and entered the legal field upon graduation. She is married with two children.

Ebadi was considered a symbol of progress in women's rights and one of the female stars under the shah's secular regime. In 1975, she became the first woman to serve as the president of the city court of Tehran and the first female judge in Iran. She held these positions until she was forced to resign in the aftermath of the Islamic Revolution in 1979 when women were barred from serving as judges. She subsequently began working as a lecturer in law at the University of Tehran and became a practicing attorney, representing people who claimed that their human rights had been violated. Her clients included street children, women subjected to domestic violence, political dissidents, and the families of intellectuals and writers killed between 1998 and 2000 by vigilantes who apparently enjoyed establishment support. The author of several books on human rights, Ebadi founded and leads the Association for Support of Children's Rights in Iran. She is an active supporter of religious freedom, including the right of Iran's Bahai minority freely to practice their religion, which many Muslims believe is heretical. She is recognized as a leading voice in the reform movement and in challenging hardliners opposed to changes to the legal and political systems. She has called for an interpretation of Islamic law that respects human rights, democracy, legal equality, freedom of speech, and freedom of religion.

Ebadi's work for human rights, particularly those of women and children, has been conducted via the channels of the legal profession. She has called for the rule of law in Iran, defining it as a system that treats men and women equally. Rather than calling for revolution from without or insisting that only Western, secular laws and standards be used in the public sphere, she was worked within the Islamic system and Islamic law to engage in a non-violent struggle for human rights and the creation of the preconditions for democracy, particularly the creation and strengthening of the institutions of civil society.

Ebadi's work defending human rights came to national attention in 1998 when she represented the family of the intellectual Dariush Farouhar who, along with his wife, was stabbed to death as part of a series of brutal murders of political dissidents that terrorized the intellectual community between 1998 and 2000. Many in Iran believe that hardliners instigated the attacks to place a check on the more liberal and democratic climate encouraged by President Khatami. Ebadi praised Khatami's support for the right of free speech and for having pressured the Intelligence Ministry, but remained concerned that the perpetrators of the crimes have not been brought to justice. In addition, the main suspect in the murders, the deputy intelligence minister, committed suicide under questionable circumstances while in prison, leading some, including Ebadi, to question whether his suicide was really a murder designed to prevent discovery of the involvement of more senior figures.

Ebadi was at the center of a July 1999 series of student demonstrations at Tehran University. The protests began after a dormitory raid by police and vigilantes who beat up students who were active in the pro-reform movement. After five days of protests, the police intervened, which led to an escalation of violence and the deaths of three people. Ebadi was accused of having inspired and encouraged the students to protest because of her own public protest at the raid and the beating of students as illegal acts. She remains convinced that the student protests were hijacked and escalated by hardliners who sought to stir up violence in order to pave the way for impeaching President Khatami on charges of failing to control the country. It remains unclear who told the police to raid the dormitory, although Ebadi has continued to work to identify those responsible for orchestrating the attacks. In the meantime, none of the police or vigilantes who took part in the raid have been prosecuted. Instead, four students accused of being the ringleaders of the demonstrations were sentenced to death by the revolutionary court in Tehran.

Ebadi herself was sentenced to fifteen months, imprisonment and was prohibited from practicing law for defaming Iranian authorities. She appealed her sentence and was fined instead.

Ebadi's work on women's rights covers a variety of issues, including marriage, divorce, travel, employment, and inheritance. Although she herself does not veil when she is abroad, in defiance of the law requiring her to veil when in Iran, she has declined to take on the legal issue of veiling out of a belief that it is more important for Iranian women to have the legal right to exist, know their rights, and start asking for them than it is to worry about the dress code. Her support for women's rights has earned her death threats for years, resulting in the constant need for police bodyguards. She was particularly singled out for her prosecution of a father charged with murdering his daughter in an honor killing, a case that was profiled on *60 Minutes*.

Ebadi points to the legal status of women in Iran as the most important issue in need of reform. Under the traditional interpretation of Islamic law followed in Iran, a woman is legally considered to be half of a man in matters of testimony and inheritance. If a man kills a woman intentionally, the woman's family has to pay half of the legal fees to put him on trial and execute him. A woman is limited in her right to divorce her husband, while the husband is not required to provide any justification for divorcing his wife. Because the wife's right to divorce is not clearly defined by the law, the judge or court alone decides whether to grant the divorce. There are no juries. Furthermore, in the event of divorce, the husband is required to pay his wife only three months' maintenance. The wife retains no claim to the family home or the husband's assets, regardless of her participation in and support for her husband's career or the length of the marriage. Believing that all of these cases represent an injustice to women, Ebadi has led the fight for the expansion of women's rights in family matters.

Ebadi has called for the awarding of alimony to reflect women's contributions to their marriages. She has also called for granting women the right to divorce their husbands as a matter of law, rather than limiting this right to prenuptial agreements and temporary legal documents pertaining to individuals. She has protested the automatic assignment of custody to the father of boys over the age of two and girls over the age of seven, as well as in cases where a divorced mother remarries, because she believes that such rulings give no consideration to the circumstances under which the divorce occurred or the characters of the parents. She has illustrated her point through a domestic violence case she prosecuted in which a woman had been beaten repeatedly by her husband. According to the law, a man can be prosecuted for physical abuse of his wife only if it occurs in public and there are witnesses to the beating. In this case, the wife had been unable to press charges until her husband struck her at a party. The children were called to testify that their father had beaten their mother so badly that she was hospitalized on more than one occasion. The judge not only disallowed their testimony, but also ruled in the man's favor because he apologized for striking his wife and promised not to do it again. For Ebadi, this case was not just about the failure of the legal system to protect the woman from violence in her own home, but also raised the questions of the capacity of a male judge to understand family dynamics from the woman's perspective and the suitability of the father as a parent.

Ironically, Ebadi has observed that such injustices perpetrated by the legal system, as based on a patriarchal interpretation of Islam, have strengthened the Iranian feminist movement as women from a variety of socio-economic classes and ideological persuasions are increasingly demanding their rights, including greater access to public space, a more active role in public life, and legal reforms that uphold the protection of women and children proclaimed by Islam. The result has been growing cooperation between secular and Islamist women in identifying common problems and seeking common solutions through legal reforms. Although she personally believes that religion and state should be kept separate, she recognizes the importance of achieving reform through the reinterpretation of Islam under the current administration.

Believing that reform, the building of democracy, and the creation of institutions of civil society are the key to increased women's and human rights in the future, Ebadi served as the unofficial spokesperson for Iranian women who played a key role in the 1997 electoral victory of the reformist president Mohammed Khatami. As of 1999, women's representation in the Majlis had increased to fourteen (a higher representation of women than exists in the U.S. Senate), more Iranian women were passing university entrance exams than men, and women had made important gains in winning jobs that had previously been considered male territory, such as driving buses. In addition, a woman serves as a jurisprudent on the Council of Guardians, which selects and supervises the Supreme Leader, a woman serves in President Khatami's cabinet, and several women have been appointed as municipal administrators. Nevertheless, it remains difficult for women to gain senior positions and some note that the presence of these token women in high-profile positions is superficial and does not represent substantive change, given that these women serve in advisory rather than decision-making positions and that they are all religious conformists who are committed to the state's official ideology and interpretation of women's rights.

Ebadi is a controversial figure in Iran not only because she has worked to promote human rights and to defend victims of violence that is either perpetrated or condoned by conservative religious figures, but also because she is a secular, rather than an Islamic, feminist who seeks to promote change through reformation of the legal system, rather than through the reinterpretation of Islam. (See also AZAM TALEGHANI.) Nevertheless, she is careful to remind people that neither Islam proper nor the fact that Iran has a religious government is responsible for the social problems faced by Iranian women. Rather, she believes that a patriarchal and incorrect interpretation of Islam combined with a government that does not understand the needs of society have prevented the changes in basic laws that she believes are necessary to resolve issues related to public need and welfare. She notes that Islam provides a legal mechanism for such reinterpretation, but that the government has failed to make use of it.

For her dedication to human rights, the rights of women and children, and the building of democracy in Iran, Ebadi has been awarded a certificate of congratulations from Human Rights Watch, the 2001 Rafto Prize from Norway, and the 2003 Nobel Prize for Peace. The Nobel committee stated that Ebadi had been chosen in order to promote human rights in Islamic countries and throughout the world. Many analysts believe that the committee also wanted to demonstrate support for moderate Muslims following the 9/11 attacks and for reform in Iran and throughout the region, particularly with respect to women's rights. Reformists hailed the award to Ebadi, seeing in it recognition of the important role Iranian women play on the political and social scenes. Although the Iranian government expressed pleasure that an Iranian had won the prize, it voiced concern that the West was using the prize to push a Western human rights agenda in Iran and interfere with Iranian national politics. The government further refused to broadcast or allow photographs of Ebadi's acceptance ceremony and speech because she was not veiled. No official celebrations were planned to recognize her achievement.

Ebadi accepted the Nobel Prize on behalf of all women – Muslim, Iranian, and other – who strive for human rights around the world and declared that she would donate the $1.4 million award to human rights groups in Iran, particularly those concerned with women and children. She remains dedicated to a vision of the world in which the human rights of every human being are recognized and enforced, regardless of gender or religious or political orientation, as the only hope for freeing the future from the cycles of violence and disaster.

Further reading

Dickstein, Cynthia. "Iran's Fighter for Women's Rights," *Boston Globe*, October 11, 2003

Ebadi, Shirin. *History and Documentation of Human Rights in Iran*. New York: U.N.I.C.E.F., 2000

—— *The Rights of the Child: A Study of Legal Aspects of Children's Rights in Iran*. Tehran: n.p., 1994

"Iranian Rights Activist Wins Nobel," www.cnn.com/2003/WORLD/europe/10/10/nobel.prize/index.html

Mahdi, Ali Akbar. "Iranian Women: Between Islamization and Globalization," in *Iran Encountering Globalization: Problems and Prospects*, ed. Ali Mohammadi. London and New York: Routledge, 2003

Mellgran, Doug. "Iranian Activist Warns West on Rights," *Boston Globe*, December 11, 2003

Moghadam, Valentine S. "The Two Faces of Iran: Women's Activism, the Reform Movement, and the Islamic Republic," in *Nothing Sacred: Women Respond to Religious Fundamentalism and Terror*, ed. Betsy Reed. New York: Thunder's Mouth Press, 2002

"Peace Laureate Blasts Denial of Candidacies," *Boston Globe*, January 30, 2004

"A Peacemaker in Iran," editorial, *Boston Globe*, October 11, 2003

Sciolino, Elaine. *Persian Mirrors: The Elusive Face of Iran*. New York: Simon & Schuster, 2000

Theodoulou, Michael. "A Tough Place to be a Woman with a Cause," *Christian Science Monitor*, October 15, 1999

www.nobel.se – website of the Nobel Prize, including biographical information and a translation of Ebadi's acceptance speech, December 10, 2003

Farid Esack (b. 1957)

A liberation theologian who is internationally recognized as one of the most important voices in progressive Islam, Farid Esack played a pivotal role in South Africa's fight to end apartheid.

Farid (also spelled Faried) Esack was born in 1957 in Wynberg in Cape Town, South Africa. His father abandoned his mother when he was three weeks old, leaving her to raise six boys on her own. Esack also has an older sister whom he did not know until after his mother's death. The family lived in such severe poverty that there was frequently not enough food to eat and Esack often went without shoes.

Esack's family was forcibly removed from Wynberg in 1961 when the government decided that the side of the road his family lived on was the "white" side. The rest of his extended family lived on the other, "black," side. Esack's family moved to Bonteheuwel, a barren township on the Cape Flats that had been reserved for blacks, Indians, and coloreds under the 1952 Group Areas Act. When his brother grew up to become the family's first gangster, Esack questioned the responsibility of the elites who uprooted the family, as well as the Muslim and black communities who had failed to stop it or support the family through its struggle. He also looked to the example of his mother who, already burdened by family responsibilities, had been rendered even more miserable by the forced move further away from her work. Before the move, she had to run for the train before sunrise and work long hours

at a factory where the administrators and supervisors were never satisfied and always demanded more production, before returning home to six children and an evening filled with housework. The move to Bonteheuwel extended the commute as she had to stand third class in two overcrowded trains and then walk through the bush to get to work and back. While she worked herself literally to death by her early fifties in exchange for a small weekly salary and a box of chocolates at Christmas, her bosses enjoyed wealth and recreation.

Esack sees his mother's history as an example of how apartheid robs the poor of their lives and well-being for the sake of elites, their power, and their money. In South Africa at that time, whites constituted only one-sixth of the population, but earned two-thirds of the national income. By contrast, blacks constituted three-quarters of the population, but earned only a quarter of the income. Watching his mother die from the combined burdens of patriarchy and economic exploitation instilled in Esack a desire to seek justice.

From a religious perspective, apartheid provided examples not only of injustice, but also of kindness, compassion, and humanity as expressed by white Christians. The family's white Christian neighbor often provided them with food or money to tide them over, giving him a practical awareness of the intrinsic value of the religious Other and the powerful experience of grace. As a result, he has never been able to accept a theology that claims salvation only for those with correct beliefs or that preaches that all Jews and Christians will go to Hell.

Esack was educated at a traditional Islamic school where he memorized the Quran. When he was about ten years old, he began an eleven-year-long formal religious commitment with the Tablighi Jamaah, an international Muslim revivalist group. Although he appreciated the group's emphasis on learning how to live one's life as a Muslim, rather than according to ritual, rules or regulations (see also RASHID AL-GHANNOUSHI), he was frustrated by the fact that he was investing enormous amounts of time and energy in religion, yet did not seem to be forming a closer relationship with God. He remained deeply unhappy and unfulfilled as a person and became increasingly concerned that the group was overly concerned about themselves and their programs to his personal detriment.

In 1974, Esack moved to Karachi, Pakistan, where he completed his undergraduate studies at Jamiah Ulum al-Islamiyya. He passed his Board of Intermediate Education Examination with distinction in 1975 and graduated in 1978. He then studied at the Darsi Nizami, Jamiah Alimiyyah al-Islamiyyah from 1978 to 1980 and engaged in postgraduate research from 1980 to 1982 in Quranic studies at Jamiah Abu Bakr. He completed a Ph.D. in Quranic hermeneutics at the University of Birmingham in the United Kingdom in 1996.

During his time in Pakistan, Esack became increasingly uncomfortable with the conservative theology he studied that reserved Paradise for Muslims alone and justified the religious and social persecution of Christians and Hindus. Pushed into recognizing the incompatibility between conservative theology and progressive real life experience, Esack concluded that the true experience of God can only come about by transcending oneself. He was strongly influenced by his contact with and participation in Breakthrough, a group of Christian liberation theologians struggling to make sense of living as Christians in a fundamentally unjust and exploitative society. Inspired by Breakthrough's commitment to social, gender, and environmental justice, Esack borrowed many of their ideas, reinterpreting them in a Muslim context as he became increasingly involved in the struggle against apartheid back in his native South Africa. He was particularly inspired by their approach to prayer which focused on content, rather than ritual perfection, and their work toward coexistence and equality with the religious Other as a matter of human survival and cultural tolerance.

Esack returned to South Africa in 1982 at the height of the struggle against apartheid, racism, and sexism. The Muslim population of South Africa had been searching for an Islamic response to apartheid since the emergence of a consciously Muslim South African identity in 1958. The 1960s had marked the nadir of repression and persecution of black South Africans in general, as the underground movement was uprooted and demoralized. The resulting rise of Black Consciousness and Black Theology of the 1970s had sown the seeds of liberation theology. However, the murder of the Black Consciousness movement's most dynamic and articulate speaker, Steve Biko, in 1977 had robbed the movement of its most gifted voice. Biko's death had not, however, led to an end to the struggle for self-respect and dignity among the oppressed. While South African Christians had begun drawing inspiration from the liberation theology of Latin America, the Muslim population had turned to the theology of revolt against neocolonialism and dictatorship that had arisen during the 1970s with the advent of Islam as a political force. Many young Muslims began to see Islam as an ideological option for South Africa.

In 1982, the major Muslim movement in South Africa was the Muslim Youth Movement (M.Y.M.). Esack joined the Executive Board to study political options for Muslims, including boycotting elections. Although he was interested in the power of religion to harness the political momentum for an end to apartheid, he became increasingly concerned that the M.Y.M.'s Islam was based on the kind of exclusivism that had led to apartheid in the first place. He believed that this model could not lead to success because it maintained a vision in which virtue was denied to all non-Muslims and no space was created for working with the religious Other. Believing that social justice and dealing with reality on the ground were more important than theological quibbling about who was going to go to Paradise and that cooperation across religious groups was vital to the future of South Africa, Esack worked to develop a theology capable of accommodating that need.

In 1984, Esack and three friends founded Call of Islam. Call became the most active Muslim movement working to end apartheid, gender inequality, and threats to the environment and encouraging interfaith work. Esack served as the national coordinator and was responsible for the personal and spiritual formation of the membership, public relations, fundraising, and networking with other anti-apartheid, ecumenical, and interfaith organizations. Call differed from the major internal liberation movement, the United Democratic Front (U.D.F.), with which it was affiliated, by promoting a spiritual and theological basis for the liberation of South Africa. Although not all Christians supported the subjugation and oppression of non-whites, religion had been invoked by all of the major political players in support of their politics and agendas, as well as for the structures and institutions of oppression. Because apartheid had been grounded in and justified by religion, Esack believed that liberation also needed to be grounded in religion.

The goal of Call was to produce a South African interpretation of Islam that reflected their experience living as an oppressed and marginalized minority under non-Muslim rule. Call focused on action, rather than theory or reading books. It became particularly well known for its use of funerals as opportunities not only to bind the community together by demonstrating care and compassion when a loved one was being buried, but also by making a political statement about the shared suffering and solidarity of Muslims and non-Muslims. Prison time was also used as an opportunity for interfaith sharing and bonding on the basis of suffering and oppression.

Call combined personal, spiritual, and religious support with political commitment. The majority of Call members were either working-class or lower-middle-class South Africans, half of whom were women. Call reinterpreted classical religious terminology to fit the contemporary South African context. For example, it reinterpreted the term jihad to refer to the struggle against apartheid, while *ummah* referred to the oppressed community. An unbeliever (*kafir*) was defined as a person who collaborated in the oppression of other people. Because Call members believed that the apartheid regime was oppressive and that anyone participating in the system became a supporter by association, the movement declared voting an act of unbelief, if not apostasy. Call's focus was not on missionary work or asserting the superiority of one religion over another, but on liberation and the relief of human suffering. It sought to win people over by folding them into the struggle for liberation, non-racialism, absolute gender equality, respect for the environment, religious freedom, ending poverty, and a more equitable distribution of wealth. Although some Call members engaged in armed struggle and many died as martyrs or in exile, it was not a jihadist organization.

Esack's main contribution to Call was the development of a Muslim liberation theology, which he defines as religiously based activism that seeks comprehensive justice. Liberation theology is based on the belief that God is active in history and desires freedom for all people. It requires practical action, rather than theoretical belief, and calls for joining with the religious Other in the pursuit of justice. Esack abandoned use of the Quran as a pretext to justify predetermined opinions in favor of using it as a text open to new interpretations that legitimize a just order that recognizes the humanity of all people. His interpretation of the Quran includes questioning what people bring to the text and its interpretation out of recognition that everyday reality plays an important role in the understanding and application of religious texts.

Esack believes that it is possible to live in faithfulness to the Quran through the development of a theological pluralism that makes space for the righteous and just of all persuasions. He believes that the Quran is most socially meaningful when applied to social conditions and certain moments of history. He has called for Muslims to do away with "stagnant" and "fossilized" interpretations of Islam focused on rituals and motions in favor of a more personally meaningful and socially relevant Islam. He believes that this is particularly important in the current social reality of expanding materialism where people may experience more comfortable lifestyles, yet also find themselves increasingly alienated from themselves, others, and God. Esack posits the humanity and compassion of liberation theology as an important foil to what he refers to as "dehumanizing fundamentalism." For Esack, the true jihad is the quest for social justice, individual liberty, and the experience and knowledge of the Divine outside of institutions and dogmatic constructions. He believes that faith cannot be separated from social responsibility.

Esack's understanding of the mechanics of apartheid recognizes the connection between emphasis on the spirituality of a faith and collaboration with the system of oppression. He came to believe that the claim that spirituality and politics must be kept separate in order to maintain neutrality was patently false because withholding religion from politics served to support oppressive socioeconomic systems. Rather than claiming that God must not care about humanity if

oppression, poverty, and starvation exist, Esack notes instead that the existence of such human tragedies represents God's call to do something to resolve them. For Esack, believing in God as a God of love means demonstrating that love to others in ways that are relevant to their daily lives. The social reality of poverty should be seen as an opportunity for engaging in charity, kindness, and the pursuit of social justice, rather than as a sign of God's lack of concern for the world. He calls for an activist approach to faith that not only identifies what is going wrong in the world, but seeks to resolve it at both the individual and community levels.

Esack's vision of brotherly and sisterly love is rooted in his belief that God considers human beings to be worthy of love and salvation. Because God's attitude is intended to serve as guidance for human beings, the refusal to recognize the inherent dignity and value of another human being dehumanizes everyone in the same manner as do poverty, racism, and sexism. Esack teaches that true concern for another is focused on that person's growth, rather than one's own personal agenda or feelings, noting that "I am" should not be rooted in "You are not." He considers faith that is focused entirely on individual spirituality to be irresponsible and unjust because it refuses to engage real-life problems and tends to maintain the status quo. He believes that because people do not have a choice about suffering the ills of oppression, they do not have a choice about engaging those ills either. Passivity is an illusion that allows the status quo to be maintained, while activism works toward bringing about a more just and humane society.

Esack's vision of liberation includes the provision of gender justice. As with other issues, he notes the important role religion has played in relegating women to second-class status. Traditional interpretations of religion tend to consider women's primary roles to be relieving male sexual tensions and producing children. Although some religious leaders have called for faithful men to demonstrate greater kindness toward women, Esack believes that this is insufficient, noting that kindness, gentleness, and compassion cannot and should not serve as substitutes for justice, freedom, and equality based on recognition of women as God's creations. He has tied the issue of gender justice directly to the end of apartheid, noting that the relegation of Second and Third World women to the home to raise children also relegates them to ignorance, hunger, and poverty.

Esack is a strong supporter of universal human rights. He challenges societies to look within themselves to see if their commitment to universal human rights is truly universal or simply a matter of demanding rights for themselves. In a particularly controversial stance, he has called for equal rights for homosexuals as a test of a society's commitment to equality.

Call became the testing ground for Esack's new contextual theology as a non-racial liberation theology seeking the large-scale mobilization of people against apartheid. Believing that peaceful coexistence was not the same as conscious religious pluralism, Call embraced Jews and Christians as brothers and sisters who were working together to end oppression. This was not a functional or utilitarian relationship, but one that involved the acceptance of the theological legitimacy and virtue of other faiths, as well as the full humanity of the religious Other. Although they were dedicated to their cause, Call members did not believe that they would achieve liberation in their lifetime. Esack resigned from Call in 1989 over differences in style and organizational discipline.

Of the aftermath of apartheid, Esack notes that the T.R.C. (Truth and Reconciliation Commission) played an important role in drawing conflict to an end, but failed to provide justice or a truly pluralist environment. He recognizes that South Africa needed someone like Desmond Tutu to reconcile the conflicting parties, but was disturbed by Tutu's tendency to stamp the whole reconciliation process with his own Christian beliefs, effectively excluding other religions or relegating them to the status of guests rather than equal participants. Despite his disagreement over the Christian overtones of the reconciliation method, Esack acknowledges that Jews, Hindus, and Muslims play disproportionately influential roles in South African life today.

Esack was appointed by President Nelson Mandela to serve a four-year term as a commissioner for gender equality, heading the Committee on Religion, Culture, Tradition, and Masculinity from 1997 until 2001. His calls for gender justice earned him a smear campaign and death threats from conservative elements who believe that traditional gender roles are an inherent part of their faith. He has been discouraged by the broad Muslim male rejection of the promotion of women's rights as part of the struggle to end apartheid, but was pleased that the new Constitutional Assembly refused to accept gender inequality in the new constitution. Recognizing how deeply ingrained patriarchy was in South African culture, the new Bill of Rights strengthened gender-equality clauses to prevent a return to discriminatory traditional or religious laws.

Esack has targeted crime and the rising H.I.V./A.I.D.S. crisis as the major issues facing South Africa for the future. He has called for strengthening individual morality, community-level activism, and the institutions of civil society as the keys to solving crime, drugs, and gangsterism. Observing that H.I.V./A.I.D.S. is a crisis of epidemic proportions across Africa, he has worked to develop a theology of compassion within Islam to encourage Muslims to embrace those who are either H.I.V. positive or who have A.I.D.S., out of recognition of their common shared humanity. In 2000, he co-founded the organization Positive Muslims to raise awareness about how H.I.V./A.I.D.S. is spread, to promote abstinence from sex outside of marriage, faithfulness during a relationship, and the use of condoms, and to offer support to Muslims who are infected, regardless of how the infection came about. Esack also served as a founding trustee of the Treatment Action Campaign, the largest H.I.V./A.I.D.S. program in South Africa that has served as a model for the rest of the world and has been nominated for the Nobel Peace Prize.

Esack's prominence as an anti-apartheid activist and progressive theologian has led to international visibility. He is the author of a number of books, including a spiritual autobiography, *On Being a Muslim*, and *Quran, Liberation and Pluralism*, both of which have been translated into numerous languages. Fluent in English, Arabic, Urdu, and Afrikaans and possessing working knowledge of German and Dutch, he writes regular columns and provides commentary for a variety of media outlets and newspapers. He is a frequent speaker at domestic and international conferences and has recorded a series of twenty-four television programs for the Dutch Muslim Broadcasting on Ethics for Young Muslims. He has taught at universities throughout the United States, Europe, and South Africa and has received funding for his work from the Human Sciences Research Council of South Africa, the Spalding Foundation of the United Kingdom and the Missiologiewissenschaft Award from Germany. Esack is the director of the Centre for the Study of Progressive Islam in Cape Town, South Africa, and holds the Besl Chair in Ethics, Religion, and Society at Xavier University, Cincinnati, OH.

Further reading

Esack, Farid. "In Search of a Progressive Islamic Response to 9/11," in *Progressive Islam*, ed. Omid Safi. Oxford: Oneworld Publications, 2003
—— *Introduction to Contemporary Islam*. Oxford: Oneworld Publications, 2004
—— *An Introduction to the Qur'an*. Oxford: Oneworld Publications, 2002
—— *On Being a Muslim: Finding a Religious Path in the World Today*. Oxford: Oneworld Publications, 1999
—— *Qur'an, Liberation and Pluralism: An Islamic Perspective of Interreligious Solidarity Against Oppression*. Oxford: Oneworld Publications, 1997
—— "Sex – the Awkard Gift from God," unpublished paper in possession of the author
—— *The Struggle: Islamists and the South African Crucible*. Johannesburg: Call of Islam, 1989
—— *Towards a Theology of Compassion – Religious Responses to H.I.V./A.I.D.S.* Forthcoming
The Muslim Vanguard, U.S. Catholic Magazine, Claretian Publications.
Interview with the author, December 3, 2003
www.positivemuslims.org.za/ – website for Positive Muslims
www.progressivemuslims.org

F

Hassan Fathy (1900–1989)

An award-winning architect who restored traditional methods, tools, and materials to modern structures, Hassan Fathy was dedicated to keeping people at the heart of his constructions and to improving the lives of the poor rural masses of the developing world while teaching them to build for themselves. He was considered one of the outstanding architects of his generation in Africa.

Hassan Fathy (also spelled Hasan Fathi) was born on March 23, 1900, in Alexandria, Egypt. His childhood musical studies served his later architectural career by focusing his attention on rhythm, patterns, and mathematical relationships. He received his secondary education at the High School of Engineering, Architectural Section, and completed his higher education at the University of King Fuad I (now the University of Cairo) in Cairo. He worked at the Department of Municipal Affairs in Cairo from 1926 until 1930, when he began teaching at the Faculty of Fine Arts in Cairo, a position that he held until 1946 and again from 1953 to 1957. He became head of the Architectural Section in 1954.

Fathy's long architectural career with an eye to development began in 1937 when he designed and exhibited his first mud-brick projects – a series of country houses built in Lower Egypt. He was then commissioned by the Royal Society of Agriculture to construct mud-brick structures incorporating an inclined vault in Bahtim, Egypt, in 1941.

Fathy's personal philosophy of building was based on the idea that the architect ought to be both the owner and the builder of his construction, rather than simply an employee of the construction system. He believed that the architect needed to have a personal stake in the construction and that architecture is necessarily a cooperative activity. While a single man can potentially design a building, it takes a team to construct it. He also believed that even the poor deserved to have aesthetic value in their structures, noting that the long-term success of housing ventures for the poor lay, in part, in the attachment the residents felt to them. Throughout his lifetime, Fathy called on the international community to put scientific and technological advances to use for the poor.

Fathy expanded his architectural vision to the construction of an entire village with the design and construction of the New Gourna Village project in Luxor, Egypt, between 1946 and 1953. The village was intended to serve people who were being moved out of the antiquities zone in Old Gourna Village.

The new village consisted of houses, a mosque, a theater, and a market. Similar to his previous constructions, New Gourna Village made use of mud bricks and traditional Egyptian decorative techniques and architectural features, including enclosed courtyards and vaulted and domed roofing. Fathy consulted with the prospective inhabitants about their needs and taught them how to make and build with mud bricks. He personally supervised the construction of the completed portions of the village, hoping that it would serve as a prototype for other projects to rehouse the rural poor in Egypt. Although the village remained incomplete due to bureaucratic and other issues, the vision and construction of New Gourna Village earned Fathy both domestic and international fame because it demonstrated how socially cooperative and environmentally friendly architecture could be developed into a major international resource. The Egyptian government appointed him director of the School Building Department for the Ministry of Education from 1949 until 1952. He also became a consultant to the United Nations Refugee World Assistance Program in 1950.

New Gourna Village came to symbolize the major themes of Fathy's architectural philosophy and style – the use of ancient design methods and materials appropriate for and faithful to the indigenous environment at minimal cost, while paying close attention to climatic conditions and public health concerns. Fathy was a pioneer of environmentally friendly buildings, using traditional methods of passive cooling and ventilation, particularly through the use of traditional courtyards, fountains, and dense brick walls. Most of his early structures were designed to house the poor while simultaneously strengthening and expanding the economy and raising the standard of living in rural areas by training the local inhabitants to make their own materials and build their own buildings.

Because much of Fathy's work was completed in Egypt, he specifically paid attention to rural Egyptian economic conditions and Egyptian architectural and urban design techniques. However, the broader method was applicable to rural areas in a variety of developing countries.

Part of Fathy's goal in reviving specifically Egyptian and Arab urban architectural themes was his desire to make his fellow Egyptians more aware of their rich architectural heritage, particularly as found in medieval Cairo. He personally drew inspiration from both Pharaonic and Islamic Egyptian styles. He worked throughout his lengthy career to convince the Egyptian state to adopt his techniques and philosophy as a means of reestablishing national and cultural pride. He also hoped that his work would lead to a renaissance of the arts in Egypt, particularly in architecture.

Fathy was a proponent of socially oriented cooperative construction techniques that restored the human scale and compass to modern architecture. He encouraged the use of natural materials and individual craftsmanship and involvement in the building of structures as the key to both conservation and sustainability. He believed that the use of natural materials offered an opportunity to reconnect human beings with their past internal balance with the environment. In the human manipulation of clay, marble, stone, and wood, he found access to historical techniques that had given expression to humanity's aspiration toward the Divine, as evidenced in the construction of mosques, cathedrals, and temples. He sought to capture the environmental harmony expressed in traditional structures that had been lost during the Industrial Revolution when the use of mechanized, energy-intensive tools replaced handmade tools and inherited techniques, casting aside the individual's personal contribution to building and the artistry it represented.

Fathy believed that the resulting emphasis on quantity over quality led to increased consumerism and materialism based on draining energy from the community and environment and disdain for local forms and products, shattering local economies.

Fathy particularly lamented the loss of traditional methods of climatization that derived their energy from the local natural environment in favor of Western expressions of progress and modernity that required the production of energy. He proposed a return to the more environmentally friendly traditional Egyptian constructions, including central, high-ceilinged upper rooms with plentiful natural light and ventilation for receiving guests and serene internal courtyards with fountains to increase air humidity and coolness. He also made frequent use of traditional Arab urban architectural structures, such as the wind catch, the lantern dome, the wooden lattice screen, walkways, pools, walls, and gardens. Prior to designing his structures, he typically studied the wind and temperature patterns in order to find the most efficient ways of capturing desert winds and channeling them through a series of baffles that increased air velocity for use as natural ventilation. This method was both economical and socially and environmentally conscious.

Fathy noted that architects in the developing world had a particularly heavy burden in designing structures because of the lack of financial resources accompanied by pressure to modernize and progress in order to push economic development forward, often at the cost not only of the environment, but also the sense of community living and working spaces. Fathy believed that the community should be at the heart of the architect's design, rather than on the periphery. He also believed that architects had a special responsibility to revive people's faith in and appreciation of their own culture. His insistence on using indigenous materials and methods was designed to restore the tradition of the village craftsman while boosting the local economy.

Fathy's success in restoring traditional methods of creating environmentally sound structures led to his working as a lecturer on climate and architecture at the Athens Technical Institute in Greece. He served as a member of the Research Project for the City of the Future from 1957 until 1962 and as the director of pilot projects for housing for the Ministry of Scientific Research in Cairo from 1963 until 1965.

Throughout the 1960s, 1970s, and 1980s, Fathy designed a variety of buildings, including private dwellings, hotels, resthouses, shops, tourist centers, casinos, refugee housing, factories, hospitals, cultural centers, farms, schools, villages, housing for the poor, mosques, conference centers, mausoleums, company buildings, and villages throughout the Middle East, Africa, Europe, and the United States. All of them included his trademark Egyptian architectural features and climate-control systems, as well as the division of private and public domestic space and the use of traditional inner courtyards. At the same time, he continued his academic and public-service careers, lecturing on town planning and architecture at Al-Azhar University, rural housing at Cairo University, consulting for the minister of tourism in Cairo, serving as a delegate for the U.N. Organization for Rural Development Project, and designing the High Institute of Social Anthropology and Folk Art for the Ministry of Culture in Cairo.

Fathy's expertise in architecture led to his service on the steering committee that developed the Aga Khan Award for Architecture. (See also AGA KHAN.) He also founded and directed the International Institute for Appropriate Technology in 1977 to develop and apply his approach to building and teaching. His work inspired the International Construction Institute, which named its

Hassan Fathy Institute for Construction Workers after him. The Institute plays a pivotal role in the U.N. Centre for Human Settlements and works closely with the Aga Khan Trust for Culture in considering how to maintain the human scale, cultural values, and aspirations of the inhabitants of future cities while encouraging them to participate in the creation of their own living environments.

Fathy's expertise in and contributions to developing-world architecture and the preservation and restoration of traditional techniques earned him broad international recognition during his lifetime. In addition to membership on the High Council of Arts and Letters of Egypt and appointment as an honorary fellow of both the American Research Center of Cairo and the American Institute of Architecture, he was awarded the Encouragement Prize for Fine Arts and gold medal in 1959 and the National Prize for Arts and Letters in 1967 by the Egyptian government. In 1980, he received the Right Livelihood Award and the Aga Khan Award for Architecture. He received a gold medal from the Union Internationale des Architectes in 1984. An exhibit of his architectural drawings and memorabilia from the American University in Cairo and the Aga Khan Trust for Culture was held at the Institut du Monde Arabe in Paris from December 2002 until February 2003.

Fathy died in Cairo in 1989. He was broadly recognized for his emphasis on the use of appropriate technologies, local materials, construction techniques, social cooperation, and environmentally conscious architecture, encouraging architects to work within their environment, rather than striving to change it, restoring a harmonious balance between nature, architecture, and human beings, and emphasizing the architect's social and cultural role in preserving the traditions and habits of the community through structures that were functional, yet served as expressions of communal art. Above all, he held that innovation, progress, and development had to be made subordinate to human needs and social values, a vision that marked him as the precursor of the concept of sustainability.

Further reading

Blair, Sheila S. and Jonathan M. Bloom. "Art and Architecture: Themes and Variations," in *The Oxford History of Islam*, ed. John L. Esposito. New York: Oxford University Press, 1999

Fathy, Hassan. "Architecture and environment." *Aridlands Newsletter*, no. 36, Fall/Winter 1994

—— *Architecture of the Poor*. Chicago: University of Chicago Press, 1973 (originally published in Egypt in 1969 under the title *Gourna: A Tale of Two Villages*)

—— "Contemporaneity in the City," in *Architecture for a Changing World*, ed. James Steele. London: Academy Editions, 1992

"Hassan Fathy," ArchNet Digital Library, archnet.org/library/parties/one-party.tcl?party_id=1

"Hassan Fathy's Elegant Solutions," *ARAMCO World*, vol. 50, no. 4, July/August 1999

Holod, Renata and Darl Rastorfer, eds. *In his Own Words*. Singapore: Concept Media, 1985

Khan, Hasan-Uddin, ed. *Hassan Fathy*. Singapore: Concept Media, 1995

Pich-Aguilera, Felipe. *Hassan Fathy: Beyond the Nile*. London: Concept Media, Ltd., 1989

Serageldin Ismail, and Samer El-Sadek, eds. *Egypt and the Aga Khan Award for Architecture*. Geneva: Aga Khan Trust for Culture, 1989

Steele, James. *An Architecture for People: The Complete Works of Hassan Fathy*. London: Thames & Hudson, 1997

—— *The Hassan Fathy Collection*. Geneva: Aga Khan Trust for Culture, 1989

Tresilian, David. "Hassan Fathy: Innovation and Tradition," *Al-Ahram Weekly On-Line*, December 19–25, 2002, issue no. 617, weekly.ahram.org.eg/2002/617/cu5.htm

www.internationalbuilders.org/hfi.html – website with examples of his structures

www.kmtspace.com/fathy.htm – website with examples of his structures www.rightlivelihood.se – website for the Right Livelihood Award

H.R.H. Sheikha Fatima bint Mubarak (b. early 1950s)

The First Lady of the United Arab Emirates, H.R.H. Sheikha Fatima bint Mubarak is an award-winning activist for women's rights and humanitarianism.

H.R.H. Sheikha Fatima bint Mubarak was married to the late H.R.H. Sheikh Zayed bin Sultan al Nahyan, the former Emir of Abu Dhabi and President of the United Arab Emirates (U.A.E.), and is the mother of the current emir. She has been a pioneer in the pursuit of women's rights and expansion of women's access to education and the workplace since the 1960s. She also set the stage for what has become a growing trend of Arab first ladies playing a public role in their countries' life and development. (See also H.R.H. SHAIKHA SABEEKA AL-KHALIFA; H.R.H. SHEIKHA MOUZA AL-MISNAD; H.M. QUEEN NOOR.) Fatima's public role, as supported by her husband, has sent the message that it is acceptable for women to be visible in Muslim and Arab societies and that women are making positive contributions to their countries' development. The image of Fatima as a strong, activist, and contributing first lady, in addition to a devoted mother and grandmother, has been particularly important in the Gulf, which historically has been the most traditional and conservative part of the Middle East. Fatima symbolizes a new trend of social and political activism for women that is expected to lead to expanded calls for democratization.

Fatima's work has been based on the twin pillars of education and job opportunities for women. She began her campaign for women's education in the early 1970s when she was pursuing her own. By setting the example, she hoped to encourage other families to enroll their daughters in school and to inspire girls to complete their educations, even in cases where, like her, they were already married. She offered her personal support to girls whose parents were opposed to their completing their educations.

Fatima established the first women's organization in the U.A.E. in 1972, the Abu Dhabi Women's Society. Sister organizations were soon founded in the other emirates, leading to the formation of the U.A.E. Women's Federation as an umbrella organization in 1975 with Fatima as its head. The federation has thirty-one branches, many of which operate in remote areas of the country. Branch activities include illiteracy eradication; vocational-training projects; nursery classes; art classes; dressmaking and handicraft classes; housekeeping; child-care advice; job-placement programs; health education; family advice; mediation services; welfare assistance; religious education; and social, sporting, and cultural activities. The federation has also worked to build strong relationships with international women's organizations, including participation in all major international conferences addressing women's issues since 1975 and organizing local and regional seminars on issues related to women and the family. By promoting women's education and providing legal support for issues of concern to professional women, it seeks to expand women's role in public and professional life in the U.A.E. Structurally, the Federation is required to participate in the formulation of and give an opinion on all draft laws concerning women and children or relating to the safety, security, and stability of society. Members are polled for their opinions, which are then sent back to the legislature for consideration and implementation.

Fatima's goals have been supported by her husband and the U.A.E. constitution which specifies that the principles of

95

social justice apply to everyone and that women enjoy the same legal status, claim to titles, access to education, and right to practice professions as men. Recognizing that such legislation remains theoretical without practical assistance, Fatima's work as head of the federation has included implementation of the legislation. She has personally supported new personal law statutes in areas pertaining to marriage, divorce, alimony, reconciliation of estranged couples, and custody of children.

During the early years, the federation focused on helping women come out of seclusion and to use their leisure time to become literate, acquire knowledge about the modern world, and obtain marketable skills in order to raise their families' living standards. The program began with the establishment of the Handmade Products and Environment Center in 1978 to revive and preserve U.A.E. heritage by training junior craftswomen in popular crafts and folklore arts, such as embroidery and wool weaving, for their own benefit. Over time, the federation's work shifted to comprehensive social planning, increasing social cohesiveness, and implementing the resolutions from the 1995 Beijing Conference on Women.

Statistics demonstrate the effectiveness of Fatima's work. In 1972–1973, there were only 19,000 female students enrolled through secondary education. The 1975 census listed only 3,005 women with a B.A. or equivalent from a university. By 1995 61,496 women had university degrees and 78.8% of university students were women. By 1996–1997, there were 270,000 female students, or 99% of girls, enrolled through secondary education. During the same period, illiteracy rates of women over the age of ten dropped to 11.3%, 18,564 women graduated from illiteracy eradication centers, and women were outperforming men at every level of education. Fatima believes that these figures prove women's desire for and success in education.

Despite the important educational achievements of women, serious attention still needs to be given to match education with the demands and needs of the workforce; as recently as 1985, women formed only 9.6% of the workforce. Although they had exponentially increased their access to education, women formed only 11.7% of the workforce by 1995. Statistics rose to about 20% by 2003. Fatima attributes this low percentage of working women to two major causes: custom and tradition; and the economic prosperity enjoyed by the country as a whole that does not require the wife's income for the family's survival. Because work has been a choice, rather than a matter of necessity, and because of the cultural pressure on women to remain at home to raise their children, educated women have not felt an obligation to work outside of the home, particularly after marriage and having children. Furthermore, there are not enough child-care facilities to provide for the needs of working mothers.

Traditionally, women in the Arab world have entered the fields of health and education. Fatima has pressed for the expansion of opportunities for women in other fields – particularly science, technology, and previously male occupations, including the military, the police force, and banking. The U.A.E. is home to the first women's army college in the Gulf and is the only Gulf country that allows women to join the armed forces and police. Major cultural changes are also occurring as women engage in the production of art, sports, acting, and singing. Fatima has particularly worked to encourage women's entry into the media and politics as a matter of public duty. She holds women equally responsible with men for serving all of society, rather than just women's rights. She has encouraged women's business initiatives by serving as the honorary president of the First Economic Business Women's Forum and by pressuring the Arab Business Women's Council to seek more active contributions by women.

Fatima's vision of development extends beyond education and participation in public life to addressing the question of environment, such as the special challenges faced by refugees. As the honorary chairwoman of the U.A.E. Red Crescent Society, she has focused on the upgrading of social and humanitarian services. She has also worked on health, social, and educational campaigns to raise living standards. In 1999, she prioritized caring for the aged and disabled. She has supported families through cooperation with the Marriage Fund.

Fatima has worked to expand bilateral and multilateral cooperation between women's organizations throughout the Arab world, including the Arab Women's Organization. Her goal is to strengthen cooperation between countries and facilitate the exchange of knowledge and experience in order to give women's issues priorty in comprehensive and sustainable development policies. She also seeks to identify practical ways of transforming ideas and goals into reality and hopes that Arab governments and organizations will cooperate in the implementation of recommendations. She notes that all solutions must be consistent with Arab and Muslim traditions, heritage, values, and identities in order to be implemented and be effective.

Fatima's work for women's rights and humanitarian projects has earned both domestic and international attention and acclaim. Her husband routinely commended her publicly for her work and held her up as an example for the rest of the country, the Gulf, and the Arab world because she serves as a living example of how women can make a contribution to their society while living in accordance with the teachings of Islam and Arab traditions. Internationally, the United Nations has frequently and repeatedly recognized her important contributions not only to the U.A.E., but also to the Arab world. In 1986, she received the U.N. Shield from the U.N. Population Fund for her efforts. This was followed in 1997 with simultaneous recognition from U.N.I.C.E.F., the World Health Organization (W.H.O.), the U.N. Fund for Population Activities (U.N.F.P.A.), the U.N. Volunteers Programme, and the U.N. Development Fund for Women (U.N.I.F.E.M.) for her more than twenty-five years of involvement in the women's movement and as an expression of recognition and commendation for the U.A.E. government and people. Other awards received by Fatima include the 1998 Humanitarian Personality of the Year Award from the Rashid Paediatric Therapy Center in the U.A.E., the 1999 Marie Curie Medal from U.N.E.S.C.O. for her efforts in spreading education and eradicating illiteracy, and a 2001 award from U.N.I.C.E.F. recognizing her as the personality most caring for children's health. Fatima has also been awarded the shield of Family Organizations in the U.A.E. and the Arab League's shield for her work in women's rights and humanitarianism. In 2003, she received the Egyptian Medal of Perfection from Egyptian First Lady Suzanne Mubarak and the International Athena Award from the Athena Foundation for her support for women's education.

Further reading

Acho, Wendy. "Behind the Veil Dwell Spirits Rebellious," *Community Bridges*, November 3, 2003, www.americanarab.com/main.cfm?location=19&release=58

Leila, Reem. "A Woman's Woman," *Al-Ahram Weekly*, May 22–28, 2003

Mitchell, Susan. "Arab First Ladies," *Sunday Business Post*, August 30, 2002

Salloum, Habeeb. "Women in the United

Arab Emirates," *Contemporary Review*, August, 2003

Soffan, Linda Usra. *The Women of the United Arab Emirates*. London: Croom Helm, 1980

dwc.hct/ac/ae/lrc/publications/arab%women/ Fatima1.htm – provides general information on women in the U.A.E. with special attention to Fatima's contributions

dwc.hct.ac.ae/lrc/publications/arab%women/ arab_women_nationality.htm – provides information about prominent Arab women by nationality

www.athenafoundation.org – website for Athena Foundation and Award

www.awc.org.jo/english/uae/downloads/ GWUKiit.doc – site for Arab Women's Congress

www.uae.gov.ae/Government/women.htm – U.A.E. government site with links to general information about the U.A.E. and the status of women

G

Tahany El Gebaly (b. 1951)

An attorney renowned for her dedication to justice and the equality of all citizens under the constitution, Tahany El Gebaly became Egypt's first female judge in 2003 when she was appointed to the Supreme Constitutional Court.

Tahany El Gebaly was born in Tanta, Egypt, in 1951. She completed her secondary education in Tanta and earned a B.A. in law at Cairo University. She also holds a diploma in Islamic law and is a specialist in international law.

El Gebaly completed her university studies in 1973, a time of political and social upheaval in Egypt. Not only were student movements at the height of their political activism, but the country itself was broadly in turmoil over Israel's occupation of the Sinai, which had begun in 1967. Encouraged by her professors to be socially, culturally, and politically aware, she became a member of the war-front service troops during her undergraduate years.

El Gebaly entered the legal profession out of concern for justice and because she was impressed by the respect accorded to a relative who served as the head of the Lawyers' Syndicate. Upon graduation, she joined a committee defending the freedom of the Lawyers' Syndicate, as well as some of those accused of participating in the labor strikes and riots of January 1978.

In her more than thirty-year-long career as a defense attorney, El Gebaly became famous for taking on big and difficult cases addressing issues of justice and equality. In the early 1990s, she defended an Egyptian youth, Ayman Hassan, who had crossed the Egyptian–Israeli border and attacked several Israelis. Hassan faced four charges, each of which carried a potential death penalty. El Gebaly won him a twelve-year sentence. In the mid-1990s, she served as a member of the committee defending Nasr Hamed Abu Zeid, an Islamic thinker accused of apostasy who was sued by Islamic extremists seeking to divorce him against his will. El Gebaly did not agree with what the man had written, but did not believe that anyone should be separated from a spouse by another party over a disagreement about that person's way of thinking. She also headed the committee organizing the 2003 case for war crimes against Israeli prime minister Ariel Sharon in Belgium.

Two of El Gebaly's most memorable cases were defenses of women accused of murder that brought broader social issues to public attention. In the first case, an old woman had killed her husband because he divorced her and removed her from their home. El Gebaly defended her out of recognition of the difficulty of divorce for women as they grow older and have nowhere to go and no one to care for them. The woman died before her case was reviewed by the court. The second woman had killed her daughter because she had committed adultery. She had received a sentence of twenty-five years imprisonment. El Gebaly defended the woman because she considered the sentence unjust. In Egypt, honor crimes are supposed to carry a maximum sentence of a few years. However, such lenient sentences are given only to men. For El Gebaly, this case was about the constitution granting all citizens equal rights, regardless of religion or gender. She has often stood before the Supreme Constitutional Court to ask for correction of constitutional breaches.

El Gebaly has long been a pathbreaker for women in the field of law. She was the first woman appointed to Egypt's Lawyers' Syndicate in 1989, as well as the first female representative to the regional Arab Lawyers' Union in 1992. A member of the minority Nasserite Party, she has successfully run against both the ruling Wafd Party and the Muslim Brotherhood in syndicate elections. She attributes her victories to public perceptions that she represents her profession well and has proven herself a capable and credible lawyer, emphasizing the capacity of performance to override political and patriarchal concerns.

In 1998, El Gebaly and twenty-four other female lawyers stirred up strong controversy by applying for judgeships. Although qualified women had been applying for judgeships since 1949, none had won the position. All of the 1998 applications were rejected. El Gebaly was informed that women were too "emotional" to serve as judges.

She responded by appealing to Islamic history and scripture to prove the permissibility of women serving as judges. First, she noted that the job of the judge is to

rule justly, a duty that she believes both men and women are capable of fulfilling. Second, she observed that there is no ban on women serving as judges in the Quran or authentic *hadith*; in fact, during the rule of the second caliph, Umar ibn al-Khattab, a contemporary of the Prophet Muhammad, a woman was appointed as judge in the marketplace. Third, she pointed out that many important early Islamic scholars unconditionally allowed women to serve as judges. Thus, El Gebaly argued that Islamic history clearly permits women to serve as judges.

El Gebaly then analyzed the function of contemporary judges, observing that their role and qualifications have changed over time. Rather than serving as interpreters of scripture and Islamic law, judges in Egypt today are responsible for applying predetermined laws supported by auxiliary institutions. Legally and constitutionally, she found nothing preventing a woman from serving as a judge, particularly given that the law does not specify that judges be male and that the constitution guarantees equality. Article 11 of the constitution specifically stipulates that the state is responsible for striking a balance between women's family duties and their work in society and for providing women with equal footing with men in the political, social, cultural, and economic domains. Therefore, in El Gebaly's opinion, the prior barring of women from the judiciary was unconstitutional. She further noted that the judiciary was unusual in its failure to have female representation. About twenty percent of lawyers in Egypt are women and women have served in a variety of official capacities, including as ambassadors and cultural ministers. In addition, despite Egypt's reputation as a pioneer in women's rights, it had lagged behind other Arab countries which had begun appointing female judges in the 1990s. In fact, eleven Arab states and thirty-nine Muslim-majority states had already appointed female judges.

El Gebaly's arguments proved effective. Although public expectation was that a woman would first be appointed to a small court, potentially in family law, El Gebaly was named to the Supreme Constitutional Court, the highest judicial authority in Egypt, on January 23, 2003. She sat on the bench for the first time on February 16, 2003. El Gebaly believes that the appointment was intended to reassert Egypt's international image as leading progress in women's rights. She also considers her appointment to be a reflection of growing political maturity in Egypt because she is not a member of the ruling party. In fact, she is usually considered to be a member of the opposition because she has voiced strong political opinions and had frequently represented clients suing the government. El Gebaly considers her appointment as judge, like her election victories, to have resulted from her proven ability and as a sign of the equal rights of all Egyptian citizens, regardless of gender or political or party affiliations.

El Gebaly's appointment occurred during the Year of the Egyptian Woman and with the support of Egypt's National Council for Women. President Hosni Mubarak stated that her appointment was a reflection of the political leadership's appreciation of women's role in society and as the crowning activity of the women's national council that set the institutional framework for women's participation at all levels of society. El Gebaly is expected to serve in her position for fourteen years until she is eligible for retirement.

Upon assuming her position as judge, El Gebaly gave up both her legal practice and her political and social affiliations. She retired from the boards of thirty three organizations and registered as a non-practicing lawyer. As a judge, she is not permitted to work on policy because it is no longer her job to comment on laws. Instead, she is expected to judge whether they are faithful to the constitution and to look at constitutional transgressions in criminal, commercial, civil, and family disputes throughout Egypt. She has used her position to help revise electoral laws and the laws of syndicates, as well as to encourage the expansion of partnership between political parties, syndicates, and women. She has refused to hear cases argued by her former law-office partners so as to avoid any potential conflicts of interest.

As the pilot program for female judges, El Gebaly has stated that she feels tremendous responsibility to perform well so as to assure the future of female judges in Egypt. She has used her appointment to declare support for women to serve at all levels of the judiciary and to encourage women to seek other high public offices, such as mayor or governor. Egyptian women's rights activists have expressed hope that her appointment will serve as a catalyst to change social attitudes and open other horizons to women.

El Gebaly's appointment was recognized with an award from the Egyptian Center for Women's Rights, accompanied by the hosting of a seminar to evaluate the significance of the appointment, its influence on future female judges, reactions to the appointment and to female judges in general, to look for ways to make female judges more socially and culturally acceptable, and to ensure that women are able to take on such roles as part of their civil rights.

Further reading

"First Woman Judge to be Appointed to Egyptian Top Court," AMAN News Center, January 6, 2003

"Interview with Tahany al Gebaly, the First Judge in Egypt," www.sis.gov.eg/women/figures/html/tahani2.htm

el-Jesri, Manal. "Their Turn Now," *Egypt Today*, March 26, 2003

Kovach, Gretel C. "After 50-Year Fight, Women get the Gavel," *Christian Science Monitor*, January 7, 2003

www.ecwr.egypt.org – site for the Egyptian Center for Women's Rights

www.sis.gov.eg – site for Egypt State Information Service

Rashid al-Ghannoushi (b. 1941)

The head of Tunisia's opposition Renaissance (EnNahda) Party, Rashid al-Ghannoushi is one of Tunisia's most prominent activists for democracy, religious pluralism, and gender equality.

Rashid al-Ghannoushi (also spelled Rachid al-Ghannouchi) was born on June 22, 1941, near Hamma, Tunisia. His father was a farmer. The only person in his village to have memorized the entire Quran, he insisted that all ten of his children, both sons and daughters, also study the Quran. Al-Ghannoushi's mother was the youngest of his father's four wives. The daughter of a merchant, she was a strong advocate for her children's education.

Al-Ghannoushi began primary school at the age of ten. Already able to read and write, he studied in both Arabic and French for several years at the village school until his father withdrew him. Believing that French was the language of the colonizers whom he regarded as the enemies of Islam, al-Ghannoushi's father insisted that he learn exclusively in Arabic and work on the family farm.

Al-Ghannoushi resumed his studies in 1956 at the traditional Islamic Zaytouna school in Gabbas. He studied the Quran, Islamic law, and theology, as well as modern sciences and subjects, in Arabic, earning a diploma in theology. He continued his studies at the faculty of theology at Zaytouna University, but withdrew in 1962 during his last year of study over concerns about the classical–traditional focus on Islam that looked only backward in time and, in his opinion, failed to engage real life. He was further concerned by the fact that program graduates were limited to becoming either teachers or religious leaders, given that university admission required a French-style education.

He taught primary school for two years and toyed with the idea of becoming a journalist. In 1964, he enrolled in agricultural studies at Cairo University in Egypt. His studies were cut short after four months when the Tunisian government withdrew its students from Egypt over concerns about the Arab socialism proclaimed by the Egyptian regime. He transferred to the University of Damascus in Syria, where he earned a B.A. in philosophy. Like many of his generation, he felt increasingly alienated from an Islam that he considered irrelevant, and stopped his daily prayers. He became involved in the Arab nationalist movement instead and spent seven months touring Europe, supporting himself by working at odd jobs and living in youth hostels.

Al-Ghannoushi's time in the West marked a turning point in his thinking. Having imagined the West as filled with only happy and prosperous people, he was surprised and disillusioned to find major social and economic problems in Europe. The experience led him to conclude that the European model was not one for the Arab world to follow. It also drew him away from Arab nationalism, which sought to pursue Western-style modernization and development. Instead, he drew inspiration from his contact with a new kind of Islamic activism that proposed Islam as an alternative to Western models and ideologies. He began to read the writings of late nineteenth and twentieth century Islamic reformers and activists, discovering a living Islam capable of adjusting to contemporary issues and concerns on the basis of a combination of faith and reason. For the first time, he saw the future of the Arab world in its own roots and civilization, rather than in importations from abroad. His belief in a return to Islam as the solution was further solidified during the 1967 Six Day War when Israel defeated the combined Arab forces of Egypt, Jordan, and Syria. Having borne personal witness to Israel's attacks on Damascus, al-Ghannoushi recognized the need for a strong and relevant ideology and faith for the Arabs.

His faith was further solidified by his involvement with the Tablighi Jamaah Islamic missionary society in Paris while he was enrolled in a Master's degree program in philosophy at the Sorbonne in 1968. Living in a foreign culture filled with individualism and unfettered freedom, particularly with respect to alcohol and sex, he found in the Tablighi Jamaah support for his faith and identity through emphasis on living a religiously observant life based on spiritual sustenance and moral purpose. (See also FARID ESACK.) He also gained his first practical experience of organized Islamic work and activism.

Al-Ghannoushi has described his time in France as one of the most difficult periods of his life. He personally observed the poor living conditions of North African workers and was appointed to teach and preach to them about Islam because of his strong educational background, despite his personal belief that he was not qualified for the job. He became the imam of a private storefront mosque in 1969. Unable to find a permanent job to support himself, he worked several part-time jobs while ministering to the poor. His own financial and moral difficulties made him realize the importance of having a faith that was relevant to daily life. As an imam, he focused on teaching the Quran, having a mosque for worship, and living a good Muslim life, rather than issues of freedom of speech or human rights within Tunisia.

In 1970, he returned to Tunisia for a visit home. The family had sent his older brother to bring him home and encourage him to end his Islamic activities in favor of pursuing a more modern lifestyle and goals. On the way, they traveled through Spain, visiting Cordoba, the former capital of Muslim Andalusia. Deeply moved by the relics of Islamic civilization they found there, al-Ghannoushi's brother, a secularist since the 1950s, returned to his faith and became one of his brother's strongest supporters until his death. Their subsequent journey through Algeria resulted in a meeting with a prominent religious scholar and activist, Malik Bennabi. Al-Ghannoushi left the meeting determined to play a role in both Tunisian politics and contemporary Islamic political thought.

Concerns about the potential repercussions of his public criticism of Tunisia's failed socialist economics and politics led him to decide to return to France. Before leaving, he stopped to visit the Zaytouna mosque. He was asked to preach at another popular mosque where he was so well received that he was asked to meet with another Islamic activist and lawyer, Sheikh Abd al-Fatah Morou. This meeting was followed by others and eventually developed into the foundation of the Islamic Tendency Movement in 1981 with al-Ghannoushi as president and Sheikh Morou as secretary general.

Al-Ghannoushi remained in Tunis, teaching philosophy at a secondary school and serving as a preacher–activist in a variety of local mosques. He joined the Quran Preservation Society out of his belief in the need to recover Tunisia's Arab–Islamic heritage. Popular among the poor working class, he particularly focused on preaching to youth, believing that they represented Tunisia's future.

From 1970 until 1978, al-Ghannoushi's Islamic movement focused primarily on promoting religio-cultural change by recovering Islamic morals, values, civilization, and identity. However, by 1978, the movement had become increasingly politicized due to the internal social situation in Tunisia combined with inspiration from Iran's burgeoning Islamic Revolution. In Tunisia, as throughout the Muslim world, Westernization, modernization, and development had failed to deliver their material promises. Like many Muslims elsewhere, Tunisians increasingly sought an Islamic alternative. Al-Ghannoushi was dedicated to finding an Islamic solution to real-life, everyday problems, such as food shortages. Believing that Islam had to be more than just a source of identity, he turned toward interpreting it as a source of personal and societal liberation.

Al-Ghannoushi's interpretation of Islam calls for the elimination of cultural alienation, economic exploitation, and moral corruption in favor of equality and gender and social justice. He has proposed reform via evolution, rather than revolution, believing that gradual social and political change are the best means of ensuring that reforms take root. The only "revolution" he envisages is one combating despotism, exploitation, and dependency. Unlike some Islamists, he has not called for the establishment of an Islamic state or the strict implementation of Islamic law. Instead, he has proposed a reinterpretation of Islamic law to reform and reconstruct Islamic principles and values for contemporary conditions and to provide a moral basis for Tunisian law. His vision of the needed moral context is one that provides freedom and equality to individuals, the judiciary, the press, and religion.

Believing that the relationship between the Muslim world and the West needs to be reevaluated and redefined, rather than rejected, al-Ghannoushi has called for Muslims to work with and accept the West selectively and critically from a position of equity, rather than dependence, toward the goal of peaceful coexistence and cooperation. He believes that the West can serve as a source of potential supplement and inspiration to Islamic doctrines. One example is his adoption of democracy, both as a philosophy and as a method of government. He notes that Islam embraces consultation (*shura*), which he interprets politically to mean mandatory consultation of the public. He believes that such consultation will prevent dictatorship, foreign domination, and anarchy in favor of independence and support for human rights, civil liberties, and political pluralism. He advocates the parliamentary system as the appropriate venue for assuring universal participation in the political process and for ensuring the rotation of authority through honest elections. He has decried as hypocritical the claims of secular and nationalistic politicians and systems to be democratic while denying Islamists the right to participate and voice their opinion. He has expressed concern that the exclusion of Islamists from the democratic process is not only likely to draw the movement into extremism, but may even kill the democratic experiment altogether. He personally has tried to work within the existing system to provide an alternative vision. He has never claimed to have the only solution.

Al-Ghannoushi believes that democracy alone can guarantee religious pluralism and grant religious minorities a voice in a Muslim majority country. He notes that pluralism is part of the Islamic heritage, citing the historical freedom of other religious groups, including Jews, to excel in their field of choice on the basis of their skill, rather than their religious affiliation. Combining this history with the Quranic principle that "there is no compulsion in religion" (Q 2:256), he has called for religious, cultural, political, and ideological pluralism in Muslim society. He supports the right of non-Muslims to practice their faith, preach, teach, write, state their opinions, think, assemble, criticize the government, and even criticize Islam, as long as such actions are undertaken within the limits of the law. He is opposed to forced conversions or violations of conscience as a matter of human rights.

He is also a strong proponent of an equal role for women in society. He supports the right of women to education, work, political participation, ownership of property, and choice of home and marriage. He believes that wearing the veil should be a matter of personal choice, rather than something imposed by the state.

In 1979, al-Ghannoushi established the Islamic Association (Jamaah al-Islamiyyah) to mark the transition of the movement from a religiocultural force to a sociopolitical movement. He served as its head, preaching a message of holistic Islam that was relevant to the political and economic needs of the people, such as workers' rights, poverty, wages, jobs, Westernization, political participation, and the development of a more authentic national and cultural identity. The association became particularly popular among students.

In 1981, the association was transformed into a political party, the Islamic Tendency Movement (M.T.I.), after Tunisian president Habib Bourguiba briefly liberalized the one-party system. The M.T.I. proclaimed the reassertion of Tunisia's Islamic heritage, life, and values while de-emphasizing its Francophile identity. It also declared the goal of working for political pluralism, democracy, and social and economic justice. It became popular among the disaffected in Tunisia, ranging from blue-collar workers and students to middle- and upper-class professionals. Recognizing the M.T.I.'s rising popularity, Bourguiba declared it illegal for combining religion and politics. He also imprisoned al-Ghannoushi, who was sentenced to eleven years in jail for operating an unauthorized association. The other leaders either went underground or into exile until 1984 when they were released under a general amnesty.

Between 1981 and 1983, the M.T.I. focused on surviving without its senior leaders and on making its ideology more suitable for its Tunisian context. When the senior leaders, including al-Ghannoushi, were released from prison

in 1984, the older and newer generations of M.T.I. leaders joined together to form Tunisia's most important opposition movement. Increasing state repression between 1981 and 1987 made it difficult for the M.T.I. to maintain its moderate stance. Although al-Ghannoushi consistently and repeatedly advised against violence, some M.T.I. members had become so radicalized by the oppression they experienced at the hands of their own government that some called for a jihad to overthrow the Bourguiba regime, demonstrating how authoritarianism, repression, and the use of violence to control Islamic movements can result in the use of violence against the system in response.

Al-Ghannoushi became a government target again in 1987 and was arrested in a crackdown on the M.T.I. As protests and clashes spread to the streets, Bourguiba decided to try to eradicate the M.T.I. Al-Ghannoushi was tried before a state security court in 1987 and was sentenced to life imprisonment with hard labor. Dissatisfied with the sentence, Bourguiba sought a new trial, demanding the death penalty. Bourguiba was overthrown shortly afterward.

Bourguiba's successor, Zine El Abedine Ben Ali, recognizing the power of the M.T.I.'s ideology, deliberately incorporated Tunisia's Arab–Islamic heritage into his political vision. He granted amnesty to al-Ghannoushi and had him released from prison in 1988. The M.T.I. offered to work with Ben Ali and changed its named to the Renaissance Party (EnNahda) to demonstrate that it was not trying to monopolize Islam. Although Ben Ali had promised official recognition of the M.T.I., he changed his mind in 1989, maintaining the ban on mixing religion and politics. The M.T.I. had proven popular during elections and had become the leading opposition group, with 13% of the vote nationally and between 30 and 40% in major urban areas. Fearing that democratization or political liberalization would expand the power and appeal of political Islam and destabilize existing regimes, as had occurred in neighboring Algeria, Ben Ali maintained the ban on EnNahda.

By the early 1990s, al-Ghannoushi was living in exile in Europe where he continues to preach and write. Although EnNahda has been driven underground, al-Ghannoushi's ideas have remained important within Tunisia and continue to inspire activism. He is considered one of the most progressive contemporary interpreters of Islam because of his flexibility and creative attention to reality and the everyday needs of Muslims. Although his ideas are considered controversial by many, Muslim activists and intellectuals nevertheless listen carefully to what he has to say and have acknowledged his impact in terms of both his intellectual contributions and his political activism.

Further reading

Esposito, John L. and John O. Voll. *Makers of Contemporary Islam*. New York: Oxford University Press, 2001 (this entry draws heavily on the biographical information presented in this book)
al-Ghannoushi, Rashid. "Again ... We and the West," *Maqalat*. Paris: Dar al-Karawan, 1984
—— "The Battle Against Islam." *Middle East Affairs Journal* 1, no. 2 (Winter 1992/1413)
—— "A Duty to Reform and a Right to Change," *Impact International* (August 14 – September 10, 1992)
—— "Islam and Democracy Can be Friends," *North African News*, January, 1992
—— "Westernization and the Inevitability of Dictatorship", *al-Marifa*, September, 1980
Jones, Linda J., trans. "Rashid al-Ghannoushi: Deficiencies in the Islamic Movement," *Middle East Report* (July–August, 1988)
"Letter from Rashid Ghannushi, Chairman of EnNahda Movement to Lord Avebury, Chairman of Parliamentary Human Rights Group," August 25, 1993
Shahin, Emad Eldin. "Ghannushi, Rashid Al-," in *The Oxford Encyclopedia of the Modern Islamic World*, editor-in-chief John L. Esposito. New York: Oxford University Press, 1995

Tamimi, Azzam S. *Rachid Ghannouchi: A Democrat Within Islamism*. New York: Oxford University Press, 2001

Jemima Goldsmith (b. 1974)

Philanthropist, fashion designer, businesswoman, and ex-wife of world champion cricket player Imran Khan, Jemima Goldsmith is a prominent spokesperson for a variety of humanitarian causes globally.

Jemima Goldsmith was born on January 30, 1974, to billionaire James Goldsmith and his then mistress Lady Annabel Vane Tempest Stewart. Although sometimes identified as Jewish due to her ancestry, Goldsmith was raised as a Christian.

As a teenager, Goldsmith was an accomplished horsewoman. She was believed to have enough talent to become a professional showjumper, but decided to pursue academia instead. She enrolled as an English major at Bristol University, but did not complete her education.

Her wealth, beauty, and upbringing among the cream of English society led to her moving in high social circles. In 1994, she met world champion Pakistani cricket player Imran Khan (see also IMRAN KHAN), at a nightclub in London. The two married in a Muslim wedding ceremony in 1995 following Goldsmith's conversion to Islam. In a statement of their commitment to charity work, the couple asked for donations to the Shaukat Khanum Memorial Cancer Hospital in Pakistan in lieu of gifts. The hospital had been established by Khan in his mother's memory to provide the best quality diagnostic and therapeutic medical care to cancer patients, regardless of ability to pay. Goldsmith later developed her own brand of ketchup to provide financial support to the hospital.

Goldsmith's conversion and marriage resulted in intense media scrutiny, in part because she was only twenty-one and Khan was forty-two. In response to the media's claim that her conversion was a prerequisite to the marriage and that converting to Islam would result in a miserable life of subservience and isolation, Goldsmith wrote an article explaining her conversion, which was widely publicized in the Muslim world and has become a mainstay on websites discussing conversions. Believing that the media scrutiny was due to broad misunderstanding in the West about Islam and Islamic culture, she sought to educate the Western public. In response to charges that she had entered into the marriage without thinking about the consequences of her conversion and moving to Pakistan, she responded that she had spent seven months studying Islam, the Quran, and the writings of a variety of Muslim scholars, and had made three trips to Pakistan to learn more about family life there. She denied claims that her conversion was a prerequisite to the marriage, noting that, under Islamic law, a Muslim man may marry a Jewish or Christian woman. She also downplayed concerns about women's status in Islam, citing the professional accomplishments and independence of Khan's sisters, and dismissed assumptions that the marriage would quickly end in divorce, citing statistics showing that divorce rates in Pakistan are much lower than they are in Europe and the United States.

Goldsmith believed that her greatest challenge in marriage would be adapting to a new and radically different culture. She gave up alcohol, nightclubs, and revealing clothing in deference to her new faith, adopting the traditional Pakistani dress of shalwar khameez (tunic and trousers). She started her own fashion line, which featured the shalwar khameez with a dappata (a five-foot-long, three-foot-wide loose veil, usually made of translucent silk), favoring white, cream, tan, vanilla, and beige as colors. She described her line as "comfort and elegance with a bit of glamour thrown in." Fashion critics characterized her designs as a "compromise between Muslim modesty and sexy femininity." Her fashions became popular in London. She was frequently photographed in Pakistani dress and was awarded the Rover People's Award for the best-dressed female celebrity at the British fashion awards in 2001. She donated profits from her clothing line to the Shaukat Khanum Memorial Cancer Hospital.

Shortly after her marriage, Goldsmith moved to Pakistan to assist Khan's political campaign to end government corruption. She also learned Urdu (the language spoken in Pakistan) and worked to improve the country's literacy levels and raise respect for animal rights. Her public actions included rescuing bear cubs from baiting sports. She remained in Pakistan until the couple divorced in 2004. She then returned to London with their two sons.

Goldsmith credits motherhood with bringing her attention to children's welfare worldwide. Increasingly aware of the stark disparity between rich and poor in Pakistan, she realized that the same levels of poverty and human suffering existed in other Third World countries. She began to support a number of campaigns designed to alleviate the suffering of children, particularly those who have witnessed or experienced extreme forms of violence, especially the loss of one or both parents. She has commented that the combination of illness, disorientation, fear, and poverty lead to the loss of any sense of what it means to be a child.

Goldsmith was appointed as the United Kingdom's Special Representative to U.N.I.C.E.F. She is a member of U.N.I.C.E.F.'s Growing Up Alone campaign, whose purpose is to raise awareness of the increasing number of children growing up without any family in some of the most war-torn countries in the world. Personally appalled by the conditions of refugee camps and the fact that one million children worldwide are growing up alone in the world as the result of conflict, Goldsmith joined the campaign to help children become children again.

Goldsmith made headlines in 2000 for her public criticism of Israel's treatment of Palestinians, marking her entrance as a public figure and voice into what has proven to be the most intractable conflict of the twentieth and twenty-first centuries. While her main focus was on the children caught in the conflict, she also rebuked the United States for its perceived uncritical and unwavering support for Israel despite human rights violations. Her criticism was sparked by an image that galvanized and resonated throughout the Muslim world: the televised broadcast of the death of twelve-year-old Mohammed al-Durra, who was shot by Israeli soldiers as his father begged them to hold their fire and tried to shield his son. Goldsmith described herself as not only "horrified" by the killing, but also "equally shocked" by the subsequent killing of the Palestinian ambulance personnel who came to help. She was particularly "appalled" that the media, rather than acknowledging the "outrageous and tragic murder of an innocent civilian child," chose instead to support Israeli claims that the child had been "caught in the crossfire," thus blaming the victim for his own death. Goldsmith asserted that such presentations were typical of biased media coverage that humanizes and sensationalizes Israeli tragedies while demonizing those of Palestinians who are condemned for supposedly sending their children out to die in order to score media points. She believes that such portrayals demonstrate a failure to distinguish between cases where children are active participants in events leading up to the tragedy, such as by throwing rocks, and cases where they are innocent bystanders, such as being passengers in cars or simply being in their own houses or gardens.

Goldsmith's article sparked strong responses. Muslims pointed to it as a statement of truth that reflected broad feelings and perceptions throughout the Muslim world. Many hoped that the fact that the criticism came from a public voice of Western origin would pressure the West into a more balanced approach to the Arab–Israeli peace process and the media into more impartial commentary. However, critics charged Goldsmith with being anti-Semitic and with having fallen into the trap of blindly supporting the Muslim perspective without consideration of the full evidence. In other words, her article reflected the polarization of public opinion and rhetoric about the Arab–Israeli conflict that typifies most discussions of the topic.

Goldsmith also took on the cause of Afghan children in 2000 through the creation of the Jemima Khan Afghan Refugee Appeal. Having visited a number of refugee camps near Peshawar, Pakistan, she found that the refugees were characterized by desperate poverty, physical exhaustion, debilitation from disease, emotional exhaustion, and grief. Almost every child in every camp had lost at least one close family member to war and many had seen a parent die in the camp. Upon learning that there are 1.5 million Afghan refugee children under the age of five at serious risk, that half of all Afghan children are undernourished, and that one in four children born in Afghanistan in the year 2000 were expected to die due to poverty, malnourishment, disease, or war, Goldsmith founded the appeal to alleviate suffering. She personally provided tents and latrines to 80,000 refugees on the border between Afghanistan and Pakistan.

Although her support for Afghan children was bolstered by the global outpouring of concern and relief for Afghanistan following the 9/11 terrorist attacks, some of her other causes were negatively impacted by the attacks due to the strain they caused on the Pakistani economy. Her clothing line particularly suffered and was terminated in 2002, resulting in the end of employment for 800 needy Pakistani women who had been paid for their embroidery and needlework. Many of the displaced women were the principal breadwinners of their families, making their income critical to family survival. Goldsmith plans to revive the clothing line when the economy recovers.

Goldsmith's dedication to charitable causes and efforts to help the poor, particularly women and children, have led many in her native Britain to compare her to her friend, the late Princess Diana. Goldsmith's willingness and ability to take on controversial political causes, regardless of the personal backlash they bring, have earned her international respect.

Further reading

Goldsmith, Jemima. "Why I Chose Islam," *Sunday Telegraph*, May 28, 1995

Khan, Jemima. "I am Angry and Ashamed to be British," Independent Digital (UK) Ltd. April 2, 2003

—— "Tell the Truth about Israel: Special Report: Israel and the Middle East," *The Guardian*, November 1, 2000

"Is Jemima Khan the New Diana?" *Guardian Unlimited*, April 11, 2001

"Jemima Khan," Profiles, *Hello!* magazine, November 5, 2001

"Jemima Khan: As she Joins U.N.I.C.E.F.'s 'Growing Up Alone' Campaign she Dedicates herself to the Children of the World," *Hello!* magazine, July 16, 2001

http://www.jemimakhanappeal.org/html – website for Jemima Khan Afghan Refugee Appeal

www.unicef.org.uk/news/Presscentre/gua19 juneJKHAN.htm UNICEF – website providing information about the Growing Up Alone Campaign

H

H.R.H. Princess Haifa Al Faisal
(b. 1952)

Founding trustee and chairwoman of the American charitable and educational organization the Mosaic Foundation, patron of the arts, and wife of the former Saudi Arabian ambassador to the United States, H.R.H. Princess Haifa Al Faisal is a prominent activist for intercultural exchange and understanding.

Born in 1952, Princess Haifa is the youngest child of Saudi Arabia's third monarch, King Faisal (r. 1963–1975), and his wife, Queen Effat. Haifa credits her parents as major role models not only for their dedication to the modernization and development of Saudi Arabia, but also for their commitment to establishing education for both boys and girls and for their support for charitable causes. She recalls her parents as having shared a common vision of how to bring Saudi Arabia into the modern era, based on their international experience. Her mother was born and raised in cosmopolitan Istanbul, while her father served as the minister of foreign affairs from the age of fourteen until he became king. Faisal and Effat were among the first Middle Eastern monarchs to rule as a couple. Haifa recalls that neither of her parents saw any conflict between Islam and the modernization and development of Saudi Arabia.

Haifa's parents were dedicated to both education and charity work. Believing that education was critical to the future of the kingdom, Faisal established the first school for boys and Effat founded an orphanage that became a school for girls – Dar al-Hanan – in 1955. Haifa's own education began at Dar al-Hanan. She completed her studies at a boarding school in Switzerland and later founded her own school in Khobar.

Haifa met her future husband, Prince Bandar bin Sultan bin Abd al-Aziz Al Saud, when she was sixteen years old. Although her mother and Bandar's grandmother thought the two might suit, they did not arrange a marriage for them. The couple met again four years later and married in 1972 of their own volition. They have eight children.

A former fighter pilot and chief acrobatics artist for the Royal Saudi Air Force, Bandar became the dean of the Diplomatic Corps and was appointed ambassador to the United States from 1983 to 2005. As the Ambassador's wife and in keeping with Saudi tradition, Haifa played a behind-the-scenes role and supported charity work. Consistent with the Arab tradition of not talking about oneself for fear of being considered boastful, she is not photographed in public and tries to keep her activities relatively private.

One of Haifa's major personal projects is the S.A.N.A. Collection, which contains over six thousand objects of Saudi material culture from the period of 1900–1975. Approximately four thousand of the collection's items are artifacts ranging from tents to toothbrushes. The collection also includes about two thousand volumes of nineteenth- and twentieth-century travel journals, anthropological studies, maps, photographs, and other works with a focus on Middle Eastern culture. Haifa's goal is to collect as many objects as possible from this time in order to preserve historical Saudi culture and identity, particularly the long historical tradition of practical art. Prior to the oil boom, Saudi Arabia was a poor country with a nomadic tradition. The combination of nomadism and poverty meant that there was little emphasis on material culture or the collection of art for its own sake. Haifa observes that this does not mean that there was no art. Rather, artistic production tended to occur in expressions of daily living, such as house decoration, embroidery on clothing, engraving, latticework, and the use of color, precious stones, metals, and mirrors in objects related to daily life, such as incense burners, utility bags, storage containers, camel trappings, tents, and rugs. The collection's significance lies not only in its assistance in recreating the material context of daily life among nomads and townspeople, but also in its documentation of weaving techniques from throughout the Peninsula; illustration of Arabian hospitality and the importance of beverages in the desert climate; documentation of living Bedouin culture; identification and recording of both the distinctions between regions and tribes throughout the Peninsula and the role of Islam in the evolution of material culture; tracing and evaluating foreign influences on Arabian traditions, particularly through pilgrims on the Hajj and international traders; and documentation of the twentieth-century transition from nomadic to city life. The collection is intended to serve as the core of a future cultural center in Saudi Arabia.

Haifa's interest in culture is not limited to Saudi Arabia but extends to the entire Arab world. Recognition of the lack of knowledge about Arab culture and the need to increase understanding of the Arab world in the United States led her and the wives of the other sixteen ambassadors of Arab countries to the United States to form the Mosaic Foundation in 1998. Both Muslims and Christians are represented on the Board of Trustees.

The Mosaic Foundation is an apolitical educational and cultural charitable organization dedicated to improving the lives of women and children, fostering deeper understanding between the Arab world and the United States, and strengthening cultural ties between the two by familiarizing Americans with Arab history and civilization. Unofficially, it also works to shatter stereotypes about Arab culture, religion, and women. As a reflection of the joint interests of the Arab world and the United States, Mosaic supports American organizations working on issues related to women and children.

Mosaic hosts one major event annually which serves as a combination cultural event and fund-raiser. The Inaugural Gala held in 1998 transformed the Atrium of the Kennedy Center into a Middle Eastern bazaar. The main cultural event was a performance of the traditional Arab dance called the *dabka* by the Caracalla Dance Theater of Lebanon. The event raised $500,000 for St. Jude's Research Hospital to establish a fund for Arab children. Subsequent events include the 1999 performance of Egyptian dances by the Cairo Opera Ballet, which raised $320,000 for the National Race for the Cure and breast-cancer research. That same year, Mosaic also began to raise funds for emergency relief projects, donating more than $200,000 to the International Kosovo Red Crescent/Red

Cross for Refugee Relief and Turkish Earthquake Disaster Relief as part of its "World Emergency Grants" initiative. In 2000, Mosaic featured a performance by the Kuwaiti Television Folklore Troupe accompanied by Arab musicians and Egyptian artists that raised $800,000 for Save the Children – the largest single private gift for Save the Children's programs in the Middle East.

Under Haifa's leadership, Mosaic has been determined to address relevant and timely issues, as well as to raise cultural awareness and appreciation. In 2001, Mosaic hosted an A.I.D.S. benefit dinner that raised $2.2 million for the United Nations Foundation for Africa. The choice of an A.I.D.S. benefit was controversial because A.I.D.S. is generally a taboo subject in Arab societies where drug use and sexual promiscuity are strongly frowned upon, if not illegal. Although the Arab world has not experienced the kind of crisis found in other countries, Haifa insisted on an A.I.D.S. benefit out of recognition that A.I.D.S. is a worldwide epidemic that touches and should be recognized and fought in every country and to show that Arabs are concerned about the entire world, rather than just their own region.

Four weeks after the 9/11 terrorist attacks, Mosaic presented a $25,000 grant to the Washington Family Relief Fund, to help local relief efforts for victims of the Pentagon attack. In keeping with its focus on education and in recognition of the rising interest in and questions about Arabs, Islam, and the Middle East, Mosaic also gave a $25,000 grant to the Washington, DC, public schools for the Youth Ambassador Program. Part of the grant was used to send eight high-school students to Egypt for a two-week educational trip. The remaining funds are to be used to develop new programs about the history, culture, religions, and people of the Arab world and to increase understanding among both teachers and students of Arab-Americans in their

communities. Other smaller charitable donations include gifts to House of Ruth, Wednesday's Child, Columbia Hospital for Women, and Children's Hospital. Planning also began in 2001 for the construction of a $40 million Arab cultural center in Washington, DC.

A series of crises occurred in 2002, resulting in the launching of the Emergency Medical Relief Campaign, which raised funds for specific projects of the International Committee of the Red Cross/Red Crescent Societies, the American Near East Refugee Association (A.N.E.R.A.), and the National Arab American Medical Association (N.A.A.M.A.) to provide assistance to women and children in the West Bank and Gaza. The year 2002 also marked an expansion of Mosaic's concern for educational issues. In the aftermath of 9/11, an annual series of three symposia was added to address issues of concern to Mosaic. The first series addressed misconceptions about Islam and Muslims, the status of women in Islam, and media stereotypes of Arabs. The second series, held in 2003, presented three women who had become legends in the Middle East through their husbands' careers as rulers, beginning with Haifa's mother. The other two women were Jihan Sadat of Egypt and H.M. Queen Noor of Jordan. (See also H.M. QUEEN NOOR.)

Although Mosaic is a charitable organization, it does not give money only to charitable causes. In 2003, the beneficiary of the major fundraiser was the Grameen Foundation U.S.A., an organization dedicated to providing financial resources to micro-financing institutions around the world to stimulate economic growth and self-sufficiency by providing small, unsecured loans to the very poor to start businesses. (See also MUHAMMAD YUNUS.) Mosaic awarded an $800,000 grant to establish the Mosaic Fund for the Arab World, which will be used to establish additional micro-credit enterprises in Djibouti, Egypt, Lebanon,

Mauritania, Morocco, and Tunisia. Mosaic also expanded its fundraising activities in 2003 with a direct-mail campaign to help the women and children of Iraq.

In the aftermath of 9/11, Mosaic recognized the need to redress the image of Islam in conflict with other cultures and religions. The 2004 major fundraising event to benefit education was a week-long celebration of al-Andalusia, or Muslim Spain. The theme was chosen to focus on a time period in which Muslims, Christians, and Jews lived and worked together peacefully and cooperatively. As Haifa noted, "It is important to show Washington that Muslims, Christians, and Jews have lived in harmony in the past – and that we can do it again." Not only was the length of this event expanded, but it also included a film festival on al-Andalusia, as well as an exhibition of Andalusian art from the Hispanic Society in New York. The intercultural exchanges of that time period are still evident in Spanish culture today, including guitar music, which evolved from the Arab string instrument the *oud*, and the popular Spanish dance, the flamenco, which evolved out of the traditional Arab dance, the *dabka*.

In many ways, the activities of Mosaic are a reflection of Haifa's dedication to building bridges of intercultural understanding between the United States and the Arab world and to supporting educational and charitable causes. Her dedication has not been without personal cost. In 2002, she came under fire for her apparent financial support for the 9/11 terrorists after a check she had written as a charitable donation ended up in the bank account of the wife of a man who helped two of the 9/11 hijackers. Haifa described herself as "horrified and deeply embarrassed" by the thought that an action of hers might have helped wreak such catastrophe on the lives of innocent people. An investigation later revealed that the check was intended for a Jordanian woman who was

in need of a medical operation. It had been endorsed to another party. Despite the negative and inaccurate publicity, Haifa did not blame the American public. She continued with her charity work and now has her accounts audited routinely.

Although the charitable environment has tightened in the aftermath of 9/11, Haifa remains Mosaic's self-described optimist. While some have expressed concern about Mosaic's viability, Haifa believes that its transformation from an ad hoc organization to a more professional one and its prominence have positioned it to remain one of the most influential charities in Washington. She also notes that the main causes Mosaic supports – women, children, and education – are causes that resonate with the broad public. The high profile and visibility of Mosaic have established it as a model for other charitable organizations.

Further reading

"Arab Ambassadors' Wives Raise $500,000 for St. Jude Hospital," *Washington Report on Middle East Affairs*, October/November, 1998, 108

Bahrain News & Information: Newsletter of the Embassy of the State of Bahrain, Washington, DC., vol. 5, no. 3, issue no. 18, 2000

Donnelly, John. "Saudis, Glitterati Add to A.I.D.S. War Chest," *Boston Globe*, November 15, 2001

"Latest News," Embassy of Egypt, www.embassyofegyptwashingtondc.org, October 2001

"Mosaic Foundation Announces $800,000 Grant to Grameen Foundation U.S.A. to Support Micro-Lending Programs in the Arab World," press release, April 16, 2003

"Mosaic Foundations' Annual Benefit Raises Funds for Charity," *Washington Notes*, Saudi embassy newsletter 5, May 2000

Roberts, Roxanne. "Women, Around the World: Arab Ambassadors' Wives Build a Foundation for Understanding," *Washington Post*, December 19, 2001

Tapper, Jake. "Cheney Supported Controversial Fundraiser," www.salon.com, July 27, 2000

Walsh, Elsa. "Profiles: The Prince," *The New Yorker*, March 24, 2003

Interview with the author, November 13, 2003

www.mosaicfound.org – website for Mosaic Foundation

Muzaffar Haleem (b. 1933)

Inspirer and motivator of the award-winning web site IslamiCity, Muzaffar Haleem is also a Muslim matchmaker, educator, social worker, poet, musician, and proponent of interfaith dialogue. She dedicates the majority of her time to developing Islamically acceptable ways for Muslim youth to explore their interests and providing support to new converts to Islam.

Muzaffar Haleem was born on June 21, 1933, in Hyderabad, which was, at that time, in India. Both of her grandfathers served as chief justices of the state of Hyderabad. Her father was a civil engineer. Her mother was a homemaker, accomplished poet, and dedicated social worker. In addition to a sister, Haleem has one brother who introduced several pioneering business concepts in Pakistan, including a drive-in theater and the first amusement park.

In 1947, Haleem's family migrated from Hyderabad to Karachi in order to live in the new state of Pakistan. She completed her high-school education there and then entered the Government College of Women, where she was active in sports, debates, dramas, and stage plays, for which she won numerous awards. She entered the law college in Karachi in 1956. During her second year, she married and decided to end her studies in order to devote her time and energy to being a homemaker and raising a family. She also worked with her brother in managing his various business activities.

Haleem's husband, Mohammed Abdul Haleem, had studied law in Karachi after completing a degree in chemistry and English literature at the University of Missouri in Kansas City. Upon completion of his studies, he placed in charge of the patent office at the Pakistan Council of Scientific Industrial Research (P.C.S.I.R.). He also served as the chief editor of the *Pakistan Journal of Scientific and Industrial Research*. The couple had four sons, one of whom died tragically at the age of ten months.

In 1964, the family moved to a small town outside of Oxford, England, where Mohammed worked for Pergamon Press. They remained in England for three years, returning to Pakistan in 1967. In 1979, the two oldest sons, Aleem and Muneeb, left for the United States to pursue their higher education. Shortly before their departure, the youngest son, Mubeen, was diagnosed with a heart defect. The family moved to Edwardsville, IL, to pursue medical treatment at St. Louis Children's Hospital. Following diagnosis with a rare medical condition called William's syndrome, which results in cardiovascular impairment and coordination weaknesses, Mubeen had open-heart surgery, followed by lengthy postoperative care and rehabilitation. Mohammed had to return to Pakistan to work. Haleem remained behind to care for Mubeen. Six months later, Mohammed was diagnosed with a tumor. He returned to the United States in 1982 and was diagnosed with a malignant, rapidly growing cancer for which there was no known cure. He lost his battle with cancer on December 11, 1983.

The loss of the man she describes as her "life companion" and a "wonderful father" with whom she had enjoyed a loving and peaceful married life left Haleem at a loss as to how to proceed. Although she returned to Pakistan in January 1984, she decided to move to the United States permanently in 1986 in order to be close to her children. She used part of the proceeds from the sale of the family home in Karachi to provide down-payments for condominiums for her sons. The extended family lives together in the same condominium building in

California. Haleem arranged marriages for all three of her sons.

In 1987, Haleem began visiting the Ventura School Prison Project in Los Angeles in pursuit of a life-long interest in helping people who wanted to study or convert to Islam. She began visiting the prison on Saturdays with the Muslim Student Association of U.C.L.A., teaching the prisoners about Islam and how to pray. She particularly reached out to those who had been deserted by their former friends and families due to their conversions. Other activities for the prison included the collection of donations, including copies of the Quran, books on Islam, prayer rugs, headscarves, and food once a month. The project also provides feasts for the Muslim festivals concluding Ramadan and the Hajj. It is supported by Human Assistance and Development International (H.A.D.I.), a California-based non-profit organization founded in 1991 by Haleem's sons and some of their friends to engage in humanitarian work.

Haleem also works with N.I.S.W.A., a Los Angeles-based women's organization that provides various services for women, including a shelter for domestic-violence victims and assistance for girls coming out of the Ventura School Prison. (See also SHAMIM IBRAHIM.) In addition to working with the social services, Haleem provides matchmaking services for Muslim boys and girls seeking marriage partners.

Haleem has also worked to promote what she calls "Islamically acceptable music." Her interest in music extends back to her youth, when she preferred socializing and composing songs to studying, and to her college days, when she sang in the choir and used to take part in music programs. Her interest was rekindled with Mubeen's medical treatments. Like many people with William's syndrome, Mubeen has special musical abilities and inclinations, including musical composition. Haleem helped Mubeen's friend and fellow composer Kacheebe

Abdullah establish a company called Sahih Entertainment which recorded its first album, *The State of the Ummah*, in 1998. Mubeen composed portions of some of the songs, one of which was sung by Haleem. Haleem, a poet with plans to publish, has also contributed some lyrics. Her support of Kacheebe's business venture reflects her long-term interest in helping young people, particularly in strengthening their faith. She believes that Sahih Entertainment allows children to explore and develop their interests, as well as to appreciate music, in an Islamically acceptable way.

Haleem's most ambitious venture began in 1995 with her inspiration and motivation in the creation of the online Muslim community known as IslamiCity, with her sons Aleem and Muneeb serving as co-founders, along with Dr. Dany Doueri and Amr Saemaldahr. An award-winning educational tool on Islam, as well as a forum connecting Muslims throughout the world, IslamiCity receives 2 million visitors per month. It has more than 65,000 registered members for its weekly newsletter. It particularly seeks to reach out to new Muslims to welcome them into the broader Muslim community.

IslamiCity was created through H.A.D.I. to use state-of-the-art technology to provide information about Islam to a global audience in a non-sectarian, comprehensive, holistic way. Its goal is to enhance awareness and knowledge in order to achieve better understanding and peaceful recognition in the rapidly shrinking global village. IslamiCity has become one of the world's leading sources of information about Islam and is the largest Muslim e-community, offering a wide range of Islamic products for all ages, including news, chat rooms, comments, e-cards, recipes, mosque information, television and radio broadcasts, prayer time, information about Islam, assistance with Quran recitation and memorization, yellow pages, multimedia products, business and investment information, shopping links, software, audio and video products, announcements, books, gifts, and organically grown ethnic foods. It is the only Islamic e-commerce site offering online sampling of audio and video products. Educationally, it maintains and updates more than 50,000 web pages related to Islam and Muslims and several thousand hours of audio and video lessons about Islam and answers 75,000 information requests annually, in addition to providing major media outlets with information about Islam and launching educational projects about Islamic history, faith, and practices. The activities are supported by a staff of nine, along with a group of volunteers dedicated to promoting understanding between civilizations.

Half of IslamiCity's visitors are from the United States, reflecting the key role played by Americans in reinterpreting Islam for a global audience. IslamiCity was declared Best Religious Site for the Month by P.B.S. in June 2000 and March 2001 and was voted #1 Religious Site by Yahoo. Yahoo also lists it in its Best 100 Websites. It has been recognized by the B.B.C., C.N.N., A.B.C., the *Washington Post*, the *L.A. Times*, and others as "a prime source of Islamic information and community services" and has been praised by *Time* for its "quality and educational content." It has been mentioned as a resource in *National Geographic* ("The World of Islam," Don Belt, January, 2002), and on N.B.C. News. *U.S.A. Today* featured IslamiCity as a "Hot Site" on its Web Guide (February 21, 2002).

IslamiCity's success is due not only to the broad array of services it proposes, but also because, in the era of electronic communication, a larger number of people are seeking faith, community, and solace online. Many people see the web as a way of reconnecting with the religion of their youth and with a broader faith community than would be possible simply through a local congregation. For many, use of the internet for religious purposes provides fellowship and connection with other people facing similar situations. IslamiCity proposes its services as an additional option to, rather than replacement of, participation at the congregational level. It also offers religious chat rooms that are sometimes visited at a rate of 150 members per minute. Post-9/11, IslamiCity's website had a tenfold increase in visitors due to the demand for accurate information about Islam and Muslims.

Haleem's involvement with IslamiCity is focused largely on the Islamic Information Network, which provides free Islamic literature upon request. Haleem communicates both with people inquiring about Islam and with recent converts. She arranges conference calls for people wishing to make the declaration of faith (*shahadah*), which marks their entrance into the Muslim community, or places them in contact with someone close to where they live. She also arranges meetings in the Los Angeles area and get-togethers for women new to Islam. Her focus on new Muslims was inspired by her own experiences as a new immigrant to a non-Muslim environment. At the time of her son's treatment and her husband's illness, she was frustrated by loneliness and feelings of isolation. This concern is reflected in a book she co-authored with Betty (Batul) Bowman: *The Sun is Rising in the West: New Muslims Tell about their Journey to Islam*, which presents interviews with new American Muslims discussing their conversions. Haleem's purpose in writing the book was to enable new Muslims to learn from each other's experiences and to realize that they are not alone.

Haleem's involvement in dialogue and understanding is not limited to the Muslim community. She is also involved in interfaith dialogue through a friendship circle called Together, which brings people from different religious backgrounds together to discuss social issues. A topic is chosen for discussion and participants share their thoughts and experiences related to it in order to gain understanding and appreciation of each other. Haleem believes that the experience of learning about other faiths and cultures, as well as presenting and teaching about one's own, is invaluable. She believes that this has been particularly important in the aftermath of 9/11 when national awareness of the need to learn more about Islam has come to center stage. Every bit as important for Haleem is the tangible symbolism of Jewish and Muslim friendship shown when she and the Jewish founder of Together, Rebecca Rona, appear together, shattering stereotypes of Jewish–Muslim hatred by reflecting the reality of mutual understanding, appreciation, and friendship.

Haleem's community activism and global outreach were rewarded with the Islamic Community Award for Dawah and Outreach in Southern California by the Council on American–Islamic Relations (C.A.I.R.) in 1999. She remains dedicated to a vision of a world in which greater mutual understanding and appreciation are made possible through education and dialogue.

Further reading

Haleem, Muzaffar and Betty (Batul) Bowman. *The Sun is Rising in the West: New Muslims Tell about their Journey to Islam*. Beltsville, MD: Amana Publications, 1999
Hidayatullah, Aysha. "Muzaffar Haleem: The Woman Behind IslamiCity," *Azizah* magazine, premier issue, winter 2001
Kaiser, Laura Fisher. "God Sitings: Searching for Faith," *Yahoo! Internet Life*, December 2001
Interview with the author, December 8, 2003
www.islamicity.com – website for IslamiCity
www.islam.org – website for IslamiCity

Asma Gull Hasan (b. 1974)

A self-described Muslim feminist and best-selling author, Asma Gull Hasan represents the "next generation" of American Muslims seeking recognition of Muslims as Americans and calling for American leadership in the interpretation of Islam.

Asma Gull Hasan was born on July 15, 1974, in Chicago, IL, to Pakistani immigrants. Her father is a renowned neurologist and entrepreneur. Her mother is a volunteer worker and fundraiser devoted to promoting musical arts. Because Hasan was born and raised in the United States, she considers being Muslim and of Pakistani descent an addition to her American identity, rather than a replacement of it. She describes herself as a "Muslim feminist cowgirl," an image that captures the independence, self-reliance, fearlessness, determination, and adventurousness that represent what being an American Muslim woman means to her.

Hasan grew up in Pueblo, CO, where she attended a private Catholic elementary school. When she was fourteen, she transferred to the Protestant Groton School in Groton, MA. She began writing fiction in high school. Her short stories have been featured in the young adult literary magazines *Merlyn's Pen* and *The Susquehanna Review*. She also had a short story published in *Taking Off: Coming of Age Stories*, which was nominated by the American Library Association as a book for young adults and was selected by the New York Public Library's list of Books for the Teen Age in 1996. She received several speaking awards in grade and high school.

Hasan was a Durant Scholar and received her B.A. in religion and American studies from Wellesley College in Wellesley, MA, in 1997. She also holds a law degree from New York University School of Law and has passed the bar exam in New York and California. While in law school, she served as staff editor for the *Review of Law and Social Change*.

Hasan's most important role models growing up were her parents whom she describes as people who set their example through their actions and daily lives, particularly their community involvement, willingness to talk about religion, and openness to attending events such as Christmas parties as a practical demonstration that religion does not have to create barriers between people. When Hasan researched and wrote her first book, *American Muslims: The New Generation*, to correct inaccurate depictions of Islam in the media by opening a window onto the American practice of Islam, her parents provided both financial and emotional support.

American Muslims was first published in 2000 and sold in small numbers. After 9/11, the book sold more than twenty thousand copies. Although pleased by the book's success, Hasan was troubled that the rising sales and requests for interviews and commentaries grew out of tragedy. Initially reluctant to speak out, she ultimately followed her father's advice and appeared on television and radio programs, served as a media resource, wrote newspaper articles and editorials, and spoke around the country.

A persuasive essay, rather than a scholarly text, *American Muslims* is written in a conversational style. The book's major contributions are the presentation of basic facts and statistics about American Muslims and Islamic principles and ways of life; historical overview of Muslim presence and involvement in the United States dating back to the time of the explorers; an optimistic first-person account of what Islam may become as American-born children of immigrants adapt their faith to American culture; and characterizations of positive examples of Muslims who have achieved success in America. The purpose of the book is to help Americans realize to what degree Muslims are already integrated into American society and that Muslims share American values. It shatters stereotypes while demonstrating the multifaceted identities of American Muslims.

Hasan notes that her multifaceted identity is typical of Americans in general – most Americans have foreign origins and have had to adapt to and adopt a new setting. In this respect, American Muslims are no different from anyone else. They are simply a continuation of the historical process of the melting pot. Generally characterizing American Muslims as people who pay taxes, build commerce, abstain from alcohol, drugs, and extramarital sex, respect women, participate in the political system, hold office, vote, pray, and spend time with their families, Hasan notes that they do not represent an inherent threat to Americans or American interests. She has called upon her fellow American Muslims to focus on their common American Muslim identity, rather than socio-economic, ethnic or national backgrounds, as the American Muslim community seeks to address the challenges of the future, such as educating Americans about Islam and Muslims in order to counteract widespread misinformation, uniting as Muslims and as Americans, overcoming the popular public image of Muslims as terrorists, and willingly becoming part of American culture. She reminds American Muslims of the advantages they enjoy because of their presence in America: freedom of speech, freedom of religion, freedom from cultures and traditions of other countries, many of which retain patriarchal values, and freedom for women to work and be part of both mosque culture and mainstream American society.

Hasan believes that because of these advantages, American Muslims have a unique opportunity to develop an interpretation of Islam that is based on the values of self-respect and gender equality. She has called for the involvement of female scholars in the process, a development that she considers to be one of the most important in contemporary Islam and for the future. She believes that this is possible in the United States because of the opportunities American culture offers to Muslim women to be active participants in religious activities, to study Arabic, and to read and interpret the Quran for themselves.

Hasan particularly holds American Muslims responsible for setting aside the gender discrimination typically found in patriarchal cultures in favor of a fresh interpretation of Islam. Her concerns about the impact of cultural traditions on the American interpretation of Islam are not abstract. Her own grandfather's interpretation of Islam long reflected patriarchal South Asian culture which asserts that, in "Islam," men are superior to women. Hasan disagreed, finding nothing in Islam or the Quran that demeans women or calls for oppressing them. In fact, she believes that Muhammad was the original feminist because he was a major advocate for women's rights, including the right to vote and participate in political affairs. While she admits that Muslim women are oppressed in some countries, she believes that this is due to cultural context, rather than "Islam."

Hasan's book is controversial for Muslims because of her frank discussion of women and women's place in American Islam. She has called for a fresh analysis of the concept of "modest dress" in the American setting, observing that, in America, wearing long, loose garments and head coverings (hijab) makes Muslim women stand out, rather than blend in. She has protested the practice of gender segregation, particularly at the mosque, as relegating women to secondary status. In order to reflect gender equality in worship, she believes that men and woman should be placed on opposite sides of the same room, so that both have an equal opportunity to hear the imam speak. Finally, she has taken on the question of dating and marriage, wondering how eligible single Muslims are supposed to meet if gender segregation is maintained. She observes that the opportunity to meet, talk, and go out does not necessarily

constitute sexual behavior. Concerned that Muslim girls who are raised in Europe often resist traditional arranged marriages, sometimes leading to violence against them perpetrated by their own families, she believes that supervised dating between Muslims should be considered an acceptable means of permitting Muslim youth to get to know each other outside of marriage proposals. A potential model already exists in the Mormon community, which provides opportunities for young people to meet each other by hosting a variety of co-educational social functions that are well supervised by adults. There are also Mormon universities, such as Brigham Young University, where young adults can meet and marry. Hasan believes that such a system, while clearly at least five to ten years in the future, could also work well for Muslims.

Hasan has raised concerns about cultural influences on American Islam through the question of Muslim leadership in the United States. Noting that the leaders of Muslim institutions and mosques in the United States are typically relatively new immigrants, rather than people who were born and raised here, she notes that these leaders tend to bring their own country's traditions and culture with them and to impose them on the American Muslim community. Believing that the time has come for American Muslims to take over the leadership of their own mosques and institutions, she has called for the raising up of American Muslim leadership capable of teaching what she describes as the common values of Islam and American culture, including self-respect, gender equality, hard work, the importance of education and family, community activism, and community involvement.

Hasan has also called on the American Muslim community to bind together politically on the basis of their shared religion, regardless of differences in ethnicity, culture, race, or national origin. She believes that American Muslims should organize and focus on the basis of internal issues, rather than allowing outside forces to determine their interests for them, beginning with issues all American Muslims agree upon: the need for greater understanding of Islam and Muslims among Americans, including official recognition of Muslim holidays; adoption of a friendlier, more understanding and tolerant diplomacy with Islamic countries; promotion of open immigration policies; and condemnation of discrimination against Muslims in any form. Once these issues have been comprehensively addressed, attention can be turned to other issues.

Hasan herself has taken on the issue of media bias against and stereotypes of Muslims as terrorists bent upon jihad against Americans. Clarifying that jihad is intended to be a matter of personal struggle, rather than armed militance, she believes that it should be reinterpreted in the American setting to mean avoiding the temptations of certain aspects of life in America, such as drug and alcohol use, extramarital sex, and failure to fulfill the required five daily prayers. She has denounced media depictions of Muslims as terrorists because they portray Islam as a religion as responsible for condoning, if not encouraging, horrific acts of hatred. Ironically, these depictions have resulted in a rising number of instances of verbal and physical harassment and assault against Muslims, acts that legally constitute hate crimes. Both Hasan and her family members received hate mail and were frightened into staying home and leaving only for special occasions in the aftermath of 9/11.

Hasan's book ends on an optimistic note, predicting the coming of the Second Golden Age of Islam. While the First Golden Age was a period of major contributions by Eastern Muslims to math, science, and civilization, Hasan believes that the Second Golden Age will be characterized by the inner growth and strengthening faith of Western Muslims

as they successfully adapt to Western life without compromising their beliefs. She expects that American Muslims will lead the way and points to the achievements of Muslims and their support for civil rights and the rights of immigrants, minorities, and women, and their work to address major social issues, such as ending inner-city violence and working in the prison systems.

Hasan is currently an associate at a law firm specializing in securities litigation. She continues to write about Islam, Islam and America, and Islam and women and to serve as a resource on Islam.

Further reading

"American Muslims: The New Generation," Publisher's Weekly, November 20, 2000

Hasan, Asma Gull. American Muslims: The New Generation. New York: Continuum International Publishing Group, 2000

―― "I Was a Catholic Schoolgirl: What Franklin Graham Doesn't Know about this Muslim Cowgirl," www.beliefnet.com

―― Why I am a Muslim: An American Odyssey. New York: Thorson Element, 2004

MacEwan, Valerie. "American Muslims: The New Generation," review, www.popmatters.com

Rhodes, Asma Jerusha. "Riding Tall: A Muslim Cowgirl," Azizah magazine, Winter 2002

Sheridan, Anne. "American Muslims: The New Generation," review for www.culture-vulture.net

Siemon-Netto, Uwe. "United Press International – Book of the Week: American Muslims: The New Generation, by Asma Gull Hasan," November 5, 2000

Young, Steve. "American Muslims: The New Generation," review, Montclair State University, Library Journal, January, 2001

www.asmahasan.com – website for Asma Gull Hasan

Farkhonda Hassan (b. 1930)

Secretary-general of Egypt's National Council for Women, member of the Egyptian parliament, and prominent geologist and environmental activist, Farkhonda Hassan exemplifies public service as a career path.

Farkhonda Hassan was born in Egypt in 1930. She earned her Bachelor of Science in geology at Cairo University in Egypt in 1952. She also received a diploma in psychology and education from Ain Shams University in Egypt. She completed a Master of Science in solid state science at the American University in Cairo and a Ph.D. in geology from the University of Pittsburgh in Pittsburgh, PA, in 1970. She has been Professor of Geology at the American University in Cairo since 1964 and is the author of many scientific articles on geology and in the field of science and technology for development and the environment for both national and international journals.

Hassan began her political career serving in the Public National Assembly from 1979 until 1984. In 1984, she was elected as a member of the Shura Assembly (the second house of the Egyptian parliament), where she served until 1989. While on the National Council for Women, she campaigned for women's rights, the environment, and scientific and technological progress. A strong supporter of environmental causes, she was instrumental in passing a number of laws concerning the protection of the Nile River from pollution, the founding of the Egyptian Environmental Affairs Agency, and the establishment and protection of a number of nature reserves. She also opposed an attempt to establish a nuclear power plant on the northern coast of Egypt.

Since 1992, Hassan has served as the chair of the Commission on Human Development and Local Administration of the Shura Assembly. In 1995, President Hosni Mubarak appointed her as the women's secretary-general of the ruling National Democratic Party, a position that she held until her resignation in 2001. Hassan's lifelong commitment to the advancement of women's causes was recognized in her inclusion as a member of the official Egyptian delegation to the 1995 Beijing Women's Conference. She is also an honorary life member of the International Parliamentary Union, the first woman from the Third World to hold such a position.

In 2001, Hassan was appointed secretary-general of Egypt's National Council for Women, a body that develops strategies for the economic empowerment of women through small enterprises, enhancing women's participation in public and political life, building relationships with N.G.O.'s, and establishing a training strategy for gender sensitization in both the workplace and broader Egyptian society. As secretary-general, Hassan declared the top priority of the council to be combating illiteracy. Other major goals included a five-year plan to expand women's rights, including passing legislation to grant Egyptian nationality to children born to Egyptian mothers and foreign fathers, and challenging the legal requirement that women have their husbands' permission to travel or be issued a passport. Arguing that the constitution proclaims the equality of men and women, Hassan has insisted that women have the right to freedom of mobility and has called on the government to recognize women as legal heads of households. Between sixteen and twenty-two percent of all Egyptian households are headed by women. The council has also recognized the need to boost women's representation in parliament in order to provide women with the practical opportunity to serve as legislators.

Hassan's work on gender and development issues extends to the international arena where she has called for the promotion of women in science and international scrutiny of the social, economic, and political processes that lead to social problems, such as poverty, segregation, and gender discrimination. Her article "Islamic Women in Science" has been widely circulated among policy makers and academics and on the internet. The article outlines major past contributions of Muslims (both men and women) to science, medicine, and technology and calls for the development of science and technology throughout the Muslim and developing worlds in order to participate again in the global advancement of science and technology. In addition to outlining initiatives that have already been taken toward this goal, the article highlights the need to address gender-based discrimination that currently discourages women from participating more actively in this scientific revival, including the emphasis on health professions to the detriment of engineering careers and socio-cultural biases that encourage consideration of women exclusively as child-bearers and rearers. Hassan has observed that women are largely absent from senior positions in scientific, science policy making, and academic institutions in the developing world.

As part of an ongoing effort to redress these inequalities, Hassan was appointed to serve as the co-chair of the Gender Advisory Board (G.A.B.) of the U.N. Commission on Science and Technology for Development (U.N.C.S.T.D.). The G.A.B. was established in 1995 to advise on gender issues in science and technology for development, to monitor and assist the implementation of U.N.C.T.S.D. recommendations, to facilitate mainstreaming gender concerns in science and technology, and to serve as a liaison with other U.N. agencies through the U.N. Development Fund for Women (U.N.I.F.E.M.). Hassan also serves as the co-chair of the Association of Women Engineers and as the vice-president of the executive board of the Third World Organization for Women in Science (T.W.O.W.S.), the first international forum to unite eminent women scientists from the Third World in order to strengthen their role in the development process, promote their representation in scientific and technological leadership, strengthen and improve their access to research, educational, and training opportunities, and increase and recognize their scientific and technological achievements.

Hassan's commitment to Third World development has included special attention to the needs of the Arab world. She was a key participant in the creation of the Arab Women's Organization (A.W.O.) in 2002, which works to grant official recognition to women's contributions to the workforce and the family in Arab societies. She has called for the A.W.O. to play a major role in amending and changing laws that discriminate against women and to work toward poverty alleviation, job creation, strengthening social welfare programs, addressing women's health concerns, expanding and promoting education for girls and women, and developing human resources.

Hassan is recognized in both Egypt and the international community as an important voice in the advancement of women's rights and in the development of science and technology in the Third World. She received the Medal of Science and Art of the First Degree from Egypt in 1980.

Further reading

"Arab Women's Summit Opens Sunday in Cairo," *Jordan Times*, November 11, 2001

"For Women and Ecology," *Al-Ahram Weekly*, October 12–18, 1995, issue no. 242

Hassan, Farkhonda. "Islamic Women in Science," *Science* 290, www.sciencemag.org/cgi/content/full/290/5489/55

Leila, Reem. "Getting Tougher on Women's Rights," *Al-Ahram Weekly*, March 29–April 4, 2001, issue no. 527

www.ictp.trieste.it/~twas/TWOWSGeneral. html – website for Third World Organization for Women in Science

www.ncw.gov.eg – website for National Council for Women, Egypt

www.unesco.org/science/women/eng/wcs_bu dapest/regional_follow_up.html – website for U.N.E.S.C.O. on Women, Science, and Technology

www.wigsat.org or www.wigsat.org/ofan/ ofan.html – website for Gender Advisory Board of the United Nations Commission on Science and Technology for Development, Africa region

Rana Ahmed Husseini (b. 1967)

An award-winning journalist and human rights activist, Rana Ahmed Husseini has harnessed the power of the media to promote public awareness of crimes against women and to call for women's and human rights.

Rana Ahmed Husseini was born on June 2, 1967, in Jordan. Her father was a civil engineer. Her mother is a librarian. She received her elementary and high-school educations in Jordan and then attended the Oklahoma City University in Oklahoma City, OK, where she completed both her Bachelor of Mass Communications in 1990 and her Master of Liberal Arts in June 1993. She worked for five months as a reporter and photographer for the *Oklahoma Gazette* covering social issues prior to returning to Jordan. She played the center position for Jordan's national basketball team from 1983 until 1999.

Husseini began working as a reporter and photographer for the *Jordan Times* in 1993. Assigned to the crime beat, she covered stories about minor cases such as thefts, fires, and accidents. In 1994, she came across a story that blossomed into a career in activism for women's and human rights: the May 1994 honor killing of a Jordanian high-school student named Kifaya.

Kifaya was murdered by her older brother. She had been raped repeatedly by her younger brother who threatened to kill her if she told anyone. Kifaya remained silent until she became pregnant. The family arranged for an abortion and married her off to a man who was fifty years her senior. When her husband divorced her six months later, she was returned to her family. It was at this point that her older brother tied her to a chair, told her to recite a verse from the Quran, and then slit her throat in order to "cleanse" the family's honor. Although Kifaya had been a victim of rape, her conservative family believed

that her loss of sexual purity was due to immoral behavior on her part. Her story came to the press's attention because the brother who had killed her turned himself in to the police, saying he was proud to have restored the family's honor. Had he not done this, the fact that an honor killing had occurred probably would not have been reported or noticed. Instead, the village would have been told that Kifaya had committed suicide or died accidentally. Social and cultural taboos on public discussions of family honor, which is considered to be a private issue, have long served to keep honor killings silent, hidden crimes.

Kifaya's case was a landmark because a public record of the crime had been made. Concerned about the broader issue of honor killings across Jordan, Husseini launched an independent investigation, beginning with Kifaya's family. She interviewed two of Kifaya's uncles, who told her that Kifaya was "not a good girl" and that she had seduced her brother. When Husseini questioned why Kifaya was to blame for having been raped and why she would have seduced her own brother when there were so many other men available, the uncles responded by stating that Kifaya had committed an impure act that tarnished the family's honor. They then shifted tactics to imply that Husseini herself was impure for investigating the killing. Husseini ended the interview, but not her investigation of honor killings.

Husseini began to analyze police files and conduct interviews with the families of other victims of honor killings. In many cases, villagers told her it would be in her best interest to leave and to stop asking questions. Police and prosecutors often asked her why she was bothering with such minor stories and offered to bring her "big" cases instead. Experience led Husseini to the conclusion that part of the problem with honor killings was a lack of institutional seriousness about such crimes.

She published her research and conclusions as a feature article in the *Jordan Times*. Although her reports were initially ridiculed, they shattered the conspiracy of silence on the topic of honor killings. She found that an average of between twenty and twenty-five Jordanian women are murdered annually in honor killings, according to official statistics. This represents a quarter of all homicides in Jordan annually and a full one-third of all female murder victims. Husseini believes that the figures may be as high as thirty percent, because this type of murder is not always reported to the authorities. In the rare cases where the killers are prosecuted, they are usually either acquitted or given very light sentences. While sentences range from three months to one year of imprisonment, the average sentence is only seven and a half months. Furthermore, according to Jordanian law, defense of the family's honor constitutes a mitigating circumstance in the crime. The law stipulates that a man's punishment for murder is to be reduced if he has found his wife or other blood relative engaged in an adulterous act and either kills her or attempts to. Minors who commit honor killings are treated even more leniently. They are sentenced only to time in a juvenile center where they can either continue their education or learn a profession until they are eighteen years old, at which point they are released with no criminal record. Because the law treats minors so lightly in these cases, honor killings are sometimes carried out by minors, although this is not a general trend.

Husseini's investigation revealed that honor killings are a problem not only because they result in the murder of the accused woman with no accompanying punishment of the man, but also because of the haziness surrounding the definition of illicit sexual activity. As proven in Kifaya's case, whether the woman was a willing or unwilling partner is irrelevant. Furthermore, it is not just the act of sexual intercourse that constitutes illicit sexual activity in the eyes of some families. In some cases, a woman's presence in the company of a strange man or even the rumor, no matter how unfounded, of the same is considered sufficient grounds for the family's loss of honor. Husseini found that leaving the family home for a time or making statements such as "This is my life," or "I am free to do as I choose" have been used as justifications for honor killings as recently as 2002.

Husseini also found that those who are pressured to kill their female family members are victimized in honor killings. The traditional, social, and cultural pressures to maintain the family honor affect both men and women. Men know that they will be considered heroes if they carry out the killing and that they will be accused of dishonoring the family if they fail. Honor crimes must therefore be understood not as acts of hatred by men against their mothers and sisters, but as acts of fear of disgrace at the very least and fear for their own lives and safety at worst. Similarly, female family members are also often pressured into helping with the killings. Fearing that they will be accused of impugning the family honor if they do not help, they also give in to pressure. Husseini recognizes that there can be no solution to the problem until the cultural and family pressure to commit honor killings is brought to an end.

Husseini learned that fear of honor killings has led to the cultural practice in some Arab countries, including Jordan, of jailing women who become pregnant outside of marriage. In these cases, the women are so afraid that they turn themselves in to the police, who imprison them in order to protect them. Once in jail, the women remain there indefinitely because they do not have the means to make bail and there are no charges against them to bring them to trial. In cases where the family comes to bail them out, it is only to kill them. Most of these women therefore remain in jail without having committed a crime. In 2003, 30–40 out of 190 inmates in Amman had been incarcerated due to threats by their brothers, fathers, and uncles to kill them.

The combination of lenient judicial treatment which implies institutional support for honor killings, the reality of women pregnant outside of marriage remaining in jail indefinitely, and the lack of public outrage over honor killings suggested to Husseini that honor killings are a culturally acceptable practice in Jordan. However, she is careful to emphasize that not all Jordanian women live under the constant threat of honor killing, and that it is not an Islamic practice: both Muslim and Christian girls have suffered honor killings in Jordan. Husseini further specifies that honor killings, while crossing both class and education boundaries, are, nevertheless, isolated and limited events. She denies any association between Islam and honor killings, observing that Islam only allows punishment of married people who commit adultery and then only where four eyewitnesses to the actual act testify to the same. Punishment in such cases is the responsibility of the community, not the family.

Despite her care to specify honor killing as a cultural rather than an Islamic tradition, Husseini's daring in publicly addressing what is considered to be a private issue has led not only to criticism of her work as anti-Islam, anti-family, and anti-Jordanian, but also to hate mail, death threats, and harassment from angry people, particularly Arab men, who feel that her work has either tarnished or threatened their honor. One man threatened to "visit her" at the newspaper if she didn't stop writing. Detractors have accused her of defending prostitutes and encouraging adultery and premarital sex because the elimination of honor killings would supposedly allow women greater sexual liberty. Others have charged that she is distracting people from other issues of "greater national importance," such as the number of illegitimate children born each year. She has even been accused of being overly influenced by her studies in the United States and of bringing Western feminism to Jordan. However, Husseini asserts that her stories do not moralize and are not overtly feminist. She simply reports the details of murders, tallies for documented honor crimes, and follows up with the sentence, if any, for the perpetrator.

Despite its controversial nature and its cost to her own personal safety, Husseini has persisted in her work because she believes that someone needs to speak out about violence against women. She refuses to listen to those who tell her that she will not be able to change anything or to take a self-defeating attitude where the safety and well-being of other human beings are at stake. She believes that exposing the truth about honor killings and other forms of violence against women is the first step to stopping such crimes. She also believes that her work contradicts neither international principles of human rights nor Islamic law. She notes that all religions support life and that no religion allows an individual to serve as judge, juror, and executioner. She has vowed to continue her investigations until these crimes stop.

Husseini's relentless outspokenness on honor killings pushed local women's groups, politicians, and the Jordanian royal family to address the issue at both the grass-roots and national levels. The press now talks more freely and openly about violence against women than in 1993 when Husseini first began reporting. Media outlets in other parts of the Arab world have also taken on discussion of the topic. Queen Noor (see also HM QUEEN NOOR) urged officials to take action to solve the problem, while King Hussein made history in a landmark 1997 address to the opening of the thirteenth parliament that marked the first time a ruling monarch addressed women's rights. King Abdullah and Queen Rania have continued the tradition of working toward the advancement of women's status, including Abdullah's introduction of a new constitution with a section dedicated to women and a request that all laws discriminating against women be amended. He was particularly supportive of a constitutional amendment to impose a harsher penalty on men who kill their daughters and sisters. The amendment was vetoed by parliament in September 2003. The day after the vote, three brothers killed their two sisters with axes in order to "cleanse the family honor."

Husseini believes that the real reason why the amendment failed was because of the way in which it was presented – a Western criticism of Jordan – rather than because of its content. The impression that the West was imposing its values on Jordanian sovereign affairs raised sensitivity and opposition to the measure. She believes that the amendment would have been successful if it had been presented as a Jordanian issue for Jordanians to decide. She continues to press for the Jordanian courts to recognize honor killings as murders. At the same time, she notes that official government recognition of honor crimes constitutes an important first step in addressing the problem, but falls short of addressing the practical issues facing women, such as the fact that many Jordanian women do not know what their rights are or that they even have rights. For example, she pressed the government to create shelters for women where they can enjoy security while receiving training and rehabilitation as opposed to seeking refuge from honor killings in jail. Although this project received support from U.N.I.F.E.M. (U.N. Development Fund for Women), it has not yet been implemented by the Jordanian government. Husseini also joined a group of activists who marched on parliament to demand

women's equality and safety. She has continued to write, transmitting the tales of the suffering of women to the broader public to raise awareness and strengthen the position of women in society.

Husseini's dedication to bringing world attention to the problem of honor killings has earned her international recognition. Her article on "Murder in the Name of Honour" won her the MEDNEWS award for the best article in 1995. She was the recipient of the 1998 Reebok Award for Human Rights for bringing attention to women's and human rights. She was granted the Human Rights Watch Award in 2000 for her overall reporting and activism against violence against women in Jordan and received the Ida B. Wells Award for Bravery in Journalism in 2003 for her ongoing coverage of honor crimes. In addition, her work has been featured in a C.N.N. documentary, a Canadian film, *Crimes of Honour*, and in magazine articles in both Europe and the United States. She has also been interviewed on a variety of television and radio stations and by magazines throughout the United States, Europe, and the Arab world.

As an activist, Husseini's approach to women's and human rights differs from the standard approach of focusing on general human rights because she has focused strictly on honor killings. She believes that a woman's basic right to life has to be guaranteed before other issues can be addressed. Her activism has been carried out through consulting work for the United Nations Development Fund for Women and Equality Now, which has involved conducting research and documentation on human rights violations and violence against women and girls and identifying priorities for the future. She has also made numerous presentations about honor crimes and gender-based violence to a variety of human rights organizations and academic institutions. Her public service includes membership in the Jordanian Women's

Union and the National Jordanian Committee to Eliminate so-called Honour Crimes, which collected over 15,000 signatures demanding the cancellation of all laws offering leniency to killers in honor crimes. She served on the panel of judges for the Amnesty International Global Award for Human Rights Journalism in 2001.

Husseini is currently writing a book about honor killing and her commitment to ending it based on her work experience and interviews with concerned parties. She continues to report for the *Jordan Times* where her colleagues have offered strong support for her ongoing work.

Further reading

Leupold, Julie. "Seven Who Till Fresh Ground," Women's E-News, January 1, 2003, www.womensenews.org

Murphy, Clare. "Jordan's Dilemma over 'Honour Killings,'" B.B.C. News Online, September 10, 2003

Prusher, Ilene. "Spotlight on Killing of Women for 'Family Honor,' " *Christian Science Monitor*, October 23, 1998

Interview with the author, November 11, 2003

www.forefrontleaders.org – short biography of Husseini and links to other pieces on honor killings

www.pbs.org/speaktruthtopower/rana.html – Husseini's PBS report on human rights in Jordan

$$\boxed{I}$$

Shams al-Din Abu Abd Allah Muhammad Ibn Battuta
(1304–1368/9)

Often called "the Marco Polo of the Muslim world," Shams al-Din Abu Abd Allah Muhammad Ibn Battuta was one of the world's greatest geographers and travelers, as well as the greatest known traveler of premodern time.

Ibn Battuta was born on February 25, 1304, in Tangiers, Morocco, a town located on what was believed to be the edge of the flat earth. A descendant of the Berber tribe of Lawata, he came from a respected family of Muslim legal scholars and judges. He followed in the family tradition of studying Islamic law, Quran recitation, and other Islamic sciences and acquiring the values, sensibilities, and manners of an educated gentleman. Although not a renowned scholar, he spoke Arabic well and was frequently found in the company of the wealthy and powerful.

Ibn Battuta's travels began in 1325 when he left his home town to make the Hajj, or pilgrimage to Mecca that is required once in a lifetime for all able-bodied Muslims who can afford to do so. Both of his parents were alive when he left. Due to insecurity on the roads, he traveled with a group of merchants. Despite the precaution, the group was followed by bandits, and was robbed by government agents. Ibn Battuta became so sick that he had to tie himself to his saddle to complete the journey.

Ibn Battuta's journey to Mecca did not follow a direct route. Throughout his travels, his journeys tended to be circuitous, rather than linear, enabling him to visit a variety of locations and frequently resulting in lengthy side trips that took him far from his original destination. His trip to Mecca took him through Morocco, Tunisia, Libya, Egypt, Palestine and Syria over a period of a year and a half. He made a point of visiting Jerusalem, then considered the center of the world, and was inspired to find that the roads from there led to everywhere on the known earth. He met and married a Moroccan woman in Damascus in 1326, although they divorced after a few weeks. Unknown to Ibn Battuta, his wife later gave birth to a son who died at the age of ten. He is known to have married at least one other wife and to have had at least one daughter. He finally completed his first Hajj in 1326, at which point he embarked on a tour of Iraq and Persia (contemporary Iran) prior to returning to Mecca.

In either 1328 or 1330, Ibn Battuta took his first major sea voyage, down the eastern coast of Africa. He traveled as far south as contemporary Tanzania and then returned to Yemen. From Yemen, he traveled to Oman and then through the Persian Gulf for another trip to Mecca.

In either 1330 or 1332, he traveled to India where he sought an official position working for the sultanate of Delhi. On the way, he went north through Egypt and Syria to Asia Minor. He crossed the Black Sea and the plains of West Central Asia, traveling west to Constantinople (contemporary Istanbul) in the company of a Turkish princess. He then returned to the Asian steppes and traveled east through Transoxiana, Khurasan, and Afghanistan, traversing the Hindu Kush mountains. As he crossed Central Asia, he was attacked by rebels mounted on rhinoceroses and was struck by an arrow. He and his companions successfully fought off their attackers and continued on their journey. He did not arrive in India until either 1333 or 1335.

Ibn Battuta remained in India for eight years, during which time he worked as a judge (*qadi*). Although his work as a judge made him materially wealthy, he was unhappy with having constantly to please the sultan. At one point, the sultan was displeased with him and sent assassins to kill him. Realizing that the assassins would not kill him while he prayed, Ibn Battuta prayed for nine straight days until they left. It was at that point that he decided to leave India for Mecca, and gave away all of his wealth. However, after forty days, he was summoned back to the sultan's court, and returned to India.

In 1341, Ibn Battuta was commissioned by the sultan to lead a diplomatic mission to the Mongol emperor of China. He set out on the trip, but was attacked and captured by rebels. He earned his release by convincing the rebels that he was just a traveler. He spent the next two years traveling through southern India, Ceylon, and the Maldive Islands with his former companions. Their experiences included encounters with man-eating tigers and personal experience of the

monsoon season. Ibn Battuta spent eight months working as a *qadi* in the Maldive Islands.

After this detour, Ibn Battuta and his companions, still anxious to see the other "edge" of the world, decided to set out for China by boat. The boats were sunk in a storm, along with Ibn Battuta's companions. Ibn Battuta himself was spared because he had stayed on shore to perform his Friday prayers. Fearing the sultan's wrath over the delay of the trip and the loss of resources, Ibn Battuta decided to travel to China as a private individual. He set out in 1345, traveling by sea and visited Bengal, Burma, and Sumatra prior to continuing to Canton. Upon arrival, he declared that he was the long-lost ambassador from India. He was honored and taken to the capital. The extent of his travels in China is unknown, but scholars believe that he remained in the southern coastal region.

In 1346–1347, Ibn Battuta returned to Mecca, traveling through South India, the Persian Gulf, Syria, and Egypt. While in Damascus, he learned that his father had passed away fifteen years previously. He passed through Jerusalem again during the plague of the Black Death which was sweeping through the Middle East. In Mecca, he performed the Hajj for a fourth and final time prior to returning home. A few miles from home, he learned that his mother had just died from the plague. He arrived in Fez, Morocco, in 1349, after an absence of twenty-four years.

Ibn Battuta made a few short trips after his return to Morocco. In 1350, he traveled across the Strait of Gibraltar to the Muslim kingdom of Granada (in contemporary Spain). He made his final trip in 1353, when he traveled with a caravan of camels across the Sahara desert to the kingdom of Mali. He completed his trip in 1355, after which he remained in Morocco.

In 1356, the Sultan of Morocco, Abu 'Inan, commissioned a young court secretary named Ibn Juzayy to record

Ibn Battuta's experiences, as well as observations about the Islamic world of this time. Ibn Juzayy had a reputation for excellence in writing law, poetry, history, and philology and was an expert calligrapher. The final product of the commission, the *rihla* account that established Ibn Battuta as "the traveler of his age," was a combined abridgment of Ibn Battuta's oral history and written notes. Because the writer's job was to prune and polish the account to make it readable, rather than simply to record it verbatim, the *rihla* includes the names of a very few places that Ibn Battuta did not actually visit. It is likely that these locations were included as a literary device intended to demonstrate that Ibn Battuta had traveled everywhere in the world that had an important Muslim population. Despite these few inventions, the account is considered to be highly accurate and has stood up well under modern scholarly scrutiny.

Ibn Battuta's *rihla* is neither a diary nor a biography. It was not written during his travels or contemporary to the events described. As a genre of Arabic literature that enjoyed immense popularity in North Africa between the twelfth and fourteenth centuries, the *rihla* typically described journeys from North Africa to Mecca for the Hajj, including impressions and descriptions of religious institutions and monuments, as well as the major personalities of the great cities of the Islamic world. Designed both to educate and to entertain the reading public, it was part autobiography and part description of people and experiences. It does not contain extensive biographical information about the author, such as when and where married and for how long or when and where children were born, because this data was not considered relevant. Similarly, it was not written as a chronology or with particular attention to dates, details of the itinerary, or the sequence of events.

Ibn Battuta's *rihla* reflects his social status as a literate, urbane gentleman who was typically concerned with the affairs, customs, and loyalties of other literate, urbane gentlemen. His travel discussions include descriptions of notable men he encountered in each city, the variety of religious monuments, the hospitality he received, and the numerous gifts with which he was showered. His main descriptions of people are of political leaders, Sufis, and religious scholars because they were likely to be of interest to his audience. Poor people and peasants were featured only when they were responsible for something negative that happened to him. The most complex *rihla* ever written, Ibn Battuta's memoirs took almost two years to write and were an object of both fascination and controversy during his lifetime. After its completion, Ibn Battuta retired to a judicial post in a provincial town in Morocco where he remained until he died in either 1368 or 1369. The original handwritten book in Arabic is housed in the National Library in Paris.

Although Ibn Battuta is often called "the Marco Polo of the Muslim world," his travels were much broader than his European counterpart's. Traveling for nearly thirty years through territories that constitute forty-four different countries in the contemporary era, Ibn Battuta covered about seventy-five thousand miles, an average of seven miles a day for almost eleven thousand days, all either by walking, caravan, horseback riding, or sailing. His account also covers a broader range of topics and is conveyed in a more personal perspective. One of the major reasons for this difference is the fact that Ibn Battuta's travels were all carried out within Muslim territories. Although there were local and regional differences in certain customs and traditions, there nevertheless remained a certain broad continuity of civilization and culture that was identifiable as Islamic. Ibn Battuta was thus always an insider in the areas he visited and was able to seek out the company of other Muslims who not only were either the majority population or the ruling parties of the countries he visited, but also shared his religion, moral values, social ideals and manners, even where differences of language, customs, and aesthetic values existed. As a result, he enjoyed friendship, hospitality, relative security, and employment throughout his travels. His experiences are a tangible example of the Muslim understanding of belonging to the broader Muslim community known as the *ummah*, in which loyalty to Islam as a set of spiritual, moral, and social values supersedes national, ethnic or tribal identities. By contrast, Marco Polo was a stranger who visited lands where few Europeans had ever been seen. He was a permanent outsider and explorer whose life was frequently at risk in the regions he visited because of that status.

The significance of Ibn Battuta's *rihla* lies not only in its description of Islamic civilization and culture, but also in its confirmation of a single intercommunicating culture extending from the Atlantic Ocean to the South China Sea. It affirms the Islamic world as a global arena, rather than a handful of trade routes. Its vision of social inclusiveness where Sunnis and Sufis alike are considered Muslims without respect to race or ethnicity offers a foreshadowing of contemporary globalization, but in a medieval setting.

Further reading

Bullis, Douglas. "The Longest Hajj: The Journeys of Ibn Battuta." *ARAMCO World*, July/August 2000, pp. 3–39

Dunn, Ross. *The Adventures of Ibn Battuta: A Muslim Traveler of the 14th Century*. Berkeley: University of California Press, 1986

Gibb, H.A.R., trans. and ed. *The Travels of Ibn Battuta A.D. 1325–1354*, 3 vols. London: Hakluyt Society, 1929; repr. 1983

Wolfe, Michael. *One Thousand Roads to Mecca: Ten Centuries of Travelers Writing About the Muslim Pilgrimage*. New York: Grove Press, 1999

www.sfusd.k12.ca.us/schwww/sch618/Ibn_Battuta_Rihla.html for a virtual tour

Abu Ali al-Hasan Ibn al-Haytham (965–1039/1040)

The "father of modern optics," Abu Ali al-Hasan Ibn al-Haytham is considered one of the greatest mathematical scientists of all time.

Abu Ali al-Hasan Ibn al-Haytham was born in 965 in Basra (in contemporary Iraq). Known in the West as Alhazen, he was also known during his lifetime as al-Basri, meaning "from Basra,"and as al-Misri, meaning "Egyptian." Ibn al-Haytham lived in Basra until young adulthood. Although he trained for a job in the civil service and was appointed minister for Basra and the surrounding region, he became disillusioned with his job because he was dissatisfied with his religious studies. After investigating the conflicting religious views of a variety of movements, he concluded that none of them represented "the truth." He therefore devoted his life to the pursuit of physics, mathematics, and other sciences. He was famous as a reputable scientist while he lived in Basra.

Ibn al-Haytham's reputation as a scientist was such that the Egyptian caliph, al-Hakim, heard about his proposal to regulate water flow down the Nile River. Although often known as a cruel ruler, al-Hakim was a major patron of the sciences who established a library in Cairo that was second in importance only to Baghdad's House of Wisdom. Al-Hakim invited Ibn al-Haytham to come to Egypt to head an engineering team to carry out his Nile River proposal. Ibn al-Haytham accepted, moving permanently to Egypt. However, after traveling a considerable distance up the Nile with the team, he realized that his proposal would not work. The team returned to al-Hakim to report that the project was not feasible. The failure of the project left al-Hakim with no confidence in Ibn al-Haytham's scientific abilities. He relegated him to an administrative position instead. Ibn al-Haytham soon realized that he could not trust al-Hakim and decided to fake madness. He was subsequently confined to his house until al-Hakim's death in 1021, at which time Ibn al-Haytham made public the scientific work he had carried out during his confinement, an act that proved that he had not been truly mad.

Ibn al-Haytham spent the rest of his life near Al-Azhar Mosque and University in Cairo, writing and copying mathematics texts and teaching. He may have made short trips to Syria and Baghdad. He completed an autobiography in 1027, specifying his intellectual formation and accomplishments. He died in either 1039 or 1040.

Ibn al-Haytham wrote approximately ninety-two major works, fifty-five of which have survived. His major topics were optics, including theories of light and vision; astronomy; and mathematics, including geometry and number theory. His most important work is *Kitab al-Manazir*, or *The Book of Optics*, a seven-volume work that methodically integrates the research work of all of the traditional themes of optics, including physical, mathematical, physiological, experimental, and psychological considerations. Translated into Latin as *Opticae thesaurus Alhazeni* in 1270, this work was the next major contribution to optics after Ptolemy's *Almagest*, in large part because it undermined the basic premises and structure of Greek optical research and rejected Greek theories of vision that considered it to be the result of contact between the eye and the object either through a ray emitted from the eye to the object or through the transmission of a form from the object to the eye. It was the most important work of physics to reach the West in medieval times and had a profound influence on Western scientists, including Leonardo da Vinci, Johannes Kepler, Roger Bacon, John Pecham, and Witelo.

Kitab al-Manazir asserted and illustrated Ibn al-Haytham's conception of optics as a theory of vision. It introduced a new methodology that focused on how vision occurs, rather than the prior approach of trying to explain what vision is. Ibn al-Haytham believed that what is sensed by the eye is not the object itself, but an image of the object formed as the result of the reflection of light from the object to the eye. His theory of vision therefore concentrated on investigating the human eye from the perspectives of its structure, an analysis of stereo vision, and the formulation of a method by which images are received. According to his theory, vision occurs when rays from the perceived object enter through the pupils, which serve as lenses, and proceed to the brain, where the faculty of sense completes the process. The eye was thus considered part of a broader optical system in which both physiology and psychology played important roles.

Ibn al-Haytham's understanding of psychology differed from those of the past because he focused on what he called "sense-perception," which occurs through documentable experimentation, rather than the psychology of perception, which remains an abstract theory with no concrete proof. He outlined four modes of sense-perception, the last of which was his original contribution: (1) perception by sensation in which the viewer's perception of an object occurs only via external stimuli, such as color or light; (2) perception by recognition, where the brain registers the presence of an object and determines what it is on the basis of comparison with other objects previously viewed; (3) perception resulting in only partial identification of the object because it fails to correspond to a specific object already viewed or the viewer fails to recall previous perceptions (such as in the case of distance); and (4) "attentive perception," which entails visual examination of various parts of an object. Ibn al-Haytham believed that knowledge could be derived from sense-perception because it entailed carrying out investigations, rather than mere contemplation of an object. He taught that the object to be sense-perceived should be set on a straight line from the surface to the surface of vision, illuminated, large enough to be visible to the naked eye, and be at a certain distance from the eye. Sense-perception was to be gained through the interrelation between these properties. Ibn al-Haytham's theory was a major theoretical advance and is close to what is believed in the contemporary era.

Ibn al-Haytham's novel approach also allowed him to study the geometric aspects of visual theories. Using studies of the physiology of the eye and integrating medical and physical research into his mathematical work, he produced a comprehensive approach and theory that enabled him to provide numerous levels of explanation and to separate the conditions of the propagation of light from physical theories of vision. The integration of Euclidean optics with the Aristotelian perception of form marked optics as a mathematical discipline.

Ibn al-Haytham's most important contribution was his insistence on experimental and mathematical support for theories, rather than reliance on abstract axioms. His experimental approach to optics allowed him to investigate virtually every aspect of light and human sight, including the way that light is refracted by air, mirrors, and water. He examined rainbows, sunlight, and aerial perspectives, correctly explaining the optical illusion that makes the diameters of the sun and moon appear to increase as they approach the horizon. He also demonstrated how the refraction of light by the atmosphere causes the sun to remain visible even after it is actually below the horizon. He came close to a theory of magnifying lenses and was the first to make use of "camera obscura" optics by studying the solar eclipse through a semi-obscured projection via a small hole in the wall onto a flat surface, an approach that anticipated modern photographic principles and provided evidence that light falls on the retina in much the same way that it falls on a surface after passing through the aperture. His experiments with parabolically shaped burning mirrors foreshadowed the lenses of future microscopes and telescopes.

Ibn al-Haytham's numerous experiments provided him with sound principles that had been proven through scientific investigation. He was the first person to observe that light is always of the same nature, regardless of its source, although he speculated that it traveled at different speeds. His examinations of the various aspects of the propagation of light led him to conceive of new problems, the most famous of which were errors of vision, such as optical illusions, and the mathematical conundrum commonly called "Alhazen's problem": finding the point of reflection on the surface of a concave or convex spherical mirror, given the fixed positions of the visible object and the eye.

The experimental method also led Ibn al-Haytham to develop theories of the reflection and refraction of light, as he observed the specular reflection of both accidental and essential light. The use of experiment to confirm theory in problems of reflection and refraction enabled him to develop precise instruments, such as a copper instrument for measuring reflections from conical, spherical, cylindrical, and plane mirrors, both concave and convex. His investigations also led him fundamentally to reappraise both basic scientific laws and universal laws about light. His work in refraction included an attempt to work out the correlation between the angle of incidence and the angle of refraction.

Ibn al-Haytham's mathematical contributions include the problem of squaring the circle, which he approached by determining the area of lunes (crescents formed from two intersecting circles) and squaring the circles using the lunes. He apparently realized that he could not solve the problem because his promised second treatise on the topic was never written. The problem remains unsolved. In number theory, he contributed the methodology of problem solving using congruences, a method now known as Wilson's theorem, which states that if p is prime, then 1 + (p-1) is divisible by p. He also considered a second methodology of problem solving using congruences that is known contemporarily as a special case of the Chinese Remainder theorem. Ibn al-Haytham's major mathematical work, *Analysis and Synthesis*, was written to study mathematical methodologies. He also did important work on isometrics, or the representation of figures with all edges drawn with true relative length and without the perspectival distortion of dimension.

One of Ibn al-Haytham's major theoretical contributions was his *al-Shuquq ala Batlamyus* (*Doubts on Ptolemy*), in which he summed up the physical and philosophical problems inherent to the Greek astronomical system and provided an inventory of the theoretical inconsistencies of the Ptolemaic models. This work presented a major challenge to astronomers of his time, who based their reworking of the Ptolemaic models on his work with varying degrees of success.

Ibn al-Haytham's contributions to optics and the fundamental nature and workings of vision and light are considered by many scientists and mathematicians to be the most original and important contributions of any Muslim scientist to modern science. His use of controlled experimentation was innovative and had a profound impact on both optics and physics, as did his care in the construction and assembly of equipment for investigations and experiments and his inclusion of dimensions as an integral part of those experiments. His willingness to modify or reject hypotheses that conflicted with the results of experimentation represented an important break

with past practices and set the stage for future scientific inquiries.

Further reading

Anderson, Margaret J. and Karen F. Stephenson. *Scientists of the Ancient World*. Berkeley Heights, NJ: Enslow Publishers, Inc., 1999

Dallal, Ahmad. "Science, Medicine, and Technology: The Making of a Scientific Culture," in *The Oxford History of Islam*, editor-in-chief John L. Esposito. New York: Oxford University Press, 1999

Hill, Donald R. *Islamic Science and Engineering*. Edinburgh: Edinburgh University Press, 1993

Syed, Ibrahim B. "Islamic Medicine: 1,000 Years Ahead of its Time," http://islam-usa.com/im4.html

Turner, Howard R. *Science in Medieval Islam: An Illustrated Introduction*. Austin: University of Texas Press, 1995

www-gap.dcs.st-and.ac.uk/~history/Mathematicians/Al-Haytham.html

Saad Eddin Ibrahim (b. 1939)

An activist for democracy, human rights, and minority rights, Saad Eddin Ibrahim is one of the most controversial voices in the Arab world.

Saad Eddin Ibrahim was born in Egypt in 1939. He received a B.A. from Cairo University in 1960 and a Ph.D. in sociology from the University of Washington in 1968. A dual American–Egyptian citizen, he has taught sociology at the American University in Cairo since 1975, as well as courses at a number of American universities.

Ibrahim was the first person to write in English about the Islamist movement, tracing its roots, development, and potential for violence. A proponent of what he calls "liberal pluralism," he is best known for his research on socio-economic problems in Egypt – overpopulation, over-urbanization, and overexpectations – that have created an atmosphere of discontent in which militant Islamism has thrived. Having found that minorities and disadvantaged groups tend to suffer disproportionately when a country is in crisis, he has called on the state to take a more active role in managing the stress and strain that accompany modernization and state building, particularly in multiethnic and multireligious societies. An outspoken critic of repression and censorship, he has called for freedom of speech and more openness and transparency in the Egyptian election process, particularly election monitoring. In 1991, he founded the Ibn Khaldun Center for Development Studies as a civil research institute to carry out his investigations into irregularities in parliamentary elections, the status of women, discrimination against the Coptic Christian minority at both the individual and institutional levels, and the normalization of relations between Egypt and Israel. Tangible results of his work include the appointment of Egypt's first female judge (see also TAHANY EL GEBALY) and the declaration of January 7, the Coptic Christian Christmas, as a national holiday.

Although he is well connected to government circles, including President Mubarak's family, Ibrahim has been accused of being a dangerous dissident working to undermine the state's authority. His critics have particularly expressed concern about Western support for his work, claiming that the United States has gained too much influence over Egyptian national affairs through Ibrahim. In June 2000, he was arrested and imprisoned on charges that he had damaged Egypt's international reputation and accepted and embezzled foreign funding without government permission. The financing in question was a $250,000 grant from the European Union (E.U.) to the Ibn Khaldun Center to fund a project encouraging voter participation. Ibrahim was accused of forging voter registration cards in order to boost his E.U. incentive pay. The defamation charge stemmed from his research into voting irregularities in eighty-eight constituencies during the 1995 parliamentary elections and his

lectures on clashes between Egyptian Muslims and Copts. Eight days after his arrest, the parliament was declared invalid by the Supreme Constitutional Court because of the electoral irregularities.

Ibrahim's case highlights the limitations on free speech and academic freedom in the Arab world, particularly the inability of citizens to criticize the government or government policies without serious personal repercussions. Many viewed Ibrahim's case as a broader case about human and civil rights. Western countries expressed surprise and dismay over the charge of illegal foreign funding. Although Egypt had passed a law prohibiting receipt of foreign funds following an earthquake in 1992 out of fear that money from abroad might be filtered to militant Islamic groups in Egypt, Western countries had not considered the potential use of the law to charge and convict a human rights activist.

Despite the E.U.'s denial of the embezzlement charge and audit that showed that the grant money had been used appropriately, the State Security Court found Ibrahim guilty and sentenced him to seven years' imprisonment for his "crimes against the state." Twenty-seven of his colleagues from the Center were also found guilty and sentenced to prison terms ranging from one to seven years. International human rights and democracy activists, including Amnesty International, immediately denounced both the trial and the sentence as politically motivated and demanded Ibrahim's release, citing the irregularities and political motivation of the trial and Ibrahim's fragile health. The Egyptian government refused to release him.

Ibrahim noted the irony of his own imprisonment. He had previously visited prisons as a researcher, working to raise conditions in Egyptian prisons to meet international standards. His sentence marked the first time he had been imprisoned himself. Undeterred, he used his prison time to reengage his fieldwork, keeping diaries and writing down stories he heard, highlighting petty corruption, strict security services, and the absurdity of life in contemporary Egypt, including his own position as a cellmate with some of his prior research subjects. He also engaged in a study of the Arab world's failure to construct a culture of self-criticism following the 9/11 tragedies. Although he had hoped that 9/11 would push Arab societies into a period of self-examination that would lead to major reforms, most countries continued to deny their internal problems. He further noted that the United States, by suspending democratic and constitutional rights and creating what he described as a "police state," could not credibly pressure Arab governments into establishing and supporting democracy and an unfettered civil society. Instead, he observed that many Middle Eastern governments were inspired by the American example to clamp down further on civil rights and society.

Ibrahim was granted a retrial in February 2002 on the basis of a procedural issue: the judges had not waited for the defense team to finish submitting all of its evidence prior to convicting and sentencing Ibrahim. His supporters expected that he would be acquitted at the new trial because of the strength of the defense's evidence. In order to demonstrate their concern about the case, a variety of international human rights organizations, academics, and diplomats from the United States, Canada, and Europe attended the session. Despite domestic and international pressure, the second trial was a repeat of the first. Although the judge indicated that he would need several days to review the defense documents after the defense completed its arguments, he issued a judgment the next day, reconvicting and resentencing Ibrahim.

Because it appeared to be politically motivated, local human rights activists, international human rights organizations, and Western governments immediately denounced Ibrahim's conviction, expressing concern about the potential repercussions for human rights organizations, including the potential for any human rights organization accepting outside funding to be vulnerable to the same accusations and treatment as Ibrahim, the reduction of staffing and operational capacity of human rights organizations, and the potential for activist organizations to be frightened into ending demands for liberalization and democratization. Activists also feared that the United States would fail to take serious action against Egypt over these issues due to the need for Egyptian support for the American-led war on terrorism, the upcoming war in Iraq, and the ongoing Arab–Israeli conflict.

In response to international demand and to protest the conviction, the Bush administration opposed increases to future aid to Egypt, representing a potential loss of approximately $100 million annually in supplemental aid. However, the measures proved counterproductive. Although it could not afford the loss of economic aid, Egypt could not appear to give in to American demands to change or commute the sentence without appearing to lose sovereignty. Instead, Ibrahim's appeal was accepted and a retrial was held.

Egypt's highest appeals court heard Ibrahim's case in March 2003 and declared him not guilty of all charges. As a free man, Ibrahim vowed to continue to fight for freedom and democracy in Egypt and to continue his work to build up civil society and institutions. He remains concerned about both the freedom of speech and academic freedom in Egypt.

Following his release from prison, Ibrahim went on a lecture tour of the United States, working with international human rights organizations to call for the worldwide repeal of emergency laws such as the Patriot Act. He also called for greater American support for democracy activists throughout the world and resolution of the Arab–Israeli conflict as requirements for the sustainable democratization of the Middle East and the most effective long-term means of combating terrorism. He has particularly encouraged tying American aid, trade, and investment to the taking of concrete steps toward full democracy, encouraging civic participation and strengthening the institutions of civil society, although he discourages the United States from controlling the development of democracy in the Arab world.

Ibrahim is a frequent consultant to the media and has appeared on major international television networks. He previously hosted a weekly television program in Egypt entitled *Off the Limelight*. He has served as the director of the Center for Arab Unity Studies in Cairo, secretary-general of the Arab Organization for Human Rights in Cairo, secretary-general and trustee of the Arab Thought Forum in Amman, Jordan, secretary-general of the Arab Council of Childhood and Development, master juror of the Aga Khan Award for Islamic Architecture (see also THE AGA KHAN, PRINCE KARIM IV), president of Sabah Publishing House, and board member and head of Arab Affairs of Al-Ahram Center for Political and Strategic Studies. He is secretary-general of the Egyptian Independent Commission for Electoral Review, president of Cairo's Union of Social Professions, and chairman of the board of the Egyptian Enlightenment Association. His international service includes membership on the World Bank's Advisory Council for Environmentally Sustainable Development, the International Board of Minority Rights Group in London, and the Board of Directors of the International Bureau for Children's Rights, and service as an advisor on civil society to U.N. secretary general Kofi Annan.

Ibrahim's work on human, civil, and minority rights has earned him international acclaim. He is the recipient of the Kuwait Award in Social and Economic Sciences (1985), the Bahrain Merit Award of Educational Research (1988), the Jordanian Order of Independence (1990), the Freedom House Award (1999), the Middle East Studies Association Academic Freedom Award (2001), the Bette Bao Lord Prize for Writing in the Cause of Freedom (2002), the Prize for International Tolerance and Human Rights, Friedrich-Schiller University, Germany (2002), the Index on Censorship Whistleblower Award (2002), the International Human Rights Awards, Lawyers Committee on Human Rights (2002), and the International P.E.N. Writers in Distress Award (2002). He was nominated for the Sakharov Prize of the European Parliament in 2002.

Further reading

Abou el-Magd, Nadia. "Activist Gets Retrial in Egypt: Foreign Diplomats Focused on Case of College Professor," *Boston Globe*, February 8, 2002

Ephron, Dan. "US, Tying Rights Case to Aid, Irks Egyptians," *Boston Globe*, September 8, 2002

Ibrahim, Saad Eddin. *The Copts of Egypt.* Cairo: Ibn Khaldun Center and Minority Rights Group, 1996

—— "A Dissident Asks: Can Bush Turn Words Into Action?" *Washington Post*, November 23, 2003

—— *Egypt, Islam and Democracy: Critical Essays with a New Postcript*, Cairo: American University in Cairo Press, 2002

Khalil, Ashraf. "Egyptian Activist is Sentenced Again," *Boston Globe*, July 30, 2002

—— "Freed Activist Fears Loss of Liberty in Terror War," *Boston Globe*, February 17, 2002

al-Rahim, Ahmed H. "US Voices Needed to Aid Arab Reformer," *Boston Globe*, January 9, 2003

Schemm, Paul. "Activist Exonerated by Egyptian Court," *Boston Globe*, March 19, 2003

Smith, Lee. "... And Why Egyptians Shouldn't," *Boston Globe*, February 16, 2003

Weaver, Mary Anne. "Mubarak Regime is Now on Trial in Egypt," New York *Times* magazine, June 17, 2001

www.democracy-egypt.org
www.ibnkhaldun.org

Shamim Ibrahim (b. 1934)

Founder of the National Islamic Society of Women of America (N.I.S.W.A.) and activist to end domestic violence and abuse, Shamim Ibrahim is one of the leading Muslim voices in the provision of social services tailored to Muslim needs.

Shamim Ibrahim was born in Pakistan in 1934. She lived in Pakistan until 1971, when she moved to Los Angeles, CA, with her husband. Ibrahim is a professional psychologist and has worked for the Los Angeles Unified School District. She served as the first female board member of the Islamic Center of Southern California and works with the Los Angeles attorney's office to organize informational sessions about the American legal system at local mosques for immigrants. She is a frequent consultant for D.S.S. cases involving Muslim families and refers both victims and batterers to the National Islamic Society of Women of America (N.I.S.W.A.) for counseling.

N.I.S.W.A. was founded in 1990 to respond to the increasing need for social services for South Asian Muslims. Following the passage of the 1965 Immigration and Nationality Act, there was a rise in the number of Indian, Pakistani, Bangladeshi, and Sri Lankan immigrants to the United States, particularly in southern California. Although many of these immigrants excelled academically and professionally, their success was accompanied by a rise in unemployment, homelessness, and domestic violence as the population diversified and adjusted to life in America. Ibrahim is careful to point out that domestic violence is not the norm in South Asia. She attributes its rise among the immigrant population to the rapid expansion and different socio-economic pressures and challenges that exist for South Asians in the United States.

Despite the rise of socio-economic problems and the proliferation of mosques, no social services met the needs of South Asians, particularly Muslims. Recognizing the serious social welfare needs of the South Asian Muslim community, particularly women, and disturbed by the rise of a culture of domestic violence and abuse among South Asian Muslims, Ibrahim invited four other women to her home for a dinner party to brainstorm about a solution. N.I.S.W.A. was the result.

N.I.S.W.A., which is also Arabic for "women", was set up as a non-profit organization to aid needy Muslim families, children, single mothers, and disaster and war victims. Because its employees possess working knowledge of South Asian culture and language, they are uniquely able to provide much-needed services for people of Middle Eastern and South Asian backgrounds that other shelters cannot. N.I.S.W.A. takes a family-oriented approach in its services, working to preserve and strengthen families by increasing awareness of legal and environmental pressures affecting them and by protecting the rights of Muslim children. Its services include counseling; referrals; food assistance; legal and financial aid; youth and senior citizen programs; moral support and information about adoption, foster care, and domestic violence. It also serves as a liaison between the South Asian community and the government and as a resource for language and cultural counseling to mainstream welfare agencies.

Statistics on domestic violence in South Asian and Middle Eastern homes suggest that about three hundred in every eight thousand reported cases involve South Asian or Middle Eastern females. However, it is also widely recognized that these statistics are flawed due to the underreporting of incidents. Ibrahim notes that South Asians are raised to observe strict family hierarchies, and a woman's identity is primarily as wife and mother. Immigrant men have played on these cultural notions combined with immigrant women's ignorance of the legal protection that exists in the United States to threaten their wives with divorce, deportation, and even death. Because family honor is considered sacred, a woman who leaves her husband for any reason is understood to disgrace both families, as well as herself. Women who report domestic violence are believed to have betrayed their culture. Because they fear being shunned by their communities, Muslim women are often careful to conceal violence against them. City attorneys have noted the difficulty of prosecuting South Asian offenders while not punishing the victims. The issue has become so serious that advocates organized the first South Asian and Middle Eastern Domestic Violence Awareness Conference in 1999.

Ibrahim defines her task as a complex balance of educating and serving her community while shattering Western stereotypes that cast all South Asian men as wife-beaters. She notes that the main issue in domestic-abuse cases is male power and control. Because South Asian culture upholds the family as sacred, teaches women to accept secondary and subservient status to men, and because the only culturally acceptable roles for South Asian women are those of either devoted daughter or loving and sacrificing mother, South Asian women do not have an individualistic outlook on life. Mothers, in particular, are expected to care for others first and therefore tend to put up with violence and abuse longer than other women. Some men exploit this cultural conditioning to control their wives, often isolating them within the family home, cutting off their contacts with the outside world, and restricting their movements. The claim of some men that their religion justifies their "disciplining" or "correcting" their wives renders the situation even more complicated.

Ibrahim believes that the foundation of N.I.S.W.A. marks only the first step in addressing domestic violence. She has called for the development of a base of men to help work on the problem as the second step, noting that the abuse of South Asian women is not limited to the husband, but is also often carried out by the husband's family. Thus, when a South Asian woman leaves a marriage, she typically gets a restraining order against the husband's entire clan. In a third step, N.I.S.W.A. opened the Amina Adaya Shelter in December 1997 to prevent domestic violence, aid victims through support services and programs designed to break the cycle of violence, and provide shelter for physically, emotionally, or mentally abused women and children. Although it serves women of all races and religions, the shelter particularly focuses on Muslim women and respects Islamic dietary laws. Ibrahim serves as the shelter's housemother, providing greatly needed friendship and information about the rights of the victims. N.I.S.W.A. works in active cooperation with state and county agencies and is recognized and respected by both mental health and social welfare professionals.

In addition to domestic-violence services, N.I.S.W.A. also provides foster-care services, assisting Muslim families with certification and ensuring that Muslim children are placed in licensed Muslim homes. It also hosts youth programs in both education and guidance and runs the only program in Los Angeles for South Asian senior citizens, including a helpline and transportation to N.I.S.W.A. programs.

Ibrahim's pioneering work in the provision and expansion of social services to the South Asian Muslim community has earned her widespread recognition in both South Asian and Los Angeles government circles.

Further reading

Ramirez, Margaret. "Sanctuary, at Last," *Los Angeles Times*, April 12, 1999
www.niswa.com

Yusuf Islam (b. 1948)

As gold-record-winning popular musician Cat Stevens, Yusuf Islam composed more than 150 songs and sold more than 45 million albums. Since converting to Islam, he has turned his musical abilities to fundraising for disaster victims and development in impoverished countries.

Yusuf Islam was born Stephen Demetre Georgiou in the West End of London, England, on July 21, 1948. His parents ran a restaurant close to the theater district. Islam began working at the family restaurant when he was ten years old.

Islam's childhood instilled in him a sense of religious difference and coexistence. Although his father was Greek Orthodox and his mother was Swedish Protestant, Islam attended a Roman Catholic school. He had his first experience of racism while in his mother's native Sweden, where his dark eyes and hair made him stand out. The children of his school there considered him to be so different that he was assigned his own section of the playground from which he could be observed from a distance.

Although initially interested in art as a child, Islam turned to music, beginning with the piano and shifting to the guitar and composition. He changed his name to Cat Stevens when he recorded his first demo tape. He had his first hit – "I Love my Dog" – when he was eighteen years old, followed by hits like "Matthew & Son," which hit the Top 20 in the United Kingdom, and "The First Cut is the Deepest." He quickly became famous as a pop musician and toured England, Belgium, and France. Although he enjoyed his popularity and the wealth and fast life that accompanied fame, he found himself empty and lacking meaning.

When he was nineteen, Islam contracted tuberculosis and was hospitalized for three months. The brush with death led him into a reflective period of searching for truth and meaning in his life. He studied different spiritual paths, including Zen, Buddhism, Hinduism, Christianity, Ching, astrology, numerology, and tarot cards, meditated and became a vegetarian, but failed to find personal peace. During the two years of convalescence that followed his hospitalization, he traveled and composed folk-style songs about his experiences. He eventually returned to his previous style, composing and recording some of his most famous songs, including "Wild World," "Morning Has Broken," and "Peace Train." His first post-hospital album, *Tea for the Tillerman*, resulted in a tour of the United States.

Following the release of *Tea for the Tillerman*, Islam returned to visual arts, including painting and photography. He designed the artwork for his album *Teaser and the Firecat*, and produced an animated short that played during performances of "Moon Shadow." As he made a greater effort to connect with the masses and share their experiences, he began to enjoy concert appearances and respond spontaneously to concert requests, often engaging in on-the-spot compositions and variations on his own music. Finding that he preferred the natural environment of the concert to the more formalized ambience of the recording studio, he redesigned his house into a private recording studio with an eight-track machine so that he could record at will. Although he enjoyed his work and the new discipline of daily writing he began at this time, he continued to feel spiritually empty.

Islam had his first contact with the religion of Islam in 1975. Although he did not convert, he found answers about life and comfort in the Quran's teachings and worldview. He described himself as particularly moved by the Quran's emphasis on prayer, charity, and kindness, respect for the Torah, Gospels, Moses and Jesus, inclusion of stories and instruction from all people, and lack of racism.

The combination of a near-drowning experience near Malibu, CA, a trip to

Jerusalem, and increasing involvement at the New Regent mosque in London led to Islam's conversion in 1977. He recorded his last pop album as Cat Stevens, *Back to Earth*, ended his pop music career, adopted the name Yusuf Islam, and abandoned his previous lifestyle in favor of charitable work. Following a conservative interpretation of Islam that considers only vocals and percussion to be permissible forms of music, he sold all of his musical instruments and gold records and donated the proceeds to his charity, Companions of the Mosque, which prints and distributes copies of the Quran and offers guidance to couples seeking to marry. He began teaching the Quran and giving college lectures. He grew a beard, wore long, flowing white clothing, sought friendships only with other Muslims and ceased making eye or physical contact, such as shaking hands, with women to whom he was not related. He also wrote a book about his conversion and gave it to anyone who asked for it. Although he wrote a few poems over the next ten years, he had little creative output during this time.

In 1979, Islam married and turned his attention to raising his family and establishing schools for Muslim children that would provide both academic training and moral guidance. He established his first school in Kilburn, North London, in 1983. After establishing a track record of academic success, he lobbied for state sponsorship for Muslim schools, similar to that given to schools run by the Church of England and Roman Catholics.

Islam's conversion took on political overtones in the late 1980s when Ayatollah Khomeini issued a *fatwa* (legal ruling) calling for the death penalty for Salman Rushdie following publication of his novel *The Satanic Verses*, which was declared blasphemous for insulting the Prophet Muhammad. As a prominent British Muslim, Islam was asked for his opinion on the matter. The media reported that Islam had endorsed killing Rushdie. However, Islam insisted that his remarks were not accurately reported and had been taken out of context. He later released a press statement clarifying his position. Although he confirmed the Quranic teaching that any person found guilty of blasphemy is to be put to death and that repentance can be accepted only under certain circumstances, he asserted that this did not mean that Muslims are free to break the law or take it into their own hands. Instead, he noted that Islamic law requires Muslims to obey the laws of the country in which they live, provided that such laws do not restrict their freedom to worship, serve God or fulfill their religious duties. Rather than killing Rushdie, he called on British Muslims to demonstrate and lobby peacefully to have the book banned in accordance with British blasphemy law. He also encouraged them to become more active in the political process in order to have a public voice. As the media continued to sensationalize the incident, Islam decided to become a public figure again. He joined the Supreme Council of British Muslims to help cure Western ignorance about Islam and to engage in a higher level of Muslim activism, while continuing his work in education and humanitarian relief work. During the first Gulf War, he was responsible for winning the release of four British hostages in Iraq. He also condemned the allied bombing and tried to set up the Gulf Peace Team to organize peace camps on the desert border between Kuwait and Saudi Arabia to curtail armed aggression by both sides.

In 1992, the eruption of the civil war in Bosnia and the genocide of Muslims that accompanied it brought a major life change for Islam. Islamic aid agencies begged him to put his musical talents to use in an international concert to help children caught in the crossfire and to raise public awareness of what was happening. Horrified by what he described as "the most shameful and sordid crime against European Muslims ever seen," as well as by the West's failure to stop them,

Islam reconsidered the role of music in Islamic culture. Listening to the hymns and songs of religious spirit and sacrifice that combined Balkan melodies with the message of Islam, he recognized for the first time that the supposed ban on music and musical instruments was more of a cultural than an Islamic issue and that music was a matter of debate among Muslims globally. Deciding for himself that "the use of certain musical instruments for the protection of the Islamic identity and culture of a nation" was "worthy of the same allowance as guns and rockets," Islam agreed to return to music. He wrote a song entitled "Father, Mother, Sister, Brother," and dedicated a poem, "The Little Ones," to the children of Sarajevo and Dunblane. In 1996, he held a concert in Sarajevo, his first in twenty years, and was awarded Bosnia's highest honor for his assistance.

The powerful experience of raising public awareness about Bosnia and helping the victims of that tragedy led to Islam's reconsideration of how his music could be put to use more broadly in educating people about Islam and in providing a cultural defense for Muslims in the face of Western media and cultural empires. He founded his own music label, Mountain of Light (see also JOSHUA SALAAM), to produce C.D.s and cassettes geared toward projecting an Islamic cultural vision. Using only vocals and percussion, he began recording again in 1993 with a musical *sirah*, or biography of the Prophet Muhammad. The two-C.D. set, *The Life of the Last Prophet*, released in 1995, was his first album in seventeen years. It earned him a mass following in the Muslim world and reached no. 1 in Turkey. Other productions under this label include *I Have No Cannons That Roar*, *Faith*, *Bismillah* (In the Name of God), and *In Praise of the Last Prophet*. One of his best-known new albums is *A is for Allah*, a two-C.D. album of children's Islamic music based on the twenty-eight-letter Arabic alphabet that is intended to be both educational and entertaining. Islam wrote the album with the goal of providing children with a practical means of learning about and loving God, as well as the fundamental teachings of Islam, through the most basic methods of education.

Islam has continued to donate his royalties to charity, particularly those supporting children, and started a charity of his own, Small Kindness. He has used his royalties and musical talents to support Muslims in Bosnia and Kosovo in the aftermath of the genocides in both places (see also MUSTAFA CERIC and IBRAHIM RUGOVA), particularly orphans and destitute families, and to provide support for building new homes for the victims of a massive earthquake in Turkey. In 2000, he released *The Very Best of Cat Stevens* for charity, earning his first gold record in more than twenty years.

Islam also proved to be a powerful voice in the aftermath of the 9/11 tragedies. Believing he had a responsibility to condemn the terrorists for their destruction of life and property, hijacking of the religion of Islam, and division of humanity, he publicly denounced terrorists and extremists for engaging in blind acts of irreligious hatred, rather than proclaiming the love and harmony Islam is supposed to stand for. He called for aid to the people of Afghanistan and called upon Christians not to pollute their faith by engaging in retaliation. Reminding the world of atrocities committed elsewhere, particularly in Bosnia, he called upon all of humanity to respond to these terrorist acts by breaking down the barriers of prejudice, ending the cycles of violence, reaching out to innocent people everywhere who suffer from war, oppression, and starvation, and carrying out deeds of charity and compassion. He made his own contribution by releasing a four-C.D. collection of his work ranging from 1965 through 1997 and including works from eleven albums – *The Cat Stevens Box Set* – on October 30, 2001.

He donated the majority of the royalties to the September 11th Fund to help victims, their families, and the communities affected by the attacks. The remainder of the royalties were given to orphans and homeless families in underdeveloped countries. He also donated personal items to be auctioned on eBay to raise money for the victims of 9/11.

Islam has noted that the idealism in which he grew up during the 1960s and 1970s has not died. He remains hopeful that the world will become more peaceful and will end war and destruction. He believes that he has a responsibility both as a Muslim and as a human being to contribute to world peace and to bring healing to countries torn by war and tragedy. During a trip to South Africa in 2003, he re-recorded his song "Peace Train," his first recorded secular pop song in more than twenty-five years, to call for a peaceful solution to the world's problems, making a further contribution by establishing a medical center in Johannesburg for A.I.D.S. patients.

Further reading

"Cat Stevens to Donate to Sept. 11 Charities," PR Newswire, September 28, 2001
"Fame, Fortune? No More, Thanks," *Rolling Stone* magazine, June 20, 1981
Fong-Torres, Ben. "Cat Stevens Out of a Bag," *Rolling Stone*, April 1, 1971
Halasa, Malu. "The Cat That Got the Koran," *Harpers & Queen* magazine, October 1, 1996
Islam, Yusuf. "Biography," www.catstevens. com
—— "Formal Statement on the Rushdie Affair," press release, March 2, 1989
—— "How I Came To Islam," press release, January 1, 1985
—— "Islam Sings," in *Taking Back Islam: American Muslims Reclaim their Faith*, ed. Michael Wolfe and the Producers of Beliefnet. Emmaus, PA: Rodale Inc. and Beliefnet, Inc., 2002
—— "Searchlighting Islam," *Mountain of Light*, October 18, 2001
Paton, John. "Islam Gives Rock Singer New Start," *Sunday Sun*, March 15, 1981
Plummer, Mark. "CAT – Interview," *Melody Maker*, January 22, 1972
Stevens, Cat. *The Great Songs of Cat Stevens.* London: Music Sales Ltd., 1994
"Yusuf Islam," www.cnn.com/2003/SHOW-BIZ/Music/10/09/malaysia.yusuf.ap/index. html
www.catstevens.com
www.yusufislam.org.uk

Lobna Ismail (b. 1962)

Founder and executive director of Connecting Cultures, Incorporated, and expert in diversity awareness training, Lobna Ismail has also developed school programs to help children respect difference and respond to bullying.

Lobna (Luby) Ismail was born on April 10, 1962, in Lafayette, IN, to Egyptian parents who emigrated to the United States to pursue their doctorates. Ismail and her two brothers were raised in Lake Alfred, FL, where her father worked at a research center.

Ismail describes Lake Alfred as a small town in central Florida where hers was the only Muslim family. Despite widespread negative stereotypes of Arabs at this time, the family was frequently invited to local churches and social clubs to speak about Egypt, the Arab–Israeli conflict, and Islam. Growing up during the end of the segregation era, Ismail recalls her classmates having been puzzled by the brown color of her skin, uncertain if she was black or white. Her best friends were Evangelical Christians who shared her love of God, desire to do good in society, belief in being religiously and spiritually conscious, and abstinence from alcohol, drugs, and dancing. Her personal experience of bridge-building between religions and cultures had a profound impact that inspired her career.

Although happy in her home town, Ismail was always aware of being part of a minority. A trip to Egypt to meet her extended family when she was fourteen years old marked her first experience of being a member of the majority. The experience of looking like everyone else, sharing the same dietary habits, and observing the same holidays was so powerful that she demanded the right to live in Egypt with her grandparents. She spent tenth grade in Egypt, learning about life in Islamic, Egyptian, and Arab culture. She returned to the United States determined to study international relations and find a way to help Egypt.

Ismail attended the American University in Washington, DC, where she completed a bachelor's degree and met her future husband, Alexander Kronemer. Torn between the Islamic culture she had learned at home and the more liberal college environment she encountered, Ismail looked to Kronemer as a big-brother figure. Although Kronemer graduated and left A.U. before Ismail, the two reconnected in 1985 while Ismail was completing a master's degree in intercultural relations at Wellesley College. The couple married after Kronemer's conversion to Islam. They have two sons.

Motherhood marked a major turning point in Ismail's life. Although her passion for understanding culture and diversity, communication, and building relations had not changed, she wanted to spend time with her children. Realizing that the only requirements for operating a business successfully were a computer and a telephone, she decided that the best way to maximize her time with the children while maintaining a career was by working from home. Connecting Cultures was the result.

Connecting Cultures was founded to fill the demand for cultural and diversity training and awareness that accompanied the push for businesses to "go global." Believing that awareness of diversity and appreciation of cultural differences are essential to communicating, working, and competing successfully, both domestically and internationally, Connecting Cultures helps clients understand, build,

and maintain relationships by addressing the fears and prejudices that arise from lack of information, misinformation, and failure to accommodate, understand, and tolerate difference. The company's major product is human resource training through a multidimensional approach to intercultural exchanges that teaches employees how to work across differences of culture, ability, race, religion, and gender. Specialized in Islamic and Arab cultural awareness, Connecting Cultures has provided training to federal and state agencies, private corporations, non-profit organizations, and educational institutions. It also provides expert commentary to the media, special events, and conferences.

From its inception, Connecting Cultures has been a partnership between Ismail and Kronemer. As the company's website notes, Kronemer brings the "Head" and depth of knowledge to the business, while Ismail brings the "Heart" – the real-life experiences of prejudice, stereotypes, and misinformation. Kronemer has won a number of writing awards, has published many newspaper and journal essays, and has appeared on radio and television as a commentator and in interviews. He also co-produced a film – *Muhammad: Legacy of a Prophet*, – that has been broadcast nationwide on P.B.S. (See also MICHAEL WOLFE.) Ismail brings experience in international cultural competency, cross-cultural communication, and Islamic awareness and cultural diversity. Like Kronemer, she is frequently cited by the national media and in international news programs.

For domestic programs, Ismail wears her hijab (head covering), using her appearance to help identify and break down stereotypes. Experience has taught her that people tend to think of a woman wearing a hijab as either a terrorist or someone who is uneducated and oppressed. Because she personally is none of those things, her appearance in hijab helps her to give her listeners a real-life example of an educated, successful Muslim woman with the expectation that their next encounter with a Muslim or Arab will lead them to remember her, rather than a stereotype. She also hopes that they will be willing to respond to hurtful remarks made by others by sharing their personal positive experience with Muslims. The physical challenges added by the multiple sclerosis with which she was diagnosed in 1996 have rendered her presentation even more powerful and have given her yet another perspective on what it means to live out diversity.

Ismail's international work has focused on pushing Middle Eastern companies to recognize their need to develop local managers and workers in order to create their own pool of global leaders and to decrease reliance on outsiders. She also encourages companies to be strategic in developing their visions and skills, particularly human resource training in intercultural exchanges.

Before 9/11, Connecting Cultures provided mostly corporate managerial training in cross-cultural diversity. However, 9/11 not only resulted in an exponential increase in demand for Connecting Cultures' services, but also a change in clientele, as police officers and government officials recognized their need for cultural sensitivity, knowledge, skills, and awareness to interface with Arabs and Muslims while pursuing investigations and interrogations. Post-9/11, Connecting Cultures' biggest client has been the Justice Department, which has contracted both training seminars and a twelve-minute video for law enforcers around the country. The aftermath of the war in Iraq also resulted in a need for increased cultural awareness for people going to Iraq to provide training for rebuilding the country.

Professionally, Ismail recognizes that 9/11 brought an unprecedented opportunity to teach about Islam and politics in the Middle East, encourage interfaith dialogue, and seek religious harmony. Although heartened by what she describes as the "concerted efforts" of both the U.S. government and companies to learn more about Islam and its message of peace and to end hate crimes, extremism, and prejudice, she was also saddened by the necessity of changing some of her presentation content. Before 9/11, she was able to shatter the image of Muslims as terrorists because Muslims and Arabs were not responsible for most of the terrorist acts committed in the U.S. Pre-9/11, the terrorist bombing in Oklahoma City was the worst act of domestic terrorism ever committed. Post-9/11, she has had to take the tough issues of terrorism and jihad head on.

At a personal level, Ismail has been both deeply touched by the outreach of members of other faiths to her and to other Muslims and deeply pained by the rising prejudice in many areas against Arabs and Muslims post-9/11. She questions whether civil rights and liberties will continue to exist for all Americans or just some of them, and recognizes the hard work ahead for American Muslims as they reclaim their hijacked faith.

Despite her busy work schedule, Ismail remains actively involved in the lives of her sons, and volunteers at their school at least once a week. Believing that children need a positive introduction to diversity at the earliest possible age and to learn to talk about prejudice and diversity, she developed a program called "Don't Laugh at Me," which provides children with tools to respond to someone who is making fun of them, allows them to practice their responses, and raises awareness of what it feels like to be on the outside, while instructing them never to laugh at another person's pain. Other school-related activities include her program "The Buddy System: One Friend at a Time," which was recognized by the National Association of International Educators in 1988, and her work for the advisory panel for *Global Visions*, a newsletter for high schools that enhances understanding of global diversity and cross-cultural communication. Ismail's volunteer work teaching about diversity and inclusion in the school system was rewarded in 1999 when she was selected as "Parent of the Year" by the National Multiple Sclerosis Society.

Ismail's work as a leader in the field of human resources and as a leading voice on the issues of Islamic awareness and religious diversity has won her both domestic and international acclaim. The author of two books, her 1997 initiative for "Building Bridges between Islam and America" received a grant from the Montgomery County Human Relations Commission. She has served as a protégé for Women Mentor Women and coordinated an art exhibition and auction for renowned Islamic calligrapher MOHAMED ZAKARIYA in 1995. She has served as a peace fellow for Seeds of Peace and as a Malone fellow in Middle East and Islamic studies for the National Council for U.S.–Arab Relations. She has been invited to speak at the Middle East Human Resources Conference in Bahrain in 2000 and 2001, at the Society of Human Resource Development's annual conference in 2000 and 2002, and at the Society for Human Resource Development's annual diversity conference in 1999 and 2001, and is a selected resource for the U.S. Saudi Arabian Business Council's Saudi Expert Guide.

Further reading

Baby, Soman. "Islam Drive Ends US Hate Crimes: Steps to Boost Awareness," *Gulf Daily News*, October 9, 2001

Britton-Warren, Claire. "They Mean Business," *Azizah* magazine, Winter 2002

"Development of Local Workers's Skills Important," *Bahrain Tribune*, October 6, 2000

La Corte, Rachel. "Connecting Cultures Group Hopes 'to Open People's Minds, Hearts,'" Associated Press, June 27, 2003

"Luby Ismail: Mother of the Year," National Multiple Sclerosis Society, *Update* newsletter, National Capital Charter, Spring 2000

Interview with the author, October 30, 2003

www.connecting-cultures.net

J

Kevin James (b. 1954)

Supervising Fire Marshal for the Fire Department of New York (retired), civil rights activist, and advocate for fire-safe cigarette legislation, Kevin James has won numerous awards for his community service and activism.

Kevin James was born in 1954 in Brooklyn, NY. His father, Walter, was of African-American and Native American descent and was raised Roman Catholic. His mother, Jeanne, was Jewish. James' parents married at a time when interracial marriages were not accepted and his father might have faced lynching for marrying a white woman had they married outside of New York. Although neither of his parents were religious, James recalls that they instilled strong ethics and values in their children and encouraged them to explore or ignore religion as they desired and at their own pace.

Growing up in a world filled with labels and racial identities, James recalls being uncertain of his place and identity as a child, particularly because people could not determine his racial heritage on the basis of his appearance. Some people thought it was acceptable to insult African-Americans in his presence because he didn't look "black." In an attempt to relate to different parts of his heritage during high school, he tried to grow an Afro and adopted Native American beadwork and a headband. Religiously, he became interested in Judaism when he was told that having a Jewish mother made him Jewish. However, when the same people who welcomed him into the Jewish community made offensive generalizations about African-Americans and lost interest in James upon learning of his own African-American heritage, his initial impression of acceptance and belonging was quickly shattered.

From his parents, James learned the importance of the only racial label that mattered: "human." He also learned from their example how to respond positively and productively to the discrimination that accompanied his racial heritage. Rather than simply being angry about injustices their families had experienced, such as the loss of some of his mother's relatives in the Holocaust, or focusing strictly on the negatives, such as the genocide and assimilation forced on Native Americans and the policy of keeping the African slave population ignorant, separate, and identifiable in order to exploit their labor, James' parents taught him that he had an obligation to fight intolerance, hatred, and oppression through activism on the basis of principle. They particularly instilled in him the moral obligation to speak out against injustice, regardless of who it is committed against. Religiously, James learned from his parents that, although racial and religious hatred are typically rooted in economic and political factors, such hatred is often supported and encouraged by religion. It was for this reason that James' father had rejected religion rooted in love for God in favor of love for his fellow human beings. He taught James that love of humanity should be carried out by social activism. It was this dedication to love and service of humanity that ultimately led James to Islam.

Both of James' parents were strong social and community activists. His mother routinely picketed for neighborhood safety issues and needed improvements, including the establishment of public libraries in underserved areas. His father, recognizing the difficulty of obtaining a quality education for many African-Americans, taught math as a volunteer. Through example, they taught their children to question and look beyond the superficial and to value the importance of the consistency between words and actions. James later discovered this message in Islam's emphasis on individual sincerity in action, struggle against personal hypocrisy, and purity of intent.

James recalls that his parents' activism did not come without cost. His father's work as a union organizer and his participation in strikes led to hardship during the McCarthy era. Although he was trained as an electrical engineer, the F.B.I. considered him a troublemaker and frequently visited his employers. He often found himself without a job, literally overnight. Unable to find engineering work, he opened a T.V. repair shop. Although times were difficult, James recalls that his family always had enough to eat, a roof over their heads, and clean clothes. Most importantly, they retained their dignity.

James completed his high-school education at Stuyvesant High School in 1972. He then took some courses in math and science at John Jay College and Brooklyn College while working in the motion-picture industry doing construction work as a member of Local 52, Motion Picture Studio Mechanics Union (Grip). When he was twenty-one, he decided that he needed to become more focused and find a way of serving people and giving something back to his community. He joined the Coast Guard from 1975 to 1977.

During his tenure in the Coast Guard, James sought spiritual truth while striving to live in conformity with spiritual principles. He initially explored Christianity, but soon began reading the Quran. Struck by the consistency between the teachings of the Quran and his upbringing, particularly the emphasis on sincerity, decency, equality, membership within the universal community of all of humanity based on faith in God rather than race or nationality, caring for the underprivileged and disadvantaged, and the responsibility to fight oppression and work for social justice, James converted to Islam in 1977 and joined the Nimatullahi Sufi order.

After completing his service in the Coast Guard, James returned to the motion-picture industry. In 1981, he joined the Fire Department both as a career change and as a way to make a constructive, positive contribution to society. For James, being a firefighter was more than just a steady-paying job; it was a calling. He liked the idea of saving lives, self-sacrifice, and helping others as a means of carrying out his Islamic ideals. He also enjoyed the physical and mental challenges, which he met through running, martial-arts training, and pursuit of merit-based promotions. James served as a firefighter for four years with the Manhattan Ladder Company 12 in Chelsea, NY. After a series of promotional exams, he became a fire marshal in 1985, adopting full police powers to conduct arson investigations. Although firefighting had been more physically dangerous, James found fire marshaling to be more stressful due to the criminal investigations and difficulty of leaving his work at work. He nevertheless became a certified fire inspector, Level II N.F.P.A., in 1988. His hard work, heroism, and determination as a criminal investigator were recognized with several merit awards: F.M.B.A. Class III in 1989 and Class B in 1989 and 1993.

The mainstay of James' work as a fire marshal was related to the epidemic of crack cocaine in New York City. The majority of fires he investigated had either been deliberately set as part of territorial disputes or were accidentally caused by people high on drugs, typically because a lit cigarette ignited something else. It was at this time that James began lobbying for "fire-safe cigarettes," which are cigarettes that do not cause fires either because they self-extinguish or because they do not burn hot enough to cause a fire. Congressional studies had already shown that the manufacture of such cigarettes was possible, but the manufacturers had chosen not to follow through with the development. At this time, non-fire-safe cigarettes were the largest cause of accidental fire fatalities not only in New York City, but also throughout the United States, causing approximately a thousand deaths annually with thousands more critically injured and disfigured from smoke inhalation and burns. They were also responsible for several billions of dollars' worth of property damage and medical expenses. James believed that fire-safe cigarettes should be mandatory. He was particularly disgusted by insider documents revealing that Philip Morris had successfully manufactured a fire-safe Marlboro cigarette around 1987, but had shelved the research until "public pressure builds unduly." James found this stance unconscionable in the face of the lives, injuries, and property that could have been spared, asserting the depravity of continuing to market a dangerous product simply for the sake of profit.

James joined forces with State Assemblyman Pete Grannis, Andrew McGuire from the Trauma Foundation in San Francisco, Russ Haven from the New York Public Interest Group, and Chris Becker, a chaplain with the Firefighter's Association, State of New York (F.A.S.N.Y.). Grannis had been pressuring New York State for fire-safe cigarette legislation since the early 1980s and, along with McGuire, convinced Congress to study the issue in 1984. James joined the effort by writing about how fires could be avoided and by publicly identifying elected officials who were complicit in allowing these fires to occur. He also wrote numerous commentary pieces on public safety and civil rights issues that appeared in major print media and staged several press conferences that appeared in major media outlets. The turning point came the week before Christmas of 1998 when three firefighters, Chris Bopp, James Bohan, and Lt. Joseph Cavalieri, were killed in a cigarette-related fire in Brooklyn. James credits the courage of Cavalieri's widow, Debbie, in setting aside her grief to join the coalition of firefighters and public safety organizations in pushing through the New York State Fire-Safe Cigarette Act, the nation's first fire-safe cigarette legislation, which was passed in 2000 and went into effect in June 2004. Other states and the federal government have also started looking into fire-safe cigarette legislation. James' contribution to the passing of this historic legislation was recognized through the F.D.N.Y. African-American Heritage Society's Community Service Award in 2000 and an Achievement Award from the Federation of African-American Civil Service Organizations in 2001.

In the midst of the fire-safe cigarette lobbying, James made other contributions to the F.D.N.Y. He founded the department's K-9 Accelerant Detection Unit in 1994 and was a member of the department's boxing team. He became a supervising fire marshal in 1995 after ranking first in a promotional exam. He also continued his professional education with courses on the Reid Interviewing Technique (1994), an F.B.I. Forensics Symposium (1995), leadership classes with the New York State Office of Fire Prevention and Control (N.Y.S. O.F.P.C.) at Camp Smith, NY (1997), the F.B.I. Photography School (1997), and the F.B.I. National Academy for law-enforcement officers in Quantico, VA, from which he graduated in 1999.

James also continued with his social activism, fighting discriminatory practices in the Fire Department. In 1997, he convinced the F.D.N.Y. to include a stipulation to implement objective criteria in the Bureau of Fire Investigations for training, transfers, appointments, and special job assignments. That year he joined with other Muslims serving in the Fire Department to form the Islamic Society of Fire Department Personnel for the dual purposes of breaking negative stereotypes of Muslims in America and serving as an interface between Muslim employees, the Fire Department, and the growing Muslim community in New York City. James also won the right for a Muslim chaplain and a prohibition against fire inspections of mosques and Muslim schools on Friday, the Muslim holy day. James' activism led him to join the Council on American–Islamic Relations (C.A.I.R.), a national civic rights advocacy group for Muslims. One of the original organizers of the New York office of C.A.I.R., he served as its director of government relations. He received C.A.I.R.'s Islamic Community Service Award in 2001.

One of James' most difficult days on the job was September 11, 2001, the day the Twin Towers of the World Trade Center were attacked and destroyed by terrorists claiming to act in the name of "Islam." James arrived on the scene about half an hour after the second tower collapsed. Surrounded by destruction that he compared to the Holocaust, he commented, "The abuse of religion to justify murder, brutality, and discrimination deeply offends me, no matter what the source." In the aftermath, James became more adamant about the need for dialogue and determination of other than violent ways to deal with problems and frustrations, noting that positions of hatred and intolerance tend to become entrenched when people stop talking to each other and become fixed in their own positions. He also became actively involved in protesting the erosion of constitutional and civil rights that followed 9/11, particularly with respect to racial profiling, the detention of Muslims without due process, detainee rights, and employment discrimination.

James retired from his position as supervising fire marshal in 2002 after twenty years of service to the Fire Department to embark on a new public-service career. In 2002–2003, he was one of ten community activists chosen as a Revson fellow at Columbia University. James had initially planned to take journalism classes, but became interested in the law school. Inspired by his classes in mediation, negotiation, and employment discrimination, he applied to the law school and was accepted for the fall 2004 class to pursue public interest law. His twenty years of experience in analyzing and identifying issues, as well as working with the district attorney in legal cases, have given him practical experience in the studies he is now approaching from a more theoretical perspective.

James remains a long-term advocate of civil rights, interfaith tolerance, and fire-safety legislation. In 2002, he was featured in the P.B.S. documentary *Muhammad: Legacy of a Prophet* (see also MICHAEL WOLFE). He has continued with his lobbying, including collaborating with the N.Y.C. Department of

Health and other tobacco control advocates to ensure that New York State implements the strongest possible standards for fire-safe cigarettes without delay. He has also worked with the Latino Workers' Center in lobbying for comprehensive immigration reform.

Further reading

"Kevin James," www.columbia.edu/cu/revson/bio02-03/james.htm
James, Kevin. "My Journey in Islam," www.pbs.org/muhammad/lt_essays.shtml
Interview with the author, November 28, 2003

Fatima Jibrell (b. c. 1950)

Recipient of the 2002 Goldman Environmental Prize and an activist who seeks to empower women and youth, Fatima Jibrell has fought against the forces of environmental and political destruction in Somalia to provide her country with a sustainable vision for the future.

Fatima Jibrell was born in what was then British Somaliland around 1950. Like seventy percent of the Somali population, Jibrell's parents were nomadic pastoralists who moved the family and their livestock constantly in search of water and grasslands. Each year, Jibrell's family migrated on foot with their livestock from their village on the coast of the Gulf of Aden over the mountains and into the grassland of the interior. Her family dried and smoked fish to be used for barter for other items, such as clothing and other types of food, rather than for money.

Jibrell's memories of her childhood environment include pulling the sand apart along the coastline and finding water close to the surface and mountains filled with springs, flowers, bees, and a variety of birds and wild animals. When she was very small, her mother tethered her to the family tent with a long rope in order to prevent her from wandering off,

getting lost in the tall grass, and potentially eaten by a lion or cheetah. Jibrell recalls hearing lions roar outside of the family tent at night.

When Jibrell was around five or six years old, her father moved to the United States. Her mother refused to move with him. Instead, she and Jibrell moved to town where Jibrell was enrolled at a private school. Jibrell's mother paid her school fees by traveling by boat to Yemen and India to trade dried, smoked fish for clothing, which she then brought back to Somalia, transported to the border with Ethiopia, and sold.

Jibrell was sent to her father in the United States to attend high school. After completing high school, she returned to Somalia, where she worked for the government, earned a degree from the Somali Institute of Public Administration, and married. She eventually returned to the United States with her husband and five daughters. She became a naturalized U.S. citizen and earned a B.A. in English from the University of the District of Columbia and an M.A. in community organizing, policy, and planning from the University of Connecticut's School of Social Work.

In the early 1990s, Jibrell decided to return to Somalia which was engulfed in conflict following the collapse of the central government. Warlordism had taken over, and violence and fighting had spread throughout the country as guns proliferated with no responsible institution to control the influx of arms or to safeguard the people. In addition, the environment had been devastated by a combination of long-term drought and human-made circumstances. The grassy, flowered, and water-filled land of Jibrell's youth had been replaced by expanding desertification. The collapse of the central government had been followed by the collapse of the traditional Somali economy, which was based on livestock. Rift Valley Fever had entered Somalia and became so widespread by

2000 that the Gulf states, which had previously been the major buyers, banned the purchase of Somali livestock. At the same time, these states had increased their demand for charcoal, which became Somalia's new "black gold." Wealthy entrepreneurs from Saudi Arabia, Yemen, and the United Arab Emirates sponsored massive logging in Somalia to meet the demand for fuel, including Somalia's last remaining equatorial rain forest. Charcoal was made by cutting down and burning Somalia's acacia trees, aged anywhere between fifty and five hundred years, with the tall grass of the grasslands serving as fuel for the charcoal kilns.

The result was disastrous for Somalia's environment. The loss of grass meant a lack of fodder for livestock. The destruction of the acacia trees not only resulted in massive deforestation, but also in the loss of the plants and animals previously sustained by the trees, as well as the grasslands which depended on the forests for their existence. As the forests, trees, and grass were cleared, the accompanying water resources dried up, resulting in the further loss of habitat. Animals such as lions, cheetahs, and elephants disappeared, as did many of the species of birds and bees that had relied on the forests for their livelihood. With the loss of animal life came the departure of the dung beetles that had played a critical role in the dissemination of animal droppings and the creation of new soil capable of sustaining and promoting plant life. With nothing left to keep the water in the land, the once-fertile soil had turned to blowing dust and desert. Without adequate water supplies, the human population also suffered. Children, pregnant women, and the elderly began to die in abnormally large numbers due to dehydration.

Deforestation was not the only environmental problem. The coastlines were also affected. Somalia is home to the second-largest coastline in Africa, making fish a potentially important food source

for people. However, with no central government capable of patrolling and policing Somalia's coastlines and waters, corporations moved in to exploit the fishing resources while destroying the marine environment, including the reefs. Ships began to flush their cleaning systems onto Somalia's coast so as to avoid paying their own coasts or port systems. Toxic waste was also dumped into the waters off Somalia. The last time Jibrell ventured into the ocean, she came out with toxic patches of blue, green, and black on her skin that took six months to remove. In the meantime, so many dead fish have washed onto Somalia's shores that the people have stopped fishing and eating fish altogether due to fears of being poisoned, limiting yet another food resource for the Somali people at a time when the previous mainstay of the food supply, cattle, was no longer sustainable.

Jibrell was driven to action by the environmental and human crises she encountered upon her return. Having known the value and use of the grasslands and marine resources as a child and having had personal experience of the symbiotic relationship between the environment and the Somali people, she was determined to stop the destruction. An additional human crisis also loomed as many Somalis were forced to leave Europe and the Gulf countries where they had been living as immigrant workers and illegal immigrants and return to Somalia – a country that could no longer sustain even their most basic human needs because of the exploitation and destruction of the environment that had occurred.

Believing that the environment was the key to resolving Somalia's problems because it is critical to the Somali way of life, Jibrell focused on the recovery of the environment and the natural resources it provides. The major obstacle she encountered was the warlords who sent armed youth to protect the charcoal manufacturers. Jibrell set ending charcoal exports as her first goal, asking Gulf countries to cease importing charcoal while pressing for domestic legislation banning charcoal exports. She also worked at the grass-roots level to educate people about the damage done by charcoal production and to prevent young people from joining the warlords. Investigation of the youth situation revealed that producing charcoal and carrying guns tended to be the only viable job options for the young. Although many of the youth interviewed stated that they would prefer to have other jobs, there were no other jobs available. It was at this time that Jibrell turned the attention of two organizations she had founded to deal with the charcoal and violence issues, the Horn of Africa Relief and Development Organization and the Resource Management Somali Network, to community building and the creation of alternative opportunities for youth.

Horn Relief was founded in 1991 in response to the humanitarian crisis and civil war engulfing Somalia. Although initially dedicated to assisting displaced persons and refugees in flight, the organization soon began to work to establish long-term peace and development strategies based on a community-led integrated social movement led by youth to address social, political, and environmental issues. Jibrell has consistently tied together broader issues of women's political participation, girls' education, youth leadership, and animal and human health as integral parts of managing the environment.

Horn Relief began by addressing the low literacy (under six percent for Somali women and only thirty-five percent for the entire country) and school attendance (less than twelve percent of all Somali youth enrolled in primary education with less than half of those actually attending) levels that prevented meaningful development in Somalia. Horn Relief runs three major education programs – Pastoral Youth Leadership (P.Y.L.), Preparing Girls for P.Y.L., and Women's

Literacy – to train women and young people in literacy and leadership skills and to promote democracy, gender equality, human rights, social justice, self-reliance, and self-esteem. Graduates of these programs are expected to become involved in the political and peace processes in Somalia at both the grass-roots and national levels.

Under Jibrell's leadership, Horn Relief spearheaded the response to the charcoal crisis by training a youth team to organize awareness campaigns about the irreversible damage of unrestricted charcoal production. A peace march was held in 1999 to stop the "charcoal wars." That same year, the government banned the export of charcoal. Horn Relief also promoted the use of solar cookers to reduce domestic demand for charcoal and taught community groups, particularly youth and women, to build small rock dams to slow the runoff during Somalia's brief rainy season and to nourish vegetation as a practical means of slowing the spread of desertification. Horn Relief also established the Buran Rural Institute (B.R.I.) to bring together women, men, youth, elders, and nomads to focus on peace, political participation, and natural resource issues. In May 2001, B.R.I. organized a camel caravan of young people with tents and equipment to travel through nomadic areas to educate people about careful use of fragile natural resources, livestock management, health care, and peace.

Jibrell's other major organization, Resource Management Somali Network (R.M.S.N.), brought together environmental groups throughout the Horn of Africa and was instrumental in creating the Women's Coalition for Peace to counter the political crisis in northeast Somalia. Much of Jibrell's work has focused on developing women's leadership due to the critical role played by women as the backbones of communities and custodians of the environment, despite the patriarchal structure of Somali society. Jibrell believes that the continued refusal to give women power at the community decision-making level was a major contributing factor to Somalia's problems. According to traditional pastoral custom, decisions are made by men under a cherry tree and women exert only indirect power by influencing men at home. Nevertheless, women are responsible for caring for children, the elderly, the handicapped, and the livestock, while men are free to leave at will. Jibrell has argued, with some success, for an empowerment of women in the decision-making processes that reflects their social responsibilities. In many villages, women have begun to attend the meetings under the cherry trees and are demanding a voice, while men have started to listen to women's ideas. Nevertheless, international aid programs and organizations, including the United Nations, have supported the traditional patriarchal structure as the appropriate format for solving Somalia's problems. Jibrell has criticized this approach because it encourages men to retain power and continue to build on past mistakes. She has called instead for a politics of inclusion that puts men and women to work together to find solutions to Somalia's problems.

Jibrell has called for continuing international support for Somalia, but in a less intrusive way that allows Somalis to identify their own problems and determine their own solutions. She believes that the most important contributions the international community can make are to refuse to provide arms to Somalia, refuse to allow other countries to poach on or destroy the few resources that remain in Somalia, end toxic waste dumps along the Somali coastline, and end forcible returns of immigrants to Mogadishu, the most dangerous place in Somalia. Limitations on arms and weaponry, in particular, would help to end violence and warlordism in favor of empowering grassroots communities seeking to establish peace, institute effective government, and

heal the environment. Jibrell has also called for a limitation on foreign aid so as to pressure Somalis into doing things for themselves. She has noted, for example, that the free food drops sponsored by the World Food Program have actually harmed farmers and the economy because the proliferation of free food has killed the domestic market for Somali-grown agricultural products.

In 2002, Jibrell was awarded the Goldman Environmental Prize. The world's richest and most prestigious grass-roots environmental award at $125,000, the Goldman Prize annually recognizes one individual from each of six continents who has made extraordinary achievements in preserving the natural environment and whose work serves as a model for others working on environmental issues around the world. Jibrell received the prize for her work through Horn Relief to incorporate education, youth, cultural programs, and economic self-sufficiency into a program that promotes the long-term health and security of the environment.

Further reading

Amosu, Akwe. "One Woman's Fight to Rescue the Environment," January 13, 2003, allafrica.com/stories/printable/20031130987.html

Dye, Alexa. "Goldman's Grassroots Heroes," April 22, 2002, www.alternet.org/story.html?StoryID=12934

Martin, Glen. "Honoring Earth's Defenders: 8 Grassroots Environmentalists Awarded Goldman Prize," *San Francisco Chronicle*, April 22, 2002

allAfrica.com – website of All Africa Global Media for current news on Africa

www.enn.com – website of the Environmental News Network for current news on environmental issues

www.goldmanprize.org – home page of the Goldman Prize

www.hornrelief.org – website of Horn of Africa Relief and Development Organization

Pearce, Fred. "Female Intuition," interview with Fatima Jibrell, www.newscientist.com/opinion/opinterview.jsp?id=ns23505

K

Ismail Kadare (b. 1936)

An award-winning poet and novelist frequently nominated for the Nobel Prize in Literature, Ismail Kadare is a recognized master of Albanian literature, the only contemporary Albanian writer to achieve international acclaim, and one of the most important literary figures of the twentieth century.

Ismail Kadare was born in 1936 in the mountain town of Gjirokastra in southern Albania, near the border with Greece. The son of a civil servant, Kadare grew up during the occupation of Albania by Nazi Germany, fascist Italy, and the communist Soviet Union. He received his primary and secondary educations in his home town before going to the capital city of Tirana to study languages and literature at the faculty of history and philology at the University of Tirana where he received his teacher's diploma in 1956. He then headed to Moscow to study at the Gorky Institute of World Literature where he remained until 1960 when relations soured between Albania and the Soviet Union.

Albania broke away from the Soviet Union in 1961. It then broke relations with all other countries, including China, beginning a period of international isolation and virtual cultural standstill. It was in this environment that Kadare began to write and became the representative of a new generation of writers and a leading figure of Albanian culture.

Kadare was initially a poet. His first two poetry collections, *Youthful Inspiration* (1954) and *Dreams* (1957) demonstrated his talent and poetic originality. His third volume, *My Century* (1961), earned high acclaim and set the pace for the renewal of Albanian verse. His next collection, *What are these mountains thinking about* (1964), is considered one of the clearest expressions of Albanian self-image under the Enver Hoxha dictatorship, which has frequently been described as a reign of terror. For Albanians, Kadare's poetry reflected both the spirit of the times and a thematic diversity previously missing from Albanian poetry. One of his most important poetic contributions was his attention to love lyrics, a traditionally neglected genre of Albanian literature that Kadare infused with sincerity and candidness. He was widely admired among Albanian youth during the 1960s for his poetry. Both his poetic and later prose works remained influential throughout the 1970s and 1980s.

Although Kadare was a committed Marxist, he was opposed to totalitarianism and socialist realism. Throughout the 1960s, he criticized the Hoxha government only through subtle allegories, because of the regime's tendency to persecute its opponents. He was nevertheless recognized as its most prominent adversary, although some critics, including the president of the League of Albanian Writers and Artists, accused him of avoiding political discussions by cloaking them in history and folklore. Kadare briefly changed tactics in 1975 with the publication of a politically satirical poem that earned him a three-year ban on publishing.

Kadare turned his literary talent to prose writing in the early 1960s. His novels made him the most popular and undisputed master of Albanian literature. His first novel, *The General of the Dead Army* (1963), became one of his most famous prose works internationally. The novel tells the story of postwar Albania through the tale of an Italian general who visits the country after the occupation and World War II in order to dig up and repatriate the bones of soldiers who died there during the war. He is so immersed in his absurd and gruesome mission in Albania that he never realizes that he himself is dead.

Kadare's works also address social and cultural issues of concern to Albanians. *The Wedding* (1968) tells the story of a young peasant girl who escapes a traditional arranged marriage by working in a factory where she meets and marries a man she loves. Although the story broke important cultural traditions, it was well received. Another very popular novel, *Broken April* (1978), traced a violent, trans-generational family feud. Although the violence is ultimately overpowered by the discovery of poetry, literature, and brotherly love in the novel, the blood feud itself reflected one of Kadare's favorite themes – the effects of the past on the present. The novel was recognized as presenting timeless and universal themes similar to those of Greek tragedies and was turned into a Brazilian film called *Behind the Sun.*

Other novels addressed Albania's historical heritage. *The Castle* (1970) told the story of Albania's struggle against the Ottoman Turks, while *The Three-Arched Bridge* (1978) used the story of the construction of a new bridge across a river to depict the rivalries and jealousies that accompanied feudal society. In this novel, which has been compared to Umberto Eco's novel *The Name of the Rose*, the bridge serves as a metaphor for modernization and development as it is intended to serve as a connection between Europe and Asia and to make the crossing of an unpredictable and powerful river easier and more secure. The novel takes place in 1377 as the Ottoman Empire was expanding and conquered Albania. The story develops through events that occur during the bridge's construction – events that divide and ultimately shatter the population as a representation of the disruption brought to Albania in particular and to the Balkans in general by the Ottoman conquest.

Kadare's novels have also ventured into the political arena. He completed *Chronicle in Stone* (1971) while he was a delegate to the People's Assembly and had more freedom to travel and publish abroad. *The Palace of Dreams* (1981) was written as a political allegory of totalitarianism. The novel tells the story of a young man responsible for the selection, sorting, and interpretation of dreams of the imperial populace in order to discover the "master dream" predicting the overthrow of the ruler. The Albanian government was highly offended by the novel and banned it almost immediately after it was published. Most Albanians found it humorous.

Kadare and his family left Albania in October 1990 and applied for political asylum in Paris, France, where they have lived ever since. Ironically, Kadare left Albania only two months before the communist regime collapsed. Living in exile gave Kadare greater freedom to write, resulting in enormous productivity in both Albanian and French. Although he continued his critiques of the Enver Hoxha regime, such as in *The Pyramid* (1992), which mocked Hoxha's fondness for elaborate statues and the love of dictators in general for hierarchy, his novels written from exile contain a stronger sentiment of bitterness and disappointment than did the novels he wrote while living in Albania.

Kadare's literary works have been translated into more than twenty languages worldwide and have been published as a ten-volume collection in both Albanian- and French-language editions. His novel *The Concert* was named the best novel of 1991 by the French literary magazine *Lire*. Kadare has been honored with membership in the Academie Française for his literary achievements.

Further reading

Elsie, Robert. "Ismail KADARE," www.alba-nianliterature.co/html/authors/bio/kadare-i.html

—— *Studies in Modern Albanian Literature and Culture.* New York: Columbia University Press, 1996

Kadare, Ismail. *Broken April.* New York: Amsterdam Books, 1978

—— *The Castle.* N.p.: University Press of the Pacific, 1970

—— *Elegy for Kosovo: Stories.* N.p.: Arcade Books, 2000

—— *The File on H.*, trans. David Bellos. New York: Arcade Publishing, Inc., 1998

—— *The General of the Dead Army.* London: Harvill Press, 2002

—— *The Three-Arched Bridge.* N.p.: Arcade Books, 1997

"Kadare, Ismail," www.booksfactory.com/writers/kadare.htm

Serafin, Steven R., ed. *Encyclopedia of World Literature in the 20th Century.* 3 vols. London: St. James Press, 1999

Terpan, Fabienne. *Ismail Kadare.* Paris: N.p., 1992

www.albanianliterature.com – provides information about a variety of Albanian writers and works

www.booksfactory.com/writers – provides biographical information about a variety of writers

M. Farooq Kathwari (b. 1944)

President, chairman, and C.E.O. of Ethan Allen Interiors, M. Farooq Kathwari has been an activist for peace and independence for Kashmir since he was a teenager.

M. Farooq Kathwari was born in Srinagar, Kashmir, on August 16, 1944. When the British Empire left what was then India in 1947, it partitioned the country into India and Pakistan, leaving the valley of Kashmir that lies between the border mountain ranges divided between the two. Both countries have claimed sovereignty over Kashmir ever since, leading to decades of hostility, violence, and diplomatic failures between the two, as well as rising militant extremism in Kashmir.

Kathwari's father fought for self-determination for Kashmir. Kathwari followed his example by becoming an activist for independence during his student years at Kashmir University where he earned a B.A. in English literature and political science in 1965. When he was jailed for showing an American journalist around during the uprising, he realized that he would likely be jailed again in the future and decided to leave for the United States.

Kathwari supported himself by working at a small printing company in Brooklyn, NY, where he learned bookkeeping, accounting, and printing. At the same time, he attended New York University's business school. He tried to study economics and accounting, but neither one appealed to him. He preferred marketing because it resonated with his heritage and culture. Kathwari's grandfather and father had run an antique shop in Kashmir. Sensing an opportunity in his grandson to expand his sales into the United States, Kathwari's grandfather sent him several boxes of Kashmiri handicrafts and accessories to sell. Kathwari sold his products on consignment and sent the proceeds back to his grandfather in Kashmir. He completed his M.B.A. in international marketing in 1968, the same year he married his wife, Farida, by telephone because it was too dangerous to return to Kashmir.

After graduation, Kathwari worked on Wall Street for Bear Stearns and then for New Court Securities, starting as a clerk and working his way up to chief financial officer within a few years. At the same time, he continued his small family business of selling wall hangings and tapestries from Kashmir. Over time, he earned some big-name customers, including Ethan Allen and Bloomingdale's. Impressed by Kathwari's business acumen, the chairman of Ethan Allen asked Kathwari to work for him. Kathwari proposed a partnership instead. Ethan Allen invested and Kathwari Ethan Allen (K.E.A.) was born, with Kathwari as majority shareholder.

Kathwari became active in sales while learning Ethan Allen's business. Realizing that the best way to earn the loyalty and respect of the sales people was to help them become better themselves, he began to take store buyers with him on shopping trips to China, Hong Kong, and India, where he helped them discover exotic accessories that would make them look visionary back in the U.S. Within several years, Ethan Allen offered to buy out the joint venture and again asked Kathwari to join Ethan Allen. Kathwari agreed to sell out his share of the business, in exchange for the chairmanship of Ethan Allen. Kathwari became president of Ethan Allen in 1985.

Kathwari took over as president at a time when Ethan Allen needed reinventing. When the company first opened in 1932, it sold early colonial American reproduction furniture. During the 1960s, it had been a leader in moving furniture sales out of department stores and into freestanding boutiques. However, by 1988, when Kathwari also became chaiman and C.E.O., Ethan Allen's sales and image had become stagnant. Not only was the company no longer growing, but it was still selling the same product line it had been selling since the 1930s.

Kathwari believed that the company needed to reinvent itself. He established an advisory group of about forty people, including retailers, manufacturers, and marketing associates, to develop ideas for solutions and a marketing plan to sell those ideas across the company. He then turned over ninety-nine percent of the senior staff and began solving problems individually. Noticing that the company advertised only four months out of the year, a time period that accounted for seventy percent of all sales, he instituted year-round advertising. He then cut delivery time from six months to four weeks, instituted the same delivery charge everywhere in the country, centralized the inventory, and created a national network of stores. These combined steps boosted sales while lowering costs.

As he was implementing the changes, Ethan Allen's parent company, Intervo, became the target of a hostile takeover. Intervo put Ethan Allen up for sale in 1989. Kathwari saw an opportunity not only for himself, but also for Ethan Allen's employees. He made a $357 million gamble on Ethan Allen's future, mortgaging his house, enlisting his management team, dealers, and employees in investing, and borrowing millions to buy the company. He offset the $330 million debt with $350 million in savings. At the same time, he changed half of the product line from colonial early American to contemporary, casual, and classic products. As consumers approved the new style, sales increased. The cash profits were used to pay back all of the debt.

Kathwari implemented his next major changes in 1993 when he took the company public on Wall Street and changed Ethan Allen's focus from selling individual furniture items to creating beautiful homes and decorating designs. Stores were changed to look more like homes or places where customers could visualize themselves living with furniture they could imagine buying. To support the concept of selling a look, Kathwari formed a team of design consultants who make free house calls to offer interior decorating advice. With more than three thousand design consultants working in more than three hundred stores and more than ten thousand employees, half of Ethan Allen's current business comes from house calls.

In 2000, Kathwari introduced another change – the simple finance plan – to make products more affordable and accessible. The plan allows customers to make their purchases through a monthly payment plan, making the purchase of an entire room at once affordable. The provision of a budget and more than $600 million in approved credit lines led to customers spending an average of fifty percent more. Ethan Allen's sales and profits continued to rise, even in 2001, the worst year in decades for the furniture industry. Kathwari reinvented the business again in 2002 not only by revamping product lines and stores, but also by introducing a media line that includes a television show and a book series.

The aftermath of the 9/11 tragedies initially had a negative impact on Ethan Allen, as store traffic was greatly reduced. However, over the long term, Ethan Allen benefited from the national period of cocooning that followed as people decided to spend more time at home with their families and focused on creating comfortable, hospitable, and inviting home decors, rather than spending money on travel or cars.

As a personal philosophy, Kathwari believes that there is more to business than profit and that companies and their leaders have an obligation to set a moral precedent by recognizing human rights and striving for justice while conducting business. Kathwari routinely recognizes dedicated and long-serving employees and insists on fairness for his dealers in having equal access to and standard pricing for merchandise, despite the opposition he encountered from larger dealers accustomed to receiving discounts for their orders. Kathwari also believes in living religious tolerance. Although he is Muslim, he has personally hosted Christmas dinners for his employees, using the opportunity to share with his Christian co-workers the Quranic history of the virgin conception and birth of Jesus. After 9/11, he put a full-page notice in the New York *Times* and the *Washington Post* calling on American leaders to continue to work for unity between people of all faiths.

Noting that a C.E.O.'s job is to manage conflict resolution, inspire creative thinking, and find solutions to difficult problems, Kathwari has encouraged C.E.O.s to take their businesses and expertise to war-torn territories. His personal cause is bringing peace and independence to Kashmir not only because of his personal connection to the region but also because he feels a personal responsiblity to resolve the escalating violence and influx of jihad fighters into the region. His oldest son, Irfan, left the United States for Afghanistan in 1992 to fight with the *mujahidin*, over the objections of his family. Having been raised on his parents' stories of the psychological frustration faced by refugees and the constant loss of people to needless death, he believed that he had a responsibility to help others in their fight for independence. Irfan was killed in a mortar attack in one of the final battles for Kabul.

Kathwari was initially bitter about the death of his son, but decided to channel his grief into working to resolve the conflict that had claimed the lives of more than thirty-five thousand people, or one percent of the total population, since 1989 when Kashmir's renewed call for autonomy from India sparked a rebellion. Hoping to spare other parents the agony of losing a child by promoting peace, he dedicated himself to ending the death and destruction in Kashmir through the formation of the Kashmir Study Group in 1996.

The Kashmir Study Group is a group of about twenty-five academics, diplomats, and politicians who bring together Indian, Pakistani, and Kashmiri perspectives on the conflict in Kashmir in order to promote dialogue toward finding a "peaceful, honorable and feasible solution" for Kashmir. The dialogue is based on three features: the equality of all participants and lack of coercion on any of them in formulating opinions; having all participants respond with empathy to the views of others; and bringing forward people's deep-rooted assumptions in order to overcome misunderstandings. Although the dialogue began with the old intractable and impractical arguments, over time the participants began to look for ways to be more practical and willing to compromise in order to find viable options by listening to various parties in the conflict, sharing ideas, looking for common ground, exploring recommendations, and urging action toward resolution of the conflict. They have published three fact-finding reports that resulted in the proposed solution of self-rule for Kashmiris within either India or Pakistan according to the choice of the Kashmiri people. The group is highly regarded in diplomatic circles and by the U.S. government as a serious body trying to help all parties by introducing constructive ideas. However, because it is the initiative of private citizens, it has no political power to enforce its solutions.

Kathwari believes that the resolution of Kashmir is an international imperative not only because of the tremendous human suffering that includes the loss of two generations and the collapse of the economy, health, and educational institutions, but also because both India and Pakistan are now nuclear powers. Noting that the Indian subcontinent is home to a fifth of the world's population, he has demanded an end to warfare and an international commitment to the reconstruction of Kashmir. He has engaged in personal diplomacy to get meaningful dialogue started between the leaders of India and Pakistan in order to build their level of mutual confidence.

Kathwari is involved in the planning of an international peace park through the University of Vermont and is on the board of directors of H.O.N. Industries. A member of the Council on Foreign Relations and the Board of the National Retail Federation, he also serves as the president of the American Manufacturers' Association, director of the Western Connecticut University Foundation, director of Refugees International, director of the Institute for the Study of Diplomacy at Georgetown University, and trustee of the National Policy Association. He is also on the international board of trustees for the World Conference of Religions for Peace, the largest international coalition of representatives from the world's great religions dedicated to achieving peace and to mobilizing the moral and social resources of religious people to' address shared problems.

Further reading

Berfield, Susan. "At Ethan Allen, Selling Furniture and Tolerance," October 22, 2001, www.businessweek.com/magazine/content/01_43/b3754076.htm

Cho, Yoon and Lee Barney. "Meet the Street: Home is Where the Spending is," *Meet the Street*, November 27, 2001, www.thestreet.co/funds/meetthestreet/10004463.html

"Farooq Kathwari, C.E.O. of Ethan Allen, Redefines American Classic," *C.N.N. Pinnacle*, April 20, 2002, www.cnn.com/TRANSCRIPTS/0204/20/pin.00.html

Kathwari, Farooq. "C.E.O.'s Can Ease Strife," *Chief Executive*, December 2003, vol. 194, www.chiefexecutive.net/depts/ceoagenda04/194f.htm

—— " 'Kashmir is an Issue that Concerns the Entire World,': The Rediff Interview," www.rediff.com/news/2000/sep/15pmus9.htm

"Resume: M. Farooq Kathwari," www.businessweek.co/magazine/content/01_43/b3754078.htm

www.ethanallen.com – website of Ethan Allen Interiors

www.wcrp.org – website of World Conference of Religions for Peace

Merve Safa Kavakci (b. 1968)

Elected to the Turkish parliament in 1999, Merve Safa Kavacki became a symbol of the quest for religious freedom in Turkey when she was booed out of parliament and stripped of both her seat and her Turkish citizenship for wearing a headscarf.

Merve Safa Kavakci was born in 1968 in Ankara, Turkey. Her father was the dean of Islamic studies and her mother taught German literature at Ataturk University. Kavakci did not complete memorization of the Quran – the most basic element of Muslim religious education – until she was twenty-seven because of a government ban against teaching the Quran to children under the age of twelve. She completed her undergraduate education at Ankara College. She then attended medical school for two years before being dismissed for wearing a headscarf in 1988.

Kavakci wears her headscarf as a matter of personal choice. Although she has frequently commented that her professional life would be easier without it, religious conviction has made her insist on her right to protect her modesty in public as a sign of her religious values and personal dignity. Like her parents, she believes that neither governments nor men should be allowed to dictate how a woman should dress. Her father's support for a woman's right to choose whether to wear a headscarf resulted in him being forced to resign as dean. Her mother was similarly barred from the classroom over her decision to wear a headscarf.

To protest the government's denial of their right to practice their religion freely, Kavakci's family left Ankara for the United States. Kavakci enrolled in computer engineering studies at the University of Texas in Dallas and married an American man, entitling her to American citizenship, for which she applied. Divorced by the time she graduated,

Kavacki returned to Turkey and entered politics, serving first as the head of the Women's Commission for the Islamist Refah (Welfare) Party and then as the head of foreign affairs for the Islamist Virtue Party. Her work brought her to the attention of Turkey's first Islamist prime minister, Necmettin Erbakan.

Kavakci ran for election to parliament in 1999 wearing her headscarf. She was elected as the deputy from Istanbul – one of only three women among the 111 Virtue Party M.P.s elected that year. Although two had campaigned wearing headscarves, Kavakci was the only one who continued to wear it after the election, believing that she had both the right and the responsibility to be consistent in her self-representation to her constituents. Her wearing of the headscarf to the swearing-in ceremony at the National Assembly on May 2, 1999, made her a national figure of controversy.

Although Turkey's population is ninety-five percent Muslim, wearing any kind of religious dress or symbol is forbidden in public buildings, such as schools, universities, courts, and government offices. Wearing the headscarf to the National Assembly was therefore illegal. Kavakci's entrance was met with such loud protests by the deputies of the Democratic Left Party (D.S.P.) over her choice of dress that the swearing-in ceremony had to be delayed. She was booed and shouted out of the Assembly. The chaos forced the session into recess. In the aftermath, a campaign emerged to enforce a strict parliamentary dress code. Previously, the code had not specifically banned headscarves for members of parliament in the assembly chamber. It simply specified that female M.P.s were to wear a two-piece outfit and male M.P.s were to wear a tie and jacket.

Kavakci was denounced for her "provocative" act, accused of being an "extremist, subversive and radical fundamentalist" and charged with wearing her headscarf as a declaration of her intent to advocate Islamic rule in Turkey. Within hours, federal prosecutors sought to try her on charges of inciting religious hatred. An investigation was launched to determine whether she and her party had engaged in anti-secular activities. The country's chief prosecutor initiated legal actions to close down the Virtue Party. The media stationed itself in front of Kavakci's house and followed her when she went out. They also went to her children's school where they photographed other children booing her children after the police and media informed them that their mother had committed a crime against the state.

Such a vehement backlash over a woman's choice to dress modestly conflicts with standard Western characterizations of Turkey as the most secular, democratic, and progressive of Muslim-majority countries. While the West has been quick to criticize Saudi Arabia and Afghanistan under the Taliban for mandating women's dress as a violation of international human rights standards, such criticism of Turkey was not forthcoming over the systematic campaign to ban women from wearing headscarves in public places, a ban that has affected the majority of Turkish women.

Historically, headscarves were part of Turkish culture, particularly in rural areas. However, the program of modernization, Westernization, and secularization that was enacted in Turkey at the turn of the twentieth century by Kemal Ataturk led many to reject rural ways, including headscarves, as backward and old-fashioned. In the contemporary era, many women have redonned headscarves to show that Islam and modernity are not in conflict. The headscarf has therefore become a symbol for those contesting what is frequently referred to as "secular fundamentalism." Women across Turkey have engaged in acts of civil disobedience ranging from attempts to enter public spaces and register for university classes while wearing headscarves to staging sit-ins and hunger strikes. The authorities have responded to these peaceful actions and the rise of popular Islamic sentiments by brutally clamping down on religious expression. Women have been killed, attacked, imprisoned, and denied education over the headscarf issue. The government has charged them with committing crimes, including "attempting to overthrow the country's secular constitution," for wearing headscarves or demanding the right to wear them. When understood within this context, the Kavakci case takes on broader meaning as a reflection of major social and political debates about religious freedom and human rights.

Because three-quarters of all Turkish women wear headscarves, Kavakci has denounced legislation banning them from schools and universities as the prerogative of an elite minority, rather than an expression of the majority public will, that ultimately denies practicing religious women the right to be teachers, doctors, lawyers, engineers or students. She believes that her example of wearing the headscarf reflects the reality of the general population which deserves visible representation in parliament. Although she was offered use of a separate office to serve her term, she refused, believing that physical separation from the parliamentary chamber would have violated the purpose for which she was elected and set a dangerous precedent for the further exclusion of headscarf-wearing women from the public sphere. Kavakci remained adamant that both the Turkish constitution and international law guaranteed her the right to wear her headscarf as an expression of her individual freedom. She accused those who prevented her swearing-in of violating both the constitution and a variety of international human rights agreements to which Turkey is a signatory. Citing her right to wear the headscarf as a matter of human rights, women's rights, and religious freedom, she charged that wearing her headscarf to parliament was a test of democracy and religious tolerance in Turkey – a test that her fellow M.P.s clearly failed. Her arguments resonated throughout the Muslim world and inspired pro-Kavakci demonstrations throughout Turkey, Iran, and other Muslim countries.

Investigations by both the government and the media into Kavakci's actions at the swearing-in ceremony revealed that the headscarf ban reflected a broad trend of trying to oust Islamists from the political system altogether. As part of the media investigation, some Turkish newspapers claimed that Kavakci had made a speech at a conference in Chicago sponsored by the Islamic Committee for Palestine calling for "jihad" and asserting herself as part of the political wing of such a holy war. The President of Turkey used this claim to denounce Kavakci as an "agent provocateur" and suggested that she might have links to several outlawed Islamist groups. The papers also reported Kavakci's opposition to Turkey's desire to join the European Union, supposedly on the basis of the Islamic awakening in Turkey. Finally, the media announced that Kavakci held dual U.S.–Turkish citizenship, a fact that she had failed to report to the Turkish government. Her failure to do so made her election illegal. The ensuing scandal gave the government further ammunition for removing her from parliament.

On May 13, 1999, less than two weeks after the swearing-in ceremony, Kavakci's Turkish citizenship was revoked on the grounds that she had failed to report her dual citizenship. She immediately appealed her case to the European Court of Human Rights, declaring her fight to be a reflection of the broader struggle for democracy and religious freedom in Turkey. The Virtue Party denounced the revocation as politically motivated. Supporters expressed concern that stripping Kavakci of her citizenship was only the first step in stripping her of her M.P.

status – a position to which she had been democratically elected, but could not hold without her citizenship, even though she had been a citizen at the time of the election and the swearing-in ceremony.

In the aftermath, additional legislation to extend bans against religious expression in public life was passed, including a 2000 bill designed to purge all Islamists from government for infractions such as being married to a woman who wears a headscarf and a 2001 dress code requiring female civil servants to wear skirts and banning women from wearing trousers in the classroom. Critics singled out the 2000 legislation as evidence of Turkey's true nature as a military dictatorship, rather than a democracy, because it was forced into law by the president in order to bypass discussion in parliament. Critics point to voting patterns, the popularity of Islamist political parties, and general social trends reflecting popular support for greater public expression of Islam as evidence that the military push to maintain secularism in power represents a suspension of democracy and the marginalization of popular opinion.

In the end, Kavakci was stripped of her seat and banned from running for public office in Turkey for five years. The Speaker of the House ordered all information – including documentation of her election, her picture, and her name – removed from the official records. No one was chosen to replace her for her term. At the same time, the Virtue Party was outlawed for violating Turkey's strict separation of church and state. The other 110 Virtue deputies were removed from parliament and banned from politics for five years, despite the fact that Virtue had been the most popular party in Turkey in 1999.

Denied her seat in parliament, Kavakci returned to the United States where she worked as a Mason Fellow at Harvard University's John F. Kennedy School of Government. She currently lives in

Washington, DC, where she has continued to fight for human rights and religious freedom in Turkey. She plans to reenter politics in Turkey as soon as it is legally permissible for her to do so.

Further reading

Bangash, Zafar. "Turkey's Secular Fundamentalists Target Muslimah M.P. Hijab," *Crescent International*, May 16–31,1999

Islamic Human Rights Commission. "The Comprehensive Repression of Human Rights in Turkish Society," London, December 7, 2000

"Kavakci Loses her Turkish citizenship," *Turkish Daily News*, May 17, 1999

"Merve Kavakci in the Hot Seat," *Turkish Daily News*, Turkish Probe Issue 331, May 16, 1999

Sanders, Bob Ray. "One Woman who Stood her Ground," *Star-Telegram*, August 3, 2003

Secor, Laura. "Covering Law: The Headscarf that Infuriated Turkey's Rulers," *Boston Globe*, February 9, 2003

Transcript from Q&A session on C.N.N., February 5, 2002

"When Secularism Clashes with Freedom of Religion: Interview with M.P. Merve S. Kavakci," *Muslim Democrat*, vol. 2, no. 3, November, 2000

Aasma Khan (b. 1971)

Co-founder of and spokesperson for the American volunteer organization Muslims Against Terrorism (M.A.T.), Aasma Khan is an attorney who defends human rights and works to educate both Muslims and non-Muslims about Islam.

Aasma Khan was born on June 1, 1971, in Peoria, IL, to Pakistani parents. Her father is an obstetrician-gynecologist. Her mother is an anesthesiologist who left her medical career to raise her children full time.

Khan is trained as a corporate lawyer. She began in litigation, working for a year for a federal judge at the Court for International Trade. She then spent two-and-a-half years in practice for Chadbourne &

Park taking pro bono cases with a human rights focus. As an attorney, Khan defines her major goals as seeking justice and representing people who otherwise would not have a voice. Two of her pro bono cases particularly reflected these goals. In the first, she represented the Kurdish Heritage Foundation, the only known museum of Kurdish artifacts in Brooklyn, against Xerox. Xerox was suing the foundation for payment for a broken machine. The foundation, a non-profit museum run out of a private home, did not have the money to pay for it. Khan presented the case as one of a major and wealthy corporation against a minority client. Xerox agreed to settle the case for $1 in order to avoid negative publicity. The second case was an asylum case for the Lawyers' Committee for Human Rights in which she defended two brothers, aged fifteen and sixteen, from Sierra Leone who had sought asylum in the United States, but were jailed as illegal immigrants. Although she lost, Khan believes that the case was important because it was widely publicized and highlighted the difficulties of seeking asylum.

Khan's dedication to justice as the key to lasting peace led her into volunteer work after the 9/11 tragedies. Outraged by a seven-page New York *Times* article declaring Islam a violent religion following the terrorist attacks, she realized the national need for accurate information about Islam and outreach by mainstream, moderate Muslims to the American population. When she went to give blood and supplies to support the victims of the tragedies, she encountered other young American Muslim professionals with whom she brainstormed about how they could make a unique contribution to national reconciliation and healing. She and twelve others decided to demonstrate leadership by forming a grass-roots volunteer non-profit educational organization, Muslims Against Terrorism (M.A.T.), to speak out against terrorism.

M.A.T. represents not only an attempt to present interpretations of Islam in a purely American setting, rather than relying on interpretations from abroad, but also reflects a broader trend in American Islam of the twenty- and thirty-something generation overtaking leadership within the Muslim community in order to stake their claim as Americans of faith who live secular lives and to demonstrate the ability of American Muslims to live completely integrated lives in American society. The group's stated mission is to raise their voices as Muslims against hatred and violence in the name of Islam in favor of peace and understanding through interfaith and intercultural coalition building. M.A.T. calls on Muslims to reflect Islam's teachings of love, tolerance, peace, and rationality in their daily lives. It is particularly committed to mobilizing the silent majority of moderate, peaceful, tolerant Muslims in order to take Islam back from extremists. With a nationwide network of more than a hundred and thirty volunteers, M.A.T. has spread its message to people from more than ninety countries. It offers adult and children's education about Islam, education of the media, education for Muslims about Islam's message of peace, and a website about Islam and its message of peace. The programs approach the topics through interfaith dialogue in order to demonstrate that Islam, like other major faiths, contains compassion, understanding, and respect for other faiths. M.A.T. has given presentations at both public and private schools, youth camps, churches, temples, synagogues, college campuses, and interfaith centers, as well as to civic organizations. The organization's main focus is community outreach.

Khan's vision of M.A.T. seeks to move beyond assigning blame and finding fault to building compassion and understanding so that Muslims can work with others to address issues of global concern. She believes that this work must begin by confronting terrorism and delegitimizing the messages of hatred and intolerance before moving to the next step of confronting the bigotry, racism, and "gender apartheid" that she attributes to "cultural Islam."

One of Khan's major goals with M.A.T. was to provide personal, accurate, and balanced answers to the questions about Islam and Muslims raised by Americans in the aftermath of 9/11. M.A.T. speakers are careful to specify that they speak simply as individuals who wish to share their beliefs and what they know about their faith. They do not claim to be religious authorities or to be "right" while their listeners are "wrong." They also make a point of telling their audiences that no single Muslim can be considered "representative" of "Islam" or "Muslims" because there are more than one billion Muslims worldwide. Khan encourages her audiences to think of Islam as a personal belief system with a number of different variations, much like Christianity has different denominations. The level of practice depends on the knowledge and dedication of the individual. She also says that the purpose of Islam is to build a personal relationship between the believer and God, to encourage Muslims to perform good deeds, and to work toward community building, particularly with Christians and Jews. She emphasizes that judgmentalism is not part of the Quranic message.

In Khan's experience, the general public is most concerned about the role of jihad in Islam and its meaning to Muslims. Most Muslims distinguish between two types of jihad on the basis of the Prophet Muhammad's example: the "greater" or "internal" jihad of personal struggle to live a good life and avoid sin; and the "lesser" or "external" jihad of self-defense of the Muslim community. Khan notes that most Muslims focus on the personal, internal struggle. However, the media tends to focus on extremists engaged in jihad as holy war. The result is a widespread misunderstanding of Islam as promoting holy war. Khan therefore makes a point of highlighting the differences between the jihad of Osama bin Laden and the guidelines for jihad specified in the Quran.

Khan's approach has proven particularly effective in her work with Jewish and Christian communities. She has worked closely with Rabbi Jerry Davidson in Great Neck, NY, and the New York Reform Jewish Action Committee. She was awarded the sixth annual Lives of Commitment Award by Auburn Seminary in New York to honor her work in using her faith to shape public discourse. *Newsweek* magazine ran a series of articles about her work in October 2001. She was profiled by the New York *Times*, featured on M.T.V. News, and participated in debates on *Politically Incorrect*.

After a lengthy period of time off to care for her mother following the removal of a benign brain tumor, Khan reengaged her interests in human rights and the role and status of women in Islam. She remains active in the nonprofit Judicial Activists Organization where she addresses immigrant issues and social justice.

Further reading

Khan, Aasma. "How Muslims Can Combat Terror and Violence," in *Taking Back Islam: American Muslims Reclaim their Faith*, ed. Michael Wolfe and the producers of Beliefnet. Emmaus, PA: Rodale Inc. and Beliefnet, Inc., 2002

Pierce-Gupta, Ellie. "Aasma Khan – Muslim Against Terrorism," *Spirituality & Health The Soul/Body Connection*, fall 2002

Scheinin, Richard and Sarah Lubman. "U.S. Muslims Seeking Vision of their Faith in Secular Land," *Mercury News*, November 14, 2001

Weaver, Carolyn. "Muslims Against Terrorism," for Voice of America, November 23, 2001

Interview with the author, August 8, 2003

www.matusa.org – website for Muslims Against Terrorism

www.mvp-us.org – website for Muslim Voices for Peace

Imran Khan (b. 1952)

A world champion cricket player who led his team to Pakistan's first World Cup victory, Imran Khan turned his attention to politics and humanitarian work following his retirement from cricket.

Imran Khan was born on November 25, 1952, in Lahore, Pakistan, to a privileged family with a long history of playing professional cricket. Both of his parents participated in Pakistan's independence movement.

As a five-year-old, Khan broke and dislocated his left arm. Because the arm was never set properly, it did not heal completely, leaving him with a weak hand and arm muscles that tire easily. As a cricket player, he had to work around his injury, batting consistently and regularly in order to maintain the full use of his hand muscles, which is critical to gripping the bat properly and maintaining proper timing. Khan had to use a bat with a special handle because of his unusual grip.

Khan began playing cricket with friends when he was seven years old. He was not naturally gifted for the game and was typically the last person to be chosen for a team. He did not begin to enjoy the game until he made his school team. He originally wanted to be a batsman because batsmen were considered the core players in Pakistan. By the time he was eleven, he was the best batsman on his prep school team. At fourteen, he became the youngest member of the Aitchison College team, where he served as the opening batsman. He quickly learned that being the best batsman at his school did not make him the best one of his age group in Pakistan. His first performance for the under-nineteen team representing Lahore against an English team was so lackluster that he was sent to the outfield.

Khan credits his experience on the under-nineteen team with providing two critical observations. First, it brought him into contact with players from poorer families who had learned to play cricket in the streets and parks. Because they had to achieve their positions on the basis of merit and depended on their positions as their sole source of income, they tended to be better players. Many of these players treated Khan with disdain because they assumed that his place on the team had been purchased by wealth and connections, rather than earned on the basis of merit. He had to work to earn their respect by proving himself and his ability. In the process, he learned to respect them and to have a more realistic view of himself as a batsman. The second major outcome was the observation that Khan had the perfect action to become a fast bowler. Although Pakistan had none at that time, all of the dominant world-class teams had fast bowlers. Khan began to work on his bowling, the skill that later propelled him into first-class cricket.

Khan began to bowl in games when he was fourteen. From the time he was sixteen until he was eighteen, he focused strictly on his bowling. By 1970–1971, he was the second-highest wicket taker at his school. His performance in an international game in March 1971 led to his inclusion on the Pakistani national team on its tour of England – his first trip abroad. While he enjoyed the discovery of the English scenery and culture, he also had his first major encounter with the remnants of English colonialism. At a banquet, the Pakistani team was made to feel inferior not only with respect to their cricket playing (Pakistan had won only one Test match against England up until that point), but also with respect to their culture and civilization. The English manager made a point of telling the Pakistani team that it was the English who had taught Pakistanis discipline through cricket and how to eat with a knife and fork. The English also insisted that their strength in bowling came from drinking beer. As a Muslim who abstains from alcohol, Khan decided to base his strength on drinking milk – an example that many other Pakistani players have followed.

The English tour ended in frustration for Khan, not only due to the racism and neocolonialism he experienced, but also because he had been unable to bowl accurately on the English pitches. One of the greatest challenges in cricket is the variety of pitches (terrains) on which the game is played because there are no international standards for their construction. The variety is due to a combination of weather conditions, soil consistencies, elevations, and buoyancies that result in the need for different bowling techniques for different pitches. Each pitch produces different results in the speed of the ball after it bounces, the height at which the ball bounces, and even in the feel of the soil when running up to make the delivery. Batting techniques also have to be varied because of the unpredictability of the action from the ball. Because matches take place over a series of days, the ball tends to deteriorate, making its response to the pitch and bowling even more unpredictable. At eighteen, Khan did not have the experience or variety of techniques to adapt to such conditions.

Khan was also discouraged by the way his teammates treated him. As the youngest player on the team, different rules were often applied to him. Although a curfew was declared for the entire team, it was applied only to the youngest players who were often turned in by their teammates for infractions. Despite his higher education, Khan was expected to be subservient to senior players and to serve as the butt of their jokes. Teamwork was generally set aside in favor of individual achievement. Later in his career when he served as captain, Khan looked back on these experiences as examples not to be repeated. Instead, he sought to build mutual respect and team spirit while fairly applying the rules to all players.

Although Khan was frustrated by his poor performance, his potential as a player was recognized by Worcestershire, which arranged for his admission to their Royal Grammar School. Khan completed the school's two-year program in nine months and entered Keble College, Oxford, in 1972, where he read philosophy, politics, and economics.

Khan began playing for the Oxford University cricket team in 1973. Improvements in his batting technique led to his election as captain in 1974. He found that the additional responsibilities of the captaincy made him a better player in general. His success at Oxford led to his inclusion on the Pakistani team touring England in 1974. Although the team emerged unbeaten and Khan himself performed adequately, many of his Pakistani teammates continued to make snide remarks about his connections and asserted that better players had been left behind. Although Khan took his cricket seriously at Oxford, he gave up the captaincy in 1975 in order to concentrate on his final exams.

Khan became Pakistan's first fast bowler in 1976, leading Pakistan to its first Test victory over Australia. During one game, he bowled for almost four hours straight without a break or change, exerting so much effort that his shirt sleeve fell off. The Test victory showed Pakistan to be a world-class team for the first time. However, the team fell apart during a later tour of the West Indies.

The 1976–1977 season highlighted for Khan some of the serious institutional problems with Pakistani cricket. Politics, rather than ability or merit, drove the selection of the team. Players tended to play for their own individual records rather than for the team, preventing strategic playing. The long-term fear of loss had led the players to give up when the going got tough and to assume that the only way to win was by focusing on batting. Most illogical of all was the placement of team management and

selection in the hands of political appointees who typically knew nothing about the game, rather than leaving such decision making to the professional athletes who played it. Khan denounced the bureaucrats for focusing more on control of the game and cheap, effective advertising than on the development of cricket, observing that little to no attention was given to the maintenance or upkeep of the pitches, teams were bribed to lose matches, player salaries were low, and players who learned cricket domestically were unprepared for international competition. He called for a complete reorganization of Pakistani cricket to address these serious structural and institutional failures.

In 1977, Khan accepted an invitation from Kerry Packer to play with the best players from the West Indies, Pakistan, and England in what came to be known as "Packer cricket." While there were many in the cricketing community who opposed Packer, Khan notes that his years playing Packer cricket were not only among the most demanding, difficult, and beneficial for him as an athlete, but also brought cricket into line with modern sports, including major salary increases; rising glamour, personalization, and marketing of individual players; and improvement of protective gear. These trends were further boosted by Pakistan's first major victory over India in 1978 which led to a cricket boom and the first widely televised cricket games in Pakistan.

Despite this important victory, the team fell apart at the World Cup in 1979. Khan experienced his first smear campaign by the press, which blamed the loss on his supposed drinking and womanizing throughout the tour. Khan insisted that the real issue behind his poor performance was a muscle injury. He also cited the recurring theme of the team's batting falling apart under pressure, a problem that was repeated during a troublesome 1981 tour in Australia. Although Khan emerged as the Man of the Series for 1981, he had not been pleased with his own performance – or that of the team. Arguments between the team and the captain led to Khan being asked to assume the captaincy.

Khan has stated that the captaincy was never one of his goals. However, recalling how holding the captaincy at Oxford had helped him to improve his game and believing that he could build team spirit, he accepted. As captain, he insisted that the cricket board allow him to select his own team, a selection that he made on the basis of merit, rather than connections. He implemented a new strategy of building an innings, rather than pursuing purely aggressive batting. He tried to treat each player as an individual, adapting his captaining style to their individual needs. He also pushed his teammates to think in terms of their long-term goals as a team, rather than individual goals or matches.

Khan's first tour as team captain began in England in the summer of 1982. When the team lost its first Test, Khan realized that he would have to lead by example, particularly in batting. His strategy paid off in the second Test when Pakistan won – only the second time that Pakistan had won in England. Khan was selected Man of the Series and earned the nickname "Lion of Pakistan."

Tremendous national pressure for a Pakistani victory against India led Khan to bowl through the 1982–1983 series, despite a stress fracture in his left shin that was not correctly diagnosed until December, 1982. Assuming initially that the problem was extreme bruising, Khan continued to push himself to play. It was an act he came to regret. In April 1983, he was diagnosed with one of the worst cases of stress fracture his treating physician had ever seen. He was told to take a year off from playing in order to heal. Reduced to batting, he helplessly watched the team lose the 1983 World Cup. Despite his break from bowling, the fracture reopened. He was told to take

four months of complete rest with no physical activity. Rather than sympathizing with the serious nature of his injury, the Pakistani press and Khan's critics launched a new smear campaign against him.

By March 1984, the bone had stopped healing altogether, threatening to end Khan's cricketing career in a position of weakness. Depressed by the thought of never playing again and angry about being humiliated by the press without an opportunity to redeem himself, Khan left Pakistan for England. For six months, he remained largely homebound. His new treatment required him to remain still for ten hours a day with his leg in a cast in order to receive therapeutic electrical treatments. He was permitted no exercise at all. Khan recalls this period as the most difficult and depressing of his life.

By October 1984, Khan's leg had healed completely. As he started to train and think about restarting his cricket career, tragedy struck again. His mother, to whom he had always been close, was diagnosed with cancer. He played for only a short time before returning to Pakistan, where he remained until her death. His mother's illness and treatment not only brought Khan face to face with her personal pain, but also exposed him to the reality that appropriate medical treatment is often beyond the reach of the poor in Pakistan. He was particularly moved by a visit to a children's ward where he saw three or four children crammed into a single bed. He vowed to do something to resolve this situation after retiring from cricket.

By 1985, Khan felt confident enough to play for Pakistan again. He led the team in a disastrous 1986 tour of Sri Lanka which was complicated not only by typical Pakistani cricket politics, but also by the domestic situation in Sri Lanka, where patriotic fervor was high following a civil war. The team redeemed itself in the West Indies where it won over one of the strongest cricket teams in the world. Khan noted that this was one of the few series in which umpiring was not an issue. He has consistently called for the use of neutral umpires during international competitions because of the immense domestic pressure for victories that many times results in questionable judgments. Only the United Kingdom has persisted in refusing to use neutral umpires, a refusal that Khan attributes to vestiges of colonialism and racism.

The most remarkable moment of 1986 for Khan was Pakistan's tour of India, which resulted in Pakistan's first victory over India on Indian soil. It was an important moment for Pakistan as a nation because of the troubled past between the two countries that included two wars, and the Pakistani team was received by a crowd of more than two hundred thousand people upon its return to Lahore. Despite this important victory, the 1987 tour of England began badly as the team was treated with disdain and overt racism by the County Cricket Board, the press, and Customs. Crippled by injuries and bureaucratic difficulties, the team initially performed poorly. However, anger over the racist treatment helped the Pakistani team pull together and become the first Pakistani team ever to win a series in England. Khan was again made Man of the Series.

Having beaten both India and England, Pakistan was favored to win the 1987 World Cup. However, they lost to Australia in the semi-finals. Khan tried to retire, but was inundated with phone calls and mail demanding that he return to the game. People demonstrated outside of his house, including some who went on hunger strikes. He was mobbed when he went out. His teammates pressured him to return. Finally, Pakistan's head of state personally appealed to him to serve his country by returning to cricket. Khan decided to return to seek the elusive World Cup.

Khan's gamble paid off in 1992 with the first-ever Pakistani victory at the World Cup, marking Pakistan as the world's greatest cricket team. It also solidified Khan's position as the greatest all-round cricket player in the world. He attributed his success to dedication, hard work, being a complete team man, and his ability to perform well consistently under pressure.

Khan retired from cricket for the second and final time after the 1992 World Cup. However, he did not retire from his criticism of Pakistani cricket at the institutional level, particularly because cricket had become a big business. He continued to call for structural reorganization, an end to corruption and abuse of power, and improvement in the quality of association officials, treatment of players, selection of umpires, and sports journalism in Pakistan. He also called for expanded resources and access to facilities for poor but talented players in order to hone and develop their skills. He has recommended the foundation of local leagues to organize and promote players and the formation of strong regional associations to strengthen cricket at the national level.

The issues that were of most concern to Khan in cricket – nepotism, inefficiency, corruption, failure to implement needed reforms, abuse of power, and constant bickering – reflected the broader political system in Pakistan. In order to fight these issues at the national level, Khan entered politics in 1996 with the foundation of his political party Tehreek-e-Insaf (Movement for Justice), to call for a "Third Way," or alternative political vision based on revolutionary changes to the economy and social structures. Khan called for greater attention to domestic issues, particularly controlling population growth, the desperate state of health care, the rising price of urban land, and greater attention to the preservation of historical treasures and environmental issues, such as massive deforestation and ecological damage. He authored a book, *Indus Journey: A Personal View of Pakistan*, both to introduce the broader public to Pakistan's landscape and to demonstrate the problems created by socialism, nationalization of the economy, redistribution of land, and diminution of feudal landlords' holdings. He called for improved relations between India and Pakistan, demanding that both invest in education and health care, rather than arms races and defense spending. He also called for an end to colonialism and racism in politics, reflecting a long-standing position he took as a cricket player in speaking out against South Africa during the apartheid era for discriminating against players on the basis of race. He frequently denounced the English cricket establishment for maintaining relations with South Africa's all-white cricket team, believing that sports should be held to the same human rights standards as political systems.

Khan was elected to parliament in 2002. He has become a strong dissident voice, raising critical issues for Pakistan's development, economy, and future. His prominence as a national sports hero has given him a wide audience for his ideas, even if this has not translated into votes for his party. As an M.P., he has tried to capitalize on the broad public desire for reform and frustration with corruption, poverty, unemployment, illiteracy, and scarcity of clean water. His call for the reduction of Pakistan's overstaffed bureaucracy in favor of putting bureaucrats to work in rural areas has proven popular.

In addition to addressing health care at the national level, Khan kept his promise to provide quality health care to the poor through the 1996 foundation of the Shaukat Khanum Memorial Cancer Hospital, the only hospital in Pakistan that provides the best quality diagnostic and therapeutic care to cancer patients, irrespective of their ability to pay. Financing for the hospital is provided by charitable contributions from the Imran Khan Cancer Appeal. One of the most prominent patrons of the hospital was the late

Diana, Princess of Wales, who was a close personal friend of both Khan and his ex-wife, JEMIMA GOLDSMITH.

Khan is the author of two autobiographies and has made a television documentary entitled *Islam and America Through the Eyes of Imran Khan.*

Further reading

Khan, Imran. *All Round View.* London: Chatto & Windus, 1988
——— *Imran: The Autobiography of Imran Khan.* London: Pelham Books, 1983
——— *Indus Journey: A Personal View of Pakistan.* London: Chatto & Windus, 1990
Magdalinski, Tara and Timothy J.L. Chandler. "With God on their Side: An Introduction," in *With God On their side: Sport in the Service of Religion,* ed. Tara Magdalinksi and Timothy J.L. Chandler. London and New York: Routledge, Taylor & Francis Group, 2002
McCarthy, Rory. "Undaunted Imran Returns to the Stump," *The Guardian,* September 27, 2002
synergye.com/cancer/main.html – website for Imran Khan Cancer Appeal

Khalid Khannouchi (b. 1971)

The fastest marathon runner in the world, Khalid Khannouchi set world records for marathon running in 1999 and 2002.

Khalid Khannouchi was born on December 22, 1971, in Meknes, Morocco. From his parents he learned the importance of being close to family and being respectful of one's elders. He was educated at the University of Mohammed the Fifth and the University of Moulay Ismail, both in Morocco.

Khannouchi began running when he was young. Despite his interest and skill in running, he struggled in his early years of training due to the lack of institutional support in Morocco. He was the Junior Moroccan Champion in the 3,000 meters, 10,000 meters, and cross country in 1990 and 1991 and placed eighth at the World Arabic Cross-Country Championships and eleventh at the World University Games in the 5,000 meters in 1991. Following this performance, he requested assistance with training expenses from the Track Federation of Morocco. When the federation declined his request, he moved to the United States. He has since refused to represent Morocco in international competition.

Khannouchi's first major competition after training in the United States was the World University Games of 1993 where he won a gold medal in the 5,000 meters. He moved permanently to the United States, sharing an apartment with three friends in Brooklyn while earning a living washing dishes and working as a busboy. At the same time, he pursued serious training and began entering American races. He met his wife and future coach and agent, American runner Sandra Inoa, at a five-kilometer race in Hartford, CT. Their September 1996 marriage enabled Khannouchi to apply for a green card and American citizenship. Grateful for American support for his running and training, he decided to represent only the United States in international competition, even though this meant waiting to become an American citizen before competing at international level.

Khannouchi's typical training regimen consists of sessions twice daily, often with friends. He drinks only water when training and running races so as not to be distracted by the potential of losing his drinks along the way. He sometimes uses races as training mechanisms, but generally does not train or race during the month of Ramadan when Muslims fast from sunrise to sundown because of the physical difficulties involved. He engages in a mix of tempo runs and track workouts, using different training styles and equipment for each. Track races require spikes and are time oriented, while road races require racing shoes and are focused on the terrain. Khannouchi prefers road races because he finds that the spikes needed for track races aggravate his calf

injuries. He trains for a variety of terrains and altitudes and particularly enjoys talking to local runners. He finds it difficult to run more than one marathon per year because of the physical demands and length of the race.

Khannouchi began entering small road races throughout the United States in 1997. At five foot five inches and only 125 pounds, he is one of the smallest marathoners. His first major marathon competition was the LaSalle Banks Chicago Marathon in 1997. He won the marathon with a time of two hours, seven minutes, and ten seconds – the fastest marathon debut in history. He repeated the Chicago Marathon in 1998, but took nine seconds longer to finish, leaving him in second place and costing him his self-confidence. He was not only disappointed in his own performance, he also feared that his fans would be disappointed in him. However, his second-best performance was not due to a lack of training or ability. He had an injury to his Achilles tendon that would require extensive medical treatment for years to come. Determined to overcome his injury, he set his sights on the 1999 Chicago Marathon and declared his intent to recover his title.

Khannouchi prepared for the 1999 marathon for four months, focusing on distance rather than speed. On the morning of the race, the temperature was thirty-five degrees farenheight, with a wind-chill factor of twenty-seven degrees. Khannouchi was so cold that he wore gloves during the warm-up and kept them on for the race. Despite the gloves, he had no mobility in his hands or jaw during the race. The wind also blurred his vision, rendering him unable to see the clock. His strategy in marathons is to set a steady pace and to remain relaxed, rather than trying to stay with the lead group. He was passed by his main competitor, Moses Tanui, about seventeen miles into the race, but decided to wait until twenty-two miles to go after

Tanui gradually. He passed Tanui with only a mile and a half to go. When Khannouchi reached the last half-mile stretch, he ran as fast as he could, crossing the finish line in victory with a world record time of two hours, five minutes, and forty-two seconds. In what was to become his hallmark style, Khannouchi credited his victory to the team effort that had made the achievement possible, thanking God for guiding him through safe training, his wife for her support, encouragement, and unwavering belief in his ability to break the record, and his fans who provided him with strength during the race and support during training. His autographed uniform and shoe from the race were placed in the Running Hall of Fame in Utica, NY.

By 2000, Khannouchi was ranked as the number one marathon runner in the United States and third in the world after placing third in the London Marathon with a time of two hours, eight minutes, and thirty-six seconds. The London Marathon left Khannouchi with hamstring injuries that complicated his goal of representing the United States in the 2000 Olympic trials, an ambition that was already hampered by the fact that he was not yet an American citizen. Despite intense pressure from his father, the Moroccan Track Federation, and the King of Morocco, Khannouchi refused to represent Morocco in the Olympics, recalling that it had failed to provide him with support for his training and running early in his career when he had needed the help. Because it had provided the needed support, he remained firm in his commitment to represent only the United States in international competitions for the rest of his career, even if that meant missing out on the 2000 Olympics because he did not yet have his citizenship. In retaliation, Morocco threatened to have Khannouchi barred from the Olympics altogether because he had once represented Morocco in some world competitions. In the end, the combination of the citizenship issue

and the injury led him to withdraw from the 2000 Olympic trials. In a press release, he stated that he believed that it would be better to wait and allow the injury to heal before pushing himself to get back into top form, a task that would require slow and gradual work if he was not to injure himself permanently.

Khannouchi became an American citizen on May 2, 2000, just days before the Olympic trials. The media accused him of using the citizenship issue as an excuse to withdraw from the trials and asserted that his citizenship had been guaranteed. Khannouchi maintained his position that the citizenship had not been a foregone conclusion and that the injury had been a major contributing factor to the withdrawal. The press additionally accused him of being greedy and taking money when he didn't win a race. Khannouchi noted that his contracts paid him regardless of how far he ran or where he placed in the competition. He also pointed to the fact that he had kept his commitment to run in the London Marathon for a fee of $175,000, despite the fact that he had received numerous other higher-paying offers due to his world-record performance in 1999. By being a man of his word, Khannouchi believed that he had proven that he was not driven by greed, but by commitment.

Although deeply hurt and embarrassed by the media attack, Khannouchi remained focused on his goal of healing. He returned to training in August, 2000, in preparation for the Chicago Marathon, which was his first race as an American citizen. He won the race with a time of two hours, seven minutes, and one second, making him the first American ever to win that marathon three times.

Energized by his victory, Khannouchi began training for the 2001 World Outdoor Championships to be held in Edmonton, Canada, marking his first international competition as an American citizen. Despite injuries that included a back spasm and blistering on his feet caused by the heat, Khannouchi began the race. He withdrew at the halfway point due to the injuries, which also caused him to withdraw from further events in 2001.

Khannouchi returned to marathon running in 2002, beginning with a victory in the Kyoto Half-Marathon. His major victory of the year came at the London Marathon where he set a second world record of two hours, five minutes, and thirty-eight seconds for a 26.2-mile-long course, winning over world champions Paul Tergat of Kenya and Haile Gebrselassie of Ethiopia. Ironically, Khannouchi had entered the race without favor and without world attention. Although he had been the most consistent marathoner in history and had the strongest record of any marathon runner, many people assumed that his injuries had ended his competitive career. He noted that the lack of attention played in his favor because he was not under tremendous pressure or intense public scrutiny. Although he had his usual nightmares about forgetting his racing shoes, his only goal that day was to prove that he was still a great marathon runner. He followed his usual strategy of maintaining a steady pace throughout the race rather than always trying to be in the lead group or engaging in fast spurts to catch up. His strategy paid off toward the end of the race as Gebrselassie fell behind at twenty-four miles, Tergat at twenty-five. Khannouchi was out in front alone for the last mile. Realizing how close he was to breaking the world record, he gave a final push, becoming the first man in thirty-three years to lower his own world record – and by a full four seconds. He crossed the finish line with a ten-second lead over his closest competitor, making it a clear and undisputed victory. Upon crossing the line, he knelt, kissed the ground, and prayed, thanking God for helping him to stay patient throughout a very difficult preceding year-and-a-half of injuries, disappointments, and

training and for providing the faith to stay patient. In his trademark style, he also expressed his appreciation to his wife for her support and to his physicians, running partners, family, and fans. He also expressed his appreciation to his sponsor, New Balance, for being patient and understanding and for not pressuring him to race or perform well, but trusting his judgment about his own pace. In recognition of his achievement, June 2, 2002, was declared "Khalid Khannouchi Day" in Westchester, NY.

Khannouchi has continued to run since his 2002 world record, but has been constrained by injuries. After a victory in the 2003 Kyoto City Half-Marathon, which he won despite being ill with tonsillitis and having spent the day before the race on antibiotics administered via I.V., a combination of illnesses and injuries prevented Khannouchi from achieving further victories. He was also forced to withdraw from the 2004 Olympic trials. He nevertheless remains focused on his goal of representing the United States in the Olympics in the future.

Further reading

Allison, Don. "An Interview with Khalid Khannouchi: Running the Race for the 2000 Olympics and USA Citizenship," www.coolrunning.com, September 5, 1999

Longman, Jere. "London Falling: Khannouchi Breaks World Record," New York *Times*, April 15, 2002

www.khannouchi.com – website for Khalid Khannouchi

Abu Jafar Muhammad ibn Musa al-Khwarizmi (c. 780–850)

Broadly considered the father of modern algebra and the first person to make algebra accessible to everyday life, Abu Jafar Muhammad ibn Musa al-Khwarizmi was one of the great early Muslim scientists. The mathematical term "algorithm," which refers to the systematic computation or system of step-by-step instructions to solve a problem or pursue a goal, is derived from his name.

Abu Jafar Muhammad ibn Musa al-Khwarizmi is believed to have been born around 780 in a district between the Tigris and Euphrates rivers in contemporary Iraq. His ancestors are thought to have come from the Central Asian city of Khwarazm (contemporary Khiva, Uzbekistan). Very little is definitively known about his personal life.

Al-Khwarizmi spent his adult life in the city of Baghdad, which was at that time both an important meeting place for the trade routes from India, Persia, and a variety of Mediterranean ports and the seat of the Abbasid caliphate. He worked for the Abbasid caliph al-Mamun at the House of Wisdom (Bayt al-Hikmah), which was responsible for acquiring and translating works of science and philosophy and making them available to researchers and translators. Al-Khwarizmi both translated scientific works and wrote important original books with new ideas about mathematics. He died around 850.

Al-Khwarizmi's most influential book, completed in 820, was his treatise on algebra, *The Book of Summary Concerning Calculating by Transposition and Reduction*. It was the first book to consider algebraic (*al-jibr*) expressions, or those that restore balance by adding or subtracting the same quantity to or from both sides of an equation or by reducing the terms. It is widely considered to be an outstanding achievement in the history of mathematics not only because of the originality of the theory it presented for solving linear and quadratic equations by radicals, but also because it provided innovative technical terminology. The book's title describes the practical purpose of the equations it presents: the completion and balancing of parts or items that had been separated. In addition to synthesizing Greek and Hindu mathematical knowledge, the book was

the first to develop a system of solutions for quadratic expressions, including geometric principles for completing the square, by reducing geometric and arithmetic problems to algebraic operations presented in normal equations with standard solutions. The two critical methods used were the transposition of terms in order to make them all positive and the reduction of similar terms. The book provides a classification system for quadratics, classifying quadratic expressions into six types: (1) squares equal to roots; (2) squares equal to numbers; (3) roots equal to numbers; (4) squares and roots equal to numbers; (5) squares and numbers equal to roots; and (6) roots and numbers equal to squares. He also provided geometric proofs of his methods and was the first to introduce the concept of using a variable to represent an unknown quantity. Modern algebra can be recognized in his work when his word descriptions of mathematical functions are replaced by symbols. His science of algebra was introduced to Europe in the twelfth century through Latin translations.

Al-Khwarizmi's mathematical work was intended for practical use in daily life, rather than as a tool to be used only by elites. He tried to translate complex abstract concepts into easily understandable numbers and equations, such as methods of addition, subtraction, fractions, and percentages for merchants. He used geometry to partition land, algebra to calculate inheritance portions according to Islamic law, and equations in matters of lawsuits, trade, digging canals, and making geometric computations. He included applications and worked examples, as well as rules for finding the areas of figures such as circles and the volumes of solids such as spheres. His practical approach to mathematics represented a major departure from the classical Greek approach that considered the discovery of the secrets of numbers to be more important than their use.

Among al-Khwarizmi's most important practical contributions to mathematics were the introduction of Arabic numerals and the concept of zero to the West. Prior to the introduction of zero, Roman, Greek, and Arabic systems which used letters to represent units plus or minus a certain amount were used. These systems had no zero. Al-Khwarizmi found great power, simplicity, and user-friendliness in the Hindu use of zero in combination with symbols for the numbers one through nine, which permitted the writing of any number, no matter how large, without the need to invent new symbols. It also made larger calculations simpler. Similarly, the use of decimals, rather than fractions, added to the ease of calculation. He explained how decimals and sexagesimal fractions were to be used and included a discussion of Egyptian fractions, showing how to find a single numerator enabling the addition of fractions, such as $\frac{1}{3} + \frac{1}{15} = \frac{2}{5}$. Egyptian fractions were introduced into Europe and rapidly became part of university courses. However, Europeans did not appreciate or understand the usefulness of zero until the late twelfth century, or 250 years after it had been introduced in Arabic mathematics.

Like many of his contemporary mathematicians, al-Khwarizmi's work was driven by the pursuit of astronomy, the oldest, most developed, and most important of the ancient sciences. Astronomy was an important science for Muslims not only because knowledge of the constellations was helpful for navigational purposes, but also because of its direct relationship to Islamic rituals, such as determining the direction of Mecca for prayer. Al-Khwarizmi served as the court astronomer for al-Mamum. His astronomical work described the movements of the sun, stars, and planets and included tables for predicting eclipses of the sun and moon. His predictions and observations were based upon records from Baghdad, as well as Hindu wisdom,

Ptolemy's tables, and commentaries by Theon and Hypatia of Alexandria, Egypt.

Al-Khwarizmi's works are important not only for their presentation of Greek, Hindu, and Arabic astronomical methodologies, but also because they provide a snapshot of the state of Arabic astronomical knowledge in the late eighth century. At this time, Hindu astronomical procedures were introduced into the Arabic-speaking world. However, their impact is difficult to measure because the methodology was transmitted to the Arabs without commentaries explaining the meanings or uses of those methods. The Arabs were left to reconstruct the meanings of the methods and their uses on their own.

Al-Khwarizmi's work *Zij al-Sindhind* is the first extant original work of Arabic astronomy. It was also the first major piece of Islamic astronomical literature to try to explain Hindu procedures, particularly the use of tables of the movements of the sun, moon, and five planets. Hindu influence is apparent in both the content and the organization of the tables, which present planetary theory prior to the discussion of eclipses. (Greek versions used an opposite presentation.) Hindu methods are also used to determine the planetary positions according to calculation of the longitude via a number of successive approximations and to calculate phases of the moon and solar and lunar eclipses. Al-Khwarizmi also based the determination of time on solar altitude and calculation of solar shadows on Hindu methods. The presentation of Hindu methodology is very close to the ancient Sanskrit texts. Only in his discussions of trigonometry did al-Khwarizmi include both the Ptolemaic and Hindu methods because the Hindus did not have the theorem of Menelaus required for solving spherical triangles. Al-Khwarizmi's work contains the first Arabic tables of sines and tangents and provides discussions of calendars and spherical astronomy.

Zij al-Sindhind was transmitted to Europe via a Latin translation.

In addition to mathematics and astronomy, al-Khwarizmi was interested in geography. He wrote a book entitled *The Book of the Form of the Earth*, which contains the latitudes and longitudes for 2,042 cities and provides detailed maps of cities, mountains, islands, rivers, and seas. His world map is one of the most accurate of its time and more accurate than that composed by Ptolemy, largely because he grouped locations according to the amount of daylight they experienced on the longest day of the year.

Al-Khwarizmi's other written works address sundial design through the preparation of tables for their construction according to latitude, the Jewish calendar, the astrolabe, and a political history of prominent people that includes their horoscopes.

Further reading

Anderson, Margaret J. and Karen F. Stephenson. *Scientists of the Ancient World.* Berkeley Heights, NJ: Enslow Publishers, Inc., 1999

Dallal, Ahmad. "Science, Medicine, and Technology: The Making of a Scientific Culture," in *The Oxford History of Islam*, editor-in-chief John L. Esposito. New York: Oxford University Press, 1999

Hill, Donald R. *Islamic Science and Engineering.* Edinburgh: Edinburgh University Press, 1993

Turner, Howard R. *Science in Medieval Islam: An Illustrated Introduction.* Austin: University of Texas Press, 1995

www.gap.dcs.st-and.ac.uk/~history/Mathematicians/Al-Khwarizmi.html

L

Amel Larrieux (b. 1977)

The star singer of Groove Theory and singer of soul whose debut album, *Infinite Possibilities*, marks her as a leader in the new generation of "conscious soul music," Amel Larrieux represents the entrance of the female Muslim voice into mainstream American music.

Amel Larrieux was born Greenwich Village, New York City, in 1977. Her mother, Brenda Dixon Gottschild, is an avant-garde African-American performer, highly acclaimed dance critic, professor of performance studies, and poetry reader. Larrieux was raised in an artists' building known as Westbeth, which is frequented by artists from throughout New York City and the United States. As a child, Larrieux frequently accompanied her mother to shows she was critiquing and was included in gatherings of her parents' artist friends and their children who came from a variety of racial and economic backgrounds. She also studied dance for twelve years. Larrieux credits being raised in an artistic environment with her choice of a career and with giving her a lifelong love and appreciation for the performing arts and racial and cultural diversity.

Larrieux's love of artistic work led her to pursue a professional music career.

She is known for an unusual level of vocal maturity, a wide vocal range, and an ability to express a variety of expressions musically. She attributes her maturity as a musician to early exposure to a broad diversity of music, as well as having been raised in a family that encouraged artistry and creativity.

Larrieux's musical career began as a member of the duo Groove Theory with former Mantronix member Bryce Wilson (A.K.A. Bruce Luvah). Larrieux served as the lead singer and co-writer for their songs. Groove Theory's debut album, *Eponymous*, was signed to Epic Records. Its first song, "Tell Me," was released in 1995. "Tell Me" broke into the top ten on the Billboard Hot 100 and the top five on the R&B charts. The album was certified as gold in October 1995 and hit the top twenty of the R&B charts. The popular song "Baby Luv" also came from this album.

Larrieux's voice and writing attracted attention from former members of Sade's backup band, Sweetback, in 1996. She starred as the vocalist on two tracks of their self-titled album. In addition to the musical exposure, Larrieux notes that the experience of working with Sade's band was an eye-opener to the music industry. Irritated by the widespread assumption that she would not be able to write or produce music on her own because she is a woman, she was determined to succeed in order to make a contribution as an African-American artist.

Larrieux co-wrote and co-produced her debut solo album, *Infinite Possibilities*, with her husband, Laru Larrieux. *Infinite Possibilities* was released by Epic/550 Music in February, 2000. The album presents a variety of musical styles, including jazz, hip-hop, rhythm and blues, Gospel, funky, as well as Middle Eastern, West African, and Indian ethnic styles. The purpose was to reflect both the variety of musical formats in which African-American artists have made contributions to music and Larrieux's personal challenge to herself – to engage in an unlimited variety of lyric, musical, and personal styles in her music. She chose the title of the album to show that diversity and creativity should not have predetermined boundaries.

Larrieux describes her music as based upon her spiritual devotion to herself and her family and her desire to uplift others. The song "I 'n' I" reflects that approach, painting a picture of a world where the individual defines what qualifies as "beautiful." The song grew out of her objection to a statement by a fashion editor responding to a question about the scarcity of black models by commenting that she knew of very few who were "pretty enough." The purpose of the song is to reject the idea of conforming to someone else's image of what is beautiful. She has stated that she believes that everyone is beautiful because they are the way God made them and encourages people not to be disappointed or embarrassed by their appearance because this constitutes an act of injustice against oneself. She urges her audiences to focus on building their character and holding fast to their own individuality, rather than conforming to someone else's standard of physical beauty – the recurrent theme of *Infinite Possibilities*. "Shine" tells the tale of broken promises and their inevitable redemption via inner strength

and faith in experiences. "Get Up" urges people to remember that "all you got's your pride" when dealing with negative people. Released in November 1999 as Larrieux's debut solo single, Get Up reached the R&B charts.

Larrieux also sought to express her personal ambitions of bringing inspiration, love, and good things to others through her choice of the title *Infinite Possibilities*. Much of the music on this album has very personal meaning. One of her most popular songs, "Sweet Misery," reminds her that she has a responsibility to live what she writes, while the poignant, Gospel-tinged ballad "Even If" was written for her daughter as a reflection of her quest to maintain the nurturing and supportive environment in which she was raised for her own children. "Makes me Whole" is an inspirational, personal ode to her husband.

Larrieux has set the advancement and development of African-American music and art as a personal goal, believing that they have not yet reached their full potential. She feels no need for labels for her own music because of the variety of musical styles and genres she incorporates in her work. She is concerned by the tendency to label the music of any African-American artist as "African-American music" because it gives the mistaken impression that the color of one's skin is more important than the music itself when categorizing its style. When asked to categorize her own music, she refers to it simply as "Amel's music," noting that there are many white people performing traditionally black musical styles, such as rock and roll, blues, jazz, and soul music, yet none of them are labeled as black artists or performers of black music.

Described by her fans as "unapologetic," "confident," and one of the "rising stars" of the "new school of conscious soul," Larrieux is renowned for her grace, maturity, strength, and determination. She has ventured into joint musical endeavors, such as collaboration with Glenn Lewis on the 2003 soundtrack for *Barbershop* and with the Roots on *Glitches* ("The Skin You're In"). She also stars as the Egyptian princess Maati on the Sci-Fi Channel's epic story *Maatkara*, an online animated series chronicling the adventures of an Egyptian princess who seeks to save the Earth and bring freedom to her people via macromedia flash animation. The narratives are a combination of Egyptian mythology and futuristic themes told through a science-fiction format.

Further reading

www.amellarrieux.com (this article draws heavily from the biography at this website)

www.rollingstone.com/artists – for more information on Larrieux's musical career and albums

www.scifi.com/maatkara

www.theblissgroup.com

www.theiceberg.com/artist – for more information on Larrieux's musical career and albums

M

Nurcholish Madjid (1939–2005)

A prominent theologian who developed an Islamic theology of religious pluralism and tolerance, Nurcholish Madjid was considered one of the most important Muslim intellectuals in Indonesia and one of the most progressive contemporary Muslim theologians in the world.

Nurcholish Madjid was born on March 17, 1939, in Mojoanyar, East Java, Indonesia, into a family of Islamic scholars. He received his early education at his father's Al-Wathoniyah *madrasah* (school) before pursuing traditional Quranic studies at Darul Ulum *pesantren* (school) in Rejoso, Jombang. He completed his Quranic studies, along with English and secular subjects, at Pondok Modern "Darus Salam" Gontor in 1960, followed by studies of Islamic literature and culture at Syarif Hidayatullah, Jakarta, Indonesia, where he earned a B.A. in Arab literature in 1968.

Madjid served as the general chairman of the Indonesian Muslim Students's Association from 1966 until 1971. He also served as president of United Islamic Students of Southeast Asia and assistant to the secretary general of the International Islamic Federation of Students Organization. His experiences as a student led him to the conclusion that Islamic thought was in need of innovation.

Madjid began as a conservative traditional modernist and wrote a pivotal essay on "Modernization is Rationalization not Westernization," in 1968. However, by the conclusion of his studies, he had gained international experience through travel in the United States, Europe, and the Middle East that led him to compare the domestic situation in Indonesia with the circumstances in other countries. He concluded that the strongest indicator of the religious nature of a society was the degree to which social justice, opportunity, and equality existed. In 1970, he presented an alternative vision – "Islamic secularization" – which called for a restoration of the spirit of *ijtihad* (independent reasoning) in order constantly to reinterpret Islam according to new circumstances and thereby to engage in an ongoing process of renewal, adjustment, and refreshment in theological interpretations focused on finding values oriented toward liberalization. He also proposed the desacralization of those aspects of life and knowledge that are not inherently religious in order to separate the religious from the worldly toward the goal of encouraging liberalization and the opening of Indonesian society.

Madjid's efforts at reinterpreting Islam for contemporary Indonesian society earned him denunciation for supposedly having strayed from Islamic teachings and being influenced by Western secular thought. Detractors pointed to his reliance on human rationality and reason for support. Some even declared him an apostate. At the same time, Muslim intellectuals were excited about his work.

Madjid decided to pursue his theological studies at the University of Chicago in 1978, where he earned a Ph.D. in 1984. His dissertation explored the theology and philosophy of the medieval Islamic scholar Ibn Taymiyyah, addressing his approach to reason and revelation in Islam. After completing his degree, Madjid returned home to Jakarta where he became a senior researcher at the Indonesian Institute of Sciences. By this time, he was recognized as a prominent and daring intellectual known for his innovative approach to social and political issues. He continued to work to develop an interpretation of Islam that would serve the spiritual needs of the modern urban population by focusing on spirituality, rather than ritual or social behavior. He became an advocate of religious pluralism and tolerance, which have since become his hallmark themes.

Madjid's theology is based on a vision of Islam that returns to the spirit and underlying principles and values of Islam as a guide for contemporary conduct, rather than adhering to the more traditional literal approach to the Quran and *hadith*. His emphasis on values and ethics reflects his opposition to sectarianism in favor of recognizing the broad Muslim community and promoting a broader vision of Islamic brotherhood that includes Christians, Jews, and other faith groups such as Hindus and Buddhists as members of the Muslim community. He called for tolerance, inclusivity, and interfaith dialogue in order to end the bigotry and intolerance that plague many religions. He has become best known for his support of religious pluralism.

Madjid's dedication to religious pluralism reflects the official government position of post-independence Indonesia. As home to more than three hundred ethnic groups and a variety of religions, the country has had to respect its diversity in order to achieve unity. In 1945, Indonesia adopted the Pancasila (five principles) that officially made it a religiously pluralist and tolerant state: upholding monotheism; following a just and civilized humanism; respecting the unity of Indonesia; democracy; and social justice. Five religions – Islam, Protestantism, Roman Catholicism, Hinduism, and Buddhism – were recognized with offices in the Indonesian Department of Religious Affairs. Passage of a 1985 law requiring all social organizations to accept Pancasila as the only basis for national and social activities and life further solidified the country's recognition of religious freedom. Religious groups have been encouraged to engage in interreligious dialogue and to work together in social ministry and in developing universal moral and ethical standards for Indonesian society. Madjid played a pivotal role in providing a solid theological basis for Muslim participation by developing a Muslim vision of religious pluralism.

Pluralism seeks to move away from the traditional pattern of approaching the religious Other with the goal of either converting the Other or challenging the Other's beliefs and teachings, in favor of encouraging mutual acceptance and dialogue in order to bring the communities closer together socially or theologically. Rather than focusing on details of belief or law, pluralism works to identify shared ethical and moral codes and concerns that provide opportunities for working together to achieve social justice, mercy, and compassion while condemning economic injustice, consumerism, materialism, greed, excessive individualism, sexual promiscuity, crime, corruption, and violence. Theologically, pluralism moves beyond the positions of absolutism (there is only one truth and I have it) and absolute relativism (it doesn't matter what you believe as long as you are sincere) to reach the position of relative absolutism (what I believe in my context is truth, but what you believe in your context also contains truth). Recognition of shared truths provides a framework for determining how society ought to operate and how human beings should interact with each other. Such a position also discourages the labeling of a different perspective as other, sinful, or evil, by recognizing the common humanity of all as creations of the same God. Mutual understanding and tolerance are expected to avoid the mistakes of the past, including the relegation of the religious Other to second-class status, intolerance, oppression, and discrimination, in favor of positive and constructive interfaith interactions as religions learn both about and from each other. Pluralism also recognizes that some theological issues cannot be resolved and must be lived with while not allowing them to block cooperation.

Madjid's vision of pluralism in a Muslim context is based on the Quranic principles of there being no compulsion in religion (Q 2:256) and the permissibility of establishing truce relationships between Muslims and non-Muslims (Q 4:90). He asserted that Islam is inherently pluralistic because it recognizes Jews and Christians as fellow "People of the Book" who share a common divinely revealed scripture and prophetic heritage that includes Abraham, Moses, and Jesus. Historically, other monotheistic religions have also been granted protected minority status under Muslim rule. Madjid believed that the commonality of humanity should be reflected in the genuine tolerance and pluralism that he asserted as the most necessary elements of religious faith and practice in an increasingly global world. His scriptural support for pluralism was based on the Quran's proclamation that God specifically created human beings as different tribes and nations so that they could come to know

one another (Q 30:22, 48:13) and the truth by seeking God and competing in virtue and good works (Q 2:251). According to the Quran, the pluralism of systems, laws, and civilizations is intended to be perman-ent (Q 5:48 and 69). Madjid believed that religious exclusivism had no place in Islam because it reflected the worship of human beings and their limited understandings, rather than worship of God in His infinite knowledge.

Madjid's approach to pluralism was rooted in his concept of Islamic secularization in which a certain amount of secularization is recognized as necessary for the religious and social vitality of Islam and for maintaining a collective sense of morality and identity between faith groups. He rejected calls for the creation of an Islamic state because he found no Quranic basis for it. Instead, he called on Muslims to repudiate ideologies that call for the insertion of religion into political initiatives both because he believed that they should be focusing on more properly religious affairs and because the social reality in contemporary Indonesia required a willingness to live with and respond to Indonesia's pluralism.

In addition to his work on pluralism, Madjid also provided the theological support for Muslim acceptance of and adherence to democracy, citing the example of the Prophet Muhammad consulting (*shura*) with his Companions and followers as a routine procedure. Madjid considered democracy to be the natural outcome of pluralism because democracy involves listening to the ideas of other people and examining them critically in order to determine which idea is the best to follow. He argued for the necessity of democracy to prevent the tyranny of an individual ruling capriciously over society. He believed that every individual has the right to freedom of expression and to be listened to and that Islam's emphasis on orthopraxy (what one does) over orthodoxy (what one believes) should lead people to question whether their society accurately reflects their faith. He believed that an unjust society where poverty, corruption, and oppression are rampant cannot be considered Islamic. Similarly, he believed that anyone working to establish a just society should be considered as a Muslim because justice is a reflection of God's will.

Madjid's support for pluralism and democracy made him a prominent public intellectual in both Indonesia and the broader Muslim world. In addition to serving as the rector of Paramadina Mulya University in Indonesia since 1998, he was also a member of the Indonesian National Commission for Human Rights and was on the board of advisors for the World Policy Institute of New School University, Dialogues: Islamic World– U.S.–the West, which was founded in the aftermath of the 9/11 attacks in order to encourage greater communication between the Islamic world and the West. Majdid died in 2005 after a long and painful illness.

Further reading

Federspiel, Howard M. *Muslim Intellectuals and National Development in Indonesia.* Cormack, NY: Nova Science Publishers, 1998

Goddard, Hugh. *Christians and Muslims: From Double Standards to Mutual Understanding.* Richmond: Curzon Press, 1995

Haddad, Yvonne. "Islamists and the Challenge of Pluralism." Occasional paper. Washington, DC: Center for Contemporary Arab Studies, Georgetown University, 1995

Hasan, M. Kamal. *Muslim Intellectual Responses to "New Order" Modernization in Indonesia.* Kuala Lumpur: n.p., 1980

Hefner, Robert W. "Modernity and the Challenge of Pluralism: Some Indonesian Lessons." *Studia Islamika* 2:4 (1995), 25

Hick, John and Paul F. Knitter, eds. *The Myth of Christian Uniqueness: Toward a Pluralistic Theology of Religions.* Maryknoll, NY: Orbis Books, 1987

Madjid, Nurcholish. "In Search of Islamic Roots for Modern Pluralism: The Indonesian Experience," in *Toward a New Paradigm: Recent Developments in Indonesian Islamic Thought*, ed. Mark R. Woodward. Tempe, AZ: Arizona State University, 1996, pp. 89–116

—— "The Issue of Modernization Among Muslims in Indonesia from a Participant's Point of View," in *What is Modern Indonesian Culture?*, ed. Gloria Davis. Athens, OH: Ohio University Center for International Studies, 1979

"Personalities in Islam: Nurcholish Madjid, Islamic Liberization Innovator," www.islamicpaths.org/Home/Engli...ry/Personalities/Content/Nurcholish.htm

Ricklefs, Merle C. *Islam in the Indonesian Social Context.* Clayton, Australia: Centre of Southeast Asian Studies, Monash University, 1991

Schumann, Olaf. "Christian–Muslim Encounter in Indonesia," in *Christian–Muslim Encounters*, ed. Yvonne Yazbeck Haddad and Wadi Z. Haddad. Gainesville: University Press of Florida, 1995

Wei-hsun Fu, Charles and Gerhard E. Spiegler, eds. *Religious Issues and Interreligious Dialogues: An Analysis and Sourcebook of Developments Since 1945.* New York: Greenwood Press, 1989

Woodward, Mark R. "Nurcholish Madjid," in *The Oxford Encyclopedia of the Modern Islamic World*, editor-in-chief John L. Esposito, vol. 3. New York: Oxford University Press, 1995

www.islamuswest.org – website for World Policy Institute of New School University, Dialogues: Islamic World–U.S.–the West

The Honorable Zakia Mahasa (b. 1955)

Master chancery in the Family Division of the Baltimore City Circuit Court, the Honorable Zakia Mahasa is the first female Muslim master chancery in the United States.

Zakia Mahasa was born in Baltimore, MD, in 1955. Her father served in the air force prior to working for the U.S. postal service. Her mother worked as a nurse, but left her profession to raise her children full time. Mahasa recalls her mother's decision to remain home full time with her children as one of the most important events of her youth and one that remains a source of warmth, peace, happiness, and security to her as an adult. Recognizing the pivotal role played by the mother within the family unit, she encourages women to give generously of themselves as mothers and to spend as much time with their children as possible, preferably staying home with them.

As a child, Mahasa was determined to be outstanding at whatever she did. She decided to be an attorney before elementary school. She completed her secondary education in Baltimore prior to earning a B.A. in business administration from the University of Maryland.

Mahasa converted to Islam on her own initiative prior to beginning her undergraduate studies. Her parents were concerned about her conversion because of a negative experience a cousin had had with Nation of Islam and because of the potential negative impact on her career. Her father questioned whether there would be a place for a Muslim woman in the American legal system, particularly one who covered her hair in observation of hijab and had a recognizably Muslim name. Mahasa believed that her performance and professional demeanor, rather than her faith, name or what she wore on her head, ought to be the determining factors in her career. She neither hid nor made an issue of her faith. At the same time, she did not compromise her faith or principles. She notes that one of the great ironies in her career is that it took longer to gain the confidence of the Muslim community in her legal skills than it did the general public. In her early years of practice, she found that Muslims typically turned to non-Muslim lawyers to handle their cases.

Mahasa's family offered their support for her law-school studies and career, providing assistance as she juggled a full-time job, marriage, and raising a small child. On a typical day, she returned home from work at 6 P.M. and had to be in class by 6:30 P.M. When she graduated

from law school, her family presented her with a "Family Pride" award in recognition of her hard work and determination. Mahasa's son has paid his own tribute to his mother by following in her footsteps as a public defender and by engaging in the political activism he has been exposed to since early childhood.

After law school, Mahasa worked as a lawyer. For the first two years, she practiced criminal and personal injury law. She then changed jobs in order to pursue her passion – the welfare of women and children. She spent the next four years representing neglected and abused children through a legal aid bureau. After this, she spent about five years representing victims of domestic violence and became the managing attorney of the legal clinic at the House of Ruth, a comprehensive domestic-violence shelter founded in 1977 to protect and provide a safe haven for women and their children to prevent and escape battering situations, facilitate rapid and effective intervention, and assure that domestic-violence is not socially tolerated. House of Ruth runs the largest domestic-violence legal clinic in the United States.

Mahasa next moved to the Baltimore City Circuit Court where she has served as master chancery since 1999. She presides over the Juvenile Court, hearing between nine and thirty cases each day. In general, the cases are very complicated and emotional because they involve abused, neglected or delinquent children. Although the cases themselves are often depressing, Mahasa finds that her work enables her to play a positive and meaningful role in the lives of those who appear before her by finding workable solutions that address the full environment of the children at the center of the cases. As a master, Mahasa makes it clear that people will be treated fairly and with respect and dignity in her courtroom. She makes certain that the people involved in the case understand the court proceedings and the repercussions of the fact that the case is being tried in court. Because the cases involve people, she tries to see the human dimension of each case, rather than thinking about cases as numbers. Aware that her decisions reflect not only upon her as a master, but also on people's perceptions and images of Islam, she is conscious of the need to be certain that her ruling is just. She believes that her faith and extensive background in family law help her to work effectively. Rejecting stereotypes of Muslim women as standoffish or reclusive, she notes that being a Muslim permits her to be accessible and approachable as befits a master. Her colleagues note that she has a reputation for caring about the people who come before her in trial. Her compassion and dedication combined with her dynamic and knowledgeable presence in the courtroom have earned her respect.

One of the hallmarks of Mahasa's judgments is her family-inclusive and family-supportive approach to rulings that recognizes the importance of finding a solution for the family unit as a whole that allows it to remain intact whenever possible. She takes seriously the family unit as the basic unit of society and civilization because experience has taught her that children who are raised without family support have little chance of success in life and are more likely to engage in misdemeanor behaviors that can rapidly escalate. She believes that the state approach often overlooks the critical element of family support in dealing with misdemeanor cases, resulting in a missed opportunity for intervention before it is too late to turn the delinquent around. Her approach has proven more effective at a practical level. The majority of delinquents she sees in her courtroom are one-time offenders, a fact that she credits to effective intervention at the appropriate time and her insistence that services be provided to both the offenders and their families. Because delinquency typically grows out of dysfunctional family units, she believes that making the

family unit whole and healthy is frequently the key to ending delinquency.

Mahasa's success and expertise in dealing with domestic abuse, homelessness, and keeping teenagers focused have led her to spearhead an effort to start services designed to address these issues at the family level with the ultimate goal of strengthening and improving communities. She serves on a committee designed to look holistically at individual juvenile cases, putting together police, educators, court systems, and groups that work with juveniles to determine cohesive solutions for targeting children in need of supervision and for strengthening community-based, family-centered programs. She is also working to resurrect a mentoring program for junior high and high-school girls. She is a member of a variety of local and state organizations, as well as the National Association of Women Judges.

In addition to her work as master, Mahasa also chairs the board of directors of Mercy U.S.A. Aid and Development, a Detroit-based emergency relief organization with satellites across the United States, Kenya, Kosovo, Albania, Somalia, and Bosnia. Founded in 1986, Mercy U.S.A. is a non-profit relief and development organization dedicated to alleviating human suffering by supporting individuals and their communities in their efforts to become self-sufficient through the provision of services and small loans that serve as seed money. The goal is to improve health and promote economic and educational growth. By focusing on development, the organization seeks to provide a "hand up" rather than a "hand out." Mercy U.S.A. has helped to build factories in Somalia and Bosnia and a school in Kenya. It also provides emergency disaster relief, such as food, tents, water, medicine, and clothing, to victims of events such as earthquakes in Mozambique, the western United States, and Iran, and the genocide in Kosovo.

Mahasa's work as a judge and community leader has resulted in numerous awards and dinners in her honor. She dedicates her spare time to community service out of belief that she has a special responsibility to earn national respect for Islam and to improve conditions for Muslims in America.

Further reading

Mahasa, Zakia. "Snapshot: A Day in the Life of Juvenile Court," *Maryland Bar Journal*, May/June, 2003, vol. 36, no. 3

Sabir, Nadirah Z. "America's First Muslimah Judge: Zakia Mahasa – Committed to Excellence," *Azizah* magazine, Premier Issue, Winter 2001

Interview with the author, February 19, 2004

www.hruth.org – website for House of Ruth

www.mercyusa.org – website for Mercy U.S.A.

Naguib Mahfouz (1912–2006)

The first Arab and Muslim writer to win the Nobel Prize for Literature, Naguib Mahfouz is broadly credited with putting Arabic literature on the international literary map.

Naguib Mahfouz was born in 1912 in Cairo, Egypt. He spent the first twelve years of his life in the al-Gamaliyah Quarter of Cairo. He then moved to the al-Abbasiya Quarter on the outskirts of Cairo. Both locations have played important roles in his novels.

Mahfouz's father was a civil servant. His mother provided him with a broad cultural and historical education through visits to museums. His work reflects an appreciation of Egyptian history from Pharaonic through Islamic civilization. Mahfouz has also been inspired by music and architecture as reflections of national culture.

Mahfouz began his education at a traditional Quran school. He completed his elementary education at Bayn al-Qasrayn Primary School and graduated from high school in 1930. He earned a B.A. in philosophy from Cairo University in 1934. He began writing as a graduate student, but left school without his degree in 1936 to become a professional writer. Although he possessed no formal education in literature, he wrote articles and short stories while working as a journalist for several newspapers.

Mahfouz's first published work was a translation of a text on ancient Egypt. His first collection of short stories was published in 1938. His role models were earlier Arabic language writers such as Taha Hussein, Abbas al-Akkad, and Salama Mousa. He credited Hussein with teaching him the meaning of intellectual revolt, al-Akkad with introducing him to the psychological novel and with instilling in him a love of democracy, individual liberty, and the arts, and Mousa with making him aware of the value of science, socialism, and intellectual tolerance.

Although Mahfouz considered himself a writer, he worked full-time as a civil servant for thirty-five years until his retirement in 1972, writing only in his spare time. Between 1939 and 1954, he worked in the Ministry of Islamic Affairs. In 1954, he became the director of the Foundation for Support of the Cinema at the State Cinema Organization. Between 1969 and 1971, he served as a consultant for cinema affairs to the Ministry of Culture and was a contributing editor of *Al-Ahram* newspaper, in which most of his novels have been serialized and for which he regularly wrote a weekly column, Point of View.

Mahfouz's first literary dream was to write a series of novels covering Egyptian history from Pharaonic times through the present. The 1919 Revolution inspired in him nationalism and a desire to probe Egyptian history for examples of rebellions against foreign occupation. The discovery of King Tutankhamen's tomb in 1922 sparked his interest in ancient Egypt when he found that certain features of contemporary Egyptian life could be traced to that time.

Mahfouz's Pharaonic novels reveal the aspirations and orientation of twentieth-century Egyptian intellectuals. Throughout the twentieth century, Egyptians were torn between their pride in the Pharaonic past and the glory of their Islamic heritage. At the same time that they found themselves unable to reconcile these two eras, they became powerfully aware of foreign interest in Egypt's heritage combined with disdain for contemporary circumstances. Mahfouz used the Pharaonic setting to criticize the contemporary political system, although he tried to avoid antagonizing it. Other writers of the time had openly rebelled against the oppression and despotism of the Egyptian monarchy, earning imprisonment and often being fired from their jobs in the process. As a result of their experiences, Mahfouz decided to make a more subtle critique of the system by developing a narrative style that implied criticism without directly stating it. The presentation of these critiques through discussions of the pre-Islamic past and criticisms of the Pharaonic era, rather than the contemporary monarchy, combined with nationalist opposition to imperialism and its servants, allowed Mahfouz the illusion of criticizing foreign imperialism and past errors while actually giving commentary on contemporary politics.

Mahfouz completed only three novels in his series – *Mockery of the Fates* (1939), *Radubis* (1943), and *Kifah Tiba* (1944) – before he turned to contemporary issues. The end of World War II and the political chaos, corruption, and threat of invasion that followed convinced him of the need both to describe contemporary circumstances and to analyze the psychological impact of social change on ordinary people. Prior to beginning his project, he engaged in an intensive self-tutorial in world literature, reading both Egyptian and Western fiction. Although Western cultural and intellectual influences are apparent in his works, particularly in their realist style and techniques, Mahfouz's novels are clearly Egyptian, representing the transformation of the Arabic novel into a highly developed art form. He is often called the "Egyptian Dostoevski," "Egyptian Dickens," and "Egyptian Balzac" as a reflection of his broad understanding of world literature.

Mahfouz's new novels took a social realist approach, using real, urban settings, rather than fictional or metaphorical ones. The settings of his works are not interchangeable. He wrote almost exclusively about the urban settings of old Cairo because this is what he personally knew, saw, and experienced. Furthermore, much of Egypt's social and political change occurred in Cairo, which was the twentieth-century center for the petite bourgeoisie, successful merchants, and civil servants. It was also an environment that witnessed first hand the effects of modernization and the temptations brought by Western values and culture. Although Mahfouz used the specific setting of Cairo, his novels from the social realist period addressed universal issues such as the human condition, the problems of change and time, loneliness, cruelty, injustice, alienation, and human suffering. His characters reflected the broad social alienation felt at that time in Egypt through their asocial and antisocial personalities, as well as their actions and frames of mind, a major departure from the anger and social commitment typically expressed by poets of this time. His social realist novels demonstrate a broad philosophical vision marked by a passion for justice and harmony, accompanied by a lack of sentimentality.

Mahfouz's personal attachment to city life came from his frequenting of cafes where he experienced life and met with friends, writers, and intellectuals. Although he gained inspiration and wrote a number of his film scripts in cafes, he did not do any literary writing there. Considering his literary writing a matter of methodical discipline, he wrote only at home at his desk. He both wrote and read on a daily basis.

One of Mahfouz's first new novels was *The Beginning and the End.* Published in

1949, it is considered a masterpiece demonstration of humanitarianism and sensitivity to human suffering with universal significance through the description of the material, moral, and spiritual problems of a petit bourgeois Egyptian family confronted with poverty during World War II. The novel reflects the major social concerns of the petite bourgeoisie – material security, the future, conformity, and the disinclination to challenge power or authority – that came to a head with the overthrow of the monarchy in 1952, which promised to return power to the people.

Mahfouz continued his social realist literature with the Cairo Trilogy, describing the political, social, and economic changes that occurred in Egypt as the result of the clash between colonialism and nationalism. The trilogy – *Palace Walk*, *Palace of Desire*, and *Sugar Street* – tells the story of the patriarch al-Sayyid Ahmad Abd al-Jawad and his descendants over three generations, from World War I until the overthrow of the monarchy in 1952, through the presentation of a variety of characters and psychological understandings. By addressing the events through their impact on the lives of a single family, Mahfouz demonstrated the personal consequences of state policies and social reform. The trilogy, which is considered a milestone in modern Arabic literary history, won Mahfouz the State Encouragement Prize for Literature in 1957 and marked him as a writer of regional importance. It also made him a popular and widely read writer throughout the Arabic-speaking world.

Mahfouz observed that winning prizes was an important part of literary life in Egypt because it guaranteed the author a readership and served as social recognition of the value of literature. Prior to the State Encouragement Prize, Mahfouz had received a variety of awards, including prizes from the Arab Language Academy and the Ministry of Education. One of the most meaningful awards he received was his first – the Qut al-Qulub al-Dimardashiya Prize – which marked the first time his work had been recognized by critics. He also received the State Merit Award, one of Egypt's highest literary honors.

Although Mahfouz had earned national acclaim for his work with the trilogy, he stopped writing for seven years due to disillusionment with the socialist Nasser regime. He began publishing again only in 1959, but in a variety of formats, including novels, short stories, memoirs, essays, screenplays, and journalistic articles. The first novel to appear after this absence was one of his most controversial, *Children of Gebelaawi*. Told through the story of the patriarch, Gebelaawi, and his children living in a Cairo alley and ostensibly looking at the issues dividing Egypt at the time, the novel was really a retelling of the lives of Adam and Eve, Cain and Abel, Moses, Jesus and the Prophet Muhammad, with Gebelaawi serving as a God figure. Mahfouz stated that Gebelaawi did not represent God, but a certain idea of God that human beings have made. The novel explored how people are constantly moving further away from both God and each other, as demonstrated by the beginning of a family feud that continues to expand over time, driving the descendants increasingly further apart until they can no longer relate to each other, despite their common origins. An allegorical novel that deals simultaneously with humanity's thirst and quest for religious faith, *Children of Gebelaawi* not only serves as a commentary on the status of Jewish–Christian–Muslim relations and contemporary Muslim understandings of Moses, Jesus, and Muhammad, but also addresses the modern question of the "death of God." The novel met with serious protests and opposition in Egypt. It was banned as blasphemous throughout the Muslim world, except in Lebanon, and was serialized in *Al-Ahram* uncut only because of Mahfouz's personal friendship with President Nasser. Ironically, the novel was intended to be an Islamic novel and concluded with the triumph of faith.

Despite the public outcry over *Children of Gebelaawi*, Mahfouz continued to write and explore the theme of humanity moving further away from God throughout the 1960s. However, he changed his writing style to one that was more modernist in technique, using freer constructions and interior monologues and emphasizing modern techniques of characterization and event sequencing. He also made increasing use of symbolism and allegory, rather than social realism, to address psychological and philosophical matters. This new methodology was reflected in his psychological and impressionistic 1961 novel, *The Thief and the Dogs*. In this story of a Marxist thief who is released from prison and plots his revenge only to be murdered in a cemetery, Mahfouz introduced a stream-of-consciousness narrative technique that was new to Arabic literature. The purpose of the technique was to show the mental anguish of the thief as he was consumed by bitterness and the desire for revenge against the individuals and society that have corrupted and betrayed him. Throughout the early 1960s, Mahfouz also took on political commentaries through his novels. His 1962 novel *Autumn Quail* reflected his reaction to the 1952 Revolution through its tale of moral responsibility, political downfall, and alienation as told by characters from different social and political backgrounds. The political-commentary approach was continued in the 1965 novel *The Beggar*, which assessed the impact of the 1952 Revolution. The use of multiple first-person narratives to represent different political views is also apparent in his 1967 novel *Miramar*.

As for many in the Arab world, the defeat of the combined armies of Egypt, Jordan, and Syria by Israel during the Six Day War of 1967 marked a period of trauma and soul-searching for Mahfouz as he sought answers as to why modernization and development had failed to deliver on their promises for the Arab world. He turned to a new literary format – playwriting – as an extension of the inner dialogues he had begun to explore in his novels. He wrote five short plays between the June 1967 loss and the October 1973 victory, which healed him psychologically. His post-1967 novels further reflect his personal soul-searching by their narrower focus on local Egyptian political and cultural life.

By the 1980s, Mahfouz had begun to mix the traditional with the contemporary, using classical Arabic narratives as subtexts in works such as *Arabian Nights and Days* (1981) and *The Journey of Ibn Fatouma* (1983). His 1985 novel *Akhenaten, Dweller in Truth*, combined old and new religious truths, demonstrating the conflict between them. During this time, his novels came to the attention of the Nobel Prize Committee due to the efforts of Jacqueline Kennedy Onassis and the expansion of scholarship on Arabic literature after 1985 which made his work accessible to a broader audience.

In 1988, Mahfouz became the first Arab and first Muslim writer to receive the Nobel Prize for Literature, marking him as a writer of global acclaim. Citing his works as "rich in nuance" and indicative of the formation of "an Arabian narrative art that applies to all mankind," the Nobel Prize not only affirmed the importance of Third World literature, but also marked the advance of contemporary Arabic literature onto the universal stage. Mahfouz was credited with opening people's minds to the human condition in Egypt and with demonstrating the forces that limit human happiness, dignity, and freedom. He was lauded for his ability as an intellectual to rebel against and reject coercion in religion, politics, and society without rejecting his cultural identity. The prize also brought world attention and prestige to

Egypt and led to English-language interest in Mahfouz's works. He has since become the most translated of Egyptian writers.

Mahfouz wrote that he was personally surprised but very proud to have received the Nobel Prize, believing that it shows that literary excellence is not limited by national boundaries. At the same time, he observed that there remain many great writers who have not been Nobel winners and are not necesssarily popular, but who nevertheless deserve attention due to the quality of their work. He held writers responsible for possessing a vision and desire to communicate all that they see based on knowledge of the works of their predecessors combined with a solid grasp of general culture, including history, politics, science, music, art, philosophy, and psychology. He believed that such knowledge of culture and appreciation of art could only be achieved where democracy is present.

Although many in Egypt celebrated Mahfouz's literary achievement, there were some who believed that he had "offended Muslims" in *Children of Gebelaawi* and denounced his support for the Camp David Accords and moderate stance on Salman Rushdie's controversial novel, *The Satanic Verses*. Mahfouz was condemned to death by Sheikh Omar Abd al-Rahman, the head of the Egyptian extremist group Islamic Jihad, and ideologue of the 1993 terrorist attack on the World Trade Center in New York City. Despite the death threat, Mahfouz refused to adapt his lifestyle or hire security guards. On October 14, 1994, as he was on his way to a weekly gathering with friends, he was stabbed in the neck by a religious opponent. The attack, which he barely survived, severed the nerve that controlled his right arm.

Following the assassination attempt, Mahfouz was forced to give up not only his beloved coffeehouses, but also his intensive daily writing schedule. Despite rigorous physical therapy, he recovered a very limited writing ability, reducing his daily writing time to about half an hour per day. Undeterred, he changed the format of his weekly newspaper column to a transcription of a conversation with a friend about a chosen topic while writing very short stories similar to Japanese haiku, encapsulating wisdom in a few words. Similarly undeterred, religious extremists unsuccessfully attempted to initiate court proceedings declaring Mahfouz an infidel and forcibly divorcing him from his wife in 1996. (See also DR. NAWAL EL SAADAWI.)

The author of fifty novels, more than a hundred short stories, thirty screenplays, and numerous theatrical plays, Mahfouz is credited with having popularized the short story and novel in the Arab literary world and with having transformed the novel into the preeminent literary form of twentieth-century Arabic and into a globally recognized standard. Although his novels have been banned in many Middle Eastern countries, he nevertheless enjoys an audience of millions in the Middle East. His novels have been translated into numerous foreign languages and he received honorary doctorates from Denmark, France, and the Soviet Union. His literary impact is evident in other novelists who have either built on his work or written in alternative styles to expand the scope of Arabic literature. One of his novels, *Midaq Alley*, was made into a film starring Salma Hayek. A documentary about Mahfouz's life and work – *Naguib Mahfouz: The Passage of the Century* – was made by Francka Mouloudi and has been presented at a variety of international film festivals. Mahfouz died in 2006 from complications from a bleeding ulcer.

Further reading

Allen, Roger. "Arabic Literature and the Nobel Prize," *World Literature Today.* Spring 1988: 201–3

—— *The Arabic Novel: An Historical and Critical Introduction.* Syracuse: Syracuse University Press, 1982

Badawi, M. M., ed. *The Cambridge History of Arabic Literature.* Cambridge: Cambridge University Press, 1983

Bear, Michael and Adnan Haydar, eds. *Naguib Mahfouz: From Regional Fame to Global Recognition*. Syracuse: Syracuse University Press, 1993

Kilpatrick, Hilary. *The Modern Egyptian Novel*. London: Ithaca Press, 1974

Mahfouz, Naguib. *Autumn Quail*, trans. Roger Allen. New York: Doubleday Anchor Books, 1985

—— *The Beggar*, trans. Kristin Walker Henry and Nariman Khales Naili al-Warriki. New York: Doubleday Anchor Books, 1986

—— *The Beginning and the End*, trans. Ramses Awad. New York: Doubleday Anchor Books, 1985

—— *Children of Gebelaawi*, trans. Philip Stewart. Washington, DC: Three Continents Press, 1981

—— *Midaq Alley*, trans. Trevor Le Gassick. New York: Doubleday Anchor Books, 1992

—— *Palace of Desire*, trans. William Maynard Hutchins. New York: Doubleday Anchor Books, 1992

—— *Palace Walk*, trans. William Maynard Hutchins. New York: Doubleday Anchor Books, 1990

—— *The Search*, trans. Mohamed Islam. New York: Doubleday Anchor Books, 1987

—— *Sugar Street*, trans. William Maynard Hutchins and Angele Botros Samaan. Cairo: American University in Cairo Press, 2001

—— *The Thief and the Dogs*, trans. Trevor Le Gassick and M.M. Badawi. New York: Doubleday Anchor Books, 1984

—— *Wedding Song*, trans. Olive E. Kenny. New York: Doubleday Anchor Books, 1984

Salmawy, Mohamed. *Naguib Mahfouz at Sidi Gaber: Reflections of a Nobel Laureate, 1994–2001, From Conversations with Mohamed Salmawy*. Cairo: American University in Cairo Press, 2001

www.kirjasto.sci.fi – index of international literary figures containing biographies and bibliographies

www.nobel.se/ – website of the Nobel Foundation and Prize

Samira Makhmalbaf (b. 1980)

The youngest film director ever to win the Jury Prize at the Cannes Film Festival, at twenty years of age, Samira Makhmalbaf is an internationally acclaimed cinematic artist.

Samira Makhmalbaf was born on February 15, 1980, in Tehran, Iran. Her father, Mohsen Makhmalbaf, is a highly acclaimed filmmaker renowned for his use of imagery, rather than violence or special effects, as a method of cinematic expression. The director of a variety of internationally acclaimed films, including *Kandahar*, he is the founder and director of Makhmalbaf Film House. Makhmalbaf's mother was killed in a house fire when she was eight years old.

Makhmalbaf's involvement in filmmaking dates to her mother's death. She began accompanying her father on his production sets when she was eight and in 1989 starred in his film *The Cyclist*, a human-interest story filmed on the border between Afghanistan and Pakistan. Makhmalbaf's experiences during the filming of *The Cyclist* had a lasting impact on her, particularly witnessing the suffering caused by war and its effects on women. Although she has taken photographs on the border areas since she was a child, she believes that still photographs cannot convey the full human tragedy of conflict. Her filmmaking seeks to address through moving imagery the tragedies of Afghanistan and Iraq, in particular. Her goal is to represent people, rather than politics.

Makhmalbaf's opportunities to observe her father on location, as well as the processes of editing and directing, led to her increasing interest in filmmaking. She left high school when she was fourteen in order to study film with her father. She persuaded him to found Makhmalbaf Film House for her, her two sisters, and her stepmother in 1996.

By the time Makhmalbaf was seventeen, she had directed two video productions. In 1998, she directed her debut film, *The Apple*, which was invited to more than one hundred international film festivals and has been screened in more than thirty countries. *The Apple* tells the story of a traditional, conservative man with a blind wife and twin twelve-year-old daughters whom he keeps locked up behind bars at home in order to observe *purdah* (seclusion of women). The film, which was based on a true-life story and in which the characters play themselves, records the first ventures of the girls into the world outside their home and their awakening to the experience of ordinary life. The film's power lies in its humanity and exploration of the lives of contemporary Iranian women. The purpose of the story is to explain the father's actions as a reflection of his belief that he is following the teachings of the Quran. He is portrayed as a tragic, rather than an evil, figure. Makhmalbaf maintained contact with the girls after the filming. Both joined Makhmalbaf Film House after the death of their mother and are supported by the film's profits.

The Apple created some controversy because it was co-written and edited by Makhmalbaf's father, leading some to question whether the film could truly be considered hers. Makhmalbaf noted that she was the director of the film and had chosen her father to edit the film not simply because he was her father, but because he was an internationally recognized filmmaker. She entered the film in the 1998 Cannes Film Festival and became, at the age of eighteen, the youngest director in the world to participate in the official competition. The film subsequently won jury prizes at film festivals in Thessalonica and Sao Paulo, as well as the International Critics Prize at the 1998 Locarno Film Festival in Switzerland, the Sutherland Trophy at the 1998 London Film Festival, and the Jury's Special Prize, the Critic's Prize, and the Audience's Prize at the 1999 Independent Cinema Film Festival in Argentina.

Makhmalbaf returned to the Cannes Film Festival in 2000 with her 1999 film *The Blackboard*, which won the Jury Prize. At twenty, she was the youngest director ever to win this prestigious prize. The film went on to win the Federico Fellini Honor from U.N.E.S.C.O., the Francois Truffaut Prize and the Giffoni Mayor's Prize at the Giffoni Film Festival in Italy, and the Grand Jury Prize from the American Film Institute in 2000. It also won jury prizes at the Moscow, Venice, and Geneva Film Festivals in 2000.

The Blackboard tells the story of a group of itinerant teachers in the mountains between Iraq and Iran. In their quest to find students, the teachers travel carrying their blackboards on their backs. Two of them break away from the group. One finds a group of boys smuggling goods across the border and offers to teach them in exchange for bread. The other meets a group of Kurdish refugees trying to return to their homeland in Iraq to die. Uninterested in studies, they hire the teacher as a guide to the border instead. Makhmalbaf has described the storyline as the result of discussions she had with her father while traveling through Kurdistan. Although the two co-wrote the screenplay and her father served as the executive producer and editor, Makhmalbaf alone was responsible for filming and directing it.

The Blackboard was filmed over a period of four months in the Kurdish mountains near the Iran–Iraq border, close to the city where Saddam Hussein unleashed nerve gas against his own Kurdish population. The region is additionally covered with landmines. Makhmalbaf used only two professional actors, preferring local villagers as more genuine in their actions, despite the fact that many of them had never seen a film. The use of local villagers presented its own challenges, including the difficulty of blending the professional actors with the locals and the tendency of the locals to stop acting in order to participate in cultural activities or to go and pray. Makhmalbaf also found herself in an unusual position of leadership with the locals. In many cases, they were reluctant to do things like get into icy water or climb mountains unless she went first.

She found that they were more likely to follow if a woman set the example. She also met with some resistance from her crew, who protested the daily two-hour trek to the Iraqi border. Makhmalbaf insisted that it was necessary to capture the energy of the bombings and the human side of the war, particularly the aftermath of chemical warfare. She spent three months away from her family with no contact by telephone during filming. Electricity had come to the region only the year before.

A metaphorical, allegorical, and surreal film, *The Blackboard* is not a documentary. Rather, Makhmalbaf describes it as an exploration of what happens to individuals who live in the midst of conflicts where violence is always close by and gunfire and helicopters are always in the background. One of the most poignant aspects of the film is that it is never clear who is carrying out the bombings that permeate it. The blurring is deliberate – not only does it demonstrate that, for the people on the ground, who carries out the bombing is not as important as the fact that it occurs, but it also suggests that no single country is responsible for it. The blurring of identity serves to show that the bombing is due to a variety of politicians and countries.

Makhmalbaf's preference for educational themes in her feature films is designed to bring attention to the susceptibility of education to geographical terrain, historical events, and religious beliefs. *The Blackboard* particularly brings this to life, as blackboards are shown being used not only for education, but also as a dowry, a partition, a clothesline, a defensive shield, a shelter, a gurney, and to make splints for Kurdish refugees injured in avalanches and battles. The blackboards challenge viewers to see that those who carry them also carry heavy mental burdens due to their life experiences. By combining reality with imagination, Makhmalbaf sought to demonstrate that even smuggling,

wandering, and living as a refugee can give birth to metaphor and be shown beautifully and artistically.

Although there is political content to her films, Makhmalbaf does not make political films and has stated in interviews that she is not interested in politics. As an artist, she is interested in universal truths and experiences. She notes that her films are much deeper than political or journalistic work because they touch on so many aspects of human existence and tragedy. Despite the rarity of her remarks on politics, she dedicated her Cannes prize to the "heroic efforts" of Iran's pro-democracy movement. She also turned her filmmaking to the aftermath of the 9/11 attacks with her filming of *God, Construction, and Destruction*, which was part of the assemblage film *11'09"1*. The film won jury prizes at the Arab Screen Independent Film Festival and the Cannes International Film Festival in 2001.

Makhmalbaf's other flirtation with politics in filmmaking occurred in *Five in the Afternoon*. Set in Afghanistan, it tells the story of a young woman who wants to become president of the Republic. The film was particularly noteworthy because it was the first to be made by a foreign director in Kabul after the fall of the Taliban. Makhmalbaf's biggest challenge for this film was finding a woman who was willing to star in it because the women of Afghanistan remained afraid of the Taliban, who had banned films and entertainment under the penalty of death for women. The film won the Jury Special Award at the 2003 Cannes Film Festival and the 2003 Grand Prize from the Society of the Churches of the World.

From a business perspective, Makhmalbaf has protested Hollywood control over the filmmaking industry, asserting that the First World monopoly over filmmaking is due to the use of political power, financial resources, and concentration of the means of production to marginalize Third World film production, giving the false impression that the Third World is incapable of expressing itself in visual terms and has nothing to say. She has particularly criticized the First World's control over how the Third World is viewed and the First World's emphasis on technical matters, rather than artistry, in filmmaking. She has called on all nations to invest in and promote national cinema and theaters, in addition to spending less on Hollywood productions, in order to prevent any single country from dominating cinema or how everyone views both themselves and the rest of the world. She has also called for greater emphasis on the human dimension of cinema, noting the power of cinema to promote human understanding. Makhmalbaf believes that cinema is as important as journalism in safeguarding democracy, noting that censorship affects both and that both filmmakers and journalists often exercise self-censorship out of fear of persecution by religious fanatics. She has expressed hope that technological advancements, particularly the digital revolution, will help cinema to become increasingly accessible to all people.

International acclaim for her films has made Makhmalbaf a role model in Iran for young people of both genders. More than a filmmaker, she shatters clichés about Iranian and Muslim women and stands for a new model of the strong Iranian woman who finds her own ways to express herself.

Further reading

Bear, Liza. "Young Director Explores Metaphors of Kurdish Dispossession, Baggage," *Boston Globe*, January 17, 2003

Makhmalbaf, Samira. "The Digital Revolution and the Future of Cinema," address to the Cannes Film Festival Forum, May 9, 2000, www.wsws.org/articles/2000/jun2000/makh-j28.shtml

Peary, Gerald. "Samira Makhmalbaf," January, 2003, www.geraldpeary.com/interviews/mno/makhmalbaf-samira.html

Sullivan, Moira. "Samira Makhmalbaf: *Five in the Afternoon,* " Special Report, *Movie Magazine International,* May 3, 2003

Weale, Sally. "Angry Young Woman," *The Guardian,* December 15, 2000

www.eskandarimakeup.com/makh/persons.asp?p=sa – website for Makhmalbaf Film House

Dr. Laila al-Marayati (b. 1962)

Past president and spokesperson for the Muslim Women's League (M.W.L.), co-founder of KinderU.S.A., presidential appointee to the Commission on International Religious Freedom, and a practicing physician, Dr. Laila al-Marayati is a prominent Muslim voice in the call for women's and children's rights and religious freedom.

Dr. Laila al-Marayati was born in Los Angeles, CA, on May 12, 1962. Her father, who had been born and raised in Palestine, was a physician and an activist for both the Palestinian and Muslim communities. Her mother was a full-time homemaker and community volunteer. From her parents, al-Marayati learned to live political activism and the quest for social justice. She is married to Salam al-Marayati, the executive director of the Muslim Public Affairs Council (M.P.A.C.) in Los Angeles.

Al-Marayati decided to pursue a medical career both to follow in her father's footsteps and because she sought an occupation that would allow her to have a positive impact on the lives of others. She attended medical school at the University of California and served both her internship and her residency at the Los Angeles County University of Southern California Medical Center. A board-certified obstetrician-gynecologist and a member of the American College of OB/GYN, she has operated a private practice in Glendale, CA, since she completed her residency in 1992. She is clinical associate professor in the department of obstetrics and gynecology at LA

County/U.S.C. Women's and Children's Hospital.

In addition to her responsibilities as a physician and the mother of three children, al-Marayati has been an advocate for women's and children's rights and a promoter of interfaith dialogue and religious freedom. In 1992, she co-founded the Muslim Women's League (M.W.L.) in response to the rape of Bosnian Muslim women by Serbs as a weapon of war and ethnic cleansing. The M.W.L. was founded to raise both public consciousness about these war crimes and money to help women affected by them. Under al-Marayati's leadership, it spearheaded the foundation of the Women's Coalition Against Ethnic Cleansing, which consisted of more than twenty women's religious and civic groups. The M.W.L. sent delegations with the coalition in 1993 and 1994 on fact-finding missions to Croatia. The delegations were responsible for convincing women to talk about their experiences to provide evidence to bring the perpetrators to justice. Many women feared telling their stories not only because of the psychological and, at times, physical damage they had sustained and would have to relive in the telling, but also out of shame for what had happened to them. The delegations also met with women's groups in Bosnia and dispensed the funds that had been raised to help them. The M.W.L.'s efforts were recognized with a Humanitarian Award from the Los Angeles Commission on Assaults Against Women in 1993.

Following the war, the group turned to highlighting women's issues, disseminating accurate information about Islam and women, and strengthening the role of Muslim women in society. The M.W.L. is dedicated to implementing the values of Islam in order to reclaim the status of Muslim women as "free, equal and vital contributors to society." Although a solid historical and scholarly grounding in the Quran, *hadith*, and Islamic law is necessary to carry authority with the Muslim community, al-Marayati believes that the time has come for a new interpretation of Islamic law that takes into consideration the needs of Muslims living in non-Muslim-majority countries – a contemporary situation that has no historical precedent of scale. Her vision of the M.W.L. is one in which the organization selects and sparks discussion on topics to which the broader Muslim community must then respond.

As a reflection of the important role played by the M.W.L. in addressing Muslim women's issues, al-Marayati and other M.W.L. members served as part of the official U.S. delegation to the U.N. Fourth World Conference on Women in Beijing in 1995. They presented the only report addressing the concerns and status of Muslim women living in the United States. They also prepared a series of position papers addressing the rights given to women by Islam and raising concerns about the selective application of Islamic law in favor of men while frequently ignoring women's rights. Although this helped to put the M.W.L. on the American map as a spokesorganization for American Muslim women, it also brought significant criticism to the participants from conservative quarters. The delegates later helped to sponsor the first Eid celebration at the White House with al-Marayati as one of the speakers.

Domestically, the M.W.L. hosts the only sports camp for Muslim girls in the United States and works on reproductive and health issues for Muslim women. It used a $70,000 grant from the Hewlett Foundation to help support the U.M.M.A. Free Clinic, the only free clinic in South Central Los Angeles that was started and is sustained by Muslim physicians; provide financial support to a domestic-violence shelter for Muslim women operated by N.I.S.W.A. (see also SHAMIM IBRAHIM); write and translate educational health brochures for Muslim women; and develop an Islamic sex-education curriculum for middle-school children at the Middle School of the New Horizon School in Pasadena, CA, as directed by al-Marayati's sister, Amira Al-Sarraf.

Al-Marayati has also taken on the controversial issue of honor killings as a matter of women's and human rights. (See also RANA HUSSEINI.) In some parts of the Muslim world, there is a cultural tradition that a man's honor lies in the sexual purity of his female family members. If a man believes that a woman has dishonored him by illicit sexual activity, whether real or imagined, tradition allows him to restore his honor by killing the woman. Al-Marayati has worked to discredit this practice among Muslims by pointing out that there is no basis in Islam for honor killings and that there is an inherent injustice in such cases because the man as an individual serves as judge, jury, and executioner while the woman is not entitled to be informed of the charges against her or to defend herself. Al-Marayati considers this procedure to be a violation of Islam's principles of justice, personal responsibility, and the requirement of witnesses to sexual crimes. She has also decried the fact that, in some countries, honor killings are treated differently from murder cases by the courts and tend to carry shorter prison sentences, if any, for the perpetrators. She has proposed a three-step process to resolve the problem. First, she calls for setting the record straight about what Islam teaches about sexual behavior, noting that, while Islam prohibits sexual relations outside of marriage for both women and men, other forms of intimacy, while sinful, are not subject to the death penalty. Second, she has called for attention to the reality that the clear guidelines of the Quran for witnessing are frequently overlooked. The result is that women are often accused of crimes they did not necessarily commit and are subjected to abuse, denigration, and death – sometimes for having been raped – while men escape trial and punishment

altogether. She has denounced this reality not only as a failure to adhere to Islam's teachings, but also as an act of gender discrimination that denies the equality between women and men proclaimed by the Quran and the God-given dignity and humanity of women. The third step in her recommended process is to address honor killings from within the Muslim community so that Muslims bear responsibility for correcting their own misperceptions about their beliefs.

Al-Marayati's work on women's issues and education of the public about Islam and religious intolerance against Muslims won her a place as a presidential appointee to the Commission on International Religious Freedom from 1999 until 2001. Prior to this, she had served as a member of the State Department Advisory Committee on Religious Freedom Abroad and had testified before Congress and as part of the U.S. delegation to the O.S.C.E. Human Dimensions meeting in Poland regarding religious intolerance against Muslims in Europe. Her experience on the commission left her disturbed by its failure to apply its policies consistently. While discrimination against the minority Coptic Christians of Egypt and Shii Muslims of Saudi Arabia was investigated and denounced, the same standard was not applied to Israel's discrimination against non-Orthodox Jews and Palestinians, both Muslim and Christian, reflecting what is frequently denounced in the Muslim world as a double standard that gives preferential treatment to Israel over Muslim countries, particularly where human rights are concerned. Al-Marayati asserts that, during a time of regional instability and rising global terrorism, this approach is counterproductive and serves not only to fuel extremist calls for hatred of the U.S., but also alienates moderate Arabs and Muslims.

Al-Marayati's concern for the human rights crisis faced by Palestinians led her to co-found and serve on the board of directors of KinderUSA, a charity organization that addresses the health and educational needs of Palestinian children living in the West Bank and Gaza through the provision of emergency food, back-to-school support including registration fees, vouchers for uniforms and shoes, and a hot breakfast for school-age children, and counseling for stress and psychological trauma. The organization also sponsors orphans, the rebuilding of kindergartens, and a voucher program for food. Al-Marayati's involvement with KinderUSA has helped her to remain focused on the people caught in the midst of the current intifada. Because she believes that all people have an obligation to advocate peacefully for those who are oppressed, she has focused her energy on encouraging Palestinian children to participate in the resistance and work for positive change by surviving, becoming educated, and being healthy.

Al-Marayati is a frequent speaker to diverse groups and is the author of numerous articles that have been published in newspapers and on the internet. She has appeared on both local and national radio and television programs addressing issues of concern to Muslims in America.

Further reading

Ali, Farkhunda and Felicity Salaam. "Muslim Women Organizations," *Azizah* magazine, Spring 2002

Al-Marayati, Laila. "The Biases of Elliott Abrams," *CounterPunch*, December 16, 2002

—— "Stand Firmly for Justice: It's Time for Muslims to Confront Honor Killings," *Azizah* magazine, Premier Issue, Winter 2001

"President Clinton Names Laila Al-Marayati, Firuz Kazemzadeh, and Charles Z. Smith as Members of the United States Commission on International Religious Freedom," White House press release, May 5, 1999

Interview with the author, October 28, 2003

www.kinderusa.org – website for KinderUSA

www.mwlusa.org – website for Muslim Women's League

Fatima Mernissi (b. 1940)

A prominent sociologist and women's rights activist, Fatima Mernissi was one of the first Arab Muslim women to insert her voice into the reinterpretation of religious texts from a feminist perspective.

Fatima Mernissi was born in Fez, Morocco, in 1940 to a middle-class family. Raised in a domestic harem, she was part of the first generation of Moroccan girls to receive a Western-style education outside of the home. She also attended the traditional Quran school where she memorized the Quran. Although she had initially held a fairly romantic image of the Prophet Muhammad due to stories passed down to her by family members, her formal studies of his sayings and deeds (*hadith*) as a teenager left her disillusioned. Much of this disillusionment came from the distortions of the Prophet's teachings introduced by male scholars, either through interpretation or selective use of certain *hadith* reflecting patriarchy and misogyny, rather than *hadith* advocating respectful treatment of women and assertion of their rights. Deeply disturbed by the negative depiction of women in the *hadith* chosen for study, she pursued graduate-level studies interrogating and analyzing the sacred texts. She received her master's degree from Mohammad V University in Rabat, Morocco, and then worked as a journalist in Paris for a short time. She completed her Ph.D. in sociology at Brandeis University in Waltham, MA, in 1973. Her dissertation was later published as *Beyond the Veil*, which became an important source on women and Islam for Westerners. Mernissi is a professor of sociology at Mohammad V University in Rabat.

Mernissi's early childhood in the harem is recounted in her autobiography, *Dreams of Trespass*. Her early childhood was defined by learning to recognize and respect boundaries marking separation: between Muslim and Christian, male and female, religious and secular, private and public. Because she was born during the French occupation of Morocco, her early childhood included the experiences of World War II and Morocco's quest for independence. Some of the boundaries of her childhood were designed to protect the prestige and honor of her household's men by preventing the women from coming into contact with the French occupying forces and by maintaining an invisible barrier between the French and Arab quarters of Fez. Mernissi's father taught her that the purpose of boundaries was to establish harmony and respect between two necessarily opposing worlds so that crossing them could only result in sorrow and unhappiness. For her father's generation, the purpose of education was to learn the boundaries and respect them. However, Mernissi consistently sought to push back the boundaries that blocked her from learning and experiencing life beyond the harem. Like many of the harem women, she perceived the boundaries as a challenge to be overcome, rather than as a protection to be respected.

Mernissi's attitude toward both boundaries and the harem were profoundly influenced by her mother and maternal grandmother. Her grandmother was one of several wives in a country harem, while her mother was her father's only wife and lived in an urban harem. From her grandmother, Mernissi learned to consider all human beings as equal regardless of their gender, religion, place of origin, socio-economic status, or language spoken, and to oppose polygyny. Her grandmother also encouraged her to pursue an education and to travel and gain greater experience of the world. For Mernissi, this became a personal quest that she sought to fulfill on behalf of all of the women of the harem.

Western images and ideas of the harem tend to focus on the supposedly erotic dimension of harem life. However, Mernissi notes that the reality of the domestic harem in which she was raised was that multi-generational families lived together, rather than a single man with multiple wives. In such situations, generational hierarchies tend to rule and individual space is neither respected nor promoted. Furthermore, a variety of experiences can exist within the social practice of maintaining a harem. She contrasts the life of her grandmother, who was one of several wives of her grandfather yet lived in the countryside with access to open space and the freedom to walk outside, swim and ride horses, with the life of her mother, who, although the only wife of her father, led a much more confined life in the city where she had to have multiple permissions and a specific purpose in order to leave the harem and then only in the company of other women and male children from the harem. She further had no access to open space or the world outside of the harem other than looking straight up into the sky, as all of the windows in the house looked out into the courtyard, rather than the street. Having been raised in the comparative freedom of the countryside, Mernissi's mother found urban harem life repressive and depressing.

Despite the confines of living within the harem, Mernissi's mother managed to assert herself as a powerful individual in several ways. Despite her father's opposition, she adopted the *djellaba*, or man's fitted robe with a hood, as her manner of dress in public, rather than the more complex traditional women's *haik*, which was cumbersome and heavy. In 1956, when Morocco declared independence from France, her mother uncovered her hair and face and participated in a nationalist march. After this, only elderly women and recent arrivals from the countryside veiled. Mernissi's mother forbade her to veil, believing that covering her hair identified her as a victim who would hide, rather than as a courageous woman capable of standing her ground. Her mother also rejected male superiority as an anti-Muslim concept and encouraged her to develop an independent spirit and rely solely on herself to solve her own problems, rather than turning to a male cousin.

Mernissi's mother was an admirer of the Egyptian feminist writer Qasim Amin. Because she was illiterate, she was dependent on her husband to read Amin's writings to her, a task he was not always willing to fulfill. The family council further denied her the right to pursue literacy classes, claiming that education was for small children and that she had no reasonable need to learn to read. It was precisely because of her own illiteracy that Mernissi's mother campaigned hard for Mernissi's right to a Western-style education. She pressured her to study well and earn a diploma so that she could live with fewer physical restrictions as an adult.

Mernissi found the contrast between the Quran school and the Western-style nationalist school striking. The Quran school had been characterized by slow-paced memorization engaged in while sitting quietly on cushions on the floor throughout the day and facing punishment by whipping for behavioral infractions or failure to memorize the material properly. The nationalist school was more modern, with chairs and tables for the children, no physical punishment, breaks for lunch, recess, and prayer, and a variety of subjects to learn. Although she enjoyed going to school and performed well, it also brought about the sad realization of the tragedy of her own mother's life.

Mernissi learned the power of words and speaking from her youth. She particularly enjoyed listening to stories and watching and participating in theatrical productions within the harem. From her aunt, she heard the tales of Scheherezade, the heroine of The Thousand and One Nights who enraptured Caliph Harun al-Rashid with her story-telling and saved her own life, as well as the lives of other women, in the process. Mernissi was fascinated by the story of Scheherezade because she was distinguished by her creativity, courage, and intelligence, rather than by more superficial qualities such as physical beauty or youth. From her example, Mernissi realized that her own future would depend on her skill with words to resolve injustice and protest discrimination. She also drew inspiration from Arab feminists who harnessed the power of words, both written and spoken, to promote women's rights and decry the cultural practices of veiling and seclusion.

Mernissi's experiences growing up, both within the harem and with religious and women's issues in general, led her to pursue historical research about interpretations of scripture and Islamic law that disturbed her. Her doctoral research marked the beginning of a number of important works that inserted the female voice into the interpretation and reinterpretation of scripture, challenging traditional patriarchal interpretations and calling for a more egalitarian interpretation of Islam. Mernissi is frequently called an Islamic feminist because she seeks to change the system by reinterpreting religious texts, as opposed to adopting Western terminology or standards. She is at the forefront of one of the most important intellectual and religious developments in the contemporary Muslim world.

Mernissi's works explore the relationship between gender identity, the status of women in Islam, sexual ideology, and socio-political organization. Although she mainly focuses on Moroccan culture and society, her works are a broader critique of political and ideological systems that silence and oppress Muslim women. The use of her own voice in her autobiography and of the voices of other women in Doing Daily Battle is a deliberate attempt to give a voice to otherwise silent women and to allow them to speak out about their struggles against sexual oppression, poverty, and illiteracy. In the process, she emphasizes that authentic Islam does not consign women to silence, obedience or passivity, placing the blame for such constructions on male scholars and jurists seeking to preserve a patriarchal system – particularly conservative Muslim men who fear that women possess an inherent sexual power capable of disrupting society if left uncontrolled. She attributes gender segregation, veiling, and the legal subordination of women to this fear, noting that they all serve as control mechanisms over women. *Beyond the Veil* explores the impact of this ideology on gender construction and the organization of Muslim domestic and political life in the contemporary era.

The Veil and the Male Elite challenges traditional Muslim discourse on women's status and gender through an analysis of the texts of the Quran and *hadith* combined with a critical examination of the historical context of Muslim law and tradition. Mernissi has argued that Muhammad called for gender equality, but that this vision was set aside in the historical development of Islam and Islamic civilization as *hadith* supportive of misogyny and patriarchy came to be considered more authoritative than *hadith* calling for greater rights and roles for women. She points to the fact that many of these *hadith* remain prominent among interpreters today as the source of continued misogyny and marginalization of women in contemporary Muslim public life.

Although most Muslim countries preserve the man's theoretical right to polygyny as part of the legal code, Mernissi believes that this is not so much a reflection of broad public acceptance for the practice as it is a message to women that their needs are not important. In her opinion, such laws ensure male dominance over society. They do not serve women or guarantee their right to emotional security or happiness. She has charged that a country's stance on polygyny is a reflection of its attitude toward democracy, observing that countries that have banned polygyny tend to be more open and democratic than countries that maintain it as a legal right for men.

Although she takes great care to differentiate between sacred scripture and governments that twist religion and religious interpretation to fit their agendas, she acknowledges that the question of cultural authenticity plays an important role in the determination of women's status as societies and individuals struggle to assimilate the rapid, uncontrolled changes in daily life that have accompanied modernization and globalization. Within this context, many have turned to religion as a source of authentic identity and stability, a phenomenon that she believes explains the popularity of Islamism (defined as those seeking a greater public role for Islam) among educated elites and high achievers. She places the conservative wave against women in the Muslim world within the broader context of the profound changes in sex roles and sexual identities as traditional roles and boundaries have been shattered and women are increasingly defined by their strength, intelligence, and accomplishments, rather than their reproductive capacities.

Mernissi's books have had an important impact in both the Muslim world and the West not only because of the novelty of her arguments and insertion of her voice into the interpretation of religion, but also because they are accessible to the general public. She writes on women's issues for the popular press and has participated in a variety of international forums encouraging public debates promoting women's issues. A recognized public figure in both Morocco and France, her major books have been translated into English, Dutch, German, and Japanese. She has been named one of the preeminent scholars of our time by *Vanity Fair*.

Further reading

Mahmada, Nog Darol. "Rebel for the Sake of Women," Liberal Islam Network, 2004, www.qantara.de/webcom/show_article.ph p/_c-478/_nr-70/i.html

Mernissi, Fatima. *Beyond the Veil: Male–Female Dynamics in Modern Muslim Society*. Bloomington: Indiana University Press, 1987

—— *Doing Daily Battle: Interviews with Moroccan Women*, trans. Mary Jo Lakeland. New Brunswick, NJ: Rutgers University Press, 1989

—— *Dreams of Trespass: Tales of a Harem Girlhood*. Reading, MA: Addison-Wesley Publishing Co., 1994

—— *The Forgotten Queens of Islam*, trans. Mary Jo Lakeland. Cambridge: Polity Press, 1993

—— "Muslim Women and Fundamentalism," in *Nothing Sacred: Women Respond to Religious Fundamentalism and Terror*, ed. Betsy Reed. New York: Thunder's Mouth Press, 2002

—— "The Satellite, the Prince and She-herezade: The Rise of Women as Communicators in Digital Islam," in *Fantasies de l'harem I noves Xahrazads*, Centre de Cultura Contemporania de Barcelona, 2003, www.mernissi.net/books/articles/rise_of_w omen.html

—— *The Veil and the Male Elite: A Feminist Interpretation of Women's Rights in Islam*. Reading, MA: Addison-Wesley Publishing Co., 1991

Rassam, Amal. "Mernissi, Fatima," in *The Oxford Encyclopedia of the Modern Islamic World*, editor-in-chief John L. Esposito, vol. 3. New York: Oxford University Press, 1995

www.mernissi.net – website for Fatima Mernissi

Shazia Mirza (b. 1976)

The world's first Muslim stand-up comedienne, Shazia Mirza marks the entry of Muslim women into the entertainment industry, challenging stereotypes and prejudices that deny Muslim women access to public space.

Shazia Mirza was born in 1976 in Birmingham, England, to Pakistani immigrants. Her father worked as a car salesman, but later was employed to help establish Asian businesses. Her mother raised the children full time before embarking on a career as a teacher.

Mirza was raised in a religiously conservative household. Her parents expected the children to become doctors or lawyers. However, Mirza wanted to be an actress. Because acting has traditionally been considered an unacceptable occupation for conservative Muslim women, she had no living female Muslim role models. She turned instead to pop singer Madonna as a woman who represented power. Madonna's example of dressing, speaking, and behaving as she pleased inspired Mirza to question why she couldn't do as she pleased and say what she wanted to say, regardless of what others said or thought.

Mirza led a sheltered life until she was nineteen. Although she attended a multicultural school where students were encouraged to learn about and appreciate each other's cultures, Mirza always felt like an outsider. She was not permitted to go to parties, take ballet or dancing classes, leave the house, or attend drama school. She also had to wear trousers under her skirt. Her father believed that she should focus on getting an excellent education and pursue a prestigious career in order to find a good husband.

In accordance with her parents' wishes, Mirza studied biochemistry at Manchester University and became a science teacher. At the same time, she rebelled against her parents' vision of her future by secretly pursuing her goal of becoming a stand-up comedienne. She put herself through the Rose Bruford School of Speech and Drama and Goldsmiths College before enrolling in a stand-up comedy writing course at the City Lit.

Mirza began making the rounds of stand-up comedy clubs in 1999, often performing two or three gigs a night in pubs and basements. She hid her profession from her parents until a week before an appearance on the TV show *Have I Got News For You* in 2001. She had already won at the London Comedy Festival, including a performance at the Palladium. Although her parents remained fearful of community criticism over her career, her mother decided to attend one of her performances. Her father proved more difficult, determined only to find her a husband. Mirza's rising international fame has eased some of the community pressure off her family, but she believes that this will last only as long as she is successful.

Although community and family pressure to marry provides material for Mirza's comedy routine, she personally does not find the pressure funny. She has commented that she would like to marry, but has little expectation of finding a husband who would share her religious beliefs and culture while allowing her to continue to perform, given the cultural expectation of wifely obedience such a man would have. At the same time, being a single Muslim woman on tour is typically lonely, given that she can safely associate only with other women. Men frequently ask her out on dates and think she is joking when she refuses because of her religious beliefs.

Mirza is a double anomaly in the world of comedy. Not only was she the first and, for several years, only Muslim comedienne, she is also one of only a few women in British comedy, which is dominated by white males cracking jokes about drinking, sex, and being white males. Mirza uses her routines to address the human condition by permitting others to see into her world in order to break clichés and stereotypes about both her faith and the status of Muslim women.

The shattering of stereotypes begins with Mirza's choice of dress: loose black pants with a long, flowing black shirt and a black headscarf, or hijab. The choice carries a dual message – it reflects her respect for her religious beliefs while challenging the prejudices of both conservative Muslims and non-Muslims about Muslim women in public space. It also pushes her audience to pay attention to what she is saying, rather than what she is wearing. Although she had originally performed without her hijab for the first nine months of her career, she decided to resume wearing it to show that Muslim women can wear the hijab without feeling oppressed. It was also a way for her to demonstrate that, in her experience, Islam gives her the freedom to choose what she wants to be.

Family dynamics form an important part of Mirza's comedy routine, reflecting her often painful reality. Her frequent jokes about her father's conservatism addressed the reality that, for years, he refused to see her perform. When she finally persuaded him to attend one of her performances in 2003, he was so fearful that she would not be successful and that no one would laugh at her jokes that he watched her performance from behind the stage curtain so that no one would know that he was there.

One of the other mainstays of Mirza's comedy routine is Islam. Although she was initially concerned that she would be misunderstood as poking fun at religion, she also believed that she had an important responsibility to correct misunderstandings about and misconceptions of Islam and Muslims. Taking inspiration from the ability of Jews and Christians to joke and laugh at themselves, she decided to include Islam and Muslims in her routine as a way of normalizing Muslims in the world community and to help Muslims understand that they need to be able to laugh at themselves and not always take themselves and Islam so seriously. She nevertheless maintains a personal policy of remaining respectful to Islam and never jokes about the Quran. Describing herself as "very devout," she takes care to distinguish between cultural issues in which she does not believe, such as arranged marriages, and her faith. She is adamant that she means no disrespect in her joking and does not seek to bring her faith or Islam into disrepute. She points instead to the ability of laughter to lead to social change and her belief that everyday people are more likely to learn something about Islam from comedy than they are from politics.

At no time did Mirza question the appropriateness of using Islam and Muslims in her comedy routine more than in the aftermath of 9/11. Out of respect for the victims, she initially canceled her shows. She was also concerned about her personal safety at this time due to threats from conservative Muslims opposed to her public appearances and to general threats against Muslim communities in non-Muslim-majority countries. However, further reflection led her to conclude that non-Muslims needed more than ever to recognize that the overwhelming majority of Muslims do not represent a threat to them and that Muslims need to continue their process of reexamining themselves and their attitudes and learning to laugh at themselves. She was also inspired by an e-mail she received from a girl working at Ground Zero who thanked her for providing laughter in the midst of such pain.

Mirza's courage in resuming her performances was rewarded by a sharp rise in her popularity post-9/11. She incorporated new material to defuse worldwide tension after the terrorist attacks, initiating a new routine beginning with a deadpan delivery of the opening line, "Hello, my name is Shazia Mirza...at least that's what it says on my pilot's license." Audiences typically reacted with an initial stunned silence, followed by laughter and applause, reflecting their recognition of their own fear of Muslims as terrorists and fanatics. Mirza believes that enabling the audience to laugh not only at her, but also at themselves, marked a critical step in shattering stereotypes and defusing often unrecognized tensions. At the same time, there were some in her audiences who did not laugh. Sensitive to the degree to which some people were unnerved by 9/11 and her performance, she offered personal reassurance to concerned individuals that she was not going to blow them up.

Some of Mirza's strongest fans are other Muslim women living in Europe, who applaud the irony in her routine and her ability to challenge stereotypes and prejudices, all while making people laugh. Mirza notes that the Muslim women in her audiences frequently laugh and cry simultaneously because they are moved not only by her comedy, but also by her courage in daring to say things that they themselves have longed to say, but could not. Many of them feel empowered simply by attending her performances. Recognizing her own role now as a powerful role model for young Muslim girls, Mirza encourages them to perform on stage in order to show that Muslim women can and should be involved in all professions, but also cautions them to know their religion and personal beliefs inside and out and to know the boundaries and truth of the Quran. Believing that the Quran grants women a great deal of freedom and power, Mirza found support for her own career choice and has successfully maintained her own personal standards of piety and devotion within that choice.

Mirza's admirers point to the importance of her routine in building cross-cultural relationships and understanding because her material incorporates both British and Muslim culture. Mirza herself is often surprised by the scope of those who appreciate her work. She performed a three-night sold-out gig in France that was attended largely by whites and Algerian Jews. A sold-out performance to two thousand people in San Francisco provided what Mirza refers to as an "amazing experience," as Muslim women sat next to gay men and laughed together, showing the power of humor to unite across seemingly impossible boundaries and offering hope for peaceful coexistence.

Mirza's strongest critics are fellow Muslims, particularly conservative men who point to her as a negative example for Muslim women because she performs in public, which some consider to be forbidden. In 2001, while performing at an all-Muslim charity event in London, she was physically attacked. Although she escaped uninjured and no arrests were made, the incident frightened her. In 2002, an Islamic fundamentalist group in Denmark threated to kill her if she performed a scheduled show there. She performed anyway, with two armed guards close by.

Mirza has won a number of awards for new comedians, including the Hackney Empire Best New Act competition at the London Comedy Festival in 2001. She won *Metro* magazine's People's Choice Best Comic Award at the London Comedy Festival in 2002 and the Young Achiever of the Year Award at the Leadership and Diversity Awards in 2003. She has given radio performances in the United Kingdom, the United States, and Australia and live stand-up comedy performances throughout Europe and the United States. In 2003, she performed at the prestigious second International Festival of Verbal Art in Berlin. She has appeared on a variety of B.B.C. productions and news and comedy shows throughout Europe, the Middle East, and the United States. She has been profiled for European and American television networks and has created films for Al Arabia T.V. and the French version of M.T.V. She was both a writer and presenter for the November 2002 B.B.C. production *Ten Things You Always Wanted to Know About Islam (But Were Afraid to Ask)*. She has also worked as an actress in the United Kingdom, including a performance at the Royal Albert Hall V Day Event in 2002, for which she wrote and performed her own monologue for Eve Ensler's *The Vagina Monologues*.

Mirza's future goals include performing in Hollywood, as well as doing theater in the West End. She hopes to appear in a sitcom and to be the first Muslim woman to receive an Oscar.

Further reading

"Ask Shazia Mirza" transcript, from *Live Chat with B.B.C. Communicate*, January 31, 2002

Bedell, Geraldine. "Veiled Humour," *The Observer*. April 20, 2003

Marcus, Aliza. "Can you Believe, a Muslim Comedian?" *Boston Globe*, February 9, 2003

Interview with the author, July 29, 2003

www.shaziamirza.org – website for Shazia Mirza

Mos Def (b. 1973)

A mainstream hip-hop musician and actor who has appeared both on television and in films, Mos Def considers himself a voice of Muslim conscience on issues of human rights and oppression.

Mos Def was born Dante Terrell Smith on December 13, 1973, in Brooklyn, NY. Although he was raised by his mother, his father has always been an important presence in his life. Mos Def credits both parents with encouraging him to steer away from negative lyrics, providing personal support and teaching him a strong sense of family and values. Both are active in managing his career. His brother, D.C.Q. of Medina Green, handles technical issues in the studio. The entire family travels together for shows.

Mos Def was formally introduced to Islam by his father when he was thirteen years old. He spent six years studying, reading, and reflecting on Islam prior to converting. Since his conversion, Islam has served as his foundation and inspiration, providing both spiritual and social themes to his music.

Mos Def grew up during what is often called the "Golden Age" of hip-hop. He drew inspiration not only from major hip-hop artists, but also from jazz, pop lyrics, cross-culturalism, and other art forms. He prefers not to be labeled as a particular type of artist, whether "black" or "hip-hop," because he does not want to be categorized and confined according to someone else's definition. Part of what he tries to communicate through his music is that there are a variety of types of "black" music and that the origins of many types of music are "black." He therefore seeks to broaden the definition of what constitutes "black" music, while setting aside the label of "alternative" that is frequently applied to him.

Mos Def describes himself as equally comfortable rhyming, singing, and playing instruments. He tends to prepare portions of his lyrics at home, but completes and adds to them in the studio in order to incorporate spontaneity and inspiration into his work. He insists that his lyrics be readable on paper, rather than simply fitting the beat. His revolutionary prose has earned him the respect of both socially conscious hip-hop fans and the music industry. It also led to his hosting the television show *Def Poetry Jam*, which serves as a pop-culture forum for poetry.

Mos Def's first professional recording was with Urban ThermoDynamics on the 1994 album *My Kung Fu*, for which he wrote the lyrics for four songs. He then made cameo appearances on Bush Babee's *Love Song* and De La Soul's *Big Brother Beat*. In 1998, he teamed with Talib Kweli to form Black Star, which released its self-titled album in 1998. Mos Def wrote the lyrics for eleven out of the thirteen songs. He has appeared as a guest artist on albums by a variety of artists.

Although Islam has a long history of association with hip-hop, including major early stars such as Afrika Bambata, Poor Righteous Teachers, Big Daddy Kane, Public Enemy, Wu Tang Clan and Busta Rhymes, Mos Def was the first hip-hop artist to articulate a complete Islamic message as part of his popular work. The opening of his debut solo album, *Black on Both Sides*, begins with "Bismillah al-Rahman al-Rahim" ("In the name of God, the Merciful, the Compassionate") – the declaration that Muslims are supposed to make before they perform a task. The booklets accompanying his C.D.'s include notations thanking God. His songs contain references to God and prayer, such as "All Praise Due." Although hip-hop generally emphasizes sex, violence, and materialism, Mos Def uses swear words and violence purposefully to reflect the social reality faced by a young African-American male living in Brooklyn, including issues of poverty, racism, conflict between blacks and whites, African-American self-esteem, and the relationship between African-Americans and law enforcement. He emphasizes the inherent value of all human beings as creations of God, refusing to portray women as sex objects or to talk trash to them in music videos. He does not permit the sale of alcohol at his concerts.

Musically, *Black on Both Sides* uses a variety of instruments, including keyboards, bass, congas, percussion, guitar, strings, piano, vibraphone, and vocals. Stylistically, the album combines soul, jazz, word chants, hard rock, and hip-hop. It received critical acclaim, leading to an invitation from M.T.V. for a recurring role on *The Lyricist Lounge Show*. His track "Umi Says" was chosen by Nike to launch Michael Jordan's Brand Jordan Nike division. As a reflection of his social consciousness, Mos Def insisted that Nike make a donation to a community-based organization of his choice in order to help redress grievances about the sweatshop conditions in some of Nike's overseas plants.

As a self-described Muslim of conscience, Mos Def has taken on issues of human rights and oppression. He has spoken out publicly about the persecution of Muslims in Bosnia, Kosovo, and Chechnya, as well as human rights violations and persecution in Sierra Leone and Colombia. Noting that black musicians historically have been social activists, he has participated in a variety of benefit concerts, including a 1999 Black August Benefit to raise money for the legal and educational campaigns of Cuban political prisoners and to create a public hip-hop library and studio in Havana, Cuba; a 2000 Anti-Proposition 21 Concert to oppose a California initiative to take funding away from minority and poor youth education; a 2000 Boarding for Breast Cancer benefit concert to promote breast-cancer awareness; concerts in 2000 and 2001 to benefit victims of police brutality, raise awareness of police brutality cases around the United States, and support the legal defense of Mumia Abu-Jamal and Jamil Abdullah Al-Amin; a 2000 benefit concert to raise money for Bridgeport, CT's Music and Arts Center for Humanity, which is dedicated to the empowerment and education of youth through music; and a 2002 Palestinian Aid Concert to aid victims of the Israeli offensive in Jenin and to demonstrate the support of hip-hop artists for the Palestinian struggle for self-determination. He also participated in the 2001 Red Hot A.I.D.S. Benefit to raise money for A.I.D.S. relief and awareness about H.I.V. and A.I.D.S. through the use of pop culture; the United Nations Children in War Festival in 2001, where he emphasized the conference's themes of children, peacemaking, and the control of small weapons; and the 2001 N.Y.C. September 11th Benefit to raise money for the victims of the 9/11 attacks.

In addition to his concert benefits, Mos Def has been a leader in social activism, including support for Not in our Name, a 2002 anti-war campaign disagreeing with President Bush's policies following the 9/11 attacks, donations to the Code Foundation Clothes Auction which auctions celebrity musician clothing to raise funds for its youth center, and participation in Hip-Hop For Respect, a group of hip-hop artists who have joined together to protest and bring attention to police brutality, particularly through a three-song benefit single entitled "Hip-Hop for Respect" in response to the shooting of Amadou Diallo (see also KADIATOU DIALLO) and an educational campaign to instruct youth on what to do and not to do if they are stopped by police. Mos Def believes that hip-hop artists have a special responsibility to speak out against police brutality because many of the victims are hip-hop fans from the ghettoes who have made hip-hop a $110 billion industry and given the artists a public voice. He believes that this public voice needs to be put to the service of fans by providing community leadership on matters of substance. Following the Diallo killing, he called upon his fellow hip-hop artists to unite in speaking out against injustice and suffering. He also participated in a concept album by Weldon Irvine entitled *The Price of Freedom … is Truth (The Amadou Project)*.

Mos Def's acting career, which began off-Broadway when he was thirteen, includes films and television appearances, with regular roles on *You Take the Kids*, *God Bless the Child*, *The Cosby Mysteries*, *The Lyricist Lounge Show*, *Reverb*, and *Def Poetry*, as well as guest appearances on *N.Y.P.D. Blue*, *Brooklyn South*, *Spin City*, H.B.O.'s *Oz*, and *The Wayne Brady Show*. In film, he has appeared as Wilt Crawley in *Where's Marlowe?*, rapper "Big Black Africa" in Spike Lee's *Bamboozled*, Lt. Miller in *Carmen: A Hip Hopera*, and Ryrus Cooper in *Monster's Ball*. He has also had roles in *Island of the Dead*, *Showtime*, and *Civil Brand* and has appeared in the Broadway play *Topdog/Underdog*.

Further reading

Asadullah, Ali. "'You're Gonna Have to Serve Somebody," in *Taking Back Islam: American Muslims Reclaim their Faith*, ed. Michael Wolfe and the Producers of

Beliefnet. Emmaus, PA: Rodale Inc. and Beliefnet, Inc., 2002

Interview on barnesandnoble.com, www.mosdefinitely.com/interview01.htm

Interview with Essence.com, Ann-Marie Nicholson, 2002, www.mosdefinitely.com/interview10.htm

www.mosdefinitely.com – website for Mos Def

Nawal El Moutawakel-Bennis (b. 1962)

The first Muslim woman to win an Olympic gold medal, Nawal El Moutawakel-Bennis is an Arab, Muslim, and Moroccan icon and sports legend.

Nawal El Moutawakel-Bennis was born on April 15, 1962, in Casablanca, Morocco. Her parents encouraged her interest and participation in sports from her childhood through their own examples. Her father was a judo artist. Her mother played volleyball. At that time, sports were viewed as a masculine occupation and it was considered unseemly for a girl to train in athletics late at night or early in the morning. Although Islam does not prohibit women from playing in sports or from becoming professional athletes, there are many cultural taboos and barriers, such as opposition to a woman exposing her bare arms or legs, that effectively bar women from sports in many countries. El Moutawakel credits her father with ignoring these taboos and encouraging her to participate in sports and to train wearing appropriate sportswear.

When El Moutawakel was eight years old, she fell down the side of a mountain and collided with a rock, shattering her left leg. The leg was not set properly and became permanently weak and unreliable. Nevertheless, she took up long-distance running, beginning competition-level training when she was fourteen. She later changed to sprints and, finally, to hurdling when she was seventeen.

El Moutawakel became the African champion in the 100-meter hurdles in 1982. However, her coach realized that she was not fast enough at that distance to qualify as a world-class hurdler. She reluctantly agreed to shift to the 400-meter event, earning a rank of twenty-sixth in the world by 1983 when she won the 400-meter hurdles at the French Championships and the gold medal in the 400-meter hurdles in both the Mediterranean Games and the African Championships, but finished ninth at the World Championships in Finland. Realizing that she was not ready for world competition, her coach encouraged her to go to the United States to train.

Although El Moutawakel knew little English (she was fluent in French and Arabic), her potential as an athlete was so remarkable that an African runner for the Iowa State Cyclones who had seen her alerted the assistant women's coach. She was offered a scholarship at Iowa State University under the Title IX program. She arrived in Des Moines in January 1983.

Eight days after El Moutawakel left Morocco, her father was killed in a car accident. Her family did not tell her immediately, but sent her brother to the U.S. six weeks later to bring her home. In what she describes as the toughest decision of her life, she decided to stay to honor her father's memory by getting a good education and better coaching in her quest to become a star athlete.

One of the major problems El Moutawakel faced with respect to her speed was her injured left leg. In hurdles, a runner who is versatile enough to change lead legs over a hurdle has an advantage, particularly on the curves. El Moutawakel had always been reluctant to use her left leg as a lead because she did not trust it not to buckle. As a result, she often had to take a choppy step before the hurdle to make sure she was leading with her right leg. The 1983 World University Games convinced her of the need to use her left leg for leading, as well, and she worked to build it up. Her performance results in 1984 proved this to be the correct strategy for her.

El Moutawakel's first year competing for the Iowa State Cyclones, was 1983–1984. Although she is five feet two and weighed only 107 pounds, she was a faster runner than her taller opponents. She won the Big Eight Conference 440-yard dash in 54.15 seconds, placed seventh in the National Collegiate Athletic Association (N.C.A.A.) 400-meters, and had a perfect outdoor collegiate hurdling season. She became only the second woman to win the same event in the same year at the Texas, Kansas, and Drake Relays, earning national collegiate records on each of the last two victories. At the Big Eight outdoor meet, she won both the hurdles with a record time of 55.75 seconds and the 400-meter run in a record 51.86 seconds. She also tried a double in the N.C.A.A. outdoor meet, where she finished fourth in the 400-meter run and set a record of 55.84 on the 400-meter hurdles. She scored 24 of Iowa state's 31 points.

Shortly after this remarkable performance, El Moutawakel was summoned back to Morocco to meet with King Hassan II. The king had supported her with telephone calls and visits throughout the years. Now, as the only woman among the nation's Olympians, he singled her out and told her, "I know you can bring a gold medal to your country." Feeling the pressure of the king's expectations, El Moutawakel sprained her ankle, missed two weeks of training before competitions began, and ran poorly in Europe and Africa. Having lost her confidence, she called her coaches for help in re-tuning her technique and regaining a proper state of mind.

1984 was the first year for a 400-meter hurdling event for women at the Olympic level. El Moutawakel met her personal goal by passing both of the test heats. She led the final race, finishing in her best time ever at 54.61 seconds, a full half-second

ahead of the runner-up, winning the gold medal and making her the first Muslim and Arab woman, as well as the first Moroccan athlete, ever to win Olympic gold. It was the only race she ever ran under fifty-five seconds. Shortly after her victory lap, she received a call from the king, who was so pleased by her performance that he declared that all girls born on the day of her victory would be named Nawal.

El Moutawakel's Olympic victory burst the barriers against women's sports in Morocco, pushing the government to recognize the benefit of investing in girls, as well as boys, at the grass-roots level. It also marked the entrance of Arabs, Africans, and Muslims into places previously reserved for Americans and Europeans. El Moutawakel became a figure of international recognition, increasing, in her eyes, her responsibility to her country to share her experiences and victory with her compatriots and to inspire young people to participate in sports. Her victory was instrumental in the development of women's sports organizations in both Arab nations and the African continent.

Like other Muslim women in prominent public positions, El Moutawakel had her detractors. There were some who were outraged by her performance, believing that she had violated Muslim traditions because of her "immodest" clothing which bared her arms and legs. While in the United States she had to register in hotels under an alias because of the many Arabs wanting to meet her, and she required a police escort while training back in her native Morocco because of her choice of clothing.

El Moutawakel's athletic career ended quickly. While running on the school golf course in 1984, she stepped on a walnut and badly sprained her left leg. Considering her a "national treasure," the king summoned her home for surgery to repair her knee. The operation proved unhelpful and cost her conditioning. A year later, her coaches and five teammates were killed in a plane crash returning from a cross country meet. An N.C.A.A. rule on age prevented her from competing for the Cyclones in her senior year. She ran for a track club instead and retired from running in the summer of 1987.

After graduation, El Moutawakel returned to Morocco where she starred in an Italian film, *Ricatto due*, married, became a mother, and began working in sports at the national level. In 1989, she was appointed national sprint and hurdle coach for both men and women, began serving on the Athletes' Commission, and became involved with Casablanca's track club. In 1991, she served as the director of the National School of Track and Field in Casablanca. In 1992, she became vice president of the Moroccan Track and Field Federation, chair of the Women's Commission, and a member of the Moroccan National Olympic Committee. In 1993 and 1994, she organized a five-mile race for women in Casablanca. She has also worked as the executive director of the B.M.C.E. (Moroccan Bank for Exterior Commerce) Foundation to improve education and the environment.

El Moutawakel became active internationally in 1995 with service on the International Association of Athletes Federation (I.A.A.F.) Council, conducting workshops in different countries and developing a subcommission for women for the Special Project for the 1998 Year of Women in Athletics. In 1997, she became the first Muslim woman to be elected as a member of the International Olympic Committee where she worked with the group on Women and Sports and the Marketing Commission. She has also served as a member of the International Committee of the Mediterranean Games, the International Committee of the Francophone Games, and the Laureus Sport for Good Foundation. She is a U.N.I.C.E.F. goodwill ambassador.

In 1997, El Moutawakel was appointed minister of sport and youth, marking the first time that a woman had served in such a high-level position in Morocco. She cited the launching of women's soccer and the organization of a major competition between Morocco and Sweden that Morocco won as her major achievements. She remained in her government position for only a short time due to her personal preference for athletics over politics. Believing that sports can eradicate barriers and taboos and change the face of the world, much as her athletic victories changed the face of sports by including Arabs and Muslims among Olympic and international champions, she has referred to sports as "the best parliament in the world" where only the most gifted and the strongest can serve, irrespective of the color of their skin, race or religion. She points to her athletic achievement as evidence of women in sports serving the causes of emancipation and national economic development. She has called for the empowerment and education of women as the key to a strong and modern Morocco.

El Moutawakel's prominence as an Arab and Muslim athlete has been recognized internationally. At the popular level, the short commuter train in Casablanca is commonly known as "Nawal." In the aftermath of 9/11, she recorded a public-service announcement promoting sports as a means of achieving international understanding and peaceful coexistence. She was inducted into the Des Moines Sunday Register's Iowa Sports Hall of Fame and was awarded the prestigious Flo Hyman Memorial Award by the Women's Sports Foundation in February 2003 in recognition of her achievement of excellence both on and off the playing field. She has called for the continuation of the Title IX Program that provided the university scholarship that brought her to the United States for training and competition. She remains a strong proponent of women's participation in sports, as well as in broader society.

Further reading

Fannuchi, Bruno. "Entretien avec Nawal El Moutawakel," *VoxLatina*, June 2000

"Flo Hyman Memorial Award Presented to Olympic Gold Medalist Nawal El Moutawakel," press release for Capitol Hill Congressional Ceremony Commemorating National Girls and Women in Sports Day, Washington, DC, February 5, 2003

Hargreaves, Jennifer. *Heroines of Sport: The Politics of Difference and Identity*. London and New York: Routledge, 2000

Jackson, Yolanda L. "Title IX – Not Just an American Right," www.womenssportsfoundation.org/c...athlestes/heroes/article.html?record=113

Magdalinksi, Tara and Timothy J.L. Chandler, eds. *With God on their Side: Sport in the Service of Religion*. London and New York: Routledge, Taylor & Francis Group, 2002

Rfaly, Linda. "Nawal El Moutawakel: 54 secondes ont crée le déclic," *Menara*, July 18, 2002

White, Maury. "Iowa State's Nawal El Moutawakel Hurdled All Obstacles," *DesMoines Register*, July 10, 1994

www2.iaaf.org – website for International Association of Athletes Federation

www.sports-academy-laureus.com

H.R.H. Sheikha Mouza bint Nasser Al-Misnad

(b. early 1950s)

> The First Lady of Qatar, H.R.H. Sheikha Mouza bint Nasser Al-Misnad has played an unprecedented public role in improving and expanding education and women's rights in the emirate of Qatar.

Sheikha Mouza bint Nasser al-Misnad is the second and most prominent wife of the Emir of Qatar, Sheikh Hamad bin Khalifa al-Thani, and the mother of the crown prince, Sheikh Jassem bin Khalifa. The emir is considered a visionary in the traditionally conservative Gulf and has introduced many important reforms, including experiments in democracy, the drafting of the first constitution, support for freedom of speech and the press, and promoting women's rights, including the right to vote, drive cars, work alongside men, run for office, and choose for themselves whether and to what degree to veil. Although these reforms have earned him the opposition of more conservative regimes in the area and restrictions on free speech remain, Qatar is widely recognized as the most progressive country in the Gulf.

Mouza has taken on a visible and vocal public presence since her husband became emir in 1995, shattering traditional Gulf cultural expectations that women should remain at home and out of public view. Mouza and the emir work as a team. The emir has declared his support for women's participation in all spheres, singling out women's education and participation in public life as critical to Qatar's continued development. Mouza works to patronize, envisage, and implement changes. The couple frequently travel together on official visits which Mouza uses to visit universities and other educational facilities to garner ideas for modernizing Qatar's education system. Her goal is to create a new generation of workers capable of adopting and adapting new technologies, ideas, and methods while remaining faithful to Qatar's Islamic principles, social teachings, and culture.

Mouza's work on women's issues has focused on the creation of an environment that encourages women to participate in public life while fulfilling their social and family obligations. Asserting that gender equality is in accordance with Islam's teachings, she believes that her work supports, rather than contradicts, her religion and culture. She notes that Islamic history records women playing an active role in public life during the lifetime of the Prophet Muhammad, including participation in wars and the workings of the court system, and that Muhammad himself consulted women about a variety of issues. She therefore believes that her work restores women to their rightful place within an Islamic framework and does not represent innovation or a break with Islamic tradition. She has commented that the banishment of women to their homes and the practice of full veiling were historical developments that occurred after, rather than during, Muhammad's lifetime, suggesting that such practices are not inherently "Islamic." She hopes, through her own example, to serve as a model for other countries of how women can have their own role in society while respecting their faith and culture.

In order to determine how the lives of Qatari women can be improved and how to make employment opportunities more accessible, Mouza has sponsored conferences to identify and recommend solutions for the challenges and problems faced by women working outside of the home. The 1997 conference on The Woman Between the Family and the Workplace sought to identify methods for achieving psychological stability while juggling career and home life and to outline approaches to support and protect the family. In 1999, Mouza and the Qatar Foundation for Education, Science and Family Development Center organized Qatar's first International Women's Conference to address Arab working women's concerns. The conference ended with the drafting of nine recommendations for creating greater flexibility for women at the workplace, well-staffed child care facilities in offices, state-run social security funds, maternity leave and pay, and the equal application of international conventions and laws to women and men. A national committee was then formed to follow up on the recommendations.

Another example of Mouza's practical support for real-life solutions is her patronage of the Qatar Ladies' Investment Company, a joint venture between a group of Qatari women and Qatar National Bank founded in 1998 to help women meet their economic, financial, and investment goals and provide them with solid knowledge of investment markets. The first organization of its kind in the region, the company is run by women for women to help them play a more important role in Qatar's economic development through the creation of an investment culture among women. It is also expected to play an important role in the process of privatization in Qatar and to provide project and venture capital mobilization. A Businesswomen's Forum was established in 2000 to increase women's contributions to small trades and industrial projects, encourage an expanded role for women in development, and enhance women's potential in making economic decisions.

Mouza's work on modernizing and expanding the education system has focused on establishing partnerships with American universities. As a graduate of the American university system, she has experience with both the educational methods and standards of American university education. Since 1996, she has served as the chairperson for the Qatar Foundation for Education, Science and Community Development, which has worked to build high-quality elementary and secondary schools in Qatar. It has also sponsored one of Mouza's most ambitious goals: the establishment of the Education City outside of Qatar's capital, Doha, to make Qatar a center for culture and education in the Gulf. Education City is intended to provide education that implements and teaches modern ideas and technology from pre-kindergarten through postgraduate studies. Mouza has particularly encouraged women to study there and to pursue fields that are not traditionally considered female, such as politics. She has also worked to attract top universities from around the world, particularly the United States, to establish branch campuses in Qatar that offer an education equivalent to that offered in their home countries.

Mouza made her first official trip for the Education City to the United States to visit

Harvard and other top colleges in 1997. Although her husband did not accompany her, she officially represented him, marking the first time a first lady officially represented a Gulf country. She recruited participation from Cornell Medical School, which officially opened its Weill Cornell Medical College branch in October 2003 in a public event that marked the appearance of the emir and Mouza together in public for the first time in Qatar. Mouza granted television cameras permission to show her face for the first time in order to demonstrate that education is at the top of her agenda. The college is the first co-educational institution of higher learning in Qatar. Other participating universities include Virginia Commonwealth University, which specializes in technical skills for women, Texas A&M, which will provide courses in chemical, electrical, mechanical, and petroleum engineering, and the RAND Corporation, which will assist with the development of improved K-12 education to build a new pool of qualified applicants for the new universities. In addition, the RAND–Qatar Policy Institute was formed to engage in research and planning projects throughout the region. Although critics have charged that the presence of American universities could potentially undermine the Muslim nature of Qatar, Mouza believes that education is the best means of disempowering extremist movements because it encourages people to think and judge for themselves. She also noted that education provides the opportunity to pursue knowledge of one's own roots, Islamic culture, and the Quran as well as of the outside world. Thus, rather than encouraging the proliferation of extremism, she believes that the expansion of education has limited it.

Statistics demonstrate the impact of reforms Mouza has sponsored and supported in expanding women's rights and access to public space. By 2000, there were more female than male students in state-run schools, illiteracy rates ran higher among men than among women (20% of men over the age of fifteen, as compared to 17% of women), and women's presence in government jobs had increased by 61%. A woman was chosen to serve on the U.N. Committee on the Rights of the Child. Women represented 52% of the workforce at the Ministry of Education and headed three sections of the Ministry of Justice: Fatwah and Research; Legislation; and Translation and Official Newsletter. In addition, five women served as legal advisors in the Fatwah and Legislation House and one in State Cases. Women were strongly present in staff and administrative positions at Qatar University, were active in the fields of literature, journalism, tourism, banking, and the arts, outnumbered men in health services, played a pivotal role in both domestic and international charitable and voluntary societies, particularly in organizing charity fairs and donation and relief campaigns, were active in the preparation of field research on needy families, and had begun attending Qatar Aeronautical College to study aviation engineering, flight and air traffic control. Although women represented only 13% of the total workforce, they challenged the status quo by demanding political, economic, and social empowerment, as well as equality in the family and society.

Mouza's work for education has received international attention and acclaim. She has addressed the United Nations and serves as U.N.E.S.C.O.'s special envoy for education. She is an activist for the disabled and has worked to establish specialized societies to care for the deaf, dumb, and blind, including the Al Noor Institute for the Blind and the National Committee for Children with Special Needs in 1998. She is actively involved in the Qatar Diabetics Association and the Family Development Center, both of which are designed to alleviate hardship among the less fortunate in Qatar.

Further reading

"Cornell University to Establish Medical School in Qatar," press release from Cornell University, April 9, 2001

Kerr, Ann Zwicker. "Arabian Days and Nights in the Twenty-first Century," November 18, 2003, www.isop.ucla.edu/article.asp?parentid=5175

El-Nawawy, Mohammed and Adel Iskandar. *al-Jazeera: How the Free Arab News Network Scooped the World and Changed the Middle East.* Boulder, CO: Westview Press, 2002

Parker, Ned. " 'The Veil is not a Barrier' in an Arab Vote," *Christian Science Monitor*, March 12, 1999

Peterson, Scott. "A First Lady Gently Shakes Qatar," *Christian Science Monitor*, January 8, 1998

"Qatar: Embracing Democracy," www.cbsnews.com/sto...3/07/25/60minutes/print-able565155.shtml

"Women in Qatar only form 13pc of Workforce, Says Study," *The Peninsula*, January 1, 2004

www.qatarembassy.net

Sahirah Muhammad
(b. early 1950s)

Founder of the International League of Muslim Women (I.L.M.W.), Sahirah Muhammad is an innovative activist in human services, social work, and educational training.

Sahirah Muhammad was born in the United States in the early 1950s. She and her husband, Abdul Rahmaan Muhammad, attended Tougaloo College in Mississippi. They began their careers as child-care workers, but quickly branched out into broader family- and community-oriented work that covers the full spectrum of ages from infants to the elderly. The couple has worked at the Abbott House for Children in Irvington, NY; Peirce-Warwick Children's Service in Washington, DC; Lakeside Residential Treatment Center in Spring Valley, NY; White Plains Middle School in White Plains, NY; Henry Street Settlement in Lower Eastside Manhattan, NY; Trinity College Child Care Centers in Hartford, CT; St. Agnes Family Center in West Hartford, CT; and the Village for Families and Children in Hartford, CT. Muhammad's work at St. Agnes House particularly emphasized the application of social services at the local level through the provision of services and educational opportunities to teenage mothers in need of parenting and life skills. St. Agnes House, a colleague of Catholic Charities, provides a supportive setting for teenage mothers and their infants irrespective of race or religion, emphasizing respect for life and recognition of the dignity and potential of every person.

Muhammad founded the International League of Muslim Women (I.L.M.W.), the largest Muslim women's organization in America, in 1981. She has served as its president since it was founded, coordinating and directing its efforts in more than twenty-five chapters around the United States and several branches in West Africa. The I.L.M.W. provides services for both individuals and families while working to create awareness and understanding of the Muslim community's needs. Its programs include running a domestic-violence shelter, food and clothing banks, providing refugee assistance, hosting foreign-exchange students, and providing parenting classes and counseling by trained social workers and mental health professionals. I.L.M.W. members act as officers of the court with the court-appointed special advocate (C.A.S.A.) program, giving impartial findings in child-abuse cases. Annual I.L.M.W. projects include a national conference, provision of fruit baskets to elderly, sick, and nursing-home residents on the two Eids (Eid al-Fitr, which occurs at the end of Ramadan, and Eid al-Adha, which occurs at the end of the Hajj pilgrimage), sponsoring Ramadan *iftars* (ends of fasts) at the mosque, and hosting a national mother–daughter–grandmother brunch honoring women.

Muhammad also founded Peace Associates in 1982 in partnership with her husband. A family-operated consulting firm capitalizing on the expertise of the Muhammads in family and social service work, Peace Associates provides training for parents, social service workers, and community workers who deal with gang violence, inmate rehabilitation, adoption and post-legal adoption issues, conflict transformation, cultural competency, and ethnic diversity. It introduced the Round Table Conversation Concept, which combines action and reflection as learning and training mechanisms. Participants learn to solve problems in a real-world organizational setting by developing new skills and insights through reflection, questioning, and collaborating. Peace Associates has produced a variety of video and audio tapes addressing the issues of racism, sexism, and "ageism."

Muhammad's pioneering work has received national attention. In 2000, she was invited to attend President George W. Bush's inaugural ceremony. She later returned to the White House with other I.L.M.W. members to dicuss crime victims and to meet with members of the Department of Justice. The Muhammads have received more than $25 million in state and federal funding through grants and proposals for their work, indicating strong public support for their methods and efforts at the local, state, and national levels.

Further reading

Ali, Farkhunda and Felicity Salaam. "Muslim Women Organizations," *Azizah* magazine, Spring 2002
www.ilmw-atl.org – website for International League of Muslim Women
www.peaceassociates44.com – website for Peace Associates
www.stagneshome.org – website for St. Agnes Homes, Inc.

Abd al-Rahman Munif
(c. 1933–2004)

One of the most acclaimed Arab novelists of the twentieth century, Abd al-Rahman Munif was an important social and political critic of the effects of modernization and the oil industry on traditional Arab societies.

Abd al-Rahman Munif (also spelled Abdelrahman Munif and Abdul Rahman Munif) was born in Amman, Jordan, around 1933. His father was from the Najd province of central Saudi Arabia. His mother was from Baghdad, Iraq. Munif's father worked in Iraq and Syria prior to settling in Jordan where Munif was born and raised. Although Munif never lived there, he was a Saudi citizen until he was stripped of his citizenship in 1963 for engaging in political activities opposing the Saudi monarchy.

Munif completed his primary and secondary educations in Jordan. He recorded his childhood memoirs in *Stories of a City: A Childhood in Amman*, not only to write a partial autobiography, but also to record and preserve the past of this important Arab city from the indigenous perspective of a person who was born and raised there and who viewed the city as a living organism filled with people who affected and were affected by events ranging from the environmental to the political. Munif objected in general to the fact that much of Arab history has been written by Western observers, rather than natives who have lived it. This theme recurs in both his factual and fictional writing.

Munif's childhood memoirs cover the transition of Amman from a traditional Arab city to a modern, developed one complete with Westerners and Western-educated Arabs. The transition is characterized through his own negative experiences in the traditional Quran school, where fear and revulsion ruled as individual students struggled to memorize a single subject perfectly. He later transferred to a government elementary school that emphasized learning through the study of a variety of subjects and building relationships with other people. Munif's memoirs also record the transition from folk medicine and superstition to reliance on modern medicine. He almost died from the measles as a child.

Munif's memoirs also document important cultural and social issues, such as the harmony he perceived between Muslim and Christian inhabitants who recognized their common membership in a broad social community despite religious differences, and the expectation that children would contribute to household economies, even when this came at the expense of their schooling. Most prominently, the memoirs give a sense of the daily lives of the inhabitants of Amman caught between World War II and the first Arab–Israeli war. At the same time that rations and poverty prevailed, he observed the sense of community that resulted from group listening to the radio, common concerns about the environment, and the need to develop other inexpensive methods of entertainment, such as kite-flying and playing marbles, to distract people from the realities of war, deprivation, and hunger.

After completing his secondary studies, Munif moved to Baghdad to pursue legal studies at Baghdad University. He earned a license in law first in Baghdad and then from Cairo University after he was deported from Iraq for his activism with the Ba'ath Party in 1955. He moved to Yugoslavia where he completed a Ph.D. in petroleum economics at the University of Belgrade. He worked briefly in politics in Lebanon before moving to Syria in 1964 to work as the director of planning for the Syrian Oil Company. He later became director of crude-oil marketing.

Munif returned to Iraq in 1975 to edit a government-run monthly periodical entitled *Oil and Development*. While there, he became a close colleague and friend of the Palestinian novelist Jabra Ibrahim Jabra with whom he co-wrote the novel *Mapless World* in 1982. Munif moved to Boulogne, France, in 1981 to write full time. In 1986, he moved to Damascus, Syria, where he remained until his death in 2004 following a lengthy battle with cancer.

When asked why he had worked in so many different professions, Munif responded that he had always been interested in political activism, but found the available political methods insufficient for what he hoped to accomplish. His main concern in life was finding different ways of connecting with others and relating to their concerns. He found that his experience in the oil industry combined with his love of reading enabled him to read societies with remarkable accuracy, particularly with respect to social and cultural issues. He put this ability to use in his novels, which depict not only individual conflicts but the broader social movements and communal conflicts that form the context for individual struggles.

Munif considered his generation to be one of transition. While burdened with the desire for and dreams of change, it lacked the political parties and power to bring change about. He was discouraged by the tendency of the political parties of his youth to focus on maintaining their own power by remaining distant from the people instead of connecting with the societies they were intended to serve. He believed that these parties were engaged in slogans, rather than politics, making their weaknesses apparent whenever they were tested and inevitably leading to decline.

As a novelist, Munif wrote broadly about the "Arab crisis," which he identified as the result of the trilogy of oil, political Islam, and dictatorship that he held responsible for the collapse, confusion, and suffering of Arab people and societies searching for modernity. He particularly lambasted the joining of oil and political Islam for enabling regimes to engage in repression and dictatorship.

Munif published his first novel in 1973, followed in 1975 by *East of the Mediterranean*, the story of a political prisoner tortured to death in an intelligence prison. A graphic portrayal of the state's techniques to control the activities of its citizens both domestically and when abroad, the novel reportedly infuriated Iraq's Ba'athist regime. Politics also dominated *Long Distance Race*, which outlined the political situation in Iran during the reign of Prime Minister Mohammed Mosaddeq.

Munif's works became more literary and social and less overtly political over time. He published *Endings* as a series of stories told in a folkloric style in the pre-Islamic literary tradition of descriptions of animals. *Endings* was his first vivid commentary on the emergence of the modern city and the urban middle class. The action centers on an enduring drought and its impact on a village on the edge of a desert. The village serves as a symbol for Arab villages facing nature without the assistance of modern technology. The novel was unique not only for its repetition of traditional themes of Arab literature – the cruelty of nature, the endless search for food and water, and the constant and imminent danger of death – but also because it occurs in a desert, rather than a city. In addition, Munif did not develop the characters of the people in the novel beyond naming their occupations, thus allowing them to represent the Everyman of the desert and to serve as a public voice.

Munif was most famous for his exploration of the impact of the oil era on traditional Arab society in *Cities of Salt*, which was published as five novels in Arabic between 1984 and 1989 and as three novels in English translation. *Cities of Salt* is the tale of the social, political, and cultural disruption and corruption of a traditional, poor oasis community in the twentieth century after the discovery of oil and Western allegiances lead to the substitution of power and money for tribal and family loyalties. The series explores how politics, power, and money corrupt traditional societies by encouraging pursuit of materialism and conquest at the expense of tribal solidarity. The detailed pictures of life in the palace provide a marked contrast to the simple piety of the common people.

The first novel in the English series, *Cities of Salt*, takes place during the early 1930s when oil was discovered, recounting the meetings between Arabs and Americans that resulted in the colonization of the region by the oil companies and the resulting confrontation that fueled superstition, history, religion, and a mutual lack of comprehension. The second novel, *The Trench*, is set in the 1950s in the royal court of a fictional monarchy and depicts the rising corruption, savagery, and wealth of the monarchy as derived from the oil industry, which grows increasingly dependent on migrant workers. The monarchy is portrayed as repressive and undemocratic, seeking its own interests and enrichment at the expense of its subjects. The final novel, *Variations on Night and Day*, depicts the rise of a fictitious sultan and the emergence of the country as a modern nation. Throughout the novel, the sultan expands and consolidates his rule by crushing rival clans and internal opposition through military means, bribes, deceit, and assassination, all as acts of holy war, while securing the influence of Western governments in the region. The sultan's ruthlessness is matched by the palace intrigues of his polygamous household as his wives vie for preeminence using similar methods of murder, gossip, and deceit.

Cities of Salt was widely acclaimed in both the Arab world and the West for its frank and sensitive portrayal of the political and social changes of Gulf countries in the twentieth century. The series was widely considered a turning point in Gulf literature because it bridged traditional and contemporary literary styles. For example, the narratives are all written in classical Arabic, but change to the colloquial Arabic of the tribes when characters speak. Munif also replicated traditional Arab storytelling techniques, such as showing an apparent lack of concern for time, as evidenced by constant jumping backward and forward in time, lengthy asides, and telling different versions of the same event.

Although *Cities of Salt* was number 1 on the list of the best 100 Arab novels of all time issued by the Arab Union of Writers, the series was banned in Saudi Arabia and most other Gulf countries for years because of the critical views it presented of tribal and religious authorities. Although Munif insisted that the series was entirely a work of fiction with no direct relation to events or characters in actual history, many have recognized the kingdom of Saudi Arabia as the fictional Arab desert land. Munif made his disclaimer out of concern that limiting the locations of his novels to a single country would have given the mistaken impression that the issues addressed were limited to individual countries. Because he sought to address what he perceived to be broad problems facing the entire Arab world, singling out one country would have meant inappropriately exonerating other countries in the process.

Munif's uniqueness as a writer lies in his successful and well-known use of literature to identify and underscore the shortcomings of Gulf societies, particularly with respect to human rights and freedoms, as they have pursued Westernized modernization and development. He is also the only Arab writer to have addressed desert rather than elite or middle-class urban environments (see also NAGUIB MAHFOUZ) and to have used fiction writing as a type of historiography of ordinary people and as a tool for change. He is one of the few writers to have challenged political taboos by writing about the stripping of human dignity and liberty in the Arab world while maintaining a remarkable degree of intellectual independence. He took his role as a Third World intellectual seriously, using his fiction as a means of political advocacy to enlighten society and call for change while maintaining focus on the people. Rather than inciting people to revolt or spouting propaganda, Munif believed that the intellectual was responsible for engaging in broad dialogue with both himself and broader society in order to be familiar with and able to express a variety of viewpoints and to move democracy forward.

Munif was widely considered one of the greatest Arab novelists of modern times and one of the most courageous writers in the Arab world. Other writers credited him with revolutionizing the Arab novel by introducing modernist narrative techniques and writing about ordinary desert people, all while serving as a "pioneer intellectual" in addressing important issues related to the renaissance of the nation. Munif received the Sultan al-Uways Award, the Arab equivalent of the Nobel Prize for Literature, in 1992 and the Cairo Award for Creative Narration in 1998 in recognition of his literary contributions.

Further reading

"Abdelrahman Munif," www.kirjasto.sci.fi/munif.htm

Allen, Roger. *The Arabic Literary Heritage: The Development of its Genres and Criticism.* New York: Cambridge University Press, 1998

—— *The Arabic Novel: An Historical and Critical Introduction*, 2nd ed. Syracuse: Syracuse University Press, 1995

Almezel, Mohammed. "Acclaimed Saudi Novelist Dies of Cancer," *Gulf News*, January 25, 2004

Habash, Iskandar. "In an Unpublished Interview, Abd al-Rahman Munif Characterizes the Crisis in the Arab Trilogy: Oil, Political Islam, and Dictatorship," *Al-Jadid*, vol. 9, no. 45; interview conducted in 1999

Munif, Abd al-Rahman. *Cities of Salt*, trans. Peter Theroux. New York: Vintage International, 1989
—— *Endings*, trans. Roger Allen. London: Quartet Books, 1988
—— *Story of a City: A Childhood in Amman*, trans. Samira Kawar. London: Quartet Books, 1996
—— *The Trench*, trans. Peter Theroux. New York: Pantheon Books, 1991
—— *Variations on Night and Day*, trans. Peter Theroux. New York: Pantheon Books, 1993
Tynes, Natasha. "Novelist Abd al-Rahman Munif Dies," *Aljazeera*, January 26, 2004, english.aljazeera.net/NR/exeres/570D32A1-2F2A-4109-8794-36EBDF020EA0.htm
www.arabworldbooks.com – provides information about Arab authors and their works
www.gulf-news.com – provides coverage of current Gulf news

Chandra Muzaffar (b. c. 1947)

Founder and president of the International Movement for a Just World (I.M.J.W.), Chandra Muzaffar has achieved international acclaim for his activism as a social critic of the injustices brought by globalization to the Third World.

Chandra Muzaffar was born around 1947 in Kedah, West Malaysia. A bout of polio when he was four years old left him with restricted mobility and a permanent partial disability. The combined experiences of physical suffering and an upbringing in a rural multiethnic environment fueled his dedication to helping the poor, weak, oppressed, and marginalized. The only son among four children, he learned to understand and empathize with women in early childhood, an experience that has translated into commitment to women's rights as an adult.

Muzaffar engaged his undergraduate studies at the University of Singapore in the late 1960s. Although he had hoped to learn about governance and power in Southeast Asia, the program emphasized mainstream American political science. Dissatisfied with his studies and what he

recalls as a mediocre faculty, Muzaffar decided to dedicate his own academic career to understanding the meaning and purpose of politics and how they relate to moral values and daily life. This pursuit was both an intellectual and a spiritual quest that drew him closer to Islam. He formally reverted to Islam in 1974.

Muzaffar began his academic career as a lecturer in political science at the Science University of Malaysia in Penang in 1970. As a student, he had been disturbed by the Western "myth of discovery" because the claim that countries such as Malaysia had been "discovered" by the West implied that these countries had not previously existed and had no history of their own. As a professor, he worked to restore the Malaysian perspective to "discovery" through a balanced approach to history that restored the indigenous perspective and discussed both the positive and negative effects of the arrival of the West in the Islamic world.

In 1975, Muzaffar returned to Singapore to pursue a Ph.D., which he completed in 1977. By this time, he was more critical of Western intellectual and cultural dominance and more committed to the spiritual and moral roots of his own philosophical tradition. His dissertation consciously sought to develop an alternative vision of human civilization that would provide justice for the weak and powerless majority.

In 1977, Muzaffar returned to his teaching position at the University of Malaysia, where he became the first director of the Centre for Civilisational Dialogue. At the same time, he and some friends formed ALIRAN, a social reform group dedicated to freedom, justice, and solidarity through the political, spiritual, and moral transformation of Malaysia. Muzaffar spent the next ten years writing and speaking about the problems of authoritarianism, religious bigotry, corruption, communalism, and disparities in opportunity and wealth. He became so involved in reforming Malaysian society that he resigned his professorship to concentrate on ALIRAN and its monthly publication.

One of Muzaffar's major themes was human rights. In 1985, he became a member of the executive committee of the Asian Commission on Human Rights. He was arrested by the Malaysian government in October 1987 and was held without trial under the Internal Security Act for two months. He was also barred from entering Singapore for having criticized the government's arrest of some professionals and social activists. Upon his release from detention, he continued his campaign for human rights and interethnic integration. In 1988, he was nominated as a monitor for Human Rights Watch.

During the late 1980s, Muzaffar began to address the broader challenges of globalization, particularly in economics, from a national perspective. In 1989, he was appointed to the National Economic Consultative Committee of the United Malaysia National Organization (U.M.N.O.). Although he resigned this position in 1990 to protest the politics of the committee, he was appointed a member of the Malaysian Economic Research Institute from 1992 until 1999.

By the early 1990s, Muzaffar was deeply involved in the economics of globalization, particularly his perception of the unidimensional and materialistic approach to development promoted by the West and its accompanying erosion of moral and spiritual values. Concluding that the challenges facing Malaysia could not be solved at the national level and were, in fact, shared by other countries in Southeast Asia, Muzaffar resigned the presidency of ALIRAN to dedicate himself full time to developing a global approach to identifying the problems of globalization and creating an alternative to the worldview that supports them. By 1992, he was challenging the omnipresent impact of "the West on the rest" and the concentration of global wealth and power in the hands of a minority elite. He established the Just World Trust to champion and give a voice to the silent majority who have become victims of this domination.

Muzaffar's approach addresses the full impact of colonization, covering the loss of control over politics, the economy, administration, and the mind. By the late twentieth century, Muslims in a variety of formerly colonized countries had become conscious of the full impact of colonization on all aspects of life and sought to reassert their indigenous history and identity as an antidote. Muzaffar believes that the awareness of the colonization of the mind has led to concerns about the cultural dimension of globalization that has captured the imagination of the youth and brought Western values, lifestyles, and ideas into Muslim societies. He believes that these values, lifestyles, and ideas in and of themselves are not necessarily negative, noting that, historically, exchanges between Islam and the West in trade, science, technology, and navigation helped both civilizations to achieve greatness. The problem as he sees it is that most of what is being adopted in terms of values and lifestyles comes from the entertainment industry, particularly dance, films, and music. Not only has this occurred at the cost of indigenous entertainment, but the values and lifestyles that are promoted are seriously at odds with Islamic culture and values.

The adoption of certain Western values and lifestyles is further complicated by the fact that many governments have focused exclusively on creating and supporting environments that are conducive to the growth and expansion of business and finance, rather than championing humanity or religion. Although he recognizes that there are benefits to globalization, such as the dissemination of knowledge; the promotion of health care; support for human rights and the rule of law; emphasis on public accountability;

and compassion for the victims of natural disasters and human-made calamities, he believes that greater attention must be given to the negative effects of globalization, such as severe environmental degradation; growing economic disparities between the wealthy and the poor; reduction of national concern for the basic needs of people in favor of profits and markets; rising unemployment; popularization of a consumer culture that pushes material wants and measures people according to their material possessions; promotion of living for the moment and instant gratification over building character and appreciating cultural diversity; restructuring education to promote skills demanded by industries; and the internationalization of crime and disease.

Muzaffar's response to these negative aspects of globalization has been to call for interfaith and intercivilizational dialogue to discover spiritual and moral worldviews and values based on religious philosophies that can offer guidance to humanity in the common quest for a just world. He founded the International Movement for a Just World (I.M.J.W.) to achieve this goal, believing that religion alone can provide the worldview and value system needed to transcend ethnic, religious, national, and regional identities and boundaries, particularly those that currently separate North from South and the First World from the Third World. He believes that developing global awareness of the injustices inherent to the existing system are necessary not only to address the poverty and powerlessness experienced by the majority of the world's people and to stem greed and selfishness, but also to create new approaches to the international order that will enhance human dignity and social justice. He believes that the promotion of greater public awareness about the injustices and inequities of the existing global system will help to nurture broader appreciation for alternative institutions and ideas that support

the creation of a universal moral and spiritual vision of life rooted in God that can guide humanity in its quest for a more just world. In order to promote this work and vision, the I.M.J.W. produces a variety of publications that are distributed to more than three thousand groups and individuals in 135 countries.

Muzaffar believes that Islam has an important role to play in the quest for justice because it calls for the elevation of humanity, the enhancement of consciousness of justice, and the unity of the brotherhood and sisterhood of the human family. Because Islam has been historically absent, if not excluded, from the process of globalization, he believes that the reassertion of the essence of Islam can serve as the key to expanding universalism and ecumenicalism. He has called for Islam to adopt a vision of reform, development, and progress that discovers and enhances humanity, rather than limits it to ritual issues and literal interpretations of Islamic law. He has particularly advocated regarding women as equals and granting minorities the same rights that are enjoyed by the majority. Muzaffar believes that women have a particularly important role to play in the progressive reinterpretation of Islam because of their demonstrated willingness to consider all human beings as equals and to address the larger challenges facing the Muslim world, building a momentum for change. He also hopes to gain the support of male clerics for changes to the current global system in order to lend authority to the proposed reforms and make them more likely to be accepted by a broader portion of the Muslim community, particularly if disseminated via the mass media.

Muzaffar believes that Malaysia can play a pivotal role in moving justice and progress forward because women already have strong rights and play an important role in running the country, particularly in business, education, and politics. Power sharing between Muslims and non-Muslims already exists and a variety of religious holidays are nationally recognized. Malaysia has also increasingly asserted a more consciously Muslim identity as it has shaken off the colonial era and sought to redefine its public image. Muzaffar is careful to point out that this reassertion of a Muslim identity should not be confused with the desire to make Malaysia into an Islamic state. He personally believes that an Islamic state would be a mistake in Malaysia because it implies a compartmentalized and "us versus them" mentality within its institutional structures: the opposite of what he is trying to achieve.

Muzaffar believes that Islam and the Islamic world can teach the West a more ethical approach to power, markets, and profits and to emphasize character rather than instant gratification. He points to Islam's comprehensive view of both individual and communal rights, as opposed to Western concepts of human rights that are based solely on the rights of the individual. He has made the expansion of dialogue and understanding between civilizations and cultures his life's mission.

In addition to leading the I.M.J.W., Muzaffar serves as a peace councilor for the International Committee for the Peace Council, a group of internationally known and respected religious and spiritual individuals who work together to demonstrate religion's capacity to relieve human suffering and promote global wholeness and healing. He also serves on the board of advisors for the World Policy Institute of New School University, Dialogues: Islamic World–U.S.–the West, which seeks to increase communication among and about the Islamic

world, the United States, and the West and to promote understanding of Muslim viewpoints and concerns. He is a member of the board of directors of the International Movement Against All Forms of Discrimination and Racism, Belgium, and deputy president of the National Justice Party. Muzaffar is the author of numerous books on human rights, religion, international relations, and Malaysian politics.

Further reading

Camilleri, Joseph A. and Chandra Muzaffar, eds. *Globalisation: The Perspectives and Experiences of the Religious Traditions of Asia Pacific*. Selangor: International Movement for a Just World, 1998

"Chandra Muzaffar," biography on www.others.com/chandra.htm

"Interview with Chandra Muzaffar," *Frontline*, October 10, 2001, www.pbs.org/wgbh/pages/frontline/shows/muslims/interviews/muzaffar.html

Knitter, Paul F. and Chandra Muzaffar, eds. *Subverting Greed: Religious Perspectives on the Global Economy*. Maryknoll, NY: Orbis Books, 2002

Muzaffar, Chandra. *Human Rights and the New World Order*. Penang: Just World Trust, 1993

—— *Muslims, Dialogue and Terror*. Kuala Lumpur: JUST, 2002

—— *Rights, Religion and Reform: Enhancing Human Dignity through Spiritual and Moral Transformation*. London: Routledge Curzon, 2002

www.islamuswest.org – website for World Policy Institute of New School University, Dialogues: Islamic World–U.S.–the West

www.just-international.org – website for International Movement for a Just World

www.peacecouncil.org – website for International Committee for the Peace Council

N

Her Majesty Queen Noor
(b. 1951)

An internationally acclaimed humanitarian and philanthropist dedicated to human rights, sustainable development, the promotion of peace and democracy, and women's and children's rights, Her Majesty Queen Noor exemplifies public service at both the national and international levels.

Queen Noor was born Lisa Halaby on August 23, 1951, to a prominent Arab-American family in Washington, DC. Her father, Najeeb, had a long and distinguished career as a public servant. Originally a test pilot for Lockheed Aviation, he worked for both the Truman and Eisenhower administrations and became the head of the Federal Aviation Administration (F.A.A.) under President John F. Kennedy. He also worked to break down racial barriers and gain acceptance for Arab Americans in the highest levels of government and commerce. Noor's mother, Doris Carlquist, was a government administrative assistant who was dedicated to community service, particularly support for the New York settlement house in East Harlem, public television, and organizations promoting U.S.–Arab relations, social welfare in the Middle East, and support for Palestinian refugees. Noor was also strongly influenced by her paternal grandmother, Laura, who taught her the power of positive thinking and the importance of living a meaningful and worthy life.

Noor moved frequently as a child, living in Washington, DC, New York City, and California. In Washington, she attended the private National Cathedral School for Girls and envisaged a career in the Peace Corps. Deeply concerned by racism and the race riots sweeping the United States during the 1960s, she supported the Kennedy administration's dedication to social justice and joined the Student Nonviolent Coordinating Committee (S.N.C.C.) in 1961 to protest and call for an end to segregation and to promote social justice. As for many of her generation, Noor's hope for the future and optimism were nearly shattered by the assassinations of President Kennedy and Dr. Martin Luther King, Jr.

In 1965, Noor's family moved back to New York. Noor was enrolled at the Chapin School, but found it difficult to adjust because discussion and debate about the civil rights movement and Vietnam were not permitted. Nevertheless, she found meaning in Chapin's community service program tutoring non-English-speaking students in a public school in Harlem, an experience that helped her to appreciate the difficulties of breaking the cycles of ignorance and poverty.

Noor spent her last two years of high school at Concord Academy in Concord, MA. She found that Concord's policy of assigning community service as punishment both helped the students be more connected to their surroundings and encouraged personal responsibility. She attended Princeton University as a member of the first class to admit women and earned a degree in urban planning in 1974.

After college, Noor worked for the British planning firm Llewelyn-Davis. She spent one year in Australia before moving to Tehran, Iran, in 1975 to work with a group of architects on building a model city center. She observed first hand the increasing religious fervor and political unrest that ultimately led to the Islamic Revolution in 1979. She also realized the fundamental lack of understanding of Islam and Middle Eastern culture in the West. These experiences sparked an interest in a career in journalism. However, she chose instead to take a position with Jordanian Airlines to establish an office responsible for the coordination, planning, and design of all of its facilities, seeing an opportunity to apply her architectural and planning training while reconnecting with her Arab roots.

Noor met her future husband, King Hussein, during a 1976 business trip for Jordanian Airlines. Other business encounters led to a courtship and a marriage proposal. Although she was concerned about the implications for Hussein of having an American wife, albeit of Arab descent, at a time of rising regional anti-American sentiment, the couple married on June 15, 1978, making Noor the youngest and only American-born queen in the world. Hussein gave her the name Noor Al Hussein, Arabic for "Light of Hussein," which she has described as the most precious gift the king gave her. The couple had four children. Noor also became stepmother to the king's eight children from prior marriages.

Noor decided to convert to Islam prior to the marriage. She has stated that it was not required or asked by King Hussein, but that she was drawn to Islam's emphasis on the individual's direct relationship with God, the fundamental equality of rights of men and women, reverence for the Prophet Muhammad and all prior prophets and messengers, proclamation of the values of fairness, honesty, justice, charity, moderation, and tolerance, and the simplicity of its beliefs with no need for a religious hierarchy or distinction between believers apart from piety. She pronounced the declaration of faith on her wedding day.

Hussein considered the marriage a partnership and supported Noor's decision to work and contribute to the building of Jordan. The couple followed a pattern of informality in governing the country, believing that it was a better reflection of the activist, hands-on role they played in Jordan than a more formal and inaccessible lifestyle would have provided. One of the major challenges of governing Jordan was the diversity of the population, a mixture of Muslims and Christians, Jordanians and immigrants. The largest sector of immigrants consists of 1.5 million Palestinian refugees. Although it placed tremendous strain on Jordan's resources, King Hussein granted citizenship to Palestinian refugees. He was the only Arab head of state to do so. He worked until he died to resolve the Palestinian issue, believing that the only path to peaceful coexistence was through a just and comprehensive peace that guaranteed the right of every state to live in peace within secure and recognized boundaries free from threats or acts of force. Noor also dedicated herself to addressing the Palestinian situation, working to dispel negative stereotypes of Arabs and Muslims, to ensure that historical accuracy takes center stage in dealing with the Palestinian cause, and to promote dialogue and understanding between all parties to the conflict. These approaches have made her a figure of both controversy and admiration.

Noor began her work in addressing the needs of Jordan and the developing world shortly after her marriage. Since 1978, she has initiated, directed, and sponsored projects and activities addressing developmental needs such as education, culture, human rights, women and children's welfare, conflict resolution, integrated community development, public architecture, urban planning, environmental and architectural conservation and planning, and drug-abuse prevention. She is known internationally as an advocate for her work in banning landmines, environmental conservation, peacemaking, economic issues in developing nations, human rights, and cross-cultural understanding. She is actively involved in a number of international organizations dealing with global peace building and conflict recovery and serves as an expert advisor to the United Nations on these issues.

Noor's first venture as queen was the assumption of an active role in the Royal Society for the Conservation of Nature in 1978. With the assistance of the International Union for the Conservation of Nature and the World Wildlife Fund, the society developed the first conservation plan in the region to identify areas of the country to be set aside as nature preserves. The most successful venture, the Dana Wildlife Reserve, paired conservation with socio-economic development, creating a tourist industry and a market for dried organic fruits and silver jewelry with nature designs. The society reintroduced the Arabian oryx into the wild in 1983, an accomplishment that was recorded in the *Guinness Book of World Records* and provided a blueprint for the World Wildlife Fund.

In 1979, Noor was appointed chair of Jordan's National Committee for the Child during the U.N. International Year of the Child. She presided over a general assessment of the state of Jordan's children and identification of short- and long-term priorities and strategies, including the inauguration of a national immunization campaign. She personally administered some oral vaccines to promote awareness of the campaign's importance. She also became involved in S.O.S. Kinderdorf International, a network of children's villages of orphans and abandoned children around the world, and oversaw the founding of several villages in Jordan, including one in Aqaba designed by architect Jafar Tukan that won the Aga Khan Award for Architecture in 2001. (See also THE AGA KHAN, PRINCE KARIM IV.) She helped to establish the Royal Endowment for Culture and Education to conduct research on the country's manpower needs and to provide scholarships, especially to women, for graduate studies in fields vital to Jordan's national development. She also worked with Jordanian engineers and architects to develop a standard building code.

In 1980, Noor joined U.N.I.C.E.F.'s child survival and development revolution to reduce infant and maternal mortality rates via low-cost interventions, such as growth monitoring, breastfeeding, immunization, and oral rehydration. By end of the 1980s, Jordan was recognized as exemplary in its advances in human development, including nutrition, school enrollment, girls' education, access to health services and water, and immunization rates above ninety percent. Noor also convened the first annual Arab Children's Congress to bring students from throughout the Arab world together to discuss and debate contemporary issues and challenges facing the Arab world and to encourage appreciation of their common historical and cultural bonds to promote understanding, tolerance, and solidarity.

Noor's advocacy and work for children's rights led King Hussein to ask her to establish and chair a national task force for children in 1995 to monitor and evaluate the condition and status of Jordan's children. In 1997, she established the National Coalition for Children, which encourages and facilitates cooperation and promotes partnerships between public, private, and non-governmental organizations and institutions involved in children's affairs. It also established a national policy and research center and a child information center on the web. The coalition has addressed issues such as child labor, urban poverty, teen smoking, youth and culture, and gaps and priorities in development research and programs. Noor's work on children's issues also includes the 1986 launching of the Children's Heritage and Science Museum, the first children's museum in Jordan and the Arab world, and the 1988 launching of the Mobile Life and Science Museum, an outreach program for children in rural areas that uses computers, books, exhibits, and hands-on educational and recreational activities to help children learn about environmental protection, health, science, and Jordanian history.

Noor began to sponsor Jordanian and Arab culture and the arts in 1981 with the foundation of the Jerash Festival for Culture and Arts, an annual festival for Arab and international performing artists. Held in the ancient Roman city of Jerash, the festival provides an opportunity for Jordanians and others to appreciate its rich architectural and cultural heritage while paying tribute to popular Arab and Muslim art forms and introducing contemporary regional and international culture. Noor also founded the National Music Conservatory in 1985 to develop musicians accomplished in classical Arabic and Western music, promote musical performances, and encourage music curricula in public schools. The conservatory encourages and offers opportunities to Jordanian children to explore both Arab and Western musical heritage, including playing instruments, choral instruction, and classes in music theory and history. The conservatory formed the first children's orchestra in

Jordan, which played at the 1986 Jerash Festival with Youth Strings in Action from the United States.

In 1984, Noor took on the issue of national education. In honor of the King's silver jubilee that year, she began planning the Jubilee School for outstanding students from the less developed areas of Jordan. The school works to develop academic and leadership potential in students by emphasizing creative thinking, leadership and conflict-resolution skills, scientific and technological expertise, and social responsibility. A Center for Excellence in Education was also established at the school to advance national and regional educational standards by developing innovative curricula and programs.

Noor's diverse development activities inspired King Hussein to establish the Noor Al Hussein Foundation (N.H.F.) by royal decree in 1985 to consolidate and integrate her initiatives. The N.H.F. initiates and supports national, regional, and international projects in integrated community development, microfinance, women and enterprise development, child and family health, and education and culture by integrating social-development strategies, such as individual and community self-reliance, grass-roots participation in decision making and implementation, and the empowerment of women, with national economic priorities. Of the N.H.F.'s programs, the Quality of Life Project, Women-in-Development Projects, Institute for Child Health Development (renamed Institute for Family Health), Jubilee School (which became part of the King Hussein Foundation), National Handicrafts Development Project, National Conservatory, Performing Arts Center, and Jordan Micro Credit Company have been recognized and supported by the United Nations and other international organizations as development models for the Middle East and the developing world.

In addition to her development work, Noor began to speak internationally about Middle East politics and U.S.–Arab relations and policy during the 1980s. Her first major speech in 1981 established her as a political figure with an important, although controversial, message. She has called upon the international community to focus its resources on human development, rather than economics or security concerns, noting that the Middle East has one of the world's highest per capita spending rates on arms, yet more than half of the region's women are illiterate and three-quarters of the population lives in poverty.

The 1990s were a mixed period for Noor. In 1992, her husband was diagnosed with a urological condition that was a precursor to the cancer that led to his death in 1999. The Gulf War of 1990–1991 resulted in a massive influx of refugees into Jordan that stretched the country's financial resources beyond its capacity to absorb at a time when outside financial assistance was also cut off because King Hussein chose to work for a diplomatic, rather than a military, resolution. Noor worked to focus world attention on the plight of refugees. The impact of the war led to a general decline in living standards in Jordan and the dwindling of the tourist industry.

Although there were some conservatives who criticized her work on women's issues as being overly Western, secular, and feminist, and thus supposedly inappropriate in an Arab and Muslim context, Noor expanded her work on education and women's causes during the 1990s. Never affiliated with the political movement for feminism in the United States, she developed her own brand of feminism from her grass-roots work in Jordan. Recognizing the importance of advancing legislation and changing societal patterns that restrain women from reaching their full potential, she worked to introduce social programs that could provide opportunities for women to transform not only themselves, but also their families and communities, through education and the strengthening of communities. She worked to expand international assistance for women through recognition of the relationship between poverty, war, and the poor treatment of women. Moved by the atrocities suffered by women during the Bosnian civil war, she served as the co-chair of the Women of Srebrenica Project in 1995 to help the victims reconstruct their lives. She also served as a member of the International Commission on Missing Persons created in 1996.

Noor's formal royal duties ended with her husband's death in 1999. She retains the title of queen and has focused her attention on international peace building, the empowerment of women, particularly in the Arab and developing worlds, human rights, cross-cultural understanding, and the work of the King Hussein Foundation, which is dedicated to implementing the late king's humanitarian vision and legacy through education, leadership, peace, and democracy. Noor's autobiography, *Leap of Faith: Memoirs of an Unexpected Life*, was written to share her memories and perspective on King Hussein's legacy, to contribute to greater awareness in the West of events that shaped and continue to shape the Middle East, Arab world, and Western understanding of Islam, and to provide financing for the foundation.

Noor's work has been recognized both nationally and internationally. She has been awarded Jordan's Grand Cordon of the Jeweled Al Nahda and the Collar of Al Hussein Bin Ali. In 1996, she was a co-recipient with Leah Rabin of the Eleanor Roosevelt Val-Kill Medal for her work for peace. She received the U.N. Environment Program Global 500 Award for environmental activism and the 2001 Distinguished Service Award from the Catholic Theological Union at the Blessed Are Peacemakers dinner for her public commitment to peace and human dignity and for her advancement of peace, reconciliation, and human development in the Middle East and throughout the world. She has also received state decorations from around the world and numerous international awards and honorary doctorates in international relations, law, and humane letters for her work in development, democracy, and peace. In 2004, she created the Najeeb Halaby Award for Public Service to honor both lifetime achievements in public service and her father's memory.

Further reading

Lafferty, Elaine. "Queen Noor: The Next Chapter," *Ms.* magazine, vol. 13, no. 3, fall 2003

Her Majesty Queen Noor. *Leap of Faith: Memoirs of an Unexpected Life.* New York: Miramax Books, 2003

"Queen Noor of Jordan to Receive Catholic Theological Union's Peacemaker Award," April 25, 2001, press release

www.icbl.org – website for International Campaign to Ban Landmines

www.landminesurvivors.org – website for Landmine Survivors' Network

www.queennoor.jo – website for Queen Noor

Thoraya Ahmed Obaid (b. 1945)

Under-secretary general of the United Nations and Executive Director of the United Nations Fund for Population Activities (U.N.F.P.A.), Thoraya Ahmed Obaid is the first Saudi Arabian national to be appointed head of a United Nations agency.

Thoraya Ahmed Obaid was born in Baghdad, Iraq, on March 2, 1945, to Saudi Arabian parents. Her father, Ahmed, was a self-taught Arabic classicist who began working for the Saudi Arabian government when he was fifteen. He ultimately became director-general of the Department of Agriculture, but left the civil service to establish the first modern printing press, the Printing and Publishing Institution, and produce the first glossy monthly magazine in Saudi Arabia, *Al-Riyadh*. Her mother, Aisha Al-Khatib, received formal education only up to the third grade, but loved learning and insisted on women's right to education. Because the first word of the Quran is "Read!," Obaid's parents believed that all Muslims, both male and female, are required to read, learn, study, and make rational decisions. They therefore insisted that all of their children, both boys and girls, be educated. Obaid's father particularly wanted his daughter

to be economically productive so as not to be dependent upon her husband. Obaid sees herself as a living example of a Muslim woman who was empowered to make her own choices in life, rendering her an important living role model for young women who face discrimination, constraints, and challenges in their quest for education and a professional career.

In keeping with her parents' wishes, Obaid began her studies with traditional religious instruction in the Quran at the age of three, followed by a modern education at the American College for Girls in Cairo, Egypt, beginning at the age of six. She was sent to boarding school because, in 1951, education for girls had not yet been established in Saudi Arabia. Girls' education was established in Saudi Arabia in 1962, the same year in which Obaid received her secondary school diploma.

Both Obaid and her parents were determined that she should pursue a college education, despite strong opposition from her father's friends who felt that a high-school education was sufficient for a girl. Obaid credits her parents for their support and protection of her, as well as their determination that she continue her education like her two oldest brothers who were both studying on government scholarships in the United States. Obaid attended Mills College, a women's college in Oakland, CA, both because it made for a smooth transition from an all-girls' boarding school and because it validated and safeguarded her father from community pressure from those who opposed her studying abroad.

That Obaid was permitted to study abroad was a remarkable achievement for this time. However, it also proved a tremendous financial burden for her family. Unable to afford the cost of her education in the United States, Obaid's father approached the minister of education and requested a scholarship for her, believing that she should be entitled to the same government support offered to boys studying abroad. The minister promised that, if she performed well the first semester, a scholarship would be forthcoming. Obaid's hard work paid off in the spring of 1963 when she became not only the first female recipient of a Saudi government scholarship to study abroad, but also became the pilot project for scholarships for other Saudi girls. The only catch was that the government wanted her to study medicine. Obaid completed two years of pre-medical education, but decided to change her major to English literature, with the approval of the government, and to take a minor in sociology. When she completed her B.A. in 1966, the Saudi government granted other women scholarships for study in the United States.

Obaid pursued graduate studies at Wayne State University in Detroit, MI, where she completed an M.A. in English literature in 1968 and a Ph.D. in English literature with a minor in cultural anthropology in 1974. Although she was supposed to return to Saudi Arabia to take a position as dean of the Women's College at King Abdul Aziz University in Jeddah, she instead married a Lebanese man toward the end of her doctoral program and decided to live in Lebanon.

In order to fulfill her commitment to the government of Saudi Arabia to work in the civil service for the same number of

years as the scholarships, Obaid joined the United Nations as a Social Affairs Officer for the Economic Commission for Western Asia (E.C.W.A.), later renamed the Economic and Social Commission for Western Asia (E.S.C.W.A.), filling one of the fourteen vacant slots allocated to her country. That year, 1975, was the International Women's Year and the United Nations was particularly interested in hiring qualified women. Obaid became responsible for women's programs, creating the first United Nations women's program in the Western Asia region. This program was instrumental in building partnerships between the United Nations and regional non-governmental organizations (N.G.O.'s). While working as a social affairs officer from 1975 until 1992, she also served as the vice president of the Staff Council from 1980 to 1982 and the coordinator of the E.S.C.W.A. Group on Women from 1989 to 1990. In addition, she was a member of the League of Arab States Working Group for formulating the Arab Strategy for Social Development from 1984 to 1985 and served on the editorial board of the *Journal of Arab Women* from 1984 to 1990. She had also been a founding member of the N.G.O., the Association for Working Mothers, in 1974. In recognition of her outstanding commitment and service to Arab women, she received an award from the General Federation of Arab Women in 1985.

Obaid took a leave of absence from E.S.C.W.A. from 1991 to 1992 when she returned to Saudi Arabia. She joined Al-Nahda, Saudi Arabia's oldest women's organization. Although it was originally designed to promote social and cultural programs from a philanthropic posture, she helped to transform it into a development-oriented organization that recognizes and engages women as actors, rather than objects for charity. Al-Nahda provides typing, language, and computer-literacy courses and lectures, guidance and income-generating ideas for businesswomen. It also maintains and produces one of the highest-quality and most diverse collections of traditional women's clothing from throughout Saudi Arabia.

In 1992, Obaid was promoted to chief of the Social Development and Population Division, where she served until 1993. She was promoted to deputy executive secretary from 1993 until 1998. She chaired the United Nations Inter-Agency Task Force on Gender in Amman, Jordan, in 1996, and was a member of both the United Nations Inter-Agency Gender Mission and the United Nations Strategic Framework Mission to Afghanistan in 1997.

In 1998, Obaid was appointed director of the Division for Arab States and Europe at the United Nations Fund for Population Activities (U.N.F.P.A.), the world's largest multilateral source of population assistance. She was promoted to executive director of the U.N.F.P.A. and under-secretary general of the United Nations on January 1, 2001. She credits her predecessors, Dr. Nafis Sadik of Pakistan and Rafael Salas of the Philippines, with setting the stage for her to carry out her work.

Made operational in 1969, U.N.F.P.A.'s mission is to support developing countries, at their request, in improving access to and the quality of reproductive health care, with special attention to family planning, safe motherhood, the prevention of sexually transmitted diseases, including H.I.V./A.I.D.S., and combating violence against women. The fund further promotes women's rights and equality and actively supports the collection and analysis of data to help countries achieve sustainable development and formulate population policies. Goals adopted at the 1994 global conference on population and development include universal access to reproductive health services by 2015, universal primary education and closing of the gender gap in education by 2015, reduction of maternal mortality by 75% by 2015, reduction of infant mortality,

increasing life expectancy, and reduction of H.I.V. infection rates in young people between fifteen and twenty-four years of age by 25% in target countries by 2005 and 25% globally by 2010.

As executive director, Obaid has worked to strengthen and expand the links between reproductive health and population and broader aspects of development, particularly poverty eradication. As part of this vision, U.N.F.P.A. has played a more leveraged and bigger role in the United Nations development system, working toward international development goals with partners such as the World Bank. It has also undertaken a staff-driven transition exercise to meet the challenges of the twenty-first century, particularly the Millennium Development Goals (M.D.G.'s), by strengthening its field presence, capacity and operations and enhancing its participation in national development dialogue. It has improved response time to development needs and humanitarian crises, such as those in Iraq, Afghanistan, the Occupied Palestinian Territory, Sierra Leone, Timor-Leste, and the Democratic Republic of the Congo.

When asked to identify the biggest threat to global health, Obaid asserted complications associated with pregnancy and childbirth, which, affecting some 20 million women annually, constitute, in her opinion, a global crisis. She believes that lack of attention to these issues reflects gender discrimination and violence based upon a lack of concern for women as they fulfill their physiological function of bearing children. She notes that maternal health represents the largest gap between rich and poor in the world, largely unnecessarily, because the medical technology and services exist to prevent death and disability. The issue is one of access – a fact that she considers unacceptable in the twenty-first century. She believes not only that women should have the right to life, safe motherhood, and freedom from gender discrimination and violence, but also that everyone would benefit from the guarantee of these rights because women play a central role in their families and communities.

In order to resolve these issues, Obaid believes that quality reproductive health, including family planning, should be considered both a public health and a human rights issue. Because births that occur less than two years apart cause infant mortality rates 45% higher than births occurring two to three years apart and because mortality rates among teenage mothers are as high as twice the normal rates due to their physical immaturity, Obaid has called for access to family-planning methods and reproductive education as a necessary step in lowering infant and maternal mortality rates and in helping families to space their children and control their fertility better. She has also called for greater attention and access to and support for the expansion of facilities providing obstetrical care and capable of providing emergency treatment in the event of medical complications, particularly obstetric fistula, which happens when a woman is in obstructed labor for too long. In most of these cases, the baby dies and the mother, if she survives, is left with extensive and permanent damage to the birth canal that leaves her incontinent. Obstetric fistula is the most preventable and treatable of all complications associated with childbirth because a caesarian section resolves the problem. Thus, she asserts the importance of guaranteeing women access to medical facilities capable of performing this operation.

Obaid has identified her central focus in her work for both E.S.C.W.A. and U.N.F.P.A. as working with governments to establish programs to empower women and develop their capacities as citizens with rights and responsibilities and working with N.G.O.'s to advocate for equality for women. She has also emphasized the importance of development that emerges from the context of each society, including the need to consider the cultural values and religious beliefs that shape people and impact on their actions. As executive director of U.N.F.P.A., she has introduced a special focus on culture and religion in the fund's development work, linking the universal values of human rights to the values of human worth promoted by all religions and found in all cultures. She does this because not only are they the context in which grass-roots people live and behave, but also because she believes that this approach facilitates and enhances the implementation of human rights principles of the Programme of Action adopted at the Cairo International Conference on Population and Development in 1994. Including sensitivity to traditions, customs, behaviors, beliefs, and faiths of the host communities when discussing population issues and reproductive health ensures that they will feel more comfortable with, and will therefore be more likely to respond positively to, the proposed programs for giving women and couples the right to choose freely the timing and spacing of their children, providing women with health services to prevent them dying during childbirth, and providing young people with appropriate information and services to maintain their reproductive health. According to this vision, culture is not perceived as a constraint, but is the context in which development work takes place.

Obaid has also applied this vision to the promotion of a human rights-based and culturally sensitive approach to dealing with the H.I.V./A.I.D.S. pandemic. Substantially scaled-up attention and resources have enabled U.N.F.P.A. to prevent infections and slow the spread of the disease, although this work is necessarily ongoing, given the scale of the spread of H.I.V./A.I.D.S. in the twenty-first century. U.N.F.P.A. has expanded its partnerships to include international organizations and broader segments of society, such as community, religious, and traditional leaders, in addressing H.I.V./A.I.D.S. Obaid's work with U.N.F.P.A. has not been without controversy. Her willingness to take on contentious issues, particularly those related to women's reproductive health and H.I.V./A.I.D.S. prevention, has earned opposition from a few extremely conservative quarters. Obaid remains unshaken in her determination to promote and meet basic human rights – social, cultural, and economic – and to focus especially on the needs of young people because she believes that they have the right to productive and dignified lives. Observing that globalization and development have interconnected people across the world as never before and given them visions of a better life, she believes that greater and more systematic attention needs to be given to making that better life possible by expanding opportunity, participation, and choices for all people, beginning with universal access to education, employment, and health care. The prevalence of conflict, poverty, and hopelessness in parts of the world where more than half of the population is under the age of twenty-five is, in her opinion, the greatest threat to world security ever known. She believes that focusing on survival is insufficient in the global era – quality of life that enables people to make their own contributions to both their families and their societies, including poverty reduction; access to adequate food, nutrition, water, and sanitation; education; employment; conflict prevention through dialogue and mutual understanding; and good and responsible governance, is critical to a peaceful future.

Obaid believes that the first step in the process of providing quality of life must be access to reproductive-health services – education, information, counseling, and medical care – in order to take control not only of death and disability for women and children, but also of unwanted pregnancies and the spread of H.I.V./A.I.D.S. She notes that young girls are at the greatest risk because of gender inequalities, the practice of early marriage, sexual violence, and the quest of older men for young women not infected by H.I.V./A.I.D.S. Historically, the U.N. focused on preventing the transmission of H.I.V./A.I.D.S. from mother to child. Obaid, however, believes that it is more important to prevent infection altogether. Only by focusing on the majority – uninfected young people – is there any hope of stopping the pandemic. She calls for prevention as the key to ending the pandemic because no vaccine against the virus exists.

Reaffirming that the basic right to reproductive health is a universal human right, Obaid and U.N.F.P.A. have identified three strategies for H.I.V./A.I.D.S. prevention: providing young people, especially adolescent girls, with information and services; ensuring that pregnant women and their children can remain H.I.V.-free; and supporting the A.B.C. approach – Abstinence, Be faithful to one partner, and Condom use. Obaid believes that there is no religious or moral problem with the U.N.F.P.A.'s stance because it is based on what was adopted by the United Nations General Assembly. She has identified overcoming "misrepresentations of and some hostility to the international consensus on women's right to make free decisions on their lives"; ensuring universal access to reproductive-health services to all couples who wish to plan their lives and protect themselves from H.I.V./A.I.D.S.; and ensuring a solid, secure, and predictable financial base for U.N.F.P.A. as the three greatest challenges of her job.

Obaid has also been an outspoken advocate of the need to empower women in order to end systematic violence against and abuse of them, whether due to conflict, refugee status, or government policy. She notes that, throughout history, women and girls have routinely suffered assaults and rapes during armed conflicts and as refugees, often as part of a systematic campaign of political domination or ethnic cleansing. Although the perpetrators are rarely apprehended or punished, the women remain forever scarred – physically, psychologically, emotionally, and, often, socially. She was heartened by the landmark February 2001 conviction of three individuals for their rape and enslavement of women in the former Yugoslavia as a crime against humanity by the International Criminal Tribunal. Recognition of these issues led to a partnership between U.N.F.P.A., the W.H.O., the U.N. Children's Fund, U.N.H.C.R., the International Federation of Red Cross and Red Crescent Societies, and other organizations to address both reproductive-health needs and sexual violence during conflicts. Emergency health projects were also begun in more than thirty countries to address family planning, including contraception; prenatal care; safe delivery and postnatal care; management of sexual violence and rape, including emergency contraception; and treatment and prevention of sexually transmitted diseases, including H.I.V./A.I.D.S.

Obaid has been particularly touched by the plight of refugee women and the women of Afghanistan under Taliban rule. She notes that one in five refugee women of childbearing age are pregnant when they arrive in refugee camps, leading to heightened risks of miscarriage, premature delivery, and complications in childbirth. She has also commented on her personal sadness and anger over the situation of Afghan women under the Taliban where the values of Islam were twisted to justify the oppression of women and the "promotion of terror." Noting that this is the same Islam that motivated her parents to educate her and that empowered her to reach where she is today, she has felt a special responsibility to ensure that Afghan women have access to education and basic reproductive-

health care, including family planning services, freedom to make decisions about marriage and childbirth, and medical care during pregnancy and childbirth. Under her leadership, U.N.F.P.A. joined with the Afghan Ministry of Health to rehabilitate the three maternity hospitals in Kabul, build schools for married women, and provide support for training midwives and other medical personnel. U.N.F.P.A. also worked with the W.H.O. to ensure that reproductive health is integrated into the emerging health-care system.

Obaid's work as executive director of U.N.F.P.A. has earned her a variety of international awards and honors. In 2001, her "outstanding commitment to global public service" was recognized by the New York Wagner School of Public Health, New York University. Her participation and contribution to the Global Philanthropy Forum: Borderless Giving was recognized in 2002 when she also received an honorary doctorate of law from Mills College and was awarded the George P. Younger Award by the Committee of Religious Non-Governmental Organizations at the United Nations. In March 2003, she was the recipient of a medal and a key to Managua and the Pedro Joaquin Chamarro Award – the highest award given by the Parliament or President of Nicaragua. The Columbia University School of Nursing awarded her the Second Century Award for Excellence in Health Care in 2003.

Further reading

Obaid, Thoraya Ahmed. "Afghan Women Today: Realities and Opportunities, Reproductive Health and Reproductive Rights," statement for International Women's Day, March 8, 2002, United Nations, New York
—— "Plenary Remarks," University for a Night 2002, Synergos at the United Nations
—— "Statement Summarizing E.C.O.S.O.C. Education Roundtable," July 1, 2002
—— "Women and Peace, Women Managing Conflict," statement for International Women's Day, March 5, 2001

—— "Women's Health and Empowerment: A Key to a Better World," statement, May 12, 2003

Interview with the author, November 5, 2003

www.alnahda-ksa.org – website for the Al-Nahda Philanthropic Society for Women

www.unfpa.org – website for U.N.F.P.A.

Hakeem Olajuwon (b. 1963)

The star center for the Houston Rockets, Hakeem Olajuwon is considered one of the greatest basketball players in N.B.A. history. He is the founder of the Dream Foundation.

Hakeem Olajuwon was born in Lagos, Nigeria, on January 21, 1963, to a family of Yoruba tribal descent. His father worked as a broker in the cement business. His mother managed the household, raised the children, and assisted with the family business. Olajuwon credits his parents with raising him with strong family and religious values through their own example and with emphasizing both his Muslim and Yoruba identities. He speaks a dialect of the Yoruba language, English, French, and three other African dialects.

Olajuwon's parents placed the highest emphasis on education for their children. All of the children were expected to win scholarships and go abroad to college. Like many Nigerians, Olajuwon's parents considered sports to be a hobby, rather than a profession. They neither encouraged nor discouraged him from pursuing athletics. They simply made it clear that he was expected to do well in school as a priority over playing.

Olajuwon's formal education began when he was six years old, and always included English. By the time he was eleven and in secondary school, he was required to speak English in class. Students who spoke local dialects were punished. The heavy English emphasis in school reflected both Nigeria's colonial heritage and the purpose of school: communication and pursuit of advanced study at university. Fluency in English was required for graduation from high school.

Like three-quarters of Nigerian children, Olajuwon was sent to a private boarding school, the Aladura Comprehensive High School, when he twelve. He spent only one year at this school, largely due to safety concerns about kidnappers targeting students for use in human sacrificial rituals. The following year, he transferred to the Muslim Teachers College, from which he graduated when he was seventeen. He played on a variety of school athletic teams, including soccer, team handball, and track. Frequently teased about his height (he was six foot nine by the time he was fifteen), Olajuwon used sports to fit in with his classmates while standing out on the basis of ability. His favorite sport in high school was team handball. He played so well that he was chosen to represent Lagos in a national tournament during his junior year. Only when the tournament was canceled due to lack of participation by other schools did he finally began to consider basketball.

Olajuwon had avoided basketball for years because of his love of team handball. Although Ganiyu Otenigbade, the head basketball coach for Lagos State University, implored him to try basketball, Olajuwon consistently refused. Coach Ganiyu persisted and finally convinced Olajuwon to come out on the basketball court and try a shot. Olajuwon tried – and missed. After missing a second shot, he spent two hours with Coach Ganiyu, finally making a basket and agreeing to join the basketball team.

Coach Ganiyu insisted that Olajuwon learn the fundamentals of the game first without worrying about how he looked when he played. He won Olajuwon's ongoing interest by pointing out that basketball was an American game, as well as a big man's game for which Olajuwon's height of six foot eleven inches would be an asset. Although Olajuwon's form, jumping, and balance were good, he did not immediately excel at basketball, partly because he did not know the rules of the game. He was strong at blocking shots, getting rebounds, and playing defense, but frequently got into foul trouble.

Olajuwon came to national attention during a team practice at the Stadium in Lagos where he was observed by Richard Mills, the head coach of the Nigerian national sports coaching institute. Mills told Olajuwon's parents that he should go to the United States to college and to play basketball. He also arranged for then-sixteen-year-old Olajuwon to play with the Nigerian national team in order to develop his talents as much as possible before applying to the United States.

Although he received letters of interest from a number of Nigerian universities, Olajuwon wanted to go to college in the United States. His appointment as Most Valuable Player in 1980 brought him to the attention of Christopher Pond, the American coach for Central Africa, who encouraged him to go to the United States to try for college on a basketball scholarship. Although visas to the United States were difficult to obtain at that time, Pond assured Olajuwon that he would arrange for the visa if Olajuwon could get his parents to pay several thousand dollars for a plane ticket to the United States. Olajuwon's father was concerned about putting all of the family's financial resources into a ticket that might not produce a scholarship. However, his mother had promised and committed herself to making her children's education a reality. She agreed to pay for the ticket, giving him all of the money she had, while his father provided spending money. Shortly afterward, Olajuwon left Nigeria with a list of universities that might be able to offer him a scholarship.

Olajuwon began and ended his quest at the University of Houston, Texas. After participating in a practice session with the team, he was offered a scholarship. Coach Lewis recognized his potential as a player,

but also realized that he was not yet ready to play college-level basketball because he did not have sufficient knowledge of the game or strength. During his first year, Olajuwon was "redshirted," which allowed him to practice with the team, but not to play in games. He used his first year to learn the game, bulk up his frame, increase his skills and strength, and learn to use his size and strength to advantage. He also learned the importance of teamwork. Although he still lacked skills, people were so excited by his raw talent that they began to call him "Hakeem the Dream" before he started playing varsity.

Despite his growing success in basketball, Olajuwon went through a difficult adjustment period to American life, food, and customs and in dealing with homesickness. During his first semester, he drank too much soda and not enough water, resulting in a serious kidney condition. At the same time, he enjoyed his studies, particularly of African history, and performed well academically.

By his sophomore year, Olajuwon's game had progressed enough for him to qualify as a backup center. His biggest problems remained a tendency to get himself into foul trouble and to tire easily. The result was that he played for an average of eighteen minutes per game. The team as a whole performed well enough to participate in the National College Athletic Association (N.C.A.A.) tournament. Olajuwon played well in the first three rounds, but got into foul trouble in the finals and was unable to help the team in the semifinals. The tournament marked the first time Olajuwon played against Michael Jordan. Although he played only twenty minutes of the game, he scored two points and grabbed six rebounds.

During the summers of his college career, Olajuwon played basketball at the Fonde Recreation Center, where N.B.A. players mixed with college and street players. The star attraction for Olajuwon was Moses Malone, the center and Most

Valuable Player for the Houston Rockets. Malone became a major role model and mentor for Olajuwon, teaching him the tougher level of competition played in the N.B.A. The result was a higher level of mental and physical confidence for Olajuwon.

By the start of the 1982–1983 season, Olajuwon had improved his game enough to start at center. That year, the Houston University team, the Cougars, became the strongest team in college basketball, winning twenty-five straight games and earning number one ranking for most of the season. The team became known as "Phi Slama Jama" due to the tendency of the star players to dunk shots. Olajuwon learned how to jam shots from the low post position. He was still awkward when it came to offense, but he became a defensive force to be reckoned with and led the nation in blocked shots. He averaged thirteen points and eleven rebounds per game that season and helped the Cougars reach the N.C.A.A. Final Four for the second consecutive year. In the semifinal matchup game, he played the best game of his college career, scoring twenty-one points, twenty-two rebounds, and eight blocked shots. Although they were favored to win the championship game, the Cougars lost at literally the last second. Olajuwon scored twenty points, eighteen rebounds, and eleven blocked shots in that game, but failed to even try to block the last-second follow-up shot from under the basket by North Carolina, believing that the game was over. Despite the loss, he was named Most Valuable Player of the tournament.

Although he was becoming more confident on the basketball court, Olajuwon was uncomfortable with his celebrity status and did not enjoy many of the activities his teammates engaged in, particularly dancing at clubs and drinking alcohol. He describes himself as particularly shocked by the attitude of his teammates and professional ballplayers toward women, as he observed them "talking trash" to them and not showing them any respect or dignity. During college, Olajuwon met Lita Spencer, with whom he had a daughter, Abisola, in 1988.

During the 1983–1984 season, the Cougars remained among the best teams in the nation, despite the loss of several key players. Olajuwon averaged sixteen points per game and led the nation in rebounding (13.5 per game average) and field goal percentage (67.5). For the third consecutive year, Houston advanced to the Final Four, but lost the championship. At this point, Olajuwon decided to enter the N.B.A. draft. In 1984, he was drafted as the first choice by the Houston Rockets, enabling him to stay in his adopted American home town. The draft was an important personal moment for Olajuwon as he was finally able to share with his parents the profits of the investment they had made in him during his first trip home to Nigeria since 1980.

The draft marked the introduction of The "Twin Towers" strategy in the N.B.A., starring Olajuwon as center and N.B.A. Rookie of the Year Ralph Sampson as forward. The two players worked together, averaging more than twenty points and ten rebounds per game. They were the most powerful duo to achieve this average since Wilt Chamberlain and Elgin Baylor in 1970. Olajuwon's performance as a rookie, averaging 20.6 points per game on 53.8 shooting from the floor and an average of 11.9 rebounds, led many to speculate that he would replace KAREEM ABDUL-JABBER as the next dominating center. Olajuwon was also recognized as one of the league's best pivot men, running the court with the speed of a guard while hitting the boards with the accuracy of the league's best rebounders. With Olajuwon on the team, the Rockets moved up to second place in the N.B.A.'s Midwest Division. Olajuwon came in second to Michael Jordan as Rookie of the Year.

Despite the excellent season, Olajuwon found professional basketball difficult and demanding. He had a volatile temper that often exploded on court. His tendency to berate officials and start fights with opponents often resulted in technical fouls that resulted in his being sidelined. Nevertheless, he worked constantly to improve his game.

Olajuwon's hard work paid off in the 1985–1986 season when his scoring rose to an average of 23.5 on 52.6 percent shooting and he continued to rank among the league's leaders in rebounds and blocking shots. He made second team All-N.B.A., losing to Abdul-Jabbar by only one vote. The Rockets made it to the playoffs in 1985–1986, facing off against the legendary Abdul-Jabbar and the L.A. Lakers. Although Abdul-Jabbar, then thirty-nine years old, was still at the top of his game, Olajuwon easily dominated him, averaging thirty points, twelve rebounds, and four blocked shots. The Rockets made it to the championship series, but lost to the Boston Celtics.

Although Olajuwon personally had an outstanding season in 1986–1987, ranking twelfth in the league in points, eighth in rebounds, and third in blocked shots, his performance could not carry a team suffering from the suspension of two players for drug use and a series of injuries for his Twin Tower, Ralph Sampson. The Rockets were eliminated in the second round of the playoffs, although Olajuwon was named to the first team All-N.B.A. for the first time.

The next few years proved frustrating for Olajuwon. Although he personally finished in the league's top ten for scoring, rebounding, blocked shots, and steals in the 1987–1988 season, the team was consistently eliminated in the first round of the playoffs. Discouraged by the loss of both Coach Fitch and Ralph Sampson, who was traded to the Detroit Pistons, Olajuwon continued to work to improve himself. During the 1988–1989 season, he dominated the game, becoming the first player to achieve more than two hundred steals (he totaled 213) and blocks (he totaled 282) in a single season. He also led the league in grabbing rebounds and became the first player in N.B.A. history to finish in the top ten for scoring, rebounding, steals, and blocks for two consecutive seasons. However, the team was again eliminated in the first round of the playoffs, a disaster that was repeated in 1989–1990, despite Olajuwon's first position in the league in rebounds and blocked shots and his achievement of a quadruple-double, defined as reaching double figures in all four offensive categories, only the fourth time this had happened in N.B.A. history.

On January 3, 1991, Olajuwon suffered an injury that almost ended his career. During a game against the Chicago Bulls, he was accidentally struck in the face by the Bulls' center, Bill Cartwright. The hit fractured the bone around Olajuwon's right eye, preventing him from playing for twenty-five games. Ironically, his injury helped to pull the team together. The Rockets won fifteen of the games he missed and had thirteen victories in a row after his return. However, in spite of this excellent performance during the season, the Rockets were again eliminated during the first round of playoffs.

Despite his outstanding performance on the court, Olajuwon was plagued by problems off it. His reputation for sniping at his teammates and arguing with management about his contracts led to an unsuccessful conclusion to his attempt to renegotiate his five-year $18.3 million contract. Early in 1991–1992, he was diagnosed with an irregular heartbeat that required medical treatment and resulted in seven missed games. He pulled a hamstring in March 1992, which led him to refuse to suit up for a game. Although a doctor later confirmed the injury, the general manager thought he was faking it to try to place himself in a better bargaining position and suspended him for three games. Olajuwon demanded to be traded, but no deal was worked out.

Discouraged and frustrated, Olajuwon returned to the faith of his childhood for refuge and inspiration. Although he had been invited to a number of mosques over the years, he had not practiced his faith in the United States. He was uncomfortable with the Nation of Islam ideology that prevailed in many mosques, particularly Nation's claim that Islam was the "black man's religion," because his own experience with Islam was that division, isolation, and racism were not in keeping with Islam's principle of absolute equality for all believers, regardless of race, tribe, color or nationality. Olajuwon had always found that Islam's strength and beauty lay in its egalitarianism.

Olajuwon found a Houston mosque in which he was comfortable in 1990, rekindling his faith. He began to pray regularly, study the Quran, and fast on Muslim holy days. His rediscovery of Islam helped him to regain both his self-confidence and control over his explosive temper. In 1991, he corrected the spelling of his name from Akeem to Hakeem and went on the pilgrimage to Mecca. He returned to the United States determined to be aggressive without being an aggressor and to back off from arguments, rather than to engage them. He stopped arguing with referees, became polite, and spoke of the need for grace and harmony between neighbors. He credited his faith with giving him a purpose and a vision for the future and with enabling him to be a positive role model.

In 1993 there were two major changes for Olajuwon: he became an American citizen; and the Rockets hired a new coach, Rudy Tomjanovich. Olajuwon credits Tomjanovich with helping him to become a better all-around player and resolving his contract issues. Tomjanovich also made Olajuwon the central figure in a new team strategy in which guards were instructed to pass Olajuwon the ball and Olajuwon was to decide whether to keep it or throw it back. The new strategy proved successful, not only for Olajuwon who posted career bests in scoring (26.1 points per game) and assists (29.1 points per game), but also in boosting team morale and building better teamwork and support for Olajuwon. That year, the Rockets won a club record of fifty-five games, finishing first in the Midwest Division for the first time since 1986. Although the team still lost in the playoffs, Olajuwon excelled in both defense and offense, leading the league in blocked shots for the third time (342 blocks) and placing fourth in rebounding (13.0 per game). He also turned in the best performace for steals (150) among centers and became only the second player in N.B.A. history to have more than 250 assists and 300 blocks in same year. As only the third player in N.B.A. history to accumulate 2,000 points, 1,000 rebounds, and 300 blocks in the same year, he was named the association's Defensive Player of the Year and finished second in Most Valuable Player voting. However, he still lacked a league championship.

The missing league championship and recognition as one of the greatest basketball players of all time finally came to Olajuwon in 1994. That year, the team won a club record of fifty-eight victories. Olajuwon averaged a career best of 27.3 points per game. After averaging 26.9 points, 9.1 rebounds, and 3.9 blocked shots for the seven championship games, he was named Most Valuable Player of the series. It was the first national championship for the Rockets, as well as for any Houston team in any sport. In recognition of the support of the entire team that enabled him to achieve his Most Valuable Player award, Olajuwon insisted that the entire team accept the trophy together. He was also awarded the Championship Series Most Valuable Player and was selected the N.B.A. Defensive Player of the Year – the only person ever to be honored with so many awards in a single year. Following their victory, the team was invited to the White House to meet President Bill Clinton. A movie about Olajuwon's life, *The Air up There*, was released that year.

Despite the victory, there were many in the basketball world who believed that Houston's victory was a fluke. Consequently, celebrity endorsements did not turn out for the Rockets or even for Olajuwon. He was not bothered by the lack of media attention because he did not believe in being a spokesperson for products that he either did not believe in or considered harmful. He was also aware of an important socio-moral dimension to celebrity endorsements, noting that a poor working mother trying to support three children cannot realistically afford $120 Reeboks or Nikes. He was concerned about the potential for his endorsement of such products to encourage children to steal, kill or find illegal ways of making money in order to buy them.

Olajuwon entered the 1994–1995 season determined to demonstrate that the Rockets deserved respect as a team. The team collectively made a commitment to excellence, despite a series of injuries. The addition of Olajuwon's former teammate Clyde Drexler brought experience, the ability to steal the ball, and excellent rebounding to the team. It also brought determination to win another N.B.A. Championship. The team improved, but was shocked in March to discover that Olajuwon was suffering from anemia and hypothyroidism due to his fasting during Ramadan. Although he was a team player, Olajuwon had placed his religious obligations as a Muslim ahead of the team's interests. He refused to stop fasting, ultimately starving himself into iron deficiency and a thyroid condition that was so severe he had to be benched for two weeks. As a result, the team's position going into the championship

playoffs was a shaky sixth – a position from which no team had ever won. However, by this point, Ramadan was over and Olajuwon was back in top form. It was his performance during the playoffs that finally changed people's perceptions of him as a center, ranking him as one of the greatest centers and basketball players of all time. When the Rockets won the championship again that year, Olajuwon was named Most Valuable Player for the second consecutive year, an achievement matched only by Michael Jordan.

This second victory brought celebrity status to Olajuwon. He appeared on television and signed contracts to represent products. He was chosen to represent the United States in the 1996 Summer Olympics as part of Dream Team III, where he put his teamwork to use in winning a gold medal. He was also selected as one of the fifty Greatest Players in N.B.A. History. By the end of the 1995–1996 season, Olajuwon had become only the ninth player in N.B.A. history to amass more than 20,000 points and 10,000 rebounds. He also became the all-time N.B.A. leader in blocked shots, with more than 3,000 to his credit. Olajuwon also achieved personal happiness in 1995, with marriage to Dalia Asafi in a traditional Muslim ceremony.

In addition to his basketball achievements, Olajuwon has taken on the role of education proponent. He created the Dream Foundation to improve educational opportunities for children in Houston and across the United States, particularly through the offering of at least five college scholarships to Houston high-school seniors. He has also become a frequent visitor to schools in each N.B.A. city, encouraging students to pursue their education, as well as their dreams, reminding them that only a few people can play in the N.B.A. each year, but that thousands of doctors and teachers are needed every day.

Further reading

Caldwell, Deborah. "A Basketball Player Finds Peace: An Interview with Hakeem Olajuwon," in *Taking Back Islam: American Muslims Reclaim their Faith*, ed. Michael Wolfe and the Producers of Beliefnet. Emmaus, PA: Rodale Inc. and Beliefnet, Inc., 2002

Christopher, Matt. *On the Court with ... Hakeem Olajuwon*. Boston: Little, Brown and Company, 1997

McMane, Fred. *Hakeem Olajuwon*. Philadelphia, PA: Chelsea House Publishers, 1997

Olajuwon, Hakeem with Peter Knobler. *Living the Dream: My Life and Basketball*. Boston: Little, Brown and Company, 1996

P

A.D. Pirous (b. 1932)

A distinguished modern artist known for his calligraphy painting and combination of classical Islamic art forms with modern artistic techniques, A.D. Pirous represents some of the most important trends in contemporary Islamic art.

Abdul Djalil (A.D.) Pirous was born in Meulaboh, Aceh, on the island of Sumatra, Indonesia, on March 11, 1932. He received the education typically available to children from the Muslim merchant community: a combination of traditional Quran memorization and recitation, Malay reading and writing, and a Western-style education. Pirous's childhood was marked both by the diverse classical Islamic influences of the Middle East, Persia, India, and the Malay Archipelago and by Western civilization and culture. He was fond of Western novels and movies, but was also raised in an environment rich in Islamic art, including poetry, literature, and his mother's embroidery. Although he was interested in all art forms, he later found himself drawn especially to Arabic script as a key form of Islamic civilization and culture.

Pirous was born in the pre-independence era when Indonesia was under Dutch rule. He was a young teenager during the Japanese occupation of 1942–1945.

Although Indonesia declared its independence on August 17, 1945, it took four years to secure it. Pirous served as a member of the Student Militia during the 1945–1949 Indonesian Revolution, which sought to unify the plurality of traditions, languages, beliefs, religions, and more than three hundred ethnicities in Indonesia into a single nation. Not limited to politics, the movement also sought to develop a cultural consciousness capable of gathering pluralism into unity without sacrificing diversity. (See also NURCHOLISH MADJID.) Art became an important public expression of this goal as well as of the new nation. Pirous was involved in the production of propaganda posters during the revolution, but did not formally join the art scene at this time.

While still colonial subjects, art students in the then-Dutch East Indies had been encouraged to study Western painting, particularly Dutch art. The result was a broad appreciation of post-Renaissance Western art. Indonesian artists of the pre-independence era had been particularly interested in natural landscape art and the use of painting to capture Indonesia's natural beauty. Pirous looks back on this period as a necessary moment in the development of contemporary Indonesian art because it provided an opportunity to study the skills and science of the West. However, rather than simply imitating or fulfilling Dutch tastes, Indonesian artists reappropriated these skills to develop their own indigenous art.

The subsequent generation of painters shifted from landscape and natural painting to more humanistic, populist, and traditional-life scenes representing the realities of society and the suffering of the people under colonization. Because Indonesian nationalism was on the rise at this time, their work was more consciously political than that of their predecessors, particularly reflecting the quest for an indigenous identity. Building on the technical expertise they had acquired under the Japanese occupation when art was used for war propaganda, Indonesian artists worked to contribute substance to their recently gained independence through their artistic and cultural achievements.

The period 1945–1960 was particularly critical for the establishment and growth of artistic organizations and studios that coordinated the efforts of artists and resulted in the foundation and development of formal art education, marking the first stage in the development of modern Indonesian art. Two institutions became particularly outstanding as modern art centers: the Faculty of Art and Design, Institute of Technology, Bandung, West Java Province, founded in 1947; and the Faculty of Art and Design, Indonesian Institute of Art (known as Yogya Art), Central Java Province, established in 1950. Both worked to clarify the Indonesian identity in art, but in different ways. The Bandung Institute became known for its abstract art, resulting in accusations that it extenuated the colonial agenda by perpetuating Western art for the first ten years of its existence. Yogya Art was oriented toward representational art. Pirous was affiliated with the Bandung Institute where he studied modern art and cubism from 1955 until his graduation in 1964.

He spent his entire professional academic career there until his retirement in 2003.

Pirous is considered one of the most important representatives of the abstract art for which Bandung became known. The 1960s marked the beginning of innovations in the kinds of art forms taught at the institutes, particularly through the inclusion of several fields of design. Hallmarks of 1960s Indonesian art include exploration of the organization of shapes and a variety of forms as students became knowledgeable about modern Western art and sought to appropriate it for their own purposes.

At this time, Pirous was offered a Rockefeller fellowship to study in the United States. Interested in starting a curriculum and lab in graphic design at Bandung, he accepted the fellowship and attended the School of Art and Design, Rochester Institute of Technology, Rochester, NY. As a student again, he began to think seriously about his work and identity as an Indonesian Muslim artist, particularly recalling his childhood in Aceh and the multitude of Islamic art forms with which he had been raised. His work was recognized in 1970 with an award for best graphic art in an art show held in Napels, NY. He completed his studies in arts and graphic design in 1970 and returned to Bandung in 1971. Back in Indonesia, he became a pioneer and leader of Decenta, a group of Bandung artists who worked to promote and design distinctively Indonesian art for Indonesia's urban elite.

Pirous became the most important producer of a new type of art, the most famous of which became known as calligraphic painting. His art combines Western abstraction with traditional Islamic forms and themes. The combination of Arabic calligraphy with Western non-figurative abstract painting visually expresses his identity as a native of Aceh who is influenced both by Islam and Arabic calligraphy and his studies of Western art forms and techniques. The use of Arabic calligraphy is intended to enhance his works, to have an ethical impact, and to proclaim his status as an Islamic artist. Pirous began producing calligraphic paintings in the 1970s. Rather than following the classic tradition of calligraphy (see also MOHAMED ZAKARIYA), he decided to establish his own form of art that combined classical Islamic artistry with modern methods and presentations in order to demonstrate the multiplicity of art forms and narratives that have formed his artistic vision.

Because he avoided political topics that would typically have resulted in censorship until 1998, Pirous was free to explore different types of art. He is considered influential because he has inspired other Muslims to take up painting and think of themselves as an art-producing community. His work has been rewarded domestically with awards for Best Painting at Biennale Indonesia I in 1974 and Biennale Indonesia II in 1976. His works were also exhibited internationally during the 1970s, including appearances at the Eighth International Biennale Exhibition of Prints at the National Museum of Modern Art in Tokyo, Japan in 1972, the Third Triennale Exhibit of India in New Delhi, India, in 1975, and the Western Pacific Prints Biennale in Melbourne, Australia, in 1978.

Some critics have dismissed Pirous's works as being strongly influenced by the West and exhibiting little indigenous originality. He responds by noting that his work is better understood as acknowledging the impact of Western art in the contemporary era to which he is indebted while remaining rooted in indigenous art forms and cultural achievements. He does not consider his art to be a shadow or imitation of Western culture, but a response to Western domination of Indonesian culture that speaks in the voice of indigenous cultures everywhere whose experience of colonization led to their devaluation and

depreciation. His work demonstrates the efforts of indigenous artists in studying and mastering the successes of Western artists as a means of catching up to modern art standards while remaining free from dependency on the West and demonstrating an ability to be independent and capable artists on their own. The very fact that innovations have been introduced demonstrates the progress and cultural advancement of Indonesian art as art, rather than imitation of Western culture or Westernization.

During the 1980s and 1990s, Indonesia experienced a boom in artistic production and in the market for art that paralleled the country's arrival on the international scene with the rise of the Asian Tigers. Indonesia began hosting more international events and activities in a variety of fields, including economics, politics, sports, culture, science, and technology, as the Asia Pacific region began to be perceived as a group of nations with important economic, cultural, and political potential. The world economic shift was accompanied by a shift in culture that was marked by an increase in art galleries, facilities, auctions, dealers, exhibitions, collections, and collectors. The public explosion of interest in art had important repercussions on artist production in Indonesia. Whereas during the 1960s artwork had been purchased mostly by embassies in Jakarta, by the late 1980s, art collectors in general were Indonesian individuals and corporations. The boom gave the artistic movement a much-needed boost as the price of artwork increased in conjunction with rising demand. A larger pool of individuals also became interested in studying and producing art. At the same time, there was a decline in creativity as topics, themes, materials, and techniques became limited according to market demands. Although the quantity of work produced increased dramatically, it was not necessarily accompanied by quality. Pirous's personal experience of the rise in public art consumption was a combination of financial rewards and problems. Not only were some of his paintings stolen, but others were falsely produced and sold under his name.

Pirous's rising prominence led to an official invitation from the United States government to visit the U.S. and tour American museums and art galleries in 1985. He was provided with a translator, Kenneth M. George, then a graduate student at the University of Michigan. George, now professor of anthropology at the University of Wisconsin-Madison, became a close friend who has helped Pirous organize and display subsequent exhibitions, including a 2002 career retrospective show in the National Gallery in Jakarta, Indonesia. George not only helped to select the works to be included, but also conducted an ethnographic study of the organization and launching of the exhibition and assisted in making a film about Pirous. As an anthropologist who specialized in the cultural politics of religion, language, violence, and art in Southeast Asia, George has observed that each of Pirous's paintings contains a story, demonstrating the intertwining of politics and art. George has worked to make Pirous's art better known in the West, considering it an important expression of Islam and Islamic art that is located outside of the Middle East. George believes that because Indonesia contains the largest Muslim population in the world, greater attention should be given to Indonesian art, culture, and politics.

Recognition of Indonesia's prominence as a Muslim country has become particularly important in light of its rapid urbanization and rising materialism that has resulted in the quest by many Indonesians for greater religious consciousness and spirituality as a source of stability and a connection with the past in a time of rapid change. A conscious artistic identification with Islam formed part of this trend, as evidenced by two major artistic festivals with Islamic features held in Jakarta in 1991 and 1995, both of which were sponsored and monitored by the Suharto government. Festival Istiqlal I, which was organized by Pirous, displayed most aspects of Indonesian Islamic culture, including arts, performing arts, literature, and science. Six million people attended the first festival, giving rise to the planning of a second festival, which was attended by nearly eleven million people.

Pirous has made important contributions to both the encouragement of a more consciously Islamic approach to art and recognition of the need to build Southeast Asia as a region through his personal collaborations with artists from other countries. His collaborations with other artists date to the 1970s when he began exhibiting his work with works by Malaysian artists. He has long-standing friendships with many senior Malaysian artists, including Sharifah Fatimah Zubir, Ibrahim Hussein, Syed Ahmad Jamal, and Latif Mohidin.

Pirous's work has been displayed in a variety of Southeast Asian countries, including appearances at the International Print Exhibition at the Taipei City Museum of Fine Arts in Taiwan in 1983, the National Cultural Museum in Kuala Lumpur, Malaysia, in 1984, the Fourth A.S.E.A.N. Exhibition of Painting and Photography in Singapore in 1985, the Third Asian Art Show in Fukuoka, Japan, in 1989, the Fifth Asian International Art Exhibition in Kuala Lumpur, Malaysia, in 1990, and the contemporary Indonesia Prints Exhibitions of the Japan Foundation at the Asian Culture Centre Gallery in Tokyo, Japan, in 1991. Pirous served as a member of the curatorial group that organized Modernities and Memories, Recent Works from the Islamic World, exhibited at the Venice Biennale in 1997. His works have also been exhibited in the West at the Third World Biennale of Graphic Art hosted by the Iraqi Cultural Centre in London, England, in 1980, and in an exhibit at the Volkenkunde Museum in Rotterdam, Holland, in 1988.

Like many Muslims around the world, Pirous was saddened and outraged over the death and destruction that occurred on 9/11. In response to these attacks and the spiraling state violence in his native Aceh, an international solo exhibition of his works entitled Words of Faith was organized by Shireen Naziree and the National Art Gallery in Malaysia in 2003 in conjunction with the annual meeting of the Organization of the Islamic Conference. This exhibition of contemporary artwork sought to encourage dialogue out of recognition of the common nature of all human beings. Although the exhibition identified with traditional Islamic values, its purpose was to use those values to demonstrate the all-encompassing spiritual context of life on earth and to point out the common universal spirituality shared by all people. Through it, Pirous hoped to inspire Muslims to unify by focusing on forgiveness and grace, using art as an opening for dialogue and discourse between the foreign and the familiar. He believes that Islamic art has an especially important role to play in the encouragement of dialogue because it is a shared cultural and spiritual element throughout Southeast Asia and because Islam's artistic legacy has long been of interest to the West. Noting that the artistic process in Islam has traditionally been considered both an act of faith and an expression of joy in being Muslim, he has asserted as one of the hallmarks of Islamic art the ability to satisfy the eye, the mind, and even the soul through the presentation of beauty. He therefore encourages Muslims to pursue the assertion of their contemporary Islamic artistic identity and to use it as a means of reattracting Western attention in a positive manner. His own work provides an opportunity to witness the reinterpretation of the theoretical and aesthetic of the Islamic perspective into what has been described as a universally appealing contemporary art.

Considered one of Indonesia's most distinguished artists, Pirous has received numerous awards for his work, including the Award for the Photographic Competition on Traditional Architecture, organized by the department of architecture, Institute of Technology, Bandung, in 1981, and a silver medal at the International Arts Exhibition I in Seoul, South Korea, in 1984. In 1985, he received an arts award from the government of Indonesia and cultural grants from the United States and Great Britain. In addition to his career retrospective held at the National Gallery in Jakarta in 2002, Pirous has also presented his work at the 1991 Calligraphy Exhibition and the 2000 Abstract Art Exhibit in Jakarta.

Further reading

George, Kenneth M. *A.D. Pirous: Vision, Faith and a Journey in Indonesia, 1955–2002.* Bandung: Yayasan Serambi Pirous, 2002

—— "Designs on Indonesia's Muslim Communities," *Journal of Asian Studies* 57, 3, 1998, pp. 693–734

—— "Signature Work: Bandung 1994," *Ethnos* 64, 2,1999, pp. 221–231

—— "Some Things That Have Happened to the Sun After September 1965: Politics and the Interpretation of an Indonesian Painting," *Comparative Studies in Society and History* 39, 4, 1997, pp. 599–634

—— *Visual Surprise and Visual Dzikir in the Work of A.D. Pirous*, exhibition catalogue for Words of Faith: Paintings and Graphic Works, Balai Seni Lukis Negara, Kuala Lumpur, Malaysia, October 6–27, 2003

Kingsbury, Damien. *The Politics of Indonesia*, 2nd ed. New York: Oxford University Press, 2002

Naziree, Shireen "A.D. Pirous: Words of Faith, 11 October–30 November 2003," official description of Words of Faith exhibition, posted on www.artgallery.org.my/html/words_of_faith.html

Pirous, A.D. and Setiawan Sabana. "Developments and Current Issues in Contemporary Indonesian Art," Bandung, 1995, users.skynet.be/network.indonesia/ni3001a32.htm

"Prof A.D. Pirous, c.v.," www.andi-galeri.co.id/a_d_pirous.htm

Wolff, Barbara. "Professor Illuminates Art of Friendship," *Arts on Campus*, University of Wisconsin-Madison newsletter, April 26, 2002, www.arts.wisc.edu/story.php?id=7354

Wright, Astri. *Soul, Spirit, and Mountain: Preoccupations of Indonesian Painters*. New York: Oxford University Press, 1994

Yuliman, Sanento. "Modern Art in Indonesia," music.dartmouth.edu/~gamelan/javafred/rd_sanento.htm

www.artgallery.org/my/html/words_of_faith.html – website for the National Art Gallery of Malaysia containing color photographs of Pirous's exhibition Words of Faith

Safi Qureshi (b. early 1950s)

Co-founder and former C.E.O. of A.S.T. Computers, Safi Qureshi is the managing partner of Irvine Ventures and honorary consul general of Pakistan to the United States.

Safi Qureshi was born in Karachi, Pakistan, in the early 1950s. He earned his B.S. in physics at Karachi University and a B.S. in electrical engineering from the University of Texas.

Qureshi began his professional career in the information technology industry in California. He worked for Documenter, Computer Automation, and Telfile Computer before co-founding A.S.T. Computers as a garage-based company engaged in the production of personal computers in 1980. As C.E.O., he played a pivotal role not only in promoting A.S.T.'s growth in emerging markets, but also in changing the PC industry from a narrow corporate enterprise into a global business. He also helped A.S.T. evolve into the digital age by developing tools to promote global and personal communications. A.S.T. rapidly became one of the best-known brand names in the P.C. industry and was, at one time, ranked as the fourth-largest computer manufacturer in the world. Qureshi was personally responsible for the creation of $300 million in wealth by 1980.

Qureshi's affiliation with A.S.T. ended when it was acquired by Samsung Electronics in the mid-1990s. He maintained his involvement with the computer industry by serving on the board of directors for I.A.F.C., Focus Software International, NetInfo, and Object Automation. He also began working as a venture capitalist, promoting education, research, and development.

Qureshi initially invested $7 million in a dozen Southern California start-up companies. He then invested $50 million in Irvine Ventures, a regionally based venture fund that works with the University of California at Irvine and local research institutions to create new companies by investing in privately held early-stage technology and internet companies. Because venture capitalism requires focusing on financial payoffs and market conditions, rather than the product or technology itself, Qureshi's position as managing partner has required a different kind of dedication and vision than he used at A.S.T.

In addition to his business initiatives, Qureshi has dedicated himself to increasing trade and cooperation in information technology between the United States and Pakistan and to improving education in Pakistan. He served as a member of President Bill Clinton's Export Council and was instrumental in convincing

President Clinton to go to Pakistan in 2000 to talk to military leaders. He has also worked to develop and expand information technology and a software export sector in Pakistan. In education, he has encouraged bright and talented Pakistani students to become entrepreneurs, particularly in technology, and to consider coming to the Silicon Valley. In an extension of this educational vision to younger children, he funded the development of A.L.I.F. (Active Learning Initiatives Facility), a Pakistani–American initiative dedicated to the promotion of creative uses of the media in education. A.L.I.F. is best known for its joint production with Pakistan Television of 104 episodes of the Urdu-language version of *Sesame Street*, which has been broadcast five days per week since 1999.

In addition to his business initiatives in Pakistan, Qureshi has worked to build commercial development in China, Thailand, India, and Indonesia. He has served on several high-level U.S. trade delegations that signed landmark agreements, including protection of intellectual property rights. He has been active in G.A.T.T., N.A.F.T.A., and A.P.E.C. issues. As president of the Southern California branch of TiE, he has worked to expand opportunities for immigrants from the Indian subcontinent to the United States.

For his efforts in building business and political relations between Pakistan and the United States, Qureshi was appointed honory consul general of Pakistan to the United States by Pakistani president Pervez Musharraf. He is rated as one of the top twenty-five executives by *Computer Resellers News*.

Further reading

Qadir, Asim. "Why Aren't There More Pakistani Professionals in the U.S.," O.P.E.N. Silicon Valley's Newsletter, *Open Forum*, Organization of Pakistani Entrepreneurs of North America, volume II, March 2003, www.opensiliconvalley.com/OPENForum Vol2.doc

Saeed, Salman. "Telecom & Software – Trends & Future in South Asia, Part II – Pakistan," www.the-south.asian.com/Dec2001/telecom %20&%20software%208.htm

"Safi Qureshi," profile on www.pakistandost. com/safi.htm

R

Radiyya bint Iltutmish (d. 1240)

Sultana of the Muslim Delhi sultanate in India, Radiyya bint Iltutmish was one of the great medieval warrior queens who successfully led her troops in battle.

Radiyya bint Iltutmish's birthdate is unknown. Historical accounts record her existence only after the death of her father, Sultan Shams al-Din Iltutmish, in 1236. Iltutmish was a Mamluk (white) slave who had risen to prominence due to his military prowess. He had been sent to India by the Ghaznavid sultan, Qutb al-Din Aybak, to claim it for Islam. He succeeded so quickly that the sultan granted him his daughter in marriage. Upon Aybak's death in 1211, Iltutmish took power and declared himself Sultan of Delhi, proclaiming his independence from the Ghaznavids. According to legend, upon hearing of Aybak's death, Iltutmish produced a document attesting to his right of succession, which he presented to the leading judges and religious scholars. These leaders recognized the document as legitimate and pledged their loyalty to Iltutmish as absolute ruler. Iltutmish in turn pledged his loyalty to the Abbasid caliph in Baghdad to solidify his position and was consecrated Sultan of India. Iltutmish's ascent was seen by many as a sign of Islam's egalitarianism, support for selection of the most qualified person as leader regardless of his origins or birth status, and lack of concern for hierarchies. This was a radical idea in majority Hindu India which subscribed to a rigid caste system in which one could not escape the circumstances of one's birth. Iltutmish ruled for twenty-six years and is considered one of the great slave kings of the Delhi sultanate.

Iltutmish died of illness in 1236, leading to a succession crisis. His oldest son, Nasir al-Din Mahmud, had been groomed as his heir apparent, but had died prematurely in 1229. Succession therefore passed to the next son, Rukn al-Din Firuz Shah, who people believed had been groomed by his father because he had accompanied Iltutmish on his return trip to Delhi during his final illness. However, Rukn al-Din proved an unfit ruler. He was largely controlled by his mother, who used her power to settle accounts in the harem. Rukn al-Din blinded and put to death one of his half-brothers and then tried to kill Radiyya. Widespread popular revolts broke out in protest.

Radiyya had contested her half-brother's accession, claiming that her father had appointed her as his political heir. Her claim was believable because she had been active in politics during her father's lifetime and clearly enjoyed his respect and favor. The daughter of his chief wife and possibly his oldest child, she had a proven talent for politics and military leadership as demonstrated by her service as her father's appointed regent during his absence on military excursions. When questioned by the local religious scholars about his choice, her father reportedly replied that he saw his sons indulging in wine, women, gambling, and flattery, all of which rendered them unfit to rule, while Radiyya had "a man's head and heart and was better than twenty such sons." Because of his own slave origins, Iltutmish found it natural to recognize a woman's merit and ability and reward it accordingly. According to some sources, Radiyya had a document signed by her father declaring her his heir.

Radiyya therefore engaged in a dramatic bid to claim the sultanate, appealing directly to the people of Delhi through a symbol created during her father's reign to protest injustice. Iltutmish had been in the habit of riding on horseback through Delhi. In order to respond to charges of injustice more efficiently, he ordered that anyone complaining of an injustice should wear colored clothing. Because the general population wore white, colored clothing stood out and was easily visible from horseback. Thus, when Iltutmish was out riding, he could see who had grievances and offer them an audience on the spot to resolve the issue. He also installed a bell near the palace that a person claiming injustice could ring as a signal to him that there was a dispute to be settled. Upon hearing the bell, Iltutmish would go out to hear the complaint and resolve it. Radiyya put this technique to use in calling for justice in her own situation. Wearing a colored habit reflecting her status as a person against whom an injustice had been committed, she publicly proclaimed her grievances to the people of Delhi and asked for their help in avenging the death of her half-brother and in deposing Rukn al-Din. She staged her performance on a Friday when the faithful were gathered at the mosque in

order to be sure of her audience. When Rukn al-Din left the palace to go to the mosque, Radiyya, in her colorful dress, mounted the palace terrace and gave her speech. In response, the people arrested Rukn al-Din and put him to death on November 19, 1236, as punishment for having murdered his brother.

Despite the removal of her brother, the path to succession was still not clear for Radiyya. Although she was enthroned, insurgents led a rebellion against her. Supported by the people of Delhi and the Mamluk military aristocracy that had put her on the throne, Radiyya ultimately quelled the rebellion and won over the insurgents.

Radiyya ruled for four years with absolute authority, adopting a male public posture. Upon acceding to the throne, she wore the imperial robes designating her as sultan and held a public audience from the throne on a daily basis, revising and confirming her father's laws, which had been abrogated by her brother, and establishing justice. She supported education and the arts, encouraged trade, and built roads and wells. She led her troops in battle and kept in touch with the people, much like her father had, by routinely walking through the marketplaces to hear people's complaints. In these capacities, she proved to be a competent and just ruler. Although she initially had coins struck in both her name and her father's, by 1237–1238, she felt confident enough to have new coins struck bearing her name alone.

However, Radiyya offended some people with her liberal behavior. She did not veil and sometimes dressed in men's clothing. She did not observe *purdah* (gender segregation) because it would have interfered with her activities as ruler. She held public, rather than private, meetings to discuss affairs of state. She extended justice to members of all religious faiths despite the fact that Hindus and Muslims were locked in bitter conflict during her reign. She rode her horse astride like a man and was armed with a bow and a quiver of arrows. She was seen in public riding an elephant. Some accounts state that she also cut her hair. Opposition to her on the basis of her "outrageous" behavior and supposed lack of morals was led by certain religious scholars and judges, who called for resistance to her rule in the name of religion.

At the same time, Radiyya failed to maintain a strong relationship with the Mamluk military elite that had brought her to power. She had sought to build her own power base, rather than relying strictly on the one she had inherited from her father. She was also reported to have fallen in love with a man who was considered inferior to her and thus unsuitable – an Ethiopian slave, Jamal al-Din Yaqut, who served as the stablemaster. Radiyya promoted him quickly through the ranks of the court, elevating him from "Emir of the Horses" to "Emir of the Emirs," an act that was resented by many in the court and military. Rumors spread that she was overly familiar with him and allowed him to run his hands underneath her clothing when she was mounting her horse. These rumors, combined with her already masculine behavior, were sufficient to convince some people that she had violated Muslim ethics of appropriate behavior. The fact that she favored a slave was also disturbing in what remained predominantly Hindu India, where the rigid caste system remained in force. The religious authorities and princes joined forces against her.

Although Radiyya raised and led an army in self-defense, she lost the battle, was deposed, and became the prisoner of a governor named Ikhtiyar al-Din al-Tuniya. Al-Tuniya fell in love with Radiyya, freed her, married her, and returned with her and a great army to reconquer Delhi and the throne in 1240. They lost the battle and the army was chased away. Radiyya fled. Hungry and exhausted, she asked a laborer cultivating his land for something to eat. When she fell asleep after eating, the laborer noticed that she was wearing a tunic embroidered in gold and pearls underneath her clothes. He decided to murder her, take her clothes, chase off her horse, and bury her in the fields. He then tried to sell the stolen clothing in the market. However, the merchants, realizing that he could not have come across such costly clothing honestly, turned him over to the police. The laborer then confessed that he had murdered Radiyya and told the police where he had buried her. Her body was exhumed, washed, placed in a shroud, and reburied.

A dome was built over Radiyya's grave. Over time, the tomb, which is located about three miles outside of Delhi, became an important site of pilgrimage and was popularly known as a place where blessing could be gained. Her shrine was visited by the great traveler IBN BATTUTA, who mentions it in his travelogue. It remains a popular site for pilgrimage in the contemporary era.

Further reading

Hambly, Gavin R.G., ed. *Women in the Medieval Muslim World*. New York: St. Martin's Press, 1998

Mernissi, Fatima. *The Forgotten Queens of Islam*, trans. Mary Jo Lakeland. Cambridge: Polity Press, 1993

Smith, Margaret. *Muslim Women Mystics: The Life and Work of Rabi'a and Other Women Mystics in Islam*. Oxford: Oneworld Publications, 2001

Ahmed Rashid (b. 1948)

An award-winning journalist and best-selling non-fiction author, Ahmed Rashid is one of the world's leading experts on Afghanistan, Pakistan, and Central Asia.

Ahmed Rashid was born in Rawalpindi, Pakistan, on September 6, 1948. His father was an engineer in the British Indian army during World War II. After the war, he established an engineering firm in England which operated until the early 1960s. The family then returned to Pakistan where his father took a land lease and engaged in coal mining. Rashid's mother was a social worker for a women's organization in Pakistan.

Because of his father's work, Rashid received part of his education in England and part in Pakistan. He attended Malvern College in England followed by Government College in Lahore, Pakistan, and Cambridge University in England. Rashid credits his cross-cultural upbringing with giving him a foot in both the Eastern and Western, Christian and Muslim worlds. This background has helped him as a journalist to explain events, societies, and cultures in Pakistan, Afghanistan, and Central Asia comprehensibly and meaningfully to a Western audience while being sympathetic to Muslim concerns.

Rashid began working as a journalist in 1978. In addition to writing for a variety of Pakistani newspapers and Western academic journals, he is the Pakistan, Afghanistan, and Central Asia correspondent for the *Far Eastern Economic Review* and the *Daily Telegraph* in London. He also writes for the *Wall Street Journal* and *The Nation* from his home base in Lahore.

Rashid has covered the various conflicts in Afghanistan since 1978. His initial goal was to expose the secretive decision-making process for Pakistan's Afghan policy. In the late 1970s and 1980s, Pakistan had supported the Afghan resistance to the Soviet invasion by hosting millions of Afghan refugees and by allowing the use of Pakistani soil and air space to bring in Western military supplies for the Afghan *mujahidin*. Pakistan had also supported Afghanistan's territorial independence and the integrity of the Afghan state. Despite this assistance, Rashid noticed an increasing hatred of Pakistanis in Afghanistan as Afghans blamed Pakistan for its contributions to extremist Islamic groups that permitted ongoing warfare. Between 1991 and 2001, Pakistan sent

munitions and logistical backing to a variety of Afghan warlords and factions. During the 1990s alone, between 50,000 and 60,000 young Pakistanis entered Afghanistan to fight, participate in ethnic and sectarian massacres, and destroy Afghan cities and villages. Rashid believes that continuing Pakistani support for the various factions, particularly the Taliban, perpetuated the civil war in Afghanistan rather than ending it.

At the same time, Rashid observed that most Pakistanis were unaware of the level of Pakistani involvement in Afghanistan because it was kept secret. Official government statements claimed that Pakistani support for various Afghan factions was necessary to acquire strategic depth in Central Asia, counter India's presence and power in the region, and promote "Islam." Rashid challenged these policies, noting that constant warfare, freezing of foreign investment, a stagnant economy, continued diplomatic isolation, and encouragement of sectarian and ethnic strife cannot be in the best interests of Pakistan for the present or future. Instead, he called for the promotion of stability, progress, and Pakistani self-respect through modern, progressive policies combined with a foreign policy geared toward making friends and creating new markets – goals that he believes can best be achieved through peaceful borders, a solid, expanding economy, better education, and the expansion of democracy and human rights. He has called upon Pakistani citizens to demand information from the government about how much money is being spent on "useless" warfare in Afghanistan rather than on necessary services at home, such as education.

In the late 1990s, Rashid called attention to the "Talibanization of Pakistan," as religious schools preaching an interpretation of Islam that supports endless jihad and continuing warfare proliferated, marginalizing historical interpretations of Islam calling for peace, tolerance, and equality between men and women. Because the majority of Pakistanis support democracy and the relegation of religion to the private sphere, Rashid argued that Pakistan should crack down on Islamic militants and offer moral, rather than logistical, support for issues such as Kashmiri sovereignty. Furthermore, rather than continuing to blame Afghanistan for militant extremism, he believes that Pakistanis should look inward, correct their own mistakes, and end support for militant, extremist interpretations of Islam. As hostilities continue to rise between Afghanistan and Pakistan, Rashid has called upon the Pakistani government to issue a formal apology to Afghanistan for its role in the perpetuation of warfare and human suffering there, particularly government support for the Taliban.

Six months prior to 9/11, Rashid had warned of rising danger in Afghanistan due to the severe humanitarian crisis there combined with rising exports of Islamic extremism, terrorism, drugs, and weapons throughout the region. He also warned of the growing control that Al Qaida and Osama bin Laden exercised over the Taliban government in Kabul and of the rising danger of extremism and terrorism in Central Asia as regimes became increasingly dictatorial and autocratic and the economies continued to plunge while birth rates skyrocketed. Although many of these regimes had enjoyed some American financial support, this was not accompanied by pressure for political and economic reforms to encourage development and Western investment.

The 9/11 attacks brought the conflicts in Afghanistan and Central Asia to international attention and Rashid to center stage as an expert. Following the Taliban's removal from power in Afghanistan, Rashid observed important progress in institutionalizing democracy, uniting previously warring factions, and recovering the education system, particularly for women and girls. However, he cautioned that the magnitude of

exhaustion and impoverishment in Afghanistan would require ongoing international financial support for the interim government and for the rebuilding of Afghanistan if peace and stability were to take root. He particularly called for expanding reforms geared toward improving the lives of citizens and preventing the expansion of support for terrorism throughout Central Asia.

Rashid's analyses of the situations in Afghanistan and Central Asia were published in two pivotal books prior to 9/11. *Taliban: Militant Islam, Oil and Fundamentalism in Central Asia* became a best-seller worldwide. Translated into twenty- two languages, it has sold more than 1.2 million copies since 9/11 and is used as a course textbook in more than 220 American colleges and universities. It was number one on the New York *Times* best-seller non-fiction list for five weeks and has been on the best-seller list in a variety of other American and European publications. It won the British–Kuwait Society for Middle Eastern Studies Book Prize in 2001. Rashid's other major book, *Jihad: The Rise of Militant Islam in Central Asia* was published simultaneously in twelve languages.

Rashid's work on Central Asia has earned him both domestic and international recognition. On March 25, 2001, he was awarded the Nisar Osmani Award for Courage in Journalism by the Human Rights Commission of Pakistan (H.R.C.P.), the only independent human rights organization in Pakistan. In his acceptance speech, Rashid noted that the award marked the first time in twenty years that his work on Pakistan, Afghanistan, and Central Asia had been recognized by a credible organization in Pakistan. In a personal gesture to rebuild Pakistan's problematic relationship with Afghanistan, Rashid offered an unconditional apology to the Afghan people for Pakistan's role in the deaths of countless Afghan civilians and the destruction of Afghan cities, culture, traditions, and freedom. He returned the entire prize of 100,000 rupees to the H.R.C.P. to be used for the benefit of Afghanistan's suffering women and children.

A man of deep faith and principle, Rashid continued his philanthropy by establishing the Open Media Fund for Afghanistan with a quarter of the royalties he received from *Taliban* in order to provide cash grants to newly starting independent print media in Afghanistan. Start-up grants typically consist of between $10,000 and $20,000 for newspapers and magazines and are intended to subsidize production for the first six months, although many publications have received a second grant for an additional six months. The first grant went to the Loya Jirga Commission in Kabul to establish a newspaper in three languages to promote the June 2002 Loya Jirga (traditional Afghan council). Other publications include a children's magazine and cultural, poetry, women's, and political weeklies that have taken on a variety of major social and political issues in Afghanistan, including warlordism, drug trafficking, and the failures of reconstruction. The fund has already distributed more than $250,000 to fourteen newspaper and magazine start-ups in Kabul and other cities. It has proven to be an important tool in the revival of the print media and the obligations of civil society as Afghanistan works toward a more democratic and peaceful future.

Rashid's work was recognized with two major awards in 2002: the Media Personality of the Year E.M.M.A. (Ethnic Multicultural Media Awards) Award in Britain for his work on the Taliban; and a joint second place for the first Daniel Pearl Award for Outstanding Story on South Asia, given by the South Asian Journalists' Association of the United States. In November 2002, he became the first journalist to address the United Nations General Assembly. In September 2003, he was invited to address N.A.T.O. ambassadors in Brussels in an all-day briefing on Afghanistan. In March 2004, he was appointed to the board of advisors for the International Committee of the Red Cross in Geneva for four years. A member of the advisory board of Eurasia Net of the Soros Foundation, a scholar of the Davos World Economic Forum, and a consultant for Human Rights Watch, he appears regularly on international television and radio programs, including C.N.N. and B.B.C. World. He is a frequent speaker at universities, think tanks, and international conferences and is regularly consulted by the United Nations and governments in Asia and Europe for his expertise on Central Asia.

Further reading

"Afghans Will Never Forgive us Easily," interview with Ahmed Rashid by Mohammed Shehzad, *Dawn* magazine, July 28, 2003
Rashid, Ahmed. Acceptance speech on receiving that Nisar Osmani Award for Courage in Journalism, from the Human Rights Commission of Pakistan, March 25, 2001
—— *Islam and Central Asia: An Enduring Legacy or an Evolving Threat?* Washington, DC: Center for Political and Strategic Studies, 2000
—— *Jihad: The Rise of Militant Islam in Central Asia.* New Haven, CT: Yale University Press, 2002
—— *The Resurgence of Central Asia: Islam or Nationalism?* London: Zed Books, 1995
—— *Taliban: Militant Islam, Oil and Fundamentalism in Central Asia.* London: I.B. Tauris, 2000
Interview with the author, October 13, 2003
www.ahmedrashid.com/ – Provides access to interviews, articles, and videos by Ahmed Rashid on Pakistan, Afghanistan, and Central Asia

S. Atiq Raza (b. 1948)

A visionary scientist and business leader of the microprocessing industry, S. Atiq Raza is the founder of Raza Foundries, a San Jose-based incubator of high-tech businesses.

S. Atiq Raza was born in Pakistan in 1948. His father was a self-taught radio engineer who inspired Raza to pursue electronic engineering. Raza attended high school at St. Anthony's and Aitchison College in Lahore, Pakistan. He earned a B.Sc. with honors in electronics at the University of London in 1972. After graduation, he returned to Pakistan, where he worked for six years at Haripur R&D Labs at Pakistan Telecoms Corp. He left Pakistan for the United States in 1978 to study at the University of Oregon. He soon transferred to Stanford University, where he earned an M.Sc. in radio electronics.

Raza was initially employed by Amdhal Corporation. He then worked for fifteen years in a variety of engineering and management jobs, including as vice president, Technology Centers, for V.L.S.I. Technology, Inc. He was considered a major star of cutting-edge semiconductor technology by the time he was thirty. A dedicated worker, he spent up to eighteen hours a day in the lab. However, he was not, by his own admission, an ideal employee. He could be difficult to work with, had a large ego, tended to be temperamental, and was not a good team player. He particularly had difficulty dealing with management because his managers were business people, rather than technical experts. As such, they not only were unable to understand his work, but were further unable to explain how his work related to the company's financial objectives. Frustrated by the inability of management and technical experts to communicate effectively with each other and to create an environment that encouraged and rewarded technical expertise, he developed his own style for managing scientific genius.

As a scientific manager and team leader, Raza found that he needed a specific type of people skills to harness and manage scientific brilliance, energy, and creativity productively. His own experience had shown him that, although they needed geniuses, businesses generally did not have management structures that

enabled them to pursue brilliant careers. Instead, he found that gifted people tended to have derailed or plateaud careers, ultimately robbing the industry of the scientific genius needed to propel it forward. Raza found this to be a serious failure in the new knowledge-based economy where a company's fortunes often depend on its collective brainpower. He therefore developed his own managerial style to resolve management shortcomings and address the needs of scientific geniuses.

In 1990, Raza became chairman and C.E.O. of NexGen, Inc., a start-up company looking to challenge Intel's domination of the microprocessor industry. NexGen's biggest challenge at that time was cash flow. Raza turned to a college friend and head of a venture capital company, Vinod Khosla, not only because the two shared common technological and business interests, but also because Khosla is Indian. Raza has always felt a personal responsibility to try to overcome the increasing hostility and suspicion between India and Pakistan. He has consistently maintained a policy of working with Indian organizations and encourages other Pakistanis to do the same.

Raza's main job at NexGen was to build a microprocessor, a task that took seven years to achieve. By 1994, NexGen had produced a solution that was fully compatible with the I386 and had a better microarchitecture than the 486. The new processor, the Nx586, was a superscaler processor capable of processing more than one instruction at a clock. It resembled the Pentium, which had just gone on the market, except that the NexGen processor had a cache for instructions and data twice the size of that of the Pentium. The NexGen processor was a higher-performance, smaller, and more compact execution unit. Once developed, the major challenge was to produce the chip in large quantities and get it to market. NexGen did not have its own factories, so it entered into a partnership with I.B.M. for chip production. By 1995, NexGen had produced the Nx586fp, which combined a processor and a coprocessor. It also included its own chipsets for shipping to keep it competitive and compatible. Although the result was cheaper than a Pentium – only $447 for a 133 MHz processor – the processor did not succeed on the market because I.B.M. did not provide sufficient production facilities to make it competitive against Intel's processor. At this point, Raza sold NexGen to Advanced Micro Devices (A.M.D.) for $850 million and set about adapting the Nx686 for the needs of A.M.D. In the process, he turned down $1.2 billion from Micron because he wanted to sell NexGen to a company that would be dedicated to bringing it to market and developing the next generation of processors while allowing him to continue to develop the management and product ramp processes that he had begun at NexGen. He achieved both at A.M.D. As president and chief operating officer, he oversaw the development of the processor roadmap and brought the AMD-K6 and Athlon family of processor products to market. He also continued successfully to use his management and product ramp processes.

Although he was responsible for ten thousand employees, most of Raza's attention went to the elite group of about a hundred scientists and engineers who were working on the K6 microprocessor chips. The chips, which featured the first 32-bit processors running at 1,000 Mhz, took three years to develop. Although these chips were not quite as fast as those made by Intel, they cost 25% less to manufacture, making possible for the first time construction of personal computers for less than $1,000. Intel had a virtual monopoly on the market until A.M.D.'s chips were brought to market in 1999.

Part of Raza's success at A.M.D. was due to his management of the production team and his ability to get them excited about and dedicated to beating Intel. His experience has shown that true scientific leaders and researchers are not interested simply in the bottom line of profit. He has found that they need to believe they are working for a bigger cause, that they are being challenged, that they are accomplishing meaningful tasks, and that their leadership possesses integrity. He has also found that scientific stars need an understanding of how their individual work fits into the broader context of the company. Raza's Best Practices Management and Fast-Track (T.M.) Engineering Methodology was so effective that, when he left A.M.D. to launch Raza Foundries in 1999, more than forty of his top staff asked either to join him or to be placed at one of the companies where he was on the board of directors.

Raza left A.M.D. due to his belief that the future of microprocessing lay in building chips for broadband communications, particularly to resolve what is called "the last mile problem," a failure in the delivery system that had been left unsolved and was causing an economic slowdown. He formed Raza Foundries (now known as Foundries Holdings, Inc.) as a special kind of venture-capital company that takes a team of engineers and rapidly brings their ideas to production and eventual buy-out. This approach has simultaneously resulted in the creation of both intellectual capital and the generation of value, setting a new standard in the field. As chairman and C.E.O. for Raza Foundries, Raza manages a staff of 100 scientists at the top of their fields. He has continued to refine his special management technique and is proud that Raza Foundries is the only company specifically tailored to the needs and understanding of engineers, providing long-term commitment and world-class resources and management training to accelerate growth and assure the partner companies' success. He believes that it is so important for scientists to be involved in the business aspect of the company that the top performers from each department routinely sit in on at least eighty percent of high-level business meetings.

Raza's personal entrepreneurial success is estimated at the creation of about $4 billion in wealth by 2001. In addition to chairing Raza Foundries, he also serves on the board of directors of Pacific Broadband Communications, Mexsi Systems, A.M.C.C., Maple Optical Systems, and several other private companies. He has also joined Pakistan's efforts to enter the software market through the O.P.E.N.-U.S. California Group.

Further reading

Qadir, Asim. "Why Aren't There More Pakistani Professionals in the U.S.," O.P.E.N. Silicon Valley's Newsletter, *Open Forum*, Organization of Pakistani Entrepreneurs of North America, volume II, March 2003, www.opensiliconvalley.com/OPENForum Vol2.doc

Raz, Tahl. "Taming the Savage Genius: The Delicate art of Managing Employees who are Way, Way Smarter Than You," *Inc.* magazine, May 2003, www.inc.com/magazine/20030501/25409.html

Saeed, Salman. "Telecom & Software – Trends & Future in South Asia, Part II – Pakistan," www.the-south.asian.com/Dec2001/telecom %20&%20software%2010.htm

"Silicon Valley Luminary S. Atiq Raza Launches Raza Foundries to Accelerate Broadband Networking and Communications Start-Ups," May 31, 2000, www.semiseek.com/news/press_release711.htm

Yashchenko, Andrei. "Atiq Raza is the Father of A.M.D. Processors: NexGen: 'Clean' Processor," August 19, 2002, www.digital-daily.com/editorial/nexgen-history/ www.razafoundries.com – website for Raza Foundries

Ibrahim Rugova (1944–2006)

Former President of Kosovo and dedicated pacifist, Ibrahim Rugova is widely recognized as the "Gandhi of the Balkans" for his refusal to engage in armed opposition to Serb aggression against the Albanian population of Kosovo and his quest to bring Kosovo to independence through peaceful means.

Ibrahim Rugova was born on December 2, 1944, in Cerrce, Kosovo. When he was five weeks old, the Yugoslav Communists executed both his father and his grandfather in their quest to re-establish control over Kosovo after the Germans withdrew. Rugova's dedication to pacifism stems, in part, from this personal history.

Rugova received his elementary and secondary education in Peja, Kosovo, and attended the University of Prishtina, where he graduated from the faculty of philosophy, department of Albanian studies in 1971. While an undergraduate, he worked as an editor for the Prishtina-based student newspaper *Bota e re* ("New World") and the magazine *Dituria* ("Knowledge"), from 1971 to 1972. From 1976 to 1977, he continued his literary studies abroad at the Ecole Pratique des Hautes Etudes in Paris. He then returned to Kosovo where he completed a Ph.D. in literature at the University of Prishtina in 1984.

Rugova taught at the Institute for Albanian Studies in Prishtina during the 1970s and 1980s, beginning as a junior research fellow in literature. He was promoted to senior research fellow and also worked as editor-in-chief of the Institute's periodical *Gjurmime albanologjike* ("Albanian Research"). In 1996, he was elected correspondent member of the Kosova Academy of Arts and Sciences, the most prestigious Kosovar institution of scholarship and science. He was the author of ten books, including an authoritative study of the works of the seventeenth-century archbishop Pjeter Bogdani.

Rugova's academic work resulted in his election as the president of the Kosovo Writers' Association in 1988, marking the beginning of his political career. Like most other Albanian professionals, he began his career as a member of the Communist Party. However, he was expelled from the party after demanding changes to Serbia's constitution. The Kosovo Writers' Association subsequently became the nucleus of the Albanian opposition movement to Serb/Yugoslav Communist rule in Kosovo.

Rugova's rise to political prominence can only be understood within the context of increasing Serb–Albanian tensions during the 1980s. Although Serbs and Albanians had lived together in Kosovo for years, the conclusion of World War II resulted in heightened tensions between the populations. These tensions had not translated into violence under the rule of Marshal Tito because Tito had refused to recognize ethnic differences among his people. He balanced ethnic rivalries by allowing all ethnicities equal opportunity to education as the stepping stone to responsible positions. Albanians had eagerly pursued educational opportunities, but Kosovo's economy could not support them all. By 1974, Albanians constituted 90% of the population, yet Serbs continued to hold a disproportionate number of the managerial positions and state jobs. Unable to break into these ranks, educated Albanians such as Rugova turned to the Communist Party and local administration for jobs. The Serb minority then complained that Albanian dominance in these positions had led to widespread discrimination against Serbs. The economic frustration began to translate into perceptions of ethnic and religious conflict. Tito's death in 1980 followed by the rise to power of extremist Serb nationalist Slobodan Milosevic exacerbated the growing tensions as Serb and Albanian nationalism reemerged.

Milosevic rose to power on his promise of rebuilding a Greater Serbia, which was to dominate Serbia, Montenegro, Bosnia, Vojvodina, and Kosovo. He turned to both religious and ethnic symbolism and rhetoric to bolster his claims of discrimination against Serbs and to justify his various campaigns of ethnic cleansing which were designed to "restore" Serbian dominance in the region. He particularly accused Albanians of engaging in demographic aggression and of forming part of an Islamic crescent of fundamentalism stretching from Bosnia to Kosovo. Claiming that the area's Muslims were determined to wage a holy war against Orthodox Serbs, Milosevic called for the defense of the seat of the Serbian Orthodox Church by reclaiming Kosovo and eradicating the Albanian population. Although ethnic tensions were generally due to competition over land, trade, and political power, Milosevic's appeal to religion was successful because the Church is a powerful source of identity for Serbs. By contrast, religion played almost no role in the political awakening of Albanians, who include both Muslims and Christians.

Milosevic tried to bolster Serbia's claim to Kosovo by claiming that Kosovo had been majority Serb up until the end of World War II when 1.5 million Albanians purportedly crossed the border from Albania into Kosovo, depicting the Kosovar Albanians as tourists rather than natives. The Serbs accused Albanians of committing crimes ranging from rapes to thefts against Serbs and deliberately played up religious, ethnic, and political concerns, making every crime against a Serb an act of political aggression to drive the Serbs out of Kosovo. Milosevic used these exaggerations to initiate a series of measures known as the Yugoslav Programme of Measures to be Taken in Kosovo to break the Albanians. Similar to apartheid in South Africa, Milosevic's measures used the tools of the state to suppress the Albanian majority, including new investment in Serb-majority areas, building of new housing for Serbs returning to Kosovo, encouraging Albanians to leave Kosovo and work elsewhere in Yugoslavia, introducing family planning for Albanians, retroactively annulling sales of property by departing Serbs to

Albanians, and forbidding Albanians from buying or selling property without official government approval. Albanian-language newspapers were closed, as was the Kosovo Academy of Arts and Sciences. Thousands of Albanian state employees were dismissed from their jobs. Even Albanian school students fell victim to Milosevic's Albanian eradication campaign when thousands of Albanian children were poisoned with either sarin or tabun (poisons used in chemical weapons) while in their schools, according to a U.N. toxicologist who examined blood and urine samples. At the same time as they were being victimized, Albanians were being conscripted into military service where some were killed by their Serb comrades. Fearing for their lives, many Albanian men of draftable age left Kosovo to go abroad, often to Germany or Switzerland, to work and support their families back in Kosovo.

In response to these acts of aggression, the Kosovar Albanians formed a resistance movement led by intellectuals belonging to the Association of Philosophers and Sociologists of Kosovo and the Kosovo Writers' Association, which was led by Rugova. The Kosovo Writers' Association soon became the center of intellectual protest against Serb policies. Dedicated to the principle of non-violent resistance espoused by Mahatma Gandhi and Martin Luther King, Jr., the protests generally took the form of public meetings and petitions. When Milosevic responded by stripping Kosovo of its autonomy, the association was transformed from an intellectual movement to a political party: the Democratic League of Kosovo (L.D.K.).

The L.D.K. was founded in December, 1989. Similar to Poland's Solidarity movement, the L.D.K. was both a mass movement and a political party. It quickly became the largest political party in Kosovo with 700,000 supporters and was the first to issue a direct challenge to the ruling Communist regime, demanding independence for Kosovo. Under Rugova's

leadership, the L.D.K. established a parallel government for Kosovar Albanians and cooperated with other Albanian political forces and the Assembly of Kosovo to establish the legal framework for the institutionalization of Kosovar independence. Kosovo was proclaimed an independent republic on July 2, 1990, and a constitution was adopted. A national referendum on independence and sovereignty was held in September, 1991 to set the stage for multiparty presidential and parliamentary elections, which were held on May 24, 1992. Voting was carried out in secret, often in private residences. The votes were then transported in secret, often by bicycle, to a center where they were counted. The L.D.K. won a sweeping majority of parliamentary seats and Rugova was elected president with an overwhelming majority of votes.

Rugova and the L.D.K. had three main goals once in power: prevention of violent revolt, internationalization of Kosovo's situation by requesting diplomatic mediation and possible U.N. trusteeship in lieu of Serb control, and systematic denial of the legitimacy of Serb rule by boycotting elections and censuses and creating the outlines of a state apparatus of a Kosovo republic. Rugova proved very successful in preventing violent revolt – a remarkable achievement throughout the 1990s as Serb oppression of Albanians intensified. Internationalization of Kosovo's situation proved more elusive. Although Rugova gained resolutions from the U.N. and the European Parliament, as well as respect for his commitment to non-violent opposition, concrete assistance was not forthcoming as the West continued to consider Kosovo an internal matter for Serbia to resolve. Rugova hoped that the long term would vindicate the L.D.K.'s commitment to the Albanian state apparatus in Kosovo, believing that the West would eventually recognize the de facto rule of Kosovo by the Albanians, even if the Serbs ruled it de jure.

Perceiving no military threat from Rugova, Milosevic concentrated his military energy on ethnic cleansing in less pacifistic Croatia and Bosnia, although he intensified the campaign of eradicating Kosovar Albanians throughout the 1990s. Tactics included the dismissal of Albanian state employees, including doctors and health workers, resulting in a decline in vaccines for Albanians and an increase in the number of deaths due to disease. Teachers were sacked for refusing to comply with a pro-Serb curriculum which eliminated teaching of Albanian literature and history. In a broad systematic campaign to destroy Albanian history and culture, Albanian-language publications were suppressed and destroyed, as were state archives and cultural institutions. Local place names were changed to the Serbian language. Albanian schools and universities were closed. Serbs and Albanians were strictly segregated in the schools, even in lavatories. Serb police routinely harassed, beat, and arrested both teachers and organizers. Arbitrary arrests and police violence by Serbs against Albanians became routine. Serbs had the right to summon Albanians to police stations for questioning for up to three days over even small matters such as "insulting the patriotic feelings" of Serbs through speech; 15,000 Albanians were questioned in this way in 1994 alone. Beatings remained illegal, but there were numerous graphic reports of severe beatings, electrical shocks to the genitals, and other forms of beatings and torture. Homes were frequently raided without explanation, and goods and money were stolen by the Serb police. In 1994, the Council for the Defense of Human Rights and Freedom in Kosovo recorded 2,157 physical assaults by police, 3,553 raids on private dwellings, and 2,963 arbitrary arrests.

Despite the rising oppression, Rugova remained a committed pacifist, combating the Serbs with alternative institutions, rather than destructive violence.

Throughout the early 1990s, he pressed forward the creation of a parallel government and institutions for Albanians, including health-care and educational facilities. Doctors and teachers were paid by the Republic through a voluntary 3% income tax, which was financed mostly by Albanians in diaspora in Germany, Switzerland, Albania, and Macedonia. Although many Kosovars believed that Kosovo should follow the example of Croatia and Bosnia in pursuing their own freedom by fighting, Rugova argued that this would be a mistake, pointing out that hundreds of thousands of people had been driven from their homes during these conflicts and that the same could happen in Kosovo. He defended his pacifism by stating that he "preferred independence for a living people, rather than a dead people," as he was certain that the results of armed conflict would be deadly. He encouraged Kosovars to be patient, believing that the international community would address Kosovo at the same time that the Bosnian crisis was resolved. When the 1995 Dayton Accords that ended the conflict in Bosnia failed to mention Kosovo, Rugova's prestige took a serious blow.

Rugova faced his greatest political challenge in the aftermath of the Dayton Accords, amidst rising public frustration and an ever-increasing campaign of eradication by the Serbs. His prime minister broke with him and criticism of his policies came under fire. The government-in-exile cut off funds as critics charged that his continued pacifism constituted passivity, if not compliance, with Serb measures. While Rugova's main political support had always come from the urban educated, the rural populations began to question how effective non-violence could be as their lives and livelihoods came under threat.

Two types of criticism of Rugova emerged. Some believed that his absolute refusal to negotiate with Milosevic was unrealistic and that Kosovo would be further ahead to become a federal unit within the new federation that included Serbia, Montenegro, Vojvodina, and Bosnia in order to begin a long-term process of emancipation. Others charged that he was not being absolute enough in his rejection of Belgrade. They sought a more active policy of protest. Rugova's stance was also undercut by Western powers who refused to intervene in Kosovo because there was no active war on the ground.

In 1996, Rugova entered into negotiations with Milosevic through the mediation of an Italian Catholic charity. The negotiations concluded with the signing of an agreement under which schools and university buildings, but not state salaries, would be made available to the Albanian parallel education system. However, the negotiated agreement was never activated, undermining Rugova's credibility. His position was further complicated by unrest in neighboring Albania, which had been one of his main supporters. The Albanian army collapsed in 1997 and its weapons stores were looted. Some of these weapons resurfaced in Kosovo among a new organization: the Kosovo Liberation Army (K.L.A.).

References to the K.L.A. first appeared in 1996 following several acts that the Serbs defined as terrorism. Because no one initially claimed responsibility, many Albanians, including Rugova, considered the actions of the K.L.A. to be yet another Serb police trick. However, by the summer of 1997, the K.L.A. was engaged in open clashes with Serb forces and was claiming credit for its actions, earning it recognition as a local resistance movement pursuing the goals of national liberation and the protection of villages under Serb attack. Some recruits joined it on this basis and it gained some popular support as an alternative to Rugova, reflecting frustration with Rugova's inability to gain international recognition of Kosovo's interests. By 1998, the K.L.A. was backed by local leaders from a variety of backgrounds, including former army officers and members of Rugova's moderate political movement. At this point, Rugova recognized it as an Albanian organization, although he did not approve of its military tactics.

Critics charged that Rugova's failure to recognize and support the efforts of the K.L.A. reflected his inability to keep up with developments on the ground. His political reputation was further damaged in October, 1997 when his pleas for postponement of a student demonstration against Milosevic fell on deaf ears. Perceptions of his loss of power and control over the population led to open disagreement between Rugova and his prime minister, Bujar Bukoshi. Although Rugova's personal standing remained high among the general Albanian population, his fellow politicians were increasingly dissatisfied with his policies. Several prominent members defected from his party.

Throughout 1997 and 1998, the Serbs escalated their use of military force, claiming the need to eradicate the "terrorist" K.L.A. Milosevic's success in portraying the K.L.A. to the West as a terrorist organization allowed him to act with relative impunity in Kosovo. Although the West threatened many times to enforce sanctions against Milosevic, these did not materialize until the end of April, 1998, by which point he had expanded his attacks on villages and increased his military build-up in the region. Milosevic was further assisted by the U.N. arms embargo on Yugoslavia and the K.L.A. because Yugoslavia was a major arms producer and had recently made large arms purchases from Russia, while the K.L.A. had only small arms that had been stolen from Albanian arms stores.

Although the K.L.A.'s attacks on Serb targets during this time period were very limited in scale, resulting in the deaths of five Serb policemen, five Serb officials, and eleven Albanian collaborators, the Serb response was hugely disproportionate. The Serbs attacked two Albanian villages with military helicopters and armoured personnel carriers. Sixteen Albanians were killed in Likoshani and fifty-one in Prekaz. Many of these victims were civilians, including women, children, and the elderly. The Serbs also looted the houses they raided. These attacks led to a series of others by Serbs on other villages, resulting in a flood of refugees and an atmosphere of terror. It was this combination of events and disproportionate response that pushed Kosovo into war and led to an increase in recruits for the K.L.A.

There was an increase in radicalization in 1998, when Vojislav Seselj was invited to join the Milosevic government. Seselj, long known for his extremist views on Kosovo, publicly advocated a policy of infecting Kosovar Albanians with the A.I.D.S. virus. Serb intellectuals published policy pieces advocating increased violence against the Albanians, such as Aleksa Djilas' article, " "Whatever Israel does to the Palestinians, we Serbs can do to the Albanians," in the Belgrade nationalist magazine, *Argument*. Foreign mediation of the conflict was repeatedly refused. Milosevic claimed that his campaign was designed to end arms smuggling by the K.L.A., yet his military forces increased their attacks on population centers, including heavy artillery and bombing campaigns. While the Serbs claimed that they were "liberating" territory from the K.L.A., the reality was that entire villages were being forcibly emptied of their inhabitants, homes, livestock, and crops in a scorched-earth campaign designed to eradicate ethnic Albanians from Kosovo altogether. Between April and September of 1998, more than three hundred Albanian villages were devastated and between 250,000 and 300,000 people were driven from their homes.

The widespread destruction led to increasingly heavy criticism of Rugova as Albanians became radicalized by their circumstances and massacres began to proliferate. Rugova continued to press the West for a mediated settlement, but the West refused to allow discussion of an independent Kosovo, insisting that it should settle for local self-government while remaining under Yugoslav autonomy and calling only for Milosevic to scale down Serb deployment in Kosovo. Rugova refused to deal.

By December, 1998, the Serb military was involved in a new offensive against the K.L.A. and 15,000 new troops were assembled outside the Kosovo border in preparation for a spring offensive. Serb authorities began to seize official documents and land-ownership registries from Albanian villages and removed Serbian Orthodox icons and artifacts from museums in Kosovo for safe-keeping in Belgrade, hinting at the destruction to come.

In January, 1999, evidence of the massacre of forty-five Albanian civilians, some of them children, by a single shot to the head at close range led to calls for an investigation by the International War Crimes Tribunal. The Serbs refused to allow the investigation and insisted on the removal of the person in charge of the verification mission. Rugova finally reluctantly agreed to negotiate a settlement leaving Kosovo under Yugoslav rule. However, Milosevic refused to reach a deal, using the negotiation process as a stalling tactic to build up military forces to pursue his campaign of ethnic cleansing, the speed, comprehensiveness, and scale of which eclipsed even the 1992–1995 ethnic cleansing of Bosnia.

By March 20, 1999, there were more than 26,000 Serb Soldiers inside Kosovo, with another 15,000 stationed on the eastern border. Studies of the troop locations indicated a strategy of creating a horseshoe of forces around Kosovo to force all Albanians to exit in a single direction from which they would be refused the right to return. The ethnic-cleansing campaign followed a standard pattern. Armed men arrived at houses and ordered people to leave within minutes. An atmosphere of terror was created in the streets as civilians were killed at random and houses were looted, set on fire, and demolished. As terrified civilians left their villages, they were funneled through a cordon of troops who robbed them of their money and possessions. The civilians were then told which route to take to the border. However, not all inhabitants were allowed to leave. Men were often separated from their families and taken away by Serb forces. U.S. satellites began to take images of newly dug mass graves. In total, up to a hundred thousand men went unaccounted for. Because the K.L.A. fighters were so heavily outmanned and outgunned, they were unable to offer much protection or assistance to the civilians.

Nearly six hundred thousand Albanian refugees fled Kosovo in a period of four weeks. Eight hundred and fifty thousand were displaced within Kosovo, making a total of 1,450,000 displaced Albanians out of a population originally numbering just under 2 million. These deportations also resulted in the confiscation of passports and identity papers. Municipal registers of births, deaths, and land ownership were destroyed. Refugees fleeing the country had to remove the registration plates of their cars and tractors before leaving. The purpose was to deprive Kosovar refugees of any and all evidence of their residence in Kosovo. Milosevic then proposed a "peace plan" which would allow refugees to return to Kosovo only in cases where they could prove they were Yugoslav citizens. Those who could not prove their citizenship would be denied reentry.

Mislosevic's campaign finally pushed the West into action in 1999. No longer willing to compromise with Milosevic and determined to break his military machine, N.A.T.O. engaged in a bombing campaign against the Serbs. As journalists were finally able to penetrate into

Kosovo and transmit images of hundreds of thousands of destitute refugees, public opinion registered outrage.

Perceptions of Rugova were mixed by this point. His adamant insistence on maintaining his pacifist stance even in the midst of Milosevic's ethnic-cleansing campaign made him a controversial figure for Albanians. His televised meeting with Milosevic at the conclusion of the war and apparent urging of an end to N.A.T.O.'s bombing campaign infuriated many Albanians. Some accused him of treason, while others claimed that he had abdicated his political position and was nothing more than a hostage of N.A.T.O. and Milosevic. Many believed that Rugova's political career was at an end and that the K.L.A. would have to fill the political vacuum.

Rugova proved resilient in the end. While it was true that he had been held by Yugoslav authorities until he signed an agreement with Milosevic as a precursor to peace talks, it was also true that, upon his release, he remained uncompromising in his vision of independence for Kosovo. He had a longer political history than the K.L.A., as well as practical experience in leading the parallel government that had been declared at the start of Milosevic's campaign. His service as the leader of the L.D.K. had earned him the long-standing trust and loyalty of his constituents. Internationally sponsored elections in 2000 confirmed his position as president, as well as the majority status of the L.D.K. in parliament with 58% of the vote. He was reelected in 2002.

Rugova's pacifist stance, even in the face of overwhelming military aggression, earned him international recognition. His peaceful policies resulted in a Peace Award from the Paul Litzer Foundation in Denmark (1995), the Sakharov Prize from the European parliament (1998), the Peace Award of the City of Munster, Germany (1999), and the Peace Prize of the Democratic Union of Catalonia "Manuel Carrasco i Formiguera" in

Barcelona, Spain (2000). He also received a honoris causa degree from the University of Paris VIII at the Sorbonne in France and was declared an honorary citizen of Venice, Milan, and Brecscia, Italy. Rugova died of lung cancer in 2006

Further reading

"Dr. Ibrahim Rugova, President of Kosova: A Short Biography," www.trepca.met, April 4, 2002
"Ibrahim Rugova: Pacifist at the Crossroads," B.B.C. News, May 5, 1999
Malcolm, Noel. *Kosovo: A Short History.* New York: Harper Perennial, 1999
McAllester, Matthew. *Beyond the Mountains of the Damned: The War Inside Kosovo.* New York: New York University Press, 2002
Rezun, Miron. *Europe's Nightmare: The Struggle for Kosovo.* Westport, CT: Praeger, 2001
"Rugova: Kosovo's Political Survivor," B.B.C. News, May 2, 2002

Jalal al-Din Rumi (1207–1273)

A mystic, poet, teacher, preacher, humanist, and visionary, Jalal al-Din Rumi has achieved international acclaim for his spiritual poetry that celebrates love as a lived experience. He is considered one of history's most profound mystical teachers and poets and is revered as a saint by people of many faiths.

Jalal al-Din Rumi was born on September 30, 1207, in Balkh, a small town west of Mazar-i Sharif that lies between contemporary Iran and Afghanistan. His father, Baha al-Din, was a preacher, jurist, mystic, and one of Rumi's most important role models. His diary of mystical experiences became one of Rumi's most treasured texts after his death.

Rumi lived a nomadic existence as a child. In 1213, his family moved to Samarkand. They fled in 1216 in the face of Genghis Khan's Mongol armies and traveled through Tajikistan and Syria en route to Mecca for the Hajj pilgrimage. Rumi's mother died along the way. In 1224, Rumi married Gowhar Khatun, a family friend from Samarkand to whom he may have been betrothed as a child. They had two sons, Ala al-Din and Sultan Valad. Rumi's family ultimately settled in Konya, Turkey, in 1229, where his father worked as a scholar. Other than a few years abroad for study, Rumi remained in Konya for the rest of his life. He was fluent in Arabic, Persian, and colloquial Turkish, the major languages of Islamic civilization.

Under his father's direction, Rumi received a traditional education that included instruction in Arabic grammar, prosody, the Quran, Islamic jurisprudence, the *hadith*, Quranic commentary, the writings of a variety of Sunni mystics, history, theology, logic, philosophy, mathematics, and astronomy. A master of all of these fields by the time he was twenty-four, he nevertheless was not considered a great sheikh. Popular belief that he had inherited his father's spiritual beauty and wisdom upon his death in 1231 led to Rumi's assumption of his father's duties as preacher and jurist. However, his studies were considered incomplete. He is believed to have traveled to Aleppo, Syria, from 1232 to 1233 and possibly to Damascus to expand his study of religious sciences. He did not return to Konya until sometime between 1237 and 1241.

While pursuing his formal studies, Rumi was initiated into his father's mystical path by one of his disciples, Burhan al-Din. As part of this initiation, Rumi engaged in forty-day retreats for fasting, meditation, and ascetic exercises, including reading and contemplating his father's spiritual notebooks. His self-mastery and progress along the Sufi path convinced Burhan al-Din that he no longer needed a mentor and was capable of assuming his father's position.

Rumi became a popular speaker and representative of an accessible and authentic mode of Islamic spirituality. He attracted many powerful followers, including the Seljuk sultan, a Georgian princess, and a variety of political leaders, artisans, and merchants – both Christian and Muslim. His lectures were attended by both women and men. Despite his powerful political connections, he demonstrated no political aspirations.

Rumi's preaching and teaching demonstrated a tolerant and inclusive interpretation of Islam. His spiritual life was guided by his desire to follow the example of the Prophet Muhammad and to actualize his potential as a perfect Muslim. In his interpretation of Islamic law, Rumi focused on the spirit that brought the law to life. Although he was ritually observant, he believed that spiritual observance was more important than the outward performance of rites and rituals. One of his favorite exercises was the composition and performance of *sama‘*, a combination of music and poetry designed to focus the listener's concentration on God and induce a trance-like state of contemplative ecstasy. The listener typically shakes his or her arms or dances in response to what is heard. The *sama‘* is a mode of worship and contemplation, rather than an incidental or chance hearing of music. *Sama‘* became a major mode of expression for Rumi from early in his life.

The early 1240s brought tragedy to Rumi's life. Burhan al-Din died in 1240/1241, followed by Rumi's wife in 1242/1243. His teenage sons, to whom he was close, left Konya for Damascus to pursue their own educations. Rumi soon remarried a widow named Kerra Khatun and had two more children.

The year 1244 marked a major transformation in Rumi's life with the arrival of Shams al-Din al-Tabrizi, who became his new spiritual mentor. Their friendship is considered one of the great mysteries of Sufism, as those who observed them together could not tell who was the teacher and who was the student. With Tabrizi as his mentor, Rumi was inspired to write many poems. He began

to externalize his internal spiritual experiences as Tabrizi encouraged him to give up his books in order to pursue the merging of souls through experience. Rumi became more ecstatic in his expressions of his love of God as the joy of music, poetry, and meditative dance replaced the self-renunciation and control he had learned from Burhan al-Din.

One of Rumi's hallmarks that was established at this time was the whirling dance that became the visible identifying characteristic of the Mevlevi Sufi order founded by his son Sultan Valad, also known as the "Whirling Dervishes." This dance is performed by planting one foot on the floor with the toes fixed around a wooden peg as an anchor. The dervishes turn at faster and faster speeds to create the phenomenon of whirling. The purpose of the whirling is to come close to God by removing the veils from one's eyes and returning to the inmost center of being which is where humans are supposed to come closest to God. The whirling is also done in imitation of the planets revolving around the sun, as well as reflecting Rumi's belief that the spiritual universe revolves around the saint who is believed to guide people in every age. The whirling ceremony is supposed to be an aesthetic expression as well as a meditation in movement. Above all, it is an act of worship.

Rumi became enamored of the ritual of turning and singing because it brought him escape from the austere ways of self-renunciation while bringing him peace, sparking his imagination and creativity, and giving him a joyous means of expressing his mystical rapture. This new approach also expanded Rumi's mass appeal, although some conservative followers felt that this new approach was beneath his dignity and education. They drove Tabrizi away from 1246 until 1247.

Without Tabrizi, Rumi declared that he had lost his inspiration. He ceased writing poetry and giving lectures until

Tabrizi was brought back. Tabrizi left permanently in 1247/1248 and was never heard from again. Rumi turned inward and began to discover Tabrizi within himself. He wrote new poems reflecting the quest of the seeker for guidance and assuming Tabrizi's voice. In many of these poems, Rumi appears as a survivor of a burning spiritual crisis and suffering that ultimately led him to inner enlightenment. The themes of grief and separation that fill this poetry reflect both the separation that Rumi experienced from Tabrizi and the one that exists between human beings and the Divine.

Tabrizi's disappearance marked the end of Rumi's preaching career to the general public. He spent the last twenty-six years of his life working with and serving his local dervish community and speaking his poetry spontaneously. This poetry was transcribed by scribes who later revised it into manuscript form.

Collections of Rumi's works reflect the diversity of his activities. *The Discourses of Rumi* is a collection of seventy-one talks and lectures given by him, which were probably collected by his students after his death to preserve his teachings. A similar collection known as *The Seven Sermons* consists of homilies about questions of ethics and faith given on ceremonial occasions. In addition, a collection of his letters known as *Maktubat* was published, revealing his status as an intercessor in the affairs of state for his family and community. The collection also includes letters of recommendation and introduction.

The most important, famous, and widely published and translated works of Rumi are his poetry collections – *Diwan-i Shams-i Tabrizi (The Collection of Shams-i Tabrizi)*, which consists of about forty thousand verses, and *Masnawi*, which consists of about twenty-five thousand verses in six books, making him one of the most prolific poets of all time. *Diwan* was composed over a period of about thirty years, from the time of

Tabrizi's arrival in Konya up until Rumi's death. It consists of individual poems arranged according to rhyme scheme. *Masnawi* was composed simultaneously, beginning in the year 1262, the same year in which his oldest son died, and ending with Rumi's own death. Unlike *Diwan*, *Masnawi* is a single work composed in a specific order and contains anecdotes and tales with moral points, in addition to poetry. Whereas *Diwan* is a work of spiritual intoxication and ecstatic lore, *Masnawi* is sober and represents a more reasoned and measured attempt to explain the dimensions of spiritual life and practice to disciples.

Love as a lived experience features prominently in Rumi's works. His purpose was to make the reader or listener surrender *(islam)* in the face of love and ecstasy. Rather than the kind of romantic love that people fall into and out of according to their emotions, Rumi's love was the kind of relationship that cannot know an end, no matter how many times one is rejected by the object of one's love. Although human beings can experience this kind of love for each other, Rumi's presentation of love is really a reflection of the relationship that human beings have with God, who is forever patient and forgiving and constantly calls human beings to Himself. It is the kind of love that requires one to give oneself over entirely in order to give life to God within oneself. It is also the kind of love that can heal human brokenness as God dissolves shame and helps people to know that they are His creation and are loved by Him despite their weaknesses, limitations, and unworthiness. In this context, the pain experienced in life on earth becomes a means of opening the spiritual door to remembering God's love.

There are two poetical ways in which Rumi wrote about spiritual experience. His classical Persian style of lyric poems express surrender to God in love through poetry and metaphor, especially references to wine and intoxication. The use of wine and drunkenness is a popular Sufi theme referring to the spiritual state of divine or mystical intoxication in which God's presence is sensed in the heart and mind of the worshiper. These symbols should not be misconstrued as support for libertinism on Rumi's part. Similarly, the apparent homoeroticism of Rumi's poetry in which Tabrizi is featured as the beloved is not an expression of homosexuality. Rather, it represents the adoption of a 300-year-old Persian literary tradition reflecting the relationship between the ruler and the ruled. Rumi condemned sexual exploitation, whether of women or young boys, on the grounds of both humanitarianism and its contradiction of Islamic law. Rumi's poetical expressions of love led his followers to call him the *qutb*, or pole, of love. His lyric poems are popular in the contemporary West.

The other type of poetry Rumi wrote was more religiously oriented and formal, yet still reflected the themes of God's love and surrender to God. He referred to Islamic law as the candle showing the way to God. Without the candle, one cannot set foot on the spiritual path. However, the candle is not enough on its own to reach the goal. The light of the law provides the light along the path that the wayfarer must travel on his spiritual quest. That path is the Sufi way. At the end of the journey, one finds truth. Rumi also compared religion to medicine because it is only by taking appropriate medicine and following a proper diet that one can pursue the Sufi path. True health can be found only by dying to the passions of the world and leaving only the face of God in the field of vision. He taught that those who wish to meet God must do good works and keep their minds focused on worship.

Rumi's teachings and works all address the interrelationship between God, human beings, and the world. His purpose is to guide, rather than explain, by encouraging people to allow them-

selves to turn toward God and devote themselves entirely to Him. Stylistically, his poetry is classified as feminine and receptive (*jamal*), rather than masculine and commanding (*jalal*). Although his symbolism and language are often complex, his message is universal and liberal enough to be applicable to all human experience.

Rumi died on December 17, 1273, at sunset, an event that was celebrated by Sufis as his union with the divine. His funeral was attended by people from all walks of life from a variety of religious persuasions and socio-economic classes. Many of his followers believed that his ability to attract and be revered and listened to by all nations and faiths was his greatest miracle. Manuscripts of his works have been collected at his shrine in Konya.

It was only after his death that the historical circumstances of Rumi's life were recorded. Because works written about him were more concerned with his spiritual influence than with the historical details of his life, Rumi has been transformed from a remarkable man to a mythical figure who has come to transcend both time and space.

Rumi's thought and writings have had a major impact on Persian, Turkish, and Urdu literature, as well as Islamic thought and philosophy. His influence can be seen in nineteenth-century Western metaphysical thought and studies of comparative religion, particularly in the writings of Hans Christian Andersen and Georg Hegel. In Iran, he is celebrated as an exponent of human liberation. Proponents of civil society point to his example of expansive and tolerant Islam as the path to be followed in the future. His works have been translated into Arabic, Turkish, French, German, Latin, English, Spanish, Italian, Swedish, Czech, Polish, Russian, Japanese, Greek, and Hebrew.

In the contemporary era, Rumi is a growth industry, particularly in the United States, where he is typically read and considered outside of his Muslim context. There are Rumi and Rumi-related websites, C.D.'s, and videos. His shrine is a major site of international pilgrimage. His books are widely recommended as inspirational reading and have been adopted by devotees of Sufism, mysticism, and New Age spirituality alike. In 1997, the *Christian Science Monitor* named him the best-selling poet in the United States. Audiobooks of his writings are particularly popular among commuters. Self-help writers such as Stephen Covey – *Seven Habits of Highly Effective People* – refer to Rumi. Yoga centers perform spiritual aerobics while listening to readings of his poetry, while dance companies have been inspired by the movements of the Whirling Dervishes. Musicians ranging from classical composers Richard Strauss and Franz Schubert to the New Age Paul Winter Consort, Buddhist composer Philip Glass, and the acoustic band Three Fish have paid tribute to and derived inspiration from Rumi. Videos about him have been narrated by Debra Winger and Vanessa Redgrave. Even the fashion world has been inspired by him: a musical version of Rumi accompanied Donna Karan's 1998 presentation.

The Whirling Dervishes also remain a source of interest in both the Muslim world and in the West. International film crews have traveled to Turkey to make documentaries about the dancers and musicians for broadcasts on British and French television. The ensemble has toured Europe, Australia, and the United States in recent years.

While some are concerned that Rumi's spirituality is being diluted and distorted by popular and secular culture in the West in favor of mass consumption, he remains for many an interfaith phenomenon whose deep spirituality overrides the boundaries normally set by differences in faith and belief systems. His thought is often quoted as an example of the ecumenical and understanding spirit that exists in Islam.

Further reading

Barks, Coleman. *Rumi: The Book of Love: Poems of Ecstasy and Longing.* San Francisco: HarperSanFrancisco, 2003

Chittick, William C. *The Sufi Path of Love: The Spiritual Teachings of Rumi.* Albany: State University of New York Press, 1983

Lewis, Franklin D. *Past and Present, East and West: The Life, Teachings and Poetry of Jalal al-Din Rumi.* Oxford: Oneworld Publications, 2000

Roumani, Rhonda "What Makes Rumi Whirl," interview with Kabir Helminski, in *Taking Back Islam: American Muslims Reclaim their Faith*, ed. Michael Wolfe and the producers of Beliefnet. Emmaus, PA: Rodale Inc. and Beliefnet, Inc., 2002

www.onelist.com/subscribe.cgi/sunlight – provides daily translations of Rumi into English

www.webcom/com/threshld – website of the Threshold Society in Vermont, the representative of the Mevlevi order in North America

S

Dr. Nawal El Saadawi (b. 1931)

A physician who has served as Egypt's director of public health and the assistant general secretary in the Medical Association in Egypt, Dr. Nawal El Saadawi is a prominent and controversial novelist and women's rights activist.

Dr. Nawal El Saadawi was born in Kafir Tahla, Egypt, in 1931. Her father was an official in the Egyptian Ministry of Education. El Saadawi completed medical school in Cairo in 1955. She has practiced public health, thoracic medicine, and psychiatry. From 1955 until 1965, she practiced medicine at University Hospital and the Ministry of Health in Egypt.

El Saadawi took on the study and analysis of the condition of Arab women with her first marriage upon the realization that she had less freedom as a wife and writer than she had experienced as a child. She soon drew a parallel between this lack of freedom within marriage and the broad lack of political and social freedom in Egypt. Her first marriage ended in divorce. She later married Dr. Sherif Youssef Hetata who has translated some of her works into English. The couple has worked together to address international human rights concerns, including service on the Commission of Inquiry for the

International War Crimes Tribunal that investigated war crimes in Iraq in 2003.

In 1966, El Saadawi became the acting director general and director general of health education for the Ministry of Health in Cairo. She held this position until 1972 when she was dismissed for having written a controversial book entitled *Women and Sex* that angered both political and religious authorities for its open and frank discussion of women and sexuality based on El Saadawi's experience as a medical doctor. She had also spoken out on the controversial practice of female circumcision, also known as excision or female genital mutilation, which is practiced by both Christians and Muslims in Egypt. About ninety percent of Egyptian women undergo this procedure to preserve their sexual purity according to custom. El Saadawi's opposition to the practice is based both on her own personal experience of the procedure and her observations, as a medical doctor and psychiatrist, of its effects on women. Her public discussion of these issues also cost her positions she had held since 1968 as the chief editor of *Health* magazine and as secretary general of the Medical Association in Egypt.

Despite the government's punitive measures, El Saadawi expanded her activism on women's issues. From 1973 to 1976, she researched women and

270

neurosis in Ain Shams University's faculty of medicine. From 1977 to 1987, she served as the founder and vice-president of the African Association for Women on Research and Development in Dakkar, Senegal. Her work on women in Africa and the Arab world led to her service as a consultant on women's programs in the United Nations in Addis Ababa, Ethiopia, from 1978 to 1979 and as United Nations Advisor for the Women's Program in Africa and the Middle East from 1979 to 1980. She also served as the head of the Women's Program in the United Nations Economic Council for West Asia (U.N.E.C.W.A.) in Beirut, Lebanon, from 1978 to 1980.

Although El Saadawi had by this time earned an international reputation for her work on women's issues, the Sadat regime considered her a domestic threat. In 1981, she and many other Egyptian intellectuals were arrested and imprisoned. She was released in 1982, shortly after Sadat's death.

Upon her release from prison, El Saadawi and 120 other women founded the Arab Women's Solidarity Association (A.W.S.A.) with El Saadawi as president. A.W.S.A. declared that the struggle for the liberation of the Arab people and freedom from economic, cultural, and media domination cannot be separated from the liberation of Arab women and their active participation in social, economic, cultural, and political life. A.W.S.A. was granted consultant status with the Economic and Social Council of the United Nations in 1985, at which point it had over a thousand members internationally and branches in a variety of Arab countries, Europe, the United States, Canada, and Australia. The Egyptian government closed A.W.S.A. in 1991, declaring it illegal, destroying its documents, and diverting its funds and assets to a religious women's association. A.W.S.A.'s major publication, *Noon* magazine, which addressed women's issues and feminist politics and for which El Saadawi

had served as editor-in-chief, was also shut down. Although El Saadawi took the Egyptian government to court, she lost the case. A.W.S.A. is currently active through its website and international branches.

El Saadawi has written a variety of types of prose, including novels, short stories, drama, and travel and prison memoirs. She wrote her first novel – *Memoirs of a Girl Called Suad* – when she was thirteen. She has published more than twenty-four books in Arabic and is one of the most controversial writers in the Arab world. She was also the first Arab woman writer to capture Western attention. Her non-fiction book *The Hidden Face of Eve* was translated into English in 1980 and became an instant classic. Interest in this book led to interest in her fiction, beginning with the translation of her novel *Woman at Point Zero* into English in 1983. The most visible of Arab women writers, she has been described as the Simone de Beauvoir of the Arab world and is widely celebrated in the West. The founder of the Egyptian Women Writers' Association, she served as an author in the Supreme Council for Arts and Social Sciences in Cairo from 1974 to 1978.

The positive reception of El Saadawi's novels in the West sparked a backlash against her by critics who claim that her success lies not in her championship of women's rights, but in her palatability for a Western audience because she confirms negative Western stereotypes about Arabs and Muslims as misogynist, backward, and violently oppressive. Some have even claimed that the promotion of her work in the West is part of the historical and systematic demotion of Arabs and Arab-Islamic culture by the West in favor of secularization and Westernization. However, her supporters note that her plots, linguistic games, literary allusions, and religious–legal intertextual references can only make sense within an Arab-Islamic context, marking her as an Arab-Islamic, rather than Western secular, writer.

One of the great ironies of Western attention to El Saadawi's work is that it has sparked Western interest in other Arab women writers, some of whom have made the same criticism that El Saadawi turns imagination and living memory into generalized social types that are not representative of Arab women's creative writing. They believe that Arab women writers should use Western attention as an opportunity to enlighten and provoke Western readers into a deeper level of thinking and analysis, rather than confirming preexisting stereotypes, prejudices, and assumptions about the harem, the veil, polygamy, and Muslim male violence against women. At the same time, Arab women writers have limited their criticisms to El Saadawi's novels. She remains widely acknowledged as a leading feminist who has conducted important and pathbreaking scientific research. They also note that her tendency to play to Western stereotypes in her novels should not be used to dismiss her achievements.

Although she is popular with English-speaking audiences and has won acclaim in the West for her literature, El Saadawi has been punished frequently by the Egyptian government both because of the topics about which she writes – women, gender inequality, sexuality, male – female relations, and the hardships endured by Arab women – and because she tackles her subjects frankly and in a straightforward manner, a departure from the traditional norm of dealing subtly with controversial topics. She is particularly known for the physical imagery of her writing, much of which revolves around the body. Although some have accused her of presenting heroines who are engaged in a biological struggle against their bodies, El Saadawi has stated that her purpose is not to encourage women to hate their bodies, but to emphasize the roots of moral, political, and social struggles in the human body. She notes the inherent contradictions of physical appearance that grant men certain rights on the basis of the presence of the male organ, while the onset of physical femininity during adolescence and puberty for women results in the loss of childhood freedoms. Believing that women have the human right to fight against such injustice, El Saadawi co-founded the Arab Association for Human Rights in 1983. Her novels also reflect her support for human rights issues through her reflections on unjust laws and social conditions that oppress women intellectually, ideologically, and sexually.

El Saadawi's visibility as a public intellectual and supporter of women's and human rights have led to the pronouncement of death sentences against her by extremist Islamist organizations. After the secularist Faraj Fawdah was assassinated by one such group in 1992, the Egyptian government instituted protection for Egypt's intellectuals, including El Saadawi. In another unusual case, a private individual accused her of apostasy in the Cairo Personal Status Court in April 2001, demanding that she be divorced from her husband. The case was dismissed twice by the prosecutor-general. Since the filing of the charges, the Egyptian Committee for Solidarity with Nawal El-Saadawi has worked to defend her and to repeal the Hisba law (law 3/1996) that allows for forcible dissolution of marriage in the case of apostasy.

El Saadawi is the recipient of several national and international literary prizes, including a 1974 Literary Award from the Supreme Council for Arts and Social Sciences in Cairo; a 1982 Literary Award from the Franco-Arab Friendship Association in Paris; a 1988 Arab Association of Australia Award; the 1988 Literary Award of Gubran; a 1989 First Degree Decoration from the Republic of Libya; and a 1994 honorary doctorate from the University of York in the United Kingdom. She also received the prestigious

Premi Internacional Catalunya Literary Award from Spain in 2003, which is presented annually to people who have made global contributions to the development of cultural, scientific or human values. An internationally known lecturer at universities and conferences, her works have been translated into more than thirty languages and are taught in college courses around the world.

Further reading

al-Ali, Nadje Sadiq. *Gender Writing: Writing Gender*. Cairo: American University in Cairo Press, 1994

Amireh, Amal. "Problems and Prospects for Publishing in the West: Arab Women Writers Today," solidarity.igc.org

Malti-Douglas, Fedwa. *Men, Women and God(s)*. Los Angeles: University of California Press, 1995

—— "Sa'dawi, Nawal al-,"in *The Oxford Encyclopedia of the Modern Islamic World*, editor-in-chief John L. Esposito, vol. 3. New York: Oxford University Press, 1995

—— *Woman's Body, Woman's Word: Gender and Discourse in Arabo-Islamic Writing*. Princeton: Princeton University Press, 1991

El Saadawi, Nawal. *The Circling Song*. London: Zed Books, 1989

—— *A Daughter of Isis: The Autobiography of Nawal El Saadawi*, trans. Sherif Hetata. London: Zed Books, 1999

—— *The Fall of the Imam*, trans. Sherif Hetata. London: Minerva, 1988

—— *God Dies by the Nile*, trans. Sherif Hetata. London: Zed Books, 1974

—— *The Hidden Face of Eve*. London: Zed Books, 1980

—— *The Innocence of the Devil*, trans. Sherif Hetata. Berkeley: University of California Press, 1994

—— *The Nawal El Saawadi Reader*. London: Zed Books, 1997

—— *Searching*, trans. Sherif Hetata. London: Zed Books, 1991

—— *Two Women in One*, trans. Sherif Hetata. London: Saqi Books, 1994

—— *Woman at Point Zero*, trans. Sherif Hetata. London: Zed Books, 1983

Tarabishi, George. *Woman against her Sex: A Critique of Nawal el-Saadawi*, trans. Basil Hatim and Elisabeth Orsini. London: Saqi Books, 1981

www.nawalsaadawi.net – website for Nawal El Saadawi

www.awsa.net – website for Arab Women's Solidarity Association

H.R.H. Sheikha Sabeeka Al-Khalifa (b. 1948)

Wife of the Emir of Bahrain, Her Highness Sheikha Sabeeka Al-Khalifa has played a prominent role in the expansion of women's rights and participation in the public sphere in Bahrain.

Sheikha Sabeeka Al-Khalifa was born in Muharraq, Bahrain, in 1948. She was raised in Riffa, Bahrain, under the patronage of her maternal grandfather, Sheikh Salman bin Hamad Al-Khalifa, the former ruler of Bahrain. Sabeeka received her elementary and secondary education in Bahrain. She then traveled abroad to the United Kingdom to pursue additional specialized courses. Fluent in Arabic, English, and French, she was married to then crown prince, Sheikh Hamad bin Isa Al-Khalifa, in 1968. She is the mother of the current crown prince.

Sabeeka became involved in issues of national importance in Bahrain upon her marriage. A patron of initiatives to improve the lives of Bahraini citizens through projects promoting the generation of family income, she has worked to revive and perpetuate traditional trades and is an advocate for the preservation of historic Bahraini architecture. She is also an environmentalist dedicated to the protection of natural life and the development of green areas in Bahrain. She is recognized as an experienced and able discerner and protector of rare breeds of Arabian horses, earning Bahrain recognition by the International Organization for Arabian Horses. A patron of both literature and the arts, she is known for her personal artistic talent, particularly in painting local scenes.

Sabeeka shattered Arab and regional stereotypes and cultural norms in 1999 when her husband succeeded his father as ruler of Bahrain. The sheikh and sheikha rule as a couple with Sabeeka taking an increasingly public role in government and politics. Their ultimate goal is the construction of a country in which all Bahrainis, both men and women, are active participants in the promotion of the country's best interests in both the private and public spheres.

Sabeeka's most prominent work has been the promotion of women's rights and advancement of the status of women in Bahrain. She was able to work from a position of strength toward this goal because of Bahrain's long tradition of educating women. Bahrain was the first country in the Gulf region to establish schools for girls prior to World War II and was one of the first to send girls abroad for a university education. In the 1950s, Bahrain also established the first organizations in the region dedicated to increasing the status of women, producing a generation of women dedicated to the promotion of women's rights and women's suffrage.

Upon achieving independence from Great Britain in 1971, Bahrain named women's equality as one of the central tenets of its national goals. Promotion of the position of women has been a central goal of the reform process begun in 1999. Forty-six members of the committee that drafted the series of political reforms known as the National Charter of Action, passed by referendum in 2001, were women, as were 49% of those who voted to approve it. In 2002, women accounted for 70% of university students.

However, although 2003 brought the appointment of the first woman C.E.O. of a bank and the first woman president of Bahrain National University, these educational achievements did not translate broadly into employment for women. In 2002, women filled only about thirty percent of the country's jobs. Helping Bahraini women break through the proverbial "glass ceiling" in employment

opportunities has therefore constituted a major component of the modernization and development plan. Programs have been instituted to provide women with better training and more specialized education, as well as opportunities for continuing education and specialization in various aspects of finance.

The broadest initiative toward encouraging greater participation by women in both the development and political processes was the establishment of the Supreme Council for Women by Emiri Order No. 44 on August 22, 2001, as an independent official body that advises the emir on women's issues. The council consists of fourteen people who are appointed on the basis of their knowledge of women's issues. Chaired by Sabeeka, the council is responsible for putting into practice the principles of women's rights outlined in the National Charter of Action by proposing public policies and recommending amendments to existing legislation, encouraging women's participation in public life, and ensuring that women are aware of their rights and duties. Sabeeka has also called for the enactment of a personal-status law in Bahrain.

The council's first major task was to draw up a national plan to review the situation of Bahraini women and propose general policies for improving it. It also sought to prepare Bahraini women to make proper use of their political rights when running for office or voting in municipal and parliamentary elections by exposing them to concepts of political independence and making sure that they understood the rules of democratic activity from the perspective of serving public interest and welfare. The council's work was put to the test in 2002 when Bahrain passed an amendment to the constitution restoring representative democracy and calling for the first democratic election in twenty-five years. Women were allowed both to vote and run for office. Six female candidates ran for office and campaigned. Sabeeka personally led the call to vote with a public plea to women to vote. Although no women were elected to parliament, Sabeeka declared that the holding of elections in which women were equal participants as both voters and candidates seeking office marked the beginning of the practical application of the democratic process in Bahrain. She also expressed hope that, over time, women will prove to be as capable and successful in politics as they are in other aspects of life. Following the elections, the emir appointed six women to his cabinet as an expression of his personal support for gender equality and the need to make Bahrain more liberal and democratic. The efforts of the council and the emir have earned international acclaim and support from both the media and the United Nations.

Sabeeka has used her work for the Supreme Council to cooperate with other civil institutions involved in women's work and the role of the family. She has been particularly active internationally, working with a variety of pan-Arab and Muslim organizations concerned with women's issues, including discussions for the formation of the Arab Women's Organization, and attending conferences of the All-China Women's Federation and the Women for Peace delegation in Egypt. She personally followed through on the implementation of the recommendations and resolutions of the Arab Women's Summit Conference in Bahrain. In another departure from past protocol, she officially represented Bahrain at the U.N. General Assembly during the 27th Extraordinary Session for the Child. In 2004, she gave a speech for Arab Women's Day in which she announced that divorced women with children to support will be legally entitled to housing and that the Supreme Council for Women had proposed a draft law to establish a family alimony fund and reconsider the criteria used to evaluate alimony.

Following the 9/11 tragedies, Sabeeka called on Muslim women and Arab women to play a public role as advocates of peace and tolerance and to engage in civilized and responsible dialogue. She also highlighted the important role of mothers and caregivers in raising a new generation capable of communicating with the world.

Like many Arab first ladies, Sabeeka is actively involved in humanitarian and philanthropic work. She presides over a variety of charitable and vocational societies, including the Bahraini Businesswomen's Society, the Yoko House for the Elderly, Al-Manar for Elderly Foster, and the Bahrain Cancer Society. Her involvement with these organizations includes direct participation in developing the quality of their services.

Sabeeka's work for raising the status of women and expanding their participation in society has been recognized both nationally and internationally. She received the Medal of Bahrain in 2002, was awarded an honorary professorship of social sciences from the China Women's University in 2002, and was named Woman of the Year by Women-Gateway in 2003.

Further reading

"Arab Women Can be Messengers of Peace, Says Shaikha Sabeeka," *Khaleej Times Online*, September 3, 2002

"Breakthrough for Women," *Gulf Daily News*, February 1, 2004

Leupold, Julie. "Seven Who Till Fresh Ground," *Women's Enews*, January 1, 2003, www.womensenews.org

"Women in Bahrain Play a Crucial Role in National Development," interview with Professor Fatima al-Belooshi, Bahrain University, by Phillip Kurata, World Economic Forum, June 21, 2003; transcript available at usinfo.state.gov/regional/nea/summit/text2003/0621women.htm

www.bahrainbrief.com.bh/english/sep-2001. htm – website for Supreme Council for Women

www.bahrainembassy.org

Joshua Salaam (b. 1973)

Leader of the American Muslim rap group Native Deen, Joshua Salaam is a pioneer in the adaptation of contemporary musical styles to religious themes, representing the vanguard of a Muslim musical movement similar to the Christian rock movement of the 1980s and 1990s.

Joshua Salaam was born Joshua Burt in Camden, NJ, on September 15, 1973. He was raised by his mother, who provided him with his earliest musical training in Motown and the Oldies. She also insisted that Salaam learn to play the violin between the fourth and ninth grades, although he never learned to read music. Always interested in playing the drums, Salaam describes himself as having an innate internal sense of rhythm and music. He wrote his first raps when he was ten years old. By the age of twelve, he was rapping at Muslim Youth of North America camps.

Salaam's public high-school years were marked by ridicule and discrimination for his conservative religious beliefs. Although he was allowed to be friendly with girls, he wasn't supposed to date or have girlfriends, which made him stand out from other boys and led to his missing out on important social events such as the prom. He also chose to dress modestly, including wearing sweat pants, rather than shorts, while running track, because he believed it was wrong for him to show his bare legs. The combination of modest dress and adherence to Muslim dietary restrictions and rituals, such as the five daily prayers, made Salaam and his Muslim friends frequent objects of derision and ridicule by non-Muslims. Salaam chose to consider these experiences as tests of strength in adhering to his beliefs and used them later in some of Native Deen's lyrics. He encourages other Muslims facing similar situations not to feel ashamed of being different and not to give in to the temptation to try and fit in with the crowd, but to try to stand strong.

Following his high-school graduation in 1990, Salaam joined Muslims Steppin' Up, which was later renamed Sonz of the Crescent. During his two years of college at Indiana University, during which he studied criminal justice, he continued to rap as Jahi and won some competitions. He then completed one year of classes at the I.T.T. Technical Institute while he worked at an H.V.A.C. company. In 1995, he joined the air force as a security police officer. He served for four years, undergoing basic training in Lackland, TX, before being stationed in North Carolina. He was deployed to Guantánamo Bay in Cuba once and to Qatar twice.

During basic training, fear kept Salaam initially silent about his religious obligations, such as praying five times daily and maintaining his modesty by not appearing naked in front of others. However, he soon requested time to pray and shower privately. When some people responded by making jokes about his being Muslim, Salaam used the jokes as opportunities to explain and clarify misconceptions about his beliefs, earning him the respect of his fellow recruits who defended him and his religion in his absence. He was also appointed dorm chief. His talent for writing and singing "jodies" (songs that are sung when the troops march) led to his training instructor calling him out of the line to march next to the other recruits and lead them in the jodies, distinguishing them from other groups of recruits.

Salaam's distinguished military service included awards for Airman of the Year and Most Outstanding Member of the police officers with whom he trained in 1997. He also served as a D.A.R.E. (drug abuse resistance education) officer for local civilian schools. He credits his faith with helping him to excel in his career, particularly in 1996 when he was stationed in Qatar about forty miles from a terrorist attack attributed to Islamic militants on the Khobar Towers in neighboring Saudi Arabia. Salaam became an important Muslim resource for his commander in dealing with the fall-out for American forces.

Honorably discharged from the military in 1999, Salaam put his criminal justice degree to work for the civil rights organization the Council on American–Islamic Relations (C.A.I.R.), while pursuing his musical career. He joined M.Y.N.A. (Muslim Youth of North America) Raps, a combined effort of various Muslim musicians, and was featured on their first album. The second, third, and fourth albums featured two other major artists: Naeem Muhammad and Abdul-Malik. All three were featured on the fifth album, after which they decided to form a group partnership, Native Deen. Salaam has commented that Muhammad brought considerable knowledge of the music industry, popular groups, and famous songs to the group, while Abdul-Malik serves as the group's most popular composer; three-quarters of the songs performed at Native Deen concerts have been composed by Abdul-Malik. The three have since traveled and performed together across the United States and the United Kingdom.

Native Deen is at the forefront of a growing trend of singing or rapping about Islam, a reflection of the adaptation of popular culture to religious needs. The rise of Muslim rap has been compared to the rise of Christian rock in the 1990s, fulfilling the desire of teenagers to have contemporary music, but with a message that reflects their faith and value systems. Salaam has commented that Native Deen seeks to help young American Muslims have fun and enjoy music without conflict with their religious beliefs.

The Muslim rap of Native Deen is very different from that of other bands such as Public Enemy and Brand Nubian which carry socio-political and sometimes racially charged messages appealing to disenchanted African-Americans.

Whereas these previous bands were affiliated with more militant black Muslim movements, particularly Nation of Islam and the Black Panthers, Native Deen's lyrics do not call for black supremacy. Rather than the sex, drugs, violence, degradation of women, crude language, and conspicuous consumption typically glorified by mainstream hip-hop, Native Deen's lyrics call for virtuous and modest behavior over vice – historically traditional Islamic messages. The lyrics also encourage being good Muslims, good students, exhortations to prayer, and warnings to avoid drugs. Careful not to swear or degrade women, the artists refer to women by praising their mothers, encouraging young Muslim women to be virtuous, and talking about how much they love their wives. The lyrics seek to reinforce positive conceptions and impressions of Islam while counteracting popular negative stereotypes that associate Islam with violence and hatred.

Native Deen's choice of rap as a musical style is based on the experience and culture of the band's members. All are African-American Muslims with exposure to American city life, making rap/hip-hop a logical musical style that reflects the fusion of African-American culture and Islam. It also highlights the fact that about a third of American Muslims are African-American.

Native Deen's music features only percussion instruments and vocal raps. No string or wind instruments are used because some Muslims believe that these are forbidden in Islam. Similarly, in accordance with conservative beliefs, dance routines are kept to a minimum. The band dresses conservatively with long pants, shirts, and skullcaps. Although some critics have labeled the group Wahhabi because of these presentation and instrumental choices, admirers believe that the presentation style is consistent with the message of the group of adhering to Islam, even when it conflicts with popular culture, and note that what is really important is the lyrics.

Popular in both the United States and the United Kingdom, Native Deen performs for audiences that range from several hundred to several thousand. They have recorded five albums, sales for which run about 3,500 per year. They perform at a variety of functions, including weddings, Eid celebrations, conventions, dinners, and baby dedications, and have been featured in newspapers, on television, and at Islamic camps. In 2003, they contracted with a new producer, Mountain of Light, which is run by YUSUF ISLAM, formerly known as Cat Stevens.

Salaam's role in the spotlight of Muslim popular culture has made him conscious of his responsibility as a role model in being faithful to his beliefs so as not to lead others astray. He believes that he can best fulfill this responsibility by continuing to write and perform raps.

Further reading

Cho, David. "Rap with Religion: D.C. Group Urges Islamic Virtue in a Hip-hop Beat," *Boston Globe*, February 25, 2002
Donaldson-Evans, Catherine. "Muslim Musicians Rap About Islam," Fox News, October 14, 2002
Interview with the author, August 6, 2003
http://www.nativedeen.com – website for Native Deen

Saladin (Yusuf Salah al-Din al-Ayyubi) (c. 1138–1193)

The Muslim general of the Crusades and founder of the Ayyubid dynasty in Egypt, Yusuf Salah al-Din al-Ayyubi, popularly known in the West as Saladin, is renowned in both Eastern and Western legends and historical accounts of the Crusades for his mercy, justice, and compassion.

Saladin (also spelled Salah al-Din) was born in Tikrit, in contemporary Iraq, around 1138. An ethnic Kurd, he was educated in both Turkish and Arab culture, as well as Arab military history and genealogy, the Quran, *hadith*, and Islamic law. He abided by the same code of chivalry followed by Europeans and was recognized as an honorable man who respected treaty relationships and kept his word, even when the terms were not favorable to him. Informal and accessible to both his soldiers and the common people, he was well known for his piety and dedication to Muslim ritual observances, particularly the five daily prayers, and for his kind treatment of servants. Although he initially gave in to demands that he dress luxuriously to demonstrate visually his wealth and power as vizier of Egypt, he soon reverted to his simpler pattern of living humbly and simply among the people. A generous man who gave away conquered wealth and palaces, as well as entire provinces, particularly to the poor, Saladin possessed only 47 drachmas when he died, yet was the most powerful man in the Middle East.

The historical Saladin is known largely through chronicles of his leadership of the Muslims during the Crusades. Highlights of his military career include the overthrow of the Fatimid caliphate and foundation of the Ayyubid dynasty in Egypt in 1171; the conquest of Damascus in 1174; the conquest of Aleppo and reunion of Egypt and Syria in 1183; and the crushing of the Crusaders at Hittin and conquest of Jerusalem and most Frankish territories in 1187. His combined military and diplomatic successes became legendary in Europe during his lifetime, as did his charisma, chivalry, heroism, and religious dedication. In one highly publicized example of his chivalry, Saladin spared an area of the castle he had been besieging after being informed that the owner's stepdaughter was celebrating her wedding night there.

Saladin was particularly known for his justice, mercy, and compassion. He held public audiences on Mondays and

Thursdays to hear cases and administer justice. Compassionate even toward his enemies and during military engagements, he treated everyone who appeared before him honorably, including women and non-Muslims. In a case where a woman from the Crusader camp asked for his assistance in recovering her daughter who had allegedly been taken by the Muslims and sold in the marketplace, Saladin sent a knight to recover the child. He returned her to her mother and sent both back to their camp.

As vizier, Saladin believed that his main responsibility was to lead Muslims in a jihad of self-defense against the invading Christian Crusaders. At the same time, he was tolerant of Jews and Christians who were not involved in the fighting, particularly Christians of Orthodox and Eastern denominations. Like other Muslim rulers, he established treaty relationships with Jews and Christians, offering them protection in exchange for payment of a poll tax. He also fulfilled the legal requirement to return the money in cases where he failed to provide the guaranteed protection.

Saladin was an unusual military leader for his time because he strictly observed the classical rules of jihad and was a man of his word. Whenever possible, he tried to engage his enemies in a treaty relationship unless they had been responsible for atrocities against Muslims. In the aftermath of battle, he tended to ransom prisoners of war, believing it inappropriate to engage in killing for the sake of killing. Although male combatants were sometimes put to death because they had directly participated in the battle, women and children, even those related to male combatants, were allowed to leave unharmed and typically with their possessions – a marked contrast to the Frankish treatment of Muslims, whose wives and daughters were routinely raped and often killed. Saladin even spared some of the distinguished male combatants, including, in one case, the

King of the Crusaders. Only in the cases of the Templars and Hospitalers was there no mercy because they were the fiercest fighters. Saladin was particularly scrupulous about respecting the prohibition against killing civilians, permitting them to go free instead.

Although Saladin believed that he was responsible for leading a jihad, he did not consider jihad necessarily to be a full-scale war. He declared all-out war against the Crusaders only after Reynauld of Chatillon had repeatedly broken his truce with the Muslims. In the most serious violation, Reynauld had attacked a caravan of pilgrims on their way to Mecca, capturing Saladin's sister. Reynauld then refused to release or ransom the prisoners. It was at this point that Saladin swore to kill Reynauld and launched a full-scale war. He eventually captured both Reynauld and King Guy. As promised, he killed Reynauld for breaking his word, but offered Guy his hospitality and freedom.

The most famous tales of Saladin's magnanimity center around the major military victories over Hittin and Jerusalem in 1187. His moderation after the capture of Jerusalem particularly marked him apart from his contemporaries. The third holiest city in Islam after Mecca and Medina, Jerusalem had been ruled by Muslims from 692 until 1099. Under Muslim rule, Christians and Jews had been permitted to worship and live in Jerusalem and had control over their own holy places. In 1099, Jerusalem was overtaken by the Christians, who proceeded to slaughter the inhabitants of Jerusalem in one of the worst massacres ever to occur there. Under Christian rule, two major Muslim holy sites, the Dome of the Rock and the al-Aqsa Mosque, were converted into a church and the headquarters of the Templars respectively, an act that has remained part of Muslim historical memory.

Hittin marked the first major victory of the Muslims over the Crusaders under

Saladin's leadership and set the stage for the reconquest of Jerusalem. In keeping with the code of chivalry, Saladin did not use the victory as an opportunity to annihilate his enemies. In fact, one of those who fought against him in Hittin, Baron Balian of Ibelin, arrived in Jerusalem at roughly the same time as Saladin. Balian sought to collect his wife, who was in the city, and take her back to Tyre. Realizing that the Muslims were preparing to attack, Balian sought an audience with Saladin in order to explain his situation and request permission to enter Jerusalem. Saladin agreed on the condition that he remain there for only one night. However, when the people of Jerusalem begged him to stay and lead them in their final battle, Balian was torn between his oath and his responsibility to his people. He sought a second audience with Saladin to ask what he should do. Understanding that Balian believed he had a religious duty to defend his people, Saladin released him from his oath and allowed him to return to Jerusalem to lead the defense. The exchange makes clear that both leaders shared the same code of conduct despite the differences in their religious faiths and that neither believed that oaths made to people of other faiths could be nullified simply on the basis of a difference in religion.

Having allowed Balian to return to Jerusalem to lead the defense, Saladin's forces prepared for the siege. In keeping with his usual pattern of engagement, Saladin first offered to withhold military engagement if the Christians would peacefully turn the city over to him. They refused, but it soon became clear that they could not win. At that time, Saladin refused to allow them to negotiate for peace, threatening instead to treat them in the same manner that they had treated the inhabitants of Jerusalem in 1099. Again, Balian offered a different solution. He told Saladin that the people were fighting only half-heartedly because they hoped that Saladin would engage in his famous

clemency and spare them. He also informed Saladin that the Christians would slaughter the 5,000 Muslim prisoners they held and destroy the al-Aqsa Mosque and the Dome of the Rock if he did not grant clemency. Saladin's religious experts ruled that he could break his oath to take Jerusalem through bloodshed if he could save the mosques in the process. Saladin therefore ended the siege of Jerusalem and granted clemency to the Christians. He kept his word that there would be no killing or plundering, despite opposition from some of his officers who were upset that he did not demand ransoms or confiscate treasures. Deeply moved by the taking of prisoners as he saw families torn apart, Saladin released many of them unconditionally. When challenged by his officers for leaving the Christian forces both intact and wealthy, thus prolonging the conflict, Saladin replied that Christians everywhere would remember the kindnesses granted to them in Jerusalem. For his mercy, Saladin was venerated as a truly chivalrous knight in the West.

Having conquered Jerusalem, Saladin first cleansed and restored the Muslim holy places. He also established the precedent of financial investment in Jerusalem, particularly in law schools and convents, that was followed by his descendants. The one major change he made was in banning the Crusaders from traveling there as a matter of political expediency. Christians who had not persecuted or fought against Muslims, such as Greek and Eastern Christians, were still allowed in Jerusalem, as were Jews who recovered the right to return, live, and worship freely there.

Saladin was also famous for his face-off against his Crusader counterpart, England's King Richard I, popularly known in the West as Richard the Lionheart. Richard and Saladin frequently saw each other from a distance during military engagements, but never met. They were known to have admired each other as knights and military leaders and both were considered exemplars of the chivalric ideal. In one military encounter in Jaffa when the Crusaders were losing to the Muslims, Richard rallied the Crusaders by leading the spearmen in a charge against the Muslims. Saladin so admired Richard's bravery that, when Richard's horse fell under him, Saladin immediately sent his groom out with two fresh horses.

Inasmuch as both Richard and Saladin represented chivalric ideals, they differed on several key points. Saladin tended to set prisoners of war free when there were too many to maintain, while Richard slaughtered them. Saladin was respected as a man of his word, while Richard came to be reviled among Muslims for his failures to keep his word to Muslims, particularly following the conquest of Acre in 1191. Already weakend by famine and disease, the Muslims offered to vacate the city in exchange for safe passage. Richard promised to allow them to leave, but changed his mind as they headed out of the city and slaughtered them instead – over three thousand men, women and children – in one of the worst violations of a treaty agreement in the history of the Crusades. Richard's behavior is not only still remembered in the Muslim world today as a demonstration of Christian hypocrisy, but it is typically contrasted with Saladin's benevolent treatment of the inhabitants of Jerusalem in 1187. Saladin and Richard eventually signed a truce in 1192, which lasted for three years and eight months.

Saladin died in 1193, after a twelve-day illness. At the time of his death, he was the head of the largest empire seen in the Muslim world for centuries. He is broadly considered the greatest Muslim leader since the Rightly Guided Caliphs and is upheld as the ideal Muslim military leader.

Further reading

Armstrong, Karen. *Holy War: The Crusades and their Impact on Today's World*. New York: Doubleday, 1991

Gabrieli, Francesco. *Arab Historians of the Crusades*, trans. E.J. Costello. New York: Dorset Press, 1957

Maalouf, Amin. *The Crusades through Arab Eyes*, trans. Jon Rothschild. New York: Schoken Books, 1984

Peters, F.E. "Jerusalem," in *The Oxford Encyclopedia of the Modern Islamic World*, editor-in-chief, John L. Esposito, vol. 2. New York: Oxford University Press, 1995

Saira Shah (b. 1965)

An award-winning journalist best known for her documentary *Beneath the Veil* about women living under the Taliban regime in Afghanistan, Saira Shah has observed first hand the wars in Algeria, Kosovo, Afghanistan, and Palestine.

Saira Shah was born in 1965 in London, England. Her father, Idries Shah, a famous Sufi short-story writer of Afghan and Scottish descent, was the subject of a B.B.C. documentary entitled *Dreamwalkers*. Shah's mother was of Indian and British descent. Her family traces its ancestry back to the Prophet Muhammad's daughter, Fatima, entitling them to use the honorary title Sayyid.

Although born and raised in Britain, Shah was raised on stories of Afghanistan as a magical, idealistic place to which she ultimately belonged and would one day return. Living in exile and caught between East and West, that sense of belonging and identity were critical to her psychological well-being.

Shah was raised in a liberal Muslim household. As a Sufi, her father taught her that Islam was a method of self-realization and spiritual guidance, rather than a religion focused on ritual perfection, literal interpretations of scripture or a mystical system. Shah describes her Islam as one of tolerance in which there is no compulsion in religion and in which the holy warrior is defined as one who struggles against him- or herself. She believes that Islam encourages the individual to think for oneself.

Shah completed her university education in London in 1986. In addition to Persian and Arabic, she studied martial arts and engaged in parachute jumping. Following graduation, she left England for Afghanistan, seeking to experience first hand the country so often described to her by her father and to discover the truth about her origins. She expected to find the country of honor and courage she had idealized as a child. A freelance journalist with no experience, she traveled to Afghanistan via Peshawar, Pakistan, where she convinced some Afghan *mujahidin* to take her by foot over and through the Hindu Kush mountains to the front line.

Rather than the Afghanistan of her father's stories, Shah encountered a country torn by war. Over the next fifteen years, she experienced first hand the fight of the Afghan *mujahidin* against the Soviet occupiers, the end of the Soviet occupation, the collapse of Afghanistan under warlord rule and conflict, and the rise and rule of the Taliban. Shah's initial impressions of Afghanistan were colored by the romanticism in which she had been raised. Although she began with a vision of the *mujahidin* as a noble fighting force, over time she realized that their purpose was to perpetuate warfare, rather than to restore peace and stability to Afghanistan.

Despite the constant danger, Shah realized that she had an instinct for journalism and spent the next three years in Peshawar. During this time, she met a scholar named Professor Majrooh who became her mentor and helped her to understand the conflict not as one of absolute good (the *mujahidin* and America) versus absolute evil (the Soviet Communists), but as shades of gray. She also met a Swiss journalist named Beat Kraettli, whom she married in 1989. The couple divorced five years later.

Shah reached a turning point in her understanding of Afghanistan in 1988 when she learned that the *mujahidin* had sold their American-supplied anti-aircraft missiles to Iran. Having corroborated the story with sources in Pakistan, she found herself torn between her Afghan romanticism and her job as a reporter. More than a journalistic coup, the story marked Shah's realization that the image of the *mujahidin* as noble was a lie. She decided to report what she had found, earning her both death threats from the *mujahidin* and ostracism by many of the American expatriates living in Peshawar who considered her report a betrayal. Her mentor, Professor Majrooh, was assassinated in his home a few weeks after the story appeared.

In 1989, Shah returned to Europe to pursue journalism, working for Swiss radio and television before returning to Britain where she worked as a foreign correspondent for Channel Four News, covering warfare in Algeria, Kosovo, Kinshasa, Baghdad, and other parts of the Middle East during the 1990s. She traveled to Rais, Algeria, in 1997 to investigate the wave of massacres that had been occurring since 1992. She found a disturbing pattern in what has become known as the "Triangle of Death." Men would come to a village from two sides and shoot at people's feet to make them fall. Those who fell then had their throats cut, except for young virgin girls who were taken away alive, presumably to provide sexual services to their captors. Those villagers who escaped usually encountered the army which, rather than helping them, shot at them and left them trapped with the killers. The killing typically lasted for several hours, after which the killers were allowed to escape. Journalists were allowed into the villages only in the company of armed guards. When Shah questioned the prime minister about why the army did not intervene and end the killing, he responded that the army had intervened as quickly as possible, but refused to allow independent investigations into the massacres that were then occurring weekly. The government preferred to blame the incidents on Islamic militants.

Even as she reported on these atrocities, Shah kept an eye on Afghanistan, watching from the sidelines as the Soviets withdrew and the warlords came to political power. The toll of the war against the Soviets was immense: 1.5 million people – nearly eight percent of the Afghan population – had been killed. Another 4 million had been displaced and were living in squalid refugee camps. An entire generation of children had been left uneducated. Agriculture had been bombed, terraced mountain fields built over centuries had been shattered, and the eroding earth was sown with mines. Many Afghans knew only war and destruction. Although it had been hoped that the *mujahidin* would bring stability to Afghanistan, they continued in their ethnic strife and warlordism. Interested in money and power, they looted Kabul, raped, kidnapped, stole from homes, and fought in the streets like gangsters. With no government powerful enough to stop them, rival political leaders began fighting each other. The prime minister shelled his own capital. Because these men had never known anything but war and many of them had no families or memories of families, they could not imagine peace. For the professional fighters, peace meant unemployment. They therefore kept the conflicts going, concerned mainly about where their supplies of ammunition and money would come from.

By 1994, the ethnic strife in Afghanistan had escalated into outright warfare. Although Amnesty International continued to document atrocities, the world community did nothing to stop it. Shah's own television company didn't think the story was worth covering at the time. The combination of ethnic wars and rampant violence led to the rise of the Taliban. Initially, the Taliban were formed to stop the marauding *mujahidin* and the warfare in Afghanistan. Uninterested in money, sex, and property, the Taliban proposed setting up a just Islamic system to resolve the rampant corruption, collapse of law and order, and major problems with abductions, rapes, and killings that had been perpetrated by the *mujahidin*. Their method was severe: restrictions against women that permitted them no access to public space or jobs, public executions of anyone violating the law, and persecution of religious and ethnic minorities. They were particularly well known for their zero-tolerance policy for anyone committing a crime against women. Although many in the world community came to decry the severity and extremism of their measures, they succeeded where everyone else had failed by stopping the shelling.

In February 2001, Shah shifted gears at Channel Four, moving from foreign correspondence to making documentaries. Channel Four also finally decided that the Taliban were worth covering. Shah was disturbed that great attention was given to the Taliban only after they blew up some ancient Buddha statues, while no one seemed to care that thousands of human lives had been lost to famine and war. She returned to Afghanistan to film her documentary *Beneath the Veil* and to investigate rumors of a Taliban massacre of a different ethnic group.

Beneath the Veil was filmed undercover by Shah in April 2001. Disguising herself as an Afghan woman, Shah donned the burqa and left her crew behind, risking her life to show the shocking ruins of Kabul, public executions, and the forbidden underground network of women struggling to survive under Taliban rule, particularly the secret classrooms for girls and the deplorable state of women's hospitals, which lacked everything from basic hygiene to medicine and food. She filmed the documentary with a camera hidden under her burqa, always aware that discovery of her activities could bring her imprisonment, punishment or death, just as attending school or working could bring imprisonment, punishment or death to the women thus engaged. The ever-present danger of discovery necessitated working and traveling undercover with members of R.A.W.A., the Revolutionary Association of the Women of Afghanistan, an underground Afghan feminist organization. Shah stayed in Kabul in a safe house for five days, at constant risk of discovery by a large network of Taliban informants.

The filming marked Shah's first encounter with the Taliban. Although she had once admired their bringing an end to the increasing corruption of the *mujahidin*, she quickly came to despise them not only because they were oppressive but also because she perceived that they had corrupted and destroyed all of the qualities she had grown up believing were quintessentially Afghan – generosity of spirit, courage, self-confidence, and humor. She found their treatment of women to be particularly shocking because she had been raised in a household where women were considered the twin halves of men – a view she had previously thought inherent to the Afghan interpretation of Islam. Although the Taliban claimed to be purifying Islamic practices in Afghanistan, some of them knew little about Islam, often confusing religion with Pushtunwali, the tribal honor code of the Pathans. One of the difficulties of dealing with the Taliban as a group was their lack of homogeneity.

Although the Taliban controlled ninety percent of Afghanistan at the time when *Beneath the Veil* was filmed, they engaged only in military battles and spent money only on arms and paying soldiers. They did not invest in the rebuilding of the infrastructure or focus on humanitarian projects, such as feeding people. Although they claimed to protect women by prohibiting them from working and going to school past the age of nine, Shah noted that the prior conflict had created more than forty thousand war widows, many of whom had no male family member to support them. These women were permitted to beg, but not to work, regardless of how many children they had to support. Shah also noted a major change in the Afghan psyche under the Taliban: with whole generations knowing nothing but war, suffering, and violence, she found evidence of mass trauma as even the Afghan sense of humor became a casualty of the ongoing conflict. She found that people were so fearful and exhausted that they no longer laughed or joked.

Shah's time in Afghanistan to film *Beneath the Veil* also had a personal dimension: her first visit to her family's seat in Paghman where her ancestors had lived for 900 years. Although she was able, through her father's word paintings, to visualize what the garden had once been, the abject destruction she encountered left her wondering how the country could ever learn to build again.

Beneath The Veil was first broadcast in the United Kingdom in June 2001. It was broadcast in the United States in August 2001 and frequently again following the 9/11 attacks. The recipient of the National Press Club Freedom of the Press Award, the Overseas Press Club Award, the George Foster Peabody Award, the Royal Television Society Journalism Award, the Monte Carlo Award, and an Edward R. Murrow Award, *Beneath the Veil* was named Programme of the Year and Shah Television Journalist of the Year at the Royal Television Society's Journalism Awards for 2002.

Encouraged by the success of *Beneath the Veil*, Shah set out to make a new documentary on the impact of terrorism on Palestinian and Israeli children for H.B.O., *Death in Gaza: Militants, Suicide Bombers, Innocent Victims*. This venture ended in tragedy when her cameraman, James Miller, was shot dead by Israeli troops in Gaza on May 2, 2003, despite carrying a white flag declaring "TV" and experience in covering more than twenty wars, including Bosnia, Chechnya, Sierra Leone, and the Congo. The Israeli government claimed that its soldiers had responded to hostile fire. However, Miller was killed with a shot to his neck, a signature sniper shot. An independent criminal investigation into his death in 2006 in London resulted in a unanimous verdict that Miller had been deliberately targeted and murdered by an Israeli soldier.

Released in 2004, *Death in Gaza* was an "Official Selection" at the 2004 Berlin International Film Festival and received a Sterling Award for a feature film at the 2004 AFI/Discovery Channel Documentary Festival and an Audience Award at the 2004 Canadian International Documentary Festival, in addition to three Emmys in 2005.

After completing the documentary, Shah dedicated herself to writing her autobiography, *The Storyteller's Daughter*. She is currently writing fiction.

Further reading

"2002 National Press Club Award Marks 13th Honor For CNN Productions, Saira Shah's Documentary 'Beneath the Veil,'" C.N.N. news release, July 9, 2002

"Algerian Violence," report by Sarah Shah for Independent Television News, London, October 21, 1997

"Discovering an Alien Homeland," Between the Lines with Saira Shah, *Boston Globe*, October 5, 2003.

"Journalist Saira Shah: Life in Afghanistan under the Taliban," CNN.com Newsroom transcript, August 24, 2001, www.cnn.com/2001/COMMUNITY/08/24/shah

Matheou, Demetrios. "Our Woman in Kabul," *The Observer*, July 20, 2003

"Saira Shah Crowned Television Journalist of the Year," Pozitiv Productions, March 1, 2002

Shah, Saira. "James Miller, the Martyr who Charmed Children," *The Observer*, May 11, 2003, www.aljazeera.info/Opinion

—— *The Storyteller's Daughter*. New York: Alfred A. Knopf, 2003

Hanan al-Shaykh (b. 1945)

An internationally acclaimed novelist, short-story writer, and playwright, Hanan al-Shaykh is considered one of the leading women writers in the contemporary Arab world.

Hanan al-Shaykh was born in Beirut, Lebanon, in 1945, to a poor, religious Shii family. Her father was a partner at a cloth shop. Her mother left the family when al-Shaykh was young, an event she recounts in her short story "The Scratching of Angels' Pens." Only fourteen when she had married, al-Shaykh's mother had been forbidden to learn to read or write. Al-Shaykh found it ironic that her father praised the pursuit of knowledge and insisted that his children be educated, but denied her mother the same right.

Al-Shaykh recalls her childhood as a time of feeling abandoned and alone. Not only did her mother leave, but one of her brothers was forced to leave Lebanon because of his political activities. Her father closed himself off from her because of his shame at betrayal by both his wife and his business partner. She also felt unconnected in Beirut because her family came from southern Lebanon.

Al-Shaykh attended the Alamillah Muslim girls' school in Beirut for her early education. She later transferred to the more sophisticated Ahliyyah school, but did not perform well. Her difficulty earning passing grades led her to question later in life whether she had a learning disability that was never diagnosed. As she grew up, her father and brothers gradually began to restrict her personal freedoms. She rebelled by writing as a release for her anger and frustration.

Al-Shaykh first experienced the desire to record her thoughts and experiences in writing when she was ten years old. She began writing more regularly and seriously when she was fourteen. Because her writing is often based on her experiences, the styles and content of her writing have changed as she has. In her early writings, she sought to convey a sense of boredom and the fact that her family didn't understand her. She began by writing newspaper essays, turning to fiction several years later. Although she is fluent in English, she writes only in Arabic.

By the time al-Shaykh was sixteen, she had published several essays in *al-Nahar* newspaper. In 1963, when she was seventeen, she made her first trip to Cairo where she completed her high-school studies and attended the American College for Girls for two years. Cairo provided her with the freedom to reinvent herself and pursue her writing. She completed her first novel, *Suicide of a Dead Man*, while studying there, examining power relations between the sexes and patriarchal control.

Al-Shaykh returned to Beirut in 1966. She worked in television and as a journalist for *al-Hasna'* women's magazine. She then worked for *al-Nahar* from 1968 until 1975. During this time, she wrote her second novel, *Faras al-Shaytan*, published in 1971. This novel included some biographical elements referring to her father, parts of her own love story, and her subsequent marriage as told through the personal development of the heroine, Sarah, against the background of southern Lebanon. Al-Shaykh left Beirut for Saudi Arabia in 1976 due to the civil war. She moved to London in 1982.

As a writer, al-Shaykh believes that her job is to write about what she feels and issues that she believes are important. She deliberately writes from different perspectives and tends to include a number of characters in her works in order to express the variety that exists in Arab societies. Some of her most controversial topics include homosexuality and prostitution, which are taboo in Muslim culture. She has also worked to expose hypocrisy and has expressed deep concern about the rise of religious extremism and its accompanying conservatism, particularly where women are concerned. She has stated that she does not write about these topics to be provocative or to showcase her writing, but to bring to light issues that tend to be hidden in Arab culture. She believes that the realities of Arab societies must be talked about in order for people to achieve freedom and true integrity.

Al-Shaykh defines her writing style as one that is straightforward, free from explanation and analysis, and focused on the creation of a mood through the provision of insightful details, meticulous descriptions, psychological depth, and cross-cultural encounters. An intuitive and spontaneous writer, rather than one with formal training, she allows her stories and characters to make their own choices about where their stories go. Because she does not set the structure of what she is going to write in advance, she has declared herself frequently surprised by the endings to her stories.

Al-Shaykh came to international attention in 1980 with the publication of her novel *The Story of Zahra*, the account of a young woman who finds her opportunity to escape patriarchal oppression in the Lebanese civil war. The novel reflects al-Shaykh's quest to understand how women surrounded by tragedy, fear, desolation, and death internalize it in their hearts, minds, and wombs while finding joy in existence. Rather than the powerless woman understood by Western readers, al-Shaykh intended Zahra to be a strong character because of her ability to set her own limits and express her will within a restrictive environment established entirely by men. She used Zahra's engagement in forbidden sexual encounters to examine how she sought freedom by defying men and patriarchal traditions. However, Zahra does not win by this method, as her body ultimately takes control back from her, breaking her spirit and personality as evidenced by madness, abortions, and nervous breakdowns. The book was so controversial that al-Shaykh was unable to find a Lebanese publisher and had to finance the publishing herself. Banned in most Arab countries for giving the wrong impression about Arab culture and feeding Western stereotypes about Arab women as oppressed victims, the novel was praised in West for its powerful portrayal of the personal human tragedy of war and madness.

Al-Shaykh's next major novel, *Women of Sand and Myrrh*, published in 1989, tells the story of four women struggling with the patriarchal order in different ways with the common goal of making their lives full in a society where their access to space is controlled by men and where sex is an unhealthy obsession. By examining the questions of freedom, tradition, and the West from a variety of perspectives and subtly questioning what freedom is, al-Shaykh describes a society torn between tradition and the West. In the end, each woman chooses a different path to accomplish her goal – returning home, experiencing sensuality, pursuing adventure, or becoming educated – all of which are expressions of freedom. *Women of Sand and Myrrh* was banned in several Middle Eastern countries, in part because it contains lesbian themes. Chosen as one of the Fifty Best Books of 1992 by *Publishers Weekly*, it was such a commercial success in English that al-Shaykh went on a twenty-two-city American book tour, the first ever for an Arab novelist.

In 1992, al-Shaykh published *Beirut Blues*, a novel in the form of ten letters written by a woman who lives in Beirut throughout the civil war to preserve her memories of the city as it existed prior to the war while she observes its destruction. As a celebration of the resilience of spirit of those who remained there, the novel reflects some of al-Shaykh's personal questions about what those experiences would have been like. The power of the novel lies in her ability to make the normally abstract and distant phenomenon of war tangible and personal while demonstrating the variety of perspectives that existed about it. The multiple levels of representation permit the writer to feel a sense of control over a situation that was completely out of control. Al-Shaykh's use of the war to provide sexual satisfaction to the heroine both celebrated the strength of Arab women and demonstrated that they are not the monolithic stereotypes bound by tradition and religion that they are

portrayed as in the West. Her choice of a letter format was intended to demonstrate that letters continue to serve as a means of maintaining contact, preserving relationships, and learning about news, as well as organizing experiences and information as they are put into writing. The letters also serve to record Beirut for posterity as a reflection of al-Shaykh's desire to preserve the old Beirut for her children and the generations to come after her.

Al-Shaykh published a collection of short stories entitled *I Sweep the Sun off Rooftops* in 1998. The major stories place the characters between East and West, or between the safety of traditional values and the lure of modernity, as highlighted by male–female roles and relationships across both genders and generations. She particularly highlights the complexity of the relationship between mother-in-law and daughter-in-law, not only as a generational interaction, but also as a reflection of the intersection of tradition with modernity at the personal level. At the same time that they criticize patriarchal notions of how women should behave, the stories praise Arab culture for giving women some power to negotiate their own realities. In each of the stories, the heroine has a goal that she tries to achieve by working within the parameters society has set for her. Although the heroines are not always successful in achieving their goals, some succeed in the way that they have chosen, despite society's failure to comprehend it. The collection continues al-Shaykh's pattern of writing stories from a variety of perspectives, including the personal voice of both men and women of varying ages and from the third person. The settings also shift between the Middle East and Europe, reflecting the theme of being between East and West.

Al-Shaykh pursued the portrayal of the lives of people caught between East and West in her 2000 novel *Only in London*. Her first novel set outside of the Arab world, it was written upon her realization that she had lived in London for nearly twenty years, during which time she had become a naturalized British citizen. She had begun writing about London with two plays about immigrants to London which were staged at the Hampstead Theatre: *Dark Afternoon Tea*, in 1995, and *Paper Husband*, in 1997. Writing the plays led her to explore the idea of place and how location influences people and makes them change, even when they are determined to hold on to their traditions. The plays also marked a new writing style. Previously, she had always worked alone and did not discuss her novels with anyone while she was writing them. However, the plays necessarily involved other people, requiring her to collaborate with a variety of professionals. They also helped her to explore a lighter side of herself and to entertain, a trait that also comes through in *Only in London*, although the issues addressed remained serious and tragic.

Of her own changes, al-Shaykh notes that she now tries to insert more humor and laughter into her writing, a task that she finds more difficult than writing about tragedy and making people cry. She frequently attends major literary festivals to promote Arabic literature and has contributed short stories to a variety of literary magazines, journals, and anthologies in order to build her recognition as a writer.

Al-Shaykh is broadly considered one of the most outspoken, daring, and important writers in the contemporary Arab world. Although they have been censored by different countries at different times, her novels now sell well throughout the Arab world where they are permitted. Popular in the United States and Europe, her novels have been translated into English, French, Dutch, German, Danish, Italian, Korean, Spanish, and Polish.

Further reading

Allen, Roger. *The Arabic Novel: An Historical and Critical Introduction*, 2nd ed. Syracuse: Syracuse University Press, 1995

"Between Two Worlds: An Interview with Hanan Al-Shaykh," interview with Paula W. Sunderman, *Literary Review*, 40, 2, winter 1997, pp. 297–309

Chalala, Elie. "Hanan al-Shaykh on Life, Dreams and Pain of Afghan Women," *Aljadid*, vol. 7, no. 37, Fall 2001

Cooke, Miriam. *War's Other Voices: Women Writers on the Lebanese Civil War*. Cambridge: Cambridge University Press, 1987

Ghazaleh, Pascale. "Hanan al-Shaykh: From the Rooftops," *Al-Ahram Weekly On-Line*, issue no. 455, November 11–17, 1999

"Hanan al-Shaykh," www.kirjasto.sci.fi/shaykh.html

"Hanan al-Shaykh (Writer)," LEBWA, Lebanese Women's Association, www.lebwa.org

"Hanan Al-Shaykh, the NI Interview," Richard Swift, *The New Internationalist*, 1996

Larson, Charles. "The Fiction of Hanan al-Shaykh, Reluctant Feminist." *Literary Quarterly of the University of Oklahoma*, 1, Winter 1991

Milani, Abbas. "A Warm, Sad Blues Riff on Life in Beirut: Novel's Letters Patch Together Haunting View of a Fractured City," review of *Beirut Blues* for the *San Francisco Chronicle*, August 13, 1995

Schlote, Christiane. "An Interview with Hanan al-Shaykh," *Literary London*, homepages.gold.ac.uk/london-journal/Schlote.html

al-Shaykh, Hanan. *Beirut Blues*, trans. Catherine Cobham. New York: Anchor Books, Doubleday, 1992

—— *I Sweep the Sun off Rooftops: Stories*, trans. Catherine Cobham. New York: Anchor Books, Doubleday, 1998

—— "My Mother, The Muslim," M.S.N.B.C. News, January 8, 2003

—— *Only in London*, trans. Catherine Cobham. New York: Anchor Doubleday Books, 2000

—— *The Story of Zahra*, trans. Peter Ford. London: Readers International, 1986

—— *Women of Sand and Myrrh*, trans. Catherine Cobham. New York: Anchor Doubleday Books, 1988

Zeidan, Joseph. *Arab Women Novelists: The Formative Years and Beyond*. Albany: State University of New York Press, 1995

www.kirjasto.sci.fi – contains biographies of international authors and references to their works

www.lebwa.org – website of the Lebanese Women's Association

Muhammad Nejatullah Siddiqi (b. 1931)

A pioneer theorist of Islamic economics, Muhammad Nejatullah Siddiqi has earned international recognition for his morally and ethically responsible approach to economics that combines traditional knowledge with modern know-how.

Muhammad Nejatullah Siddiqi was born in Gorakhpur, India, in 1931. His father was a physician who worked both in a government dispensary and in his own private practice. His mother was a descendant of a family of religious scholars who also served as spiritual guides. He recalls his childhood as one in which religion and community activism played central roles.

Siddiqi completed his secondary education in Arabic and Islamic learning in Rampur, India, and at the Madrasatul Islam, Saraimir, in Azamgarh, India, in 1953. He expected to pursue a career in science and technology. However, while in high school he read and was inspired by the writings of Mawlana Abu al-Ala Mawdudi. His resulting interest in combining Islamic scholarship with modern studies in order to Islamize knowledge led him to serve as the editor of *Islamic Thought* from 1954 until 1959 while pursuing his undergraduate studies at Aligarh Muslim University. He changed his major to economics, completing a B.A. in 1958 and an M.A. in 1960. He then taught economics at Aligarh University while working on a Ph.D. in which he explored the development of an Islamic approach to contemporary economics. He completed his degree in 1966. He served as professor of Islamic studies and director of the Institute of Islamic Studies at Aligarh Muslim University from 1977 until 1978, when he transferred to the Centre for Research in Islamic Economics at King Abdulaziz University in Jeddah, Saudi Arabia. He served there until June, 2000. In 2001, he became a fellow at the Center for Near Eastern Studies at the University of California, Los Angeles. During the 2002–2003 academic year, he was a visiting scholar at the Islamic Development Bank in Jeddah. In addition to his work in economics, he has written critiques of terrorism and the use of unauthorized violence by Muslims.

Islamic economics was conceived in the early twentieth century as an alternative to secular economic doctrines such as capitalism and Marxism. It grew out of concerns that Western economic doctrines and patterns were lacking in moral and ethical guiding values to prevent the exploitation of the masses to the benefit of a minority of elites. Historically, Islamic economics has been characterized by its dedication to deriving inspiration and guidance from the Quran and *Sunna* (example of the Prophet Muhammad) and by its search for economic perspectives and insights in Islamic history and civilization, rather than in secular philosophical traditions. Although, as a discipline, it has sought to rediscover and revive the economic values, priorities, and mores of the early seventh-century Muslim community, this has not been done in order to recreate exactly that early community. The development of a distinct, independent, and self-consciously Islamic economic tradition is a modern phenomenon that addresses modern economic concerns and challenges.

The movement to create a distinctively Islamic discipline of economics began in pre-partition India as part of a broad program to establish a variety of Islamic disciplines as alternatives to Western doctrines and patterns and to demonstrate the practicality of Islam as a complete way of life. The early writings of this genre tended to be descriptive and prescriptive, rather than theoretical or practical, explaining how Islamic disciplines differed from Western systems. As such, they tended to provide principles and values, rather than a blueprint for an

Islamic economy or the nuts and bolts of how such an economy would operate.

Siddiqi represents the second phase in the development of Islamic economics: the formulation of Islamic economic theory; the incorporation of modern analytical techniques; and the addressing of real-life problems. He can best be described as a realist in his approach to Islamic economics. Although he encourages Muslims to behave in an ideal fashion, he recognizes the impracticality of building an Islamic political economy or economic agenda on the basis of such ideal behavior. He has further recognized the reality of modern banking as a necessity of modern economics, finance, and trade. He encourages Muslims to see reality as it is, not as they want it to be, and to make reality their starting point in working toward the Islamic ideal in a practical fashion now, as opposed to waiting for a perfect ideal to come into existence at some undefined point in the future. Although he believes that history does contain some important lessons, he cautions Muslims against allowing themselves to be trapped by it. He has called for a contemporary, universal, and dynamic approach to economics.

Islamic economic theory is based on recognition that individuals need to be part of a society in order to survive because no individual is capable of producing everything necessary for existence. At the same time, this theory recognizes the innate selfishness of humanity which requires a downplaying of individualism accompanied by morally informed human behavior in consumption, exchange, and production in order to maintain control over human self-interest. This recognition of a necessarily social dimension to human life is reflected in Siddiqi's works which exhort the Muslim to engage in religiously appropriate – i.e. unselfish, altruistic, principled, and morally pragmatic – economic behaviors in order to avoid destructive competitive behaviors and immoral

activities such as speculating, hoarding, gambling, extravagance, and waste. Siddiqi charges Muslims with supporting economic activities that encourage fair prices, respect for others, and hard work.

The connection between the law and morality is central to Islamic economics. Recognizing that good moral behavior cannot remain a matter of individual choice alone if it is to have a broad social impact, the institutionalization of the will to morality has become a goal for many Muslim societies. Islamic banking is one means of accomplishing this goal. While free will still plays an important role in determining human behavior, the existence of institutions that encourage moral behavior by promoting human welfare, eradicating corruption, and ensuring justice, equality, and reciprocity not only makes such moral behavior more concrete, but also serves to ensure the dignity of all members of society.

Rather than focusing strictly on limitations set by morality, Siddiqi encourages the motivation of the individual economic actor through the provision of opportunities, resources, and spiritual growth, as well as political empowerment through a democratic process of consultation (*shura*). He believes that a change of government does not mean necessarily changing the government in the sense of overthrowing or replacing it. In fact, he considers confrontation to be counterproductive, as trade and global interdependence are current economic realities. Rather than dividing the world into East versus West, he encourages recognition of pluralism in faith, ethnicity, and heritage as global realities that must be incorporated into an Islamic vision of economics. Believing that no individual knows all of the answers to the world's questions, he encourages constant dialogue as the most productive and effective means of solving problems and implementing solutions.

Siddiqi's early works focused on ideas and contracts found in early Islamic literature, such as trade, sharing, and barter. Although he believed that it was important to use these simple transactions as the basis for the framework for an Islamic economy, he recognized that they were insufficient for the actual economic needs of and challenges facing contemporary Muslims. Asserting that Islamic economics must adapt to the constantly changing financial and economic context in order to remain relevant and applicable to daily life, he addressed issues such as finance, banking, credit, and currency exchange in order to find Islamically acceptable methods of engagement. He began by working on issues of concern for countries that had made a formal commitment to Islamic banking – Saudi Arabia, Sudan, and Pakistan – where the financial sectors and economic affairs needed to be reorganized in accordance with Islamic law. These countries were particularly concerned about the need to establish a banking sector that did not operate on the basis of interest and the development of Islamic insurance and partnerships.

Although Islamic law permits and even encourages profit-making and commercial activity on the basis of the Prophet Muhammad's own example of having worked as a businessman, it does not allow for the exploitation of the needy or of borrowers. Siddiqi has noted that the Quran prohibits charging interest on loans because it demeans and diminishes the lenders, corrupts society, improperly appropriates the property of other people, results in negative economic growth, and is unjust. The injustice occurs through the imbalance of the relationship between the borrower and the lender. In an interest-charging loan, the lender makes a guaranteed profit over time without carrying any risk while retaining all of the power in the relationship because the need for the loan rests solely with the borrower. The borrower is left to carry the full burden of responsibility and risk, while paying out a set profit to

the lender, regardless of the outcome of the use of the loan. Siddiqi believes that the interest paid out by banks on savings accounts is not Islamically permissible because it does not come out of the bank's profits nor is it proportional to such profits. Instead, the interest is paid by the entire society as higher prices are charged for services and goods due to the charging of interest, regardless of the profitability of the venture.

By contrast, the Islamic vision of lending calls for the lender and the borrower to share the risk. In the case of the purchase of a commodity for personal consumption, the Islamic lending institution engages in buying the commodity and reselling it to the borrower at a marked-up price. Because there is no profit or charging of interest over time, there is no exploitation of the borrower's need. The lender engages in risk by converting capital into a commodity that the borrower may fail to buy or may default on. Once the borrower takes possession of the commodity, it is up to him to bear all profits or losses on the basis of use. There is therefore no imbalance or injustice in the relationship. In the case of a business venture, the lender hopes that the venture he is lending money to will make a profit, but profit is not guaranteed. The purpose of the money is to facilitate the transaction, not to make a guaranteed return. Because it is based on moral principles, Islamic financing is intended to rid the market of corrupt practices such as fraud, interest, gambling, coercion, hoarding, raising prices by making false bids, exploitation of need, and withholding information.

Islamic banking continues the trend of having depositors lend their money to the bank for the purpose of investing it. The depositors earn a percentage of the profits from the investment, rather than a set rate of interest. Islamic banks do not guarantee repayment of the capital invested because this would absolve the depositor from risk. Siddiqi believes that not having a guaranteed return results in greater competition and efficiency among banks because investors must monitor the bank's performance in order to make the most out of their investment. The successful transformation of Islamic economic theory into practice is evident in the expansion of Islamic financial services globally. The first Islamic banks were established in the private sector during the 1970s. The early 1980s brought Islamic investment companies offering a percentage of non-guaranteed profits in exchange for payment of a management fee. Islamic mutual funds appeared in the late 1980s. The Dow Jones developed an Islamic Market Index. Although Islamic financial institutions remain relatively small compared to conventional institutions, the sector is expected to continue to grow as more investors choose to borrow and invest in Islamically permissible ways.

Siddiqi has also been in the forefront of the development of Islamic insurance. He has applied the same concept of risk to insurance in order to demonstrate that the concept of insurance is Islamically permissible. The critical definition of risk with respect to insurance is that the risk is involved in carrying out the ordinary business of life, such as owning a house or driving to work, rather than the kind of risk involved in gambling or playing a game of chance where the risk could be avoided simply by refusing to engage in the activity. In Islam, financial gain is supposed to be based on work, should serve a social purpose, and is intended to encourage fairness and cooperation across the community. Insurance provides for protection against risk to those engaged in such activities because it bonds together a group of individuals facing similar risks and uncertainties as a mechanism for coping with the catastrophe when it occurs at an individual level. Were the individual to face the catastrophe alone, financial collapse could occur. Bonding together collectively prevents

that individual disaster, thus promoting public welfare. Because the purpose of benefits is to replace what was lost, thus restoring the pre-catastrophic status, no profit is earned from Islamic insurance. Fire, house, and auto insurance are considered Islamically acceptable because they provide protection against such potential situations. Siddiqi has further endorsed Islamic life insurance policies that are based on mutual cooperation.

In keeping with his concern for moral and ethical values and behavior, particularly in economic life, Siddiqi has addressed the disparities between rich and poor and social injustices brought about by communism, socialism, and capitalism, particularly rising crime, tensions, and threats to peace. Believing that the Islamic vision of life must encompass economic and financial matters, as well as morality and personal conduct, he has called for the strengthening of the moral commitment of both individuals and the social environment in order to build families and societies, as well as economies in the future. He has denounced terrorism and violence as unethical and inhuman distortions of a faith that has historically stood for dialogue, communication, compassion, love, tolerance, gentleness, and forgiveness. He has called for an interpretation of jihad that focuses on the restoration of human freedom, choice, and democracy in order to alleviate human suffering.

Siddiqi's pioneering work in economics was recognized with the King Faisal International Prize for Islamic Studies in 1982 and the American Finance House Award in 1993. He has served on the editorial board of the *Journal of King Abdulaziz University: Islamic Economics* since 1983 and is a member of the International Board of Review of Islamic Economics, *IQTISAD Journal of Islamic Economics and of Humanomics*. He has served on the boards of the *American Journal of Islamic Social Sciences*, the *Journal of Islamic Sciences*, the advisory board of Islamic economic studies at the

Islamic Research and Training Institute at the Islamic Development Bank in Jeddah, and the board of trustees of the Accounting and Auditing Organization for Islamic Financial Institutions in Bahrain. Many of his English-language books have been translated into Arabic, Persian, Turkish, Bengali, Hindi, Malay, and Indonesian.

Further reading

"Interview with a scholar: Prof. Nejatullah Siddiqi," www.soundvision.com/Info/money/nejatullah.interview.asp

Kuran, Timur. "The Economic System in Contemporary Islamic Thought: Interpretation and Assessment." *International Journal of Middle East Studies*, 18, May, 1986, pp. 135–164

—— "Economics: Economic Theory," in *The Oxford Encyclopedia of the Modern Islamic World*, editor-in-chief John L. Esposito, vol. 1. New York: Oxford University Press, 1995

Siddiqi, Mohammed Nejatullah. *Banking Without Interest*. Leicester: Islamic Foundation, 1983

—— *Economics, an Islamic Approach.* Leicester: Islamic Foundation, 1999

—— "Evolution of Islamic Banking and Insurance as Systems Rooted in Ethics," paper presented to the College of Insurance, New York, April 26, 2000, www.soundvision.com/Info/money/islamicbanking.asp

—— *Insurance in an Islamic Economy.* Leicester: Islamic Foundation, 1985

—— "Islamic Finance & Beyond: Premises and Promises of Islamic Economics," paper presented to Harvard University Forum on Islamic Finance, Islamic Finance: Challenges and Global Opportunities, Cambridge, MA, October 1–2, 1999, islamic-finance.net/islamic-economics/eco2.html

—— *Issues in Islamic Banking.* Leicester: Islamic Foundation, 1983

—— "Nature and Methodology of Islamic Political Economy in a Globalized World Environment," paper presented to International Workshop on Islamic Political Economy in Capitalist Globalization: An Agenda for Change, School of Social Sciences, University Sains Malaysia, December 12–14, 1994, islamic-finance.net/islamic-economics/eco5.html

—— *Partnership and Profit-Sharing in Islamic Law.* Leicester: Islamic Foundation, 1985

—— *Riba, Bank Interest and the Rationale of its Prohibition.* Jeddah: Islamic Research and Training Institute/Islamic Development Bank, 2004

—— *Role of the State in the Economy.* Leicester: Islamic Foundation, 1996

—— *Teaching Economics in Islamic Perspective.* Jeddah: Centre for Research in Islamic Economics, 1996

—— "Violence and Muslims," *Zindagi* (Urdu-language magazine published in New Delhi), April 2004. An abridged version of this paper appeared in the *American Journal of Islamic Social Sciences*, 2004

Vogel, Frank E. and Samuel L. Hayes, III. *Islamic Law and Finance: Religion, Risk, and Return.* The Hague: Kluwer Law International, 1998

Series of interviews with the author, May, 2004

www.dowjones.com/islamic – website for Dow Jones Islamic Market Index

www.islamic-economics.com/ – website providing a variety of information about Islamic economics and links to other relevant sites

www.islamic-finance.net/ – website for School of Islamic Business Education and Research, including a link to its International Journal of Islamic Financial Services

www.kff.com/english/kfip/selectionproc.html – website for the King Faisal International Prize

www.siddiqi.com/mns – Siddiqi's website

www.soundvision.com/Info/money/nejatbio.asp – contains c.v. for and articles by Siddiqi

M. Osman Siddique (b. 1950)

The first Muslim and the first person born in South Asia to represent the United States abroad as an ambassador, M. Osman Siddique served as U.S. ambassador to the Republics of Fiji and Nauru and the Kingdoms of Tonga and Tuvalu from August 1999 until June 2001.

M. Osman Siddique was born in 1950 in Dhaka, Bangladesh. He moved to the United States in 1971 to attend

Indiana University. He completed his M.B.A. in 1974.

Siddique is a businessman by profession. In 1976, he founded I.T.I./Travelogue, Inc., a corporate travel management company that services the metropolitan Washington, DC area. As president and C.E.O. of the company, Siddique developed it into one of the largest travel-management companies in the United States. In 2000, it was rated the sixth-largest travel agency in metropolitan Washington, and was valued at $40 million, making it one of top minority-owned businesses in the metropolitan area. In 1994, the company was awarded the Arthur Andersen and *Washington Business Journal*'s FasTrack Award for the fastest growing companies in the Washington, DC area. Siddique has twice been named as a finalist for *Inc.* magazine's Entrepreneur of the Year Award sponsored by Ernst & Young.

Siddique has been active in politics since the 1990s. He has been a member and supporter of the American Muslim Council since it was founded and served as a member of the National Democratic Institute's international observer delegation to the Bangladesh parliamentary elections in 1996.

Siddique's combined political and business expertise came to the attention of the Clinton administration, leading to his inclusion on several presidential delegations, the most important of which were the White House Conference on Travel and Tourism and the First Hemispheric Trade and Commerce Forum. This work ultimately led to his nomination for the position of ambassador to Fiji, Nauru, Tonga, and Tuvalu by President Clinton on May 27, 1999, marking the first time that a Muslim had been nominated for an ambassadorship in the United States. The appointment was intended to fill a vacancy that had existed since the departure of the prior ambassador in July 1997 for personal reasons. The nomination was announced one week after general elections had taken place in Fiji in order to demonstrate American support for the democratic process. The four countries agreed to Siddique's appointment, pending his confirmation.

Siddique was confirmed as ambassador by the U.S. Senate on August 5, 1999, and was sworn in on August 17, 1999. He took his oath with his right hand on the Holy Quran, rather than the Bible, the first American ambassador ever to take the oath in this manner. For American Muslims, the swearing-in marked an important achievement in the long-term goal of the emergence and full inclusion of American Muslims in American political life. Siddique held the ambassadorship from August 1999 until June 2001. During this time, Fiji experienced a period of major civil unrest that led to Siddique's recall in 2000, although he later returned.

Siddique has continued with his business activities following the conclusion of his ambassadorship. He is a member of the board of trustees of Bryant College and a member of the board of directors of Partners for Development. He was previously a member of the board of directors for the National Center for New Americans. He currently serves on the board of directors of CryoBanks International, an umbilical-cord blood-storage and donation company.

Further reading

"Clinton Nominee as Ambassador to Tuvalu Expected to be Confirmed Shortly," PAC-News, July 16, 1999

"First American Muslim Ambassador to be Sworn in," A.M.C. Update, August 12, 1999, posted on www.muslims.org/web-news/messages/90.html

"M. Osman Siddique Sworn in as U.S. Ambassador to Fiji," *U.S.I.S. Washington File*, August 19, 1999, posted on usembassy-australia.state.gov/hyper/WF990819/epf407.htm

www.cryo-intl.com – website for CryoBanks International

Dr. Pratiwi Pujiliestari Sudarmono (b. 1952)

A medical doctor and specialist in microbiology who has served as Indonesia's Deputy Assistant Minister of State for Science and Technology, Dr. Pratiwi Pujiliestari Sudarmono was selected to be Indonesia's first astronaut and the first Muslim woman in space.

Dr. Pratiwi Pujiliestari Sudarmono was born in Indonesia on July 31, 1952. She completed her Bachelor of Science in 1976, her M.D. in 1977, and her Master of Science in microbiology in 1980, all from the University of Indonesia, Jakarta. She completed her Ph.D. in molecular biology at the University of Osaka, Japan, in 1984.

Sudarmono began her career in public health in 1984 with a grant from the W.H.O. for research on the biology of *salmonella typhi* in a quest for develop a faster and cheaper diagnostic tool and vaccine candidate. Her research led to collaboration with the Infectious Disease Hospital in Jakarta and primary health stations throughout Indonesia. She worked to develop health systems and health management in rural areas and to combat tropical diseases through better disease management, including prevention methods and early diagnosis and efficient therapeutics. The results of her lab research were applied in Indonesia's Mother Friendly Movement campaign, which seeks to reduce both infant and maternal mortality rates through better management of infectious disease in rural populations. As part of a national campaign to introduce safe motherhood programs throughout Indonesia, the Mother Friendly Movement became a national policy that has been implemented in all villages in Indonesia. Its purpose is to enhance the welfare of women and children by preventing disease, promoting health, and reducing health burdens caused by gender inequalities, poverty,

traditional/local cultures and ways of life, geographic conditions, and the limited skill and knowledge of traditional birth attendants and village midwives. The campaign has taken a multidisciplinary approach and has integrated gender roles. A joint collaboration between the government and N.G.O.s, it has also called for women to participate in the "family welfare post/center" at the grassroots level.

Sudarmono was appointed Indonesian astronaut to the N.A.S.A. space-shuttle mission from 1985 until 1995. She was selected for a N.A.S.A. mission on October 30, 1985, for which she was to serve as a payload specialist accompanying an Indonesian communications satellite into orbit. On a more personal and cultural level, she also developed plans to perform a classic Indonesian dance in zero gravity. Sudarmono's flight to outer space was scheduled for June, 1986, and would have made her the first Muslim woman astronaut. The tragic explosion of the space-shuttle *Challenger* earlier in 1986 led to cancelation of the mission.

Disappointed by the cancelation of the mission, but determined to pursue her scientific and public health research, Sudarmono taught microbiology in the medical school at the University of Indonesia, Jakarta, from 1985 until 1999. She served as the head of the microbiology department from 1994 until 2000 and then as the director of research and community services. Her academic work continued her research in science and technology policy and research and development in medicine and health. She has served as an adviser to the Bandung Institute of Technology and is a member of the board of trustees of the P.P.M. Institute of Management in Indonesia.

Sudarmono's academic performance led to her receiving a grant from the World Bank to continue research on medical microbiology and tropical diseases. She has been a visiting scientist at the N.A.S.A. Space Biology Laboratory in Houston, TX, the Walter Reed Army Institute for Research in Washington, DC, and the Tsukba Medical School in Japan. In addition to being a member of many national and international scientific and medical organizations, she has chaired the Indonesian Society of Microbiology since 1990.

Sudarmono pursued her work in public health as a Fulbright scholar, conducting research on the use of information technology to decrease maternal and infant mortality rates in Indonesia, which are higher than those of most A.S.E.A.N. countries. Her objective was to increase Indonesia's participation in the global health issues project by developing a model for the use of information technology to improve preventive and promotive measures in community-health development, focusing on two districts: (1) West Nusa Tenggara (traditional Muslim communities with limited gender participation, specific cultural practices, and very high rates of maternal and infant mortality); and (2) East Nusa Tenggara (traditional Christian communities with large gender participation, but moderate maternal and infant mortality rates). The model included women, N.G.O.s, and health personnel and officials working in a variety of aspects related to safe motherhood, and child health and welfare programs. Sudarmono sought to develop a health policy designed for specific areas in Indonesia where public participation is necessary for the improvement of health and welfare, especially for women and children. The ultimate goal was to create bottom-up initiatives, rather than the traditional government top-down public-health policy.

Sudarmono's publications include a book entitled *The Gender Role in Community Base Development in Indonesia* (2000), which has become a standard reference for government projects related to women in health, gender in social development, family planning programs, and

national vaccination programs. She is also the author of *Challenges of Health in a Borderless World* (2002), which addresses public-health issues in the era of globalization.

Sudarmono's service in public-health issues led to her appointment as a national point of contact representative for the U.N.E.S.C.O. Regional Network for Microbiology and Microbial Technology in Southeast Asia. This network, established in 1974 to link existing institutes for advanced studies in microbiology and microbial technology in developed and developing countries in Southeast Asia, works to promote communication and development cooperative programs to improve research and training programs in the region.

Sudarmono's research and scientific contributions earned her the Bintang Jasa Pratama, the Indonesian national medal for outstanding achievement in science and technology. They also resulted in her appointment for eleven years as the deputy assistant minister of state for science and technology and to service on the United Nations Information and Communications Technology Task Force, which focuses on women in public life and education.

Sudarmono currently serves as the director of the Agency for Agricultural Research and Development, where she works on biosafety protocol for the regulation of genetically engineered agricultural biotechnological products and the development of national policies on biotechnology.

Further reading

"Fulbright New Century Scholars Program: Sudarmono, Pratiwi," www.cies.org

Sudarmono, P. "Biofilm Formation and its Impact on Bacterial Resistance to Antibiotics in Hospital Environment in Indonesia." *Indonesian Journal of Medicine* (no further information available)

—— *The Gender Role in Science and Technology Development in Indonesia.* Jakarta: Bina Askara Press, 2000

Sudarmono, P. and I. Suhadi. "The Management of Typhoid Fever and other Salmonellosis in Indonesia." *Proceedings of 4th Asia Pacific Symposia on Typhoid Fever and other Salmonellosis.* Taiwan, 1999 www.unesco.biotec.or.th/ – website for U.N.E.S.C.O.

Suleyman the Magnificent (1494–1566)

Known in the Muslim world as Suleyman Kanuni (Suleyman the Lawgiver) and in the West as Suleyman the Conqueror, Suleyman the Magnificent was the most powerful sixteenth-century ruler in the world.

Suleyman (also spelled Suleiman and Sulayman) the Magnificent (r. 1520–1566) was born on November 6, 1494, in Trabzon on the coast of the Black Sea in Turkey. The only son of Sultan Selim I, he was the tenth Ottoman sultan. Suleyman is considered one of the most important Ottoman sultans because he ruled the Ottoman Empire (c. 1300–1919) at its zenith during the Ottoman renaissance. His reign marked the peak of Ottoman power and prosperity, the highest development of the Ottoman government, law, military, and economy and an increase in the power exerted by the imperial harem in the political affairs of the empire. A contemporary of the Holy Roman Emperor Charles V, King François I of France, and Henry VIII of England, Suleyman was considered the most significant ruler in the world by both contemporary Muslims and Europeans.

Suleyman's numerous accomplishments included the transformation of the Ottoman army into a major fighting force and power, the codification and revision of the judicial system, and the construction of a variety of architectural and artistic projects that made Istanbul both the political and cultural capital of the Ottoman Empire and the most active and innovative city in the world architecturally. As a military leader, he expanded the empire to

double its previous size. His multilingual empire stretched from Vienna in the west to the Arab Peninsula in the east and from the Crimea in the north to the Sudan in the south. His conquest of Belgrade (1521), Rhodes (1522), Buda (1529), and Transylvania (1562) placed him in control of most of Greece, Hungary, and large portions of the Austrian Empire. He was responsible for the exile of the Knights of St. John to Malta and the defeat and death of King Lewis of Hungary at Mohacs in 1526. His unsuccessful siege of Vienna in 1529 stirred great fears in Europe.

European fears of Suleyman were due in part to religious concerns. He was the most powerful Muslim leader in the world, outranking the ruler of the Safavid Empire based in Persia. As part of his foreign policy of destabilizing Europe, particularly the Holy Roman Empire and the Roman Catholic Church, he provided generous financial support to Protestant countries and formed an alliance with France in 1525 against the Austrian Habsburgs, who were the most powerful rulers in Europe at the time, thus ensuring that Europe would remain politically and religiously unstable and open to invasion. Suleyman's policy was not driven by a personal desire for endless conquest or a hatred of Christianity. In fact, many of his subjects were Christians and Jews who enjoyed official recognition and protection of their faith in accordance with the Islamic principle of recognizing and protecting fellow "People of the Book" (those claiming possession of a divine revelation). His policy of expansionism is best understood within the broader world historical context of the time. Europe was aggressively expanding, both militarily and commercially, presenting a serious threat to the hegemony of the Muslim world. European–Ottoman battles were fought largely in Eastern Europe and the Mediterranean Sea. Suleyman's naval commander, Admiral Barbarossa, won important victories against the Venetians that gave the Ottomans control over the Mediterranean. Barbarossa became infamous for his wars on the coasts of North Africa, Italy, and Dalmatia and was typically portrayed in the West as a pirate.

Suleyman offered support to Muslim countries threatened by European expansion because he believed that it was his duty as the defender of Islam to protect Muslims throughout the world. He used this duty, combined with his role as the protector and defender of the holy cities of Mecca and Medina, to declare himself Caliph of the World. He believed that this status gave him the right to annex and/or conquer nominally Muslim regions that were deemed by religious authorities to have abandoned orthodox beliefs or practices.

Suleyman's position as caliph not only marked him as a military defender of Islam and Muslims, but also meant that he had a responsibility to provide justice and protect the masses from the corruption of government officials. His place in history comes largely from his role as a lawgiver and provider of justice. He is sometimes referred to as the "second Solomon" of Islamic history in recognition of the fact that he was named for King Solomon of the Old Testament who was known for his wisdom in providing justice. Suleyman's reign is broadly considered to have marked the greatest harmony and justice in any Islamic state in history.

Suleyman's title "Kanuni" reflects his propagation of the *kanun* law, which is distinct from the Sharia, or Islamic law proper as found in the Quran and *Sunna* (example of the Prophet Muhammad). Originating in Turkish and Mongol traditions that considered the law pronounced by the monarch as sacred, the first *kanun* had been collected by Mehmed the Conqueror (r. 1451–1481). By 1501, the *kanun* had been set in fairly final form as a complete and independent set of laws. As the most important practical law in the empire, the *kanun*

addressed issues including the status, dress, and duties of functionaries; economic regulations; administrative and military matters; the disciplining of officials; the implementation of landholding and taxation systems; the organization of religious affairs; and criminal justice.

Suleyman was known as the Lawgiver not because he made major revisions to the legal code (although he made a few), but because the laws took their final form during his reign. No revisions were made after his rule. His main contribution was the compilation and organization of the criminal code by offenses, rather than penalties, between 1539 and 1541. This code contained all of the sections of the earlier criminal codes, combining them with other provisions.

During his forty-six years as sultan, Suleyman reconstructed Istanbul into a city befitting the status of the center of the empire and of Islamic civilization. New fountains, aqueducts, dams, bridges, public baths, caravanserai, botanical gardens, and religious schools were built. Sulayman's favorite and most talented architect and engineer, Sinan, designed and built a variety of monuments, mosques, and public buildings, many of which are still standing with little or no damage. Among the most important structures completed during Suleyman's reign are the Suleymaniye Mosque and annexes, the Sehzadebasi Mosque and establishments, the Sultan Selim Mosque and establishments, the Cihangir Mosque and Haseki establishments, and some baths built for his favorite and most influential wife, Roxalena/Hurrem Sultan. The Suleymaniye Mosque in particular is considered one of the greatest architectural achievements of Islam. Coffee-houses were introduced to Istanbul at this time and the Port of Golden Horn became a major port and source of surveillance. As caliph, Suleyman also replaced the mosaics on the outside of the Dome of the Rock in Jerusalem with tiles.

Suleyman was a major patron of the arts and scholarship, including visual art, music, literature, religious thought, and philosophy. Most of the cultural forms associated with the Ottoman Empire date from his reign, including miniature paintings. He had a palace studio that employed twenty-nine painters, half of whom were Europeans, to produce miniatures. A master goldsmith, Suleyman was recognized as an excellent poet. His court was considered on a par with, if not more magnificent than, the major courts in Europe of this time.

Suleyman died on September 6, 1566, during a war with Austria outside of Sziget in contemporary Romania. He was buried in the mausoleum complex of the Suleymaniye Mosque in Istanbul.

Further reading

Clot, Andre. *Suleiman the Magnificent*, trans. John Howe. Chicago: New Amsterdam Books, 1993

Inalcik, Halil. *The Ottoman Empire: The Classical Age, 1300–1600*. London and New York: Praeger Publications, 1973

Itzkowitz, Norman. *Ottoman Empire and Islamic Tradition*. Chicago and London: University of Chicago Press, 1972

Kunt, Metin and Christine Woodhead, eds. *Suleyman the Magnificent and his Age: The Ottoman Empire in the Early Modern World*. Reading, MA: Addison-Wesley, 1995

Lapidus, Ira M. "Sultanates and Gunpowder Empires," in *The Oxford History of Islam*, ed. John L. Esposito. New York: Oxford University Press, 1999

Peirce, Leslie P. *The Imperial Harem: Women and Sovereignty in the Ottoman Empire*. New York: Oxford University Press, 1993

Shaw, Stanford J. "Ottoman Empire," in *The Oxford Encyclopedia of the Modern Islamic World*, editor-in-chief John L. Esposito, vol. 3. New York: Oxford University Press, 1995

Video: *Conquerors: Suleyman the Magnificent*, The Discovery Channel

www.allaboutturkey.com – website with a variety of information about Turkey and Turkish history, including a biography of

Suleyman the Magnificent with links to his monuments and accomplishments www.osmanli700.gen.tr/english/ – Ottoman history website

H.R.H. Prince Sultan bin Salman bin Abd al-Aziz Al Saud (1956)

The first Muslim and Arab astronaut, Prince Sultan bin Salman bin Abd al-Aziz Al Saud has dedicated his life to the promotion of science, medical research, and the rights of the disabled. He has also made important contributions to reviving and appreciating Saudi urban heritage.

Prince Sultan was born on June 27, 1956, in Riyadh, Saudi Arabia. His father is the governor of the Riyadh region. He credits his parents with raising him in a household where public and charitable work and service were emphasized and expected.

Sultan attended elementary and secondary school in Riyadh. He earned a bachelor's degree in mass communications from the University of Denver and a master's degree in social and political science from the Maxwell School of Citizenship and Public Affairs at Syracuse University, Syracuse, NY.

A certified civil pilot in both Saudi Arabia and the United States since 1976, Sultan has served in the Royal Saudi Air Force as a colonel and fighter pilot (now retired). He trained at the King Faisal Air Force Academy in Riyadh from 1985 to 1986 and at the King Abd al-Aziz Airbase in Dhahran in 1990. He flew in the Gulf War of 1990–1991 as part of the Saudi Air Force contingent, participating in the defense of his country and the liberation of neighboring Kuwait. His service was recognized with the Participation in the Gulf War and the Liberation of Kuwait Medal, Second Class, from Kuwait and the Liberation of Kuwait Medal from the Saudi armed forces. He is certified as an airline transport pilot for multi-engine land jet aircraft G-1159, Lear Jet, and GIV, commercially for airplane single engine land and Glider Aero Tow, and privately for airplane single engine Sear, Rotorcraft-Helicopter, Jet Aircraft HS-125, and CE 500. He has nearly five thousand hours of flight time.

Sultan served as a payload specialist on the STS-51-G *Discovery* mission in 1985 as part of a seven-member international crew, which included American and French astronauts. His mission was to launch an Arabian communication satellite, the ARABSAT 1-B. He also conducted three scientific experiments designed by the Saudi Arabian King Fahd University of Petroleum and Minerals which provided data on the diffusion of gas in space; the behavior of oil and water when mixed in zero gravity using Saudi, Kuwaiti, and Algerian oil; and measuring the effects of weightlessness on the human body in space. The oil and water experiment provided important data on combating oil-spill pollution and improving oil-recovery techniques. In addition to his scientific work, Sultan also gave a guided tour of the shuttle's interior in Arabic, which was broadcast to Arab television viewers back on earth. He spent a total of 7.07 days in space, circling the earth 111 times on his 2.9 million-mile journey.

Sultan's activities in space were reported to have included recitation of the entire Quran and prayers for all of humanity. He was surprised by the media attention given to his private religious activities in space because his was a scientific, not a religious, mission. The media heard about his prayers when he sent a message through mission control to his mother to let her know that he was praying three times a day. (Although five daily prayers are the normal standard, the five can be combined into three during travel.) While in space, he prayed according to Florida time, performing the required prostrations in zero gravity by fastening his feet to the floor with assistance from his fellow crew members.

From a personal perspective, space travel and working with N.A.S.A. were the "opportunity of a lifetime" for Sultan. As a pilot, he appreciated the technological wonder of space travel and the view of Earth, "the Home Planet," from space. He described the view of the earth from space as being "like if you had built your house from the inside and had never seen it from the outside" (the traditional method of house construction in Saudi Arabia). The view gave him a new perspective on what it means for all of humanity to coexist on a single tiny planet, as well as new appreciation for the unprecedented power of hindsight today due to the cataloguing and accumulation of historical data, combined with the capacity for knowledge and communications. Most powerful of all was the realization that the political problems that seem so insurmountable on earth are impossible to see from space. Although all of the astronauts spent the first day identifying countries and areas they had visited, it proved impossible to maintain such a narrow vision of earth. As he said in a comment from space, "The first day or so we all pointed to our countries. The third or fourth day we were pointing to our continents. By the fifth day, we were aware of only one Earth." Mentally, none of the astronauts was able to focus on geographic borders by the end of the trip, despite their different backgrounds. Their new perspective of the most important element – a single Earth – made the crises on Earth seem as infinitesimal as the human beings living there, engaged in endless squabbles about boundaries and the distribution of resources. It imbued in Sultan a tremendous sense of responsibility for working to resolve the problems that threaten to destroy the Earth, as well as to ensure that all people are able to live productive, healthy lives. He returned inspired to pursue environmental causes and the development of science and research.

Sultan's space travel was a historic moment not only for the Arab and Muslim worlds, but also for developing countries, all of whom identified with his accomplishment and the arrival of the developing world into this most exclusive and technologically advanced form of science. He was widely decorated for his achievement, receiving not only the N.A.S.A. Space Flight Medal, a certificate of appreciation from the Lyndon B. Johnson Flight Center, and a resolution by the House of Representatives of the Massachusetts State House "commending on the Historical achievement as the first Saudi Arabian Astronaut to be launched into space" in 1985, but was decorated with medals and sashes from Saudi Arabia, Tunisia, Bahrain, Pakistan, Sudan, the United Arab Emirates, Lebanon, Oman, Qatar, Kuwait, Yemen, China, Iraq, Morocco, and Syria. France appointed him an Officier De La Legion D'Honneur and he was granted the keys to the County of Los Angeles and the City of Dallas in the United States. He received an Acknowledgment for Leading the Arabs into the Space Era from the American-Arab Anti-Discrimination Committee in the United States and was made a Commandeur de l'Ordre de la Grande Etoile de Djibouti. He also received an honorary doctorate in science from the King Fahd University of Petroleum and Minerals.

The historic flight was also an important moment for Saudi Arabia as a country. The launching of the satellite served as a validation of the country's scientific progress and the culmination of an enormous joint project reflecting the achievements of important national goals: increased investment in education, particularly at the university level; and the material development of the country. The entire team of scientists who participated in the launching of the satellite returned to Saudi Arabia to the accolades of crowds of people expressing their pride in the achievement. Sultan believes that this is the future Saudi Arabia needs to look to.

Particularly in the aftermath of 9/11 and the subsequent wars against terrorism, including on Saudi soil, Sultan retains hope that the philosophers, artists, architects, and scientists Saudi Arabia has produced will continue to propel the country forward constructively, rather than allowing it to fall into the hands of terrorists bent on destruction. On a global level, he believes that space offers an opportunity for different countries, cultures, and religions to find common ground for working together to the benefit of all.

Upon his return to Earth, Sultan became a founding member and served on the board of directors of the Association of Space Explorers, an international organization comprising all astronauts and cosmonauts who have traveled to space. He remains involved in the local development of a space program in Saudi Arabia, as well as in a variety of space programs in the United States and Europe, including the Association of Space Explorers, the British Interplanetary Society, the American Astronautical Society, the Young Astronauts Program (U.S.A.), National Space Society (U.S.A.), Space Studies Institute (U.S.A.), the Planetary Society (U.S.A.), and International Academy of Astronautics (France). He is also involved in organizations dedicated to air travel, including the Aircraft Owners and Pilot Association (U.S.A.) and the Saudi Aviation Club, which he founded and chairs. The Saudi Aviation Club is a national non-profit organization to introduce personal aviation to the young community and to encourage competitions. His other scientific activities include service as the head of the advisory committee for the construction of the Prince Salman Science Oasis Project for the Riyadh Science Foundation and as the honorary chairman of the board of directors of the Saudi Computer Society. He is a member of the National Geographic Society in the United States and the Saudi Geographical Society in Saudi Arabia.

Sultan has taken an active role in the preservation and development of Saudi history, heritage, and architecture. He established the Prince Sultan bin Salman Award for Built Heritage and served as the honorary president of the Al-Umran Saudi Association, which consists of specialists in the field of built environment and urbanism. He also founded al-Turath to preserve and develop the heritage of both Saudi Arabia and the broad Arab and Islamic heritage, both culturally and academically. The organization's activities include the collection of historical documents from around the world, particularly photographs, videos, and film footage of regions of Saudi Arabia and photographs of unknown travelers to the Arabian Peninsula for the National Archives for Historical Photographs. Al-Turath is active in the preservation of the architectural heritage of Saudi Arabia, encouraging the use of local materials in construction and documenting and renovating buildings and neighborhoods of historical value, most importantly the main old Hijaz railway station in Medina, the 1938 al-Murabaa palace, and the eighteenth-century mosque of Imam Saud bin Abd al-Aziz bin Muhammad. Al-Turath was also part of a team that proposed the development scope of work for the restoration of the town of al-Diri'yyah, which is important to both the political and religious history of Saudi Arabia as the seat of the Al Saud family. It publishes guides to areas and buildings of historical significance in the kingdom and books on Saudi history and heritage, as well as building models of old Saudi towns based on historical research.

In addition to his scientific and historical work, Sultan is an advocate for the disabled. Elected as the chairperson of the Disabled Children's Association in 1986, he highlights the association as an important model in Saudi Arabia because of its history of elections and institutionalized system of checks and balances between elected officials, supervising government ministries, and the board of directors, and continuity with Saudi political culture and social structures including consultation, discussion, and agreement. Business achievements of the organization include financial solvency, implementation of cost controls, encouragement of women's participation, and charitable endowment work, including the construction of the first human-engineered environmentally friendly office space in the Middle East. Concerned by the cultural tendency to hide the disabled as though they were something to be ashamed of, Sultan led a major public campaign to address their rights and needs and to use science to treat and prevent disabilities while educating and rehabilitating the disabled and their families.

Sultan's work with the disabled expanded in 1989 when he was reelected chairman of the Saudi Benevolent Association for Handicapped Children. In 1990, he was elected chairman of the Prince Salman Center for Disability Research, a project of the Disabled Children's Association that has grown to be the first independent national organization of its kind in the Middle East. Dedicated to becoming an international institution of excellence at the forefront of disability research on the global level, the center seeks to attract and train the highest-caliber research staff to engage in research covering the life span from birth to death in order to gain increased knowledge of illnesses and treatments, particularly the reduction and prevention of disabilities, and to improve the quality of life and opportunity for achievement of disabled people. Sultan also served as the chairman of the steering committee to work on a national code for the disabled, which was later passed into legislation, and has worked to bring media attention to disability in order to raise funds and set an example of how to build with charitable donations. He has been particularly supportive of low-cost but environmentally friendly buildings. He has worked internationally with the World Planning Group to Revise the Charter of the Disabled and is the founder and patron of the Prince Sultan bin Salman Prize for the Holy Quran for the Disabled Children.

Sultan's work for the disabled has received international recognition. *Al-Majallah* magazine named him Man of the Year for Benevolent Work in 1997. He received a certificate of recognition "for outstanding leadership and inspiration dedicated to improving the quality of life for the mentally and physically challenged" from Temple University's School of Podiatric Medicine in 1999. He currently serves as the minister of tourism in Saudi Arabia.

Further reading

Facey, William. *Back To Earth: Adobe Building in Saudi Arabia*. Riyadh: al-Turath in association with the London Centre of Arab Studies, 1997

Lawton, John and Patricia Moody. "A Prince in Space," *ARAMCO World*, vol. 37, no. 4, January/February 1986

"Play 'Space Card' Against Source of Islamic Terrorism," James Oberg, *Space News*, December 3, 2001

"Tradition is Modernity's Future," interview with H.R.H. Prince Sultan ibn Salman ibn 'Abd al-'Aziz, *ARAMCO World*, vol. 50, no. 4, July/August 1999

Interview with the author, December 6, 2003

www.dca.org.sa – website for the Disabled Children's Association

www.jsc.nasa.gov – N.A.S.A. website that keeps biographies of all N.A.S.A. astronauts

www.pscdr.org.sa – website for the Prince Salman Center for Disability Research

www.sct.gov.sa and wwww.sauditourism.gov.sa – websites for the Supreme Commission for Tourism

www.al-turath.com – website for al-Turath

Zainab Al-Suwaij (b. 1971)

Founder and executive director of the American Islamic Congress (A.I.C.) and the only woman to have participated in the uprising against Saddam Hussein in 1991, Zainab Al-Suwaij is a member of an American team charged with rebuilding the education system in Iraq.

Zainab Al-Suwaij was born in Basra, Iraq, in 1971, into a prominent Shii family claiming direct descent from the Prophet Muhammad. Her great-grandfather played a major role in shifting Iraqi Shiism from a literal interpretation of scripture to one that was more modern and context based. She was raised in the home of her grandfather, a leading religious cleric.

Although al-Suwaij was raised in a religious household, Iraq was an avowedly secular society. She learned to keep religion and politics separate as a matter of survival from her early childhood. She began wearing the hijab in the third grade as a reflection of her grandfather's position, but learned to keep her religious opinions and identity private so as not to provoke the ruling regime. Saddam Hussein was suspicious of Shiis because of their potential affiliation with Iran – an issue of national security during the 1980–88 Iran–Iraq War. Al-Suwaij learned the harsh necessity of not criticizing the government in the fourth grade when one of her classmates asserted that the Ayatollah Khomeini and Iran were not as terrible as the Iraqi government portrayed them to be. The girl, along with her entire family, disappeared from the neighborhood the next day. Al-Suwaij never saw them again. Similar situations occurred with the expulsion of families of Iranian origin and Iraqi Jews whose houses were subsequently taken over by government officials.

Al-Suwaij describes life under Saddam as harsh and restricted. People were unable to gather and openly discuss issues such as democracy, freedom, and civil society. Students were forced to participate in political demonstrations either supporting Saddam or denouncing Iran, Israel, and/or the United States. Those who refused to participate were beaten by police. Students were also pressured to join the ruling Ba'ath Party and to report on their parents' political views. Classroom instruction included the teaching of loyalty to Saddam and hatred of his enemies.

Al-Suwaij attended Karbala High School and holds a certificate in Islamic studies and Arabic literature from the Islamic Institute in Basra. She was denied her high-school diploma because she refused to join the Ba'ath Party. As a result, she was unable to go to college or get a job in Iraq. Having completed high school, she left to visit family in Kuwait in 1990 and was present during the invasion by Iraq. She personally witnessed the accompanying killing and destruction, including soldiers beating both men and women, zoo animals running in the streets, and the literal tearing apart of the country. She returned to Iraq just as the Allied bombing began.

Al-Suwaij holds the distinction of being the only female participant in the popular uprising against Saddam that was encouraged by President George Bush following the American victory in the Gulf War. Although she normally veils, she removed her headscarf and donned pants and boots to join with the men of Karbala in their quest for freedom. When the group was fired on by Saddam loyalists, Al-Suwaij was struck on the cheek by a bullet. Within a week, the popular uprising had liberated fifteen of the eighteen provinces in Iraq. Al-Suwaij helped treat wounded people at the hospital and liberate a prison filled with thousands of prisoners, including Iraqis, Kuwaitis, other Arabs, and Europeans. One of the prisoners showed her a torture chamber equipped with a human meat grinder into which were placed live prisoners who refused to confess their crimes against the government. There were also chemical baths in which people were dissolved, ovens, sexual torture chambers, and a variety of torture tools, including hooks, electrical wires, and nail-plucking devices.

Although American assistance had been promised to those leading the uprising, it did not materialize. As a result, the uprising failed and the majority of the participants, including many of Al-Suwaij's friends and neighbors, were executed. Her memories of the aftermath include seeing dogs chewing on the corpses of opponents that had deliberately been left in the streets to discourage would-be rebels. Not only was the uprising crushed, but Iraqis emerged from the experience bitter against and distrustful of the United States and its values. Fearing for her life, Al-Suwaij fled to Iraq's border with Jordan where she went into hiding for two months. She eventually bribed a border guard into overlooking her name on a blacklist and crossed into Jordan.

Al-Suwaij left Jordan for the United States in 1992. She enrolled at Gateway College in New Haven, CT, where she earned a bachelor's degree. She became the first woman in her family to work while living in the United States and has been a teaching fellow in Arabic at Yale University. She has maintained her personal tradition of wearing the hijab, although her husband does not believe it necessary for her to wear it. She believes that every woman should be free to make her own choice about the hijab.

Al-Suwaij's new life in the United States provided her with first-hand experience of freedom, diversity, and tolerance. She has described 9/11 as a watershed for her because she saw the terror she thought she had left behind in Iraq follow her to the United States and threaten her children and friends. Fearful that her new-found freedom, safety, and peace would become casualties of growing hatred and suspicion of Muslims in the United States, she founded the American Islamic Congress (A.I.C.) in November, 2001 to lead American Muslims in rejecting Islamic radicalism, promoting democracy in the Muslim world, and building tolerance, peace, and interfaith and interethnic understanding in support of pluralism, diversity, and the rights of minorities. The A.I.C. has particularly called on American Muslims to defend and promote the rights of Muslims abroad, including the building of civil society, free labor unions, fair courts, and schools that teach tolerance. She believes that immigrant Muslims have a particularly important role to play because they have personal experience of life without freedom of speech and freedom of the press, as well as state control over everything from the school systems to the preaching of hatred.

Al-Suwaij has used her position with A.I.C. as a platform for writing opinion pieces, helping bureaucrats at Boston's City Hall to grapple with the post-9/11 issue of Arab racial profiling, lecturing at schools, and imploring the American Muslim community to police itself against radicalism. She has appeared on C.N.N., regularly grants newspaper interviews, and writes editorials and articles about Iraq, Muslim women, and Islam. She was a leading voice in the Iraqi expatriate support for the American toppling of the Saddam Hussein regime because of her personal experiences of growing up under that regime and her participation in the failed uprising of 1990. In response to anti-war critics, she noted that years of diplomacy did not bring about tangible results for the people of Iraq who continued to suffer under Saddam's regime throughout the Clinton administration. She argues that her stance was supportive of the innocent people of Iraq because it addressed the "real situation" there, noting that Saddam had not hesitated to use chemical weapons against his own people. In a meeting with President Bush in April, 2003, she implored him not to let the Iraqi people down a second time if he promised them freedom.

Saddam's ouster brought mixed feelings for Al-Suwaij. Although she was relieved that the regime was finally out of power, she felt overwhelmed by the work required to rebuild the country. Observing that Iraq is a multireligious and multiethnic society, she has called for tolerance and respect for diversity, as well as the separation of religion and state, as the keys to rebuilding a peaceful and cohesive society. She believes that national unity will be possible post-Saddam because all religions and ethnicities suffered under and were persecuted by him when they did not support him.

As part of the rebuilding process, Al-Suwaij was appointed by President Bush to serve on a team funded by the U.S. Agency for International Development to rebuild Iraqi schools and redesign the national curriculum to teach skills ranging from math and writing to free thinking. Recognizing the vital role schools play in the functioning of civil society, the team has worked to make schools centers for social and health services, such as vaccination, health education, and nutritional assistance, as well as academic institutions.

The team began by surveying about four-and-a-half thousand schools across Iraq, compiling an inventory and building a database of the number of students and teachers, as well as the assets and facilities at each school. They found that most of the schools were in desperate need of physical rehabilitation – particularly functioning bathrooms. They then surveyed the children who were not in school, often because they had gone to work to support their families. This involved meeting with the parents, trying to help them understand the importance of education, and encouraging them to have their children return to school. In recognition of the need to help children who have fallen behind their age groups, the team set up a series of centers for accelerated learning projects, such as providing two years of schooling in a single year, with the goal of rematriculating the students into their regular schools. The final step was the overhaul of the curriculum and rebuilding of the schools. Recalling her school days when images of Saddam Hussein and the Ba'ath Party were omnipresent in textbooks for every topic studied from math to art, such as ordering students to draw pictures of war or the government, learning to count AK-47 assault rifles, and solving word problems referring to Saddam, Al-Suwaij was adamant that both the Saddam personality cult and the military themes had to end. The A.I.C. has helped to train more than thirty-three thousand teachers. New science and math curricula supplied by U.N.I.C.E.F. have also been implemented.

Al-Suwaij's work in Iraq has also included the empowerment of Iraqi women. Although Iraqi women in general are well educated, they have been crushed between political and religious parties, culture, and tradition. Although Al-Suwaij has found that they want to participate and speak out, they are often ignored and prevented from playing a role in the building of Iraq's future. Her own experience of freedom of thought and expression in the United States has made her determined to help Iraqi women participate in all aspects of society. She has arranged workshops and training seminars for women in Iraq, called for the development of women's organizations, and has spoken to American leaders about the importance of involving Iraqi women in Iraq's reconstruction. She has also taken her message of the right of women to participate in government and society to the grassroots level. When visiting her grandfather in Basra, she often goes out to sit with poor women and talks to them about their rights as wives, mothers, daughters, and citizens.

In all of her work, Al-Suwaij sees reason for optimism. She believes that the presence of Iraqi-Americans is most critical to the ultimate success of the reconstruction because of the assistance they can provide in helping Iraqis establish a free press, gain technology, open doors to education and cooperation between universities, help build labor unions, help people write about and publish their experiences under the Saddam regime, and establish artistic and musical groups. At the same time, she cautions that the psychological damage of the Saddam era will take longer to address, in large part because of the national period of self-questioning and self-definition that has taken place since the overthrow of the regime. Although she finds her lengthy absences from her children difficult, she feels obligated to help to create a safe and free future for all Iraqi children.

Further reading

Cassidy, Tina. "Keeping Up the Fight," *Boston Globe*, April 7, 2003

"The Opportunity Before Us: A Conversation with Zainab Al-Suwaij," Ethics and Public Policy Center event, April 4, 2003

Pappano, Laura. "Rebuilding Iraqi Schools Lets U.S.-Led Team Rewrite History," *Boston Globe*, May 11, 2003

Al-Suwaij, Zainab. "Op-Ed," *Wall Street Journal*, September 11, 2002

Interview with the author, November 11, 2003

www.aicongress.org – website for American Islamic Congress

www.womenforiraq.org – for projects on which Al-Suwaij has worked

T

Azam Taleghani (b. c. 1945)

Politician and Islamic feminist, Azam Taleghani represents the rising trend among Iranian women of working within the religious framework of the Islamic Republic for the expansion of women's rights and access to public space.

Azam Taleghani was born in Tehran, Iran, around 1945. Her father, Ayatollah Mahmoud Taleghani, was one of the most progressive and famous Iranian clerics in the twentieth century. A strong supporter of women's rights, he was not a political figure. He was concerned about the potential for despotism under Ayatollah Khomeini and the Islamic Republic, and died under suspicious circumstances in 1980.

Taleghani was taught by her father to think for herself, argue and claim and use her rights. Although she starting wearing the chador (full-length covering) when she was six years old, she discarded it as a young woman. When she confronted her father with her actions, he told her that she had the right to make up her own mind about the veil. She ultimately chose to resume wearing it several years before the revolution, and has worn it ever since.

Taleghani has a long history of political activism geared toward challenging the status quo. Before the Islamic Revolu-

tion, she was a clandestine distributor of anti-shah literature, for which she served a two-year prison sentence. After the revolution, her anti-shah activism earned her political legitimacy and revolutionary credentials that helped her to win a seat in the Majlis (parliament). She was one of three women elected to the body of 217 members. In 1980, she represented Iran at the United Nations Conference on Women held in Thailand.

With the support of the Khomeini regime, Taleghani became the head of the Women's Society of the Islamic Revolution, which was formed to encourage women's support of the new order. The post-Revolutionary period set the foundation for a religiously oriented regime to take power, partially by insisting on a separation between the family and civil society and by returning women to the more traditional roles of caregiver and mother within the family and professions supporting those roles, such as nursing, teaching, and sewing. Women were barred from the judiciary, singing, engineering, and agriculture and were segregated from men in institutions of higher education. Compulsory veiling was introduced to nurture and preserve Islamic morality and modesty, while the concept of women's rights was delegitimized as a Western and un-Islamic development. Secular women were removed from public positions, particularly in political institutions.

Although these measures were strongly supported by conservative men, women were not as accepting, not only because they were directly affected by the measures, but also because women had played an important role in the revolution and the formation of the new nation. They were concerned by the fact that, despite their contributions to the revolution's success, no woman had participated in the framing of the new constitution, women's issues were left largely unaddressed in light of the need to stabilize the country, and women were generally treated as objects of state policy, rather than participants in its formulation. The Islamic feminist movement, of which Taleghani is a part, has its origins in this formative period because it was at this time that women's equality and rights were curtailed in favor of traditional, conservative, and often literal interpretations of Islam. Taleghani herself, while supporting the implementation of Islamic law, cautioned authorities against compulsory veiling and spoke out against the stoning of women for adultery. Over time, Islamic feminists began to use the compulsory veil as a means of empowerment by demanding access to public space for women who obeyed the dress code.

As a member of the Islamic feminist movement, Taleghani has worked to fight discrimination and prejudice against women, as well as women's relative powerlessness under the new regime. Working in conjunction with secular feminists, the Islamic feminists have reinterpreted and presented modern ideas through religious language and a religiously inspired and guided worldview, while questioning the logic of gender segregation and the traditional Islamic model of the family, denouncing violence against women, and calling for reforms of discriminatory laws. Together, the secular and Islamic feminists have supported legal reforms, been active in the women's print media, and called for women's access to work in the government and media. In the process, they have met with resistance from conservatives who fear the erosion of both the previously unquestionable authority of clerics and the traditional family unit.

Taleghani took center stage in the discussion about the appropriate place for women in 1997 when she declared herself a candidate for the presidency of Iran. She was the first woman to do so since the revolution. Although she did not expect to be elected or to be taken as a serious candidate, she sought to raise the issue of a woman's right to hold the office and its compatibility with Islamic teachings, as well as to raise awareness of the gap between the state's theoretical proclamation of equality between men and women and the practical reality as lived out in Iran. Taleghani's candidacy was based on the premise that the constitution specifies that only a *rejal* can run for president. Fluent in both Arabic and Farsi, Taleghani argued that, although *rejal* in Arabic refers to men, in Farsi (the language spoken in Iran) it is a more generic term for the political elite. Because she had served as a member of the political elite in the past, she believed that she had a right to run for office. She further noted that, although the constitution does not specify that women are qualified to be political leaders, women have served in the Majlis since the revolution. She believes that women should serve as political leaders because the Quran teaches that society, groups, and individuals are responsible for changing themselves in order to achieve social change and because, in her opinion, Muslim women are particularly sensitive to the reality of what it means to bear the burden of morality for an entire society given that women are the culture bearers of Islam.

To bolster her claim, Taleghani sought the opinions of religious scholars in Qom and Tehran who had helped to draft the 1979 constitution. Serious debate about the terminology ensued in religious circles and led to split opinions. Although some clerics believed that *rejal* had to mean men, thus barring women from the presidency, others found Taleghani's interpretation to be correct, making men and women equally eligible for the position. Still others allowed theoretically for the possibility of women serving as judges, clerics or Supreme Leader, but not as president. Taleghani's candidacy was vehemently opposed by conservative clerics who were upset that she dared to raise the issue. One ayatollah informed her that the presidency was too high-level and high-pressure for a woman to handle because of the strain it would place on her nerves. As a mother of four who was imprisoned by the shah when her children were young, the primary caregiver to a severely disabled child, and someone who has always worked for a living, Taleghani noted the absurdity of the argument in her case, commenting that her nerves had already withstood a great deal of pressure. Her candidacy also sparked an important debate among Iranian women. The feminist magazine *Zanan* featured a series of articles addressing the "natural" and "Islamic" right of women to head government offices.

In the end, Taleghani's candidacy, like those of most potential candidates, was disqualified. However, she believes that she won a major victory because she was not disqualified on the basis of her gender. Rather, she was not considered a sufficiently religious or political personality for the job. She believes that this sets an important precedent because it proves that a woman can run for president. She then tried to run for the Majlis in 2000, as she has tried to do in every election cycle since her term, but was rejected by the Guardian Council. Again, her disqualification was concern over her affiliation with the Freedom Movement her father had co-founded in opposition to the shah, rather than her gender.

Taleghani has taken her activism in religious reinterpretation to the grassroots level. She runs a small clothing-making business in Tehran that also serves as a night school for women to read and interpret the Quran. She opened the school out of frustration that seminaries in Qom, the religious heart of Iran, were exclusively for men. Opening the school was her way of providing women with the intellectual tools to succeed in the republic, as well as to insert themselves into religious interpretation.

Taleghani also founded and directs the Islamic Women's Institute of Iran, which works to improve the status and standard of living for Iranian women by implementing income-generating projects, providing legal counseling, conducting literacy and training programs and assisting women in entrepreneurial ventures. It also seeks to end violence of all types against women, including rape, prostitution, domestic violence, and the smuggling of women and girls; has called for the development of a legal system that protects and advises women; and engages in research on women's employment, family legal and economic conflicts, and the difficulties facing housewives.

In addition to her political and religious campaigns, Taleghani has engaged in human rights activism, including an address to the United Nations Commission on Human Rights in April, 2003 and the staging of a sit-in in front of Evin prison in August, 2003 to protest the treatment of political prisoners.

Since the early 1980s, Taleghani has published the weekly newspaper *Payam-e Hajar*. Initially supported by the new Islamic state to politicize and publicize Islamic feminine virtues, the paper has evolved into a voice for Islamic feminism, challenging patriarchal and clerical interpretations of Islam that promote male supremacy in favor of a feminist interpretation of the Quran that seeks to change the culture, norms, and guidelines of power and morality in order to increase women's access to public space and insert women's voices into both the decision-making process and the official interpretation of religion. *Payam-e Hajar* has particularly promoted the idea that the reinterpretation of religious texts can serve as the basis for the revision of laws affecting women while providing for their daily needs.

Taleghani is an important symbol for Iranian women because she represents a small elite group of women with impeccable revolutionary and Islamic credentials who are working for change in Iran from within the system. She has received death threats from both conservative elements and vigilantes, but remains an active participant in the reinterpretation of Islam in Iran through a variety of activities.

Further reading

Gheytanchi, Elham. "Post-Revolutionary Iran: Islamic Feminism and the Crisis of Civil Society," www.sscnet.ucla.edu/soc/groups/ccsa/gheytanchi.htm

Kar, Mehranguiz. "Women's Strategies in Iran from the 1979 Revolution to 1999," in *Globalization, Gender, and Religion: The Politics of Women's Rights in Catholic and Muslim Contexts*, ed. Jane H. Bayes and Nayereh Tohidi. New York: Palgrave, 2001

Mahdi, Ali Akbar. "Iranian Women: Between Islamization and Globalization," in *Iran Encountering Globalization: Problems and Prospects*, ed. Ali Mohammadi. London and New York: Routledge/Curzon, 2003

Mir-Hosseini, Ziba. *Islam and Gender: The Religious Debate in Contemporary Iran.* Princeton: Princeton University Press, 1999

Moghadam, Valentine S. "The Two Faces of Iran: Women's Activism, the Reform Movement, and the Islamic Republic," in *Nothing Sacred: Women Respond to Religious Fundamentalism and Terror*, ed. Betsy Reed. New York: Thunder's Mouth Press, 2002

Sciolino, Elaine. *Persian Mirrors: The Elusive Face of Iran.* New York: Simon & Schuster, 2000

www.unhcr.ch – website for U.N. Commission on Human Rights

www.zan.org – provides news on women's issues in Iran in English

Tayyibah Taylor (b. 1952)

Editor-in-chief of *Azizah* magazine, the first American magazine published by Muslim women for Muslim women, Tayyibah Taylor is a leader in reshaping the image of Muslim women in the media.

Tayyibah Taylor was born in San Fernando, Trinidad, in 1952. Her parents were both natives of Barbados. Her father worked as a chemist for the Texaco oil refineries in Trinidad. Her mother was a full-time mother and homemaker. As a child, Taylor lived in Trinidad, Barbados, and Toronto, Canada.

Taylor was raised in a practicing Christian home and attended church regularly several times a week. Her first encounter with Islam occurred during high school when she was studying world history and world religions. She pursued her interest in religions, particularly Islam, in her studies at the University of Toronto. As a college student, she underwent the kind of self-questioning and reflection that were hallmarks of youth in the 1960s. Concerned with exploring the universe and her place in it, she dropped out of the university and returned to Barbados for a year. It was during this time that she "found herself" in Islam and made the conscious decision to change herself. Taylor describes the change as both physical and spiritual. She left Toronto in a pair of short shorts with a big Afro and a bohemian look. She returned wearing a long, flowing dress and with her hair wrapped and covered.

Shortly after her return to Toronto, Taylor married a professional basketball player and moved first to Texas and then to Seattle where she set the foundations for an Islamic school. Following retirement, her husband became a coach for the Saudi Arabian basketball team. They lived in Jeddah, Saudi Arabia, for six-and-a-half years, where Taylor gained first-hand experience of gender segregation and limitations on her personal freedoms, such as not being allowed to drive. At the same time, she encountered a diversity of Islamic practices that demonstrated how people can be sincere in their faith despite interpreting it in a variety of ways. Her studies of the Quran and Arabic at King Abd al-Aziz University had a profound influence on her faith and her appreciation of diversity within unity. The women with whom she studied came from a variety of national backgrounds and differed in some of their rituals, yet Taylor found them to be equal in their piety and in their striving for God-consciousness.

After their return to Seattle, Taylor and her husband divorced. A mother of five, Taylor began teaching at the Islamic school she had helped to found for several years and eventually became its administrator. She worked at the school until 1999 when she moved to Atlanta, GA. While working at the school, she began to think about a magazine for Muslim women that would bring together Islam, women's issues, and communication.

Taylor's upbringing in Canada and subsequent move to the United States had made her aware of the power of the media in creating images and impressions. As a child in Toronto, she had noticed that there were no people of color in the media, in textbooks or on billboards. Their only presence was in the race riots broadcast from the United States, meaning that the only public images she had of people of color were negative. This reinforced the internalization of a feeling of inferiority. Her discovery of *Ebony* magazine at the age of twelve marked her first encounter with positive public images of people of color, helping her to realize that they were not "bad" people.

Taylor realized that Muslims, particularly women, shared this problem of having only negative images of themselves. She found that Muslim women were portrayed by the media as voiceless nonentities or terrorists, dressed entirely in black, and Arab, making them people to pity, hate, or suppress. Her goal with *Azizah* was to present a more positive and accurate image of Muslim women, both visually and through articles, all of which were to be written by Muslim women, with the ultimate goal of demonstrating Muslim women as active agents, rather than as objects of someone else's analysis.

Taylor founded *Azizah* magazine in 2001 as "a tool for empowerment." Its readership of about 25,000 includes both men and women, public and university libraries. A typical issue includes feature articles highlighting American Muslim women in a variety of professions; a feature article on a major social issue of interest, such as family dynamics, financial investments, and legal rights in the workplace; poetry; book reviews; fiction; recipes; articles on religious issues, home interior decorating, travel, health, sports, and fashion; and advertisements for everything from Islamic investment services to Islamic fashions. By showing the national, ethnic, and racial diversity of American Muslim women and their choice of dress, covering everything from Western dress to traditional, loose-fitting clothing to uniforms, with some women veiled and others not, *Azizah* demonstrates that there is no single way that Muslim women dress, not all Muslim women are Arabs, and some do not choose to identify themselves as Muslim through their clothing because they consider their faith to be a private matter.

Although *Azizah* targets Muslim women, Taylor believes that it can also help to shatter the negative stereotypes of Muslim women often held by non-Muslims and to educate the American public about Islam and Muslim women, particularly post-9/11. For many non-Muslims, *Azizah* marks their first positive encounter with American Muslim women as they define themselves. It is consciously American Muslim in presentation because Taylor wants to show the empowerment that the American legacy of critical thinking and freedom of movement and being gives to women. She hopes that the combination of this American legacy with Islam's encouragement for the pursuit of knowledge and autonomy will inspire American Muslim women to become more involved in community activities and American culture.

Taylor takes her role as a media leader seriously, believing that she has a responsibility to create an appetite for substantive issues and discussions, rather than feeding appetites that she believes degrade women, such as representing women only as physical bodies and emphasizing sexual gymnastics as the best means for catching men. She focuses instead on connecting Muslim women to each other, giving them their own voices, and highlighting female Muslim accomplishment in order to encourage other Muslim women to break out of their own physical and mental boundaries to seek their own accomplishments. Although many Muslim men and women support and applaud this approach, there are others who object to Taylor's work because they believe that good, pious Muslim women should be silent and invisible. Some have expressed concern that focusing on Muslim women in American public life could lead American Muslim women to neglect their roles as wives and mothers. Still others are disturbed by the photographs, fearing that featuring attractive women, sometimes wearing make-up – although frequently they are veiled – could lead to sexual desire on the part of men viewing the magazine.

Taylor responds to these criticisms by noting that the photographs are necessary to *Azizah*'s goal of encouraging Muslim women to better themselves intellectually, physically, and spiritually and to contribute to their communities by providing self-affirmation among them. Because *Azizah*'s purpose is to reflect who American Muslim women are, rather than what some people might want them to be, showing them in their diversity of races, ethnicities, and styles of dress is necessary. Finally, she has commented that one of *Azizah*'s most important purposes is to encourage critical thinking. She has deliberately chosen controversial topics in order to discuss them from a variety of perspectives and to demonstrate that there is no single opinion or "correct" answer on the topic.

In the aftermath of 9/11 in which negative stereotyping of Muslims, limitations of Muslim civil rights, and hate crimes against Muslims have become more frequent and pronounced, Taylor believes that *Azizah*'s work in presenting accurate information, critical thinking, and a variety of perspectives is more important than ever. She is particularly concerned that the prevalence of negative stereotyping of Muslims not only tends to internalize feelings of inferiority among Muslims, but also sends a message to the majority population of America that it is okay to dominate, feel superior to, ridicule, and even inflict harm upon Muslims, particularly Muslim women who are often easy targets because of their dress. Taylor has denounced the use of images of Muslim women in both the United States and abroad not only to fulfill political agendas, but also to prove how "Islamic" a government's rule is or is not. She believes that such use does not reflect women's interests or needs.

Taylor has called upon Muslims to continue to develop their own media, through journalism, magazines, and television, so as to make their voices heard and to take control over their image in America. She believes that the time has come for Muslims to be participants in, rather than spectators of, their own destiny.

Further reading

Jones, Vanessa E. "One Faith, Many Faces," Boston Globe, April 19, 2003

El-Mosli, Samia. "Azizah Rising," ARAMCO World, vol. 55, no. 2, March/April 2004

Taylor, Tayyibah. "How Media Forms Perceptions," Keynote address to Muslim Women's League, 2003

—— "Praises in the Sky," Azizah magazine, winter 2002

Interview with author, July 7, 2003

www.azizahmagazine.com – website for Azizah magazine

Richard Thompson (b. 1949)

An accomplished electric and accoustic guitar player and songwriter, Richard Thompson has been a prominent musician on the alternative music scene since the late 1960s.

Richard Thompson was born on April 3, 1949, in West London, England. His father was a military veteran who also worked as a policeman. His mother was a housekeeper. Thompson was born into a family of broad musical tastes, including jazz, early rock, rhythm and blues, and the traditional music of the United Kingdom, particularly Scottish folk and bagpipe music.

Thompson began school at the age of five. Always artistic, he enjoyed painting and reading literature and poetry. He earned the highest marks in his school in junior high and attended the prestigious William Ellis School for high school.

Thompson began playing the guitar when he was ten years old. He learned by ear, from friends, and by taking classical guitar lessons that helped him to develop his technique. He had mastered fingering and chords by the time he was twelve, roughly the same time he received his first electric guitar. He began playing in bands with his peers during his last year of high school, including with a group known as Emil and the Detectives. It was also during this time that he began writing songs. He had his first serious engagement at his sister's birthday party when he was sixteen years old.

Thompson has always been known for having his own style and playing what he wants to play, rather than focusing on what is commercially successful or pleasing to his audience. He came into friction with his father over this tendency in his early years, a tension that was exacerbated by his decision to pursue a professional musical career, rather than going to college. He completed his exams and then worked as an apprentice for a local design partnership making mosaics and stained glass.

Thompson first came to public attention in his role as a founding member of the folk-rock band Fairport Convention in 1967. One of the first groups to feature material by Joni Mitchell, Fairport made its debut supporting Pink Floyd and created a name for itself through a series of live performances. In his early years, Thompson was a shy performer who hid behind the amplifiers and was weak on vocals. However, his guitar playing attracted the attention of American producer Joe Boyd, who engineered the band's first self-titled album, featuring folk, jazz, and instrumentals. Popularly dubbed "the new Jefferson Airplane," Fairport was particularly recognized for its lyrics.

Fairport took on a stronger folk orientation in 1968 with the addition of vocalist Sandy Denny. It was also at this time that Thompson began to introduce his songs to the group, including one of their most famous – "Meet on the Ledge" – written when he was still a teenager. He quickly became recognized for his ability to compose contemporary songs that drew upon traditional genres, particularly English folk ballads. His status as a songwriter was solidified on the 1969 album What we Did on our Holidays, which included Fairport's biggest hit, "Si Tu Dois Partir," which reached number twenty-one on the U.K. singles chart in 1969 and brought Richard his only Top of the Pops appearance.

By 1969, Fairport had moved toward electric folk music and was playing a variety of live gigs. One gig ended in tragedy when the van driver fell asleep and the car ran off a hill, killing drummer Martin Lamble and Thompson's girlfriend, Jeannie Franklyn, in whose memory he composed the song "Never Again." A variety of benefit concerts were held by groups such as Pink Floyd and Yes to help Fairport recover. In shock following the accident, Thompson made his American debut at the Troubadour in Los Angeles, CA. Although Fairport was uncertain what the future held, the U.K. edition of *Rolling Stone* magazine considered Fairport sufficiently newsworthy to place them on the October 1969 front cover.

Fairport turned a new musical corner with the addition of fiddler Dave Swarbrick and the recording of its best-selling album *Liege & Lief*, which marked Fairport as the first English band to make English folk-rock a success. Considered a milestone in defining British rock, the album sold 100,000 copies. Although it marked the band's split with the departure of Sandy Denny in 1970, the album brought Fairport to the attention of other folk artists, including Odetta and Linda Ronstadt. The combination of Thompson's guitar playing with Swarbrick's fiddle became a hallmark of Fairport's live performances. Thompson and Swarbrick wrote only a handful of songs together, but those songs shaped two major Fairport albums and are considered among the group's finest.

Despite Fairport's success, which included an American debut tour with Traffic and Crosby, Stills, Nash, and Young, Thompson decided to leave the group to pursue a solo career as a guitarist. His debut solo album, *Henry the Human Fly*, appeared in 1971. Although his fans consider it a classic that established his solo talent, it was Warner Brothers' lowest-selling album of all time at about fifteen thousand copies worldwide.

During the 1970s, Thompson found increasing musical success and personal happiness. In 1972, he married folk singer Linda Peters with whom he went on to record six albums. He toured extensively, received good musical reviews, and saw his record royalties rise. The Thompsons released one of their most important albums together in 1974: *I Want to See the Bright Lights Tonight*. Although it sold only 15,000 copies in the United States, the album is considered a Thompson masterpiece, reflecting uniquely pre-punk English rock and roll. The title track earned Thompson a U.K. hit single. The album was voted eighty-sixth best album of the past twenty years by *Rolling Stone* in 1987 and made number seventy on the list of 100 Greatest Albums Ever Made by *Mojo* magazine in 1995.

Despite the couple's musical success, Thompson remained filled with emptiness. In 1973, he discovered Sufism, the mystical interpretation of Islam, finding in it a joining of spirituality with discipline, self-confirmation, a sense of purpose, and a solid grounding from which to face an increasingly materialistic world. The Thompsons' conversion was reflected in their 1975 album *Pour Down Like Silver*, which featured them wearing Islamic attire and included Islamic references and lyrics. Dedicated to following the Islamic lifestyle preached by their sheikh, the Thompsons moved into an Islamic commune in 1976. They made the Hajj pilgrimage and adhered to a strict and often austere lifestyle.

Musically, the conversion to Islam led to the Thompsons' absence from the music scene between 1975 and 1978. The one exception was Thompson's 1976 instrumental release, *Guitar, Vocal*, which received critical acclaim. His dedicated to his new faith led to a general loss of interest in music, despite having been listed on *Zig Zag*'s 1975 British Guitarist Poll as second only to Eric Clapton and ahead of Jimmy Page, Paul Kossoff, and

Keith Richard. He gave up his electric guitar in favor of accoustic.

Although they remained dedicated to their faith, the Thompsons left the commune in 1978. Determined to recover his career, Thompson experimented with Arabic and Islamic texts in his songwriting. Their first post-commune album, *First Light*, reflected a greater attempt to be commercial, but was not very successful, selling less than twenty thousand copies. Thompson returned to his prior approach to music – writing and performing what he wanted to write and perform, rather than focusing on commercial success. The result was what is considered the Thompsons' best album together, *Shoot out the Lights*, released in 1982. The album sold about a hundred and twenty thousand copies.

Shoot out the Lights earned the Thompsons major attention in both the U.K. and the U.S., resulting in their first – and last – American tour together. *Rolling Stone* listed it as the ninth-best album of the 1980s and the twenty-fourth-best record released during the magazine's history. Thompson had a successful solo tour in 1981 that led to his acclamation as Rock's Best-Kept Secret by *Rolling Stone* for his guitar playing. A joint tour in 1982 was considered a musical success that included some of Linda's best performances, but was personally difficult and painful for both as it marked the end of their marriage and musical partnership.

Thompson's first post-Linda album was *Hand of Kindness*, released in 1984. He was always interested in experimenting with new musical forms, and the album introduced a brass section with saxophones trading solos with Thompson's guitar. Considered by fans to be a goodbye to Linda and an apology for the heartache, the album sold only half as well as *Shoot out the Lights*.

By 1986, alternative music had become more popular in the United States and Thompson had become a bigger name. By

then married to American Nancy Covey, he ventured into composing film tracks for a few years, most notably for *Sweet Talker* in 1991.

In 1991, Thompson was invited by Bob Dylan to participate in the Guitar Greats celebration in Seville, Spain. The same year brought the release of Thompson's best-selling album *Rumor & Sigh*, which sold about two hundred and fifty thousand copies worldwide and resulted in a major tour. The album earned Thompson a Grammy nomination for Best Alternative Music Album and included his most famous and most requested song, "1952 Vincent Black Lightning." A traditional ballad with a decidedly modern (motorcyle) theme that includes Appalachian-style guitar playing, "1952 Vincent Black Lightning" is frequently at the top of internet polls and college radio station "most requested song" lists. It reached number thirty-two on the U.S. charts. The album was declared one of the Best of the Year by *Q* magazine, which also awarded Thompson its Best Songwriter Award in 1991.

The 1990s brought Thompson a partnership with fellow Muslim musician Danny Thompson. They recorded *The Industrial Project* together as a tribute to the Industrial Revolution and the social issues it raised through the decline in the mining industry in Britain. The album served as the basis for a 1997 B.B.C. documentary on the Industral Revolution. Thompson also began to release "official" live recordings during the 1990s, as well as a boxed set covering his thirty years of musicianship, *Watching the Dark*, and a double album – *you?me?us?* – that included one disc for accoustic guitar and one disc for electric guitar. Releases of Greatest Hits albums followed, including *Best of Richard & Linda Thompson – The Island Record Years* in 2000 and *Action Packed – The Best of the Capitol Years* in 2001.

By 1999, Thompson was considered a sufficiently important musician for

Playboy magazine to ask him to submit a list of what he considered to be the ten greatest songs of the millenium. Although *Playboy* then declined to publish the list, the project was picked up by the Getty Museum, which asked him to contribute "something out of the ordinary" to a concert series. The result was the beginning of Thompson's popular 1,000 Years of Popular Music live tour in which he engages in a music history lesson with his listeners. He includes pieces like "Barbara Allen," a perennial favorite with folk clubs and schools, and Gilbert and Sullivan pieces in his performances. Although the songs are not as well known as other ballads such as "Greensleeves," Thompson believes that his selections have merit because the songs themselves serve as the stars. He also notes the universality and timelessness of the themes of his chosen pieces: love, lost love, death, and the fleeting joys of life.

The timeless and universal themes of these songs are directly related to Thompson's own goals as a lyricist. He has consciously sought to continue the historical tradition of using music to provide entertainment, news, and bedtime stories and to address political and social concerns, particularly the need to heal and diffuse contentious issues such as racism. He is one of the few contemporary musicians apart from rap artists to do so. He has stated that he writes about the larger concerns of life and the extremes of human nature because these are the experiences that resonate with all people. Although he acknowledges that many of his songs are based on observations that have angered or upset him, particularly the decay of social values, he insists that he always sets out to write fiction. Over the course of his career, he has written nearly three hundred songs, including both lyrics and music.

Thompson's lengthy career includes playing support for artists such as Suzanne Vega, REM, Randy Newman, Bonnie Raitt, and Crowded House, while receiving tribute from artists including REM, Bonnie Raitt, Los Lobos, David Byrne, June Tabor, Martin Carthy, Maddy Prior, Syd Straw, the Blind Boys of Alabama, and Bob Mould who performed cover versions of Thompson's songs in the 1995 album *Beat the Retreat*. His songs have been performed by Emmy Lou Harris, Nancy Griffith, Lee Konitz, the Golden Palominos, Loudon Wainwright III, and David Byrne of Talking Heads. He appeared at the 2002 Cropredy Festival to commemorate the thirty-fifth anniversary of Fairport Convention. He reunited with his ex-wife, Linda, to appear with her on an album that also starred their son Adam. In 2003, *Rolling Stone* named Thompson number nineteen on its list of the top hundred guitar players in pop music.

Further reading

Heylin, Clinton. *Gypsy Love Songs and Sad Refrains: The Recordings of Richard Thompson and Sandy Denny*. Manchester: Labour of Love Productions, 1989

Humphries, Patrick. *Richard Thompson: The Biography*. New York: Schirmer Books, 1997

Menin, Bruce. "October Ends with a Visit from British Folk-Rocker Richard Thompson," *Merrimack River*, October 24, 2003

The Rolling Stone Index: Twenty-Five Years of Popular Culture, 1967–1991. Ann Arbor, MI: Popular Culture, Ink, 1993

Thompson, Richard. "My Favourite Songs of the Past 1,000 Years," *The Guardian Unlimited*, September 16, 2003

www.richardthompson-music.com – website of Richard Thompson

Abu Jafar Muhammad ibn Muhammad ibn al-Hasan Nasir al-Din al-Tusi (1201–1274)

The father of non-Euclidean geometry and a major scientist, physician, astronomer, mathematician, philosopher, theologian, and ethicist, Abu Jafar Muhammad ibn Muhammad ibn al-Hasan Nasir al-Din al-Tusi is considered one of the great intellectuals of his age and one of the most versatile Muslim thinkers of all time.

Abu Jafar Muhammad ibn Muhammad ibn al-Hasan Nasir al-Din al-Tusi (also known as Khwaja Nasir and Khvaja) was born on February 18, 1201, in Tus, Khurasan (contemporary Iran). His father was a Twelver Shii jurist who served both as a member of the local religious establishment and as al-Tusi's first teacher, teaching him law, science, logic, metaphysics, mathematics, geometry, algebra, philosophy, and the religious doctrines of a variety of schools and sects. Upon completion of his education with his father, al-Tusi traveled to Nishapur to pursue advanced studies in philosophy, mathematics, and medicine. He studied with the famous astronomer Kamal al-Din ibn Yunus and became known as an outstanding scholar in his own right.

In 1220, al-Tusi's hometown was sacked by the Mongol armies that were conquering the East. He was taken by agents of the Nizari Ismaili leader, Nasir al-Din Abd al-Rahman, to the Nizari Ismaili stronghold of Alamut. It is unclear whether his departure and stay were voluntary or forced. He became a highly regarded member of the court and wrote major theological, mathematical, astronomical, and philosophical works in both Arabic and Persian. He also contributed to a revival of peripatetic philosophy, particularly the works of the Muslim philosopher Ibn Sina (Avicenna). He dedicated his major work on ethics, *Akhlaq-i Nasri*, to Abd al-Rahman in 1232.

Al-Tusi's political and religious loyalties are unclear. When the Mongols conquered Alamut in 1256, he not only was instrumental in negotiating the surrender of the Grand Ismaili Master to the Mongols, but he also joined Hulagu Khan's forces and returned to the Twelver Shiism of his youth. He was with the Mongol forces when they sacked Baghdad, massacred its inhabitants, and ended the Abbasid caliphate in 1258. Impressed by al-Tusi's scientific knowledge and abilities, Hulagu Khan made him the scientific adviser to the Mongols and offered him material and financial support for his research. Al-Tusi later served as the administrator of *awqaf* (charitable endowments) for the Mongols.

The most important result of al-Tusi's collaboration with the Mongols was the construction and operation of a major astronomical observatory in Maragha (in contemporary Azerbaijan) for which al-Tusi served as chief scientist. The observatory became operative in 1262 and counted both Persians and Chinese among its scholars. The preeminent observatory of its time, Maragha was equipped with the most technologically advanced instruments of the day, including those collected by the Mongol armies from Baghdad and other major Islamic centers, such as astrolabes, representations of constellations, shapes of spheres and epicycles, a four-meter wall quadrant constructed of copper, and an azimuth quadrant invented by al-Tusi. The observatory also contained a mosque and a library with books on a wide range of scientific topics. It became a major research center for science, mathematics, astronomy, and philosophy. Al-Tusi also continued his theological work, reformulating Twelver Shiism in philosophical terms. His theological work remains influential among contemporary Shiis. He traveled to Baghdad during the last year of his life and died there on June 26, 1274.

Al-Tusi wrote between fify-five and sixty-five treatises, a quarter of which were about mathematics, a quarter about astronomy, a quarter on philosophy and religion, and the remaining quarter on a variety of other subjects, including logic, medicine, minerals, color, metaphysics, perfume, and poetry. His books were originally written in either Persian or Arabic, but were translated into Latin and other European languages during the Middle Ages. His most important works were those addressing mathematics and astronomy.

Al-Tusi's work on astronomy challenged the limits of the Ptolemaic worldview that had ruled astronomy for the past thousand years. In a major work entitled *al-Tadhkira fi-ilm al-hay'a* or *Memoir on Astronomy*, he outlined the serious shortcomings of Ptolemy's theory of planetary motions and set forth his own comprehensive structure of the universe. Ptolemy had tried to explain scientifically what appeared to be non-uniform motions of the sun and planets with respect to the earth by pointing to corrections of epicycles (orbits within orbits) and geometrical modifications. Al-Tusi's model of the universe varied the distance of the epicyclic center from a given point by having it oscillate in a straight line. Each motion was uniform with respect to its own center, but could be combined with other motions, a resolution that became known as the "Tusi couple." The "Tusi couple" presents two circles, one having half the diameter of the other and the smaller being tangential to the larger. Although the two circles move in simple uniform rotation, they do so in opposite directions, giving the smaller circle a speed of rotation that is twice that of the larger. Any point on the smaller circle describes a straight line from point A to point B on the larger circle. This model was applied to all of the planets, except Mercury and the Moon. Al-Tusi's work was considered so important during the Middle Ages that at least fifteen commentaries were written about it. His ideas are also believed to have influenced Copernicus who, in 1530, completely overturned the Ptolemaic model by theorizing that the planets revolved around the Sun, rather than the Earth.

Al-Tusi's other contributions to astronomy include the invention of an instrument called a "turquet" that contained two planes, the calculation of the value of 51' for the precession of the equinoxes, written works on the construction and use of a variety of astronomical instruments, including astrolabes, and the production of his own astronomical tables based on twelve years of observations in a book entitled *al-Zij Ilkhani*, which he dedicated to Hulagu Khan. These tables rapidly became the most popular tables among astronomers and were used until the fifteenth century.

Al-Tusi's major contribution to mathematics was the treatment of trigonometry as a separate discipline, independent of spherical astronomy. He wrote the first extant exposition of the whole system of spherical and plane trigonometry, including the famous sine formula for plane triangles: $a/\sin A = b/\sin B = c/\sin C$, and the six fundamental formulae for the solution of spherical right-angled triangles. His work challenged the objections of earlier mathematicians to the comparison of the lengths of straight and curved lines. He also completed a manuscript outlining the methodology for the calculation of nth roots of integers and the determination of the coefficients of the expansion of a binomial to any power giving the binomial formula and the Pascal triangle relations between binomial coefficients. He wrote a major commentary on Ptolemy's *Almagest*, which introduced a variety of trigonometrical techniques for the calculation of the tables of sines to three sexagesimal places for each half degree. He also added refinements to the problem of infinite regress used in standard forms of cosmological arguments and arguments about the possible division of matter into atoms. As a scientist, he accepted the notion of "potential" rather than "actual" infinity, except in the case of God's infinite existence.

Al-Tusi's other varied works include a major work on ethics, *Akhlaq-i Nasri*, which made the Islamic ethical tradition and the ethical writings of Plato and Aristotle available to Persian readers and proposed justice as the key virtue that should guide philosophical ethics and religious law. He wrote commentaries on a variety of Greek texts and five major works on logic that explain the use of inference, or the use of two logical connectives to build up molecular propositions, such as "if–then" and "either–or." His philosophical works asked important questions about the nature of space and advocated an early and possibly first version of "soft determinism," which denies both absolute determinism and pure free will. According to this theory, the universe is the best of all possible worlds and each entity has an assigned role in it. The self-conscious belief in free will allows human agency to be a factor in a set of causes that collectively determine an effect.

Al-Tusi has been credited with a revival of Islamic science, mathematics, astronomy, philosophy, theology, and the peripatetic tradition of Ibn Sina. His students went on to major accomplishments, – for example, Qutb al-Din al-Shirazi, who wrote the first satisfactory mathematical explanation of the rainbow.

Further reading

Anderson, Margaret J. and Karen F. Stephenson. *Scientists of the Ancient World*. Berkeley Heights, NJ: Enslow Publishers, Inc., 1999

Dallal, Ahmad. "Science, Medicine, and Technology: The Making of a Scientific Culture," in *The Oxford History of Islam*, editor-in-chief, John L. Esposito. New York: Oxford University Press, 1999

Hill, Donald R. *Islamic Science and Engineering*. Edinburgh: Edinburgh University Press, 1993

Overbye, Dennis. "How Islam Won, and Lost, the Lead in Science," New York *Times*, October 30, 2001

Turner, Howard R. *Science in Medieval Islam: An Illustrated Introduction*. Austin: University of Texas Press, 1995

www-gap.dcs.st-and.ac.uk/~history/Mathematicians/Al-Tusi_Nasir.html

Baroness Pola Manzila Uddin (b. 1959)

The first Muslim and Asian woman to serve in the British House of Lords, Baroness Pola Manzila Uddin of Bethnal Green is a peer of the realm.

Baroness Pola Manzila Uddin was born in 1959 in Bangladesh. She migrated to Britain with her family as a young child. Raised in the East End of London, she was educated at the University of North London where she earned a degree in social work.

As a young adult, Uddin became involved in local politics, lobbying for the rights of the growing Muslim community. She joined the Labour Party of Tony Blair and was a major supporter during the 1990s because she believed that Blair was sincere about reaching out to Muslims and welcoming them into politics. Because he was known to have personally engaged in study of the Quran and to have cultivated a special relationship with Muslims, the Muslim community believed that he would protect Muslim interests and work to resolve the Palestinian situation.

In addition to her political activities, Uddin was deeply involved in social work. She worked as a youth and community worker at a Y.W.C.A., a liaison officer for Tower Hamlets Social Services, and manager of Tower Hamlets Women's Health Project. Her special interests are education, health, children, local government, and equal opportunities.

Uddin has called for recognition of the Muslim community of Great Britain as a British Muslim community, rather than an immigrant community. Because she believes that British Muslims have a stake in the community, country, and education system, she has worked to improve education for Muslim youth, particularly teenage boys. A supporter of women's causes, she was one of three key people involved in the construction of a Muslim women's center that offers a variety of activities, including English classes, computer classes, and a children's center, as well as sanctuary.

Uddin's social activism on issues such as youth and education combined with her work as a local councilor led to her appointment to the House of Lords. She was appointed as one of Prime Minister Blair's working peers in 1998 and was raised to the peerage as Baroness Uddin of Bethnal Green in the London Borough of Tower Hamlets, 28% of which is Bangladeshi, in 1998. Her swearing-in oath reflected her Muslim faith and served as a declaration that the House of Lords belongs to Muslims as well as Christians. At her swearing-in, she used the name Allah both to pay her homage

320

to Allah as God and to demonstrate that they are one and the same. She also wanted to highlight Britain's status as a tolerant society that has welcomed a variety of faiths to participate in the government.

Uddin's work as a peer involves membership on the E.O.P. Implementation Committee and service as a trustee of St. Katherine's and Shadwell Trust. As a spokesperson for Muslim issues, she has particularly worked for greater participation in the public sphere by Bangladeshi immigrants and their descendants. She played a pivotal role in the campaign by St. Bartholomew School of Nursing and Midwifery to attract East London's ethnic communities, particularly Bengalis, into midwifery and nursing careers. Recognizing the need for increased Bangladeshi training, she observed that nursing has long been considered an acceptable and valued occupation for Muslim women and that there is a strong need for health services to be more responsive to the needs of the Bangladeshi community. At the same time, she considers ethnic recruitment as an opportunity for greater ethnic engagement in making changes within the health-care system, as well as in broader British society.

The events of 9/11 brought major changes to the status of Britain's Muslim community and to Uddin's politics. The combination of the war on terrorism in Afghanistan and the toppling of the Saddam Hussein regime led to a breakdown in the relationship between the Muslim community and the Labour government. Although both Blair and President George W. Bush repeatedly stated that the war in Iraq had nothing to do with Islam or Muslims, the Muslim community remained highly sensitive to the popular linkages between Islam and terrorism and experienced an erosion of trust and confidence toward both governments. Uddin warned the Labour government of the widespread belief in the Muslim world that the war against terrorism was actually a war against Islam, leading some to support the idea of a pan-Muslim defense against imperial aggression. She further predicted that the war in Iraq would lead to an increase in suicide bombings beyond Palestine due to Muslim anger not only over the war in Iraq, but also over the failure of the United States and United Kingdom to implement a just solution to the Palestinian situation. She was particularly concerned that both the U.S. and the U.K. appeared not to recognize the intensity of anger in the Muslim world over these issues.

Uddin objected to claims that the war in Iraq was justified on moral grounds and the presence of weapons of mass destruction. She noted that the evidence provided was both old and questionable and that the U.N. did not fully back the military action. She also commented that the killing of civilians, particularly women and children, and the flouting of international law can never be moral and declared the proclaimed need to enforce U.N. resolutions in Iraq hypocritical when the same stance was not made with respect to Israel and Palestine. Uddin spoke directly of her concerns in a speech to the House of Lords, asserting that reminders of the evil of Saddam Hussein were unnecessary for Muslims because Hussein had been responsible for the deaths of more Muslims than any other person in history.

Uddin's stance on the war in Iraq was a departure from her usual approach to politics, which is one of building relationships on the basis of shared history. While many have decried the British colonial past as being responsible for poor relations between Britain and certain countries today, Uddin notes that this special history has enabled Britain to cultivate strong and positive relationships with Asians, Muslims, and Arabs. She points to that ability as Britain's special strength and has served on a committee for building community cohesion on the basis of greater understanding between different groups of people.

Uddin is frequently used as a media commentator and Muslim spokesperson.

Further reading

Clay, Laraine. "Baroness's Peace Call," September 30, 2002, www.towerhamlets.gov.uk/templates/news

Harrison, Roger. "Blair has Failed Dismally to Check Bush," www.aljazeerah.info/Opinion%20ed...0Roger%20Harrison%20aljazeerah.info.htm

"School Launches Major Ethnic Recruitment Drive in East End," *News from St. Bartholomew School of Nursing & Midwifery*, November 5, 2002, www.city.ac.uk/barts/news

www.mcb.org.uk – website for the Muslim Council of Britain

www.towerhamlets.gov.uk – website for Tower Hamlets

Hajjah Maria Ulfah (b. 1955)

One of the most influential and popular Quran reciters in Southeast Asia, Hajjah Maria Ulfah has been an international celebrity and acclaimed artist since the mid-1980s.

Hajjah Maria Ulfah was born on December 21, 1955, in Lamongan in the East Java province of Indonesia. Her father was a trader. Her mother was a housewife.

Ulfah received her elementary and secondary education in her native Lamongan. Her formal education occurred in a *pesantren*, or traditional private Islamic boarding school with a curriculum centered on traditional Islamic knowledge. After completing her secondary education, she attended the Islamic Teacher School in Lamongan, graduating in 1972. She then pursued religious studies at the State Institute for Islamic Studies in Surabaya, East Java, from which she graduated in 1977, followed by studies at the Institute for Quranic Studies in Jakarta, from which she received a Master of Arts in 1981.

Ulfah was initially a reluctant reciter. She began intensive training in Arabic Quran recitation when she was in the first grade, although she did not like it. Her father recognized her talent and encouraged her to memorize the Quran and recite it at home. She so disliked public recitation that she ran away to a friend's house every evening when she was supposed to be studying. Her parents, rather than forcing the issue, addressed her behavior for the first week and then ceased to mention it. It was only then that Ulfah began to have the desire to study the Quran. She won her first recitation competition at the district level in 1967 at the age of twelve.

Age and experience helped Ulfah develop her technique into an art form. By the age of eighteen, she had already attained a high degree of technical excellence in Quran recitation and had won her first province-level championship. Because her personal interest in artistic recitation (*tajwid*) continued to grow, she enrolled at the Institute for Quranic Studies in Jakarta where she was able to work with teachers with both national and international reputations, as well as a variety of methods of reading. Although she began performing Quranic recitation on both radio and television beginning in 1977 (a task that she has continued ever since), she won major national acclaim only in 1980, when she became the first-place champion in the National Competition in Quranic Recitation in Jakarta. Part of the reward for winning the competition was an all-expenses paid trip to Mecca to perform the Hajj pilgrimage, an accomplishment that resulted in the honorific title of Hajjah. (A man who has completed the Hajj is known as "Hajji.") A first-place win at the International Competition in Quranic Recitation in Kuala Lumpur, Malaysia, that same year led to international acclaim. She was invited to recite on Jeddah Radio in Saudi Arabia, followed by honored guest recitations in the

International Competition in Quranic Recitation in Kuwait and at the Competition in Quranic Recitation in Sabah, Malaysia, in 1981.

Quran recitation (*tajwid*) is one of the greatest artistic, musical, and cultural accomplishments for Muslims. It differs from the general Quran memorization expected of all Muslims. It takes longer to learn and must be perfect, including punctuation, because Muslims believe it is the divine Word of God exactly as it was revealed orally to the Prophet Muhammad. Tampering with the text or recitation method is not permitted. The Quranic text itself is considered so sacred that students who are learning the methods of recitation typically practice with classical Arabic literature first in order to master the technique before they are permitted to work with the sacred text.

Quran recitation in the Muslim world enjoys the kind of popularity associated with pop music, opera, and sports stars in the West. Talented Quran reciters are believed to bring great prestige to their families and are considered national treasures. They typically engage in performance, teaching, and judging, thereby promoting high standards of musicianship, virtuosity, and technical ability. In Indonesia, Quran-recitation competitions are held at the school, village, district, provincial, and national levels for both boys and girls, men and women, and are sponsored by both businesses and the government. Most schools have special Quran-recitation clubs. Competitions are festive events, often attended by thousands, and are frequently accompanied by parades and a variety of cultural and social events. Winners typically receive cash prizes, certificates, trophies, and/or other prizes, as well as fame.

The fact that both men and women are recognized as equally capable and efficient Quran reciters and recite at a variety of government, business, social, educational, and cultural events reflects the prominent role women play in Indonesian public life. It also sets Indonesia apart from the Arab world where reciters are typically male. Female Arab reciters are rare and are generally not well known because they are sometimes excluded from the public sphere and are often segregated from men. Religious scholars in some parts of the Muslim world consider the voice of a woman to be forbidden and thus relegate it to the private realm. In Indonesia, Quran recitation is considered an important national artistic and cultural expression for both men and women. Recitations are broadcast from local mosque sound systems and national radio and television stations. High standards for recitation are maintained by formal training schools and the presence of premier reciters in the public realm. Reciters of Ulfah's caliber, who are capable of moving their listeners to tears, are only about one in ten million.

Ulfah has popularized the Egyptian style of Quran recitation, reflecting a broad trend in Indonesia away from the traditional Meccan style beginning in the 1950s. She spreads her knowledge through a combination of recitations and teaching. She began recording her Quran recitations on cassette in 1981, including not only recitation, but also some Indonesian translation and discussion of recitation methods. The cassettes were sold commercially both in Indonesia and internationally and are played in public places. Ulfah received a Gold Plate Record Award in 1984 from Musica Studio's for her recording.

The achievement of champion status led to Ulfah's inclusion on the board of judges for the National Competition for Quranic Recitation beginning in 1983, as well as for local mosques and government ministries. Judging is an important professional activity for reciters. Judgments are made according to a variety of criteria, including voice; timing; rhythm; tempo; regulation and control of breath; sectioning and treatment of text; eloquence and fluency; comportment and good manners. In longer competitions, total number of melodies heard, choice of opening and closing melodies, transitions, overall tempo, styles and variations in rhythm and timing are also added. Judging is thus not just an aesthetic issue of the sound of a voice, but also includes the technical aspects of recitation. The power of sound, rather than physicality, gender or showmanship, is considered the most important element to judge.

Ulfah has worked as a lecturer at the Institute for Quranic Studies, a women's college in Jakarta, since 1982 and at the Islamic State University in Jakarta since 1996. She has served as vice-dean of Ushuluddin faculty, assistant rector of administration and finance, and rector at the Institute for Quranic Studies. Her professional experience includes service as the manager of the Central Institute for the Development for Quranic Recitation, Education and Training Department, manager of the Central Institute for Quranic Recitation, Territory of the Capital City, Jakarta, Department of Judging and Evaluation (at both the provincial and national levels), and manager at the Association for the Fellowship of Qari and Qariah, Hafidz and Hafidzah, for which she has served as the head of department IV, Women's Issues and Cooperation, since 1988. She took over the positions of manager and expert director of the Institute for the Development for Quranic Recitation in 1999.

In addition to serving as a premier reciter, Ulfah teaches recitation at the Institute for Quranic Studies in order to produce women scholars of the Quran and *hadith* capable of critical, systematic and scientific oral and written thought and communication. Also an expert on the history of Quran recitation in the Indonesian archipelago, Ulfah oversees about eight hundred women who seek to become Quran teachers. Her students are required to memorize the Quran, broken down into thirty parts. Incoming students are required to possess reading knowledge of Arabic and to have a certain copy of the Quran for memorization purposes. Each day, the student is required to memorize four pages. The memorization process takes four years to complete at this pace. Some students are able to learn it faster. Memorization is achieved by walking around repeating the text. Once memorized, two students at a time sit with the teacher for correction. The student recites and the teacher corrects the method of recitation according to the rules. Melodic recitation occurs in a separate class. Yet another class provides instruction in the meaning of the text. Upon completion of the program, the student earns the title of *hafiz*, which means "memorizer of the Quran." Graduates often become teachers or judges in their villages.

In addition to her scholarly work in Quranic recitation, Ulfah has published a variety of articles on the role of national competition in missionary work in Indonesia, the law of female voice in Quranic recitation, the law of Quranic recitation in chorus, the role of Muslim women in Indonesian society, and the art and methodology of Quranic recitation. She has served on the Committee of the Fatwa of the Central Majelis Ulama Indonesia (M.U.I.) in Jakarta since 1996. The committee is responsible for determining aspects of Islamic law, such as the legal implications and solutions to problems or cases presented by the people and the government, and giving opinions about social and financial problems. Ulfah's participation in the Majelis reflects the broad role that women play in public life in Indonesia, where they routinely serve as teachers, physicians, members of parliament, and judges, as well as in other capacities.

Ulfah became the head of the Cultural Foundation for the Religious Boarding School (*pesantren*), Al-Mudhoffar, in Lamongan in 1997. She founded the Cultural Foundation for the Al-Qur'an Boarding School (*pesantren*), Baitul Qurra in Ciputat, Tangerang, Banten province in 2000, for which she also serves as head.

Ulfah has performed as a honored guest reciter in Brunei, Egypt, the Netherlands, France, Belgium, Switzerland, Australia, the United States, Malaysia, Canada, Austria, Denmark, and Germany, as well as in Indonesia. She has appeared on European television and at a variety of American universities and has been recorded in the Phonogrammarchiv at the Austrian Academy of Sciences.

Further reading

Denny, Frederick Mathewson. "Qur'anic Recitation," in *The Oxford Encyclopedia of the Modern Islamic World*, editor-in-chief John L. Esposito, vol. 3. New York: Oxford University Press, 1995

Durkee, Noura. "Recited from the Heart," *ARAMCO World*, May/June 2000, pp. 32–35

Nelson, Kristina. *The Art of Reciting the Qur'an*. Austin: University of Texas Press, 1985

Rasmussen, Anne K. "The Qur'an in Indonesian Daily Life: The Public Project of Musical Oratory," *Journal of the Society for Ethnomusicology*, vol. 45, no. 1, Winter 2001, pp. 30–57

Rippin, Andrew, ed., *Approaches to the History of the Interpretation of the Qur'an*. Oxford: Clarendon Press, 1988

Sells, Michael A. *Approaching the Qur'an: The Early Revelations*. Ashland, OR: White Cloud Press, 1999

Interview with the author, January 11, 2004

Series of personal communications with Anne K. Rasmussen, December 2003 through February 2004

www.mariaulfah.com – website for Hajjah Maria Ulfah

Information about judging competitions and observations about recitation styles are drawn from the ethnographic fieldwork of Anne K. Rasmussen and are gratefully acknowledged as such.

Umm Kulthum (1904–1975)

Widely acclaimed as the most popular and influential performing artist in the history of the Arab world, Umm Kulthum cultivated an international audience of millions and became a cultural icon and symbol of Egypt.

Umm Kulthum was born around May 4, 1904, in a small rural village in Egypt. Her father was an imam at the local mosque. Her mother was a full-time housewife and mother. Both parents were devout Muslims who taught her to trust God, be faithful to her ideals, and respect herself.

Umm Kulthum was raised in poverty and simplicity in a small mud-brick home, an upbringing that she later credited with helping her to remain connected to the Egyptian masses. Because her father's salary was insufficient for the family's needs, he supplemented his income by reading the Quran and singing with her brother at various religious occasions. She overheard their rehearsals and learned the songs by rote, which she then sang to her rag doll. One day, her father overheard her singing. Recognizing the power of her voice, he started to include her first in rehearsals and then in performances. During her early years, she sang by imitation, rather than understanding.

Umm Kulthum received a classical religious education at a Quranic school beginning at the age of five. These studies, which were focused on the memorization and correct pronunciation and phrasing of the Quran, not only marked her participation in the most basic education any Muslim is expected to receive, but also provided her with a common heritage and style that she incorporated into her musical career. It was partly because her singing reflected an important cultural expression common to all Muslims that she developed broad public acceptance and acclaim.

Umm Kulthum did not enjoy performing as a child. Her father had to bribe her with promises of milk pudding to get her to sing. Her first public performance occurred when her brother fell ill and was unable to perform at the house of the local village leader. Although she was only between the ages of five and eight, her voice was so powerful that she was immediately asked to sing at another function. Additional invitations to sing quickly followed, often a fair distance away, enabling her to set higher fees, in addition to which she frequently received gifts of jewelry, silk, and money. The family began to travel to performances by boat, train or donkey, rather than strictly on foot.

Recognizing her potential, Umm Kulthum's father began to make family decisions with her career needs in mind. He studied the habits of other singers and insisted that she receive the same courtesies at her performances, such as transportation to and from the train station and a bottle of soda water during the performance. His major concern was to maintain her respectability while pursuing a career in entertainment, an occupation that was generally considered inappropriate for women at that time. Concerned by the popular association of entertainment with loose living, alcohol, drug consumption, gambling, prostitution, and the presence of foreign soldiers, her father insisted that her appearance, demeanor, and environment reflect modesty. In the early years, he dressed her as a Bedouin boy and forbade the serving of alcohol when she was singing.

As Umm Kulthum found herself in increasing demand, she became frustrated by the realization that, although she had learned many songs, she did not know how to interpret them to convey emotion. She credits Sheikh Abu al-Ila, the leading religious singer in Egypt and preeminent singer of classical Islamic music of that time, with teaching her to understand the lyrics and express emotion. She also considered him to be the greatest and most important musician she ever met. It was the Sheikh who convinced her father to take her to Cairo.

Umm Kulthum was an established performer in Cairo by 1922, appearing at benefit concerts, downtown theaters, weddings, and in the homes of the wealthy. She sang both Arab religious songs and popular love songs, but not obscene pieces. Unwilling to sacrifice her standards or sing songs she considered unworthy, she worked to cultivate an audience capable of appreciating her music. Between 1922 and 1928, she became a major star, deliberately creating a repertoire and professional identity that declared and empowered her as a self-consciously upper-class Egyptian performer. She discarded the Bedouin dress in favor of long, flowing classic dresses, adopted elite manners, and learned to speak intelligently about politics and literature. She wore her hair in either a bun or a chignon and developed the trademark of holding a silk scarf while singing. The result was a combination of traditional elegance, dignified bearing, and contemporary style.

During the early years, Umm Kulthum was admired for her natural talent and powerful voice, but was frequently criticized for her lack of artistic expression. Her father hired private teachers to help her develop greater vocal flexibility, lightness of tone, vocal control, and the virtuosic skills that helped her to heighten the meaning of both the tune and the text. This pursuit of formal musical training distinguished her from her peers and demonstrated the dedication to self-improvement and self-discipline that also became hallmarks of her career. She became renowned not only for her vocal strength, but also for her stamina in singing well over long periods of time with a uniform quality from the lower to the upper ends of her register without noticeable shifts or breaks. She also mastered the use of vocal ornamentation, such as head and chest resonance, clarity of pitch and tone, and the ability to produce a variety of sounds, including hoarseness, nasality, falsetto, trilling, and vibrato. Her clarity of diction was repeatedly noted and set her apart from most other singers who either did not enunciate clearly or did not recite the lines properly and broke phrases in inappropriate places. She was recognized as both a premier interpreter and a pacesetter of Arabic musical culture. Her style remains actively studied in the contemporary era by both Arab musicians and Quran reciters.

Like other popular singers, Umm Kulthum became active in the commercial sphere of music, including managing and directing her own career. During the 1920s, a revolution occurred in the entertainment industry with the foundation and expansion of commercial recordings, beginning with phonograph records and developing into audio cassette tapes and radio broadcasts. The result was a shifting of patronage of musicians from individuals and families to theaters and recording companies. The relatively low cost of recordings and equipment to play them made the entertainment industry accessible to the general public. Middle-class families could afford to purchase their own equipment and recordings, while the poorer classes were able to listen to recordings and radio broadcasts in public places such as coffee-houses and restaurants.

Umm Kulthum was recruited by Odeon Records in 1923. They released fourteen recordings by her between 1924 and 1926, all of which were new compositions with religious themes. She credited the high sales of these recordings to the fact that she had performed at weddings and celebrations throughout the countryside, giving her a popular base outside of Cairo that distinguished her from other recording stars. The success of the early recordings not only established her as a major Egyptian star, but also gave her the needed leverage to negotiate increasingly lucrative contracts. After 1926, she released an average of four or five new recordings each year, each of which sold very well. In 1926 alone, more than fifteen thousand copies of her records were sold, setting a new record for sales.

Two major changes to Umm Kulthum's career occurred in 1926. First, she left Odeon for Gramophone Record, which had offered her a large annual retainer fee that permitted her to secure her income at an economically volatile time, while allowing her to select her other performance opportunities. Like other recording artists of the time, she received a set fee for her recordings, rather than a percentage of the sales. She maintained this payment arrangement until 1959 when, having repeatedly experienced financial losses, she elected to take a percentage of sales. The second major change was the replacement of her accompanists. Up until this point, members of her family had served in this capacity, leading some to express concern that the accompanists did not fit the professional image she sought to project and made her appear overly traditional and stern. She therefore hired a prestigious professional orchestra, which included some of the most accomplished performers in Cairo, some of whom were more famous than she was. The move marked her advance into the ranks of highly respected professional musicians, as well as her new emphasis on artistic sophistication and an attempt to be more modern. Symbolically, it marked her transition from community performer to artistic star.

The type of music Umm Kulthum sang required a gifted poet to compose the lyrics, a composer of the main musical line of the piece, and an ensemble of players of a variety of instruments who could easily adapt to her style of performance, which typically involved interruption of the flow of the piece in order to repeat lines and passages numerous times in varied forms. Her favorite poet was Ahmad Rami. Some of the most important composers with whom she collaborated were Muhammad Abd al-Wahhab, Zakariyya Ahmad, Muhammad al-Qasabji, and Riyad al-Sunbati, who was her favorite and most favored composer. Al-Sunbati was the composer of "Atlal," one of her best-loved songs which she performed in almost every concert series she gave in the Arab world. It became a signature composition and to this day evokes her memory. Her collaboration with Abd al-Wahhab, the other major performing artist of the twentieth century, resulted in the song "Inta 'Umri" ("You are my Life"), which was released in 1964 and became one of her most popular and famous songs, with profits exceeding $750,000. At the same time, Umm Kulthum herself was always a dominant and active part of the creative process that resulted in a song. The composers of the lyrics and music represented only the first step in musical production. She typically required that the musical composer produce at least three different introductions to a given piece so that she would have a choice. She chose and sometimes rearranged lines and words of the written texts to make them easier to understand or to sing as she desired.

Although Umm Kulthum's professional success marked her as a highly accomplished musician, it also brought about her first major scandal as other female singers became jealous of her success and their own falling popularity. In 1926, a popular journalist suggested that her habit of receiving guests in her home suggested lewdness on her part. Her father was so outraged over the scandal that he threatened to take the entire family back to their village and end her career. He changed his mind only after the personal intervention of Sheikh Abu al-Ila. After this incident, she never again received visitors in her home. She remained wary of the press for the rest of her life and became conscious of the need actively to manage her public image in order to counteract characterizations of herself as either lewd or demanding, imperious, and hard to please. For years, she refused to talk about her personal life and declined broadcast interviews.

By the 1930s, Umm Kulthum was sufficiently well established and powerful to exercise choice in her artistic direction and venues and to assert herself more powerfully in financial arrangements and in her relationships with new entertainment institutions. She continued to expand her audience, performing her first concert abroad in Syria in 1931. She also began to include more romantic tunes in her repertoire. Her unique ability to express the emotion of the text through both her music and her enunciation made her as the singer the center of attention, highlighting her individual artistry and discouraging the audience from singing along or focusing on the accompanists or chorus. The combination of religious and popular pieces in her repertoire earned her an increasingly broad audience.

The 1930s brought the advent of what was to become Umm Kulthum's most enduring and successful venture: her Thursday night concerts. These concerts grew in part out of the decline of the commercial recording industry and the expansion of radio stations that accompanied the Great Depression and World War II. She began performing live for Egyptian radio in 1934. "Umm Kulthum Night" became an important cultural institution for the vast majority of Egyptians and had a tremendous impact on the social and musical life of the Middle East. More than entertainment events or musical expressions, these broadcast concerts were distinctive social events that made her a cultural icon for nearly forty years. They were so popular that they remain reflected in the telling of historical events, such as "General so-and-so postponed a military maneuver because Umm Kulthum was singing."

In addition to her Thursday night concerts, Umm Kulthum also gave series of concerts at a theater on Thursdays and Saturdays. By the mid-1930s, she was able to produce her own concerts without the aid of an intermediary agent.

While this meant more work for her in terms of negotiating the theater rental and conducting her own advertising, it also gave her greater control over both the performance and the profits. Management of her own productions was a strong indicator of her success and power in a field that had traditionally belonged to men. She was one of the two most highly paid and famous performing artists in Egypt.

Umm Kulthum was widely respected for her hard work in connecting with her audiences. She tried to arrive for concerts at least an hour early to give her time to get a feel for the theater, the stage, and her audience. She liked to watch the audience from behind the stage curtain because it was at that moment that she made her final decisions about what to sing. During her lifetime, Arab music was performed through improvisation on the basic lines of composition, rather than by playing exactly what was written. Because both the singer and the accompanists were expected to engage in constant improvisation during the performance, both had to feel the music and work by ear, with the singer directing and controlling the musical production and the accompanists following. The singer was typically guided by the tradition of audience participation, which consisted of listening to and encouraging the singer, particularly by calling for repetitions of particular lines, which then had to be presented in a variety of ways. Her concern for her audience explains in part both her longevity and her cross-generational appeal.

Umm Kulthum's songs were very long, sometimes lasting for an hour. Contemporary artists who sing her songs typically sing only portions of them because they lack her stamina. Her rehearsals typically lasted between two and five hours apiece, while concert performances lasted anywhere between three and six hours. Her longest concert – a 1967 performance in Paris – lasted a record seven hours. Although the commercial production of a single new song typically took a year or longer, she recorded about three hundred songs during her lifetime. By the mid-1950s, she began to make studio recordings of new songs prior to performing them so that they could be sold immediately following their first public performance.

Umm Kulthum began a series of film appearances during the 1930s. She made six films, playing the lead singing role in each. Her first movie, Widad (1935), was the first Egyptian entry in an international film festival in London. The second, Nashid al-Amal (Song of Hope, 1937), included "The University Song," which called upon students to rouse themselves for the sake of progress and country. It became very popular because it was composed and performed at a time of increasing student demonstrations for independence from Britain and greater government responsibility. A third film, Dananir, opened in 1940, with a fourth, Ayida, following in 1942. Ayida was her only film failure, in part because she starred as an Ethiopian princess and wore black makeup, which proved too shocking for the audience. In addition, the romantic situation was left unresolved. A revised version was released nine months later, but did not do well. Her most popular films were Sallama (1945) and Fatma (1947). Fatma told the story of a poor nurse who, following illtreatment by the son of a wealthy pasha, was defended by the collective action of the neighborhood and the judicial system. This film, more than any other, reflected major social themes of the time: the flagrant misbehavior and perfidy of the wealthy at the expense of ordinary people, the importance of solidarity between neighbors and friends, and the value of the virtuous woman who successfullly resists temptation.

The 1940s are often described as "the Golden Age of Umm Kulthum." During the earlier years of her career, she had sung twenty-three different styles of music, reflecting the complexity and sophistication of her musical abilities. Over time, she decreased the number of styles to maintain a broad audience. She entered her neoclassical stage in 1946 when she introduced a new style of poetic texts that were more easily accessible to the public, featuring Muslim religious expression and old Arabic and Muslim forms and cultural practices, while introducing new musical gestures that nevertheless maintained the familiar Arab foundation of musical composition. Her success in making her audience appreciate this style marked her as a true artistic leader capable of elevating the tastes and sophistication of her listeners. She became known as the singer who "taught poetry to the masses" and as "the voice of Egypt." Even the illiterate were able to recite poetry after they heard her sing it.

Umm Kulthum continued with her new musical and poetic style through the mid-1950s because it resonated powerfully with the cultural interests and needs of Egyptians as they sought a more Arab and Islamically rooted identity. Her songs portrayed themes of national and patriotic interest, as well as Sufi musical styles. She did not adopt Western instruments and styles as openly as other musicians of the time, preferring to emphasize her authentic Egyptianness, although in a modern way. Public support for "Egypt for Egyptians" was very prominent during her career, and support for Arab art was a way of making a political statement for many. Her conscious Egyptianness made her an icon in the 1940s and 1950s as Egypt gained independence and searched for an authentic identity. Between 1952 and 1960, she sang more national songs than at any other time – at least half of her repertoire. Her reputation as a singer of national songs earned her an increasing number of invitations to provide national songs for other countries. She recorded songs for National Day for Kuwait twice during the 1960s,

as well as an anthem for Iraq. During the 1950s, she recorded a radio program on the Sufi saint RABIA AL-ADAWIYYA, which was later turned into a film.

In addition to her artistic work, Umm Kulthum became increasingly engaged in the institutions of cultural production in Egypt. She joined the Listening Committee, which selected appropriate music for radio broadcasts, and steered the creation of Studio 35, the most modern recording facility in Egypt. In 1945, she was elected president of the Musicians' Union, a position that she retained for seven years. In addition, she served as a cultural emissary from Egypt to other Arab nations and was a member of several government committees on the arts.

During the late 1940s and 1950s, Umm Kulthum began to fashion herself as a public spokesperson for a variety of political and social causes. By the 1960s, she spoke openly and publicly about issues of national importance, including support for Egyptian soldiers who fought in the Sinai in 1948, the need for government funding for musical institutions, and the importance of appreciating Egyptian national heritage. Political themes were also expressed in the romantic poetry of her new love songs in the 1960s. Many Egyptians understood these songs to reflect common emotions about the Arab–Israeli conflict and concerns about President Gamal Abd al-Nasser's government. The fact that these texts lent themselves to multiple and varied interpretations accounts, in part, for their popularity.

After Egypt's defeat by Israel in 1967, Umm Kulthum embarked on the biggest benefit fundraising effort of her life: concerts for Egypt benefiting the Egyptian government. Between 1967 and her death in 1975, she gave more than $2,530,000 to the government, having performed in Paris, Tunisia, Libya, Morocco, Lebanon, Sudan, Iraq, Pakistan, Abu Dhabi, Syria, and Kuwait, as well as within Egypt. She created a special song for each country in which she was invited to sing, based on the texts of well-known national poets. Her trips took on the characteristics of state visits, as she made highly publicized visits to local places and events of cultural and historical interest.

Suffering from ill health, Umm Kulthum gave her last concert and recorded her last new song in 1973. On January 21, 1975, she suffered a kidney attack that led to her death on February 3, 1975. Cairo Radio chanted the Quran following the announcement of her death, an honor usually reserved for heads of state. Her funeral not only drew dignitaries from throughout the Arab world, but was also the most massive demonstration ever seen in Cairo, with millions of mourners filling the streets. Her body was taken from the hands of the official bearers and passed around for three hours before being taken to the mosque for prayers and finally buried. Numerous periodicals and newspapers throughout the Arab world devoted entire issues to her life after she died. Her villa in Cairo was converted into a national museum.

Umm Kulthum has enjoyed unparalleled longevity in the Arab world. During the 1980s and 1990s, Egypt had a radio station dedicated entirely to her music. Compact discs of her music are still marketed worldwide and her work is broadcast, played, produced, and reproduced throughout the Arab world. In Cairo, the Umm Kulthum Coffee-house plays her music throughout the day. Her life story appears internationally in books written for children. A variety of web pages are available for those interested in learning more about her or looking for specific recordings. She remains a powerful presence in Egyptian culture and a symbol of national strength who is credited with the production of twentieth-century Egyptian musical culture. She is also credited with having raised the level of respect for musicians and for serving as a role model for young women aspiring to both entertainment careers and public professions. A strong proponent of Arab, Egyptian, and Muslim heritage, she became part of that heritage herself. Her struggle to achieve high standards in her art and personal life earned her awards, medals, and decorations from Egypt and throughout the world.

Further reading

Danielson, Virginia. "Artists and Entrepreneurs: Female Singers in Cairo during the 1920s," in *Women in Middle Eastern History: Shifting Boundaries in Sex and Gender*, ed. Nikki R. Keddie and Beth Baron. New Haven: Yale University Press, 1991

—— *The Voice of Egypt: Umm Kulthum, Arabic Song, and Egyptian Society in the Twentieth Century*. Chicago: University of Chicago Press, 1997

"Umm Kulthum, Famed Egyptian Singer," interviews with Mahmud Awad, in *Middle Eastern Muslim Women Speak*, ed. Elizabeth Warnock Fernea and Basima Qattan Bezirgan. Austin: University of Texas Press, 1977

Documentary film: *Umm Kulthum: A Voice Like Egypt*, 1997, Michal Goldman

www.almashriq.hiof.no/egypt/700/780/umkoulthoum/ – provides links to Umm Kulthum's music, films, biography, discography, and songs, as well as a bibliography of materials related to her

Amina Wadud (b. 1952)

A feminist Muslim theologian and professor of philosophy and religion, Amina Wadud is one of the most influential and controversial contemporary interpreters of Islam.

Amina Wadud was born on September 25, 1952, in Maryland. Her father was a Methodist minister who also worked as a custodian. Her mother was a housewife. From her father, Wadud learned the importance of integrity and individual responsibility for her own spiritual destiny.

Wadud converted to Islam during her undergraduate studies at the University of Pennsylvania, where she completed a B.S. in Education in 1975. She taught English at the University of Qar Younis in Libya from 1976 to 1977 and then returned to Philadelphia where she taught fifth grade and created an Islamic studies curriculum for grades 3–12 at the Islamic Community Center School from 1979 until 1980. From 1980 until 1984, she taught an Islamic studies course for adults. She completed an M.A. in Near Eastern Studies in 1982 and a Ph.D. in Islamic studies and Arabic in 1988 at the University of Michigan. From 1989 to 1992, she taught at the International Islamic University in Malaysia.

Shortly after her arrival in Malaysia, Wadud met with Sisters in Islam, a voluntary group of professional women dedicated to developing and promoting a method of reform for expanding Muslim women's rights. She soon became a core member, bringing an inclusive interpretation of women in Islam based on her hermeneutical study of the Quran. She had undertaken her study to discover the divine intent toward women. She has stated that, had she found that the intent toward women was backwardness, prohibitions, subservience, and narrow confines, she would have left the faith. However, her analysis of the Quranic text in its original Arabic led her to conclude that historical contextualization of Quranic revelations is critical to understanding why certain actions have been undertaken at certain times, such as gender segregation in the mosque. Challenging patriarchal interpretations of the divine text as only one – and not necessarily the best – way of reading and interpreting the Quran, she stripped them from the text, discovering instead liberation and equality for women. Because she believes that the Quran's insistence on justice obligates Muslim women to experience justice in their lives, she has called for the inclusion of women as active and equal participants in Quran interpretation.

Wadud's findings helped Sisters in Islam assert women's rights and dignity from within the Islamic tradition, rather than having to look for outside support. It also gave them both the right and the obligation to work for policy reforms, women's equality and dignity, and an end to women's oppression, particularly domestic violence. They called for Muslim women's participation as full and equal partners in the socio-economic development and progress of the Muslim community, contending that female experience, thought, and voice are needed in the interpretation and administration of religion throughout the Muslim world. Although the group consists of less than twenty-five members, it has received extensive media coverage in Malaysia and enjoys the support of both men and women, as well as the government. Although detractors point to members' failure to adhere to certain cultural norms, such as veiling, as evidence of their supposed lack of dedication to Islam, supporters praise the group's role in debating issues of both religious and national importance in a democratic and intellectually honest manner.

Since 1992, Wadud has taught philosophy and religious studies at the Virginia Commonwealth University. In addition to her academic work, she has chaired the Women's Coordinating Committee of the World Conference on Religion and Peace since 1999. She has served on the national board of advisers of the Islamic Cultural Preservation and Information Council since 1999 and as honorary director and member of the Advisory Council of the Islamic Supreme Council of America since 1998.

Wadud's theological work stresses what she calls the gynocentrism of the Quran, or the presentation of women and women's issues with compassion and justice. Because God cares for women, she believes that conflict resolution should also include care for women. She asserts woman's unique role in the creation of human life as a mechanism for recognizing and appreciating the humanity of every person. Because women, as mothers, tend to see the human dimension of conflicts and death, she believes that they should be included in the decision-making processes of conflict resolution in order to ensure a focus on humanity and decrease the choosing of war, terror, and violence as solutions. She has examined Islamic ethical theory, Islamic concepts of the family and family and personal law codes, and the development of pro-faith feminism from an Islamic perspective. At the forefront of contemporary debates and discussions within Islam about the status of women and gender, she has also researched progressive Islam in the United States, Muslim women's empowerment, Muslim women as agents of peace and human rights, and the Quranic concepts of race, class, and gender.

Despite her progressive work within the Islamic tradition, Wadud's personal and professional lives became casualties of the 9/11 tragedies. Teaching classes that day, she had not been aware of the extent of the attacks until she encountered personal harassment because of her choice to veil. Concerned for her personal safety and well-being, she wore her scarf wrapped around her shoulders, rather than her hair, for her commute home. From this point on, 9/11 was about erasure for her: erasure of her freedom of choice, her identity, and her freedom to practice her religion safely. Feeling stripped of her choice of dress – an issue that is critically important to her as an African-American, a Muslim, a human rights activist, and a woman – Wadud described herself as feeling kinship with her slave ancestors who had been stripped of their dignity and modesty to be sold on auction blocks. She chooses to wear the hijab as a symbol of her sisterhood with other Muslim women around the world, preferring brilliant colors that recall both her time in Malaysia and her African ancestry. She believes that all Muslim women should be free to dress as they wish and that no one should have the right to dictate their manner of dress.

Wadud considers her personal experience of 9/11 to be a reflection of the collective general experience of African-Americans and Muslim women, noting that issues such as ethnic profiling have long constituted part of the experience of African-Americans and Muslim women who wear the hijab in the United States. Struggling to retain her dignity and remain whole post-9/11, she reaffirmed her personal identity by resuming the veil. She reasserted herself as a Muslim by participating in interfaith activities focused on healing and through public and professional service. Her public speeches often mark the first experience with a Muslim for audience members. Many are surprised by her openness to interfaith work. Wadud believes that every person should be free to choose their own faith system, including those who were raised as Muslims and converted to other faiths. She believes that the level of faith in a person's heart and how that faith is lived out is more important than the particular faith system to which one adheres. Although many non-Muslims admire her for this belief, it has made her a figure of controversy for some Muslims.

Wadud is also a figure of controversy due to her feminism and progressive stance. She defines a progressive Muslim as one who believes that Islam needs to be allowed to progress and develop historically to address contemporary concerns, including H.I.V./A.I.D.S., pluralism, and diversity, and to allow both men and women to participate in the formulation of Muslim identity and the interpretation of Islam. She has called for a more inclusive and equitable interpretation of Islamic law based on Quranic values such as justice, equality, human well-being, and human dignity. She believes that American Muslims, particularly African-Americans, who constitute the largest single ethnic group of American

Muslims, have particularly important contributions to make because they have a long history of opposition to mainstream American ideology, policies, culture, and perspectives, particularly where racism is concerned. Although they have not played a prominent role in defining American Islam historically, Wadud believes that they are increasingly poised to take on a leadership role in the future so that past experiences can help to guide future policies and emphases, particularly with respect to racism and discrimination. She has decried the past tendency of the American media to exclude the voices of both African-Americans and women in their depictions of American Islam, despite the fact that Muslim women are the most frequent targets of public harassment.

Since 9/11, Wadud has become a more active Muslim voice in the United States as she and her work have received broader coverage in the media. She was interviewed by the History Channel for the documentary *Inside Islam: History Channel* and has appeared on a variety of national and international radio and television broadcasts. Her articles have appeared in both scholarly journals and the mainstream American media. Her book *Qur'an and Woman: Rereading the Sacred Text from a Woman's Perspective* has been translated into Persian, Dutch, Spanish, Arabic, Turkish, and Indonesian.

Further reading

"Can Muslims Handle the Truth? Amina Wadud Talks about Islam, A.I.D.S., and Tolerance," interview by Ahmed Nassef, Muslim Wakeup!, June 6, 2003

"Muslims: Interviews: Amina Wadud," P.B.S. Frontline, March 2002

Wadud, Amina. "Belonging: As a Muslim Woman," in *My Soul is a Witness*, ed. Gloria Wade-Gayles. Boston: Beacon Press, 1995

—— "My Relationship with Sisters in Islam," for Mosaic's Religions for Peace Women's Program, WCRP Religions for Peace, New York, Spring/Summer 2001

—— "Point of View: Erasures – The Events of September 11th Changed our World Forever," *Azizah* magazine, Spring 2002

—— *Qur'an and Woman: Rereading the Sacred Text from a Woman's Perspective*, expanded ed. New York: Oxford University Press, 1999

Interview with the author, October 25, 2003

www.muslimtents.com/sistersinislam/home-mission.htm – website for Sisters in Islam

Sheikh Hasina Wazed (b. 1947)

A prominent activist for democracy and world peace, Sheikh Hasina Wazed is the head of the Awami Muslim League of Bangladesh. She served as prime minister from 1996 until 2001.

Sheikh Hasina Wazed was born on September 26, 1947, in the village of Tungipara, in what was then East Pakistan. Her father, Sheikh Mujibur Rahman, was a founding member of the Awami ("People's") Muslim League that became Bangladesh's largest political organization and led Bangladesh to independence. Her mother spent her adult life as a political wife and mother.

Hasina grew up during the formative political years in Bangladesh. Like her father, she became politically active as a student. She received her education at Keralcopa primary school and attended secondary school at Narishikhma Mandir girls' school and Azimpur girls' school for secondary education. She passed her Secondary School Certificate examination in 1966 at Kamrunnessa Girls' High School and was admitted to Eden Girls' College, the leading women's college in Bangladesh.

Hasina's political career began in 1966 when her father declared his six-point program for independence. She became a leader in the Student League, a branch of the Awami League, maintaining contact between her father and political and student leaders throughout her father's imprisonment in the late 1960s. She rose to the position of president of the Eden College branch and also served as the vice-president of the Student Union. Although she had intended to become a doctor or teacher, she found herself drawn by events into politics. She completed her B.A. with honors in Bengali literature at Dhaka University in 1973. At that time, she was the president of the Student League for her hall.

Hasina began her public-level engagement in politics in 1969 as a participant in the independence movement. That same year, her father met with the President of Pakistan and demanded the establishment of a federal parliamentary democracy and full regional autonomy. The 1970 national parliamentary elections resulted in an absolute majority victory for the Awami League. However, the military junta refused to hand over power. Mujib responded by organizing a noncooperation movement against the government to demand democracy. Although the political movement was temporarily interrupted by a cyclone that resulted in the deaths of a million Bangladeshis, politics returned to the forefront in 1971 when Mujib declared Bangladesh's independence from Pakistan. He was charged with treason, tried under martial law, and sentenced to death by hanging. In response, armed rebellion broke out and a war for independence began. Hasina and other family members were placed under house arrest. The family was liberated only when Mujib was released from prison in Pakistan and was permitted to return to now-independent Bangladesh in January 1972.

Elected as prime minister, Mujib worked to enact a secular constitution and declared a second revolution to eradicate poverty, eliminate corruption, and control population growth. At that time, Bangladesh had a population of 75 million and the lowest per capita income in the world. The combination of the war for independence and natural disaster had resulted in the destruction of most of Bangladesh's infrastructure, a situation that was exacerbated by a massive famine in 1974 that killed about a million and a half people and resulted in widespread political instability, corruption, political infighting, mismanagement of the economy, and loss of popular support. The experiment in democracy ended on August 15, 1975, when Mujib and twenty-one others, including Hasina's mother and brothers, were assassinated in a military coup. Hasina and one sister survived because they were abroad. The military pardoned and, in some cases, promoted the killers. No independent judicial commission was permitted to investigate the assassinations.

Hasina spent the next six years in exile in India and London, launching her formal political career in 1979 when she began to reconsolidate the Awami League and presented her first political speech. By 1980, she was meeting with Awami League leaders in London, calling for the trial of her family's assassins. She returned to Bangladesh as the unanimously elected head of the Awami League on May 17, 1981. Welcomed by a crowd of 1.5 million supporters, she pledged to restore the democratic rights of the people and led the opposition to the military rule of General Ziaur Rahman. She accused the general of ending democracy, socialism, and secularism in favor of military rule and of introducing religion into the public sphere through government sponsorship of Islam and the foundation of a variety of Islamic institutions. Shortly after her return, Zia was assassinated.

Despite strong popular pressure to stand for the presidency in 1981, Hasina declined to run for office at that time. Discrediting of the elections due to vote rigging led to another military coup, the suspension of constitutional rights, and a continuation of martial law. Hasina called for an end to military rule and the restoration of democracy,

leading a major protest against the military government.

As the opposition leader, Hasina was repeatedly arrested and confined to her home throughout the 1980s. In 1983, she supported the protests by students against military rule in the capital city of Dhaka, publicly condemning the arrest of 400 students and the killing of others. She joined forces with Zia's widow, Khaleda, to protest martial law and demand that a parliament be established. She also led a variety of civil protests calling for an end to martial law through elections. Despite frequent house arrests, she and Khaleda worked to end martial law, although they disagreed as to what should happen once it was ended. The two ended their partnership temporarily in 1986, but resumed it in 1987 to continue their opposition to military rule.

In March 1986, Hasina declared her intent to participate in the general election for parliament. Although she won, she was arrested again in November 1987. She claimed that her arrest was unconstitutional because she was a member of parliament and the leader of the opposition. The constitution required that the Speaker of the Parliament consent to her arrest – which he had not. General Ershad responded by dissolving the parliament. Hasina refused to participate in the 1988 elections, believing that they would be neither free nor fair.

In addition to numerous house arrests, Hasina was frequently targeted for assassination. In one attempt in 1988 in a public meeting in Chittagong, fifty workers of the Awami League were killed and 200 others were shot. General Ershad used the chaos that ensued to declare a state of emergency, expand press censorship, halt public demonstrations, and increase the illegal arrests of lawyers, journalists, and political workers. After another attempt on her life in 1989 during a sit-down strike that resulted in the killing of five people and the injury of 200 others, Hasina called for a country-wide strike to demand the trial of those responsible for the killings. The movement earned enough momentum for her to call for a caretaker government in 1990. The country united under the joint leadership of Hasina and Khaleda Zia to call for Ershad's ouster. When he responded by arresting the women again, the people erupted into a combination of student protests and civil demonstrations that culminated in Ershad handing power over to the caretaker government. Hasina proclaimed the restoration of democracy to Bangladesh and called for elections.

In the subsequent election, the Awami League received only 38% of the votes, leading many to raise questions about fraud and forgery. Khaleda became Bangladesh's first female prime minister, while Hasina again served as the opposition leader in parliament. Shortly after taking office in 1991, another assassination attempt was made against her. When Khaleda's government continued the old pattern of dependence on civil servants and military bureaucrats, Hasina called for the institutionalization of democracy and asked the international community to refuse to deal with the government. A political stalemate took hold by 1995 and resulted in the dissolution of parliament. Although elections were scheduled for 1996, Hasina called on the public not to participate, claiming that Khaleda was leading the country into conflict, civil war, and destruction. She called on the president to take over all powers as a caretaker government in order to oversee fair and free elections. Her success in uniting the opposition parties against the government led to Khaleda's resignation in March 1996, although her party elected her leader of the house. When Hasina began a hunger strike in protest, negotiations between Hasina and Khaleda were reopened. Hasina demanded the release of opposition leaders and workers from prison, the closing and rejection of the mock

processes of elections, the resignation of the current government, renewed talks between the president and the opposition parties, compensation for those killed or injured during protests, and guarantees of the security of the lives and property of the people through the restoration of law and order. She then declared a non-cooperation movement until these demands were met. The resulting paralysis of the government over the next twenty days of non-cooperation, demonstrations, and conflict led to the passing of the Caretaker Government Bill and the resignation of Khaleda at the end of March. This peaceful civil process of implementing a caretaker government was hailed as a model for Third World countries seeking democracy.

General elections were held in June 1996 with 73% of the population voting. Although Khaleda's Bangladesh Nationalist Party (B.N.P.) received more votes than had been anticipated, the Awami League had won a workable majority of the vote, enabling Hasina to form a national government of consensus. As a gesture of her support for true democracy, she invited the B.N.P. and Jatya Party (J.A.P.A.) to join the government and became prime minister. As prime minister, she called for an end to the illegal arms trade, expanded public spending on education, an end to media censorship, and support for economic development through a free market economy and aid to farmers. Critics were concerned by her immediate requirement that her father's photograph be placed in all institutions and offices and declaration of August 15 as a day of national mourning in memory of her family. She is frequently compared to Pakistan's BENAZIR BHUTTO and Myanmar's Aung San Suu Kyi for this deliberate self-association with the policies and legacy of her father.

As prime minister, Hasina committed herself to ending poverty and developing Bangladesh, most notably through the construction of the Bangabandhu Jamuna Bridge which connects the two geographic parts of Bangladesh and is the eleventh-largest bridge in the world and the largest bridge on the Indian subcontinent. She also established a water-sharing agreement between India and Bangladesh for use of the Ganges River to boost irrigation and canals in an effort to expand agricultural production and introduced an old-age pension for poor men and women. Believing that economic development was a priority for Bangladesh, she declared that Bangladesh would not engage in arms races so that public funds could be saved for eradicating poverty and illiteracy.

Hasina declared justice, law, and order to be priorities for her administration. She worked to repatriate Pakistani families, bring the killers of her family and political protestors to justice, implement local elections, ensure respect for human rights, and enforce the law. Internationally, she took on the role of peacemaker between India and Pakistan following nuclear-weapons testing by both countries and has worked to promote bilateral relations in South Asia. She established herself as a peacebroker within Bangladesh through the implementation of the Chittagong Hill Tract Peace Agreement, which ended tribal conflicts through the provision of a regional council to coordinate and supervise general administration, law, order, and development in tribal areas. The agreement has been replicated in other countries as a model for ending ethnic conflicts. Recognizing that women have been particularly hard hit by poverty, illiteracy, unemployment, and high maternal and child mortality rates, she especially dedicated herself to women's development and the promotion of women's rights. Although she is known to be personally devout, she has projected a largely secular–socialist image.

Hasina's government was the first to complete its five-year tenure. Although she lost the 2001 election to Khaleda Zia,

she resumed her position as leader of the opposition in parliament, where she continues to serve. Her tenure is remembered in Bangladesh for economic growth, the achievement of self-sufficiency in food production, and the decrease in both poverty and birth rates.

Hasina is recognized internationally for her dedication to peace and democracy and the promotion of development in Bangladesh. She has addressed the World Food Summit, the United Nations General Assembly, the Inter-Parliamentary Union Conference in India, the Micro-Credit Summit of 1997, U.N.E.S.C.O.'s Fifth International Conference on Adult Education, and the Organization of the Islamic Conference. The author of several books and numerous articles, she is also a founding member of Bangladesh's leading sports club, Abahani Krira Chakra, and is a member of Culture and Literature Sangha. She is a frequent speaker at universities. Her work for peace, democracy, and fraternity in the Indian subcontinent has been recognized in Bangladesh with the 1997 awarding of the Nejati Memorial Award and internationally with honorary doctorates from Boston University in the United States, Waseda University in Japan, and the University of Abertay in Scotland.

Further reading

Ahmed, Rafiuddin. "Awami League," in *The Oxford Encyclopedia of the Modern Islamic World*, editor-in-chief John L. Esposito, vol. 1. New York: Oxford University Press, 1995

Ahmed, Sirajuddin. *Sheikh Hasina, Prime Minister of Bangladesh*. New Delhi: U.B.S. Publishers' Distributors Ltd., 1998

Bayes, Jane H. and Nayereh Tohidi, eds. *Globalization, Gender, and Religion: The Politics of Women's Rights in Catholic and Muslim Contexts*. New York: Palgrave, 2001

Bertocci, Peter J. "Bangladesh," in *The Oxford Encyclopedia of the Modern Islamic World*, editor-in-chief John L. Esposito, vol. 1. New York: Oxford University Press, 1995

Bhuiyan, Md. Abdul Wadud. *Emergence of Bangladesh and Role of Awami League.* Delhi: Vikas Publishing House, 1982

Matin, Abdul. *Sheikha Hasina: The Making of a Prime Minister.* N.p.: Radical Asia Publications, 1997

www.albd.org/ – website of the Bangladesh Awami League

Michael Wolfe (b. 1946)

A writer of both fiction and non-fiction, film producer, and leading voice of American Muslims, Michael Wolfe has worked to make mainstream Islam more accessible and comprehensible to the American public while calling upon American Muslims to reinterpret their faith in its contemporary context.

Michael Wolfe was born in 1946 in Hamilton, OH. His father had been an Orthodox Jew, but converted to liberal Reform Judaism. His mother was a Christian. Wolfe's family celebrated both Jewish and Christian holidays. He learned to read Hebrew and was "confirmed" in the Reformed Jewish version of the bar mitzvah, but sang in the high-school Christmas choir and dated a Christian girl. Although he learned to respect both Judaism and Christianity as faiths, he found meaning in neither.

Wolfe began what he describes as "serious writing" when he was fourteen years old. Inspired by Ezra Pound's biography and dedication to the written word, he wrote in verse. When he was fifteen, he sent some of his poems to *Saturday Review* and began corresponding with an editor there. The following summer, he participated in the Bread Loaf Writers' Conference at Middlebury College where he met Robert Frost, John Berryman, and Dudley Fitts. The recipient of numerous awards for his poetry, including the Academy of American Poets Award in 1968, the Glascock New England Poetry Prize, Holyoke College, in 1968, the Marin County Arts Council

Writer Award in 1983 and 1990, and the California State Arts Council Writers' Award in 1985, his writings are recognized by the National Endowment for the Arts, the California Arts Commission, and the American Travel Writers' Association. He has taught writing at Phillips Exeter Academy, Phillips Andover Academy, California State Summer School for the Arts, and University of California at Santa Cruz. In 1998, he received the Lowell Thomas Award for Best Cultural Tourism Article, 1998, from the Society of American Travel Writers.

Wolfe earned a B.A. in classics from Wesleyan University in 1968. Having made his first trip to Tangier, Morocco, after graduation, he returned in 1970 after winning the Amy Lowell Traveling Poets Scholarship. Several renewals enabled him to spend the subsequent three years traveling throughout North and West Africa. He had his first encounters with Muslims there, including black Africans from a variety of tribes, Berbers, Arabs, and Europeans. Struck by their ability to judge people on the basis of their merit, rather than their race, Wolfe was attracted by the egalitarianism he saw practiced by Muslims, an attitude that he gradually came to realize was due to their faith, rather than their geographical location.

Wolfe left North Africa in 1974 and settled in Northern California where he started a small publishing company, Tombouctou Books, with which he published three volumes of poetry – *World Your Own, How Love Gets Around,* and *No, You Wore Red* – and a short travel journal called *In Morocco.* He began to explore prose writing during the 1980s and completed a book-length work of fiction, *Invisible Weapons.* Despite his writing success, Wolfe became increasingly dissatisfied with the spiritual void he felt within. Believing that a spiritual foundation was necessary to his understanding of the world, he sought a faith that did not require intermediaries to navigate incomprehensible mysteries, or substitute dogma for reason, was not inherently racist, and that considered sex to be a natural and healthy part of life, rather than a sinful behavior to be resisted or something to be disdained. Most importantly, he sought clarity and freedom of belief accompanied by rituals designed to discipline his mind and sharpen his senses. He talked to other Americans about his spiritual quest, but found that most of the educated Westerners he knew considered religion to be either a medieval concept best left to the past or political manipulation. They tended to suggest secular humanism and its accompanying support for democracy and freedom as a more appropriate contemporary worldview.

Wrestling with his need for spiritual fulfillment, Wolfe recalled his time in Africa where he had come into contact with Islam as both a faith and a culture. He returned to Morocco in 1981 and 1985, interested in learning more about Morocco's traditional, rather than sectarian, interpretation of Islam. He spent two years thinking about and studying Islam and joined a mosque prior to converting in 1989. Most of his American friends expressed dismay at his conversion, perceiving Islam as an autocratic political function, rather than a spiritual practice. Barraged with negative American media portrayals of Islam, Wolfe adopted the correction of such misperceptions as a personal quest.

Wolfe decided to make the Hajj pilgrimage to Mecca in 1990 not only out of a spiritual desire, but also out of personal curiosity and the desire to continue his travels. He prepared for his trip by reading scholarly accounts of the Hajj and a variety of topics related to Islam. Having decided to record his journey, he spent three months prior to the Hajj in Morocco where he set the framework for the book, combining the style of a Western travel book with the deeper expression of spirituality. He returned from the Hajj profoundly moved by the experience of membership in a global spiritual community where millions of believers simultaneously engage in the same act of obedience and profession of belief.

Wolfe spent the next three years writing a book about his experiences entitled *The Hadj: An American's Pilgrimage to Mecca*. Published in 1994, it has been translated into Indonesian. A travelogue, rather than a handbook on Islam, pilgrim's guide, missionary tract, or autobiography, it was the first travel account of the pilgrimage to be written by an American for both Muslims and non-Muslims. A description not only of what Wolfe saw, but also of what his expectations of the Hajj had been and how the experience differed from those expectations, it sold well in the United States. Combining historical explanations and references to explain the rituals with a modern perspective, the book includes descriptions of the physical stamina required to make the Hajj and places Islam within the monotheistic tradition, explaining its continuity with Judaism and Christianity.

After completing *The Hadj*, Wolfe spent four years researching and editing an anthology of Hajj travelogues entitled *One Thousand Roads to Mecca: Ten Centuries of Travelers Writing about the Muslim Pilgrimage*. Published in 1997, it has also been translated into Indonesian. A literary anthology including excerpts from travelogues written by Muslim pilgrims over a thousand years, the book includes accounts that provide a description of the mechanics of Hajj rituals, along with contextualization.

Wolfe's books on the Hajj led to his writing, producing, narrating, and hosting an unprecedented half-hour special report on the Hajj broadcast from Mecca for A.B.C.'s Nightline with Ted Koppel in 1997. The project marked the first live broadcast by an American from Mecca. The show was nominated for Peabody, George Polk, Overseas Press Club, and

Emmy awards and received the Muslim Public Affairs Council's Media Award that year.

Wolfe's success with this broadcast led to his co-production with Alexander Kronemer of a two-hour documentary film entitled *Muhammad: Legacy of a Prophet* for P.B.S. that was first broadcast in 2002. (See also LOBNA ISMAIL.) The film was produced by the Unity Productions Foundation, a non-profit organization dedicated to the fair, balanced, and accurate representation of the world's spiritual and cultural traditions in media and print for which Wolfe serves as executive producer and president. In February 2003, Wolfe worked with C.N.N.-International television news reporter Zain Verjee to produce a new half-hour documentary on the Hajj. As a recognized media expert on Islam, Wolfe is frequently interviewed on radio and lectures regularly at a variety of Islamic centers and American universities. He also writes occasional columns for Beliefnet, the leading multifaith internet site and media company for religion, spirituality, and inspiration that won the 2002 Webby Award for Best Spirituality Site and was a finalist for the National Magazine Award for General Excellence Online.

As for many American Muslims, 9/11 was a crisis for Wolfe, in large part because he believes Muslim failure to claim and define their faith for themselves allowed fanatical extremists to define "Islam" and "Muslims" for the American public. Believing that Muslims need to take the threat of terrorism seriously because they have the most to lose if terrorists succeed in carrying out another attack or taking control over Islam, he has called on American Muslims to speak out about their faith, teach others about Islam, and make the moral character of Islam more visible in the public sphere. Disturbed by the definitions and descriptions of Islam by non-Muslims he heard on television and in religious institutions,

classrooms, and Congress, as well as by Osama bin Laden, he decided to take on a public role in explaining Islam as a faith of peace, progress, forgiveness, and compassion. He believes that the post-9/11 period may be looked back on as the defining moment when American Muslims found their voice.

As part of his contribution to this process of self-definition and reclamation of faith, Wolfe edited a book entitled *Taking Back Islam: American Muslims Reclaim their Faith*, including excerpts from men and women who are committed to both Islam and democratic pluralism. The purpose of the book was to provide a forum for American Muslims to reclaim and reframe the moral character of their faith as a religion of tolerance, wisdom, and peace, rather than enraged, intolerant, suicidal, and destructive. The book won the Wilbur Award, Best Book of the Year on Religion, in April 2003.

Wolfe continues to educate the American public about Islam and to push American Muslims to reinterpret their faith in the contemporary pluralist American context. He points to American social and political traditions, particularly the civil rights movement and the U.S. Constitution and Bill of Rights, as guides for the American Muslim community for the future. He believes that Islam and democracy are compatible and that women and homosexuals should enjoy equal rights. He has called for understanding and practice of Islam as a faith, rather than a political system, and an end to the racism typically experienced by Muslims of non-European origin. A strong critic of racism and discrimination, he has denounced the disproportionate discrimination against Muslim workers that requires court orders to enforce their right to work and practice their religion, including the right to pray five times daily, attend Friday prayers at the mosque, and, for those women who choose to do so, to cover their hair. As an

American, Wolfe believes that these rights and freedoms ought to be considered a matter of course, rather than battles that have to be fought in the courts. He remains hopeful that Muslims will continue to expand their active participation in American public life in the future and that they will seize the social and economic opportunities that are supposed to be available to all Americans.

Further reading

Wolfe, Michael. "From a Western Minaret, http://www.beliefnet.org/story/82/story_82 81.html

—— *The Hadj: An American's Pilgrimage to Mecca*. New York: Atlantic Monthly Press, 1993

—— "Michael Wolfe's Story of Conversion to Islam," http://www.islamfortoday.com/ wolfe1.htm

—— "A New Year's Resolution for American Muslims," http://www.beliefnet.org/story/ 96/story_9657.html

—— *One Thousand Roads to Mecca: Ten Centuries of Travelers Writing about the Muslim Pilgrimage*. New York: Grove Press, 1999

Michael Wolfe and the Producers of Beliefnet, eds. *Taking Back Islam: American Muslims Reclaim their Faith*. Emmaus, PA: Rodale Inc. and Beliefnet, Inc., 2002

Interview with the author, September 9, 2003

www.beliefnet.com – internet magazine with articles by members of a variety of religions

www.upf.tv – website for Unity Productions Foundation

Y

Nadia Yassine (b. 1958)

Spokesperson for Morocco's most important Islamist organization, al-Adl wa-al-Ihsan (Justice and Spirituality), Nadia Yassine is expected to become the first female leader of an Islamist movement in the Arab world.

Nadia Yassine was born in 1958 in Morocco. She received her secondary education at Descartes High School, in Rabat, Morocco, and pursued university studies in political science in Paris, France. An accomplished painter and student of Western culture, she projects the public image of a traditional Muslim woman, wearing a headscarf and loose clothing, yet articulates the ideas of a modern feminist. She is frequently featured in both domestic and international print media, radio, and television.

Yassine is the daughter of Sheikh Abdessalam Yassine, a long-time political dissident and the founder and leader of al-Adl wa-al-Ihsan, a moderate Islamist movement that seeks to expand the role of Islam in Moroccan public life through legal, non-violent means. Widely recognized as Morocco's only real opposition party, it is supported by about twenty percent of the population, making it the largest non-parliamentary Islamic movement in Morocco. It is particularly strong on university campuses and in city slums. Although Sheikh Yassine has consistently preached a message of compassionate Islam, the redressing of social problems through good works, and working within the system for change, he earned former King Hassan II's disfavor when he accused him of tolerating corruption and encouraging Western-style moral decay. Placed under house arrest for ten years, the sheikh continued to preach and advise. His daughter became the party's official spokesperson.

As the official spokesperson, Yassine has defended her father's reforms, while presenting her own voice. An articulate, charismatic, and gifted speaker, she has worked to educate people through dialogue and debate while remaining sensitive to issues of cultural authenticity and justice. Her leadership of al-Adl wa-al-Ihsan represents a cultural revolution for Moroccans accustomed to male leadership. Conservatives and traditionalists consider her leadership "heretical" and "contrary to Islam," yet Yassine notes that there are many feminists in the movement, particularly in Casablanca where women hold 20% of the leadership positions, and that women in Morocco already serve as judges and ministers, as well as in other high civil and military positions. She believes that the time has come to modernize and reform both Moroccan law and the image of the female Islamist.

One of al-Adl wa-al-Ihsan's major themes is the rejection of Westernization and Western culture due to the perception that the removal of religion from the public sphere has brought problems, as well as benefits, in the West, particularly the absence of moral and ethical guidance that explains some of the excesses of Western culture, such as drug addiction, skinheads, heavy metal music filled with violence and hatred, and the loss of spirituality in favor of secularization and alternative spiritualities, such as black magic. Thus, rather than destroying or rejecting modernity, Yassine seeks to Islamize it by giving the liberating message of Islam back to humanity and using the Quran as a source of guidance in both individual and communal life.

It is precisely because it calls for returning Islam to the public sphere that al-Adl wa-al-Ihsan is opposed by secularists and Westernized elites. Equating Islamism with extremism, fanaticism, repression, and backwardness, particularly where women's rights are concerned, opponents have claimed that Islamism can only lead to a puritanical and austere regime like that of the Taliban. However, Yassine notes that both she and her father have called for the Islamization of modernity to take place through democratic means and without violence. She denies the charges that implementation of Islamic law will necessarily lead to the negation of modernity and democracy.

Yassine believes that Islam will lead to progress because it provides the moral, ethical, and legal framework for expanding women's rights in ways that are relevant to the majority of women. She describes her position as a combination of feminism and Islamism that provides cultural authenticity while addressing real-life issues. She supports reforms that reinterpret Islam to improve women's status and rights in practical and relevant ways, such as reforms of the personal

status code that would raise the status of women so that they do not remain perpetual legal minors. She has not supported Western-style reforms focused on personal freedoms that are relevant only to wealthy women, such as the right to obtain passports for travel abroad without their husbands' permission.

Yassine was widely criticized for leading the opposition to reforms to the personal status code proposed by King Mohammed VI in 2000. The previous Mudawana, or Personal Status Code, was a mixture of Moroccan custom and Islamic law that placed women in a subordinate and subservient position to the husband even before marriage. The king had proposed the reforms on the basis of his personal recognition of the injustice to women the prior code represented. Women's rights organizations charged that the prior code constituted a type of juridical violence against women by denying them the right to participate in the political, social, cultural, and economic development of Morocco. The king's proposed reforms met with parades of support by tens of thousands of women in Rabat, but were opposed by hundreds of thousands in Casablanca who, led by Yassine, claimed that the law was in need of reform, but that those reforms should be made within a Muslim, rather than Western, context. Yassine was arrested for her participation in the protests, but was later released. A variety of critics denounced her, claiming that she sought to prevent Moroccan women from gaining justice. She maintains that her opposition was due to the fact that the reforms were based on Western legal codes, rather than Islamic law.

In a reflection of his responsiveness to public opinion, the King withdrew his proposed reforms and appointed a royal commission to restudy the law and propose reforms that would leave the Quranic prescriptions in place while allowing for the expansion of social justice. The resulting new version of the

Mudawana is one of the most progressive codes for women's rights in the Arab world. For example, men are now required to go to court to make repudiation of their wives binding, and women have been released from the legal requirement to be "obedient" to their husbands. The custodial parent maintains the right to the marital home, thus recognizing the mother's contribution and care for the children and hopefully redressing the serious problem of abandoned women and children living on the streets in Morocco. Although the concept of marriage guardianship was maintained, the law states that a woman eighteen years of age or older has the right to serve as her own marriage guardian and to determine her own marriage. Yassine has found that this reform better reflects the spirit of the original Quranic requirement.

Although Yassine has been a major supporter of the revised Mudawana, she remains critical about two aspects. First, she believes that the new Mudawana does not go far enough because it has not changed the status of women as perpetual legal minors under the penal code. Second, she believes that the liberation of women is only a first step in the process of survival, noting that an illiterate and unemployed woman who cannot support herself will not realistically be able to make use of her right to divorce. In Yassine's opinion, the next major step to be taken by the government should be the implementation of practical measures to resolve real social problems, rather than just passing legal reforms.

Yassine spoke out against the 9/11 attacks, and dismissed bin Laden as a "son of Islam who has got lost" and missed out on the essence of Islam. She defines Islam as a religion of peace, tolerance of other religions, respect for women's rights, including divorce and contraception, and the ability to take inspiration from Western parliamentary systems. She remains disturbed by the ability of people such as bin Laden to tarnish the reputations of other Islamist groups that have deliberately followed a path of non-violence. She has also been clear that Islamism should not be equated with the state systems of Iran, Saudi Arabia, and Afghanistan under the Taliban because their goals and methods are different from those of other Islamist groups. She highlights the fact that Islamists have increasingly demanded political and civil freedoms, but within the framework of existing governments, rather than through calls for violence or revolution. She believes that the most important lesson for Muslims in the aftermath of 9/11 is the need to modernize Islamism, particularly with respect to making it more supportive of women's rights.

Further reading

Harter, Pascale. "Changing Status of Morocco's Shunned Wives," B.B.C. News, January 28, 2004

McNaught, Anita. "The King and the Sheikh's Daughter," B.B.C. News, March 28, 2002

"Moroccan Female Fundamentalist Challenges Osama bin Laden," *Daily Excelsior*, November 1, 2002

"Nadia Yassine, l'égerie islamiste," www.humanite.press.fr/journal/ 2000-04-01/ 2000-04-01-222821

"Nadia Yassine, l'héritière du Cheikh," *Maroc Hebdo*, December 24, 2003, www.bladi.net/modules/qui/imprimer_12.html

Talbi, Mohamed. "Maroc: Nadia Yassin, une Oriana Fallaci islamiste," *Jeune Afrique L'Intelligent*, November 28, 2003

Muhammad Yunus (b. 1940)

The founding visionary of the Grameen Movement and the micro-credit Grameen Bank and winner of the 2006 Nobel Prize for Peace, Muhammad Yunus has changed the face of rural economic and social development by melding capitalism with social responsibility to eradicate poverty.

Muhammad Yunus was born in Chittagong, in what was then East Bengal, India, in 1940. His father was a goldsmith. His mother taught him through her own example to help the poor.

Yunus received his early education in Chittagong. An outstanding student who was already teaching economics at the age of twenty-two, he was awarded a Fulbright scholarship in 1965 which he used to attend Vanderbilt University in Nashville, TN. He earned a Ph.D. in economics in 1969. He then worked as an assistant professor of economics at Middle Tennessee State University until 1972, when he returned to the newly independent nation of Bangladesh to teach economics at Chittagong University.

Yunus initially found beauty in the economic theories he taught. However, in 1974, Bangladesh experienced a widespread, human-made famine that resulted in the deaths of approximately 1.5 million Bangladeshis. Struck by the absurdity and emptiness of teaching economic theories at a time when people were literally dying in the streets from hunger, Yunus realized his theories did not address the poverty surrounding him. He found it obscene that a person could work twelve hours a day seven days a week and still die of starvation. Believing that the poor held the answers to their own salvation, he decided to study them.

Yunus's first project was a 1974 pilot program of rural people participating in self-government known as Gram Sarker. The program was adopted nationally in 1980. In 1978, Yunus received the President's Award for his system of cooperative three-share farming known as Tebhaga Khamar which had been adopted as the Packaged Input Program in 1977. Although these programs, which emphasized improving rice-farming techniques and forming farmers' cooperatives for irrigation during the dry season, helped farmers, the truly destitute – the landless, assetless, rural poor – remained out of reach.

Seeking to understand the underlying causes of destitution, Yunus embarked on a series of field trips to a nearby rural village in 1975 and 1976. During one of those trips, he met a woman weaving bamboo stools. She had no capital to buy the raw bamboo she needed. Because she had no collateral, she had to borrow money from a middleman to purchase the materials. The middleman subsequently took most of her profit, leaving her with only about four cents profit for a full day's work. When he found forty-one other villagers with similar problems, Yunus realized that the poverty of the destitute was not due to laziness, a lack of intelligence, or a lack of will to save. It was due to a structural issue: the lack of capital. Forced to pay as much as 10% interest per month, per week or even per day, people simply could not break the subsistence barrier, no matter how hard or long they worked. Horrified by the exploitation, suffering, and denigrated human existence he found, he surveyed the families to find out how much capital they would need to borrow in order to break free from the middleman and become self-sustaining. Upon discovery that a total of $30 was needed, he extended personal loans to them without interest or a set repayment date.

Realizing that his personal, emotional response was insufficient for addressing widespread poverty, Yunus sought to develop a long-term institutional solution capable of expanding beyond a single village. Based on his interviews and studies of the village, he believed that the best approach would be a rural bank lending money for a variety of projects, including trade, small manufacturing, retail and door-to-door sales, rather than the traditional approach of providing assistance only to farmers. He tried to generate interest in local commercial banks to lend money to the destitute without collateral, but the banks refused to issue credit to people they considered too much of a risk. Yunus decided to launch his own program: the Grameen ("Rural") Project.

Yunus's vision was based on an understanding of the rural poor as hardworking, trustworthy people who sought an opportunity to break out of poverty. He believed that they would work hard to make their ventures successful because they could not afford to fail. In order to break the psychological barrier of having to amass a large lump sum at the conclusion of the loan period, he had people repay the loans in tiny increments on a daily basis. Not only did this make the repayment seem more manageable psychologically, but he found that it enhanced the self-discipline and confidence of the borrowers in their ability to manage a loan. Once the initial loan is repaid, the borrower has the option of taking out another, larger loan. Over time, the loan portfolio is expanded to finance the projects of the seasoned borrower's entire family, as well as to address the development needs of the community, such as building sanitary latrines, installing tubewells to provide drinking water and irrigation for gardens, and extending credit for purchasing agricultural inputs for seasonal cultivation and leasing equipment and machinery.

The concept of micro-credit was revolutionary. Traditional aid and development programs have focused on donations of large sums of money to be invested by governments and organizations in large infrastructure ventures to promote development from the top down. Grameen approached poverty eradication from the bottom up by providing small loans – typically less than $100 and often as little as $20 – to destitute individuals for the purchase of an income-earning asset such as a cow for milking or raw materials for weaving or craft production. The extension of a loan, rather than charity, was designed to promote personal effort and responsibility, as well as to build peer pressure and peer support that could then translate into greater community leadership and activism.

In keeping with its community focus, Grameen uses peer pressure and peer support as collateral for the loans by requiring individuals to form groups of five in order to borrow money. The five must come from different families and decide among themselves the order in which they will take out the loans and what the loans will be used for. The ventures must begin earning income quickly because the repayment period begins one week after the loan is extended. Initially, loans are extended to two people. The extension of loans to two more people depends on the ability of the first two borrowers to repay their loans, as proven over a six-week period. When all four prove their creditworthiness, the fifth person is also allowed to borrow money. If one person defaults on the loan, the entire group is penalized. The borrowers thus become responsible for policing themselves. Grameen does not use the police or judicial systems to enforce loan repayment. In cases where a person defaults, the bank does not vilify the person, recognizing that the personal circumstances of some individuals, such as infirmity or illness, may be so hard that they cannot pay the loan back. Bad debt accounts for only about 0.5% of the cost of doing business and only about 2% of the loans issued.

Grameen has focused on lending to women as the key to resolving Bangladesh's poverty because women tend to be the most vulnerable to poverty, illiteracy, and lack of work experience. They are also the least likely to be considered for loans by commercial banks. By economically mobilizing women, Grameen hoped to shift the position of women from one of complete dependence on the family to one of self-sufficiency. Yunus found through experience that women tended to be the most careful about their debts because they had the most to gain by successfully repaying their loans. Loans to women also tended to benefit entire families, rather than individual borrowers, because of women's family responsibilities. Although many in the West have hailed Grameen's focus on women, that focus has rendered it controversial among many Bangladeshis, particularly husbands, religious leaders, government officials and others who feared that women's financial independence and self-sufficiency would lead to the breakdown of families. However, Yunus has observed that these successful women are valued more highly and are less likely to be divorced by their husbands, have invested in their children's welfare and education, and are more likely to vote. They also tend to have fewer children, an important concern in Bangladesh where the birth rate remains one of the highest in the world despite widespread poverty.

The first Grameen Project, run between 1976 and 1979 in the village of Jobra, resulted in about five hundred micro-loans, 98% of which were repaid. Armed with tangible proof of the program's success, Yunus persuaded the Central Bank of Bangladesh and some nationalized commercial banks to adopt his program in 1979, resulting in the foundation of Grameen Bank. Similar to the Grameen Project, Grameen Bank charges 16% simple interest on one-year loans. Repayment begins during the second week of the loan. No education, training or infrastructure is required for borrowers because the loans are intended to enable them to practice skills they already possess. The only requirements for borrowing are destitution and proven understanding of the "16 Decisions" by which borrowers pledge to abide. The methodology has proven most successful in areas where social life is based on solidarity, particularly rural areas with strong communities, because it depends on peer support and discipline.

By 1983, Grameen had 59,000 clients in eighty-six branches and was incorporated as a separate legal institution with Yunus as its managing director. By the

late 1980s, it had shifted investment from irrigation and fisheries into other business sectors and non-banking activities, including venture capital, textiles, and internet service provision. New organizations, including the Grameen Fisheries Project, the Grameen Krishi Foundation for irrigation projects, and the Grameen Trust for international replication and health programs, were founded in 1989 to support new programs. Grameen also began to provide training and support in its methodology to other Third World countries seeking to replicate its model.

By 1998, Grameen had become the largest rural bank in Bangladesh with more than 12,000 employees and 1,112 branches serving 2.3 million borrowers in more than 35,000 villages for loans and payments exceeding $35 million. It was estimated that about ten percent of the Bangladeshi population was living directly on benefits brought about through Grameen loans. Group savings have proven as successful as group lending, totaling about $162 million by 1998, $152 million of which has been saved by women.

Grameen's approach has proven so successful in Bangladesh that replica micro-credit programs have been established in fifty-eight countries worldwide, including Malaysia, India, Nepal, the Philippines, Sri Lanka, Poland, and the United States, forming an $8 billion industry. The Grameen Foundation U.S.A. was founded in 1997 to provide financing, technical assistance, and technology support to grass-roots institutions replicating Grameen Bank's success around the world. Grameen's positive impact has been documented in independent studies by the World Bank, the International Food Research Policy Institute, and the Bangladesh Institute of Development Studies. About half of Grameen's borrowers pull themselves above the poverty line within five years with another quarter coming close. Yunus attributes the failure of the remaining quarter to break out of poverty to the lack of social infrastructure to care for the ill and infirm.

Yunus believes that access to credit should be considered a fundamental human right, along with food, clothing, health, education, and shelter, because credit has proven to be both the most cost-effective weapon in fighting poverty ever found and a catalyst for the socioeconomic development of the poor. He believes that emphasis should be given to the eradication of poverty, rather than to making it more tolerable through foreign aid or engaging in large infrastructure projects that tend to enrich the already wealthy. This philosophy of self-help has resulted in criticism from traditional aid and development agencies that microloans and micro-credit have distracted governments from bringing water, sanitation, health care, and schools to desperate communities. They particularly criticize Grameen's status as a profit-making institution, arguing that the alleviation of human suffering should be a humanitarian matter, not a profit-making venture. Muslim critics have denounced Grameen's charging of interest as un-Islamic. Detractors have also claimed that Yunus's ideas could not work on a large scale and that the quality of services would deteriorate if the numbers grew too large.

In response to his critics, Yunus notes that 92% of the bank's shares are owned by its borrowers, thus creating a loop in which borrowers pay interest to themselves. Every person who borrows money from Grameen is issued one nontradeable share upon taking out the loan. Borrowers are also required to begin a savings plan to provide insurance against disaster. He denies charges that Grameen is un-Islamic, pointing to the broader social good of encouraging self-employment within families, self-sufficiency from donors, and Grameen's service to more than 60% of all villages in Bangladesh by 2002. He has pledged to reduce interest rates when and if he can. His ultimate goal is to reach a critical mass of 100 million people, or about ten percent of the world's poor, through the extension of micro-credit.

Since the 1990s, Yunus and his revolutionary ideas have come to the attention of world policy makers. Many of his admirers believe that he should win the Nobel Peace Prize for his practical and result-oriented work. International acclaim for his work includes appointment by the U.N. secretary general to serve on the International Advisory Group for the Fourth World Conference on Women in Beijing from 1993 to 1995, the Global Commission of Women's Health from 1993 until 1995, the U.N. Expert Group on Women and Finance, and the Advisory Council for Sustainable Economic Development since 1993. He is the chair of the policy advisory group of the Consultative Group to Assist the Poorest and serves on the boards of Amanah Ikhtiar Malaysia (a Grameen replication project), the International Rice Research Institute in the Philippines, Credit and Savings for the Poor in Malaysia, the Calvert World Values Fund, the Foundation for International Community Assistance, the National Council for Freedom from Hunger, R.E.S.U.L.T.S., and the International Council of Ashoka Foundation. His expertise is sought on education, health, disaster prevention, population, development, and banking programs. The World Bank appointed him head of the advisory committee to propagate his vision worldwide.

Yunus is frequently interviewed by the international press. *Asiaweek* named him one of the twenty-five most influential Asians and he was named Man of the Week by A.B.C. T.V. In addition to the President's Award in 1978, the Central Bank Award in 1985, and the Independence Day Award in 1987 from Bangladesh, Yunus has received the Roman Magaysay Award from the Philippines (1984), the Aga Khan Award for Architecture (1989), the Mohamed

Shabdeen Award for Science from Sri Lanka (1993), the Case Humanitarian Award, the World Food Prize from the United States (1994), and the Volvo Environmental Prize (2003). In 2006, he was awarded the Nobel Prize for Peace for his work to end global poverty.

Further reading

"Banking on the Poor: A Bangladeshi Lesson for the World," *The Times*, editorial, October 31, 1998

Counts, Alex. *Give us Credit: How Muhammad Yunus's Micro Lending Revolution is Empowering Women from Bangladesh to Chicago*. New York: Random House, 1996

Gibbons, David S. *The Grameen Reader*. Dhaka: Grameen Bank, 1994

Iqbal, Munawar. *Distributive Justice and Need Fulfillment in an Islamic Economy*. Leicester: Islamic Foundation, 1988

Jain, Pankaj S. "Managing Credit for Rural Poor: Lessons from Grameen Bank," *World Development*, January 1996

Jolis, Alan. "The Good Banker," *The Independent on Sunday Supplement*, May 5, 1996

"Muhammad Yunus," *The Guardian*, October 31, 1998

Righter, Rosemary. "Bangladesh's Famous Financier Uses Micro-credit to Bring Wealth to the Underprivileged of Many Nations," *The Times*, October 31, 1998

Todd, Helen. *Women at the Centre: Grameen Bank Borrowers after One Decade*. Boulder, CO: Westview Press, 1996

"Twenty Great Asians: The Lender – Muhammad Yunus," *Asiaweek*, 1998

Yunus, Muhammad. *Jorimon and Others: Faces of Poverty*, 3rd ed. Dhaka: Grameen Bank, 1991

Yunus, Muhammad and Alan Jolis. *Banker to the Poor*. London: Aurum Press, 1998

www.grameen-info.org/ – website for Grameen Bank

www.gfusa.org/ – official site for Grameen Foundation U.S.A.

Z

Abu al-Qasim al-Zahrawi
(936–1013)

The father of modern surgery, Abu al-Qasim al-Zahrawi was the most renowned physician and surgeon of his age.

Abu al-Qasim al-Zahrawi was born in 936 in Zahra, a neighborhood of Cordoba, which was the capital of al-Andalus (Muslim Spain). He was educated at the University of Cordoba. Also known in the West as Abulcasis, Bucasis, and Alzahravius, he served as court physician to King Abd al-Rahman III of al-Andalus at the zenith of Islamic culture and science in Europe when Muslims, Christians, and Jews lived and worked together in interfaith harmony. Al-Zahrawi spent his life practicing medicine, particularly surgery, and writing medical treatises. He died in 1013.

The most important of al-Zahrawi's works was the thirty-volume *al-Tasrif li-Man Ajizan al-Ta'lif*, (*Manual for Medical Practitioners*). Considered the best medieval surgical encyclopedia in existence as well as a synthesis of the medical knowledge available during his lifetime, the work details both symptoms and treatments. The most popular, influential, and widely copied part of the book is the section on surgery. Translated into Latin and used in Europe until the seventeenth century, it stressed the importance of basic sciences, particularly anatomy and physiology, in recognizing and understanding the functions of the organs and their shapes, connections, and borders. Al-Zahrawi also recommended knowledge of the bones, nerves, and muscles, their numbers, origins, and insertions, and knowledge of the arteries and veins, particularly where they start and end. He described the ligature of arteries long before Ambrose Pare in the West, believing that this was the most basic knowledge any physician or surgeon should possess because a mistake could lead to the death of the patient.

Al-Zahrawi was a pioneer in many surgical specialties and in general procedures. His book contains detailed descriptions of medical operations and illustrations of about two hundred surgical instruments, many of which he invented. Among his most important inventions were instruments for internal examination of the ear, for the internal inspection of the urethra, and for applying or removing foreign bodies from the throat. He encouraged physicians to invent their own tools.

Al-Zahrawi's observations about surgical manipulations and technologies covered obstetrics, fractures, cauterization, mouth hygiene, artificial teeth, paralysis, treatment of wounds, and dislocations. He devoted a chapter to midwifery, offering tips to midwives and addressing topics such as obstructed labor and obstetrical maneuvering. Surgical procedures outlined in detail include the innovative removal of a kidney stone through the bladder, the dissection of animals, surgery of the eye, ear, and throat, and stypics. Among his most delicate operations were amputation and the removal of a dead fetus. He was the first to describe surgical treatment in the specializations of ophthalmology and otorhinolaryngology (E.N.T.).

Al-Zahrawi's work is particularly important in its presentation of two very delicate types of procedures: liver and cranial surgery. He correctly asserted that treatment of an abscess of the liver must take place in two separate procedures. In the first, adhesions are to be made around the abscess in order to close it off from the peritoneal cavity and prevent pus from spreading throughout the abdomen, which would kill the patient. Once this first step is complete, an incision to remove the abscess can be made. On cranial surgery, he began by identifying different types of skull fractures, depending on the strength of the blow received and the type of instrument with which it was delivered. He taught that the type and severity of the fracture determined the type of surgical procedure to be used. He identified five different types of cranial fractures: axial fractures (the complete splitting of the skull); incomplete axial fractures (the partial splitting of the skull); comminuted fractures (typically caused by being hit by a rock or stone and varying in size); hairy fractures (so-called because they are tiny and linear like a hair and, consequently, are often hard to see); and depressed fractures, which typically occur when the skull is soft and is indented, rather than breaking. This last type of fracture was most frequently seen in children.

In order to diagnose the type of fracture, al-Zahrawi recommended examination of the wound, which involved removing debris, exposing the skull, and feeling it. This was to be done by shaving the patient's head and removing bone fragments as needed. He did not recommend such an examination in cases where the patient had a high fever, experienced repeated vomiting, exhibited exophthalmos or convulsions or was comatose, because the patient was likely to die due to the severity of the injury. He recommended the use of ink when a hairy fracture was suspected because the ink would stain the fracture, making it easily visible. In the event of bleeding during the examination or surgery, he recommended applying pressure on the wound with towels soaked in alcohol or wax.

In addition to the descriptions of medical procedures and surgical instruments, al-Zahrawi's book included an important list of pharmaceutical drugs and descriptions of how to prepare a variety of substances, including litharge, white lead, lead sulphide, copper sulphide, cadmia, vitriols, and crocus of iron. This list was translated into Latin in the thirteenth century and was widely used in Europe.

Al-Zahrawi was the first physician to use cauterization to control bleeding and to use wax and alcohol to stop bleeding from the skull during cranial surgery. He used cauterization in fifty different types of surgery. He was the first to describe hemophilia; distinguish between goiter and thyroid cancer; teach the lithotomy position for vaginal operations; describe a tracheotomy operation and perform it successfully as emergency surgery on one of his servants; and use cotton in surgical dressings to control hemorrhage and as padding for splints and in fractures of the pubis and dentistry. He introduced what is known today as Kocher's method of reduction of shoulder dislocation and patelectomy – a thousand years before it was reintroduced by Brooke in 1937. He was also the first known person to perform the surgical stripping of varicose veins. Although he wrote ten centuries prior to the modern performance of this procedure, he carried it out almost exactly as it is currently practiced, including the location of the incisions, the manner of keeping the skin open with hooks, and hanging the veins on hooks while conducting the procedure.

In addition to being a pioneer in clinical medicine, al-Zahrawi was the first person to write about orthodontia. An expert in dentistry, he included in his *Tasrif* sketches of various dental instruments, as well as descriptions of important dental operations, the preparation of artificial teeth, and the replacement of defective teeth. He was the first to discuss the problems of non-aligned and deformed teeth, as well as how to rectify these defects. He recommended the reimplantation of fallen teeth and the use of dental prostheses carved from cows' bones – a major improvement over wooden dentures. His descriptions of dental operations included extractions, fixation, reimplantation, and artificial teeth. He was the first known person to describe referred tooth pain, cautioning physicians against removing a healthy tooth to which pain was referred. He also instituted the use of gold thread in fixing teeth due to the tarnishing of other metals and their tendency to cause adverse reactions.

Al-Zahrawi had a profound influence on the fields of medicine and surgery for five centuries, surpassing the influence of Galen in the European modern curriculum. During his lifetime and largely because of his work, surgery became a respected practice in the Islamic world and was regularly carried out by reputable physicians. By contrast, at that time in Europe, surgery was typically practiced by barbers, butchers, priests, and monks until 1163 when the Council of Tours issued a declaration calling on all priests and monks to abandon surgery. The principles laid down by al-Zahrawi are still recognizable in contemporary medical science, particularly surgery.

Further reading

Abouleish, Ezzat, M.D. "Contribution of Islam to Medicine," www.imamreza.net/ old/eng/islam/Sciences/islamic-medicine02.htm

Anderson, Margaret J. and Karen F. Stephenson. *Scientists of the Ancient World.* Berkeley Heights, NJ: Enslow Publishers, Inc., 1999

Dallal, Ahmad. "Science, Medicine, and Technology: The Making of a Scientific Culture," in *The Oxford History of Islam,* editor-in-chief John L. Esposito. New York: Oxford University Press, 1999

Hill, Donald R. *Islamic Science and Engineering.* Edinburgh: Edinburgh University Press, 1993

Menocal, Maria Rosa. *The Ornament of the World: How Muslims, Jews and Christians Created a Culture of Tolerance in Medieval Spain.* Boston: Little, Brown & Company, 2002

Syed, Ibrahim B. "Islamic Medicine: 1,000 Years Ahead of its Time," on http://islamusa.com/im4.html

Turner, Howard R. *Science in Medieval Islam: An Illustrated Introduction.* Austin: University of Texas Press, 1995

www.ummah.net/history/scholars/ZAHRAWI.html

Mohamed Zakariya (b. 1942)

The only American master Islamic calligrapher, Mohamed Zakariya is an internationally renowned artist and builder of medieval scientific instruments.

Mohamed Zakariya was born in Ventura, CA, in 1942. His father was an artist who made W.P.A. murals prior to World War II, spent the war mapping the fronts and reporting troop movements in North Africa from a B-17, and worked in the movie industry. His mother was a homemaker who also designed elegant household arrangements. Zakariya credits his parents with teaching him about color, design, and taste. His wife, Sally, the editor of *American School Board Journal,* is his sounding board for new ideas and texts.

Zakariya was educated in the United States. In his late teens, he traveled to Morocco where he spent most of his time in mosques. He returned to the United States when he was nineteen and formally converted to Islam, teaching himself Arabic at night while working as a factory machinist during the day. He became interested in calligraphy when he realized its importance in Arabic and Islamic life as both a religious exercise and an art form used to write beautiful and elaborate manuscripts of the Quran, which Muslims believe to be the literal Word of God. Although he appreciated calligraphy's role as "music for the eye" offering both spiritual reflection on the Divine and expansion of one's vision and understanding of the meaning of the text, he did not pursue it formally until he met Egyptian calligrapher Abdussalam Ali-Nour during a second trip to Morocco. Ali-Nour became Zakariya's first calligraphy teacher in 1964.

Zakariya spent the mid-1960s traveling through Europe, working at odd jobs such as restoring houses and performing with a British comedy troupe, while studying calligraphy in his spare time. His favorite location was the Oriental Reading Room of the British Museum in London, where he was able to study calligraphy texts. At that time, visitors were permitted to handle books and works, including some eighth-century texts that had been made within a century of the Prophet Muhammad's lifetime. He learned about the properties of ink and paper by handling the texts and holding them up to the light.

Zakariya returned to California in 1968. While working for an antique dealer in West Hollywood, he learned to restore and build reproductions of antiques. The combination of his love of working with his hands and fascination with ancient and medieval science led him to make sundials and astrolabes. His success in making reproductions of Renaissance scientific and musical instruments, illuminated manuscripts, and celestial globes led to his being named artist-in-residence at Scripps College in 1970.

In 1972, Zakariya moved to the suburbs of Washington, DC, to pursue calligraphy seriously. In the eight years that followed, he completed his first functioning astrolabe, and published two books on calligraphy that met with critical acclaim. The books were not only the first written by an American Islamic calligrapher, but also marked the first time that an Islamic calligrapher had written about calligraphy as an art in a language other than a Muslim language. Despite this success, he was discouraged by the plateau he felt he had reached in his calligraphy by 1980. Believing that his art was one in which he should see constant improvement, he was frustrated by the impression that he was no longer progressing as an artist.

It was at this time that, unknown to Zakariya, Dr. Esin Atil, an Islamic art historian at the Smithsonian Institution's Freer Gallery of Art, sent samples of Zakariya's calligraphy to the Research Center for Islamic History, Art, and Culture in Istanbul, Turkey. Atil saw in Zakariya's work the major elements of traditional master calligraphers: composition in a traditional manner, the use of more than a dozen types of script, and mastery of illumination. Believing that Zakariya was an important prospect because of his talent and because he was the only person in the United States working on Islamic calligraphy, Atil hoped that the Research Center would be interested in having him as a student. The Research Center quickly confirmed the skill and enthusiasm inherent in Zakariya's work, but realized that it was the product of a calligrapher who had not received formal training. In a compromise solution, the Research Center invited Zakariya to come for instruction, but under the proviso that he set aside everything he had learned previously and start over from the beginning.

Zakariya responded with enthusiasm, in part because the Turks are considered to have perfected the art of calligraphy during the Ottoman Empire and because contemporary Turkish calligraphers are broadly recognized as the world's last great calligraphers. Beginning in 1984, he engaged in an unconventional learning program – one carried out through the mail. Learning the art of calligraphy generally requires that the student and teacher be together to practice visually. Zakariya notes that the lessons are not so much about how to work as they are about how to see. Because calligraphy takes years to master and because Zakariya resided and worked in the United States, a move to Turkey for such a lengthy time was not possible. Instead, he began a correspondence course with Turkish master calligraphers Hasan Çelebi for *sulus / nesih* script and with Ali Alparslan for *ta'lik* script. He spent one month in Istanbul in 1984 meeting daily with his teachers. The lessons began with individual letters and then moved to two letter combinations. Full sentences were not approached until several years into the program. The main work of learning calligraphy involves constant practice of writing exercises in order to achieve the precision and certainty essential to the art of beautiful writing. Learning good calligraphy typically involves reviewing and copying the works of great masters. Zakariya notes that it took longer for him to become a master calligrapher than it takes for a surgeon to be trained, in part because one must master everything that one expects to teach others.

Zakariya received his *icazet* (diploma) from Çelebi in 1988 and from Alparslan in 1997, making him the first American ever to receive *icazet*s in calligraphy and the only recognized Islamic calligrapher in the United States. It also marks his ability both to duplicate the works of other masters and to write Quranic texts and Islamic sayings independently. He has maintained relationships with his teachers, noting the importance of having other experts with whom to discuss ideas and provide guidance for new directions for his art. Because calligraphy requires constant practice and improvement of method, study never ends. It simply moves in different directions. Zakariya both writes and illuminates his own work.

Zakariya came to international attention during the 1980s when he began to exhibit his work in the United States and abroad. In the early 1980s, he exhibited his work in Doha, Qatar, and taught at the Doha Free Art School. He visited the Gulf again in 1986 for exhibitions and lectures in Saudi Arabia, Qatar, Bahrain, Oman, and Abu Dhabi. That same year, he won his first calligraphy prize in a competition sponsored by the Research Center in Istanbul where he had studied.

At the same time, interest in Zakariya's astrolabes grew. The astrolabe, an engraved brass plate on which brass discs and pointers rotate to simulate the apparent rotation of the stars around the celestial pole, was an important medieval navigational and surveying tool that also served as a daily clock and calendar for predicting seasons and calculating astronomical problems. With as many as nine parts that move in relation to each other, the design requires a wealth of knowledge, extensive geometrical calculations, and precision engraving with specially designed tools. Zakariya has made thirteen functioning astrolabes, each of which took between three and six months to construct. Although many of the undocumented techniques, including the engraving process, have been lost, Zakariya was able to extract enough of the mathematical and scientific principles from old Arabic manuscripts to build his astrolabes, some of which are on permanent display at the Aramco Science Museum in Dhahran, Saudi Arabia, and the King Abdul Aziz International Airport in Jeddah, Saudi Arabia. Others have been exhibited at the Ornamental

Metal Museum in Memphis, TN, and the Adler Planetarium in Chicago, IL. He also has sundials on display in the National Museum in Doha, Qatar, and the Time Museum in Rockford, IL. Zakariya also makes compasses and is a master woodworker whose woodturning has been exhibited at the American Craft Museum in New York.

By the 1990s, Zakariya was spending less time on instruments and machine work and more on calligraphy. His calligraphy had generated so much interest in the United States that the American Arab Affairs Council sponsored him for a ten-state, two-year tour of the United States in 1990. He then designed and produced nine large calligraphy panels using texts from the Quran and poetry for an exhibition on Images of Paradise in Islamic Art that traveled to five states in 1992. Since then, his calligraphy has been exhibited at the Smithsonian Institution's Renwick Gallery and S. Dillon Ripley Center, the Klutznick National Jewish Museum in Washington, DC, the Metropolitan Museum of Art in New York City, and the Walters Gallery in Baltimore, MD. His work was featured as part of the Al-Andalus: The Art of Islamic Spain exhibition at the Metropolitan Museum of Art. He has given demonstrations at the Milwaukee Art Museum, the Detroit Institute of Art, the Albuquerque Museum of New Mexico, and the Sackler Gallery at Harvard University in Cambridge, MA. He has also participated in exhibitions and symposia in Turkey, Kuwait, Iraq, Qatar, Bahrain, Oman, Saudi Arabia, and Abu Dhabi.

In addition to producing beautiful calligraphic art, Zakariya has sought to educate the public about Islamic art, including its history and development. He has presented a variety of workshops and lectures about Islamic calligraphy and is the author of numerous articles and monographs, including *Music for the Eyes*, published by the Metropolitan Museum of Art and the Los Angeles Museum of Art, in conjunction with the 1998–1999 exhibition of Ottoman calligraphy from the Sakip Sabanci collection. In addition, he has translated the exhibition catalogues *Letters in Gold*, and *Art of Calligraphy in the Islamic Heritage* by Ugur Derman from the Turkish.

Zakariya's mastery of calligraphy is more than an art form. It also requires a certain technical and mechanical expertise. A traditional calligrapher in every sense of the word, he is not only able to work in all major script styles, but also carves his own pens, makes his own ink and paper, and illuminates his own texts. For many calligraphers, such details and ancillary crafts are frequently relegated to an apprentice. Zakariya, however, considers them to be a critical component in the production of his art.

Zakariya's calligraphy pays tribute to the classical methods and traditions of calligraphy while introducing his own original ideas. Rather than trying to push the boundaries of calligraphy into a contemporary American idiom, he has worked within the tradition to honor and revitalize the past while recognizing the variations in calligraphy across time, space, and cultures. He has found the greatest personal inspiration in the Ottoman style not only because it tends to be more modern and rigorous than the Hispanic/Maghribi scripts, but also because it speaks to him as a Muslim of American/European descent. Like American society, Ottoman civilization was both international and multicultural. Zakariya claims inspiration from the intelligence, appreciation, tolerance, and humanistic thought of Ottoman society and civilization that produced a sense of personal, individual responsibility while permitting broad religious and artistic freedom. The Ottomans also provided strong state support for the arts and raised calligraphy to a fine art. (See also SULEYMAN THE MAGNIFICENT.) Zakariya's own work makes use of historical Turkish methods, such as the production of marbled papers according to the Turkish ebru method and use of Turkish Baroque illumination schemes to produce Islamicized ornamental themes. At the same time, he uses different color schemes and patterns, so that his work is not derivatively Turkish. He uses Turkish Baroque illumination both because of its European origins and because it is a simple and bold style of ornamentation that leaves space for experimentation.

As with any artist, Zakariya has his detractors. There are some who believe that, as an American, he has no "birthright" to works of art written in Arabic, Turkish or Farsi because he does not share those ethnicities. He dismisses such attitudes, noting that Islam, as a religion of equality, is not concerned by ethnicity and that ethnic exclusivity has no place in religion or the arts. He believes that Islamic art and language are the heritage of all Muslims and that Muslim artists could spend their time far more productively by presenting the truth of their beliefs through sincere, authentic, and superb workmanship in their art and by combining loyalty to the traditions of the past with new, fresh, and vital interpretations that allow the ancient texts to speak for themselves. He is particularly concerned with the need to keep calligraphy free from the cultural and political constraints that have hampered other visual Islamic art forms in the contemporary era, particularly the destruction of Ottoman-era mosques and cemeteries in the Balkans out of belief that the ornamentation, color, and local flavor somehow violate Islamic standards of art and architecture. Because calligraphy is the reproduction of a perfect and infallible text, the calligrapher should not have to be concerned about or constrained by cultural prohibitions against representational art or imagery. He firmly believes that the calligrapher must be free to give the text meaning through its visual presence and to allow the art of the word to live and evolve in ways that reflect the unchanging nature of the text itself while

encouraging the viewer to discover what it means.

As for many American Muslims, 9/11 raised concerns for Zakariya about the future of Islam in the United States and about the acceptance of Muslims as part of the fabric of American life. The attacks came at a particularly awkward time for Zakariya as his long-planned "Eid Greetings" stamp designed for the US Postal Service had just been released ten days earlier. The stamp, which features gold calligraphy of the Arabic phrase "Eid Mubarak" against a lapis lazuli background, had been released after a five-year campaign by the American Muslim community for a holiday stamp similar to those already issued for the Christian celebration of Christmas and the Jewish celebration of Hanukkah. In order to persuade the Postal Service to issue the stamp, a variety of American Muslim organizations had repeatedly lobbied Congress and American Muslim schoolchildren had written more than five thousand letters to the postmaster general. The stamp was intended to be a symbol of the acceptance of Muslims in the United States and a reflection of their participation in American society. In the aftermath of 9/11, many feared that the stamp would fail, symbolizing rejection of Islam and Muslims by their fellow Americans.

The Muslim community began a campaign, including e-mails and letters, to request that people buy the stamps so that the post office would not drop them. In what Zakariya has described as a "remarkable demonstration of American spirit," many Americans from diverse backgrounds chose to make their own statement in the aftermath of 9/11 by buying the stamps. All 75 million stamps of the initial issue were sold out in the first year, making them part of the U.S.P.S. permanent collection that are to be reissued during the appropriate seasons.

Zakariya also experienced a groundswell of interest in his calligraphic work in the aftermath of 9/11. Possessing knowledge of Islam as both a religion and an ethic, he became an important spokesperson for Islam. The fact that his Islam is a faith, rather than a political ideology or system, enables him to take a realistic, rather than apologetic, approach to his discussions. His lectures are frequently filled to over capacity and tend to run longer than planned because of public interest.

While teaching his own students, Zakariya has continued to present his calligraphic works in exhibitions around the United States and in the Muslim world, including Saudi Arabia, Qatar, and the United Arab Emirates. At the request of Muslim students, he remodeled the mosque at Georgetown University, complete with a *mihrab* indicating the direction of Mecca for prayer, seven original calligraphic works, pine bookcases, and a vacuum cleaner with a case in order to encourage the students to take care of their place of worship. In keeping with his own understanding of Islam as a religion of equality, he made no separation of space between men and women. He also donated some classical literature in the hope that the students will retain their vision of Islam as a faith, rather than a political ideology. He also provided calligraphy for the Muslim Community Center Mosque in Maryland.

In his own contribution to interfaith dialogue, Zakariya organized a joint exhibition with Jewish calligrapher Neil Yerman and Christian calligrapher Karen Gorst entitled Writing the Sublime: The Art of Calligraphy in the Religions of Abraham, designed to demonstrate the shared heritage and scriptural foundations for peace of the Abrahamic faiths. The exhibition debuted in November, 2003 at the Interfaith Center of New York, the Onisaburo Gallery, before traveling to other American cities.

For his dedication to community service and the promotion of a kinder, gentler face of Islam, Zakariya was profiled in the P.B.S. production *Muhammad: Legacy of a Prophet* (see also MICHAEL WOLFE and LOBNA ISMAIL) and received a community service award from a Los Angeles mosque. He has been profiled by *Psychology Today*. In 2004, he won a prestigious award in *celi ta'lik* script in the Sixth International Competition from the Research Center for Islamic History, Art, and Culture in Istanbul, where he learned his art. He shared the prize with a Syrian and a Persian.

Further reading

Goodstein, Laurie. "U.S. Muslims Push Stamp as Symbol of Acceptance," New York *Times*, November 20, 2001

Kesting, Piney. "Calligrapher at Work," *Saudi Aramco World*, vol. 43, no. 1, January/February, 1992

—— "The World of Mohamed Zakariya," *Saudi Aramco World*, vol. 43, no. 1, January/February 1992

"Writing the Sublime: The Art of Calligraphy in the Religions of Abraham," www.interfaithcenter.org/writing/shtml

"Writing the Sublime: Mohamed Zakariya Heals with the Pen," November 10, 2003, www.altmuslim.com/art_comments/php?id=1112_0_13_0_C

Zakariya, Mohamed. The *Calligraphy of Islam: Reflections on the State of the Art*. N.p, n.d.

—— *Music for the Eyes*. New York and Los Angeles: Metropolitan Museum of Art and the Los Angeles Museum of Art, 1998

—— *Observations on Islamic Calligraphy: An Introduction to Islamic and Ottoman Calligraphy*. Washington, DC: Library of Congress, 1978

Interviews with the author, October 23, 2003, and March 26, 2004, and series of personal correspondence

www.interfaithcenter.org – website for the Interfaith Center of New York

www.mideasti.org/library/islam/zakaria.html – website featuring statements by Zakariya about his work

www.nlm.nih.gov/exhibition/islamic_medical/calligraphy/calligraphy.html – presentation of Islamic Calligraphy with Mohamed Zakariya, sponsored by the National

Library of Medicine; includes film coverage of Zakariya engaged in his work with explanations of the tools, materials, and styles he uses
www.zakariya.net – Zakariya's personal website

Dr. Elias Adam Zerhouni
(b. 1951)

Head of the National Institutes of Health (N.I.H.), Dr. Elias Adam Zerhouni is the first Arab-American and first American Muslim to serve in this capacity. He is one of the highest ranking Arab-American and American Muslim officials in the U.S. government.

Dr. Elias Adam Zerhouni was born on April 12, 1951, in Nedroma, Algeria. His father was a math professor. He was educated at the University of Algiers and received his medical degree in 1975. A specialist in radiology, he met his wife, pediatrician Nadia Azza, in high school when both were competing to be on Algeria's national swim team.

In 1975, Zerhouni and his wife left Algeria for the United States, where they became naturalized citizens. Zerhouni completed his residency in diagnostic radiology at Johns Hopkins University in Baltimore, MD, in 1978 as chief resident. He served as assistant professor of radiology at the university from 1979 until 1985, when he was promoted to associate professor of radiology. He also worked in the department of radiology at Eastern Virginia Medical Schools and its affiliated DePaul Hospital from 1981 until 1985. He was appointed director of the M.R.I. division at Johns Hopkins in 1988. In 1992, he was promoted to professor of radiology and professor of biomedical engineering at Johns Hopkins, where he remains on the faculty. He was promoted to chairman of the department of radiology and radiological science in 1996 and to the position of executive vice dean of the School of Medicine in 1997,

both of which he retains. He has also served as the vice dean for research at Johns Hopkins.

Zerhouni's administrative achievements at Johns Hopkins include the development of a comprehensive strategic plan for research, a reorganization of the school's academic leadership, and a restructuring of the clinical practice association in the School of Medicine. He also planned a major biotechnology research park and urban revitalization project near the medical campus, helped obtain a center on informatics, and led a successful effort to establish the Institute for Cell Engineering, for which he obtained an anonymous donation of $58.5 million. The institute's purpose was to develop and advance Johns Hopkins' expertise in stem-cell research.

Zerhouni's academic achievements include serving as the principal investigator on three N.I.H. grants and co-investigator on two others. He holds, singularly and jointly, eight patents and has authored or co-authored more than a hundred and fifty peer-reviewed publications and eleven book chapters. His medical and research achievements include the development of high resolution computed axial tomography (C.A.T. scanning) densitometry techniques for anatomic and physiologic studies of the lung that can determine, for example, whether nodules found on the lung are malignant or benign, and the adaptation of magnetic resonance imaging (M.R.I.) technology to take moving pictures of the heart by using magnetic fields to create a grid (described as a three-dimensional tic-tac-toe board) capable of tracking the heart. This technique, known as myocardial tagging, is widely used to diagnose heart problems. The most important aspect of these methods is that all of them are either non-invasive or minimally invasive, making them less hazardous and painful for the patients. Zerhouni's pioneering work is geared toward what he calls the reinvention of the role of radiology in medicine. He is particularly concerned by the challenge of a constantly growing population and the need for earlier detection of cancer which will significantly reduce medical expenses and mortality. The goals of reducing expenses and detecting cancer earlier were pivotal in his development of new technologies that combine radiology and endoscopy.

In addition to his academic and administrative achievements, Zerhouni is a businessman. His personal experiences with developing medical technology includes creation of his own companies, founding or co-founding five companies that sell his inventions. During his tenure as chair of radiology at Johns Hopkins, Zerhouni and other local radiologists established a company specializing in the delivery of outpatient, high-tech imaging services. This company was later acquired by the American Radiology Services Corporation. He helped to establish Surgi-Vision, Inc., a company which has licensed novel, image-guided clinical technology from his laboratories. He was also engaged in a collaborative effort with General Electric to develop innovative high-speed M.R.I. technology.

Zerhouni is a figure of both admiration and controversy. His medical colleagues credit him with being a creative thinker capable of finding solutions outside of standard procedures and a skilled negotiator capable of bringing together a variety of talents and interests for the common good. He is known as a man of integrity and someone who is willing to abide by collective decisions, even if he personally disagrees with them. Although he is trained in radiology, he has proven able accurately to assess medical issues outside of his own field. He is considered a visionary capable of seeing where the health-care system is heading and what needs to be done, operating in the reality of medical practice while maintaining high academic standards. At the same time, he has generated

controversy over his support for stem-cell research, as these are sometimes, although not always, obtained from human embryos. While he has not commented specifically on his opinions about embryo research, he has affirmed his respect for the preciousness of human life and is known to oppose abortion.

Zerhouni's combination of medical expertise, research creativity, and managerial prowess led to his nomination for the directorship of the N.I.H., a $27 billion federal agency that conducts research on some of the most challenging scientific and medical questions facing the nation. Consisting of twenty-seven centers and institutes and employing 15,000 people, the N.I.H. oversees more than 45,000 research grants in a variety of fields, including biotechnology, genetics, and disabling diseases such as Alzheimer's, Parkinson's, diabetes, mental illness, and cancer. Zerhouni was nominated for the directorship at a White House ceremony on March 26, 2002. At a time when the United States was addressing critical decisions about cloning, stem-cell research, and bioterrorism in the aftermath of the 9/11 terrorist attacks, the nomination had symbolic, as well as medical, importance. President George W. Bush made a veiled reference to concerns about a Muslim and Arab-American being appointed to such an important position when he referred to Zerhouni as a "quadruple threat: a doctor who excels at teaching, researching, patient care and management." Zerhouni began his tenure as director on May 20, 2002, after confirmation by the Senate.

Zerhouni's accomplishments as N.I.H. director include the establishment of a road map for science for 2003, including expansion of the successful control of acute, short-term lethal diseases, such as coronary heart disease and stroke. Recognizing the broad increase of life expectancy, he noted that the landscape of diseases that need to be addressed in the contemporary era has changed from what it was in the past. Of most importance is the shift of expenditure from acute diseases to chronic diseases. He has called for novel experiments, innovations, and approaches to address this shift and to address new fields such as biological complexity and genetics in dealing with diseases such as cancer, Parkinson's disease, and Alzheimer's, all of which are caused by a variety of factors, some of which precede the disease. Because proximate causes are known, he believes that the next major step is the determination of the factors leading to proximate causes, such as the body's inability to produce insulin, which causes diabetes. He has also called for greater interaction and assimilation between biological, physical, information, and behavioral sciences, so that a multidisciplinary approach is taken to address medical issues. He has named the conducting and funding of medical research as N.I.H.'s top priority, seeking to achieve new knowledge to prevent, detect, diagnose, and treat diseases and disabilities, from A.I.D.S., diabetes, cancer, and heart disease to the common cold and other enduring illnesses. Confronting the threats of bioterrorism has also been named as an important goal.

Zerhouni has initiated the creation of a new research vision for the N.I.H. focusing on biomedical research as a new pathway for discovery and for reengineering clinical medical research. He has completed the doubling of the N.I.H. budget and named directors to the National Institutes for Mental Health, Alcohol Abuse and Alcoholism, Drug Abuse, Neurological Disorders and Stroke, and General Medical Sciences. A member of the National Academy of Sciences' Institute of Medicine since 2000 and the board of scientific advisers of the National Cancer Institute since 1998, Zerhouni was a consultant to the White House under President Ronald Reagan in 1985 and to the World Health Organization in 1988.

Further reading

Brown, Laura J. "Arab-American Doctor Named to Senior Medical Post in Bush Administration: Algerian-born Elias Zerhouni to lead National Institutes of Health," U.S. Department of State Office of International Information Programs, March 28, 2002.

Mazar, M. "Bush nomme Elias Zerhouni a la tete de l'Institut americain de la sante," *Le Quotidien d'Oran*, March 28, 2002

Stolberg, Sheryl Gay. "From Algeria to a Dream: Elias Adam Zerhouni," New York *Times*, March 27, 2002

"Zerhouni Assumes Leadership of the National Institutes of Health," N.I.H. news release, May 20, 2002

www.nih.gov – website for the National Institutes of Health

Ahmed Hassan Zewail (b. 1946)

Winner of the unshared Nobel Prize for Chemistry in 1999, Ahmed Hassan Zewail is the founder of the field of femtochemistry and the first Egyptian, first Arab, and first Muslim to win the Nobel Prize for Chemistry. He is the only living Muslim Nobel laureate in science.

Ahmed Hassan Zewail was born in Damanhur, Egypt, on February 26, 1946. His father ran a business importing and assembling motorcycles and bicycles before becoming a government official. His mother was a full-time mother and homemaker who, although uneducated herself, encouraged her children to succeed in their educations.

Zewail began his education at the Sidi Ibrahim al-Desuqi Mosque in Damanhur. Because university studies were generally limited to the elite, he knew that his dream of a university education could be achieved only through merit. He received his secondary education in Desuq, excelling in his studies, particularly science and math, preparing him for national exams in which he competed with all other students in Egypt. The results of the national exams determined who would continue on to university studies and in which disciplines. Students with the highest scores were chosen for the most prestigious professions, so he focused on physics, chemistry, mechanics, and mathematics. His scores on the national exams made him eligible for the university. Although his father believed that he should earn a B.S. in agricultural engineering, his mother and uncle supported his determination to continue in science. Zewail applied and was admitted to the faculty of science at Alexandria University.

Zewail entered the university in 1963. Because there were no dormitories, he lived with an uncle and took the train to Alexandria daily. University studies in Egypt were approached with seriousness and respect by both students and professors. Professors served as role models and were expected to be prompt and to have their lessons prepared in advance. Students were expected to arrive on time for classes and not to disrupt instruction. Although freshman classes typically had 500 students, professors made certain that all students could see and hear and were meticulous about their problem solving, presenting all steps of the solution, integration, differentiation, and equations with precision and thoroughness. Zewail received what he describes as a quality education under this system, although his research often required him to copy articles by hand from the library sources because there were no photocopy machines.

Zewail's studies at the faculty of science required him to choose four subjects to study during his freshman year. He was expected to drop one subject per year until he had one main subject left. He began with mathematics, chemistry, physics, and geology, reluctantly dropping mathematics after his first year. His high grades earned him his first newspaper notice and photograph, as well as a monthly stipend. His performance during his second year earned him a position as one of only seven "specials" in

chemistry, marking him as one of the top students and putting him on track for graduate school. He completed his university studies in 1967, earning the distinction of excellent with the rank of first-class honor – the highest recognition offered by the university. He was ranked first in his science class.

Zewail's studies for his master's degree at the University of Alexandria sparked his interest in spectroscopy. Laboratories in Egypt at that time were modest and most of the equipment was not very advanced. The exception was the new spectrophotometer, which Zewail quickly learned to use. Although the master's program was supposed to take between two and four years to complete, Zewail completed his thesis and had it approved within eight months, enabling him to apply for a Ph.D. program abroad and to publish his research, which appeared between 1969 and 1971.

Zewail was accepted by the University of Pennsylvania for August of 1969, complete with full tuition remission and a stipend. His initial excitement about the acceptance was soon tempered by the bureaucratic hurdles he faced in Egypt. Officially, he was not permitted to graduate from his master's program before the end of the two-year period. The University of Alexandria also had a policy that did not allow direct offers to be made to students; an offer had to be made to a department, which then chose the person to receive the appointment. Realizing that the University of Pennsylvania could not make such an offer, Zewail wrote to his new mentor for help. His professor sent the requested letter to the department, but with the proviso that he would not accept anyone other than Zewail. Even with this letter, Zewail still had to collect signatures from all of the other students in his group stating that they had no interest in the scholarship. He also had to request an official leave of absence in order to bypass the two-year regulation and then go through several levels of government bureaucracy, culminating with the Ministry of Higher Education in Cairo, personally presenting his request, before he was able to obtain all of the necessary paperwork to go abroad. He got married three days before he left Egypt.

Zewail asked for a research assignment upon his arrival in the U.S. He was assigned to work on the Stark effect on large biological molecules. Having always preferred quantitative to qualitative science, he asked to work on a smaller system. Within a few months, he was conducting experiments. He submitted his first paper within a year and became competent in quantum mechanics, lasers, electricity, and magnetism within two years, despite his lack of experience in working with complex instrumentation. During this time, he also began several of his trademark tendencies, including a multidisciplinary approach combining chemistry and physics and working on several research projects at once, typically involving spectroscopy of solids, magnetic and electric field effects on crystals, optical detection of magnetic resonance, and the behavior of molecules in an electric field. He completed his Ph.D. in 1972 with more than ten co-authored publications.

Zewail decided to pursue a postdoctoral position at the University of California, Berkeley, in 1974. Because he had no teaching responsibilities, he was able to dedicate himself to research. Access to expensive, state-of-the-art equipment there led him to realize that what keeps the United States at the forefront of science is a handful of outstanding institutions. He became convinced of the need to develop similar centers of excellence in Egypt to improve the science base and attract the best researchers.

In 1976, Zewail was invited to the California Institute of Technology (Caltech) where he began research into the coherence of molecules through the use of lasers. He published his first paper within

two months of his arrival and was considered for tenure in 1978. He became full professor of chemical physics, as well as a U.S. citizen, in 1982.

Between 1976 and 1978, Zewail worked on real-time motion at the atomic and molecular levels, seeking to understand coherence and catch both small and large molecules in action. Although some critics expressed concerns about his concept of coherence and protested that his work was not true chemistry, Zewail remained confident in his idea. He ultimately discovered that coherence is the key element in probing and controlling molecular dynamics on the atomic scale, a concept that was fundamental to his later development of the sub-discipline of femtochemistry.

Zewail became increasingly convinced that the best method of monitoring dynamics was through the use of coherent laser techniques, rather than an apparent spectral feature. Lasers would also allow for the direct measurement of the energy redistribution rates among all atomic motions. In order to test his theory, he had to build new equipment: a vacuum chamber for molecules coming out of the source as a collimated beam at supersonic speed. He designed a system that included a molecular beam interfaced with a picosecond laser system.

At first, Zewail sought directly to measure the rate of vibrational energy redistribution for an isolated molecule using a picosecond laser that deposited energy into the molecule in nuclear vibrational motion. He hoped to see an evolution to other motions, expecting to find a decrease in time in the population of molecules in the initially excited vibrational stage. However, rather than decay, he found that the population was oscillating coherently back and forth with well-defined periods and phases, a phenomenon that reflected the rebirth of molecular motion, rather than a decay. The results confirmed the significance of coherence and its existence in complex molecular systems. Knowing that his findings were likely to receive considerable attention and skepticism, he carried out many experiments to confirm them.

Zewail's findings resulted in a paradigm shift in science and physics as new theories and methods had to be developed to explain the vibrational-energy redistributions and to adjust for shorter time resolutions for molecules exhibiting different chemical processes and undergoing rotational motions. Zewail also developed a method for observing the full period of coherent rotational motion (recurrences) by aligning the molecules with one polarized ultrafast laser and probing the rotating molecules with another. The method, known as "rotational coherence spectroscopy" (R.C.S.), initially met with skepticism, but was proven accurate through repeated experimentation. It is currently used in many labs.

Believing that further discoveries remained in learning to control the phases, Zewail turned next to nuclear magnetic resonance (N.M.R.) experiments in the optical domain using lasers. The use of lasers proved to be more difficult because the phases were harder to control when using optical pulses of light than they had been using the radiofrequency pulses in N.M.R. Nevertheless, within a year, he had developed a laser technique capable not only of exciting and probing molecules coherently, but also of controlling the phases at optical frequencies when using pulsed lasers.

Having mastered control of the phases, Zewail turned to better time resolution. He had picosecond lasers, but wanted to go into the domain of subpicoseconds (10^{-12} second). He borrowed a pulsed laser setup that allowed him to observe the bond breakage in a molecule containing three atoms at the subpicosecond time scale. Although he had not yet resolved the transition states, he published his observations in 1985 while searching for a pulsed laser of another single order of magnitude improvement in time resolution. He had

already received the Alexander von Humboldt Award for senior U.S. scientists in 1983 and an N.S.F. award of extended funding for especially creative research in 1984. He received his first national recognition in 1985 when he was awarded the Buch-Whitney Medal.

Zewail's breakthrough occurred in 1986 through the development of femtochemistry. His goal was to see the transition states of atoms in motion in real time, or a femtosecond, which is one millionth of one billionth of a second (10^{-15} second). Femtochemistry requires the probing of between millions and billions of molecules for each initiation pulse and then repeating the experiment numerous times to provide a signal strong enough for analysis. The timing of the laser pump and probe pulses must be of femtosecond precision and the launch configuration must be of sub-angstrom resolution in order to synchronize the motion of the independent molecules so that they have all reached a similar point in their structural evolution at the moment when the probe pulse arrives to capture the impression. Achievement of this goal required years of building the experimental and theoretical foundations of femtochemistry, more years of experimentation to prove that the theories were correct, and the development of new instrumentation with unprecedented time resolution and the interfacing of femtosecond lasers with molecular beam technology, as well as massive funding.

Zewail conducted his first successful experiment in 1986, witnessing the breaking of molecular bonds in real time for the first time in history. The experiment also showed that molecules experienced multiple cycles of bonding prior to coming apart at the end. The results, particularly with respect to dynamics and motion, were so different from what was accepted as standard knowledge at the time that Zewail had not only to question the key concepts involved, but also to formulate the theoretical framework for the physics involved. His pioneering work in the new field of femtochemistry was recognized with a John Simon Guggenheim Foundation fellowship in 1987.

Zewail's pioneering work led to his being awarded the King Faisal International Prize in Science in 1989. Founded in Saudi Arabia in 1977 to recognize outstanding work in science, medicine, literature, and Islamic studies, the prize is awarded on the basis of merit and continuous support from academic institutions both nationally and internationally. Historically, the science and medicine awards had gone to non-Arabs, although Arabs and Muslims typically received the awards for literature and Islamic studies. Zewail was the first Arab to receive the prize in either science or medicine, making that year a particularly proud moment for the Arab world. Many winners of the King Faisal prize go on to win the Nobel Prize.

By the 1990s, femtochemistry was recognized as a new sub-discipline and was being applied to the study of gases, fluids, and solids, and on surfaces and in polymers. Zewail's group addressed organic chemistry with molecules of more than ten atoms. As they worked to develop new instrumental methods, other labs began to apply the techniques to medicine, including studying the transformation of a photon of light into a nerve impulse, as occurs in the eye, and studying the process of photosynthesis in plants in real time. By the late 1990s, femtochemistry was being used to determine how molecular electronic components should be designed, understand the mechanisms of a variety of life processes, and develop the medicines of the future. Medical applications include use for the imaging of tumors and for the direct view of cells and how they change over time. In the future, Zewail expects that femtochemistry will grow in the areas of control of reactions, biology/medicine, and greater observation of structural transitions, particularly in biological molecules.

Zewail's breakthroughs in femtochemistry generated interest from both the scientific community and the general press. Caltech announced the discovery in late 1987 after Zewail's scientific papers had passed scrutiny. By 1988, femtochemistry was being featured on the covers of professional journals. In 1994, the prestigious U.S. journal *Science* announced femtochemisty as a new field of study. In 1998, *The Journal of Physical Chemistry* ran a special issue on Ten Years of Femtochemistry. Femtochemistry also became the subject of a variety of books and conferences, including the 1995 Solvay Conference and the 1996 Nobel Foundation Symposium on Femtochemistry and Femtobiology. The Nobel conference was particularly prestigious as it is used to judge the importance of a topic and whether it might be worth the Nobel Prize. Zewail also won major scientific awards, many of which are considered steps on the ladder to the Nobel Prize. He won the Wolf Prize in 1993 and the Robert A. Welch Award in Chemistry in 1997. Although the Welch Award typically recognizes "lifetime achievements," it was given to Zewail at a relatively young age for his "outstanding contributions in chemistry for the betterment of humankind." In 1998, he was awarded the most important and distinguished award in science in the United States, the Benjamin Franklin Medal in Chemistry.

The Benjamin Franklin Medal not only increased American attention to Zewail's work, but also resulted in the first official recognition of his work from Egypt. When he went to Egypt to receive the honor, he was welcomed by thousands of people in the streets who wanted to celebrate his achievements. In addition to the Order of Merit, First Class, in Sciences and Art from President Hosni Mubarak, stamps bearing Zewail's likeness were issued in ten-piaster and one-pound denominations, an honor that is usually granted only posthumously. The major street in his home town of Damanhur was named after him and his high school in Desuq was renamed for him, along with a street. So enthusiastic were the Egyptian people for his achievement that the police lost control of the crowds seeking to give him a hero's welcome.

On October 12, 1999, it was announced that Zewail had won the unshared Nobel Prize in Chemistry, the first Egyptian, first Arab, and first African ever to win. Although Egyptians had won the Nobel Prize for Peace in 1979 (Anwar al-Sadat) and the Nobel Prize for Literature in 1988 (see also NAGUIB MAHFOUZ), Zewail was only the second Muslim ever to win a science prize. (See also ABDUS SALAM.) For Zewail, winning the Nobel was important not only as a personal achievement, but also because it demonstrated that developing countries are capable of producing genius recognizable by the rest of the world and that science is not limited by time or space. It marked the return of Arabs and Muslims to great scientific achievements comparable to those of the past and continued the trend of Third World scientists earning a place in the most exclusive realms of scientific and technological achievement. (See also SULTAN BIN SALMAN BIN ABD AL-AZIZ AL-SAUD.) In his acceptance speech, which was broadcast live on Egyptian television and radio and was watched by millions of people around the world, Zewail commented that he hoped that the award would inspire the young generations living in developing countries with the knowledge that they have a contribution to make to world science and technology.

After the Nobel, Egypt awarded Zewail its highest state honor, the Order of the Grand Collar of the Nile, ranking him behind only the president, living former presidents, and vice-presidents in Egypt. He was awarded the keys to a variety of cities and many shields and medals from Egyptian organizations. A third stamp was issued, showing his portrait next to the pyramid. In 2000, the city of Alexandria dedicated Dr. Ahmed Zewail Square.

Egypt's recognition of his work, combined with his own recognition of the importance of his Egyptian background in his accomplishment, encouraged him to push forward with his idea of the creation of a center of excellence in science and technology in Egypt. In a meeting with President Mubarak, Zewail outlined Egypt's need for such a center. A groundbreaking ceremony for the University of Science and Technology (U.S.T.) was held a few days later. Zewail hopes that the U.S.T. will become the center of scientific research and development in Egypt that will enable Egypt not only to participate in globalization through the development of critical technologies, but also help it to retain its best university graduates. He has encouraged the continued strengthening of democratic institutions, the expansion of freedom of speech, and the minimization of bureaucracy as necessary corollaries to the U.S.T.'s work.

Zewail had worked to improve the science base in Egypt since the 1980s through a variety of lectures, conferences, and direction of research at the United Nations Alexandria Research Center (U.N.A.R.C.). Winning the Nobel Prize led him to greater contemplation of his responsibility to the progress of developing nations. He decided to pursue three major areas where he felt that he could be effective: the continuation of his scientific research; the popularization of science in order to continue to inspire young people and keep the public interested in science and new knowledge; and expansion of his involvement in science for the have-nots. He is particularly dedicated to creating partnerships between the Arab and Muslim worlds and the West, disagreeing with those who claim that conflicts over issues of civilization or culture are inevitable. He points instead to the economic and political forces at play in the creation of world instability, such as poverty, illiteracy, and the unjust division of the world into a minority of "haves" and a majority of "have-nots." He believes that differences of living standards, rather than religions or culture, are responsible for the creation of dissatisfaction, violence, and racial and ethnic conflict and that the answers to the world's problems lie not in slogans such as globalization or a new world order, but in addressing the four major issues that plague the developing world: illiteracy; incoherent policies for science and technology; restrictions on human thought and constitutional laws; and fanaticism. He has proposed that these issues be resolved through the restructuring of education and science, the creation of centers of excellence, and the commitment of national resources by developing countries, accompanied by the commitment of developed countries to focusing their aid programs toward more specific goals, the comprehensive inclusion of solutions to problems, a minimization of politics in aid, and dedication to being partners in the success of developing countries.

Zewail has used portions of his prize monies to establish merit-based prizes and awards of his own. He established the Ahmed Zewail Prize at the American University in Cairo in 2000 for the best graduating students. He also established a prize to honor the best student graduating from his high school and directed that a portion of the endowed fund be used to help the school with equipment and infrastructure. He established the Ahmed Zewail Fellowships for creative work in the arts in 2004.

Zewail has received honorary degrees and awards around the world. An elected member of the National Academy of Sciences, the American Academy of Arts and Sciences, the American Philosophical Society, and the American Academy of Achievement, he is a fellow of the American Physical Society and a member of the Pontifical Academy of Sciences, the European Academy of Arts, Sciences, and Humanities, the Indian Academy of Sciences, the Royal Danish Academy of Sciences and Letters, the Royal Society of the United Kingdom, the Russian Academy

of Sciences, the Royal Swedish Academy of Sciences, and the Royal Academy of Belgium. He serves on the boards of trustees for a variety of educational institutions. He received the Insignia of the Pontifical Academy from Pope John Paul II and was featured on a B.B.C. documentary entitled *The End of the Race Against Time*, in 2001. A frequent speaker at conferences on science and world affairs, editor of *Chemical Physics Letters*, and author of both books and articles, his autobiography has been translated into twelve editions and languages, including Chinese.

Zewail is the first Linus Pauling Chair professor of chemistry and professor of physics and the director of the National Science Foundation Center's Laboratory for Molecular Sciences (L.M.S.) at Caltech.

Further reading

Browne, Malcolm W. "Snapshots Taken as Chemicals Bond," New York *Times*, December 4, 1987

Maugh, Thomas H., II. "Unprecedented Step: Scientists Able to See 'Birth' of New Molecules," *Los Angeles Times*, December 3, 1987

Zewail, Ahmed H. "The Birth of Molecules," *Scientific American*, 263 (6), December, 1990

—— "Femtochemistry – Atomic-scale Dynamics of the Chemical Bond Using Ultrafast Lasers," in *Les Prix Nobel*. Stockholm: Almqvist & Wiksell, 2000

—— *Femtochemistry: Ultrafast Dynamics of the Chemical Bond*, 2 vols. River Edge, NJ: World Scientific, 1994

—— "The New World Dis-Order – Can Science Aid the Have-Nots?" In *Proceedings of the Jubilee Plenary Session of the Pontifical Academy of Sciences* (Vatican), 99, 2001

—— "Science for the Have-Nots," *Nature*, 410, April 12, 2001

—— *Voyage Through Time: Walks of Life to the Nobel Prize*. Cairo: American University in Cairo Press, 2002

Zewail, Ahmed H. ed. *The Chemical Bond: Structure and Dynamics*. Boston: Academic Press, 1992

Interview with the author, March 31, 2004

www.aquanet.co.il/wolf/ – website for the Wolf Foundation and Prize www.its.caltech.ed/~femto/ – home page for Ahmed Zewail

www.kff.com/english/kfip/selectoinproc.html – website for the King Faisal International Prize

www.nobel.se/ – website for the Nobel Foundation and Prize

www.thersa.org/rsa/bf_medal.asp – website for the R.S.A. and the Benjamin Franklin Medal

www.welch1.org/ – website for the Robert A. Welch Award

Zinedine Zidane (b. 1972)

The soccer star who led the French team to the World Cup Championship in 1998 and three-time winner of the Player of the Year Award from the Fédération Internationale de Football Association, Zinedine Zidane has put his star athletic abilities to work raising money for children living in poverty in Asia, Africa, and Latin America.

Zinedine Zidane, popularly known as "Zizou," was born on June 23, 1972, in Marseille, France. Originally from the Kabyle region of Algeria, his parents immigrated to France before he was born. Zidane is close to his family and credits his parents with teaching him hard work, honesty, and a love of soccer and games filled with spontaneity and fun.

Like many young people in Marseille, Zidane began playing soccer at an early age at the U.S. Saint Henri club. From there, he moved on to the Septemes Sports Olympiques. Zidane left Septemes after participating in the first-year junior selection for the league championship at the age of fourteen. He was professionally discovered that same year by the recruiter for Cannes. Following an invitation for a one-week stay in Cannes in 1986, Zidane remained for six years, playing with professionals from the age of sixteen. Determined to exceed expectations, he played his first game in the First Division in 1989 when he was seventeen. He played midfield for

Cannes, scoring his first goal as a professional on February 8, 1991, at the age of eighteen. His first season was capped by a fourth-place finish that qualified the team for the U.E.F.A. Cup.

Zidane's second season with Cannes did not go as well as the first. He switched to the Bordeaux team the Girondins in 1992 and signed a four-year contract. He scored ten goals in his first year. Every year that he played for the team, they qualified for the U.E.F.A. Cup, although he scored only six goals per year for the remaining three years. He made his international debut in an August 17, 1994, game against the Czech Republic, earning him international recognition and a place on the French World Cup team for the first time. He was sent in to play sixty-three minutes into the game when the team trailed 2–0. Although he scored two goals, the team did not win the cup. The team made it to the finals again in 1995–1996, but lost to Bayern Munich.

In 1996, Zidane's contract with Bordeaux was fulfilled. He signed with the Italian team Juventus, and moved to Turin, Italy, where he spent the next four years. He quickly became an international star. The team was the runner-up for the U.E.F.A. Cup in 1996 and won the 1996 European Super Cup, the 1996 European/South American Cup, the 1996 Toyota Cup, and the 1997 League Super Cup. Zidane was named the Italian Champion in 1997 and 1998 and was the runner-up in the 1997 and 1998 Champions League. He was also awarded the Golden Ball by France Football as the French Player of the Year in 1998 and was named World Player of the Year by F.I.F.A. in 1998, 2000, and 2003.

Zidane's acceptance of the Golden Ball award reflected many of the characteristics that have made him a soccer champion. The importance of family was demonstrated by the presence of his extended family at the presentation ceremony in Paris. Also present were about twenty childhood friends, reflecting his attitude as a team player. Zidane is renowned for playing for the benefit of his team, rather than his own personal glory. Individual moves he attempts are done in order to develop a maneuver or to make an opening advantageous to his side. He is particularly skilled at making complicated moves look simple. Known by both fans and players as "extraordinarily humble," he is widely recognized as one of the most successful soccer players in the world and in history.

One of the most important events in Zidane's professional career was the 1998 World Cup tournament. Zidane led the French team in its first ever appearance in the final rounds of the tournament. The team beat South Africa, but the next game, against Saudi Arabia, brought trouble for the team when Zidane and the Saudi captain became involved in a dispute. Zidane's retaliation against the Saudi captain resulted in his being banned from the next two games. The French team struggled without Zidane, scoring the winning goal with just seven minutes left. His teammates commented that it was not just Zidane as an individual player with consistency and strong technical skills who was missed, but Zidane as a leader and innovative thinker. He returned in the quarter-final game against Italy. He showed his full repertoire of skills in the semi-final and final games against first Croatia and then Brazil, which was widely expected to win the tournament. In the final part of the game against Brazil, Zidane scored two rare headed goals to win the game and the tournament – a first ever win for France.

France burst into a national celebration, culminating in a parade in Paris. The Arc de Triomphe was draped with a banner declaring, "Merci, Zizou" ("Thank you, Zizou"). A moment of tremendous national pride for the French, the celebration occurred at a time when France was being split from within over the question of the proper status of Muslim – particularly Algerian – immigrants and concerns that France was being "overtaken" by immigrants due to a combination of high immigration rates and low birth rates among French nationals. Having Zidane as a national hero raised questions about the supposed dangers of this "reverse colonization" and rising racism in France. At the time of the victory, the extremist right-wing National Front Party was supported by 20% of the population.

Zidane as a national symbol carries different meanings for different interpreters. As the son of Algerian immigrants, he was part of the first generation of his family to be born and raised in France. As such, most French would normally consider him Algerian, rather than French. However, many French do not consider Zidane to be Algerian or "a typical Algerian," both labels that tend to carry pejorative associations and meanings. For his French fans, including some who vote for Jean-Marie LePen and the National Front, Zidane does not represent any particular race or religion. However, his Algerian fans and fans of Algerian descent point with pride to his Algerian and Kabyle origins, as well as his Muslim faith. Zidane himself does not volunteer opinions about race or religion, fueling the belief of many of his French fans that he is different from his fellow Algerian immigrants and descendants of immigrants because he appears to be more French than Algerian. He speaks French, rather than Arabic, and often refers to his pride in being French, giving the impression that he has assimilated into French culture, rather than remaining apart from it in favor of another culture or national identity. French fans thus point to him as living proof of how assimilation can work to the benefit of the nation, while immigrants, particularly Algerians, look to him as a beacon of hope for acceptance and a better life for immigrants. Immigrants, in particular, saw the 1998 World Cup championship as an opportunity for French society to back away from the fascism of the National Front Party in favor of recognition of the social and cultural revolution France has experienced since the end of World War II and the collapse of the French Empire. Although Zidane clearly symbolizes different things to different people, he enjoys universal respect and popularity in France both for his athleticism and because he lives courteously and humbly. He has not provided any front-page gossip.

Zidane is considered to have demonstrated his best level of professional performance in the European Championships in 2000. His mastery of control over the game and ability constantly to revise and reevaluate the game while playing it in order to organize the team's offensive were considered hallmarks of his playing style.

The most expensive soccer player in the world, Zidane left Juventus for the Spanish team Real Madrid in 2001 for a world record fee of £46 million (roughly $66 million). His team won the European Champion Cup in 2002 and the World Championship Cup in 2003, despite a thigh injury that kept Zidane out of two games.

Since 2003, Zidane has become increasingly involved in humanitarian work. Recognizing that he is both a hero and a role model to young people, particularly Algerians, he has put his stardom and popularity to use raising money for causes related to children. In 2003, he co-launched and co-sponsored charity games to raise money for Children of the Sahara who live in extreme destitution in southern Algeria and for children who were orphaned by a May 2003 earthquake that devastated Algiers. At each of the games, some of the children who benefited from the proceeds were present and had the opportunity to meet him. Another charity game was held later that same year, featuring the Friends of Zizou against the Friends of Ronaldo. This game was organized by the U.N. Development Program to finance projects to fight poverty in Africa, Asia, and Latin America. Promoters believe they could have sold three times as many tickets due to popularity of the team leaders. Zidane scored the first two goals of game. He was named ambassador for the 2005 Mediterranean Games in Almeria, Spain, and became the first male model for Christian Dior.

In July 2003, Zidane announced his intent to retire in 2005 at the conclusion of his contract with Real Madrid in order to focus on his humanitarian work.

Further reading

"An Ambassador called 'Zizou'," *Reports*, March 2003, www.almeria2005.es

Brewin, John. "World Cup Legends – Zinedine Zidane (France)," December 21, 2001, www.soccernet.com

Chaumier, Denis. "FIFA World Player of the Year Zidane, in the Name of All his Near and Dear," March 19, 1999, www.fifa.com/en/display/article,4992.html

Farrar, David. "Zinedine Zidane – Whose Hero?" June, 2002, www.footballculture.net/players/profile_zidane.html

Garcia, Fernando. "Zinedine Zidane: Biographie," July 31, 2003, zidane.fr.free.fr/biografia-fr.html

Magdalinski, Tara and Timothy J.L. Chandler. "With God on their side: An introduction," in *With God on their Side: Sport in the Service of Religion*, ed. Tara Magdalinksi and Timothy J.L. Chandler. London and New York: Routledge, Taylor & Francis Group, 2002

Silverstein, Paul A. "Stadium Politics: Sports, Islam and Amazigh Consciousness in France and North Africa," in *With God on their Side: Sport in the Service of Religion*, ed. Tara Magdalinksi and Timothy J.L. Chandler. London and New York: Routledge, Taylor & Francis Group, 2002 www.zidane.net – website for Zinedine Zidane

Appendices

APPENDIX 1: ENTRIES BY PROFESSION

Architecture

Hassan Fathy, 91

Art

A.D. Pirous, 242
Mohamed Zakariya, 359

Business/Economics

Muzaffar Haleem, 114
Lobna Ismail, 143
M. Farooq Kathwari, 157
Safi Qureshi, 248
S. Atiq Raza, 255
Muhammad Nejatullah Siddiqi, 293
Muhammad Yunus, 345

Environmentalism

Fatima Jibrell, 151

Film

Moustapha Akkad, 21
Samira Makhmalbaf, 192

Human rights

Kadiatou Diallo, 72
Shirin Ebadi, 81

Saad Eddin Ibrahim, 134
Chandra Muzaffar, 219

Judiciary

Tahany El Gebaly, 99
Zakia Mahasa, 184

Literature

Assia Djebar, 74
Ismail Kadare, 155
Naguib Mahfouz, 187
Abd al-Rahman Munif, 215
Jalal al-Din Rumi, 265
Dr. Nawal El Saadawi, 270
Hanan al-Shaykh, 285

Media/Journalism

Mohammed Jasim al-Ali, 25
Rana Ahmed Husseini, 123
Ahmed Rashid, 252
Saira Shah, 281
Tayyibah Taylor, 310
Michael Wolfe, 339

Music/Entertainment

Yusuf Islam, 140
Amel Larrieux, 178
Shazia Mirza, 202

APPENDIX 2: ENTRIES BY DATE OF BIRTH

717

Rabia al-Adawiyya, 14

780

Abu Jafar Muhammad ibn Musa
  al-Khwarizmi, 174

930

Abu al-Qasim al-Zahrawi, 351

965

Abu Ali al-Hasan Ibn al-Haytham, 131

973

Abu Rayham Muhammad al-Biruni, 50

1138

Saladin (Yusuf Salah al-Din
  al-Ayyubi), 278

Thirteenth century

Shajarat al-Durr, 78
Radiyya bint Iltutmish, 250

1201

Abu Jafar Muhammad ibn Muhammad
  ibn al-Hasan Nasir al-Din al-Tusi, 316

1207

Jalal al-Din Rumi, 265

1304

Shams al-Din Abu Abd Allah
  Muhammad Ibn Battuta, 128

1494

Suleyman the Magnificent, 297

1900

Muhammad Asad, 41
Hassan Fathy, 91

1904

Umm Kulthum, 325

1912

Naguib Mahfouz, 187

1926

Abdus Salam, 11

1930

Farkhonda Hassan, 120

1931

Dr. Nawal El Saadawi, 270
Muhammad Nejatullah Siddiqi, 289

1932

A.D. Pirous, 242

1933

Muzaffar Haleem, 114
Abd al-Rahman Munif, 215

1934

Shamim Ibrahim, 138

1935

Moustapha Akkad, 21

1936

The Aga Khan, Prince Karim IV, 18
Assia Djebar, 74
Ismail Kadare, 155

1937

Djamila Bouhired, 54

1959

Oussama Cherribi, 64
Kadiatou Diallo, 72
Baroness Pola Manzila Uddin, 320

1962

Lobna Ismail, 143
Dr. Laila al-Marayati, 195
Nawal El Moutawakel-Bennis, 208

1963

Hakeem Olajuwon, 235

1965

Saira Shah, 281

1967

Rana Ahmed Husseini, 123

1968/1969

Rina Amiri, 38

1968

Hassiba Boulmerka, 56
Merve Safa Kavakci, 161

1971

Yaphett El-Amin, 35
Aasma Khan, 164
Khalid Khannouchi, 171
Zainab Al-Suwaij, 303

1972

Zinedine Zidane, 368

1973

Mos Def, 205
Joshua Salaam, 276

1974

Jemima Goldsmith, 106
Asma Gull Hasan, 117

1976

Shazia Mirza, 202

1977

Amel Larrieux, 178

1980

Samira Makhmalbaf, 192

APPENDIX 3: ENTRIES BY COUNTRY
(some names appear in more than one category)

Afghanistan

Rina Amiri, 38
Jalal al-Din Rumi, 265

Albania

Ismail Kadare, 155

Algeria

Djamila Bouhired, 54
Hassiba Boulmerka, 56
Assia Djebar, 74
Dr. Elias Adam Zerhouni, 359

Austria

Muhammad Asad, 41

Bahrain

H.R.H. Sheikha Sabeeka Al-Khalifa, 273

Bangladesh

M. Osman Siddique, 293
Baroness Pola Manzila Uddin, 320
Sheikh Hasina Wazed, 335
Muhammad Yunus, 345

Saudi Arabia

H.R.H. Princess Haifa Al Faisal, 110
Abd al-Rahman Munif, 215
Thoraya Ahmed Obaid, 229
H.R.H. Sultan bin Salman bin Abd
al-Aziz Al Saud, 299

Somalia

Fatima Jibrell, 151

South Africa

Farid Esack, 85

Spain

Abu al-Qasim al-Zahrawi, 351

Switzerland

The Aga Khan, Prince Karim IV, 18

Syria

Moustapha Akkad, 21
Saladin (Yusuf Salah al-Din al-Ayyubi),
278

Trinidad

Tayyibah Taylor, 310

Tunisia

Rashid al-Ghannoushi, 102

Turkey

Tansu Ciller, 68
Merve Safa Kavakci, 161
Suleyman the Magnificent, 297

United Arab Emirates

H.R.H. Sheikha Fatima bint Mubarak, 95

United Kingdom

Jemima Goldsmith, 106
Yusuf Islam, 140
Shazia Mirza, 202
Saira Shah, 281
Richard Thompson, 313
Baroness Pola Manzila Uddin, 320

United States

Kareem Abdul-Jabbar, 5
Moustapha Akkad, 21
Muhammad Ali, 28
Yaphett El-Amin, 35
Rina Amiri, 38
Muzaffar Haleem, 114
Asma Gull Hasan, 117
Shamim Ibrahim, 138
Lobna Ismail, 143
Kevin James, 147
M. Farooq Kathwari, 157
Aasma Khan, 164
Khalid Khannouchi, 171
Amel Larrieux, 178
Zakia Mahasa, 184
Dr. Laila al-Marayati, 195
Mos Def, 205
Sahirah Muhammad, 214
H.M. Queen Noor, 223
Hakeem Olajuwon, 235
Safi Qureshi, 248
S. Atiq Raza, 255
Joshua Salaam, 276
M. Osman Siddique, 293
Zainab Al-Suwaij, 303
Tayyibah Taylor, 310
Amina Wadud, 332
Michael Wolfe, 339
Mohamed Zakariya, 353
Dr. Elias Adam Zerhouni, 359
Ahmed Hassan Zewail, 361

Uzbekistan

Abu Rayham Muhammad al-Biruni,
50

APPENDIX 4: ENTRIES BY CONTINENT, ACCORDING TO WHERE BORN

Africa

Djamila Bouhired, 54
Hassiba Boulmerka, 56
Kadiatou Diallo, 72
Assia Djebar, 74
Shajarat al-Durr, 78
Farid Esack, 85
Hassan Fathy, 91
Tahany El Gebaly, 99
Rashid al-Ghannoushi, 102
Farkhonda Hassan, 120
Shams al-Din Abu Abd Allah
    Muhammad Ibn Battuta, 128
Saad Eddin Ibrahim, 134
Fatima Jibrell, 151
Khalid Khannouchi, 171
Naguib Mahfouz, 187
Fatima Mernissi, 198
Nawal El Moutawakel-Bennis, 208
Hakeem Olajuwon, 235
Dr. Nawal El Saadawi, 270
Umm Kulthum, 325
Nadia Yassine, 343
Dr. Elias Adam Zerhouni, 359
Ahmed Hassan Zewail, 361

Asia (including Middle East)

Abdus Salam, 11
Rabia al-Adawiyya, 14
Moustapha Akkad, 21
Mohammed Jasim al-Ali, 25
Rina Amiri, 38
Benazir Bhutto, 46
Abu Rayham Muhammad al-Biruni, 50
Tansu Ciller, 68
Shirin Ebadi, 81
H.R.H. Sheikha Fatima bint Mubarak, 95
H.R.H. Princess Haifa Al Faisal, 110
Muzaffar Haleem, 114
Rana Ahmed Husseini, 123
Abu Ali al-Hasan Ibn al-Haytham, 131
Shamim Ibrahim, 134
M. Farooq Kathwari, 157
Merve Safa Kavakci, 161

Imran Khan, 166
Abu Jafar Muhammad ibn Musa
    al-Khwarizmi, 174
Nurcholish Madjid, 181
Samira Makhmalbaf, 192
H.R.H. Sheikha Mouza bint Nasser
    Al-Misnad, 211
Abd al-Rahman Munif, 215
Chandra Muzaffar, 219
Thoraya Ahmed Obaid, 229
A.D. Pirous, 242
Safi Qureshi, 248
Radiyya bint Iltutmish, 250
Ahmed Rashid, 252
S. Atiq Raza, 255
Jalal al-Din Rumi, 265
H.R.H. Sheikha Sabeeka Al-Khalifa,
    273
Saladin (Yusuf Salah al-Din al-Ayyubi),
    278
Hanan al-Shaykh, 285
Muhammad Nejatullah Siddiqi, 289
M. Osman Siddique, 293
Dr. Pratiwi Pujiliestari Sudarmono, 295
Suleyman the Magnificent, 297
H.R.H. Sultan bin Salman bin Abd
    al-Aziz Al Saud, 299
Zainab Al-Suwaij, 303
Azam Taleghani, 307
Abu Jafar Muhammad ibn Muhammad
    ibn al-Hasan Nasir al-Din al-Tusi, 316
Baroness Pola Manzila Uddin, 320
Hajjah Maria Ulfah, 322
Sheikh Hasina Wazed, 335
Muhammad Yunus, 345

Europe

The Aga Khan, Prince Karim IV, 18
Muhammad Asad, 41
Mustafa Ceric, 61
Oussama Cherribi, 64
Jemima Goldsmith, 106
Yusuf Islam, 140
Ismail Kadare, 155
Shazia Mirza, 202

Ibrahim Rugova, 258
Saira Shah, 281
Richard Thompson, 313
Abu al-Qasim al-Zahrawi, 351
Zinedine Zidane, 368

North America

Kareem Abdul-Jabbar, 5
Muhammad Ali, 28
Yaphett El-Amin, 35
Asma Gull Hasan, 117
Lobna Ismail, 143

Kevin James, 147
Aasma Khan, 164
Amel Larrieux, 178
Zakia Mahasa, 184
Dr. Laila al-Marayati, 195
Mos Def, 205
Sahirah Muhammad, 214
H.M. Queen Noor, 223
Joshua Salaam, 276
Tayyibah Taylor, 310
Amina Wadud, 332
Michael Wolfe, 339
Mohamed Zakariya, 353

APPENDIX 5: ENTRIES BY WHERE EDUCATED

Canada

Tayyibah Taylor, 310

Europe

Abdus Salam, 11
Muhammad Asad, 41
Benazir Bhutto, 46
Oussama Cherribi, 64
Assia Djebar, 74
Farid Esack, 85
Rashid al-Ghannoushi, 102
Jemima Goldsmith, 106
H.R.H. Princess Haifa Al-Faisal, 110
Imran Khan, 166
Shazia Mirza, 202
Abd al-Rahman Munif, 215
Ahmed Rashid, 252
S. Atiq Raza, 255
Ibrahim Rugova, 258
H.R.H. Sheikha Sabeeka Al-Khalifa, 273
Saira Shah, 281
Richard Thompson, 313
Baroness Pola Uddin, 320
Nadia Yassine, 343
Zinedine Zidane, 368

United States

Kareem Abdul-Jabbar, 5
The Aga Khan, Prince Karim IV, 18

Moustapha Akkad, 21
Muhammad Ali, 28
Yaphett El-Amin, 35
Rina Amiri, 38
Benazir Bhutto, 46
Mustafa Ceric, 61
Tansu Ciller, 68
Asma Gull Hasan, 117
Farkhonda Hassan, 120
Rana Husseini, 123
Saad Eddin Ibrahim, 134
Shamim Ibrahim, 138
Lobna Ismail, 143
Kevin James, 147
Fatima Jibrell, 151
M. Farooq Kathwari, 157
Merve Safa Kavakci, 161
Aasma Khan, 164
Amel Larrieux, 178
Nurcholish Madjid, 181
Zakia Mahasa, 184
Dr. Laila al-Marayati, 195
Fatima Mernissi, 198
Mos Def, 205
Thoraya Ahmed Obaid, 229
Hakeem Olajuwon, 235
A.D. Pirous, 242
Safi Qureshi, 248
S. Atiq Raza, 255
Joshua Salaam, 276
Osman Siddique, 293

Select bibliography

Abdul-Jabbar, Kareem. *Giant Steps*. New York: Bantam Books, 1983.

—— *A Season on the Reservation: My Sojourn with the White Mountain Apache*. New York: William Morrow & Company, 2000.

Abdul-Jabbar, Kareem and Alan Steinberg. *Black Profiles in Courage: A Legacy of African-American Achievement*. New York: Avon Books, 1997.

Aga Khan Foundation International Strategy, 1991–1999. Geneva: Aga Khan Foundation, 1992.

Ahmed, Leila. *Women and Gender in Islam: Historical Roots of a Modern Debate*. New Haven: Yale University Press, 1992.

Ahmed, Sirajuddin. *Sheikh Hasina, Prime Minister of Bangladesh*. New Delhi: U.B.S. Publishers' Distributors Ltd., 1998.

Akhund, Iqbal. *Trial and Error: The Advent and Eclipse of Benazir Bhutto*. New York: Oxford University Press, 2000.

Ali, Muhammad with Richard Durham. *The Greatest: My Own Story*. New York: Random House, 1975.

al-Ali, Nadje Sadiq. *Gender Writing: Writing Gender*. Cairo: American University in Cairo Press, 1994.

Allen, Roger. *The Arabic Literary Heritage: The Development of its Genres and Criticism*. New York: Cambridge University Press, 1998.

—— *The Arabic Novel: An Historical and Critical Introduction*, 2nd ed. Syracuse: Syracuse University Press, 1995.

Anderson, Margaret J. and Karen F. Stephenson. *Scientists of the Ancient World*. Berkeley Heights, NJ: Enslow Publishers, Inc., 1999.

Arberry, A.J., trans. *Muslim Saints and Mystics*. New York: Oxford University Press, 1966.

Armstrong, Karen. *Holy War: The Crusades and their Impact on Today's World*. New York: Doubleday, 1991.

—— *Muhammad: A Biography of the Prophet*. San Francisco: HarperCollins, 1993.

—— *Jerusalem: One City, Three Faiths*. New York: Alfred A. Knopf, 1996.

Asad, Muhammad. *Islam at the Crossroads*. Chicago: Kazi Publications, 1995.

—— *The Message of the Qur'an*. Gibraltar: Dar al-Andalus, 1980.

—— *Principles of State and Government in Islam*. Berkeley: University of California Press, 1961.

—— *The Road to Mecca*. New York: Simon & Schuster, 1954.

Badawi, M.M., ed. *The Cambridge History of Arabic Literature*. Cambridge: Cambridge University Press, 1983.

Barks, Coleman. *Rumi: The Book of Love: Poems of Ecstasy and Longing*. San Francisco: HarperSanFrancisco, 2003.

Bayes, Jane H. and Nayereh Tohidi, eds. *Globalization, Gender, and Religion: The Politics of Women's Rights in Catholic and Muslim Contexts*. New York: Palgrave, 2001.

Bear, Michael and Adnan Haydar, eds. *Naguib Mahfouz: From Regional Fame to Global Recognition*. Syracuse: Syracuse University Press, 1993.

Bhuiyan, Md. Abdul Wadud. *Emergence of Bangladesh and Role of Awami League*. Delhi: Vikas Publishing House, 1982.

Bhutto, Benazir. *Daughter of Destiny: Benazir Bhutto, an Autobiography*. New York: Simon & Schuster, 1989.

Camilleri, Joseph A. and Chandra Muzaffar, eds. *Globalisation: The Perspectives and Experiences of the Religious Traditions of Asia Pacific*. Selangor: International Movement for a Just World, 1998.

Charrad, Mounira M. *States and Women's Rights: The Making of Postcolonial Tunisia, Algeria, and Morocco*. Berkeley: University of California Press, 2001.

Cherribi, Oussama. "The Council of Europe's Human Rights Perspective on the Media," in *Studies in Communications*, vol. 6: *Human Rights and Media*, ed. Diana Papademas. New York: Elsevier Science Publishers, 2003.

—— "The Global Aspects of the Internet," in *Encyclopedia of International Media and Communications*, ed. Donald H. Johnston. New York: Academic Press, 2003.

—— "The Growing Islamization of Europe," in *Modernizing Islam: Religion in the Public Sphere in Europe and the Middle East*, ed. John L. Esposito and Francois Burgat. Newark and London: Rutgers University Press & Hurst, 2003.

Chittick, William C. *The Sufi Path of Love: The Spiritual Teachings of Rumi*. Albany: State University of New York Press, 1983.

—— *Sufism: A Short Introduction*. Oxford: Oneworld Publications, 2000.

Christopher, Matt. *On the Court with ... Hakeem Olajuwon*. Boston: Little, Brown and Company, 1997.

Clot, Andre. *Suleiman the Magnificent*, trans. John Howe. Chicago: New Amsterdam Books, 1993.

Cooke, Miriam. *War's Other Voices: Women Writers on the Lebanese Civil War*. Cambridge: Cambridge University Press, 1987.

Counts, Alex. *Give us Credit: How Muhammad Yunus's Micro Lending Revolution is Empowering Women from Bangladesh to Chicago*. New York: Random House, 1996.

Dallal, Ahmad. "Science, Medicine, and Technology: The Making of a Scientific Culture," in *The Oxford History of Islam*, editor-in-chief John L. Esposito. New York: Oxford University Press, 1999.

Danielson, Virginia. "Artists and Entrepreneurs: Female Singers in Cairo during the 1920s," in *Women in Middle Eastern History: Shifting Boundaries in Sex and Gender*, ed. Nikki R. Keddie and Beth Baron. New Haven: Yale University Press, 1991.

—— *The Voice of Egypt: Umm Kulthum, Arabic Song, and Egyptian Society in the Twentieth Century*. Chicago: University of Chicago Press, 1997.

Davis, Gloria, ed. *What is Modern Indonesian Culture?* Athens, OH: Center for International Studies, Ohio University, 1979.

DeLong-Bas, Natana J. *Wahhabi Islam: From Revival and Reform to Global Jihad*. New York: Oxford University Press, 2004.

Diallo, Kadiatou and Craig Wolff. *My Heart will Cross this Ocean: My Story, my Son, Amadou*. New York: One World Ballantine Books, 2003.

Djebar, Assia. *Love and Fantasia*. Paris: Albin Michel, 1995 [1985].

—— *The Mischief*, trans. Frances Frenaye. New York: Simon & Schuster, 1958.

—— *So Far from Medina*. London: Quartet Books, 1994.

—— *Sultana's Shadow*. London: Quartet Books, 1989.

—— *Women of Algiers in their Apartment*. Charlottesville, VA: University Press of Virginia, 1992.

Dunn, Ross. *The Adventures of Ibn Battuta: A Muslim Traveler of the 14th Century*. Berkeley: University of California Press, 1986.

Ebadi, Shirin. *History and Documentation of Human Rights in Iran*. New York: U.N.I.C.E.F., 2000.

—— *The Rights of the Child: A Study of Legal Aspects of Children's Rights in Iran*. Tehran: n.p., 1994.

Elsie, Robert. *Studies in Modern Albanian Literature and Culture*. New York: Columbia University Press, 1996.

Esack, Farid. "In Search of a Progressive Islamic Response to 9/11," in *Progressive Islam*, ed. Omid Safi. Oxford: Oneworld Publications, 2003.

—— *Introduction to Contemporary Islam*. Oxford: Oneworld Publications, 2004.

—— *An Introduction to the Qur'an*. Oxford: Oneworld Publications, 2002.

—— *On Being a Muslim: Finding a Religious Path in the World Today*. Oxford: Oneworld Publications, 1999.

—— *Qur'an, Liberation and Pluralism: An Islamic Perspective of Interreligious Solidarity Against Oppression*. Oxford: Oneworld Publications, 1997.

—— *The Struggle: Islamists and the South African Crucible*. Johannesburg: Call of Islam, 1989.

—— *Towards a Theology of Compassion – Religious Responses to H.I.V./A.I.D.S.* Forthcoming.

Esposito, John L. *Islam and Politics*, 4th ed. Syracuse, NY: Syracuse University Press, 1998.

—— *Islam: The Straight Path*, 3rd ed. New York: Oxford University Press, 1998.

—— *The Islamic Threat: Myth or Reality?* 3rd ed. New York: Oxford University Press, 1999.

—— *Unholy War: Terror in the Name of Islam*. New York: Oxford University Press, 2002.

—— *What Everyone Needs to Know About Islam*. New York: Oxford University Press, 2002.

Esposito, John L., editor-in-chief. *The Oxford Encyclopedia of the Modern Islamic World*. New York: Oxford University Press, 1995, 4 vols.

—— *The Oxford History of Islam*. New York: Oxford University Press, 1999.

Esposito, John L., ed. *Political Islam: Revolution, Radicalism, or Reform?* Boulder, CO: Lynne Rienner Publishers, Inc., 1997.

Esposito, John L. and Francois Burgat, eds. *Modernizing Islam: Religion in the Public Sphere in Europe and the Middle East*. Newark and London: Rutgers University Press & Hurst, 2003.

Esposito, John L. and John O. Voll. *Islam and Democracy*. New York: Oxford University Press, 1998.

—— *Makers of Contemporary Islam*. New York: Oxford University Press, 2001.

Esposito, John L. with Natana J. DeLong-Bas. *Women in Muslim Family Law*, 2nd ed. Syracuse: Syracuse University Press, 2001.

Esposito, John L., Yvonne Yazbeck Haddad, and Jane I. Smith. *Immigrant Faiths: Christians, Jews and Muslims Becoming Americans.* Walnut Creek, CA; Alta Mira Press, 2002.

Facey, William. *Back To Earth: Adobe Building in Saudi Arabia.* Riyadh: Al-Turath in association with the London Centre of Arab Studies, 1997.

Fakhry, Majid, trans. *The Quran: A Modern English Version.* Berkshire: Garnet Publishing, 1996.

Fathy, Hassan. *Architecture of the Poor.* Chicago: University of Chicago Press, 1973 [1969].

Fathy, Hassan. "Contemporaneity in the City," in *Architecture For A Changing World,* ed. James Steele. London: Academy Editions, 1992.

Federspiel, Howard M. *Muslim Intellectuals and National Development in Indonesia.* Cormack, NY: Nova Science Publishers, 1998.

Fernea, Elizabeth Warnock and Basima Qattan Bezirgan, eds. *Middle Eastern Muslim Women Speak.* Austin: University of Texas Press, 1977.

Gabrieli, Francesco. *Arab Historians of the Crusades,* trans. E.J. Costello. New York: Dorset Press, 1957.

George, Kenneth M. *A.D. Pirous: Vision, Faith and a Journey in Indonesia, 1955–2002.* Bandung: Yayasan Serambi Pirous, 2002.

George, Kenneth M. *Visual Surprise and Visual Dzikir in the Work of A.D. Pirous,* exhibition catalogue for Words of Faith: Paintings and Graphic Works, Balai Seni Lukis Negara, Kuala Lumpur, Malaysia, October 6–27, 2003.

Gibb, H.A.R., trans. and ed. *The Travels of Ibn Battuta A.D. 1325–1354.* London: Hakluyt Society, 1929; repr. 1983, 3 vols.

Gibbons, David S. *The Grameen Reader.* Dhaka: Grameen Bank, 1994.

Goddard, Hugh. *Christians and Muslims: From Double Standards to Mutual Understanding.* Richmond: Curzon Press, 1995.

Haddad, Yvonne Yazbeck, ed. *Muslims in the West: From Sojourners to Citizens.* New York: Oxford University Press, 2002.

Haddad, Yvonne Yazbeck and John L. Esposito, eds. *Islam, Gender and Social Change.* New York: Oxford University Press, 1998.

—— *Muslims on the Americanization Path.* Atlanta: Scholars Press, 1997.

Haddad, Yvonne Yazbeck and Wadi Haddad, eds. *Christian–Muslim Encounters.* Gainesville: University Press of Florida, 1995.

Haleem, Muzaffar and Betty (Batul) Bowman. *The Sun is Rising in the West: New Muslims Tell about their Journey to Islam.* Beltsville, MD: Amana Publications, 1999.

Hambly, Gavin R.G., ed. *Women in the Medieval Muslim World.* New York: St. Martin's Press, 1998.

Hargreaves, Jennifer. *Heroines of Sport: The Politics of Difference and Identity.* London and New York: Routledge, 2000.

Hasan, Asma Gull. *American Muslims: The New Generation.* New York: Continuum International Publishing Group, 2000.

—— *Why I am a Muslim: An American Odyssey.* New York: Thorson Element, 2004.

Hasan, M. Kamal. *Muslim Intellectual Responses to "New Order" Modernization in Indonesia.* Kuala Lumpur: n.p., 1980.

Heylin, Clinton. *Gypsy Love Songs and Sad Refrains: The Recordings of Richard Thompson and Sandy Denny.* Manchester: Labour of Love Productions, 1989.

Hick, John and Paul F. Knitter, eds. *The Myth of Christian Uniqueness: Toward a Pluralistic Theology of Religions,* Maryknoll, NY: Orbis Books, 1987.

Hill, Donald R. *Islamic Science and Engineering*. Edinburgh: Edinburgh University Press, 1993.

Holod, Renata and Darl Rastorfer, eds. *In his own Words*. Singapore: Concept Media, 1985.

Horne, Alistair A. *A Savage War of Peace: Algeria, 1954–1962*, rev. ed. New York: Penguin Group U.S.A., 1987.

Humphries, Patrick. *Richard Thompson: The Biography*. New York: Schirmer Books, 1997.

Ibrahim, Saad Eddin. *The Copts of Egypt*. Cairo: Ibn Khaldun Center and Minority Rights Group, 1996.

—— *Egypt, Islam and Democracy: Critical Essays with a New Postcript*. Cairo: American University in Cairo Press, 2002.

Inalcik, Halil. *The Ottoman Empire: The Classical Age, 1300–1600*. London and New York: Praeger Publications, 1973.

Iqbal, Munawar. *Distributive Justice and Need Fulfillment in an Islamic Economy*. Leicester: Islamic Foundation, 1988.

Itzkowitz, Norman. *Ottoman Empire and Islamic Tradition*. Chicago: University of Chicago Press, 1972.

Kadare, Ismail. *Broken April*. New York: Amsterdam Books, 1978.

—— *The Castle*. N.p.: University Press of the Pacific, 1970.

—— *Elegy for Kosovo: Stories*. N.p.: Arcade Books, 2000.

—— *The File on H*, trans. David Bellos. New York: Arcade Publishing, Inc., 1998.

—— *The General of the Dead Army*. London: Harvill Press, 2002.

—— *The Three-Arched Bridge*. N.p.: Arcade Books, 1997.

Kar, Mehranguiz. "Women's Strategies in Iran from the 1979 Revolution to 1999," in *Globalization, Gender, and Religion: The Politics of Women's Rights in Catholic and Muslim Contexts*, ed. Jane H. Bayes and Nayereh Tohidi. New York: Palgrave, 2001.

Keddie, Nikki R. and Beth Baron, eds. *Women in Middle Eastern History: Shifting Boundaries in Sex and Gender*. New Haven: Yale University Press, 1991.

Khan, Hasan-Uddin, ed. *Hassan Fathy*. Singapore: Concept Media, 1995.

Khan, Imran. *All Round View*. London: Chatto & Windus, 1988.

—— *Imran: The Autobiography of Imran Khan*. London: Pelham Books, 1983.

—— *Indus Journey: A Personal View of Pakistan*. London: Chatto & Windus, 1990.

Khan, S.S. and M.H. Khan. *Rural Change in the Third World: Pakistan and the Aga Khan Rural Support Program*. New York: Greenwood Publishing Group, 1992.

Kilpatrick, Hilary. *The Modern Egyptian Novel*. London: Ithaca Press, 1974.

Kingsbury, Damien. *The Politics of Indonesia*, 2nd ed. New York: Oxford University Press, 2002.

Knapp, Ron. *Top Ten Stars of the N.C.A.A. Men's Basketball Tournament*. Berkeley Heights, NJ: Enslow Publishers, Inc., 2001.

Kneib, Martha. *Kareem Abdul-Jabbar: Basketball Hall of Famers*. New York: Rosen Publishing Group, Inc., 2002.

Knitter, Paul F. and Chandra Muzaffar, eds. *Subverting Greed: Religious Perspectives on the Global Economy*. Maryknoll, NY: Orbis Books, 2002.

Kunt, Metin and Christine Woodhead, eds. *Suleyman the Magnificent and his Age: The Ottoman Empire in the Early Modern World*. Reading, MA: Addison-Wesley, 1995.

Lai, C.H. and Azim Kidwai, eds. *Ideals and Realities: Selected Essays of Abdus Salam*, 3rd ed. Singapore: World Scientific Publishing Co. Pte. Ltd., 1989.

Lapidus, Ira M. *A History of Islamic Societies*, 2nd ed. Cambridge: Cambridge University Press, 2002.

Lewis, Franklin D. *Past and Present, East and West: The Life, Teachings and Poetry of Jalal al-Din Rumi*. Oxford: Oneworld Publications, 2000.

Maalouf, Amin. *The Crusades through Arab Eyes*, trans. Jon Rothschild. New York: Schoken Books, 1984.

Magdalinski, Tara and Timothy J.L. Chandler, eds. *With God on their Side: Sport in the Service of Religion*. London and New York: Routledge, Taylor & Francis Group, 2002.

Mahdi, Ali Akbar. "Iranian Women: Between Islamization and Globalization," in *Iran Encountering Globalization: Problems and Prospects*, ed. Ali Mohammadi. London and New York: Routledge/Curzon, 2003.

Mahfouz, Naguib. *Autumn Quail*, trans. Roger Allen. New York: Doubleday Anchor Books, 1985.

—— *The Beggar*, trans. Kristin Walker Henry and Nariman Khales Naili al-Warriki. New York: Doubleday Anchor Books, 1986.

—— *The Beginning and the End*, trans. Ramses Awad. New York: Doubleday Anchor Books, 1985.

—— *Children of Gebelaawi*, trans. Philip Stewart. Washington, DC: Three Continents Press, 1981.

—— *Midaq Alley*, trans. Trevor Le Gassick. New York: Doubleday Anchor Books, 1992.

—— *Palace of Desire*, trans. William Maynard Hutchins. New York: Doubleday Anchor Books, 1992.

—— *Palace Walk*, trans. William Maynard Hutchins. New York: Doubleday Anchor Books, 1990.

—— *The Search*, trans. Mohamed Islam. New York: Doubleday Anchor Books, 1987.

—— *Sugar Street*, trans. William Maynard Hutchins and Angele Botros Samaan. Cairo: American University in Cairo Press, 2001.

—— *The Thief and the Dogs*, trans. Trevor Le Gassick and M.M. Badawi. New York: Doubleday Anchor Books, 1984.

—— *Wedding Song*, trans. Olive E. Kenny. New York: Doubleday Anchor Books, 1984.

Malcolm, Noel. *Kosovo: A Short History*. New York: Harper Perennial, 1999.

Malti-Douglas, Fedwa. *Men, Women and God(s)*. Los Angeles: University of California Press, 1995.

—— *Woman's Body, Woman's Word: Gender and Discourse in Arabo-Islamic Writing*. Princeton: Princeton University Press, 1991.

Matin, Abdul. *Sheikha Hasina: The Making of a Prime Minister*. N.p.: Radical Asia Publications, 1997.

McAllester, Matthew. *Beyond the Mountains of the Damned: The War Inside Kosovo*. New York: New York University Press, 2002.

McMane, Fred. *Hakeem Olajuwon*. Philadelphia, PA: Chelsea House Publishers, 1997.

Menocal, Maria Rosa. *The Ornament of the World: How Muslims, Jews and Christians Created a Culture of Tolerance in Medieval Spain*. Boston: Little, Brown and Company, 2002.

Mernissi, Fatima. *Beyond the Veil: Male–Female Dynamics in Modern Muslim Society*. Bloomington: Indiana University Press, 1987.

—— *Doing Daily Battle: Interviews with Moroccan Women*, trans. Mary Jo Lakeland. New Brunswick, NJ: Rutgers University Press, 1989.

—— *Dreams of Trespass: Tales of a Harem Girlhood*. Reading, MA: Addison-Wesley Publishing Co., 1994.

—— *The Forgotten Queens of Islam*, trans. Mary Jo Lakeland. Cambridge: Polity Press, 1993.

—— *The Veil and the Male Elite: A Feminist Interpretation of Women's Rights in Islam*. Reading, MA: Addison-Wesley Publishing Co., 1991.

Mills, Nicolaus and Kira Brunner, eds. *The New Killing Fields: Massacre and the Politics of Intervention*. New York: Basic Books, 2002.

Mills, Paul S. and John R. Presley. *Islamic Finance: Theory and Practice*. New York: St. Martin's Press, 1999.

Mir-Hosseini, Ziba. *Islam and Gender: The Religious Debate in Contemporary Iran*. Princeton: Princeton University Press, 1999.

Moghadam, Valentine S. "The Two Faces of Iran: Women's Activism, the Reform Movement, and the Islamic Republic," in *Nothing Sacred: Women Respond to Religious Fundamentalism and Terror*, ed. Betsy Reed. New York: Thunder's Mouth Press, 2002.

Mohammadi, Ali, ed. *Iran Encountering Globalization: Problems and Prospects*. London and New York: Routledge/Curzon, 2003.

Munif, Abd al-Rahman. *Cities of Salt*, trans. Peter Theroux. New York: Vintage International, 1989.

—— *Endings*, trans. Roger Allen. London: Quartet Books, 1988.

—— *Story of a City: A Childhood in Amman*, trans. Samira Kawar. London: Quartet Books, 1996.

—— *The Trench*, trans. Peter Theroux. New York: Pantheon Books, 1991.

—— *Variations on Night and Day*, trans. Peter Theroux. New York: Pantheon Books, 1993.

Musallam, B.F. *Sex and Society in Islam*. Cambridge: Cambridge University Press, 1983.

Muzaffar, Chandra. *Human Rights and the New World Order*. Penang: Just World Trust, 1993.

—— *Muslims, Dialogue and Terror*. Kuala Lumpur: JUST, 2002.

—— *Rights, Religion and Reform: Enhancing Human Dignity through Spiritual and Moral Transformation*. London: Routledge Curzon, 2002.

Nasr, S.V.R. "Islamic Opposition in the Political Process: Lessons From Pakistan," in *Political Islam: Revolution, Radicalism, or Reform?* ed. John L. Esposito. Boulder, CO: Lynne Rienner Publishers, Inc., 1997.

El-Nawawy, Mohammed and Adel Iskandar. *al-Jazeera: How the Free Arab News Network Scooped the World and Changed the Middle East*. Boulder, CO: Westview Press, 2002.

Nelson, Kristina. *The Art of Reciting the Qur'an*. Austin: University of Texas Press, 1985.

Nielsen, Jorgen. *Muslims in Western Europe*, 2nd ed. Edinburgh: Edinburgh University Press, 1995.

Her Majesty Queen Noor. *Leap of Faith: Memoirs of an Unexpected Life*. New York: Miramax Books, 2003.

Olajuwon, Hakeem with Peter Knobler. *Living the Dream: My Life and Basketball*. Boston: Little, Brown and Company, 1996.

Pedersen, Lars. *Newer Islamic Movements in Western Europe* (Research in Migration and Ethnic Relations). London: Ashgate, 1999.

Peirce, Leslie P. *The Imperial Harem: Women and Sovereignty in the Ottoman Empire*. New York: Oxford University Press, 1993.

Pich-Aguilera, Felipe. *Hassan Fathy: Beyond the Nile*. London: Concept Media, Ltd., 1989.

Rashid, Ahmed. *Islam and Central Asia: An Enduring Legacy or an Evolving Threat?* Washington, DC: Center for Political and Strategic Studies, 2000.

—— *Jihad: The Rise of Militant Islam in Central Asia*. New Haven, CT: Yale University Press, 2002.

—— *The Resurgence of Central Asia: Islam or Nationalism?* London: Zed Books, 1995.

—— *Taliban: Militant Islam, Oil and Fundamentalism in Central Asia*. London: I.B. Tauris, 2000.

Rasmussen, Anne K. "The Qur'an in Indonesian Daily Life: The Public Project of Musical Oratory," *Journal of the Society for Ethnomusicology*, vol. 45, no. 1, Winter 2001, pp. 30–57.

Remnick, David. *King of the World: Muhammad Ali and the Rise of an American Hero*. New York: Random House, 1998.

Rezun, Miron. *Europe's Nightmare: The Struggle for Kosovo*. Westport, CT: Praeger, 2001.

Ricklefs, Merle C. *Islam in the Indonesian Social Context*. Clayton: Centre of Southeast Asian Studies, Monash University, 1991.

Rippin, Andrew, ed. *Approaches to the History of the Interpretation of the Qur'an*. Oxford: Clarendon Press, 1988.

The Rolling Stone Index: Twenty-Five Years of Popular Culture, 1967–1991. Ann Arbor, MI: Popular Culture, Ink, 1993.

El Saadawi, Nawal. *A Daughter of Isis: The Autobiography of Nawal El Saadawi*, trans. Sherif Hetata. London: Zed Books, 1999.

—— *The Fall of the Imam*, trans. Sherif Hetata. London: Minerva, 1988.

—— *God Dies by the Nile*, trans. Sherif Hetata. London: Zed Books, 1974.

—— *The Hidden Face of Eve*, trans. Sherif Hetata. London: Zed Books, 1980.

—— *The Innocence of the Devil*, trans. Sherif Hetata. Berkeley: University of California Press, 1994.

—— *The Nawal El Saawadi Reader*. London: Zed Books, 1997.

—— *Searching*, trans. Sherif Hetata. London: Zed Books, 1991.

—— *Two Women in One*, trans. Sherif Hetata. London: Saqi Books, 1994.

—— *Woman at Point Zero*, trans. Sherif Hetata. London: Zed Books, 1983

Saeed, Abdullah. *Islamic Banking and Interest: A Study of the Prohibition of Riba and its Contemporary Interpretation*. Leiden: E.J. Brill, 1996.

Safi, Omid, ed. *Progressive Islam*. Oxford: Oneworld, 2003.

Salmawy, Mohamed. *Naguib Mahfouz at Sidi Gaber: Reflections of a Nobel Laureate, 1994–2001, From Conversations with Mohamed Salmawy*. Cairo: American University in Cairo Press, 2001.

Sciolino, Elaine. *Persian Mirrors: The Elusive Face of Iran*. New York: Simon & Schuster, 2000.

Sedgwick, Mark J. *Sufism: The Essentials*. Cairo: American University in Cairo Press, 2000.

Sells, Michael A. *Approaching the Qur'an: The Early Revelations*. Ashland, OR: White Cloud Press, 1999.

Serafin, Steven R., ed. *Encyclopedia of World Literature in the 20th Century*. London: St. James Press, 1999, 3 vols.

Serageldin, Ismail and Samer El-Sadek, eds. *Egypt and the Aga Khan Award for Architecture*. Geneva: Aga Khan Trust for Culture, 1989.

Shah, Saira. *The Storyteller's Daughter*. New York: Alfred A. Knopf, 2003.

Shaheen, Jack. *Reel Bad Arabs: How Hollywood Vilifies a People*. N.p.: Interlink Publishing Group, 2001.

al-Shaykh, Hanan. *Beirut Blues*, trans. Catherine Cobham. New York: Doubleday Anchor Books, 1992.

—— *I Sweep the Sun off Rooftops: Stories*, trans. Catherine Cobham. New York: Anchor Books, Doubleday, 1998.

—— *Only in London*, trans. Catherine Cobham. New York: Anchor Doubleday Books, 2000.

—— *The Story of Zahra*, trans. Peter Ford. London: Readers International, 1986.

—— *Women of Sand and Myrrh*, trans. Catherine Cobham. New York: Doubleday Anchor Books, 1988.

Siddiqi, Mohammed Nejatullah. *Banking Without Interest*. Leicester: Islamic Foundation, 1983.

—— *Economics, an Islamic Approach*. Leicester: Islamic Foundation, 1999.

—— *Insurance in an Islamic Economy*. Leicester: Islamic Foundation, 1985.

—— *Issues in Islamic Banking*. Leicester: Islamic Foundation, 1983.

—— *Partnership and Profit-Sharing in Islamic Law*. Leicester: Islamic Foundation, 1985.

—— *Riba, Bank Interest and the Rationale of its Prohibition*. Jeddah: Islamic Research and Training Institute/Islamic Development Bank, 2004.

—— *Role of the State in the Economy*. Leicester: Islamic Foundation, 1996.

—— *Teaching Economics in Islamic Perspective*. Jeddah: Centre for Research in Islamic Economics, 1996.

Smith, Margaret. *Muslim Women Mystics: The Life and Work of Rabi'a and Other Women Mystics in Islam*. Oxford: Oneworld Publications, 2001.

Smith, Maureen. "*Muhammad Speaks* and Muhammad Ali: Intersections of the Nation of Islam and Sport in the 1960s," in *With God on their Side: Sport in the Service of Religion*, ed. Tara Magdalinksi and Timothy J.L. Chandler. London and New York: Routledge, Taylor & Francis Group, 2002.

Soffan, Linda Usra. *The Women of the United Arab Emirates*. London: Croom Helm, 1980.

Steele, James. *An Architecture for People: The Complete Works of Hassan Fathy*. London: Thames & Hudson, 1997.

—— *The Hassan Fathy Collection*. Geneva: Aga Khan Trust for Culture, 1989.

Tamimi, Azzam S. *Rachid Ghannouchi: A Democrat Within Islamism*. New York: Oxford University Press, 2001.

Tarabishi, George. *Woman against her Sex: A Critique of Nawal el-Saadawi*, trans. Basil Hatim and Elisabeth Orsini. London: Saqi Books, 1981.

Terpan, Fabienne. *Ismail Kadare*. Paris: n.p., 1992.

Todd, Helen. *Women at the Centre: Grameen Bank Borrowers after One Decade*. Boulder, CO: Westview Press, 1996.

Trimingham, J. Spencer. *The Sufi Orders in Islam*, with foreword by John O. Voll. New York: Oxford University Press, 1998.

Turner, Howard R. *Science in Medieval Islam: An Illustrated Introduction*. Austin: University of Texas Press, 1995.

Vertovec, Steven and Ceri Peach, eds. *Islam in Europe: The Politics of Religion and Community*. London: Macmillan, 1997.

Vogel, Frank E. and Samuel L. Hayes, III. *Islamic Law and Finance: Religion, Risk, and Return*. The Hague: Kluwer Law International, 1998.

Voll, John Obert. *Islam: Continuity and Change in the Modern World*, 2nd ed. Syracuse: Syracuse University Press, 1994.

Wade-Gayles, Gloria, ed. *My Soul is a Witness*. Boston: Beacon Press, 1995.

Wadud, Amina. *Qur'an and Woman: Re-reading the Sacred Text from a Woman's Perspective*, expanded ed. New York: Oxford University Press, 1999.

Wei-hsun Fu, Charles and Gerhard E. Spiegler, eds. *Religious Issues and Interreligious Dialogues: An Analysis and Sourcebook of Developments Since 1945*. New York: Greenwood Press, 1989.

Welch, Anthony and Stuart Cary Welch. *Arts of the Islamic Book: The Collection of Prince Sadruddin Aga Khan*. Ithaca: Syracuse University Press, 1982.

Wolfe, Michael. *The Hadj: An American's Pilgrimage to Mecca*. New York: Grove Press, 1998.

—— *One Thousand Roads to Mecca: Ten Centuries of Travelers Writing about the Muslim Pilgrimage*. New York: Grove Press, 1999.

Wolfe, Michael and the Producers of Beliefnet, eds. *Taking Back Islam: American Muslims Reclaim their Faith*. Emmaus, PA: Rodale Inc. and Beliefnet, Inc., 2002.

Woodward, Mark R., ed. *Toward a New Paradigm: Recent Developments in Indonesian Islamic Thought*, Tempe, AZ: Arizona State University, 1996.

Wright, Astri. *Soul, Spirit, and Mountain: Preoccupations of Indonesian Painters*. New York: Oxford University Press, 1994.

Yunus, Muhammad. *Jorimon and Others: Faces of Poverty*, 3rd ed. Dhaka: Grameen Bank, 1991.

Yunus, Muhammad and Alan Jolis. *Banker to the Poor*. London: Aurum Press, 1998.

Zakariya, Mohamed. *The Calligraphy of Islam: Reflections on the State of the Art*. N.p, n.d.

—— *Music for the Eyes*. New York and Los Angeles: Metropolitan Museum of Art and the Los Angeles Museum of Art, 1998.

—— *Observations on Islamic Calligraphy: An Introduction to Islamic and Ottoman Calligraphy*. Washington, DC: Library of Congress, 1978.

Zeidan, Joseph. *Arab Women Novelists: The Formative Years and Beyond*. Albany: State University of New York Press, 1995.

Zewail, Ahmed H., ed. *The Chemical Bond: Structure and Dynamics*, Boston: Academic Press, 1992.

—— *Femtochemistry: Ultrafast Dynamics of the Chemical Bond*. River Edge, NJ: World Scientific, 1994, 2 vols.

—— *Voyage Through Time: Walks of Life to the Nobel Prize*. Cairo: American University in Cairo Press, 2002.